# Sustainable Applications for Machine Learning

# Sustainable Applications for Machine Learning

Guest Editors

**Danial Javaheri**
**Hassan Chizari**
**Amir Masoud Rahmani**

MDPI

Basel • Beijing • Wuhan • Barcelona • Belgrade • Novi Sad • Cluj • Manchester

*Guest Editors*
Danial Javaheri
School of Computing,
Engineering and Physical
Sciences
University of the West of
Scotland
London
UK

Hassan Chizari
School of Business,
Computing and Social
Sciences
University of Gloucestershire
Gloucester
UK

Amir Masoud Rahmani
Future Technology Research
Center
National Yunlin University of
Science and Technology
Douliou
Taiwan

*Editorial Office*
MDPI AG
Grosspeteranlage 5
4052 Basel, Switzerland

This is a reprint of the Special Issue, published open access by the journal *Machine Learning and Knowledge Extraction* (ISSN 2504-4990), freely accessible at: https://www.mdpi.com/journal/make/special_issues/554E537Y52.

For citation purposes, cite each article independently as indicated on the article page online and as indicated below:

| Lastname, A.A.; Lastname, B.B. Article Title. *Journal Name* **Year**, *Volume Number*, Page Range. |
|---|

**ISBN 978-3-7258-7176-6 (Hbk)**
**ISBN 978-3-7258-7177-3 (PDF)**
**https://doi.org/10.3390/books978-3-7258-7177-3**

# Contents

**Preface** . . . . . . . . . . . . . . . . . . . . . . . . . . . . . . . . . . . . . . . . . . . . . . . . . . vii

**Zoja Anžur, Klara Žinkovič, Junoš Lukan, Pietro Barbiero, Gašper Slapničar, Mohan Li, et al.**
A Review of Methods for Unobtrusive Measurement of Work-Related Well-Being
Reprinted from: *Mach. Learn. Knowl. Extr.* **2025**, *7*, 62,
https://doi.org/10.3390/make7030062 . . . . . . . . . . . . . . . . . . . . . . . . . . . . . . . . 1

**Joan D. Gonzalez-Franco, Alejandro Galaviz-Mosqueda, Salvador Villarreal-Reyes, Jose E. Lozano-Rizk, Raul Rivera-Rodriguez, Jose E. Gonzalez-Trejo, et al.**
Revolutionizing Cardiac Risk Assessment: AI-Powered Patient Segmentation Using Advanced Machine Learning Techniques
Reprinted from: *Mach. Learn. Knowl. Extr.* **2025**, *7*, 46,
https://doi.org/10.3390/make7020046 . . . . . . . . . . . . . . . . . . . . . . . . . . . . . . . . 23

**Suset Vázquez-Aveledo, Rosenberg J. Romero, Lorena Díaz-González, Moisés Montiel-González and Jesús Cerezo**
Optimizing a Double Stage Heat Transformer Performance by Levenberg–Marquardt Artificial Neural Network
Reprinted from: *Mach. Learn. Knowl. Extr.* **2025**, *7*, 29,
https://doi.org/10.3390/make7020029 . . . . . . . . . . . . . . . . . . . . . . . . . . . . . . . . 45

**Elias Dritsas and Maria Trigka**
Exploring the Intersection of Machine Learning and Big Data: A Survey
Reprinted from: *Mach. Learn. Knowl. Extr.* **2025**, *7*, 13,
https://doi.org/10.3390/make7010013 . . . . . . . . . . . . . . . . . . . . . . . . . . . . . . . . 76

**Yajing Chen, Urs Liebau, Shreyas Mysore Guruprasad, Iaroslav Trofimenko and Christine Minke**
Advancing Life Cycle Assessment of Sustainable Green Hydrogen Production Using Domain-Specific Fine-Tuning by Large Language Models Augmentation
Reprinted from: *Mach. Learn. Knowl. Extr.* **2024**, *6*, 122,
https://doi.org/10.3390/make6040122 . . . . . . . . . . . . . . . . . . . . . . . . . . . . . . . . 118

**Masoumeh Hashemi, Richard C. Peralta and Matt Yost**
Balancing Results from AI-Based Geostatistics versus Fuzzy Inference by Game Theory Bargaining to Improve a Groundwater Monitoring Network
Reprinted from: *Mach. Learn. Knowl. Extr.* **2024**, *6*, 92,
https://doi.org/10.3390/make6030092 . . . . . . . . . . . . . . . . . . . . . . . . . . . . . . . . 139

**Ray-I Chang, Chih-Yung Tsai and Yu-Wei Chang**
Enhancing Visitor Forecasting with Target-Concatenated Autoencoder and Ensemble Learning
Reprinted from: *Mach. Learn. Knowl. Extr.* **2024**, *6*, 83,
https://doi.org/10.3390/make6030083 . . . . . . . . . . . . . . . . . . . . . . . . . . . . . . . . 162

**Mustafa Pamuk and Matthias Schumann**
Towards AI Dashboards in Financial Services: Design and Implementation of an AI Development Dashboard for Credit Assessment
Reprinted from: *Mach. Learn. Knowl. Extr.* **2024**, *6*, 85,
https://doi.org/10.3390/make6030085 . . . . . . . . . . . . . . . . . . . . . . . . . . . . . . . . 188

**Dina A. Alabbad, Shahad Y. Ajibi, Raghad B. Alotaibi, Noura K. Alsqer, Rahaf A. Alqahtani, Noor M. Felemban, et al.**
Birthweight Range Prediction and Classification: A Machine Learning-Based Sustainable Approach
Reprinted from: *Mach. Learn. Knowl. Extr.* **2024**, *6*, 36,
https://doi.org/10.3390/make6020036 . . . . . . . . . . . . . . . . . . . . . . . . . . . . . . . . . **230**

**Sakorn Mekruksavanich and Anuchit Jitpattanakul**
Effective Detection of Epileptic Seizures through EEG Signals Using Deep Learning Approaches
Reprinted from: *Mach. Learn. Knowl. Extr.* **2023**, *5*, 94,
https://doi.org/10.3390/make5040094 . . . . . . . . . . . . . . . . . . . . . . . . . . . . . . . . . **249**

# Preface

This Reprint brings together recent research on the sustainability of machine learning across critical domains. As AI and smart systems grow, vast amounts of data and complex decision-making raise concerns around reliability, efficiency, security, privacy, and societal impact.

The contributions examine sustainability from both theoretical and practical perspectives—they delve beyond computational efficiency to include dependability, robustness, ethics, and governance. These works present approaches to achieve trustworthy and resilient ML in real-world settings.

Topics include dependable learning, deep neural network optimization and acceleration, privacy-preserving and federated learning, security in generative models, ethical AI, and sustainability of NLP systems. The applied studies presented span the topics of healthcare, smart cities, Industry 4.0, sustainable supply chains, and circular economy.

Combining methodological and application-driven research, this Reprint offers a valuable reference for researchers, practitioners, and decision-makers focused on sustainable ML in high-impact and mission-critical contexts.

**Danial Javaheri, Hassan Chizari, and Amir Masoud Rahmani**
*Guest Editors*

*machine learning & knowledge extraction*

MDPI

*Review*

# A Review of Methods for Unobtrusive Measurement of Work-Related Well-Being

**Zoja Anžur [1,2,*], Klara Žinkovič [1], Junoš Lukan [1,2], Pietro Barbiero [3], Gašper Slapničar [1,2], Mohan Li [3], Martin Gjoreski [3], Maike E. Debus [4], Sebastijan Trojer [1,5], Mitja Luštrek [1,2] and Marc Langheinrich [3]**

1 Jožef Stefan Institute, 1000 Ljubljana, Slovenia
2 Jožef Stefan International Postgraduate School, 1000 Ljubljana, Slovenia
3 Faculty of Informatics, Università della Svizzera Italiana, 6900 Lugano, Switzerland
4 Institute of Work and Organizational Psychology, University of Neuchâtel, 2000 Neuchâtel, Switzerland
5 Faculty of Computer and Information Science, University of Ljubljana, 1000 Ljubljana, Slovenia
* Correspondence: zoja.anzur@ijs.si

**Abstract:** Work-related well-being is an important research topic, as it is linked to various aspects of individuals' lives, including job performance. To measure it effectively, unobtrusive sensors are desirable to minimize the burden on employees. Because there is a lack of consensus on the definitions of well-being in the psychological literature in terms of its dimensions, our work begins by proposing a conceptualization of well-being based on the refined definition of health provided by the World Health Organization. We focus on reviewing the existing literature on the unobtrusive measurement of well-being. In our literature review, we focus on affect, engagement, fatigue, stress, sleep deprivation, physical comfort, and social interactions. Our initial search resulted in a total of 644 studies, from which we then reviewed 35, revealing a variety of behavioral markers such as facial expressions, posture, eye movements, and speech. The most commonly used sensory devices were red, green, and blue (RGB) cameras, followed by microphones and smartphones. The methods capture a variety of behavioral markers, the most common being body movement, facial expressions, and posture. Our work serves as an investigation into various unobtrusive measuring methods applicable to the workplace context, aiming to foster a more employee-centric approach to the measurement of well-being and to emphasize its affective component.

**Keywords:** affective computing; ambient intelligence; facial expressions; gestures; well-being; sensors

## 1. Introduction

Well-being measurement has become an increasingly prominent research topic across various disciplines due to its impact on numerous aspects of life. As per the American Psychological Association (APA) Dictionary of Psychology, well-being is defined as a state characterized by happiness, low levels of distress, good physical and mental health, a positive outlook, and high quality of life [1]. In the psychological literature, however, various definitions of well-being exist, and despite extensive research, open questions regarding them persist. Similarly, there is a large body of literature on the definition of work-related well-being. Wijngaards et al. [2], for example, define well-being at work as the experience or state of well-being in the work setting or when working ([2], p. 798).

Within the organizational context, workplace practices and work-related well-being are linked to several organizational improvements [3], such as employee performance [4].


https://doi.org/10.3390/make7030062

Researching well-being has its origins in psychology, where a wide range of instruments exist for measuring it (e.g., [5–7]). However, most of them rely on self-reports, which are impractical and obtrusive for employees, as filling out questionnaires is time-consuming and disruptive to their workflow. Recently, however, researching well-being has garnered interest in other fields, such as computer science, where sensing technologies that have a less disruptive nature have increasingly been employed. Research is available utilizing a variety of sensors in diverse contexts, such as support tools for chronic disease management [8]. In this review, we therefore focus on the use of unobtrusive sensors, which are designed to collect data without requiring active participation or causing disruption to normal activities. In consequence, unobtrusive sensors are subtle and can be easily integrated into daily scenarios [8]. Given their numerous advantages, unobtrusive sensors are increasingly featured in the scientific literature and are being integrated into novel research methods.

When utilizing unobtrusive methods, researchers can focus on either (or both) behavioral or physiological signals. Significant challenges arise when measuring physiological signals in naturalistic environments where conditions are highly variable (e.g., movement, changing lighting, makeup, and eyewear). These conditions often lead to decreased accuracy and stability of the measurements. For instance, Slapničar et al. [9] conducted a study in which they estimated blood pressure using a modified red, green, and blue (RGB) camera, which required stable environmental conditions (e.g., consistent lighting, minimal movement). This suggests that remote physiological monitoring may not be practical for large-scale naturalistic applications. In contrast, behavioral signals are more directly observable, making them more robust and less dependent on environmental variables. Furthermore, monitoring physiological signals often relies on wearable devices, which would mean increased obtrusiveness for employees. Given the aforementioned limitations of physiological signal measurement in settings such as the workplace, we will investigate behavioral markers instead of physiological signals in this review.

A variety of studies have been conducted across diverse contexts, such as the well-being of residents in long-term care facilities [10] and the well-being of students in educational settings [11]. In this review, we will focus on investigating well-being in the workplace. We do this because, as mentioned in the previous paragraphs, work-related well-being is linked to several organizational improvements [3], such as employee performance [4], making it an important topic of investigation. Furthermore, monitoring well-being in the workplace using methods such as questionnaires is obtrusive to employees' workflow, emphasizing the importance of investigating alternative methods such as unobtrusive sensors. Given the significant variations among workplaces, we decided to focus on the workplace of knowledge workers, making our approach context-specific.

To the best of our knowledge, there is currently a lack of research that focuses on monitoring well-being in the workplace using unobtrusive sensors. Additionally, well-being is frequently used as an umbrella term, which often hinders the comparability of existing studies. For example, Wallace et al. [12] investigated the potential of a pressure-sensitive mat for assessing well-being, which is particularly suitable for deployment in the homes of aging adults. However, the presented method focuses mainly on assessing the physical aspect of well-being, which is not suitable in the context of knowledge workers, where other (i.e., psychological) aspects are equally important. Because of these issues, we decided to define multiple aspects of well-being, as presented in the following paragraphs.

To tackle the challenges related to defining the dimensions of well-being and to ensure clarity, we draw on the definition of health provided by the World Health Organization (WHO) [13], by refining it and proposing a conceptual framework of well-being. We do this by defining the dimensions and sub-dimensions of well-being based on the existing psychological literature and explaining the relevance of each sub-dimension to the overall construct. Then, we present the most suitable and developed unobtrusive methods for measuring each sub-dimension and discuss how these methods can be applied in the context of the workplace. Lastly, we mention the limitations of our approach and the general issues that this field is facing.

## 2. Conceptualizing Well-Being

As already mentioned, various definitions of well-being exist in the psychological literature, and despite extensive research, open questions regarding them persist. The complexity and variability of well-being have prevented a consensus on its definition [14]. Nevertheless, the importance of its affective components is well-recognized (e.g., [15,16]). A model (with proposed dimensions of well-being) reaching high agreement among professionals that could be used in practice remains to be established [5]. Furthermore, well-being is often used as an umbrella term [16], leading to ambiguous interpretations and questionable comparability among studies.

### *2.1. Taxonomies of Well-Being*

Well-being is a complex construct with numerous influencing factors. Due to its dynamic structure that changes over time and fluctuates within a person [17], an extensive body of literature explores the factors that lead to well-being and the outcomes it is connected to. In this section, we review several highly influential studies on well-being from psychology with the aim of introducing the reader to the main approaches in this field.

First, in 1984, Diener [15] investigated well-being, including happiness, life satisfaction, and positive affect, highlighting that various factors influence well-being at different analytical levels. Second, another early work was presented by Ryff and Keyes [18], who focused specifically on psychological well-being and empirically investigated the construct's six-factor structure: autonomy, environmental mastery, personal growth, positive relations with others, purpose in life, and self-acceptance. By comparing this approach to others and using empirical data for validation, the authors reported that the proposed structure effectively captured the main aspects of psychological well-being. Third, the WHO provided a broader framework [13] by introducing a definition of health in 1995 as not only the absence of disease but also a state of physical, mental, and social well-being. This conceptualization indicated three important aspects of well-being, which remain some of the most widely investigated today.

Fourth, emphasizing its dynamic and changing structure [17], in their proposed framework, Dodge et al. [14] viewed well-being as the interplay between an individual's resources and challenges. Both resources and challenges can be psychological, social, or physical. Well-being is achieved when resources and challenges are in equilibrium, meaning the individual has the resources to meet their challenges. Fifth, Sonnentag [17] complemented this work by gathering empirical evidence supporting the fluctuating nature of well-being, particularly in the workplace, where it manifests in various on-the-job behaviors, including performance. She investigated the role of job stressors, job resources, interpersonal factors, personal resources, and work–home interface in relation to work-related well-being and its variability.

Sixth, Fisher [16] focused more on the context of the workplace and proposed a conceptualization of work-related well-being, defining three major components: social, eudaimonic, and subjective. Social well-being involves satisfaction with peers, leaders, etc. Eudaimonic well-being includes job involvement, engagement, flow, and intrinsic motivation. Lastly, subjective well-being pertains to attitudes toward work and experiences of both positive and negative affect.

In summary, various taxonomies have been proposed, yet the field still lacks a consensus due to the complexity of well-being. For the purpose of our research, we use the definition of health provided by the WHO [13], specifically the three aspects of well-being, because it captures the broadness of the construct and is well-known and established in the field. We further divide the three proposed dimensions into sub-dimensions to create a clearer and more defined framework because the definition provided by the WHO [13] is too general for the purpose of our review. We do this by combining the findings of the presented taxonomies, as certain proposed dimensions are shared. Refining the three proposed dimensions in a more concrete and precise manner allows us to partially bridge the gap between the different terminologies used to assess well-being in psychology and computer science.

In this review, we therefore adopt a pragmatic approach by proposing a concept of well-being that not only focuses on affect but also highlights the importance of engagement, fatigue, stress, physical comfort, sleep deprivation, and social interactions, as further described in the next section. Our approach is pragmatic in that, instead of conducting an exhaustive and systematic review of various well-being taxonomies from the psychological literature, we selectively reviewed some of the most prominent ones and used them to shape our own conceptual framework. The proposed conceptualization with clearly defined components should help us investigate the available methods for the unobtrusive measurement of well-being.

### 2.2. Proposed Concept of Well-Being

As highlighted in the previous section, well-being is a broad and complex construct and is often used as an umbrella term. In our review, we decided to use the definition provided by the WHO [13], which we further divided into sub-dimensions. In our concept, we focused on affect while also emphasizing the importance of other dimensions. It is important to note, however, that certain dimensions now serve as predictors, while others act as indicators of well-being. As this falls outside the scope of the current review, it will not be explored further. The dimensions and sub-dimensions that we adopt in our work are presented in Figure 1. We define each of the sub-dimensions as follows:

- **Psychological well-being:** As per Ryff [19], psychological well-being includes happiness (the experience of pleasure) and eudaimonic well-being (referring to flourishing, engagement, feeling a sense of purpose):
  - **Affect:** Affect is defined as the experiences of negative and positive affect. As per the circumplex model [20], each affect can be described as a combination of two independent dimensions: pleasure and arousal. Negative affect is a negative well-being indicator, whereas positive affect is a positive well-being indicator.
  - **Engagement:** Engagement is defined as a state where an employee has a high level of energy, is enthusiastic, and is immersed in their work. Engagement is composed of vigor, dedication, and absorption. Vigor refers to high energy and resilience levels, dedication refers to being strongly involved in one's work, and absorption refers to being focused on and immersed in one's work [21]. Engagement is a positive well-being indicator.
  - **Fatigue:** Fatigue is defined as a state that happens as a consequence of long periods of demanding cognitive activity [20]. Fatigue is a negative well-being indicator.
  - **Stress:** As per the APA dictionary [22], stress is recognized as the physiological or psychological response to stressors, which can be either internal or external. The physiological response can manifest in sweating, a dry mouth, accelerated speech, etc., and influences how people behave and feel. Stress is a negative well-being indicator.

- **Physical well-being:** As per Seligman [23], physical well-being extends beyond the absence of sickness, capturing an individual's capability to realize their fullest wellness potential:
    - **Physical comfort:** As defined by Kölsch et al. [24], the physical comfort zone is composed of postures and motions that are voluntarily adopted, as opposed to those that are avoided. Physical comfort positively impacts well-being.
    - **Sleep deprivation:** Sleep deprivation occurs when there is either a total absence of sleep or a reduction in sleep duration [25]. Sleep deprivation negatively impacts well-being.
- **Social well-being:** As per Pressman [26], social well-being is experienced when various social needs, such as the feeling of support and belonging, are met:
    - **Social interactions:** A social interaction is defined as a process that entails mutual interaction or responses between two or more individuals [27]. There is evidence of the link between frequent and deeper social interactions and well-being [28], indicating that enriching interactions and social support can contribute to increased well-being.

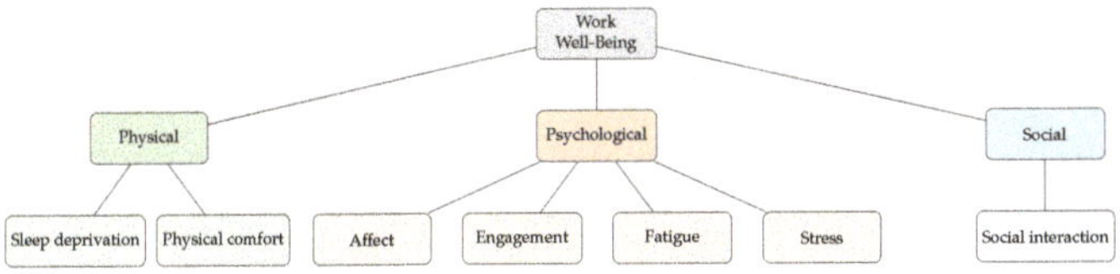


**Figure 1.** Proposed concept of work-related well-being.

All sub-dimensions were defined by us based on the existing literature. Affect is crucial in investigating well-being, as evidenced by the research of Diener [15] and Fisher [16], with the latter also emphasizing the importance of engagement. Fatigue is linked to occupational safety through its impact on cognitive and motor performance [29], while stress is associated with various negative organizational outcomes, including turnover intentions and job burnout [30]. Physical comfort, particularly posture, is recognized as a significant aspect of workplace experience and well-being [31]. Furthermore, the importance of sleep in various domains of our lives is extensively documented in the literature [32]. Lastly, social interactions and related elements are incorporated into the taxonomy proposed by Fisher [16], since studies such as [33] indicate that quality connections can be sources of energy and well-being at work.

## 3. Paper Selection Method

For our review, we adopted an exploratory approach. We primarily limited our search to two databases, IEEE Xplore and the ACM Digital Library, chosen for their rich collections of relevant articles from computer science. Our search focused on articles published in the last five years, covering each sub-dimension that comprises well-being, as portrayed in Figure 1. Consequently, we conducted seven different keyword-based searches of both libraries, as presented in the Appendix A, Table A1. Our interest in methods for unobtrusive sensing guided our keyword selection. Each study had to meet two criteria for inclusion in our review:

- Focus on one of the identified sub-dimensions of well-being.
- Focus on unobtrusive sensing methods.

Due to the large number of reviews already conducted on sensing affect and stress, we introduced an additional criterion for these sub-dimensions: to include only review studies.

As presented in Table 1 and Figure 2, our initial search resulted in 644 articles investigating the various identified sub-dimensions. We then screened each article to determine its relevance and quality and decided whether to include it in the subsequent analysis. Specifically, we focused on whether each article met our inclusion criteria, as specified above, and excluded articles with poor grammar.

**Table 1.** Number of articles included.

| Sub-Dimension | No. of Articles After the Keyword Search | No. of Articles After the Screening |
|---|---|---|
| Affect | 55 | 6 |
| Engagement | 98 | 7 |
| Fatigue | 112 | 2 |
| Stress | 32 | 3 |
| Physical comfort | 176 | 3 |
| Sleep deprivation | 34 | 8 |
| Social interactions | 162 | 6 |
| Sum | 644 | 35 |

After this process, the number of relevant articles decreased greatly, and sometimes, we could not find many suitable articles using the described methodology. In such cases, we conducted manual searches, including studies found on Google Scholar or in the cited literature from already included articles. Additionally, highly relevant papers older than five years were also considered where necessary.

Overall, the screening process resulted in 35 articles, which were thoroughly reviewed by the authors and included in the analysis. In the following sections, we provide an overview of the relevant papers related to the unobtrusive measurement of the sub-dimensions of well-being we proposed in Section 2.

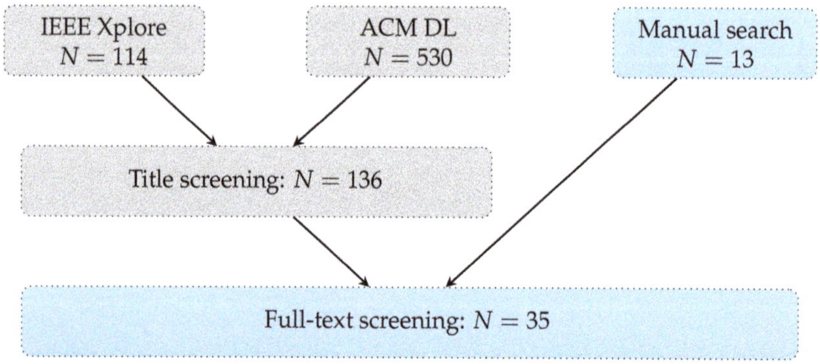


**Figure 2.** Review steps.

## 4. Psychological Well-Being

### 4.1. *Affect*

Because emotion and affect are widely researched, we decided to only investigate existing reviews from the chosen libraries. Six reviews were deemed relevant, as they focused on detecting current or short-term emotions and affect using unobtrusive sensors. In the reviewed articles, affect was most often investigated through facial expressions and facial motions [34,35] and speech [34,36,37]. Additionally, manifestations through different auricular positions (positions of the ear) [38] and facial temperature changes [39] were investigated. The most commonly used sensors were an RGB camera [34,35], a microphone [34,36–38], a thermal camera [39], and radar sensors [40]. It is important to highlight the extensive body of literature focused on monitoring physiological signals associated with affect (e.g., [41]). However, these methods have various limitations, as discussed in Section 1. Notably, some studies complement behavioral markers with physiological signals, which we include in this section due to their high relevance.

In a systematic literature review of wearable sensors by Rödigger et al. [36], the use of wearable devices for detecting emotions and other physiological states was investigated. Specifically, for capturing emotions, an electroencephalogram (EEG), an accelerometer, and a microphone were mentioned. Furthermore, a system for measuring the ear position using reflected sound was mentioned, indicating a relationship between auricular positions and emotions [38]. Gong et al. [35] investigated the use of inertial data from smartphones and wearables to capture characteristic facial motions.

In addition to Röddiger's findings, Stampf et al. [42] presented a review in which various sensor modalities for detecting emotions and physiological states in highly automated vehicles were investigated for monitoring stress and arousal levels. The review mentioned a study that explored auditory signals like paralinguistic cues, where an automated emotion recognition system was created using multiple microphones to infer seven different emotion categories, such as boredom, sadness, happiness, etc. [37]. The model used various acoustic features processed using a neural network classifier and reached accuracies between 70% and 90% for the classification of different groups of emotions [43]. Similarly, a survey of Ambient Intelligence by Dunne et al. [44] addressed various methods for emotion detection, emphasizing the role of computer vision and physiological signals. Techniques such as gesture analysis and body language interpretation were discussed, most often for recognizing basic emotions (e.g., anger, joy, pleasure, sadness, fear) and focusing on the upper body, hands, and arms.

In a review by Braun et al. [34], the contactless detection of drivers' emotional states was investigated. The review discussed various methods for emotion recognition, including facial expressions, speech, physiological states, and body gestures, emphasizing the potential for combining these techniques to enhance the accuracy of emotion detection. Differences in body temperature in some facial regions were also mentioned as an indicator of emotional reactions, therefore demonstrating the potential of using thermal imaging technology for emotion detection [39]. Additionally, Souondariya et al. [45] proposed a visual method for emotion recognition: eye-tracking with electrooculography (EOG) signals, which detects changes in eye positions and recognizes affective states using the valence-arousal model and multi-class SVM classifier. Although this method is not inherently unobtrusive, it can be adapted to reduce its level of intrusion.

Lastly, Nocera et al. [40] provided an overview of radar-based methods for the unobtrusive measurement of various signals, which are then used to build machine learning (ML) models. Despite focusing primarily on studies detecting physiological signals, the review also mentioned methods for affective computing. Highlighting the high potential of emotion recognition, the review summarized various use cases from recognizing the emotional response of patients to recognizing the responses of consumers. One of the studies included in this review was conducted by Zeng and Liu [46], who proposed a method for emotion recognition based on millimeter-wave radar. Their unobtrusive method reached an accuracy of 86.50% when detecting emotional states.

In this section, a wide range of methods and sensors for detecting and recognizing various emotions and types of affect were presented. Covering different approaches, some of the studies mentioned relied on both physiological signals and behavioral markers in their research, making it challenging to assess the contribution of the latter. Furthermore, the review by Rödigger et al. [36] focused on investigating wearable sensors, and the unobtrusiveness of these methods is questionable. The wearable sensors are not contactless, but due to their resemblance to earphones (which are used by numerous people every day in the office), they were nevertheless deemed unobtrusive in the context of the workplace and therefore included in our review. Reviewing such methods highlighted the potential and accuracy of unobtrusive techniques for emotion recognition.

### 4.2. Engagement

We included a total of seven studies focusing on measuring engagement in our review. In the reviewed studies, engagement was most often investigated via its manifestation through facial expressions [47–52] and posture [47,48]. Manifestation through hand gestures [47], upper-body motion [53], gaze estimation, and head rotation [52] was also investigated. Accordingly, the most commonly used sensor in these studies was an RGB camera [47,49,50,52], followed by a microphone array [48], wearables with inertial sensors [51], and a depth camera [53].

Ashwin et al. [47] investigated student engagement unobtrusively using an RGB camera. They utilized various features derived from facial expressions, hand gestures, and posture. Employing a convolutional neural network, they classified engagement into four categories, achieving a classification accuracy of 71%. Similarly, Whitehill et al. [49] investigated student engagement using an RGB camera and features based on facial expressions. They tested various ML approaches, and their binary classification algorithm (high vs. low engagement) achieved a classification accuracy comparable to human annotators. The most discriminating feature referred to the in-plane rotation of the face, which was negatively associated with high engagement. The second most discriminating feature referred to the raising of the upper lip (positive correlation with engagement), followed by the features referring to the raising of the inner brow and eye closure (negative correlation with engagement). Aslan et al. [50] proposed another approach using an RGB camera to infer student engagement based on facial expressions. In addition to video data, the approach incorporated student-specific performance data. The authors introduced a platform for monitoring student engagement to aid teachers in making their teaching methods more engaging. The platform monitored engagement at both individual and group levels, proving to be a promising and beneficial tool in supporting teachers' roles.

Gao et al. [48] introduced another method for monitoring engagement using a device equipped with a speaker and a microphone array to track user engagement based on facial expressions and emotional gestures (i.e., hand gestures that accompany emotions). The signals emitted by the speaker, also included in the setup, are near-ultrasound (16 kHz to 20 kHz). The signal is directed toward the user's face and upper body, and the reflected echo is received by the microphone array, enabling unobtrusive and contact-free monitoring of the user.

A depth camera is also an effective sensor for monitoring engagement [53]. Huynh et al. demonstrated its use in inferring features related to upper-body motion. They described a protocol for predicting player engagement using data from a mobile phone, depth camera, and wristband. Besides upper-body motion, physiological data and touchscreen events were utilized to predict engagement. Evaluated across six different games, random forest (RF) emerged as the most promising ML approach among the ones investigated, achieving classification accuracies of 85% in cross-sample evaluation and 77% in cross-subject evaluation, thus successfully classifying player engagement into three categories.

As seen in previous studies, engagement can not only be monitored directly but also through inferring facial expressions. There is extensive work in this field, but given its indirect connection to engagement, we limit our review to only some of the most relevant ones that came up in our search. A study by Verma et al. [51] introduced a system for recognizing 32 facial action units using wearables with inertial sensors, achieving an accuracy of 89.9% using deep learning. Similarly, the work presented by Vedernikov et al. [52] used facial expressions to detect the engagement of participants during online meetings using non-contact sensors (i.e., an RGB camera and a remote pulse oximeter). Vedernikov et al. [52] used a fusion of various physiological and behavioral features to predict engagement, with the latter including facial expressions and motion features such as gaze tracking, gaze direction, eye landmarks, and head rotation. Using an ensemble of KNN and RF, their model predicted engagement with an accuracy of 96% when using the fusion of both types of features.

As outlined in the previous paragraphs, various methods and sensors are suitable for measuring and predicting engagement. However, most available studies focus on investigating engagement in specific scenarios (e.g., in the classroom or while watching a video clip), raising questions about the generalizability of these results to different contexts. This also prompts inquiry into the specificity of engagement as a construct, questioning whether employee engagement significantly differs from student engagement. Furthermore, most of the aforementioned studies focus on detecting behavioral engagement, focusing less on the emotional and cognitive aspects of it, therefore deviating slightly from our definition of engagement presented in Section 2. Nonetheless, the presented methods allow for the unobtrusive and comprehensive measurement of engagement, and they can be easily adapted for use in the workplace, making them relevant for the aim of this review.

### 4.3. Fatigue

Our search revealed that the literature often lacks clear distinctions between different types of fatigue. Additionally, there is sometimes a poor distinction between different constructs, e.g., mental fatigue, cognitive load, and effort. We reviewed two studies that focused on measuring and/or predicting mental fatigue using unobtrusive sensors. The methods used relied on an analysis of blinking behavior, namely the blink rate, duration, pupil measurement, gaze point, etc. [54]. Another relevant method found in the literature relied on an analysis of breathing frequency and respiratory cycle duration [55]. The sensors used in these works were an eye tracker [54] and a radar [55].

Li et al. [54] investigated the accuracy of various ML approaches in predicting the mental fatigue of construction industry operators. They used eye-movement data obtained with a wearable eye tracker and self-report questionnaires as ground truth for training the models. The proposed approach resulted in the highly accurate classification (accuracies between 79.5% and 85.0%) of operators' mental fatigue into three distinct categories. Among the evaluated methods, support vector machine (SVM) and linear discriminant analysis (LDA) yielded the most accurate results.

Furthermore, Turetskaya et al. [55] investigated the differences in respiratory patterns detected by two radars under different conditions: resting state and mental fatigue/effort. Although the study did not directly investigate mental fatigue, the proposed methods remain relevant for exploring it, provided they are appropriately adapted. The authors of [55] used bioradiolocation, a non-contact radar method for detecting organisms, to gather data. Their study concluded that significant differences in breathing patterns exist between the two conditions, making the proposed method suitable for detecting respiratory pattern changes due to mental effort.

Our search revealed a variety of unobtrusive methods available for measuring mental fatigue, as summarized in the previous paragraphs. However, there is a poor distinction between the different types of fatigue. Many studies from our initial keyword search focused on physical fatigue [56] or driver fatigue/drowsiness [57,58]. Adão Martins et al. [29] conducted a literature review on monitoring fatigue using wearable sensors and similarly found a low number of studies investigating mental fatigue (8 out of 59). These studies spanned various domains such as healthcare and transportation, using diverse fatigue-inducing tasks and types of input data, achieving generally good model performance.

### 4.4. Stress

Stress is a construct often present in the literature, and there are three main methods used to measure stress [59]: self-reports, either using standardized questionnaires, interviews, or diaries; observational methods of behavior and emotional expressions; and measurements of physiological correlates.

Stress physiology has been of central importance ever since the introduction of the term [60] and plays an important role in automatic stress detection (see related reviews [61–65]), especially since it is seen as an objective measure of stress. As such, we can reduce the problem of unobtrusive stress monitoring to the non-intrusive detection of vital signs. As a good example of an overview of one such technique, namely millimeter-wave sensing technologies, we refer the reader to the work of Wu et al. [66]. However, using physiological markers to monitor stress is often affected by motion artifacts, making it challenging to implement in workplace settings [65].

Due to the limitations of the unobtrusive monitoring of physiological signals described in Section 1, in this work, we focus instead on behavioral manifestations of stress, which are crucial, since they can mediate affective and physiological responses [59]. They are often framed in terms of coping with stress and thus alleviating it, but some dysfunctional behaviors, such as drinking, smoking, or aggressive behaviors, can even exacerbate stress. Behavioral stress responses have received less attention in stress detection studies (see [61]) but lend themselves well to unobtrusive monitoring. In fact, observational methods are widely used by psychologists when studying the stress responses of very young children and adults with cognitive impairments. When traditional pen-and-paper techniques are employed for this purpose, observation is an expensive and time-consuming method. This highlights the motivation for developing unobtrusive and automatic monitoring methods for behavioral stress responses.

We identified three studies that approached stress detection by unobtrusively observing people's behaviors. The reviewed studies employed a variety of methods, relying on body movements [67], activity information [68], communication patterns, phone usage, and location [69]. The sensors used included a millimeter-wave sensor [67], a WiFi-based localization system [68], and a smartphone [69].

Using a millimeter-wave sensor, Ha et al. [67] implemented a system to monitor stress in a contact-free manner. Their approach was based on both physiological signals and behavioral markers. Besides measuring heart rate variability and breathing rate, they also included body movements as features that captured activities such as shaking the leg or stretching the neck. These features were described by the movement intensity, number of high-activity occurrences, and mean intensity of high activity. Motion features were used alongside heartbeat interval and respiratory features to predict stress levels. This approach allowed for a classification of stress into three classes, reaching a median accuracy of over 84% when trained and tested across different subjects. Zakaria et al. [68] made use of a passive WiFi-based localization system to track students' locations and the presence of other people. With these features, they heuristically mapped the locations to activities, broadly classified into work, non-work, and group activities. In their main study, they compared the logistic regression (LR), SVM, and RF classifiers. Among the three classifiers, the latter achieved the highest area under the ROC curve (AUC) score of 0.97, demonstrating that activity information can be successfully used to differentiate between severely and normally stressed students. However, the subsequent validation study encountered numerous false positives, likely due to the low number of severely stressed participants. Nosakhare and Picard [69] used a mobile application in addition to a smartwatch to determine communication patterns (call and SMS exchanges), phone usage, and locations (time spent on campus, indoors, and outdoors). They used these features to uncover latent behavioral patterns using supervised latent Dirichlet allocation (sLDA), from which they were able to detect stress. Using sLDA, they were able to classify low vs. high stress levels with an accuracy of approximately 60%.

In the studies described, body movements, student activity derived from locations, phone usage, and communication patterns were all behaviors that were monitored and related to stress. It should be noted, however, that the relationship between stress and behavior is highly dependent on the population being studied. While predicting stress based on physiological signals could offer more opportunities for generalization, the same cannot be concluded for behavioral markers. For example, the features in [68,69] were developed with students as participants and would be difficult to generalize to other populations. Some behaviors, such as phone usage, might show more consistent patterns, while others, such as student activity derived from locations, are only applicable to the particular population with whom the method was developed. Thus, it is paramount to consider whether a feature or method is appropriate for the population or the culture it is employed in [59].

## 5. Physical Well-Being

### 5.1. Physical Comfort

Our search initially revealed several methods for the unobtrusive measurement of employee physical comfort. We discovered a high number of studies focusing on health monitoring and various physiological signals, but the prevalence of research specifically addressing employee physical comfort remained rather low. This resulted in a decrease in the number of relevant studies compared to the initial pool of identified studies. We included three studies that focused on measuring physical comfort in our review, even though one study only partially met our criteria for inclusion. Specifically, the method was not entirely non-contact, and its unobtrusiveness was not clear-cut.

Two of the reviewed studies used posture as a descriptor of physical comfort [31,70], and one study used repetitive strain injuries of the wrists and elbows [71]. The sensors used included inclinometers [70], an RGB camera [31], and resistive flex sensors [71].

Olsen et al. [70] proposed a system for monitoring the posture of dentists using three inclinometers positioned on the dentist's coat to ensure unobtrusiveness. The system required individual calibration and was assessed in a user study in which multiple ML algorithms were used for posture classification. The $k$-nearest neighbor (kNN) algorithm was reported as being the most suitable approach in terms of accuracy and other characteristics, namely simplicity and speed.

Chen et al. [31] proposed a system for monitoring the health and well-being of employees using an RGB camera, offering personalized recommendations to improve well-being and productivity. The system addressed multiple aspects of well-being, including posture. It utilized semi-Markov models to learn user behavior, habits, and preferences, after which ergonomic recommendations were given. Consisting of two layers, the model incorporated the influence of contextual information on the current states, thereby improving its ability to accurately identify user behavior and deliver more relevant recommendations.

Lastly, Wac et al. [71] proposed a prototype for monitoring and assessing users' hand and elbow movements to prevent repetitive strain injuries, which are increasingly common due to the rise in office work. Three resistive flex sensors were implemented in a sleeve—two of them on the wrist and one on the elbow. Although this was only preliminary work, the initial evaluation showed that 91% of users would use the system again. Although the system was not non-contact, as it was implemented in a sleeve, its obtrusiveness can be debated.

Nevertheless, due to its high relevance to the context of knowledge workers, we include it in our review.

In summary, there are few studies investigating the measurement of employee physical comfort, as outlined in the previous paragraphs. Despite not being entirely unobtrusive, the presented methods are beneficial for measuring the physical comfort of knowledge workers.

### 5.2. Sleep Deprivation

Among the articles initially identified, eight were relevant. The reviewed studies mainly focused on detecting a lack of sleep, either as micro-sleep events or drowsiness during a specific activity [57,72–74]. This was often measured through eye blinking [72–75], facial expressions with an emphasis on yawning [72–74], and nodding [74]. For these manifestations, an RGB camera was the most utilized sensor. Despite our focus on behavioral markers, we included studies that complement them with physiological signals due to their high relevance, similar to the approach taken in Section 4.1.

Jan et al. [72] developed a method for detecting driver drowsiness, in which they recorded ten drivers with two RGB cameras—one facing the driver and the other facing the road. They concluded that the behaviors that can define a driver's behavior or drowsiness are closing the eyes (for at least 3 s), turning the head or distractions, yawning, using a smartphone, crossing lanes, and being too close to another car. Their approach, evaluated using jackknife cross-validation, resulted in a mean accuracy of 88.75%.

Next, Soleymanpour et al. [57] compared behavior to physiological signals for detecting driver drowsiness. They monitored metrics like the percentage of eyelid closure (PERCLOS) and sleepiness ratings via the Karolinska Sleepiness Scale (KSS) and observed yawning and head movements with a front RGB camera. Additionally, they used a Neuro-Bio Monitor (NBM) to detect driver drowsiness using non-intrusive sensors located in the headrest. The NBM detects the brain's electromagnetic field from neuronal activity and detects fatigue thresholds by analyzing the ratio of theta and alpha to beta brainwave activity. In the evaluations, the authors achieved an accuracy of 78.79% and a detection rate of 95% compared to the KSS. The NBM also exhibited trends similar to the PERCLOS and blink-duration measurements, indicating the comparable performance of behavioral markers and physiological signals. In the study, eye-tracking glasses were utilized to measure the PERCLOS, which raises concerns about the method's unobtrusiveness. However, we included this study in our review due to its potential for adaptation to a less intrusive approach. Additionally, the other behavioral markers examined were derived using unobtrusive methods, ensuring the overall relevance and applicability of the findings to the focus of our review.

Yamamoto et al. [75] introduced a novel method for estimating blink duration using a Doppler sensor, which is a device that uses the Doppler effect to measure the velocity and movement of objects based on changes in frequency or wavelength, and spectrogram analysis, focusing on the dynamics of eyelid movement. The method detects eyelid movements using Doppler-shifted microwaves, avoiding the privacy and low-light issues of camera-based systems. The system uses a Doppler sensor to monitor the speed and direction of eyelid movements, with the blink duration estimated from the timing differences between the onset of eyelid-closing and eyelid-opening energies on the spectrogram. The method successfully detected drowsiness, achieving an average root mean squared error (RMSE) of 49.3 milliseconds across the tests.

Zhang et al. [73] proposed another method for detecting driver drowsiness using second-order blind identification, relying on smartphone-based videos. This method simultaneously separates multiple physiological sources, such as blood volume pulse, and certain behaviors, such as eye blinks and yawning, directly from facial video streams without needing detailed localization of the eyes or mouth. Additionally, by analyzing these separated signals in parallel, driver drowsiness is determined. The research confirmed that integrating multiple physiological signals and behaviors using this method effectively enhances the accuracy and reliability of drowsiness detection.

Another method combining behavioral markers and physiological signals was introduced by Kundinger et al. [74], who utilized an RGB camera to obtain data on micro-sleep events and observer ratings to assess driver drowsiness. Trained observers analyzed video recordings to rate the driver's level of drowsiness on a six-item scale based on facial expressions and visible behaviors such as eye closure and nodding off. Concurrently, micro-sleep events were identified using an image-processing method when the driver's eyes closed for at least one second, indicating significant lapses in attention. The observer ratings and detected micro-sleep events were then combined into an assessment of the drowsiness level of each participant. Additionally, heart rate data was collected from wrist-worn sensors and an electrocardiogram. Using the assessment of the drowsiness level as ground truth, a binary classification of drowsiness (drowsy vs. not drowsy) was performed based on physiological signals. A range of classifiers, including RF, random tree, decision stump, decision table, and $k$-nearest neighbor, were compared for developing both person-specific and person-independent models. The results indicated that the person-specific models generally achieved higher accuracy, with some classifiers reaching approximately 90%. This suggests that tailoring models to individual users can significantly enhance classification performance, highlighting the importance of personalized approaches in achieving optimal accuracy.

Our review of methods for the unobtrusive measurement of sleep deprivation revealed a lack of diversity in studies that focus on this construct. The majority of articles identified in the initial search predominantly examined sleep quality recorded during the night. These methods cannot be directly applied to the workplace environment because they would not be relevant, as people do not sleep during work hours. Therefore, we decided not to include such studies in our review. Moreover, a large body of literature on driver drowsiness was examined, which primarily involved recording participants for any signs of sleepiness or drowsiness. These findings are promising for potential application to workplace research, suggesting that similar methods could be adapted to measure employee alertness.

## 6. Social Well-Being

*Social Interactions*

From the initial search, six studies were found to be relevant, as they focused on using unobtrusive sensors to track and record social interactions. All of the reviewed studies utilized microphones to record different types of interactions. The reviewed studies predominantly focused on detecting spoken conversations and analyzing aspects such as their content and duration [76–78], frequency [79], and the frequency of different content categories [79]. Moreover, some studies investigated texting and calling, where the frequency and duration of calls [80,81] and the number of texts [81] were recorded. Consequently, the two devices most often used were microphones [76–79] and smartphones [80,81].

Tan et al. [79] investigated team communication as a measure of cohesion in preformed League of Legends teams. Using the microphones in participants' smartphones, they recorded voice communication and analyzed two measures: communication frequency (words per minute) and category frequency (instances per category per minute). Categories included commands, suggestions, disagreements, social interactions, encouragement, and emotional expressions. The results indicated that word frequency and the sequence of communication categories could serve as proxies for team cohesion, with social interactions emerging as the key predictor.

Jo et al. [77] developed an application called MAMAS for monitoring parent–child mealtime conversations and food intake. The MAMAS app records a dialogue between a parent and child using the phone's microphone and creates an analysis report based on the interactions, using speech recognition software and a self-report survey. Bi et al. [78] similarly used microphones, among other sensors, to log conversations and other activities during family mealtimes.

Shash et al. [76] extracted voice conversations from the phone's microphone data and used them to infer the duration of students' social interactions during the day and to assess their behavioral patterns involving smartphones.

Furthermore, in the study by Sefidgar et al. [80], social interactions were tracked using phone call data to understand the short-term behavioral impact of discrimination. The researchers analyzed the number and duration of incoming, outgoing, and missed calls, leveraging these metrics as one of the indicators of social support and interactions.

Similarly, Maxhumi et al. [81] used smartphones to continuously record and classify human voice interactions and to analyze phone call logs and SMS logs. They examined the number, duration, and frequency of calls and messages to investigate their correlation with perceived stress levels, aiming to enhance stress prediction models based on objective smartphone data.

In summary, our review identified many studies that focused on detecting and logging social interactions, predominantly using (smartphone) microphones. These studies employed various methods, such as analyzing voice conversations, phone call data, and SMS (text message) logs to infer social behaviors and psychological states. Despite the diversity in the methods, the (smartphone) microphone consistently proved to be a crucial tool, helping achieve state-of-the-art performance in these studies. It is important to note, however, that some of the approaches discussed are still in the early stages of development. Additionally, the complexity and diversity of social interactions make this area of research particularly challenging. As a result, providing a straightforward overview of the algorithms and methods employed was not always feasible. These challenges highlight the need for continued investigation in this field to better understand and model social dynamics. Furthermore, our review found no studies that specifically addressed the detection of social interactions in the workplace, but the approaches discussed could be adapted and applied in the context of the workplace.

## 7. Privacy-Aware Sensing

Data privacy has long been a primary concern in mobile sensing systems, as the use of unobtrusive sensing technologies, such as video and audio data collection methods, can significantly intrude on users' privacy [82]. One of the main issues is that, despite their convenience, physically unobtrusive technologies often collect personal and sensitive data, such as video and audio recordings. For the purpose of analyzing well-being in research, users are typically more willing to participate in controlled studies but may hesitate when asked to participate in field studies. Thus, to develop a well-being measurement approach that users are likely to accept, experimenters must establish trust through the implementation of robust privacy measures. A critical first step in ensuring privacy is risk assessment, which identifies the primary risks and vulnerabilities of sensing systems and guides the prioritization of privacy measures. These measures typically require ad hoc customization, as privacy is both user- and context-dependent, meaning that what one user considers private may not be a concern for another [83,84]. To improve user privacy, particularly in safeguarding third parties, several methods have been developed, including statistical and ML approaches, to automatically detect privacy-sensitive situations and ensure that only users with valid consent are sensed. These techniques also allow users to set their preferences regarding when sensing occurs, such as only during video calls or when actively using the device. Privacy-sensitive situations can be detected using methods like identifying sensitive scenes in videos (e.g., bathrooms) [85,86], sound shredding or subsampling for audio [87], and applying differential privacy [88] to eye-tracking data [88, 89]. In recent years, privacy-by-design approaches have also included deep learning-based strategies, such as encoding raw data in non-interpretable, low-dimensional representations (known as embeddings) or using federated learning [90], where user data is stored in model weights rather than in raw format. This ensures that user identification remains infeasible even when data is processed by state-of-the-art deep learning technologies.

## 8. Proposed Setup

As highlighted in the previous sections, a variety of methods exist for measuring different sub-dimensions of well-being. Based on our analysis of the most common methods, we chose the most frequent ones from Table 2 that would be suitable for measuring well-being in the workplace without interfering with the employee's work. The most suitable setup is presented in Figure 3. It is composed of an RGB camera with a microphone, an eye tracker, and a radar. The RGB camera and microphone can be utilized to measure engagement, physical comfort, sleep deprivation, social interactions, and affect. The eye tracker and radar can be utilized to measure fatigue. Furthermore, collecting data from the individual's smartphone should be included with the aim of measuring stress.

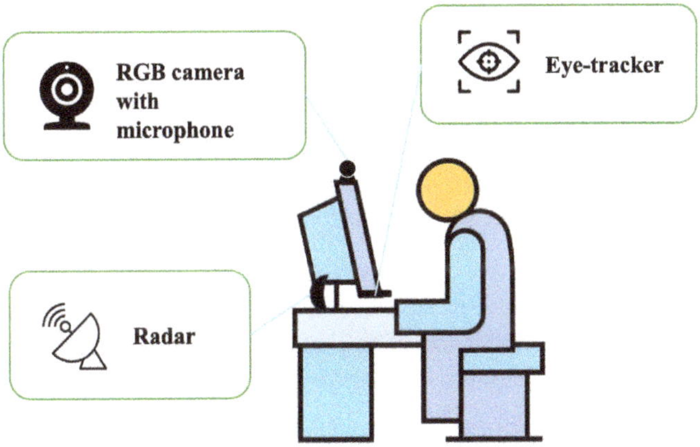


**Figure 3.** Proposed setup for the unobtrusive measurement of work-related well-being.

**Table 2.** Framework for inferring work-related well-being from behavior.

| Sub-Dimension | Behavioral Marker | Sensors | Relevant Literature |
|---|---|---|---|
| Affect | Facial expressions | RGB camera, microphone | [34,35] |
| | Speech | Microphone | [34,37] |
| | Auricular positions | RGB camera | [38] |
| | Facial temperature changes | Thermal camera | [39] |
| | Eye movement and position | RGB camera, EOG signals | [45] |
| Engagement | Facial expressions | RGB camera, microphone array | [47–52] |
| | Posture | RGB camera, microphone array | [47,48] |
| | Hand gestures | RGB camera | [47] |
| | Upper-body motion | Depth camera | [53] |
| | Gaze tracking and direction | RGB camera | [52] |
| | Head rotation | RGB camera | [52] |

**Table 2.** *Cont.*

| Sub-Dimension | Behavioral Marker | Sensors | Relevant Literature |
|---|---|---|---|
| Fatigue | Eye movement | Eye tracker | [54] |
| | Respiratory pattern | Radar | [55] |
| Stress | Body movements | Millimeter-wave sensor | [67] |
| | Activity information | WiFi-based localization system | [68] |
| | Communication patterns | Smartphone | [69] |
| | Phone usage | Smartphone | [69] |
| | Location | Smartphone | [69] |
| Physical comfort | Posture | Inclinometer, RGB camera | [31,70] |
| | Hand and elbow movement | Wearable sleeve | [71] |
| Sleep deprivation | Eye blinking | RGB camera | [72–74] |
| | Distraction | RGB camera | [72] |
| | Yawning | RGB camera | [57,72–74] |
| | Head movement | RGB camera | [57,72] |
| | Blink duration | Doppler sensor | [75] |
| | Micro-sleep events | RGB camera | [74] |
| | Nodding | RGB camera | [74] |
| Social interactions | Communication frequency | Microphone | [79] |
| | Category frequency | Microphone | [79] |
| | Spoken conversations | Microphone | [77,78] |
| | Duration of interaction | Microphone | [76] |
| | Number and duration of phone calls | Smartphone | [80,81] |
| | Number of SMSs | Smartphone | [81] |

## 9. Discussion

As highlighted in this review, measuring work-related well-being using unobtrusive sensors is a promising field, yet it is still in its early stages of development. In this article, we aimed to provide a framework to guide research in this field. As outlined in Section 1, there is a lack of consensus among professionals regarding the definition of well-being [14], which is also often an issue in the broader field of ML in mental health [91]. Due to this gap, we decided to use the definition provided by the WHO [13] and refine it based on the relevant literature, as presented in Section 2. By explicitly defining what we mean by well-being and corroborating it with related works, we showed how insights from studies across various domains can be combined to contribute to the measurement of well-being. Our definition aims to provide a foundation for developing methods that effectively capture work-related well-being in a non-invasive manner, thereby advancing the field and improving practical applications in workplace settings.

The sensors and behavioral markers used to monitor each sub-dimension of well-being we defined are summarized in Table 2, illustrating various approaches used to infer well-being from behavior. The most commonly used sensors include different types of cameras (RGB, depth), microphones, and smartphones. These sensors capture a range of behavioral markers, with the most common being facial expressions, posture, and body movements.

There are several limitations of our work. Specifically, we did not follow robust guidelines for reporting systematic literature reviews, such as the PRISMA 2020 guidelines [92], which are widely used in the literature to ensure that systematic reviews are valuable, transparent, and complete. Although this might have influenced our analysis, adhering to these guidelines was challenging due to the lack of consensus regarding the definition of well-being and the scarcity of relevant articles. Consequently, we could not always strictly apply our inclusion criteria (see Section 3 above). We faced challenges regarding the unobtrusiveness of certain methods and included some older articles if we deemed them still highly relevant. While we focused on behavioral markers, many studies also included physiological signals. In those cases, we reported both to give a complete picture, which sometimes made it difficult to highlight the specific impact of behavioral markers. Additionally, workplace-specific studies were limited, so we examined studies from other settings that could be adapted to the context of knowledge workers.

Thieme et al. [91] pointed out that most studies in the field of ML in mental health are proof-of-concept studies that "focus on technical or algorithmic development of (initial) ML models" ([91], p. 21). The same can be said of the studies included in our review. This means that the insights should be considered preliminary and are not necessarily immediately applicable to real-world scenarios.

Another challenge in the field of unobtrusive well-being measuring is that, to the best of our knowledge, most studies tend to investigate only specific aspects of the construct, rarely approaching it in a holistic manner. Given that well-being consists of a broad range of states [93], this narrow focus may overlook important dimensions that contribute to its comprehensive understanding. Adopting a more holistic approach could potentially lead to a more accurate and complete measurement of the construct, capturing the full spectrum of factors that influence it.

## 10. Conclusions

Our review is an initial attempt to explore existing methods for measuring work-related well-being in an unobtrusive, privacy-aware, and holistic manner. Despite the challenges posed by an ill-defined and complex field, as mentioned above, we provide an overview of possible approaches for addressing this issue. Our findings suggest that a wide variety of methods can provide insight into well-being without disrupting daily work activities.

However, the field remains in an early stage, with most studies focusing on isolated well-being components (e.g., stress or fatigue), often within narrow experimental contexts. Current research, therefore, rarely approaches well-being holistically, which limits its applicability to real-world organizational settings. With our review, we hope to facilitate the establishment of integrated, multi-dimensional frameworks and cross-disciplinary collaboration between psychology and computer science. Future work in this field should aim to validate existing methods and approaches across diverse contexts, with the aim of making them more applicable and generalizable. Furthermore, diverse cultural backgrounds should also be considered. More longitudinal studies would also be beneficial for obtaining a more in-depth understanding of the studied constructs.

In terms of broader implications, our work provides a framework that can guide the future development of mature, privacy-aware, and unobtrusive systems, as this could facilitate the early detection (and possible prevention) of decline in employee well-being. Considering the unobtrusiveness of the proposed framework, our approach could also be extended to studies involving vulnerable populations, such as individuals with physical, cognitive, or other disabilities. Because the framework and the proposed setup rely on unobtrusive sensing that does not require active user participation or the wearing of any devices, it is particularly well-suited for populations who may have reduced mobility or increased sensitivity to monitoring technologies. Therefore, this approach can facilitate the inclusive research of vulnerable populations and enable well-being assessment in contexts where traditional methods may be impractical or ethically problematic. Future studies are necessary, however, to explore how such unobtrusive methods can be tailored to accommodate the specific needs of various populations.

Our work also lays the foundation for applications in the increasingly common context of remote work. Naturally, such applications require careful ethical consideration to avoid the risk of worker exploitation or excessive pressure to boost productivity. Nonetheless, they have the potential to enhance employee well-being, particularly in remote settings where supervisors have limited direct contact and insight into workers' mental (and physical) states due to reduced direct contact. This underscores the value of unobtrusive sensing technologies, which can support the remote monitoring of well-being without being invasive. Recent studies, such as [94], have demonstrated how sensors can be integrated into home environments for non-intrusive monitoring. Although applied primarily in clinical populations, such studies indicate promising directions for future applications.

To conclude, by laying this foundation, we aim to facilitate further research into unobtrusive and user-centric well-being measurement methods. As workplace well-being becomes an increasingly critical concern for both employees and employers, scalable technological solutions will be essential for fostering sustainable and healthy work environments.

**Author Contributions:** Conceptualization, Z.A., K.Ž. and J.L.; methodology, Z.A., K.Ž. and J.L.; validation, J.L.; investigation, Z.A., K.Ž. and J.L.; writing—original draft preparation, Z.A., K.Ž., J.L. and P.B.; writing—review and editing, P.B., G.S., M.L. (Mohan Li), M.G., M.E.D., S.T., M.L. (Mitja Luštrek) and M.L. (Marc Langheinrich); visualization, Z.A. and J.L.; supervision, M.L. (Mitja Luštrek) and M.L. (Marc Langheinrich); project administration, P.B., G.S., M.G., M.L. (Mitja Luštrek) and M.L. (Marc Langheinrich); funding acquisition, J.L., P.B., G.S., M.G., M.L. (Mitja Luštrek) and M.L. (Marc Langheinrich). All authors have read and agreed to the published version of the manuscript.

**Funding:** This study was funded by the TRUST-ME project, jointly supported by the Swiss National Science Foundation (SNSF) (grant agreement 205121L_214991) and the Slovenian Agency of Research and Innovation (ARIS) (grant agreement N1-0319). Dr. Gjoreski's work was funded by the SNSF through the XAI-PAC project (PZ00P2_216405).

**Institutional Review Board Statement:** Not applicable.

**Data Availability Statement:** No new data were created, as this is a review study.

**Conflicts of Interest:** The authors declare no conflicts of interest.

## Abbreviations

The following abbreviations are used in this manuscript:

| | |
|---|---|
| APA | American Psychological Association |
| ML | machine learning |
| PERCLOS | percentage of eyelid closure |
| RGB | red, green, and blue |
| WHO | World Health Organisation |

## Appendix A

**Table A1.** Keywords used in paper selection.

| Sub-Dimension | Keywords Used |
|---|---|
| Physical comfort | ("comfort" OR "physical comfort") AND (("unobtrusive" OR "non-contact" OR "contact-free" OR "contact free") AND ("sensors" OR "sensing")) |
| Sleep deprivation | ("sleepiness" OR "sleep deprivation") AND (("unobtrusive" OR "non-contact" OR "contact-free" OR "contact free") AND ("sensors" OR "sensing")) |
| Engagement | ("engagement") AND (("unobtrusive" OR "non-contact" OR "contact-free" OR "contact free") AND ("sensors" OR "sensing")) |
| Affect | ("emotions" OR "emotion" OR "affect" OR "affects") AND (("unobtrusive" OR "non-contact" OR "contact-free" OR "contact free") AND ("sensors" OR "sensing")) AND ("review" OR "literature review" OR "survey") |
| Fatigue | ("fatigue") AND (("unobtrusive" OR "non-contact" OR "contact-free" OR "contact free") AND ("sensors" OR "sensing")) |
| Stress | ("stress") AND (("unobtrusive" OR "non-contact" OR "contact-free" OR "contact free") AND ("sensors" OR "sensing")) AND ("review" OR "literature review" OR "survey") |
| Social interactions | ("social interaction" OR "social relations" OR "relationships") AND (("unobtrusive" OR "non-contact" OR "contact-free" OR "contact free") AND ("sensors" OR "sensing")) |

## References


1. American Psychological Association. Well-being. In *APA Dictionary of Psychology*; American Psychological Association: Washington, DC, USA, 2018.
2. Wijngaards, I.; King, O.C.; Burger, M.J.; van Exel, J. Worker well-being: What it is, and how it should be measured. *Appl. Res. Qual. Life* **2021**, *17*, 795–832. [CrossRef]
3. Grawitch, M.; Gottschalk, M.; Munz, D. The Path to a Healthy Workplace A Critical Review Linking Healthy Workplace Practices, Employee Well-being, and Organizational Improvements. *Consult. Psychol. J. Pract. Res.* **2006**, *58*, 129–147. [CrossRef]
4. Isham, A.; Mair, S.; Jackson, T. Worker wellbeing and productivity in advanced economies: Re-examining the link. *Ecol. Econ.* **2021**, *184*, 106989. [CrossRef]
5. Pradhan, R.K.; Hati, L. The Measurement of Employee Well-being: Development and Validation of a Scale. *Glob. Bus. Rev.* **2022**, *23*, 385–407. [CrossRef]
6. Czerw, A. Diagnosing Well-Being in Work Context—Eudemonic Well-Being in the Workplace Questionnaire. *Curr. Psychol.* **2019**, *38*, 331–346. [CrossRef]
7. Chari, R.; Sauter, S.L.; Petrun Sayers, E.L.; Huang, W.; Fisher, G.G.; Chang, C.C. Development of the National Institute for Occupational Safety and Health Worker Well-Being Questionnaire. *J. Occup. Environ. Med.* **2022**, *64*, 707–717. [CrossRef]
8. Guo, Y.; Liu, X.; Peng, S.; Jiang, X.; Xu, K.; Chen, C.; Wang, Z.; Dai, C.; Chen, W. A review of wearable and unobtrusive sensing technologies for chronic disease management. *Comput. Biol. Med.* **2021**, *129*, 104163. [CrossRef]
9. Slapničar, G.; Wang, W.; Luštrek, M. Feasibility of Remote Blood Pressure Estimation via Narrow-band Multi-wavelength Pulse Transit Time. *ACM Trans. Sen. Netw.* **2024**, *20*, 77. [CrossRef]
10. Carucci, K.; Toyama, K. Making Well-being: Exploring the Role of Makerspaces in Long Term Care Facilities. In Proceedings of the 2019 CHI Conference on Human Factors in Computing Systems, Glasgow, UK, 4–9 May 2019; CHI '19, pp. 1–12. [CrossRef]
11. Ola, O.; Harrington, B. Exploring Lightweight Practices to Support Students' Well-being. In Proceedings of the 53rd ACM Technical Symposium on Computer Science Education V. 2, Providence, RI, USA, 3–5 March 2022; SIGCSE 2022; pp. 1070–1071. [CrossRef]
12. Wallace, B.; Larivière-Chartier, J.; Liu, H.; Sloan, T.; Goubran, R.; Knoefel, F. Frequency Response of a Novel IR Based Pressure Sensitive Mat for Well-being Assessment. In Proceedings of the 2020 IEEE 20th International Conference on Bioinformatics and Bioengineering (BIBE), Cincinnati, OH, USA, 26–28 October 2020; pp. 481–486. [CrossRef]
13. World Health Organization. *Constitution of the World Health Organization*; World Health Organization: Geneva, Switzerland, 1995.
14. Dodge, R.; Daly, A.; Huyton, J.; Sanders, L. The challenge of defining wellbeing. *Int. J. Wellbeing* **2012**, *2*, 222–235. [CrossRef]
15. Diener, E. Subjective well-being. *Psychol. Bull.* **1984**, *95*, 542. [CrossRef]
16. Fisher, C. Conceptualizing and Measuring Wellbeing at Work. In *Work and Wellbeing*; Wiley Blackwell: Hoboken, NJ, USA, 2014; pp. 1–25. [CrossRef]
17. Sonnentag, S. Dynamics of well-being. *Annu. Rev. Organ. Psychol. Organ. Behav.* **2015**, *2*, 261–293. [CrossRef]
18. Ryff, C.D.; Keyes, C.L.M. The structure of psychological well-being revisited. *J. Personal. Soc. Psychol.* **1995**, *69*, 719. [CrossRef] [PubMed]
19. Ryff, C.D. Happiness is everything, or is it? Explorations on the meaning of psychological well-being. *J. Personal. Soc. Psychol.* **1989**, *57*, 1069. [CrossRef]
20. Russell, J. A Circumplex Model of Affect. *J. Personal. Soc. Psychol.* **1980**, *39*, 1161–1178. [CrossRef]
21. Bakker, A.B.; Demerouti, E. Towards a model of work engagement. *Career Dev. Int.* **2008**, *13*, 209–223. [CrossRef]
22. American Psychological Association. Stress. In *APA Dictionary of Psychology*; American Psychological Association: Washington, DC, USA, 2018.
23. Seligman, M.E. Positive health. *Appl. Psychol.* **2008**, *57*, 3–18. [CrossRef]
24. Kölsch, M.; Beall, A.C.; Turk, M. An objective measure for postural comfort. In *Proceedings of the Human Factors and Ergonomics Society Annual Meeting*; SAGE Publications Sage CA: Los Angeles, CA, USA, 2003; Volume 47, pp. 725–728.
25. Orzeł-Gryglewska, J. Consequences of sleep deprivation. *Int. J. Occup. Med. Environ. Health* **2010**, *23*, 95–114. [CrossRef]
26. Pressman, S.D.; Kraft, T.; Bowlin, S., Well-Being: Physical, Psychological, Social. In *Encyclopedia of Behavioral Medicine*; Gellman, M.D., Turner, J.R., Eds.; Springer: New York, NY, USA, 2013; pp. 2047–2052. [CrossRef]
27. American Psychological Association. Social interaction. In *APA Dictionary of Psychology*; American Psychological Association: Washington, DC, USA, 2018.
28. Sun, J.; Harris, K.; Vazire, S. Is well-being associated with the quantity and quality of social interactions? *J. Personal. Soc. Psychol.* **2020**, *119*, 1478. [CrossRef]
29. Adão Martins, N.R.; Annaheim, S.; Spengler, C.M.; Rossi, R.M. Fatigue Monitoring Through Wearables: A State-of-the-Art Review. *Front. Physiol.* **2021**, *12*, 790292. [CrossRef]
30. Salama, W.; Abdou, A.H.; Mohamed, S.A.K.; Shehata, H.S. Impact of Work Stress and Job Burnout on Turnover Intentions among Hotel Employees. *Int. J. Environ. Res. Public Health* **2022**, *19*, 9724. [CrossRef]

31. Chen, C.W.; Määttä, T.; Wong, K.B.Y.; Aghajan, H. A collaborative framework for ergonomic feedback using smart cameras. In Proceedings of the 2012 Sixth International Conference on Distributed Smart Cameras (ICDSC), Hong Kong, China, 30 October–2 November 2012; pp. 1–6.
32. Forrester, N. How better sleep can improve productivity. *Nature* **2023**, *619*, 659–661. [CrossRef] [PubMed]
33. Dutton, J.E. *Energize Your Workplace: How to Create and Sustain High-Quality Connections at Work*; John Wiley & Sons: Hoboken, NJ, USA, 2003; Volume 5.
34. Braun, M.; Weber, F.; Alt, F. Affective Automotive User Interfaces–Reviewing the State of Driver Affect Research and Emotion Regulation in the Car. *ACM Comput. Surv.* **2021**, *54*, 137. [CrossRef]
35. Gong, J.; Zhang, X.; Huang, Y.; Ren, J.; Zhang, Y. Robust Inertial Motion Tracking through Deep Sensor Fusion across Smart Earbuds and Smartphone. *Proc. ACM Interact. Mob. Wearable Ubiquitous Technol.* **2021**, *5*, 62. [CrossRef]
36. Röddiger, T.; Clarke, C.; Breitling, P.; Schneegans, T.; Zhao, H.; Gellersen, H.; Beigl, M. Sensing with Earables: A Systematic Literature Review and Taxonomy of Phenomena. *Proc. ACM Interact. Mob. Wearable Ubiquitous Technol.* **2022**, *6*, 135. [CrossRef]
37. Jones, C.; Jonsson, I.M., Using Paralinguistic Cues in Speech to Recognise Emotions in Older Car Drivers. In *Affect and Emotion in Human-Computer Interaction: From Theory to Applications*; Peter, C., Beale, R., Eds.; Springer: Berlin/Heidelberg, Germany, 2008; pp. 229–240. [CrossRef]
38. Huang, D.Y.; Seyed, T.; Li, L.; Gong, J.; Yao, Z.; Jiao, Y.; Chen, X.A.; Yang, X.D. Orecchio: Extending Body-Language through Actuated Static and Dynamic Auricular Postures. In Proceedings of the 31st Annual ACM Symposium on User Interface Software and Technology, Berlin, Germany, 14 October 2018; UIST '18; pp. 697–710. [CrossRef]
39. Abdelrahman, Y.; Schmidt, A. Beyond the visible: Sensing with thermal imaging. *Interactions* **2018**, *26*, 76–78. [CrossRef]
40. Nocera, A.; Senigagliesi, L.; Raimondi, M.; Ciattaglia, G.; Gambi, E. Machine learning in radar-based physiological signals sensing: A scoping review of the models, datasets and metrics. *IEEE Access* **2024**, *12*, 156082–156117. [CrossRef]
41. Koelstra, S.; Muhl, C.; Soleymani, M.; Lee, J.S.; Yazdani, A.; Ebrahimi, T.; Pun, T.; Nijholt, A.; Patras, I. DEAP: A Database for Emotion Analysis; Using Physiological Signals. *IEEE Trans. Affect. Comput.* **2012**, *3*, 18–31. [CrossRef]
42. Stampf, A.; Colley, M.; Rukzio, E. Towards Implicit Interaction in Highly Automated Vehicles—A Systematic Literature Review. *Proc. ACM Hum.-Comput. Interact.* **2022**, *6*, 191. [CrossRef]
43. Jones, C.; Sutherland, J. Acoustic Emotion Recognition for Affective Computer Gaming. In *Affect and Emotion in Human-Computer Interaction: From Theory to Applications*; Peter, C., Beale, R., Eds.; Springer: Berlin/Heidelberg, Germany, 2008; pp. 209–219. [CrossRef]
44. Dunne, R.; Morris, T.; Harper, S. A Survey of Ambient Intelligence. *ACM Comput. Surv.* **2021**, *54*, 73. [CrossRef]
45. Soundariya, R.; Renuga, R. Eye movement based emotion recognition using electrooculography. In Proceedings of the 2017 Innovations in Power and Advanced Computing Technologies (i-PACT), Vellore, India, 21–22 April 2017; pp. 1–5. [CrossRef]
46. Zeng, K.; Liu, G. Emotion recognition based on millimeter wave radar. In Proceedings of the 2023 3rd International Conference on Bioinformatics and Intelligent Computing, Sanya, China, 10–12 February 2023; BIC '23; pp. 232–236. [CrossRef]
47. Ashwin, T.S.; Guddeti, R.M.R. Unobtrusive Behavioral Analysis of Students in Classroom Environment Using Non-Verbal Cues. *IEEE Access* **2019**, *7*, 150693–150709. [CrossRef]
48. Gao, Y.; Jin, Y.; Choi, S.; Li, J.; Pan, J.; Shu, L.; Zhou, C.; Jin, Z. SonicFace: Tracking Facial Expressions Using a Commodity Microphone Array. *Proc. ACM Interact. Mob. Wearable Ubiquitous Technol.* **2021**, *5*, 156. [CrossRef]
49. Whitehill, J.; Serpell, Z.; Lin, Y.C.; Foster, A.; Movellan, J.R. The Faces of Engagement: Automatic Recognition of Student Engagementfrom Facial Expressions. *IEEE Trans. Affect. Comput.* **2014**, *5*, 86–98. [CrossRef]
50. Aslan, S.; Alyuz, N.; Tanriover, C.; Mete, S.E.; Okur, E.; D'Mello, S.K.; Arslan Esme, A. Investigating the Impact of a Real-time, Multimodal Student Engagement Analytics Technology in Authentic Classrooms. In Proceedings of the 2019 CHI Conference on Human Factors in Computing Systems, Glasgow, UK, 4–9 May 2019; CHI '19; pp. 1–12. [CrossRef]
51. Verma, D.; Bhalla, S.; Sahnan, D.; Shukla, J.; Parnami, A. ExpressEar: Sensing Fine-Grained Facial Expressions with Earables. *Proc. ACM Interact. Mob. Wearable Ubiquitous Technol.* **2021**, *5*, 129. [CrossRef]
52. Vedernikov, A.; Sun, Z.; Kykyri, V.L.; Pohjola, M.; Nokia, M.; Li, X. Analyzing Participants' Engagement during Online Meetings Using Unsupervised Remote Photoplethysmography with Behavioral Features. In Proceedings of the 2024 IEEE/CVF Conference on Computer Vision and Pattern Recognition Workshops (CVPRW), Seattle, WA, USA, 17–18 June 2024; pp. 389–399. [CrossRef]
53. Huynh, S.; Kim, S.; Ko, J.; Balan, R.K.; Lee, Y. EngageMon: Multi-Modal Engagement Sensing for Mobile Games. *Proc. ACM Interact. Mob. Wearable Ubiquitous Technol.* **2018**, *2*, 13. [CrossRef]
54. Li, J.; Li, H.; Umer, W.; Wang, H.; Xing, X.; Zhao, S.; Hou, J. Identification and classification of construction equipment operators' mental fatigue using wearable eye-tracking technology. *Autom. Constr.* **2020**, *109*, 103000. [CrossRef]
55. Turetskaya, A.; Anishchenko, L.; Ivanisova, E. Non-Contact Detection of Respiratory Pattern Changes due to Mental Workload. In Proceedings of the 2020 Ural Symposium on Biomedical Engineering, Radioelectronics and Information Technology (USBEREIT), Yekaterinburg, Russia, 14–15 May 2020; pp. 125–127. [CrossRef]

56. Zhou, L.; Fischer, E.; Brahms, C.M.; Granacher, U.; Arnrich, B. Using Transparent Neural Networks and Wearable Inertial Sensors to Generate Physiologically-Relevant Insights for Gait. In Proceedings of the 2022 21st IEEE International Conference on Machine Learning and Applications (ICMLA), Nassau, Bahamas, 12–14 December 2022; pp. 1274–1280. [CrossRef]
57. Soleymanpour, R.; Shishavan, H.H.; Heo, J.S.; Kim, I. Novel Driver's Drowsiness Detection System and its Evaluation in a Driving Simulator Environment. In Proceedings of the 2021 IEEE International Conference on Systems, Man, and Cybernetics (SMC), Melbourne, Australia, 17–20 October 2021; pp. 1204–1208. [CrossRef]
58. Chen, H.; Han, X.; Hao, Z.; Yan, H.; Yang, J. Non-contact Monitoring of Fatigue Driving Using FMCW Millimeter Wave Radar. *ACM Trans. Internet Things* **2023**, *5*, 3. [CrossRef]
59. Ice, G.H.; James, G.D. Conducting a field study of stress. In *Measuring Stress in Humans*; Ice, G.H., James, G.D., Eds.; Cambridge University Press: Cambridge, UK, 2006; Chapter 1, pp. 3–24.
60. Selye, H. The general adaptation syndrome and the diseases of adaptation. *J. Clin. Endocrinol. Metab.* **1946**, *6*, 117–230. [CrossRef]
61. Alberdi, A.; Aztiria, A.; Basarab, A. Towards an automatic early stress recognition system for office environments based on multimodal measurements. *J. Biomed. Inform.* **2016**, *59*, 49–75. [CrossRef]
62. Arsalan, A.; Anwar, S.M.; Majid, M. Mental Stress Detection using Data from Wearable and Non-wearable Sensors: A Review. *arXiv* **2023**, arXiv:2202.03033. [CrossRef]
63. Gedam, S.; Paul, S. A Review on Mental Stress Detection Using Wearable Sensors and Machine Learning Techniques. *IEEE Access* **2021**, *9*, 84045–84066. [CrossRef]
64. Taskasaplidis, G.; Fotiadis, D.A.; Bamidis, P.D. Review of Stress Detection Methods Using Wearable Sensors. *IEEE Access* **2024**, *12*, 38219–38246. [CrossRef]
65. Masri, G.; Al-Shargie, F.; Tariq, U.; Almughairbi, F.; Babiloni, F.; Al-Nashash, H. Mental Stress Assessment in the Workplace: A Review. *IEEE Trans. Affect. Comput.* **2024**, *15*, 958–976. [CrossRef]
66. Wu, Y.; Ni, H.; Mao, C.; Han, J.; Xu, W. Non-intrusive Human Vital Sign Detection Using mmWave Sensing Technologies: A Review. *ACM Trans. Sens. Netw.* **2023**, *20*, 16. [CrossRef]
67. Ha, U.; Madani, S.; Adib, F. WiStress: Contactless Stress Monitoring Using Wireless Signals. *Proc. ACM Interact. Mob. Wearable Ubiquitous Technol.* **2021**, *5*, 103. [CrossRef]
68. Zakaria, C.; Balan, R.; Lee, Y. StressMon: Scalable Detection of Perceived Stress and Depression Using Passive Sensing of Changes in Work Routines and Group Interactions. *Proc. ACM Hum.-Comput. Interact.* **2019**, *3*, 37. [CrossRef]
69. Nosakhare, E.; Picard, R. Probabilistic Latent Variable Modeling for Assessing Behavioral Influences on Well-Being. In Proceedings of the 25th ACM SIGKDD International Conference on Knowledge Discovery & Data Mining, Anchorage, AK, USA, 4–8 August 2019; KDD '19. [CrossRef]
70. Olsen, G.F.; Brilliant, S.S.; Primeaux, D.; Najarian, K. Signal processing and machine learning for real-time classification of ergonomic posture with unobtrusive on-body sensors; application in dental practice. In Proceedings of the 2009 ICME International Conference on Complex Medical Engineering, Tempe, AZ, USA, 9–11 April 2009; pp. 1–11. [CrossRef]
71. Wac, M.; Kou, R.; Unlu, A.; Jenkinson, M.; Lin, W.; Roudaut, A. TAILOR: A Wearable Sleeve for Monitoring Repetitive Strain Injuries. In Proceedings of the CHI '20: CHI Conference on Human Factors in Computing Systems, Honolulu, HI, USA, 25–30 April 2020; CHI EA '20; pp. 1–8. [CrossRef]
72. Jan, M.T.; Hashemi, A.; Jang, J.; Yang, K.; Zhai, J.; Newman, D.; Tappen, R.; Furht, B. Non-intrusive Drowsiness Detection Techniques and Their Application in Detecting Early Dementia in Older Drivers. In *Proceedings of the Future Technologies Conference (FTC) 2022, Volume 2*; Arai, K., Ed.; Springer International Publishing: Berlin/Heidelberg, Germany, 2023; pp. 776–796.
73. Zhang, C.; Wu, X.; Zheng, X.; Yu, S. Driver drowsiness detection using multi-channel second order blind identifications. *IEEE Access* **2019**, *7*, 11829–11843. [CrossRef]
74. Kundinger, T.; Sofra, N.; Riener, A. Assessment of the Potential of Wrist-Worn Wearable Sensors for Driver Drowsiness Detection. *Sensors* **2020**, *20*, 1029. [CrossRef]
75. Yamamoto, K.; Toyoda, K.; Ohtsuki, T. Doppler Sensor-Based Blink Duration Estimation by Analysis of Eyelids Closing and Opening Behavior on Spectrogram. *IEEE Access* **2019**, *7*, 42726–42734. [CrossRef]
76. Shah, D.; Upasini, A.; Sasidhar, K. Findings from an experimental study of student behavioral patterns using smartphone sensors. In Proceedings of the 2020 International Conference on COMmunication Systems & NETworkS (COMSNETS), Bengaluru, India, 7–11 January 2020; pp. 768–772. [CrossRef]
77. Jo, E.; Bang, H.; Ryu, M.; Sung, E.J.; Leem, S.; Hong, H. MAMAS: Supporting Parent–Child Mealtime Interactions Using Automated Tracking and Speech Recognition. *Proc. ACM Hum.-Comput. Interact.* **2020**, *4*, 66. [CrossRef]
78. Bi, C.; Xing, G.; Hao, T.; Huh-Yoo, J.; Peng, W.; Ma, M.; Chang, X. FamilyLog: Monitoring Family Mealtime Activities by Mobile Devices. *IEEE Trans. Mob. Comput.* **2019**, *19*, 1818–1830. [CrossRef]
79. Tan, E.T.S.; Rogers, K.; Nacke, L.E.; Drachen, A.; Wade, A. Communication Sequences Indicate Team Cohesion: A Mixed-Methods Study of Ad Hoc League of Legends Teams. *Proc. ACM Hum.-Comput. Interact.* **2022**, *6*, 225. [CrossRef]

80. Sefidgar, Y.S.; Seo, W.; Kuehn, K.S.; Althoff, T.; Browning, A.; Riskin, E.; Nurius, P.S.; Dey, A.K.; Mankoff, J. Passively-sensed Behavioral Correlates of Discrimination Events in College Students. *Proc. ACM Hum.-Comput. Interact.* **2019**, *3*, 114. [CrossRef] [PubMed]
81. Maxhuni, A.; Hernandez-Leal, P.; Morales, E.F.; Sucar, L.E.; Osmani, V.; Mayora, O. Unobtrusive Stress Assessment Using Smartphones. *IEEE Trans. Mob. Comput.* **2020**, *20*, 2313–2325. [CrossRef]
82. Langheinrich, M. Privacy by design—Principles of privacy-aware ubiquitous systems. In *Proceedings of the International Conference on Ubiquitous Computing*; Springer: Berlin/Heidelberg, Germany, 2001; pp. 273–291.
83. Du, W.; Li, A.; Zhou, P.; Niu, B.; Wu, D. Privacyeye: A privacy-preserving and computationally efficient deep learning-based mobile video analytics system. *IEEE Trans. Mob. Comput.* **2021**, *21*, 3263–3279. [CrossRef]
84. Hoyle, R.; Templeman, R.; Anthony, D.; Crandall, D.; Kapadia, A. Sensitive lifelogs: A privacy analysis of photos from wearable cameras. In Proceedings of the 33rd Annual ACM Conference on Human Factors in Computing Systems, Seoul, Republic of Korea, 18–23 April 2015; pp. 1645–1648.
85. Korayem, M.; Templeman, R.; Chen, D.; Crandall, D.; Kapadia, A. Enhancing lifelogging privacy by detecting screens. In Proceedings of the 2016 CHI Conference on Human Factors in Computing Systems, San Jose, CA, USA, 7–12 May 2016; pp. 4309–4314.
86. Templeman, R.; Korayem, M.; Crandall, D.J.; Kapadia, A. PlaceAvoider: Steering First-Person Cameras away from Sensitive Spaces. In Proceedings of the NDSS, Citeseer, 2014, San Diego, CA, USA, 23–26 February 2014, Volume 14, pp. 23–26.
87. Kumar, S.; Nguyen, L.T.; Zeng, M.; Liu, K.; Zhang, J. Sound shredding: Privacy preserved audio sensing. In Proceedings of the 16th International Workshop on Mobile Computing Systems and Applications, Santa Fe, NM, USA, 12–13 February 2015; pp. 135–140.
88. Dwork, C. Differential privacy. In *Proceedings of the International Colloquium on Automata, Languages, and Programming*; Springer: Berlin/Heidelberg, Germany, 2006; pp. 1–12.
89. Dedovic, K.; Rexroth, M.; Wolff, E.; Duchesne, A.; Scherling, C.; Beaudry, T.; Lue, S.D.; Lord, C.; Engert, V.; Pruessner, J.C. Neural correlates of processing stressful information: An event-related fMRI study. *Brain Res.* **2009**, *1293*, 49–60. [CrossRef]
90. McMahan, B.; Moore, E.; Ramage, D.; Hampson, S.; y Arcas, B.A. Communication-efficient learning of deep networks from decentralized data. In Proceedings of the Artificial Intelligence and Statistics, Lauderdale, FL, USA, 20–22 April 2017; pp. 1273–1282.
91. Thieme, A.; Belgrave, D.; Doherty, G. Machine Learning in Mental Health: A Systematic Review of the HCI Literature to Support the Development of Effective and Implementable ML Systems. *ACM Trans. Comput.-Hum. Interact.* **2020**, *27*, 34. [CrossRef]
92. Page, M.J.; McKenzie, J.E.; Bossuyt, P.M.; Boutron, I.; Hoffmann, T.C.; Mulrow, C.D.; Shamseer, L.; Tetzlaff, J.M.; Akl, E.A.; Brennan, S.E.; et al. The PRISMA 2020 statement: An updated guideline for reporting systematic reviews. *BMJ* **2021**, *372*, n71. [CrossRef]
93. VanderWeele, T.J. On the promotion of human flourishing. *Proc. Natl. Acad. Sci. USA* **2017**, *114*, 8148–8156. [CrossRef]
94. Menniti, M.; Laganà, F.; Oliva, G.; Bianco, M.; Fiorillo, A.S.; Pullano, S.A. Development of Non-Invasive Ventilator for Homecare and Patient Monitoring System. *Electronics* **2024**, *13*, 790. [CrossRef]

machine learning & knowledge extraction

MDPI

*Article*

# Revolutionizing Cardiac Risk Assessment: AI-Powered Patient Segmentation Using Advanced Machine Learning Techniques

**Joan D. Gonzalez-Franco [1], Alejandro Galaviz-Mosqueda [2], Salvador Villarreal-Reyes [1], Jose E. Lozano-Rizk [3], Raul Rivera-Rodriguez [1,*], Jose E. Gonzalez-Trejo [3], Alexei-Fedorovish Licea-Navarro [4], Jorge Lozoya-Arandia [5] and Edgar A. Ibarra-Flores [6]**

1 Department of Electronics and Telecommunications, CICESE Research Center, Carretera Ensenada-Tijuana 3918, Playitas, Ensenada 22860, BC, Mexico; joandavid@cicese.edu.mx (J.D.G.-F.); svillar@cicese.mx (S.V.-R.)
2 Monterrey CICESE Research Center, Alianza Centro 504, Apodaca 66629, NL, Mexico; agalaviz@cicese.edu.mx
3 Division of Telematics, CICESE Research Center, Carretera Ensenada-Tijuana 3918, Playitas, Ensenada 22860, BC, Mexico; jlozano@cicese.edu.mx (J.E.L.-R.); gtjose@cicese.edu.mx (J.E.G.-T.)
4 Department of Biomedical Innovation, CICESE Research Center, Carretera Ensenada-Tijuana 3918, Playitas, Ensenada 22860, BC, Mexico; alicea@cicese.mx
5 Department of Data Science, CUChapala, Universidad de Guadalajara, Av. Juárez 976, Col. Americana, Americana, Guadalajara 44100, JA, Mexico; jorge.larandia@academicos.udg.mx
6 Head of Education and Research, Ensenada ISSSTE Hospital Clinic, Calle Delante, Militar, Ensenada 22890, BC, Mexico; edgar.ibarra@issste.gob.mx
* Correspondence: rrivera@cicese.edu.mx

**Abstract:** Cardiovascular diseases stand as the leading cause of mortality worldwide, underscoring the urgent need for effective tools that enable early detection and monitoring of at-risk patients. This study combines Artificial Intelligence (AI) techniques—specifically the k-means clustering algorithm—alongside dimensionality reduction methods like Principal Component Analysis (PCA) and Uniform Manifold Approximation and Projection (UMAP) to identify patient groups with varying levels of heart attack risk. We used a publicly available clinical dataset with 1319 patient records, which included variables such as age, gender, blood pressure, glucose levels, CK-MB Creatine Kinase MB (KCM), and troponin levels. We normalized and prepared the data, then we employed PCA and UMAP to reduce dimensionality and facilitate visualization. Using the k-means algorithm, we segmented the patients into distinct groups based on their clinical features. Our analysis revealed two distinct patient groups. Group 2 exhibited significantly higher levels of troponin (mean 0.4761 ng/mL), KCM (18.65 ng/mL), and glucose (mean 148.19 mg/dL) and was predominantly composed of men (97%). These factors indicate an increased risk of cardiac events compared to Group 1, which had lower levels of these biomarkers and a slightly higher average age. Interestingly, no significant differences in blood pressure were observed between the groups. This study demonstrates the effectiveness of combining Machine Learning (ML) techniques with dimensionality reduction methods to enhance risk stratification accuracy in cardiology. By enabling more targeted interventions for high-risk patients, our unsupervised segmentation approach focuses on intrinsic data patterns rather than predefined diagnostic labels, serves as a powerful complement to traditional risk assessment tools.

**Keywords:** artificial intelligence; k-means clustering; heart attacks; dimensionality reduction; troponin; patient segmentation; machine learning

## 1. Introduction

Cardiovascular diseases (CVDs) represent one of the most significant public health challenges of the 21st century. According to the World Health Organization (WHO), CVDs are the leading cause of death globally, accounting for approximately 31% of all deaths worldwide [1]. These conditions encompass a wide range of disorders affecting the heart and blood vessels, including coronary heart disease, cerebrovascular disease, rheumatic heart disease, and other conditions. The high prevalence and mortality associated with CVDs underscore the urgent need to improve strategies for prevention, diagnosis, and treatment.

The impact of CVDs extends beyond mortality; they also affect patients' quality of life and impose a considerable economic burden on healthcare systems. Risk factors such as high blood pressure, elevated blood glucose, high cholesterol levels, smoking, obesity, and physical inactivity significantly contribute to the development and progression of these diseases [2]. Moreover, the complex interplay between genetic, environmental, and lifestyle factors makes early identification of at-risk individuals challenging.

In this context, early detection and effective monitoring of patients at risk of heart attacks are crucial to reducing the incidence and mortality associated with CVDs. Preventive interventions and timely treatments can substantially improve clinical outcomes and alleviate the strain on healthcare systems. However, traditional risk assessment methods often fail to capture the full complexity of the factors involved, limiting their effectiveness.

Artificial Intelligence (AI) and Machine Learning (ML) emerge as promising tools to address these challenges. AI enables the analysis of large volumes of data and the discovery of hidden patterns that may go unnoticed using conventional statistical methods. ML, as a subfield of AI, focuses on developing algorithms capable of learning from data and improving their accuracy over time without being explicitly programmed for each task [3]. These techniques have proven effective in various medical applications, such as computer-assisted diagnosis, prediction of clinical outcomes, and treatment personalization [4,5].

Specifically, the use of unsupervised learning algorithms, such as clustering, allows for the identification of patient groups with similar characteristics without the need for predefined labels. The k-means algorithm is one of the most widely used methods in this field due to its simplicity and efficiency in handling large datasets [6]. By combining it with dimensionality reduction techniques like Principal Component Analysis (PCA) and Uniform Manifold Approximation and Projection (UMAP), it is possible to simplify high-dimensional data and better visualize relationships between variables [7,8].

The present study aims to apply AI techniques—specifically the k-means clustering algorithm along with PCA and UMAP—to identify groups of patients with different levels of risk for heart attacks. By analyzing clinical and laboratory variables such as age, gender, blood pressure, glucose levels, and troponin levels, we seek to detect patterns and groupings that may not be evident through traditional analyses. This approach can contribute to improving risk stratification and developing more effective prevention strategies in cardiology. Particularly, our unsupervised segmentation approach, by focusing on these intrinsic data patterns rather than being constrained by predefined diagnostic labels, can serve as a powerful complement to traditional risk assessment tools [9,10].

The main contributions of this study are as follows:

- **Effective Dimensionality Reduction Using UMAP**: We successfully applied the nonlinear dimensionality reduction technique UMAP to the clinical dataset, reducing complexity while preserving essential data structures. This allowed for clearer visualization and better handling of nonlinear relationships between medical variables.
- **Identification of Patient Groups with Varying Cardiac Risk Levels**: By utilizing the k-means clustering algorithm on the reduced dataset, we identified two distinct

groups of patients with different levels of risk for heart attacks. This highlights the potential of unsupervised ML methods in uncovering hidden patterns in medical data.

- **Insights into Critical Biomarkers for Heart Attack Risk**: We identified troponin, CK-MB Creatine Kinase MB (KCM), and glucose levels, along with gender, as significant factors in stratifying cardiovascular risk among patients. This finding can aid clinicians in focusing on key biomarkers for early detection and intervention.
- **Contribution to Personalized Medicine and Preventive Cardiology**: Our approach demonstrates how AI and machine learning techniques can enhance risk stratification accuracy, leading to more targeted interventions for high-risk patients and improved prevention strategies in cardiology.

These results can benefit healthcare professionals by providing advanced tools for patient risk assessment and supporting the integration of AI in clinical decision-making processes.

The rest of this article is organized as follows: Section 2 details the methodology employed, including a description of the dataset and the analytical techniques used. Section 3 presents the results obtained and their interpretation. In Section 4, we discuss the clinical implications of our findings. Finally, Section 5 concludes by highlighting the main contributions of the study and suggesting directions for future research.

## 2. Materials and Methods

In this section, we detail the process we followed to evaluate the effectiveness of the clustering model and identify significant patterns in the medical variables of each patient. To achieve the study's objectives and validate our hypothesis, we developed a methodology that integrates several techniques, including Exploratory Data Analysis (EDA), dimensionality reduction, and machine learning algorithms. The focus of the study was to identify hidden patterns and natural groupings in a clinical dataset, aiming to classify patients into different risk groups for heart attacks.

Figure 1 presents a block diagram illustrating the workflow of the methodology used in this study. This diagram allows us to visualize the interrelationships between each stage of the process, facilitating replication of the methodology by other researchers. The implementation was entirely coded in Python 3.11.12 using open-source libraries (e.g., scikit-learn for UMAP and k-means, Matplotlib/Seaborn for visualizations).

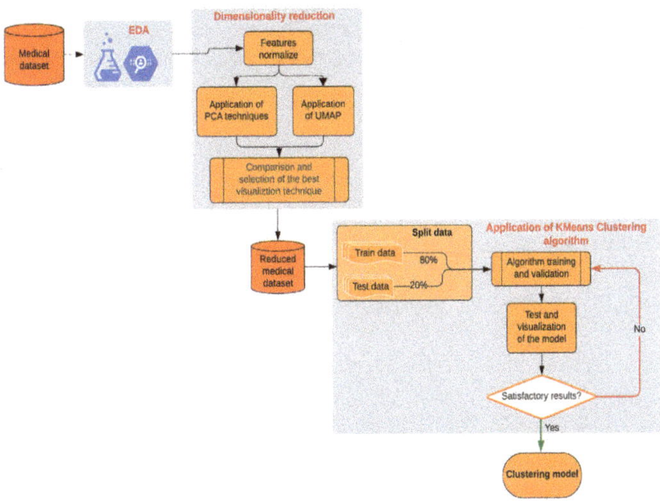


**Figure 1.** Block diagram of our proposal methodology.

We explain each of the phases in detail below, highlighting the key contributions and aspects of each process.

1. **Exploratory Data Analysis (EDA)**: We began the study with a thorough analysis of the medical data, identifying the most relevant features for subsequent analysis. During this phase, we evaluated the distribution of variables, checked for missing data, and explored possible relationships between variables. Our goal in the EDA was to gain a clear understanding of the data and prepare the dataset for the next phases of analysis. Detecting outliers and normalizing variables were critical steps to ensure data homogeneity and readiness for modeling. By thoroughly understanding the data's characteristics, we aimed to minimize biases and enhance the accuracy of our modeling efforts.
2. **Dimensionality Reduction**: The original dataset contained multiple medical features that could have nonlinear relationships. To facilitate clustering and pattern visualization, we implemented dimensionality reduction techniques. We applied the Uniform Manifold Approximation and Projection (UMAP), a nonlinear dimensionality reduction method ideal for preserving both local and global data structures. We initially applied Principal Component Analysis (PCA) for dimensionality reduction, but observed overlapping clusters due to its linearity assumption, which failed to capture critical nonlinear interactions (e.g., troponin's exponential relationship with glucose levels in high-risk patients). Switching to UMAP, which models local and global structures, improved cluster separation and revealed two distinct risk phenotypes. This phase reduced the dataset's complexity to a two-dimensional space, simplifying the subsequent clustering stage and enhancing pattern discernibility.
3. **K-means Clustering Algorithm**: After reducing the data to two dimensions using UMAP, we applied the k-means clustering algorithm to identify natural groupings among the patients. K-means partitions the data into a predefined number of clusters, aiming to minimize intra-cluster distances and maximize separation between clusters. In this study, we chose to establish two clusters after evaluating several options and determining that this number provided the most meaningful segmentation of patients based on critical biomarkers like troponin, KCM, and glucose levels. This decision was guided by methods such as the elbow method and silhouette analysis, ensuring that our clustering approach was both data-driven and clinically relevant.
4. **Validation and Visualization**: After applying k-means, we validated the model using internal validation metrics and visual inspection of the clusters. We adjusted based on the cluster cohesion and separation observed in the visualization. Once satisfied with the cluster quality, we proceeded to interpret the clusters clinically, identifying relevant patterns and differences between patient groups that could inform risk stratification and intervention strategies.

This methodological approach enabled us to achieve a meaningful classification of patients based on their cardiac risk, highlighting the utility of AI techniques in the early identification of risk factors in the clinical setting. By combining UMAP and k-means, we effectively segmented the patient population and achieved a clear visualization of the results, providing valuable insights that could enhance clinical decision-making and patient outcomes.

Although PCA and UMAP are established techniques for dimensionality reduction, their application to explore linear patterns and nonlinear relationships has seen growing interest in recent years, with emerging studies applying these techniques to explore clinical data. Prior studies have focused on linear methods (e.g., PCA + k-means) for clinical data visualization [11], but these approaches fail to capture nonlinear interactions between biomarkers, which are critical for identifying subclinical risk patterns. Our work addresses this gap by proposing a workflow that prioritizes UMAP over PCA when data exhibit nonlinear relationships, demonstrating its superiority in cohorts with complex metabolic profiles. Table A1 in Appendix A provides a comparative analysis of related works, highlighting this study's main contribution and the research gap addressed by our novel integration.

### 2.1. Medical Dataset and EDA

This work uses the clinical dataset **Heart Attack Analysis & Prediction Dataset**, provided by Rashik Rahman Pritom, available on Kaggle under the CC BY 4.0 license. The dataset contains 1319 patient records, each containing eight relevant variables selected based on their significance in cardiovascular health assessment. These variables are [12,13]:

- Age: Patient's age in years.
- Gender: Male or Female (represented as 0 and 1, respectively).
- Pulse Rate: Heart rate measured in beats per minute.
- High Blood Pressure (Systolic Pressure): Maximum arterial pressure during heart contraction.
- Low Blood Pressure (Diastolic Pressure): Minimum arterial pressure between heartbeats.
- Glucose Level: Blood glucose concentration in mg/dL.
- CK-MB (Creatine Kinase MB) (KCM): an enzyme primarily found in the heart and, to a lesser extent, in skeletal muscles.
- Troponin Level: Blood troponin concentration in ng/mL, a specific biomarker for myocardial damage.

The dataset's dimensions (1319 samples $\times$ 8 features) provide a robust foundation for applying ML techniques. The data were retrospectively collected from electronic medical records of local hospitals, ensuring diversity and representativeness within the sample population.

We conducted an observational, descriptive, and cross-sectional study. No direct interventions were made with the patients; instead, we analyzed existing data to identify groupings based on similarities in clinical and laboratory variables.

Although the dataset is publicly available, its application in this context (stratification based on troponin/glucose levels) is novel. Previous studies using these data have focused on supervised models [14], while our unsupervised approach uncovers hidden patterns without the bias of prior labeling. An excerpt of the first ten rows of the dataset is presented in Table A2 of Appendix A, illustrating the structure and type of data used in this study.

Before proceeding with the modeling phase, we performed an extensive EDA to understand the underlying patterns and distributions within the dataset. This step was crucial for identifying data quality issues, uncovering relationships between variables, and informing subsequent analytical choices.

We conducted an EDA to understand the distribution and relationships among the variables. Using histograms, box-and-whisker plots, and correlation matrices, we identified patterns and potential outliers in the data.

Since the variables were on different scales, we applied normalization using the *StandardScaler* method. This process allowed us to standardize the data, ensuring that each variable contributed equally to the analysis and enhancing the effectiveness of the clustering algorithms.

We identified and analyzed outliers to determine whether they should be excluded or if they provided relevant information. Outliers can offer valuable insights into extreme or unusual cases that might significantly influence the study's results (see Figure A1 in Appendix B). We decided to retain these outliers because they could represent patients with higher risk and are essential for the integrity of the analysis.

To identify linear relationships between variables, we calculated the Pearson correlation matrix. We observed a moderate correlation between systolic and diastolic blood pressure ($r \approx 0.59$), suggesting that patients with high systolic pressure tend to have high diastolic pressure. The other variables showed low correlations, indicating that each contributes unique information to the dataset and is valuable for the clustering process.

By thoroughly understanding and preprocessing the data, we ensured that the dataset was suitable for dimensionality reduction and clustering. The insights gained from the EDA guided our methodological choices and helped us interpret the results within a clinical context.

### 2.2. Dimensionality Reduction

In clinical datasets with multiple variables, it is common for some variables to correlate with each other, leading to redundant information that can complicate analysis. Dimensionality reduction techniques help simplify high-dimensional data while preserving as much relevant information as possible. This simplification facilitates data processing, enhances the performance of machine learning algorithms, and makes data visualization more manageable [15].

Although the dataset contains only 8 variables, dimensionality reduction was essential to visualize nonlinear patterns in an interpretable 2D space. This allowed groups of patients to be identified who, although not highly linearly correlated, share similar risk profiles when complex multivariate interactions are considered.

Principal Component Analysis (PCA) is a widely used statistical method that transforms a set of possibly correlated variables into a set of uncorrelated variables known as principal components [16]. These components are linear combinations of the original variables and are ordered so that the first principal component captures the maximum possible variance in the data, the second component captures the next highest variance, and so on. We selected the initial components that explained at least 95% of the total variance, aiming to reduce dimensionality while retaining most of the information [17].

Uniform Manifold Approximation and Projection (UMAP) is a nonlinear dimensionality reduction technique that constructs a high-dimensional graph based on probabilistic distances between data points and optimizes a low-dimensional representation preserving both local and global data structures [8]. Mathematically, UMAP minimizes the cross-entropy cost function between two fuzzy sets, one representing high-dimensional similarities, $v_{ij}$, and the other low-dimensional similarities, $w_{ij}$:

$$C = \sum_{i \neq j} [v_{ij} \ln\left(\frac{v_{ij}}{w_{ij}}\right) + (1 - v_{ij}) \ln(\frac{1 - v_{ij}}{1 - w_{ij}})] \tag{1}$$

where $v_{ij}$ is the probability of association between points $i$ and $j$ in high-dimensional space, and $w_{ij}$ is the corresponding probability in the reduced space [8]. This formulation, derived from fuzzy set theory and Riemannian geometry, allows UMAP to capture nonlinear relationships between clinical variables (e.g., troponin–glucose interactions), which often exhibit non-additive relationships in cardiovascular risk assessment [18].

Compared to linear methods like PCA [15], UMAP better preserves both local and global structures in biomedical datasets, a critical advantage for visualizing natural patient groupings [19]. We used UMAP to visualize the data in a two-dimensional space, facilitating the identification of natural groupings among patients.

### 2.3. Application of K-Means

The k-means algorithm clusters data into **k** groups by iteratively minimizing the sum of squared distances between data points and the centroid of their assigned cluster [20,21].

This method aims to partition the dataset into distinct, non-overlapping subsets where each data point belongs to the cluster with the nearest mean value. Formally, given a dataset X containing $n$ x-dimensional data points $X = \{x_i\}$, where $i$ = 1, 2, . . ., n, X is partitioned into '**k**' clusters $C = \{c_j\}$, where $j$ = 1, 2, . . ., **k** such that:

$$J(C_k) = \sum_{x_i \in c_k} ||x_i - \mu_k||^2 \quad (2)$$

The primary goal is to minimize the total within-cluster variance ($J$), ensuring that data points within each cluster are as homogeneous as possible while maintaining separation between clusters. That is, minimize Equation (3):

$$J(C) = \sum_{k=1}^{K} \sum_{x_i \in c_k} ||x_i - \mu_k||^2 \quad (3)$$

where $\mu_k$ denotes the centroid (mean) of cluster $C_k$. The algorithm proceeds as follows [21]:

1. **Initialization**: Randomly select $k$ initial centroids from the dataset.
2. **Assignment**: For each data point, compute its Euclidean distance to all centroids and assign it to the nearest cluster.
3. **Update**: Recalculate each centroid as the arithmetic mean of all points assigned to its cluster.
4. **Iteration**: Repeat steps 2–3 until cluster assignments stabilize (i.e., centroids no longer change significantly between iterations).

To identify the optimal number of clusters or groups (**k**), we employed the elbow method and the silhouette coefficient:

1. **Elbow Method**: This technique involves running k-means clustering on the dataset for a range of k values and computing the within-cluster sum of squares (WCSS). By plotting WCSS against the number of clusters, we look for an "elbow" point where the rate of decrease sharply changes, indicating diminishing returns with additional clusters [22]. In our analysis, the elbow point suggested that k = 2 was optimal.
2. **Silhouette Coefficient**: This metric measures how well each data point fits within its assigned cluster compared to other clusters. It ranges from −1 to 1, where a higher value indicates better clustering quality [23]. We calculated the silhouette scores for different k values and found that the highest average silhouette score occurred at k = 2, reinforcing the result from the elbow method.

By combining these two methods, we confidently determined that dividing the patients into two clusters was the most meaningful approach for our dataset. This allowed us to effectively group patients based on critical biomarkers such as troponin, KCM, and glucose levels, which are significant indicators of cardiac risk.

## 3. Simulation Results

In this section, we explain the steps taken to execute the entire process outlined in the block diagram of Figure 1. The process is divided into three main parts: EDA, dimensionality reduction, and application of ML algorithms. Each subsection provides a detailed account of the methodologies employed and the results obtained, offering insights into how each step contributes to identifying patient groups with varying levels of cardiac risk.

We begin with the EDA to understand the dataset's characteristics and prepare the data for analysis. Next, we apply dimensionality reduction techniques to simplify the dataset while preserving essential information. Finally, we utilize machine learning algorithms to cluster the patients and interpret the results within a clinical context.

### 3.1. EDA Application

In this subsection, we present the correlation matrix between the features in the dataset. Also, we show a statistical summary of all variables in the dataset and the outlier analysis.

We plotted the correlation matrix to understand how closely related the variables are to each other. In a correlation matrix, values closer to 1 indicate a stronger positive correlation between variables, meaning they tend to increase together. Correlation matrices are fundamental tools in exploratory data analysis, helping to identify relationships between variables and detect potential multicollinearity issues [24].

From the correlation matrix (see Figure 2), we observed that the variables *pressurehigh* (systolic blood pressure) and *pressurelow* (diastolic blood pressure) have a correlation coefficient of approximately 0.59. Although this correlation is not extremely high, it indicates a moderate relationship between the two variables. This makes clinical sense, as patients with higher systolic pressure also have higher diastolic pressure [25]. This correlation reflects the physiological relationship between the two measures of blood pressure, influenced by factors such as arterial stiffness and vascular resistance.

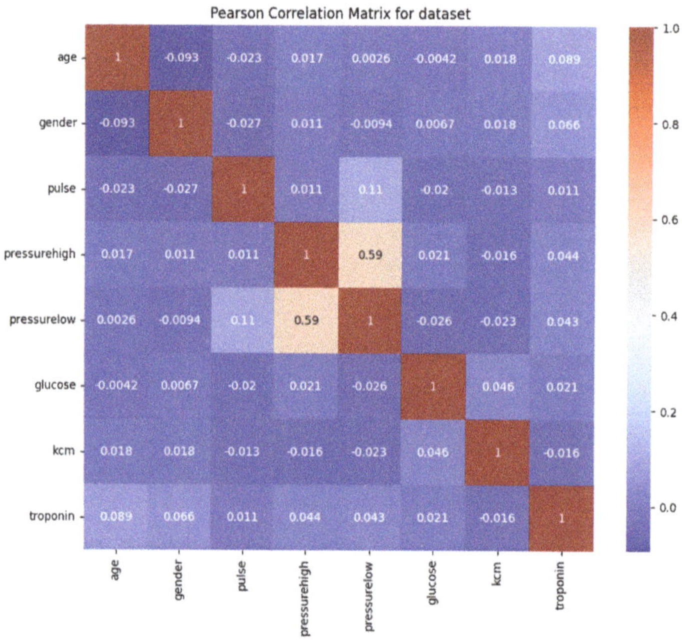


**Figure 2.** Correlation matrix of the features.

Depending on the analytical approach, one might consider whether both variables are necessary or if one could suffice. However, since the correlation is moderate rather than strong, both variables may still provide unique information and contribute valuable insights to the analysis.

The other variables did not show significant correlations with each other (see Figure 2), suggesting that there is no strong collinearity in the dataset. This lack of high correlation among most variables is advantageous for clustering purposes because it indicates that each variable contributes distinct information. When variables are not highly correlated, clustering algorithms like k-means can more effectively utilize the unique characteristics of each variable to segment patients into meaningful groups.

Understanding the correlations between variables helped us ensure that the dataset was suitable for clustering without the need to remove or combine variables due to redundancy [26]. It also provided confidence that each variable could potentially influence the formation of clusters, aiding in the identification of patient groups with different risk profiles.

To further understand the dataset, we performed a statistical analysis of all variables, focusing on measures such as mean, standard deviation (std), minimum and maximum values, and quartiles. Table 1 below presents a comprehensive summary of these statistical metrics, offering deeper insights into the distribution and variability within the data.

**Table 1.** Statistical summary of dataset variables.

| | Age | Pulse | Pressurehigh | Presurrelow | Glucose | KCM | Troponin |
|---|---|---|---|---|---|---|---|
| **mean** | 56.19 | 78.34 | 127.17 | 72.26 | 146.63 | 15.27 | 0.36 |
| **std** | 13.65 | 51.63 | 26.12 | 14.03 | 74.92 | 46.33 | 1.15 |
| **min** | 14 | 20 | 42 | 38 | 35 | 0.32 | 0.001 |
| **25%** | 47 | 64 | 110 | 62 | 98 | 1.66 | 0.006 |
| **50%** | 58 | 74 | 124 | 72 | 116 | 2.85 | 0.014 |
| **75%** | 65 | 85 | 143 | 81 | 169 | 5.81 | 0.086 |
| **max** | 103 | 1111 | 223 | 154 | 541 | 300 | 10.3 |

From the statistical data, we notice that the *pulse* variable exhibits a high standard deviation (51.63) relative to its mean (78.34). Additionally, the maximum value of *pulse* is 1111, which is significantly greater than the third quartile (85). This disparity suggests the presence of outliers that could be affecting the distribution of this variable.

Similarly, the variables *glucose*, *KCM*, and *troponin* show maximum values considerably higher than their respective third quartile values. This indicates the presence of outliers that might influence the interpretation of these variables.

By carefully analyzing these statistical summaries, we gained valuable insights into the dataset's characteristics, which guided our subsequent steps in the analysis. Recognizing the presence of outliers and understanding their potential significance helped us make informed decisions about data preprocessing and ensured that our clustering results would be meaningful in a clinical context. Appendix B shows all the outliers presented in the features of this dataset (see Figure A1).

Given that our objective is to identify groups of patients, we decided to retain these outliers because they could represent a specific subgroup within the dataset. These extreme values might correspond to patients with higher risk profiles, and excluding them could lead to a loss of critical information.

By maintaining the outliers, we aim to ensure that the clustering algorithm captures the full spectrum of patient data, potentially revealing important patterns associated with elevated cardiac risk.

### 3.2. Dimensionality Reduction Applications

In this section, we normalized all the data to the same scale. This step is essential because the algorithms need to interpret and differentiate the meaning of each numerical variable, given that they were originally on different scales. By standardizing the data using *Standardscaler* normalization, we ensured that each variable contributed equally to the analysis, preventing variables with larger scales from dominating the results.

With all data on the same scale, we proceeded to visualize the variance distributed among each principal component. PCA operates by transforming the original variables into a new set of uncorrelated variables called principal components, ordered by the amount of variance they capture from the data [16]. In other words, the more variance a component captures, the more it contributes to the segmentation and separation of the data.

In our study, since we have eight variables, we can obtain a maximum of eight principal components. However, the human eye can only visualize up to three dimensions effectively, making it challenging to interpret more than three components visually. Therefore, we focused on the first few components that capture the most variance.

Ideally, the first two or three principal components should capture a substantial portion of the total variance to allow for meaningful visualization and analysis [7]. In Figure 3, we present the variance of each principal component individually and how they accumulate to reach 100% of the total variance.

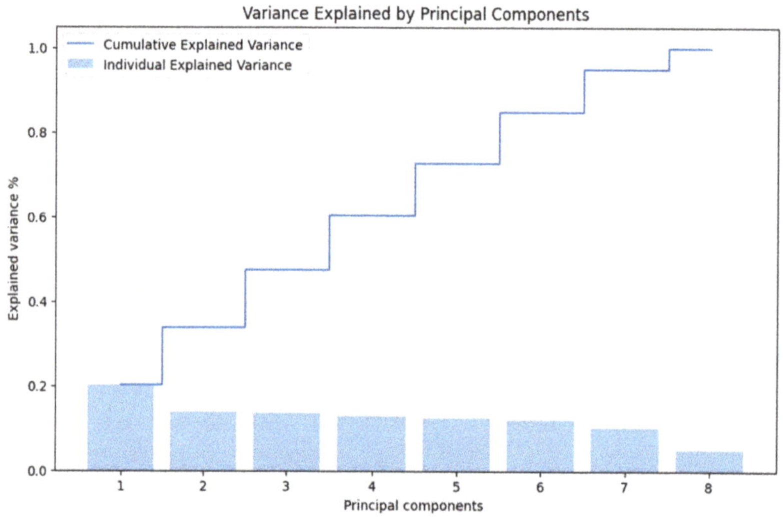


**Figure 3.** Variance explained by each principal component.

Observing the figure, we notice that the sum of the first two components barely reaches 40% of the accumulated variance. This low percentage indicates that the data are not well represented in just two dimensions using PCA, as a significant amount of information (variance) remains in the higher components.

The limited variance captured by the first two principal components suggests that PCA may not be the most effective dimensionality reduction technique for our dataset, especially if nonlinear relationships exist between variables [27]. This finding led us to consider alternative methods better suited for preserving complex data structures.

In Figure 4, we present the plot of the data distributed using the first two principal components, which account for almost 40% of the total variance. The figure shows a high concentration of data points clustered together, with a few points scattered away from this dense area. The points are quite dispersed overall, and there do not appear to be evident clusters indicating a natural separation between groups in the data.

This observation is consistent with our earlier findings, where we noted that the first two principal components capture a relatively small portion of the total variance. Because these components do not explain a significant amount of variance, important information may be lost when projecting the data onto this lower-dimensional space. This loss of information makes it difficult to distinguish distinct groups or patterns within the dataset using PCA.

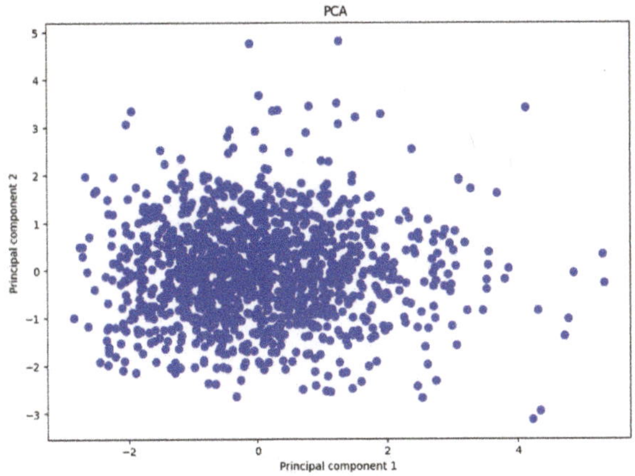


**Figure 4.** Representation of the first two principal components.

Based on these insights, we conclude that PCA is not effective for reducing the dimensionality of our dataset in this specific problem. The ineffectiveness of PCA may be attributed to the data not exhibiting linear relationships among variables. Since PCA is a linear dimensionality reduction technique, it struggles to capture the complex, nonlinear structures that may exist in the data [16,27]. This limitation suggests the need for alternative methods that can handle nonlinear relationships more effectively.

UMAP

We decided to apply the UMAP technique, which proved to be more effective for our problem due to two main reasons [8,28]:

1. **Preservation of Local and Global Structure**: UMAP is specifically designed to preserve both the local and global structures of the data. This means it attempts to maintain close relationships between similar data points as well as the broader relationships among groups of points in the high-dimensional space. By doing so, UMAP provides a more faithful representation of the data's intrinsic geometry in a lower-dimensional space. This characteristic is crucial when dealing with complex datasets where important patterns may exist at different scales.
2. **Manifold Approximation**: UMAP operates under the assumption that the data lie on a low-dimensional manifold within the high-dimensional space. It seeks to find a representation of this manifold in a lower-dimensional space. This approach can result in a clearer separation of clusters or patterns, making it easier to identify distinct groups within the data. UMAP's ability to capture nonlinear relationships enhances the visualization and interpretability of data.

After applying UMAP to the normalized data, we obtained Figure 5. From this figure, we can clearly observe two distinct groups of patients, one on the left and one on the right. This outcome indicates that UMAP successfully reduced the dimensionality of the dataset while preserving meaningful structures relevant for clustering.

Using UMAP, we achieved our objective of dimensionality reduction for this dataset. The technique effectively unveiled the underlying structure of the data, showing the presence of two natural groupings among the patients. This result sets a strong foundation for the next step, which involves applying the k-means algorithm to divide the patients into clusters and interpret the findings.

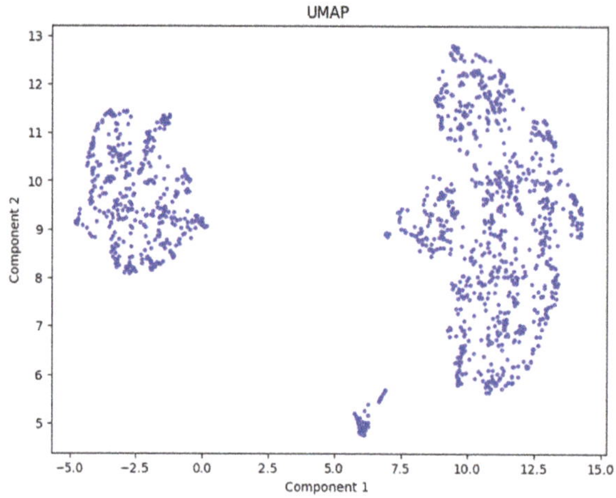


**Figure 5.** UMAP representation by two components.

### 3.3. K-Means Application

Although Figure 5 suggests the presence of two distinct patient groups, we verified this observation using the elbow method and the silhouette score, as explained in the methodology section. These methods helped us determine the optimal number of clusters (k) for our dataset.

After calculating and plotting these indicators, as shown in Figure 6, we found that both methods indicated that k = 2 is the optimal number of clusters. This finding aligns with our initial hypothesis based on the UMAP visualization.

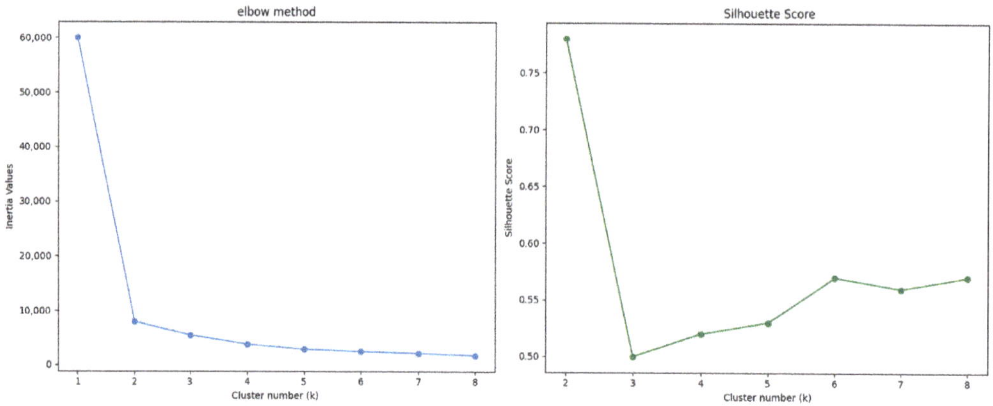


**Figure 6.** Elbow method and Silhouette score.

With the optimal number of clusters determined, we applied the k-means algorithm to divide the patients into two groups. By confirming the optimal number of clusters through these methods, we ensured that our clustering approach was robust and data-driven. The resulting clusters provided a foundation for analyzing the characteristics of each group and interpreting their clinical significance. The clustering results are presented in Figure 7.

Our unsupervised approach offers key advantages over traditional supervised models. First, it allows us to uncover hidden patterns that escape label-based methods: we identify high-risk patients with moderate elevation of troponin combined with severe hyperglycemia, a profile that supervised models might ignore by focusing only on binary diagnoses of infarction. Second, by not relying on predefined clinical labels, this approach is ideal for analyzing retrospective data with incomplete or biased diagnoses, common in hospital registries. This allows emerging risks to be detected in subclinical populations, offering opportunities for preventive interventions before major cardiovascular events occur.

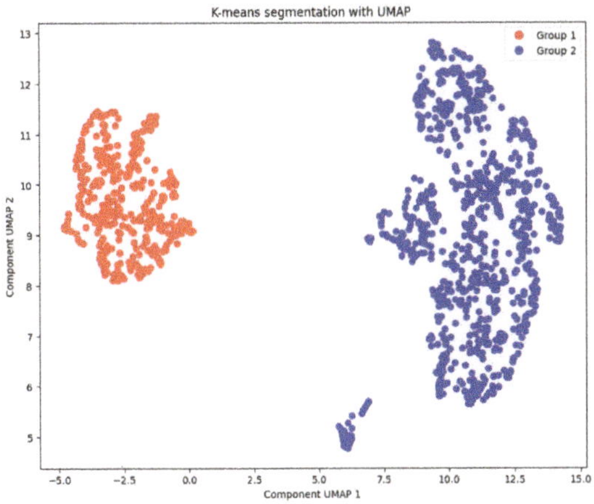


**Figure 7.** Patients' segmentation with k-means (k = 2).

The k-means algorithm has two key limitations in the context of clinical data. First, it assumes that the clusters are spherical and homogeneously sized (convex clusters), a simplification that may not reflect the complexity of biomedical patterns with irregular shapes or asymmetric distributions. Second, although we base the choice of k = 2 on the elbow method and silhouette coefficient, this decision could underestimate the heterogeneity of subpopulations in large-scale studies, where a higher k value could reveal more granular risk stratifications. These limitations were partially mitigated by clinical validation of the identified groups, prioritizing medical relevance over purely statistical criteria.

## 4. Discussion

In this section, we present a summarized comparison of the two patient groups identified and discuss the main differences observed. It is important to preface this discussion by noting that our primary aim was not to replicate a supervised classification of a single outcome (such as the presence or absence of a past heart attack), but rather to leverage UMAP and k-means to uncover potentially more nuanced patient segments that reflect the risk for a broader spectrum of cardiovascular risk profiles based on their comprehensive data signatures. This aligns with a growing body of research demonstrating the power of unsupervised learning to identify novel signatures of health and disease from complex biomedical data, even without explicit diagnostic labels [9], and to delineate cardiovascular risk patterns in populations [29].

The dataset's 'positive/negative' labels, referring to the occurrence of a heart attack, represent a crucial clinical endpoint; however, cardiovascular health encompasses a wider array of conditions and risk gradations, and AI, including unsupervised methods, is increasingly recognized for its potential to enhance clinical value across this entire spectrum [30,31]. Our methodology sought to identify these underlying data-driven patient groupings, which may offer insights beyond the binary classification of a single outcome. Table 2 shows the average values of key variables for each group.

**Table 2.** Average Values of Key Variables in the Segmented Groups.

| | Group 1 | Group 2 |
|---|---|---|
| **age** | 58 | 55 |
| **gender** | Only 3% are men | 97% are men |
| **pressurehigh** | 127 | 127 |
| **pressurelow** | 73 | 72 |
| **glucose** | **143** | **150** |
| **KCM** | **8.18** | **18.65** |
| **troponin** | **0.1186** | **0.4761** |

The results obtained using UMAP and k-means clustering suggest that patients in Group 2 are at higher risk due to elevated levels of *troponin*, *KCM*, and *glucose*, three significant indicators for cardiac issues. Although Group 1 has a slightly higher average age, it does not exhibit the same elevated levels of these critical biomarkers.

The stark difference in gender distribution between the two groups is noteworthy; Group 2 consists of 97% male patients, whereas only 3% of Group 1 are male. This disparity could be clinically significant and may relate to gender-specific risk factors for cardiovascular diseases. Existing literature indicates that men have a higher risk of certain cardiac events compared to women, potentially due to differences in hormonal profiles, lifestyle factors, and prevalence of risk behaviors [32]. Exploring this aspect further would be valuable in future studies.

Interestingly, both groups have similar average blood pressure readings, implying that blood pressure may not be the distinguishing factor between these clusters. Instead, biomarkers like troponin and glucose appear to play a more pivotal role in differentiating patient risk profiles in this dataset.

Applying UMAP as a dimensionality reduction technique was crucial for clearly identifying the differences between the groups. By preserving both local and global data structures, UMAP facilitated the effective use of the k-means algorithm for patient segmentation. The combination of these AI techniques allowed us to uncover patterns that might not have been apparent using traditional linear methods like PCA.

### *4.1. Quantitative Alignment of Data-Driven Clusters with Heart Attack Labels*

This data-driven segmentation, free from the constraints of predefined outcome labels for a single condition, allows for the discovery of emergent patient profiles that may represent different points along the cardiovascular risk continuum or distinct etiological pathways. Indeed, unsupervised learning has proven effective in identifying clinically relevant subgroups in conditions like coronary artery disease [33] and in discovering groups in patients with subclinical cardiac dysfunction before evident clinical progression [34], highlighting its utility for personalized prevention and early risk stratification.

To address the need for quantitative validation against available ground truth, we evaluated how our two k-means clusters align with the dataset's binary 'positive'/'negative' labels for historical heart attack. A contingency analysis (Table 3) revealed the following distribution: Cluster 2 contained 308 'negative' and 586 'positive' patients, while Cluster 1 comprised 201 'negative' and 224 'positive' patients.

**Table 3.** Contingency analysis of clusters and labels.

| Cluster \ Class | Negative | Positive |
|---|---|---|
| **1** | 201 | 224 |
| **2** | 308 | 586 |

However, when we compared these clusters against the original clinical labels (positive/negative for cardiac event), we observed a purity of 60%, indicating substantial overlap rather than a clean separation (see Figure 8). The high-risk aligned Cluster 2 demonstrated a sensitivity (recall) of 72.3% in capturing patients with a 'positive' heart attack label, and a precision (positive predictive value) of 65.5%.

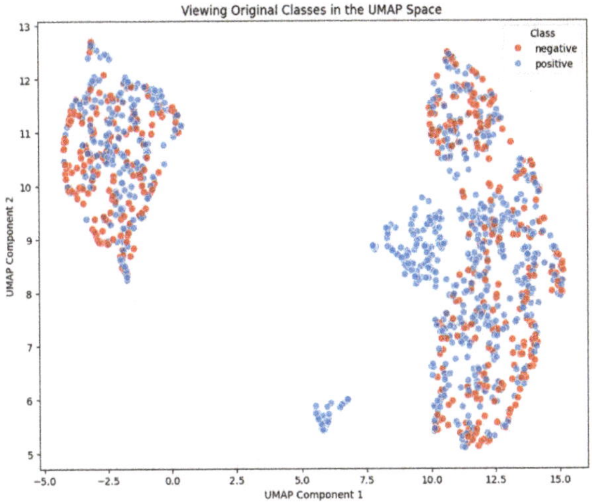


**Figure 8.** Mapping of the classes into the clusters.

It is crucial to emphasize that k-means in this context is not intended as a supervised classifier for predicting cardiac events, but rather as an exploratory tool to reveal latent structure in the biomarker space reduced by UMAP. Thus, a 60% purity and a precision of 65.5% (which is only marginally above the baseline prevalence of 'positive' cases) should not be viewed as a 40% "error rate", but as a measure of concordance between unsupervised groupings and predefined clinical categories [35].

This divergence highlights that the UMAP + k-means clusters capture a different, potentially orthogonal, structure from the binary labels. The fact that both clusters contain a majority of 'positive' cases yet are clearly distinguished by the k-means algorithm based on UMAP-transformed biomarker (as shown in Figure 7 and Table 2), strongly suggests that our unsupervised approach is identifying distinct patient phenotypes even within a population with a high prevalence of the 'positive' historical heart attack label.

In cardiovascular medicine, disease phenotypes are often heterogeneous and multifactorial. Patients labelled "negative" may share subclinical biomarker profiles with those labelled "positive", reflecting intermediate or early-stage pathophysiology not encoded in a simple dichotomy. The observed overlap and 60% purity, therefore, suggest the existence of intermediate subpopulations or a continuous risk spectrum beyond the scope of the labels used [30].

Critically, the clinical utility of our clusters is further underscored by their distinct biomarker profiles (Table 2). For example, Cluster 2 not only captured 72.3% of patients with a prior heart attack label but also contained 308 patients labeled 'negative'. These individuals, despite lacking a documented past event, share a high-risk biomarker signature (elevated troponin, KCM, glucose) with many 'positive' patients. This is precisely the type of subclinical risk profile that our unsupervised approach aims to uncover, potentially identifying individuals who could benefit from proactive monitoring or preventive strategies before an overt event occurs. Therefore, the quantitative alignment with the binary 'heart attack' label, while providing one dimension of evaluation, must be interpreted alongside the rich clinical and biomarker distinctions that define the clusters and point towards a broader cardiovascular risk assessment.

### 4.2. Clinical Implications and Pathway to Personalized Cardiology and Improved Outcomes

The findings of this study, stemming from an unsupervised, biomarker-driven patient segmentation, offer several compelling clinical implications and pave the way for impactful future research directions. The ability of our AI-powered approach to discern distinct patient groups, particularly Group 2, characterized by its high-risk biomarker profile (elevated troponin, KCM, and glucose), holds a significant and actionable promise for transforming proactive cardiovascular risk management. This approach aligns with the principles of personalized medicine, where interventions are customized to individual patient profiles [36].

As a possible clinical implication, the statistical and clinical analysis of key biomarkers may offer clinical significance, such as *troponin* is a highly specific biomarker of myocardial injury and is widely used in the diagnosis and prognosis of acute coronary syndromes. In this study, Group 2 patients show an average troponin level of 0.4761 ng/mL, significantly higher than the 0.1186 ng/mL observed in Group 1. This finding suggests possible underlying ischemia or latent myocardial damage in these patients, which could correlate with a higher risk of coronary events in the short to medium term [37].

The clinical and prognostic implications: The elevated troponin levels in Group 2 support the hypothesis of a high cardiovascular risk profile. Recent studies indicate that even moderately elevated troponin levels are associated with increased all-cause and cardiovascular mortality [38]. Thus, patients in this group may benefit from close monitoring and intensive preventive interventions, such as angiotensin-converting enzyme inhibitors (ACEIs) or beta-blockers, to mitigate the risk of cardiac events.

On cross-check data, glucose levels and metabolic risk: Hyperglycemia is a key marker of insulin resistance and metabolic dysfunction, factors closely linked to cardiovascular risk [39]. In this study, Group 2 shows an average glucose level of 150 mg/dL, compared to 143 mg/dL in Group 1. Although both groups present hyperglycemia, the elevated levels in Group 2 suggest a possible coexistence of prediabetes or type 2 diabetes, conditions that exacerbate the risk of atherosclerosis and other adverse cardiovascular events [40].

Implications for metabolic health and cardiovascular risk: Sustained hyperglycemia, as observed in both groups, is a risk factor for microvascular and macrovascular complications. Studies indicate that dysglycemia promotes a chronic inflammatory state and increased oxidative stress, pathological processes that contribute to endothelial damage and atherosclerosis [41]. The combination of elevated troponin and glucose levels in Group 2 may indicate an increased risk of metabolic syndrome and coronary artery disease.

To continue the comparison of metabolic repercussions between groups, Group 1 can be defined as having a lower risk profile. Clinical and risk profile: Patients in Group 1 exhibit moderately elevated glucose levels but relatively low troponin levels, suggesting a lower cardiovascular risk burden. Moderate hyperglycemia, in the absence of myocardial injury markers, may indicate an early phase of metabolic dysfunction without significant cardiovascular involvement. Intervention strategies: Recommendations for these patients may focus on primary prevention strategies, such as lifestyle modifications (healthy diet, regular exercise) and the use of metformin to improve insulin sensitivity and reduce the risk of progression to type 2 diabetes and cardiovascular events [42].

Group 2 can be defined as having a high-risk profile. Implications of high cardiovascular and metabolic risk: The co-elevation of troponin and glucose in Group 2 suggests more severe metabolic dysregulation and a substantially increased cardiovascular risk. This clinical profile is consistent with metabolic syndrome and a state of low-grade chronic inflammation, conditions that increase the risk of atherothrombosis and cardiovascular events [43]. Priority clinical interventions: For patients in this group, intensive management is essential, which may include optimizing glycemic control through insulin therapy or newer antidiabetics (such as SGLT2 inhibitors or GLP-1 agonists) and the use of statins to reduce cardiovascular risk. Moreover, troponin monitoring could provide valuable information on the response to interventions and the risk of short-term cardiac events [44].

## 5. Conclusions

This study demonstrates the feasibility of using machine learning techniques to identify groups of patients with different levels of relevant cardiovascular risk profiles specific to this cohort of 1319 patients. While this study introduces a novel, data-driven segmentation of individuals based on real-time biomarkers such as troponin, without incorporating labeled clinical outcomes like documented cardiovascular events.

In evaluating the alignment of these data-driven segments with the dataset's 'heart attack (positive/negative)' labels, we observed a quantitative correspondence accuracy of 60% when mapping clusters to these binary outcomes. Notably, both identified clusters contained a majority of patients with a 'positive' heart attack label, yet were distinctly separated by our UMAP + k-means approach based on their comprehensive biomarker profiles. This underscores that while the clusters capture a significant portion of patients with a documented past event (e.g., the higher-risk biomarker cluster encompassed 72.3% of 'positive' cases), their primary utility lies in identifying nuanced patient phenotypes including individuals labeled 'negative' but exhibiting high-risk biomarker signatures that reflect a broader spectrum of cardiovascular risk beyond a single historical event.

Our unsupervised segmentation approach, by focusing on these intrinsic data patterns rather than being constrained by predefined diagnostic labels, can serve as a powerful complement to traditional risk assessment tools [9,10]. It can reveal "hidden risk" in patients whose biomarker profiles suggest underlying myocardial distress or metabolic derangement not yet clinically apparent or fully weighted in standard risk calculators.

In a clinical context, these insights can guide proactive screening and personalized monitoring strategies for patients who, despite being labeled "negative", may share a biomarker signature with higher-risk individuals, thereby enabling truly precision-driven interventions beyond conventional diagnostics [30,35].

Group 2, characterized by high troponin (0.4761 ng/mL), KCM (18.65 ng/mL), glucose levels (150 mg/dL), and a predominance of male patients (97%), requires prioritized medical attention and specific intervention strategies such as Sodium-Glucose Transport Protein 2 (SGLT2) inhibitors [45,46] or troponin-guided monitoring [47,48]. In contrast, patients in Group 1, although older (mean age 58 vs. 55 years), appear to have a lower risk based on these biomarkers, suggesting reduced acute risk despite advanced age.

The extreme gender disparity in Group 2 (97% male) highlights potential sex-specific risk factors, such as hormonal or behavioral differences, warranting tailored prevention strategies. Notably, blood pressure, a conventional risk metric, showed no significant variation between groups (127/73 vs. 127/72 mmHg), emphasizing the primacy of biomarkers like troponin and glucose in risk stratification.

Applying the k-means clustering algorithm alongside dimensionality reduction techniques like PCA and UMAP allowed us to effectively group patients and clearly visualize the data. These findings can assist healthcare professionals in clinical decision-making and in designing prevention and treatment programs.

While PCA, UMAP, and k-means are individually established techniques, our work uniquely integrates them into a clinical decision-support pipeline that (1) prioritizes UMAP to model nonlinear biomarker interactions critical for risk stratification, and (2) delivers actionable, patient-specific interventions (e.g., SGLT2 inhibitors for high-risk groups). This two-tiered approach—bridging nonlinear ML and therapeutic targeting—represents a critical advance over purely algorithmic applications, translating unsupervised learning into real-world cardiology practice.

Segmenting patients using AI techniques offers a promising avenue for improving the diagnosis and prevention of cardiovascular diseases. It provides significant advantages:

- Early Risk Identification: Enables the detection of patterns and risk factors that might go unnoticed in traditional analyses.
- Personalized Treatments: Facilitates patient stratification, potentially leading to more personalized and effective interventions.
- Impact on Precision Medicine: Incorporating biomarker analysis into risk assessment offers an opportunity to implement targeted and evidence-based interventions. For instance, patients in Group 2 could benefit from comprehensive management programs to reduce cardiovascular risk and improve long-term clinical outcomes, aligning with the principles of personalized medicine [5].
- Optimization of Healthcare Resources: Helps prioritize medical care toward patients at higher risk, enhancing efficiency in resource allocation.

However, this study has some limitations. This study focused on unsupervised methods to uncover subclinical patterns without relying on diagnostic labels. While a supervised model could predict infarctions with high accuracy, it would not identify subgroups of patients with emerging risk profiles, which are critical for proactive preventive strategies. As such, future work will focus on a supervised validation phase, where clinical outcomes will be integrated to assess the prospective value of these subgroups in predicting cardiovascular events. Additionally, longitudinal data will be crucial to evaluate the temporal stability and progression of these phenotypic clusters, potentially guiding personalized preventive interventions.

We recommend expanding this study by incorporating more clinical variables and utilizing different clustering algorithms to validate and enrich the results. Additionally, future work should consider variables related to lifestyle habits, such as smoking, diet, physical activity, and cholesterol levels, among others.

**Author Contributions:** Conceptualization, J.D.G.-F., R.R.-R. and J.E.L.-R.; Methodology, J.D.G.-F., S.V.-R. and A.G.-M.; Software, J.D.G.-F., J.E.G.-T. and J.E.L.-R.; Validation, S.V.-R., A.-F.L.-N. and E.A.I.-F.; writing—original draft preparation, J.D.G.-F., R.R.-R. and J.E.L.-R.; writing—review and editing, R.R.-R., J.E.L.-R., A.G.-M., A.-F.L.-N., J.L.-A. and E.A.I.-F.; funding acquisition, R.R.-R.; Investigation, J.E.G.-T. and E.A.I.-F.; Formal Analysis, E.A.I.-F. All authors have read and agreed to the published version of the manuscript.

**Funding:** This research received no external funding.

**Data Availability Statement:** The data that support the findings of this study are available from the corresponding author upon reasonable request.

**Acknowledgments:** The authors would like to thank the CICESE Research Center and the Secretariat of Science, Humanities, Technology and Innovation (Secihti) for their support.

**Conflicts of Interest:** The authors declare no conflicts of interest.

# Appendix A

**Table A1.** Related works.

| Previous Work | Contributions | Opportunity |
|---|---|---|
| Unsupervised Learning for Heart Disease Prediction: Clustering-Based Approach [10] | Comparison of unsupervised models (k-means, DBSCAN, etc.) for patient stratification. Web interface for clinical use. | Lack of integration with lifestyle variables. It is mainly based on age and gender. |
| Detecting cardiovascular diseases using unsupervised machine learning clustering based on electronic medical records [11] | Robust model with EMR (155k patients) using k-means and PCA. High accuracy (~86%) in CVD detection. | It does not include advanced biomarkers (e.g., troponin). Linear PCA: Reduction to 2D mixes nonlinear clusters, limiting visual/clinical separation. |
| Machine learning-based prediction models for cardiovascular disease risk using electronic health records data: systematic review and meta-analysis [49] | Meta-analysis demonstrates superiority of ML (AUC 0.86) over traditional models. Identifies methodological heterogeneity as a clinical barrier. | Lack of standardization in metrics and external validation. |
| Our study | Combines k-means with UMAP (not just PCA) for better visualization/clustering. Focus on specific biomarkers (troponin, CK-MB) for accurate stratification. Identifies at-risk groups with significant differences in biomarkers (not just demographic variables). | Could be scaled with temporal data to predict dynamic risk. It could include more variables related to lifestyle habits, such as smoking, diet, physical activity, and cholesterol levels. |

**Table A2.** Fragment of ten entries of the medical dataset.

| Age | Gender | Pulse | Pressurehigh | Pressurelow | Glucose | KCM | Troponin |
|---|---|---|---|---|---|---|---|
| 64 | 1 | 66 | 160 | 83 | 160 | 1.80 | 0.012 |
| 21 | 1 | 94 | 98 | 46 | 296 | 6.75 | 1.060 |
| 55 | 1 | 64 | 160 | 77 | 270 | 1.99 | 0.003 |
| 64 | 1 | 70 | 120 | 55 | 270 | 13.87 | 0.122 |
| 55 | 1 | 64 | 112 | 65 | 300 | 1.08 | 0.003 |
| 58 | 0 | 61 | 112 | 58 | 87 | 1.83 | 0.004 |
| 32 | 0 | 40 | 179 | 68 | 102 | 0.71 | 0.003 |
| 63 | 1 | 60 | 214 | 82 | 87 | 300 | 2.370 |
| 44 | 0 | 60 | 154 | 81 | 135 | 2.35 | 0.004 |
| 67 | 1 | 61 | 160 | 95 | 100 | 2.84 | 0.011 |

# Appendix B

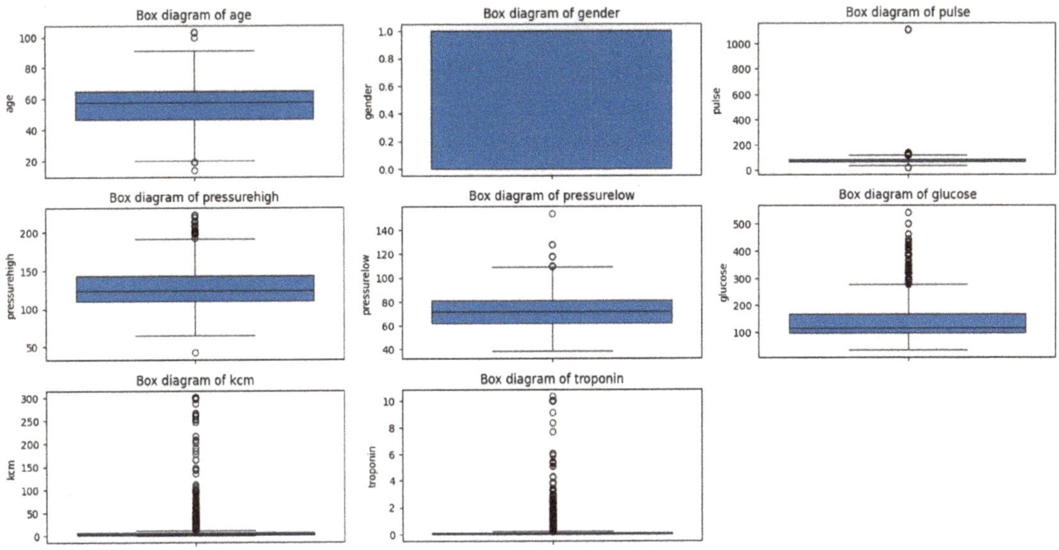


**Figure A1.** Outliers in the medical dataset.

## References

1. World Health Organization (WHO). Cardiovascular Diseases (CVDs). Available online: https://www.who.int/news-room/fact-sheets/detail/cardiovascular-diseases-(cvds) (accessed on 23 October 2024).
2. Chen, Y.; Tang, M.; Yuan, S.; Fu, S.; Li, Y.; Li, Y.; Wang, Q.; Cao, Y.; Liu, L.; Zhang, Q. Rhodiola rosea: A Therapeutic Candidate on Cardiovascular Diseases. *Oxidative Med. Cell Longev.* **2022**, *2022*, 1348795. [CrossRef] [PubMed]
3. Heaton, J. Ian Goodfellow, Yoshua Bengio, and Aaron Courville: Deep learning. *Genet. Program. Evolvable Mach.* **2018**, *19*, 305–307. [CrossRef]
4. Esteva, A.; Robicquet, A.; Ramsundar, B.; Kuleshov, V.; DePristo, M.; Chou, K.; Cui, C.; Corrado, G.; Thrun, S.; Dean, J. A guide to deep learning in healthcare. *Nat. Med.* **2019**, *25*, 24–29. [CrossRef]
5. Topol, E.J. High-performance medicine: The convergence of human and artificial intelligence. *Nat. Med.* **2019**, *25*, 44–56. [CrossRef]
6. Capó, M.; Pérez, A.; Lozano, J.A. An efficient approximation to the K-means clustering for massive data. *Knowl.-Based Syst.* **2017**, *117*, 56–69. [CrossRef]
7. Jolliffe, I.T.; Cadima, J. Principal component analysis: A review and recent developments. *Philos. Trans. R. Soc. A Math. Phys. Eng. Sci.* **2016**, *374*, 20150202. [CrossRef]
8. McInnes, L.; Healy, J.; Melville, J. UMAP: Uniform Manifold Approximation and Projection for Dimension Reduction. *J. Mach. Learn. Res.* **2020**. [CrossRef]
9. Shomorony, I.; Cirulli, E.T.; Huang, L.; Napier, L.A.; Heister, R.R.; Hicks, M.; Cohen, I.V.; Yu, H.-C.; Swisher, C.L.; Schenker-Ahmed, N.M.; et al. An unsupervised learning approach to identify novel signatures of health and disease from multimodal data. *Genome Med.* **2020**, *12*, 7. [CrossRef] [PubMed]
10. Jetty, J.; Sk, S.S.; Polepalle, R.B.; Parusu, V. Unsupervised Learning for Heart Disease Prediction: Clustering-Based Approach. *ITM Web Conf.* **2025**, *74*, 01005. [CrossRef]
11. Hu, Y.; Yan, H.; Liu, M.; Gao, J.; Xie, L.; Zhang, C.; Wei, L.; Ding, Y.; Jiang, H. Detecting cardiovascular diseases using unsupervised machine learning clustering based on electronic medical records. *BMC Med. Res. Methodol.* **2024**, *24*, 309. [CrossRef]
12. Apple, F.S.; Sandoval, Y.; Jaffe, A.S.; Ordonez-Llanos, J. Cardiac Troponin Assays: Guide to Understanding Analytical Characteristics and Their Impact on Clinical Care. *Clin. Chem.* **2017**, *63*, 73–81. [CrossRef] [PubMed]
13. Shah, A.S.V.; Griffiths, M.; Lee, K.K.; A McAllister, D.; Hunter, A.L.; Ferry, A.V.; Cruikshank, A.; Reid, A.; Stoddart, M.; Strachan, F.; et al. High sensitivity cardiac troponin and the under-diagnosis of myocardial infarction in women: Prospective cohort study. *BMJ* **2015**, *350*, g7873. [CrossRef] [PubMed]
14. Ayushi; Sethi, S.; Jyoti. Heart Disease Prediction Integrating UMAP and XGBoost. *Int. J. Recent Technol. Eng.* **2020**, *9*, 2449–2457. [CrossRef]
15. Cunningham, J.P.; Ghahramani, Z. Linear Dimensionality Reduction: Survey, Insights, and Generalizations. *J. Ma-Chine Learn. Res.* **2015**, *16*, 2859–2900.
16. Abdi, H.; Williams, L.J. Principal component analysis. *WIREs Comput. Stat.* **2010**, *2*, 433–459. [CrossRef]
17. Gonzalez-Franco, J.D.; Preciado-Velasco, J.E.; Lozano-Rizk, J.E.; Rivera-Rodriguez, R.; Torres-Rodriguez, J.; Alonso-Arevalo, M.A. Comparison of Supervised Learning Algorithms on a 5G Dataset Reduced via Principal Component Analysis (PCA). *Future Internet* **2023**, *15*, 335. [CrossRef]
18. Gale, C.P.; Kashinath, C.; Brooksby, P. The association between hyperglycaemia and elevated troponin levels on mortality in acute coronary syndromes. *Diabetes Vasc. Dis. Res.* **2006**, *3*, 80–83. [CrossRef] [PubMed]
19. Becht, E.; McInnes, L.; Healy, J.; Dutertre, C.-A.; Kwok, I.W.H.; Ng, L.G.; Ginhoux, F.; Newell, E.W. Dimensionality reduction for visualizing single-cell data using UMAP. *Nat. Biotechnol.* **2019**, *37*, 38–44. [CrossRef] [PubMed]
20. Xu, D.; Tian, Y. A Comprehensive Survey of Clustering Algorithms. *Ann. Data Sci.* **2015**, *2*, 165–193. [CrossRef]
21. Ikotun, A.M.; Ezugwu, A.E.; Abualigah, L.; Abuhaija, B.; Heming, J. K-means clustering algorithms: A comprehensive review, variants analysis, and advances in the era of big data. *Inf. Sci.* **2023**, *622*, 178–210. [CrossRef]
22. Bholowalia, P.; Kumar, A. EBK-Means: A Clustering Technique Based on Elbow Method and K-Means in WSN. *Int. J. Comput. Appl.* **2014**, *105*, 17–24. Available online: https://citeseerx.ist.psu.edu/document?repid=rep1&type=pdf&doi=5771aa21b2e151f3d93ba0a5f12d023a0bfcf28b (accessed on 20 March 2025).
23. Arbelaitz, O.; Gurrutxaga, I.; Muguerza, J.; Pérez, J.M.; Perona, I. An extensive comparative study of cluster validity indices. *Pattern Recognit.* **2013**, *46*, 243–256. [CrossRef]
24. Schober, P.; Boer, C.; Schwarte, L.A. Correlation Coefficients: Appropriate Use and Interpretation. *Anesth. Analg.* **2018**, *126*, 1763–1768. [CrossRef]

25. Whelton, P.K.; Carey, R.M.; Aronow, W.S.; Casey, D.E.; Collins, K.J.; Dennison Himmelfarb, C.; DePalma, S.M.; Gidding, S.; Jamerson, K.A.; Jones, D.W.; et al. ACC/AHA/AAPA/ABC/ACPM/AGS/APhA/ASH/ASPC/NMA/PCNA Guideline for the Prevention, Detection, Evaluation, and Management of High Blood Pressure in Adults. *J. Am. Coll. Cardiol.* **2018**, *71*, e127–e248. [CrossRef]
26. Everitt, B.S.; Landau, S.; Leese, M.; Stahl, D. *Cluster Analysis*, 5th ed.; Wiley Series in Probability and Statistics; John Wiley & Sons, Inc.: Chichester, UK, 2011. [CrossRef]
27. Van Der Maaten, L.; Hinton, G. Visualizing Data Using t-SNE. Netherlands, Aug 2008. Available online: https://jmlr.csail.mit.edu/papers/volume9/vandermaaten08a/vandermaaten08a.pdf (accessed on 25 October 2024).
28. McInnes, L.; Healy, J.; Saul, N.; Großberger, L. UMAP: Uniform Manifold Approximation and Projection. *J. Open Source Softw.* **2018**, *3*, 861. [CrossRef]
29. Segar, M.W.; Rao, S.; Navar, A.M.; Michos, E.D.; Lewis, A.; Correa, A.; Sims, M.; Khera, A.; Hughes, A.E.; Pandey, A. County-level phenomapping to identify disparities in cardiovascular outcomes: An unsupervised clustering analysis. *Am. J. Prev. Cardiol.* **2020**, *4*, 100118. [CrossRef]
30. Saba, P.S.; Al Kindi, S.; Nasir, K. Redefining Cardiovascular Risk Assessment as a Spectrum. *Circ.* **2024**, *83*, 574–576. [CrossRef]
31. Gill, S.K.; Karwath, A.; Uh, H.-W.; Cardoso, V.R.; Gu, Z.; Barsky, A.; Slater, L.; Acharjee, A.; Duan, J.; Dall'Olio, L.; et al. Artificial intelligence to enhance clinical value across the spectrum of cardiovascular healthcare. *Eur. Heart J.* **2023**, *44*, 713–725. [CrossRef]
32. Regitz-Zagrosek, V.; Kararigas, G. Mechanistic Pathways of Sex Differences in Cardiovascular Disease. *Physiol. Rev.* **2017**, *97*, 1–37. [CrossRef]
33. Flores, A.M.; Schuler, A.; Eberhard, A.V.; Olin, J.W.; Cooke, J.P.; Leeper, N.J.; Shah, N.H.; Ross, E.G. Unsupervised Learning for Automated Detection of Coronary Artery Disease Subgroups. *J. Am. Heart Assoc.* **2021**, *10*, e021976. [CrossRef]
34. Kaptein, Y.E.; Karagodin, I.; Zuo, H.; Lu, Y.; Zhang, J.; Kaptein, J.S.; Strande, J.L. Identifying Phenogroups in patients with subclinical diastolic dysfunction using unsupervised statistical learning. *BMC Cardiovasc. Disord.* **2020**, *20*, 367. [CrossRef] [PubMed]
35. Gordon, M.M.; Moser, A.M.; Rubin, E. Unsupervised analysis of classical biomedical markers: Robustness and medical relevance of patient clustering using bioinformatics tools. *PLoS ONE* **2012**, *7*, e29578. [CrossRef]
36. Ashley, E.A. The Precision Medicine Initiative. *JAMA* **2015**, *313*, 2119–2120. [CrossRef]
37. Thygesen, K.; Alpert, J.S.; Jaffe, A.S.; Chaitman, B.R.; Bax, J.J.; Morrow, D.A.; White, H.D. Fourth Universal Definition of Myocardial Infarction (2018). *Circulation* **2018**, *138*, e618–e651. [CrossRef]
38. Daccord, N.; Celton, J.-M.; Linsmith, G.; Becker, C.; Choisne, N.; Schijlen, E.; van de Geest, H.; Bianco, L.; Micheletti, D.; Velasco, R.; et al. High-quality de novo assembly of the apple genome and methylome dynamics of early fruit development. *Nat. Genet.* **2017**, *49*, 1099–1106. [CrossRef] [PubMed]
39. American Diabetes Association. Standards of Medical Care in Diabetes—2021 Abridged for Primary Care Providers. *Clin. Diabetes* **2021**, *39*, 14–43. [CrossRef]
40. Swinburn, B.A.; Kraak, V.I.; Allender, S.; Atkins, V.J.; Baker, P.I.; Bogard, J.R.; Brinsden, H.; Calvillo, A.; De Schutter, O.; Devarajan, R.; et al. The Global Syndemic of Obesity, Undernutrition, and Climate Change: The Lancet Commission report. *Lancet* **2019**, *393*, 791–846. [CrossRef]
41. Brownlee, M. The Pathobiology of Diabetic Complications. *Diabetes* **2005**, *54*, 1615–1625. [CrossRef]
42. Knowler, W.C.; Barrett-Connor, E.; Fowler, S.E.; Hamman, R.F.; Lachin, J.M.; Walker, E.A.; Nathan, D.M.; Diabetes Prevention Program Research Group. Reduction in the incidence of type 2 diabetes with lifestyle intervention or metformin. *N. Engl. J. Med.* **2002**, *346*, 393–403. [CrossRef]
43. Grundy, S.M.; Cleeman, J.I.; Daniels, S.R.; Donato, K.A.; Eckel, R.H.; Franklin, B.A.; Gordon, D.J.; Krauss, R.M.; Savage, P.J.; Smith, S.C., Jr.; et al. Diagnosis and management of the metabolic syndrome: An American Heart Association/National Heart, Lung, and Blood Institute Scientific Statement. *Circulation* **2005**, *112*, 2735–2752. [CrossRef]
44. Kumar, V.; Thakur, J.K.; Prasad, M. Histone acetylation dynamics regulating plant development and stress responses. *Cell Mol. Life Sci.* **2021**, *78*, 4467–4486. [CrossRef] [PubMed]
45. Zannad, F.; Ferreira, J.P.; Pocock, S.J.; Anker, S.D.; Butler, J.; Filippatos, G.; Brueckmann, M.; Ofstad, A.P.; Pfarr, E.; Jamal, W.; et al. SGLT2 inhibitors in patients with heart failure with reduced ejection fraction: A meta-analysis of the EMPEROR-Reduced and DAPA-HF trials. *Lancet* **2020**, *396*, 819–829. [CrossRef] [PubMed]
46. McMurray, J.J.V.; Solomon, S.D.; Inzucchi, S.E.; Køber, L.; Kosiborod, M.N.; Martinez, F.A.; Ponikowski, P.; Sabatine, M.S.; Anand, I.S.; Bělohlávek, J.; et al. Dapagliflozin in Patients with Heart Failure and Reduced Ejection Fraction. *N. Engl. J. Med.* **2019**, *381*, 1995–2008. [CrossRef] [PubMed]
47. Allen, B.R.; Christenson, R.H.; Cohen, S.A.; Nowak, R.; Wilkerson, R.G.; Mumma, B.; Madsen, T.; McCord, J.; Veld, M.H.I.; Massoomi, M.; et al. Diagnostic Performance of High-Sensitivity Cardiac Troponin T Strategies and Clinical Variables in a Multisite US Cohort. *Circulation* **2021**, *143*, 1659–1672. [CrossRef]

48. A Byrne, R.; Rossello, X.; Coughlan, J.J.; Barbato, E.; Berry, C.; Chieffo, A.; Claeys, M.J.; Dan, G.-A.; Dweck, M.R.; Galbraith, M.; et al. 2023 ESC Guidelines for the management of acute coronary syndromes. *Eur. Heart J.* **2023**, *44*, 3720–3826. [CrossRef]
49. Liu, T.; Krentz, A.; Lu, L.; Curcin, V. Machine learning based prediction models for cardiovascular disease risk using electronic health records data: Systematic review and meta-analysis. *Eur. Heart J. Digit. Health* **2025**, *6*, 7–22. [CrossRef]

machine learning & knowledge extraction

MDPI

*Article*

# Optimizing a Double Stage Heat Transformer Performance by Levenberg–Marquardt Artificial Neural Network

**Suset Vázquez-Aveledo [1], Rosenberg J. Romero [2,*], Lorena Díaz-González [3], Moisés Montiel-González [4] and Jesús Cerezo [2]**

[1] Postgraduate in Science, Autonomous University of Morelos State, Av. Universidad 1001, Cuernavaca 62209, Morelos, Mexico; suset.vazquez@uaem.edu.mx
[2] Engineering and Applied Research Centre, CIICAp, Autonomous University of Morelos State, Av. Universidad 1001, Cuernavaca 62209, Morelos, Mexico; jesus.cerezo@uaem.mx
[3] Research Center in Sciences, Autonomous University of Morelos State, Av. Universidad 1001, Cuernavaca 62209, Morelos, Mexico; ldg@uaem.mx
[4] Faculty of Chemical Sciences and Engineering, Autonomous University of Morelos State, Av. Universidad 1001, Cuernavaca 62209, Morelos, Mexico; moises.montiel@uaem.mx
* Correspondence: rosenberg@uaem.mx; Tel.: +52-777-329700 (ext. 6233)

**Abstract:** Waste heat recovery is a critical strategy for optimizing energy consumption and reducing greenhouse gas emissions. In this context, the circular economy highlights the importance of this practice as a key tool to enhance energy efficiency, minimize waste, and decrease environmental impact. Artificial neural networks are particularly well-suited for managing nonlinearities and complex interactions among multiple variables, making them ideal for controlling a double-stage absorption heat transformer. This study aims to simultaneously optimize both user-defined parameters. Levenberg–Marquardt and scaled conjugated gradient algorithms were compared from five to twenty-five neurons to determine the optimal operating conditions while the coefficient of performance and the gross temperature lift were simultaneously maximized. The methodology includes R2024a MATLAB© programming, real-time data acquisition, visual engineering environment software, and flow control hardware. The results show that applying the Levenberg–Marquardt algorithm resulted in an increase in the correlation coefficient (R) at 20 neurons, improving the thermodynamic performance and enabling greater energy recovery from waste heat.

**Keywords:** absorption heat pump; absorption heat transformer; artificial neural networks; automatic control; water–lithium bromide

## 1. Introduction

Waste heat recovery has established itself as an essential strategy to optimize energy consumption and mitigate greenhouse gas emissions in industry [1]. In parallel, the use of renewable energy continues to grow rapidly, and it is projected that by the end of 2025, it will account for approximately 30% of global energy consumption [2]. In this context, absorption heat transformers (AHTs), considered a type of absorption heat pump [3], stand out as thermodynamically efficient equipment, capable of adapting to renewable sources such as solar and geothermal [4] and converting waste energy into a valuable resource, boosting sustainability and industrial efficiency [5,6].

The circular economy promotes waste heat recovery as a fundamental practice to optimize energy use, minimize waste, and reduce the environmental impact of industrial processes [7]. The integration of absorption heat pumps, with circular economy principles, is becoming increasingly important to improve energy efficiency and reduce environmental impacts in various industrial sectors. Recent studies highlight the central role of absorption heat pumps in the recovery and reuse of waste heat, as well as in the efficient conversion of energy resources supporting the circular economy model [8,9]. These applications encourage the reuse of resources and reduce dependence on primary sources.

In addition, research on efficient cogeneration systems [10] and latent heat recovery technologies in wet biomass flows [11] underlines the importance of absorption heat pumps to close energy cycles in industrial processes. Likewise, the integration of renewable energies, such as concentrated solar power for low-pressure steam generation [12], or the optimization of hydrogen-integrated energy centers [13], reinforces the transition to sustainable models, demonstrating that AHT can be a key catalyst for the synergy between energy efficiency and economic sustainability.

Due to the multiple variables present in the thermodynamic cycle of an AHT, the need arises for an automatic control that considers in its strategy both the multiple variables present in the cycle as well as the associated disturbances that can guarantee its correct operation. Proposals for automatic control related to classical control methods, such as PID (proportional–integral–derivative) controllers, have been published in the literature [14]; however, these approaches are limited to nonlinear and multivariable systems such as AHTs. This study was limited to calculating the flow ratio; however, the control response in the two cycles was not characterized.

On the other hand, artificial intelligence (AI) technologies, such as artificial neural networks (ANNs) and fuzzy logic (FL), have become key tools for the development of advanced control systems. These methodologies stand out for their ability to efficiently manage nonlinearities, multivariable interactions, and uncertainty scenarios, making them ideal for applications in complex and dynamic systems [15].

Several scientific publications have reported the use of ANN applied to thermal processes. Ref. [16] uses ANN in heat pumps to improve demand response, achieving high precision and optimizing energy consumption. Ref. [17] apply reinforcement learning to optimize control in a heat pump, achieving greater efficiency in energy management. Ref. [18] uses ANN to control a heat pump to improve energy efficiency and thermal comfort. Sajadi predicts real-time temperature fields in manufacturing processes using ANN [19]. In addition, Yarahmadi proposes the ANN in a laser powder bed fusion process to predict the distribution of the temperatures present [20]. On the other hand, in pyrolysis processes, Muravyev focuses on the application of ANN for thermal analysis [21]. Also, Zhang combines ANN and genetic algorithms to maximize heat transfer and minimize pressure loss of finned heat exchangers with elliptical tubes [22], but there is no ANN for a double-stage absorption heat transformer (DSHT) for maximizing simultaneously coefficient of performance (COP) and gross temperature lift (GTL).

This study is based on the premise that no reports in the literature on applications of double-stage absorption heat transformers that use artificial intelligence for automatic control. This system presents multiple variables with high nonlinearity, such as enthalpy, which are essential for the calculation of the thermal power of the eight heat exchangers that make up the thermodynamic cycle. Furthermore, the double-stage absorption heat transformer requires centralized automatic control that considers all the present variables and the associated disturbances. The measured data can be trained by artificial neural networks, allowing for greater accuracy compared to previously published idealized models [6].

The objective of this work is the fusion of the technology of R2024a ANN-Matlab© software with a commercial mass flow control system to obtain the maximum value of the temperature desired by the user simultaneously with the maximum value of the performance coefficient as a function of the surrounding temperatures (condenser temperature in

AHT (TCO) associated with that of the environment, generator temperature in AHT (TGE) associated with the temperatures of the waste heat source) for circular economy thermal processes. This work is a continuation of our previous publication [3], in which only the control strategy based on maximizing the COP × GTL product separately for each stage of the AHT was presented.

## 2. Materials and Methods

This section identifies the software, hardware, and flowchart used for fluid flow control (MEV1), as well as the methodology used to obtain the maximize the COP × GTL using artificial intelligence techniques.

### 2.1. Signal Characterization

A computer-aided simulator was developed based on experimental data obtained in the prototype of the double stage heat transformer (DSHT) physically installed in the Laboratory of Applied Thermal Engineering of the Center for Research in Engineering and Applied Sciences (CIICAP) of the Autonomous University of the State of Morelos, Mexico. Based on experimental data, this simulator was developed with the main objective of analyzing the system's behavior under different operating conditions. Additionally, it determines the time required to reach a desired state from the transient heating stages. In Appendix C, an actual photograph of the DSHT is shown on the entire page.

To this end, in each test, the temperature variations during the heating stage were recorded and the coefficients of the function that presented the highest correlation in each case were obtained. These coefficients, together with temperature variations, allowed the generation of a third-degree polynomial function that describes the variation in temperature over time. This tool enables the analysis of temperature behavior in each DSHT channel at any given time. Tables 1 and 2 present the 44 temperature channels of the equipment and the functions obtained for each of them. Additional uncertainty analysis was calculated for each temperature channel at operating conditions of each by error propagation theory.

**Table 1.** DSHT stage 1 channel temperature variation function.

| Canals | Stage 1 | Uncertainty (°C) |
|---|---|---|
| C101 | $\Delta T(t) = -0.0000001t^3 + 0.00002t^2 + 0.0235t + 37.075$ | ±0.002419 |
| C102 | $\Delta T(t) = -0.000000002t^3 - 0.000017t^2 + 0.0167t + 25.993$ | ±0.001718 |
| C103 | $\Delta T(t) = -0.000000002t^3 - 0.000017t^2 + 0.0167t + 25.993$ | ±0.001718 |
| C104 | $\Delta T(t) = 0.00000082t^3 - 0.00034t^2 + 0.0679t + 32.918$ | ±0.003738 |
| C105 | $\Delta T(t) = 0.00000002t^3 - 0.000036t^2 + 0.0961t + 24.398$ | ±0.002805 |
| C106 | $\Delta T(t) = 0.00000005t^3 - 0.000027t^2 + 0.0099t + 28.052$ | ±0.001371 |
| C107 | $\Delta T(t) = 0.00000029t^3 - 0.00012t^2 + 0.0476t + 30.241$ | ±0.003054 |
| C108 | $\Delta T(t) = 0.0000002t^3 - 0.00005t^2 + 0.0431t + 32.702$ | ±0.002042 |
| C109 | $\Delta T(t) = -0.00000015t^3 - 0.00008t^2 + 0.0417t + 30.954$ | ±0.002312 |
| C110 | $\Delta T(t) = -0.00000023t^3 + 0.00005t^2 + 0.0128t + 37.794$ | ±0.002249 |
| C111 | $\Delta T(t) = 0.0000004t^3 - 0.0001t^2 + 0.043t + 32.630$ | ±0.002514 |
| C112 | $\Delta T(t) = -0.0000002t^3 + 0.00003t^2 - 0.0175t + 37.067$ | ±0.001987 |
| C113 | $\Delta T(t) = -0.00000018t^3 + 0.00001t^2 + 0.0119t + 25.705$ | ±0.001621 |
| C114 | $\Delta T(t) = 0.000001t^3 - 0.0002t^2 + 0.0436t + 31.177$ | ±0.002579 |

**Table 1.** *Cont.*

| Canals | Stage 1 | Uncertainty (°C) |
|---|---|---|
| C115 | $\Delta T(t) = 0.0000005t^3 - 0.00001t^2 + 0.0419t + 33.636$ | ±0.002276 |
| C116 | $\Delta T(t) = 0.000001t^3 - 0.00003t^2 + 0.0388t + 31.291$ | ±0.002324 |
| C117 | $\Delta T(t) = 0.0000008t^3 - 0.00002t^2 + 0.0361t + 33.784$ | ±0.002256 |
| C118 | $\Delta T(t) = 0.00000008t^3 - 0.00014t^2 + 0.1292t + 38.650$ | ±0.002324 |
| C119 | $\Delta T(t) = 0.000004t^3 - 0.001t^2 + 0.0761t + 31.838$ | ±0.004383 |
| C120 | $\Delta T(t) = 0.0000014t^3 + 0.0004t^2 + 0.0469t + 29.98$ | ±0.00347 |
| C201 | $\Delta T(t) = 0.0000001t^3 - 0.00001t^2 + 0.0181t + 18.348$ | ±0.002162 |
| C202 | $\Delta T(t) = -0.00000028t^3 + 0.00008t^2 + 0.002t + 21.133$ | ±0.001306 |

**Table 2.** DSHT stage 2 channel temperature variation function.

| Canals | Step 2 | Uncertainty (°C) |
|---|---|---|
| C203 | $\Delta T(t) = 0.0000002t^3 - 0.0001t^2 + 0.0692t + 31.320$ | ±0.006216 |
| C204 | $\Delta T(t) = 0.0000003t^3 - 0.0003t^2 + 0.1043t + 31.274$ | ±0.008174 |
| C205 | $\Delta T(t) = -0.00000002t^3 + 0.000016t^2 + 0.0033t + 23.536$ | ±0.0004484 |
| C206 | $\Delta T(t) = 0.000035t^3 - 0.0001t^2 + 0.117t + 37.989$ | ±0.02224 |
| C207 | $\Delta T(t) = -0.00000006t^3 - 0.00003t^2 + 0.0513t + 31.670$ | ±0.004116 |
| C208 | $\Delta T(t) = 0.0000015t^3 - 0.0006t^2 + 0.0726t + 40.735$ | ±0.01304 |
| C209 | $\Delta T(t) = 0.00000018t^3 - 0.00025t^2 + 0.0731t + 33.368$ | ±0.005832 |
| C210 | $\Delta T(t) = -0.000001t^3 + 0.0001t^2 + 0.0665t + 28.387$ | ±0.002836 |
| C211 | $\Delta T(t) = 0.00000018t^3 - 0.0002t^2 + 0.0989t + 31.699$ | ±0.006024 |
| C212 | $\Delta T(t) = -0.0000008t^3 - 0.00012t^2 + 0.0412t + 31.705$ | ±0.002128 |
| C213 | $\Delta T(t) = 0.00000024t^3 - 0.0002t^2 + 0.088t + 31.186$ | ±0.007064 |
| C214 | $\Delta T(t) = 0.0000004t^3 - 0.000206t^2 + 0.0551t + 38.891$ | ±0.003068 |
| C215 | $\Delta T(t) = -0.0000009t^3 + 0.00032t^2 + 0.0132t + 25.676$ | ±0.00176 |
| C216 | $\Delta T(t) = -0.0000022t^3 + 0.00006t^2 + 0.0992t + 35.135$ | ±0.003712 |
| C217 | $\Delta T(t) = -0.00000018t^3 + 0.00002 + 0.031t + 33.645$ | ±0.000284 |
| C218 | $\Delta T(t) = -0.00002t^3 + 0.00079 + 0.081t + 34.799$ | ±0.00628 |
| C219 | $\Delta T(t) = -0.00000006t^3 - 0.00003 + 0.0346t + 33.694$ | ±0.001092 |
| C220 | $\Delta T(t) = -0.00000016t^3 - 0.000284t^2 + 0.1538t + 26.957$ | ±0.010864 |
| C301 | $\Delta T(t) = 0.00000424t^3 - 0.000964t^2 + 0.1363t + 34.480$ | ±0.015544 |
| C302 | $\Delta T(t) = 0.000006t^3 + 0.0002t^2 + 0.0673t + 30.036$ | ±0.002456 |
| C303 | $\Delta T(t) = 0.0000001t^3 - 0.00005t^2 + 0.0196t + 19.538$ | ±0.000656 |
| C304 | $\Delta T(t) = 0.00000003t^3 + 0.000012t^2 + 0.013t + 19.715$ | ±0.000112 |

### 2.2. *Artificial Neural Networks*

The control strategy applied to operate the DSHT under conditions that maximize the COP × GTL product is based on determining the first stage working fluid flow value (MEV1) using MLP-ANN [3]. The developed ANN consists of 9 input variables and 9 output variables forming a MIMO (multiple-input and multiple-output) system. The names and units of measurement of inputs and outputs are shown in Table 3. See Appendix C to identify from right to left in the photograph of the laboratory's prototype, the condenser 1 (CO1 label), generator 1 (GE1 label), evaporator 1 (EV1 label), absorber 1 (AB1 label), condenser 2 (CO2 label), generator 2 (GE2), absorber 2 (AB2) and evaporator 2 (EV2 label).

**Table 3.** Input and output variables of the ANN model.

| Inputs | Outputs |
|---|---|
| TGE1: Generator temperature AHT [°C] | QGE1: Thermal power of generator AHT [kW] |
| TGE2: Generator temperature DSHT [°C] | QGE2: Thermal power of generator DSHT [kW] |
| TCO1: Condenser temperature AHT [°C] | QEV1: Evaporator thermal power AHT [kW] |
| TCO2: Condenser temperature DSHT [°C] | QEV2: Thermal power of evaporator DSHT [kW] |
| TEV1: Evaporator temperature AHT [°C] | MEV1: Working fluid flow AHT [kg/s] |
| TEV2: Evaporator temperature DSHT [°C] | XGE1: Generator concentration AHT [%] |
| TAB1: Absorber temperature AHT [°C] | XGE2: Generator concentration DSHT [%] |
| TAB2: Absorber temperature DSHT [°C] | FR1: Flow ratio AHT [dimensionless] |
| QAB2: Thermal power of absorber DSHT [kW] | FR2: Flow ratio DSHT [dimensionless] |

The range of the input variables is adjusted to the operating conditions evaluated for the DSHT, with a variation of 1 °C. Although the absorber in AHT (AB1) provides a higher thermal level available for the evaporator in DSHT (EV2), EV2 operates at the equilibrium temperature required for the concentration feed of the Stage 2 system. Any excess energy supplied by AB1 to EV2 results in increased pressure. The output variables were normalized within the range of 0.0 to 1.0 and the accuracy is reported. The range of these values is presented in Table 4 which has 10 input variables and 10 output variables, making it a MIMO system (multiple input–multiple output).

**Table 4.** Variables and values of input and output variables.

| | Variables | Values | Accuracy |
|---|---|---|---|
| Inputs | TGE1 [°C] | 60–65 | ±0.1 °C |
| | TGE2 [°C] | 60–65 | ±0.1 °C |
| | TCO1 [°C] | 20–25 | ±0.1 °C |
| | TCO2 [°C] | 20–25 | ±0.1 °C |
| | TEV1 [°C] | 67–72 | ±0.1 °C |
| | TEV2 [°C] | 80–85 | ±0.1 °C |
| | TAB1 [°C] | 97–102 | ±0.1 °C |
| | TAB2 [°C] | 103–108 | ±0.1 °C |
| | QAB2 [kW] | 1 | ±0.01 kW |
| Outputs | QGE1 [kW] | 0–1 | ±0.01 kW |
| | QGE2 [kW] | 0–1 | ±0.01 kW |
| | QEV1 [kW] | 0–1 | ±0.01 kW |
| | QEV2 [kW] | 0–1 | ±0.01 kW |
| | MEV1 [kg/s] | 0–1 | ±0.001 kg/s |
| | XGE1 [%] | 0–1 | ±0.01 %w |
| | XGE2 [%] | 0–1 | ±0.01 %w |
| | FR1 [dimensionless] | 0–1 | ±0.01 |
| | FR2 [dimensionless] | 0–1 | ±0.01 |

The neural network learning algorithm adjusts the weights and biases to obtain the desired outputs minimizing the error [23]. There is no single method to determine the optimal number of neurons or layers in the network, so a trial-and-error approach is employed [24]. In this study, the number of neurons in the hidden layer was established by ensuring that the correlation between the output generated by the network and the expected values was greater than 0.9998.

The ANN was programmed using the MATLAB © nftool (Neural Fitting) tool that facilitates data selection, the creation and training of neural networks, as well as the evaluation of their performance by calculating mean square error and regression analysis [25]. Several networks with different neurons in the hidden layer were tested, ranging from 5 to 25. To train the networks, the data were randomly divided into three sets as follows: 70% was used for training, 15% was used for validation, and the remaining 15% was used as a completely independent test of the generalizability of the network [3].

The MATLAB© toolbox (nftool) allows you to develop an artificial neural network (ANN) with a predetermined feedforward architecture, in which the number of neurons in the hidden layer can be adjusted. To evaluate the model's performance during the training, validation, and testing phases, the toolbox uses metrics such as the correlation coefficient (R) and the mean square error (MSE).

During ANN training, a mechanism called validation checks (early stopping) is used to monitor the validation error. Its function is to stop training when the validation error begins to increase after several iterations, thus avoiding overfitting and improving the model's generalization capabilities.

Appendix A (Figure A1) presents a flowchart explaining how the number of neurons in the ANN hidden layer is determined, following the criterion of maximizing R. The process begins in MATLAB's nftool, where the input and output data are first imported. The nftool randomly determines 70% of the data for training, and the user defines the percentage for validation and testing, in our case 15% for each. Next, the number of neurons (N) in the ANN hidden layer is initialized. After training the ANN, the R values (training, validation, and testing) are obtained, and these data are saved in Excel.

The number of neurons is then increased, and the network is retrained to calculate the new R values (training, validation, and testing), and these data are saved again. If the current values of R (training, validation, and test) are greater than the previous ones, the number of neurons in the hidden layer is increased again. This process is repeated until the current values of R (training, validation, and test) no longer exceed the previous values of R (training, validation, and test), at which point the cycle ends, obtaining the neurons needed to configure the ANN and completing the cycle.

Two optimization algorithms for ANN training were tested: the Levenberg–Marquardt method (LM) and the scaled conjugate gradient (SCG). According to [26], the LM method is accurate, but computationally expensive, especially for large networks. On the other hand, the SCG method is faster, although its accuracy is lower, especially in complex networks. In this study, the LM algorithm was chosen, since even though its computation time is longer than that of SCG, this aspect is not relevant, since the DSHT operates in a steady state for long periods, requiring maximum accuracy for its control.

To ensure the reliability of this database, experimental data from the DSHT were used, with a total of 155,520 samples. Of these, randomly, 108,864 samples were used in the training phase, 23,328 values for validation, and the remaining were used for testing. Training the ANN, using both the Levenberg–Marquardt and scaled conjugate gradient algorithms, leads to the optimal point, defined as the maximum value of the product COP $\times$ GTL, allowing both maximum possible values to be achieved simultaneously for the desired condition.

### 2.3. Hardware and Software

#### 2.3.1. Automatization for Flow Control

The devices were used to collect data on the variables (temperature and flow) as well as to control the MEV1 flow are shown in Figure 1. These include a Model 34970A Data Acquirer with three 34901A modules, thermocouples, a flow sensor, an Arduino UNO, a servo valve, and a computer.

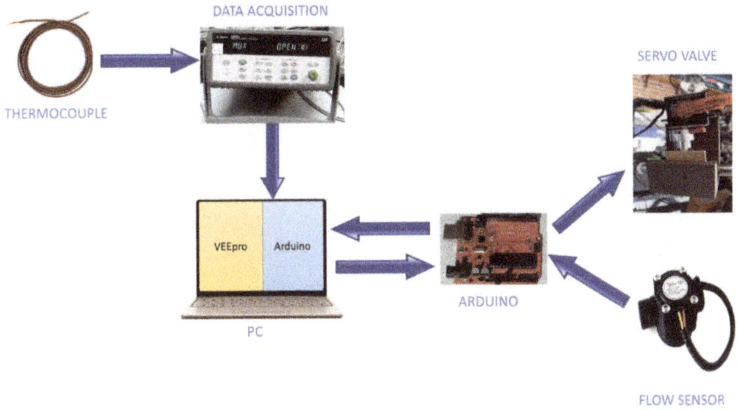


**Figure 1.** Hardware implemented for signal acquisition and control of the DSHT.

For the control of the MEV1 flow of the DSHT, a 1/2-inch manual ball valve (on/off) coupled to a servo motor was used as the final control element. According to a previous study carried out by [27] the torque necessary for the opening and closing of this valve is around 1.57 Nm. It was decided to use the SAVOX SB2290SG servomotor with 4.41 Nm of torque, since this is higher than what is needed to rotate the valve, which operates with a voltage of 6 V to 7.4 V, velocity of 6 V: 0.16/60 °s and 7.4 V: 0.13/60 °s. Besides, its outstanding feature lies in its ability to receive a PWM (pulse width modulation) control signal, which facilitates the manipulation of its angular position in a simple way.

For the coupling of the servo motor to the manual valve, a piece that fits onto the top of the valve was used, in addition to another part that was 3D printed to keep the servo motor fixed; both allow the valve to adjust its rotation from 10 to 85 degrees as shown in Figure 2a.

(a) (b)

**Figure 2.** *Cont.*

(c)

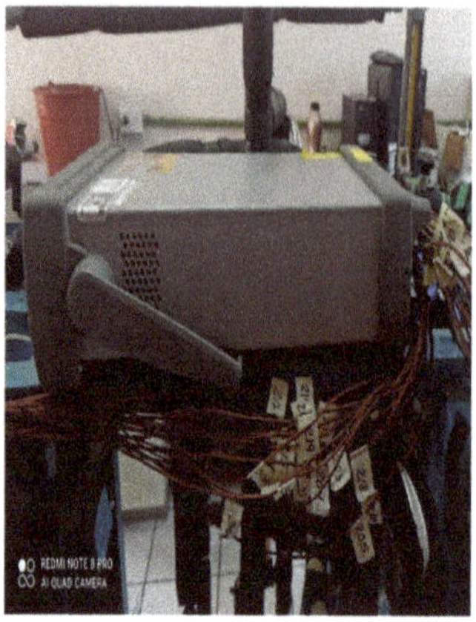

(d)

**Figure 2.** This figure describes devices used in control: (**a**) servo valve used for MEV1 flow control; (**b**) flow sensor coupled to the DSHT; (**c**) connecting the Arduino® UNO to the flow sensor and servo valve; (**d**) acquisition system 34970A, 34901A modules, and thermocouples.

### 2.3.2. Flow Sensor

The acquisition of the DSHT MEV1 flow rate was carried out using a 1/2-inch YF-S20 flow sensor, allowing the measurement of water flow to determine consumption (Figure 2b). This sensor operates at a voltage of 4.5 V to 18 V DC, working flow rate of 1 to 30 L/min, and accuracy of $\pm 10\%$. It operates thanks to the flow of water that activates a turbine connected to a magnet; when turned, this magnet activates a Hall effect sensor. The electrical impulses generated by this sensor can be interpreted by a digital input from an Arduino.

The sensor generates a square wave, with a frequency proportional to the flow rate [28]. The conversion factor from frequency (Hz) to flow rate (L/min) varies between models and depends on pressure, density, and even the flow itself, Equation (1), where $Q$ [L/min] represents the flow, $f$ [Hz] the frequency, and $k$ is the conversion factor; in the case of this sensor, the average conversion factor provided by the manufacturer is 7.5.

$$Q = \frac{f}{k}, \tag{1}$$

### 2.3.3. Arduino® UNO Interface

The Arduino® UNO features in its configuration 14 digital input/output pins, 6 analog inputs, a 16 MHz quartz crystal, a USB connection, a power connector, and a reset button [29]. The Arduino UNO microprocessor was used, because with the digital input pins you can acquire the MEV1 digital flow signal provided by the flow sensor mentioned above. In addition, it has a PWM output that serves to send the necessary signal to the servomotor.

Figure 2c illustrates the physical connection of the Arduino to a breadboard, thus linking the flow sensor and servo valve. The 5V (Vdc) and ground (GND) pins of the Arduino are connected to the microboard using cables. The microboard, in turn, is connected to the flowmeter and the servo valve. The flowmeter data signal is linked to pin 2 of the Arduino, configured as a digital signal, while the servo valve is linked to pin 3 of the Arduino, intended for the PWM signal.

The MEV1 flux generated by the ANN, which corresponds to the maximum product of COP $\times$ GTL, represents the flux necessary for the DSHT to operate in its best scenario according to the input vector introduced in the ANN. According to [3] one of the important parameters of the DSHT is the flow ratio (FR), a dimensionless value that is calculated as the ratio between the concentration of lithium bromide in the generator and the difference in concentrations between the generator and the absorber. This value is also equal to the ratio of the dilute lithium bromide solution flow to the refrigerant flow. According to [14], a variation in concentration causes alterations in the FR, which initially impacts the flows of the evaporator and the absorber, and later those of the generator, in accordance with the conservation of matter. These changes are restricted by thermodynamic equilibrium conditions, which consider parameters such as pressure, temperature, and concentration.

The control stability under operating conditions was evaluated, and the standard deviation was 0.002245 kg/s.

The correspondence between the MEV1 flow and the opening or closing angle of the servo valve ($\alpha$) is shown in Table 5, according to Equation (2). Using the R2 metric, the variations of the MEV1 flow in each test performed in the laboratory were analyzed for the variation of the rotation angle of the servo valve with a range of 10 to 85 degrees, resulting in second-degree polynomial functions. These equations correspond in each case for a unit of QAB2.

$$M = F(\propto), \tag{2}$$

where

M: Flow [kg/s];

$\alpha$: Servo valve angle [°C]

**Table 5.** Ratio of the MEV1 flow to the opening or closing angle of the servo valve.

| Test | Function |
|---|---|
| 1 | $M_{EV1}(\propto) = 9 \times 10^{-09}\ \alpha^2 + 3 \times 10^{-07} \propto + 0.0006$ |
| 2 | $M_{EV1}(\propto) = 1 \times 10^{-08}\ \alpha^2 + 3 \times 10^{-07} \propto + 0.0006$ |
| 3 | $M_{EV1}(\propto) = 2 \times 10^{-08}\ \alpha^2 + 3 \times 10^{-07} \propto + 0.0006$ |
| 4 | $M_{EV1}(\propto) = 1 \times 10^{-08}\ \alpha^2 + 2 \times 10^{-07} \propto + 0.0006$ |
| 5 | $M_{EV1}(\propto) = 9 \times 10^{-09}\ \alpha^2 + 3 \times 10^{-07} \propto + 0.0006$ |
| 6 | $M_{EV1}(\propto) = 4 \times 10^{-09}\ \alpha^2 + 2 \times 10^{-07} \propto + 0.0005$ |
| 7 | $M_{EV1}(\propto) = 1 \times 10^{-08}\ \alpha^2 + 3 \times 10^{-07} \propto + 0.0006$ |

#### 2.3.4. Data Acquisition

The Agilent Acquirer model 34972A was used, which supports the insertion of several modules for various functions, with a maximum capacity of three modules. In this instance, three 34901A modules were used, to which J-type thermocouples were connected. It has an operating temperature range of −210 °C to 760 °C, with a standard accuracy of ±2.2 °C or ±0.75% of the measured value. The total number of thermocouples connected to the data acquisition system is 44, representing the different physical temperatures of the DSHT (Figure 2d).

#### 2.3.5. Visual Engineering Environment Software

For the development of the MEV1 flow control, Visual Engineering Environment (VEE) Pro-9.33 was used as the main program in parallel with the Arduino software (IDE). Appendix B (Figure A2) shows the flow diagram that begins by acquiring the temperature and absorption power provided by the user, as well as the acquisition of the data through the data acquirer. Once these data are obtained, if this condition is not met, the program ends. If the condition mentioned above is true, it means that the necessary entry vector is available to enter the ANN.

The ANN generates the necessary output values that respond to the increased product of COP × GTL, leading to the first-stage fluid flow ($M_{EV1}$). This flow value is sent to the IDE software via serial port, and with the PWM signal of the same, the value of the degree of opening or closing of the corresponding servo valve is sent.

Once the servo valve varies the necessary degrees, the physical ($M_{EV1\_physical}$) flow value sensed by the flow sensor is acquired through the digital input of the Arduino. With this feedback, a comparison is made between the $M_{EV1\_ANN}$ and the $M_{EV1\_physical}$ and if the condition that they are different is met, it means two things:

1. Changes in the vector of operating conditions of the DSHT.
2. Acquiring the $M_{EV1\_physical}$ value before detecting the valve rotation value.

Therefore, the program must follow this same dynamic, and if the condition is not achieved, $M_{EV1\_ANN}$ and $M_{EV1\_physical}$ are the same. In this condition, the program continues sending the same angle value to the valve. The iterative process continues until the input vector's operating conditions change.

## 3. Results

A search was carried out to determine the value of the R greater than 0.9998 and an MSE as close to zero as possible, using the Levenberg–Marquardt method as an optimization algorithm. To do this, five to twenty-five neurons were tested in the occult layer (Table 6). The results indicate that when using 20 neurons in the hidden layer, the lowest values of MSE and the highest values of R were obtained for training, validation, and testing. Thus, the ANN was configured with 20 neurons in its hidden layer.

**Table 6.** MSE and R referring to neurons present in the hidden layer of the ANN.

| Neurons | | 5 | 10 | 15 | 20 | 25 |
|---|---|---|---|---|---|---|
| MSE | Training | $4.18619 \times 10^{-4}$ | $5.16531 \times 10^{-5}$ | $4.43622 \times 10^{-5}$ | $1.78592 \times 10^{-5}$ | $2.84184 \times 10^{-5}$ |
| | Validation | $4.18619 \times 10^{-4}$ | $5.83722 \times 10^{-5}$ | $4.47101 \times 10^{-5}$ | $1.97765 \times 10^{-5}$ | $2.78101 \times 10^{-5}$ |
| | Testing | $4.18619 \times 10^{-4}$ | $5.49637 \times 10^{-5}$ | $4.88679 \times 10^{-5}$ | $1.77207 \times 10^{-5}$ | $2.78455 \times 10^{-5}$ |
| R | Training | $9.99630 \times 10^{-1}$ | $9.99545 \times 10^{-1}$ | $9.99611 \times 10^{-1}$ | $9.99841 \times 10^{-1}$ | $9.99751 \times 10^{-1}$ |
| | Validation | $9.99630 \times 10^{-1}$ | $9.99486 \times 10^{-1}$ | $9.99660 \times 10^{-1}$ | $9.99826 \times 10^{-1}$ | $9.99754 \times 10^{-1}$ |
| | Testing | $9.99627 \times 10^{-1}$ | $9.99516 \times 10^{-1}$ | $9.99571 \times 10^{-1}$ | $9.99844 \times 10^{-1}$ | $9.99755 \times 10^{-1}$ |

The ANN was designed with twenty neurons (Ns = 20) in the hidden layer (Figure 3), resulting in 180 weights, Wi{k,s} = 180 as shown in Table 7 and Wo{l,s} = 180 according to Table 8. Two bias vectors were used: one with twenty values (b1) and another with nine values (b2), detailed in Table 9. This configuration was used to predict the output values associated with the maximum product of COP × GTL, considering a vector of input conditions corresponding to the DSHT.

Using trial and error, MSE minimums of $1.78592 \times 10^{-5}$, $1.97765 \times 10^{-5}$, and $1.77207 \times 10^{-5}$, respectively, were achieved by employing 20 neurons in the hidden layer. These low MSE values indicate optimal network performance in predicting the maximum COP × GTL output based on input operating conditions. In addition, the regression plots confirm the effectiveness of the model, showing a strong fit for all datasets with correlation values (R) greater than 0.9998 (Figure 4).

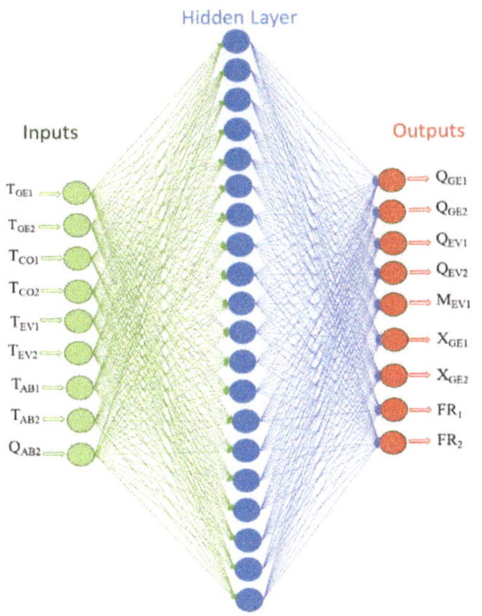


**Figure 3.** Model of the neural network perceptron multilayers.

**Table 7.** Weights of the input vector with respect to the hidden layer of DSHT ANN.

| $\mathbf{Wi}_{\{20,1\}}$ | $\mathbf{Wi}_{\{20,2\}}$ | $\mathbf{Wi}_{\{20,3\}}$ | $\mathbf{Wi}_{\{20,4\}}$ | $\mathbf{Wi}_{\{20,5\}}$ | $\mathbf{Wi}_{\{20,6\}}$ | $\mathbf{Wi}_{\{20,7\}}$ | $\mathbf{Wi}_{\{20,8\}}$ |
|---|---|---|---|---|---|---|---|
| −0.9707 | −0.0100 | 66.9167 | 0.1637 | 0.0076 | 0.0877 | −6.900 | −13.2861 |
| −0.0009 | 0.0052 | −0.0022 | −0.0435 | $-3.1913 \times 10^{-6}$ | 0.0257 | 0.0022 | −0.0016 |
| 0.0949 | 0.0124 | −0.5066 | −0.0889 | −0.0001 | −0.0504 | 0.5886 | 0.1221 |
| −0.4572 | 0.0067 | 2.8211 | −0.0352 | $-6.70806 \times 10^{-6}$ | −0.0248 | −2.1403 | 0.3929 |
| $-2.1437 \times 10^{-6}$ | −0.0477 | 0.0018 | 0.2589 | $2.8521 \times 10^{-5}$ | 0.2241 | −0.0013 | −0.2146 |
| 0.0894 | 0.0014 | 0.3448 | −0.0027 | $-7.9386 \times 10^{-6}$ | $6.9341 \times 10^{-6}$ | 0.0025 | −0.0101 |
| −11.9317 | 0.0046 | 10.4245 | −0.0067 | 0.0004 | 0.0009 | 0.0084 | 0.0024 |
| −0.4420 | 0.0039 | 2.5667 | −0.0183 | $8.2110 \times 10^{-5}$ | −0.0135 | −2.1589 | 0.2142 |
| 0.0896 | −0.2134 | −1.0210 | 0.0259 | −0.0006 | 0.0180 | 0.2981 | −0.4800 |
| 0.4522 | −0.0021 | −2.5038 | 0.0083 | $-6.7576 \times 10^{-5}$ | 0.0067 | 2.2680 | −0.1020 |
| 0.2536 | 0.0036 | −0.7549 | −0.0269 | 0.0003 | −0.0185 | 1.5020 | 0.4725 |
| 0.0186 | −0.0069 | 0.0844 | 0.0090 | $3.9038 \times 10^{-5}$ | 0.0401 | −0.0191 | −0.1288 |
| −0.0810 | −0.010 | 0.9629 | −0.0256 | 0.0006 | −0.0176 | −0.2602 | 0.4636 |
| 0.0342 | $9.3861 \times 10^{-5}$ | −0.0417 | −0.0027 | $-3.5353 \times 10^{-5}$ | −0.0019 | 0.2101 | 0.0832 |
| −0.0001 | −0.1266 | 0.0005 | −0.2631 | $-5.4257 \times 10^{-6}$ | −0.0027 | 0.0013 | 0.0068 |
| −0.0884 | −0.2005 | 1.0147 | −0.0266 | 0.0006 | −0.0181 | −0.2937 | 0.4786 |
| −0.0001 | 12.7505 | 0.0013 | −11.0696 | 0.0002 | −0.0064 | 0.0051 | 0.0199 |
| −0.0003 | −0.0362 | −0.0012 | 0.1264 | $-3.1597 \times 10^{-5}$ | 0.2452 | 0.0002 | −0.1554 |
| −0.0163 | 0.0157 | −0.0733 | 0.0036 | $-4.1376 \times 10^{-5}$ | −0.0614 | 0.0194 | 0.0995 |
| 0.4804 | −0.0089 | −3.0714 | 0.0488 | 0.0001 | 0.0338 | 2.1814 | −0.5268 |

**Table 8.** Hidden layer weights with respect to the DSHT ANN output vector.

| $\mathbf{Wo}_{\{1,20\}}^T$ | $\mathbf{Wo}_{\{2,20\}}^T$ | $\mathbf{Wo}_{\{3,20\}}^T$ | $\mathbf{Wo}_{\{4,20\}}^T$ | $\mathbf{Wo}_{\{5,20\}}^T$ | $\mathbf{Wo}_{\{6,20\}}^T$ | $\mathbf{Wo}_{\{7,20\}}^T$ | $\mathbf{Wo}_{\{8,20\}}^T$ | $\mathbf{Wo}_{\{9,20\}}^T$ |
|---|---|---|---|---|---|---|---|---|
| 0.0004 | 0.0002 | −0.0176 | −0.0001 | −0.0177 | 0.0110 | 0.0004 | −0.032 | 0.0012 |
| −3.7721 | −8.7448 | −1.9396 | −3.5883 | −2.1171 | −0.4420 | 0.4999 | −0.0232 | −5.0740 |
| −0.0420 | 0.0070 | 0.4734 | −0.0079 | 0.4689 | −0.0004 | −0.0007 | 0.0286 | 0.0029 |
| −0.4764 | −0.0370 | −17.8683 | 0.1040 | −18.1554 | −0.1674 | −0.0064 | −34.7524 | −0.0367 |
| −13.8912 | 9.5971 | −5.3957 | −14.5236 | −5.4037 | −0.0018 | 0.0114 | 0.0015 | −4.8584 |
| 0.0928 | −0.0247 | −0.7126 | 0.0491 | −0.7224 | 2.4011 | 0.0602 | −1.4565 | 0.1608 |

**Table 8.** *Cont.*

| $Wo_{\{1,20\}}^T$ | $Wo_{\{2,20\}}^T$ | $Wo_{\{3,20\}}^T$ | $Wo_{\{4,20\}}^T$ | $Wo_{\{5,20\}}^T$ | $Wo_{\{6,20\}}^T$ | $Wo_{\{7,20\}}^T$ | $Wo_{\{8,20\}}^T$ | $Wo_{\{9,20\}}^T$ |
|---|---|---|---|---|---|---|---|---|
| 0.0094 | 0.0033 | −0.0463 | 0.0042 | −0.0498 | 0.3983 | 0.0006 | −0.1071 | 0.0020 |
| 0.4411 | 0.0346 | 17.1188 | −0.1085 | 17.3914 | 0.0354 | 0.0064 | 33.2782 | 0.0292 |
| 0.0973 | −0.0270 | 2.7412 | 0.0510 | 2.7751 | −0.0103 | −0.0034 | 5.9217 | 0.0063 |
| 0.1712 | 0.0131 | 6.8628 | −0.0482 | 6.9711 | −0.0132 | 0.0034 | 13.2644 | 0.0109 |
| −0.0102 | −0.0029 | −0.3632 | −0.0054 | −0.3668 | 0.0013 | 0.0020 | −0.7578 | 0.0044 |
| −2.9476 | 4.7769 | −0.0253 | −2.9086 | −0.1114 | −0.6306 | 0.1526 | 3.7563 | −0.8020 |
| 0.2159 | −0.0590 | 6.0166 | 0.1114 | 6.0922 | −0.0135 | −0.0077 | 13.0098 | 0.0174 |
| 0.2276 | 0.0147 | 3.2497 | 0.1522 | 3.2809 | −0.0734 | −0.0355 | 9.2639 | −0.1304 |
| 0.9963 | −0.2739 | 0.4570 | 0.9941 | 0.4801 | 0.0119 | −3.1836 | 0.1462 | 1.0923 |
| −0.1132 | 0.0298 | −3.2395 | −0.0587 | −3.2797 | 0.0107 | 0.0049 | −6.9881 | −0.0069 |
| 0.1847 | −0.0599 | 0.0833 | 0.1828 | 0.0884 | 0.0050 | −0.5951 | 0.0096 | 0.1743 |
| −0.8833 | −5.3522 | −0.4634 | −0.9178 | −0.4692 | −0.0146 | −0.0175 | 0.0721 | −8.2437 |
| −3.1361 | 5.6090 | −0.8346 | −3.0348 | −0.9597 | −0.5852 | 0.4277 | 2.3422 | 0.0072 |
| −0.2099 | −0.0166 | −7.6677 | 0.0454 | −7.7924 | −0.1153 | −0.0033 | −14.9043 | −0.0184 |

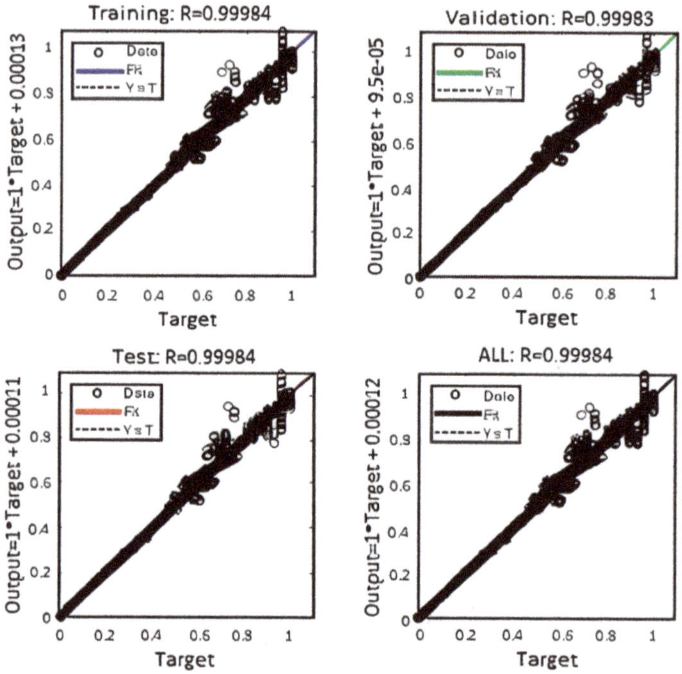


**Figure 4.** Regression of the proposed ANN for DSHT.

**Table 9.** Biases of the DSHT ANN model.

| b1 | b2 |
|---|---|
| 54.4937 | 12.8656 |
| −0.3201 | −6.7723 |
| −1.0302 | 7.3636 |
| 2.5434 | 13.5084 |
| 2.2253 | 7.3384 |
| −0.1183 | 0.0796 |

**Table 9.** *Cont.*

| b1 | b2 |
|---|---|
| −0.3830 | 0.4253 |
| 2.3015 | 6.6770 |
| −0.5007 | 10.5917 |
| −2.2028 | |
| −2.5434 | |
| −0.0039 | |
| 0.4887 | |
| −1.2356 | |
| 0.0896 | |
| 0.5003 | |
| 0.3915 | |
| 1.9931 | |
| −0.0084 | |
| −2.7692 | |

*Transient State Simulator and DSHT ANN*

After the creation of the computer-aided simulator to produce the transient states of each temperature variable present in the DSHT (Tables 1 and 2), and with the support of the ANN, an analysis was carried out based on the experimental data of seven trials previously documented by [27], with the aim of graphically replicating its behavior and verifying that TAB1 is superior to TEV2 due to the efficiency of the heat transfer

Figures 5–17 show the behavior of the temperatures corresponding to the generator, condenser, evaporator, and absorber in the first and second stages of the AHT over time. From time 0 to t0, the dynamic state of each variable is observed until the steady state is reached. Subsequently, during the t0–t1 interval, the operating conditions are entered into the ANN, generating the condition that maximizes the COP × GTL product in each case. The DSHT will remain in this optimal condition until the user modifies the TAB2. In response, the ANN will again adjust the system at t1–t2 to ensure the new maximum value of the COP × GTL product.

Test 1:

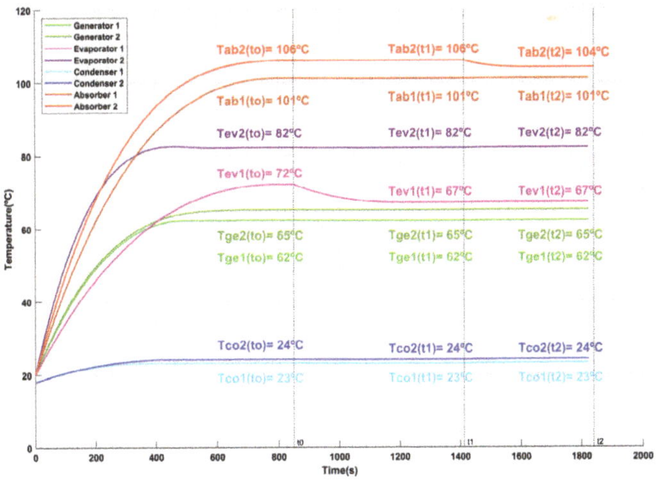


**Figure 5.** Behavior of DSHT temperatures over time for Test 1.

During the t0–t1 interval in Test 1, when entering the operating conditions into the ANN, a reduction in the temperature of the first stage evaporator (TEV1) from 72 °C to 67 °C is observed, which optimizes the COP × GTL product. The relationship can be seen in Figure 6, where the pink line represents a TAB2 of 106 °C, and the purple diamond indicates a COP × GTL of 9.3546. The optimal point, identified by the ANN, corresponds to a maximum value of 10.1213 (violet square). This state will be maintained until TAB2 is reduced to 104 °C (a variation of 2 °C) at the user's discretion, at which point the ANN will adjust the system in the range t1–t2 to reach a new maximum of COP × GTL.

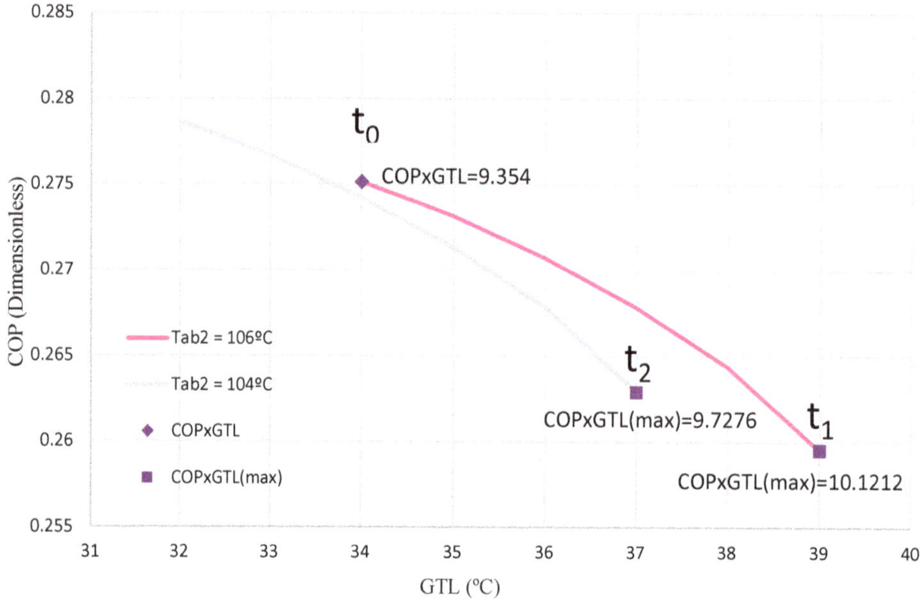


**Figure 6.** COP with respect to the GTL for Test 1.

Test 2:

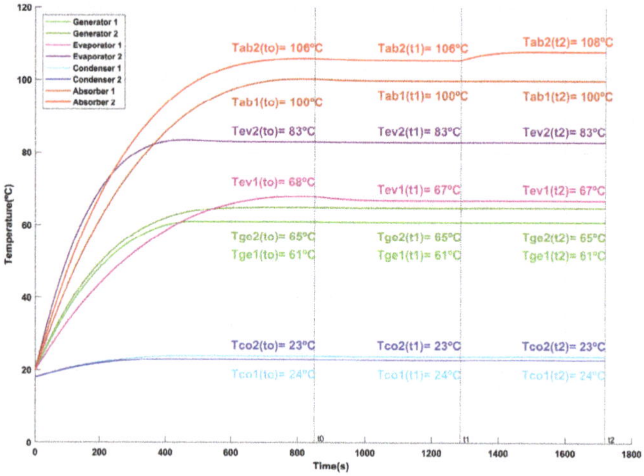


**Figure 7.** Behavior of DSHT temperatures over time for Test 2.

In Test 2, the operating conditions introduced into the ANN during the t0–t1 interval cause a decrease in TEV1, maximizing the COP × GTL product. According to Figure 8, the pink line represents TAB2 at 106 °C, while the purple rhombus shows a COP × GTL of 9.9512. The ANN points out that the optimal scenario occurs when the product reaches a maximum value of 9.9899 (violet square). This DSHT status will be maintained until TAB2 is increased to 108 °C, at which point ANN will adapt the system at t1–t2 to achieve the new maximum of the COP × GTL product.

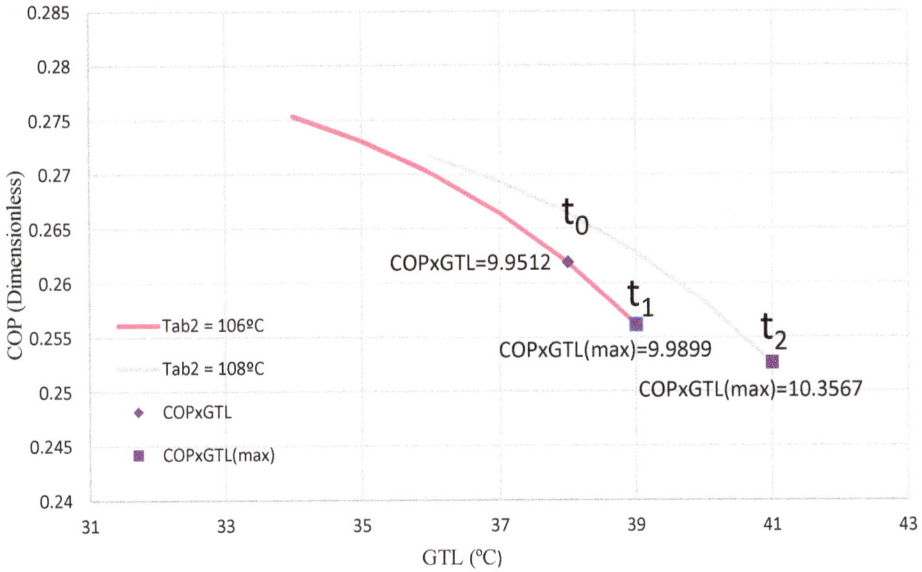


**Figure 8.** COP with respect to the GTL for Test 2.

Test 3:

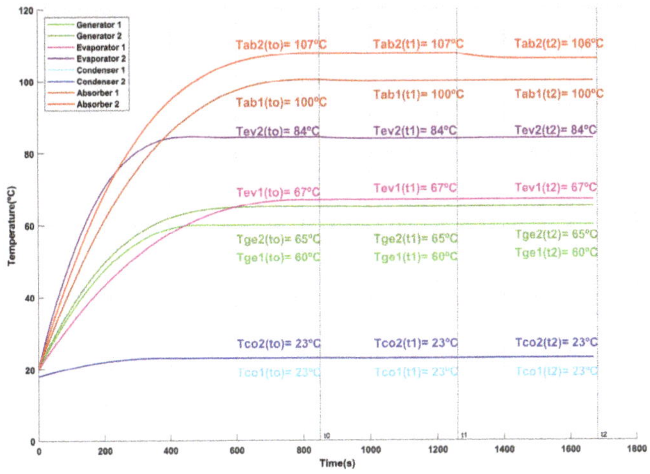


**Figure 9.** Behavior of DSHT temperatures over time for Test 3.

During Test 3, between times t0 and t1, the operating conditions processed by the ANN determined that the DSHT remained in an optimal configuration, reaching a maximum

COP × GTL of 9.9959. This value, represented by a purple circle and a pink line (with TAB2 set at 107 °C), is illustrated in Figure 10. This condition will be maintained until the user adjusts the TAB2, reducing it by 1 °C. Subsequently, in the t1–t2 interval, the ANN will readjust the system to reach a new maximum value of COP × GTL.

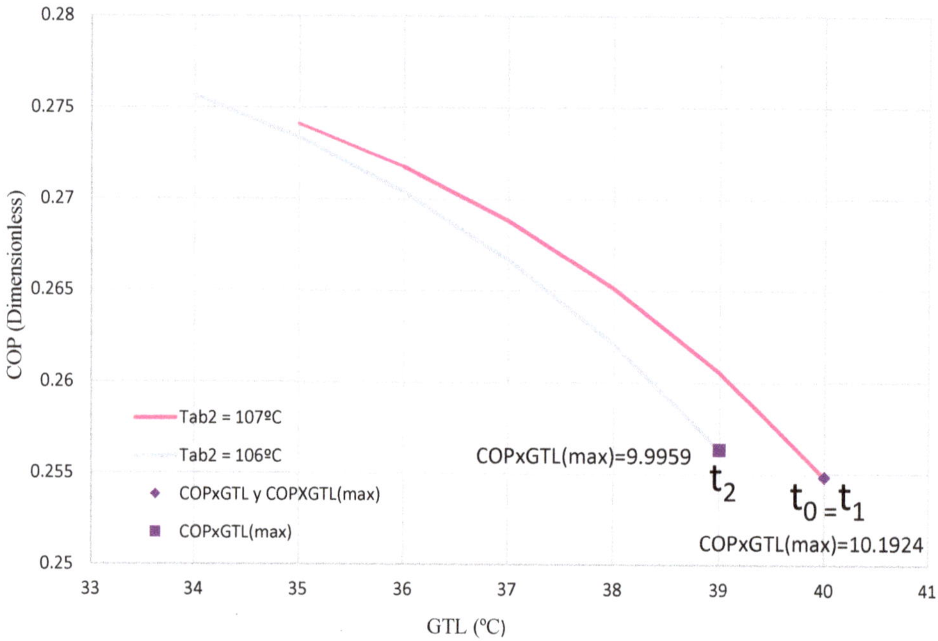


**Figure 10.** COP with respect to the GTL for Test 3.

Test 4:

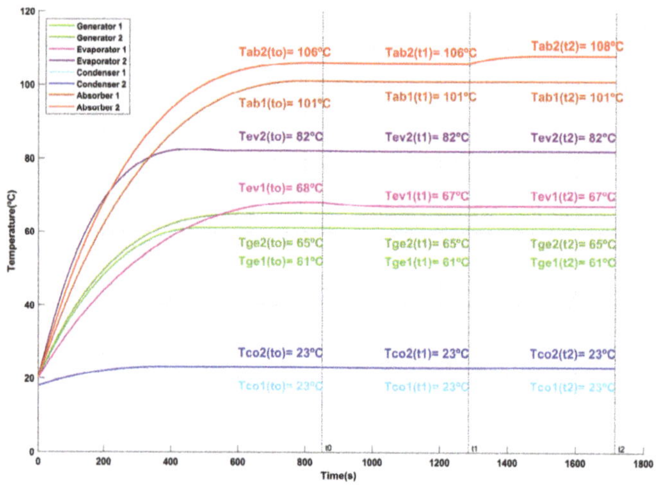


**Figure 11.** Behavior of DSHT temperatures over time for Test 4.

During Test 4, in the t0–t1 interval, the conditions entered into the ANN generate a decrease in TEV1 that maximizes COP × GTL. As Figure 12 shows, the pink line reflects TAB2 at 106 °C, and the purple diamond indicates a COP × GTL of 9.9247. The ANN calculates the optimal scenario when this value reaches a maximum of 9.9441 (violet square). The DSHT system will remain in this condition until TAB2 is increased to 108 °C, which will cause the ANN to adjust the system to t1–t2 to reach the new maximum of COP × GTL.

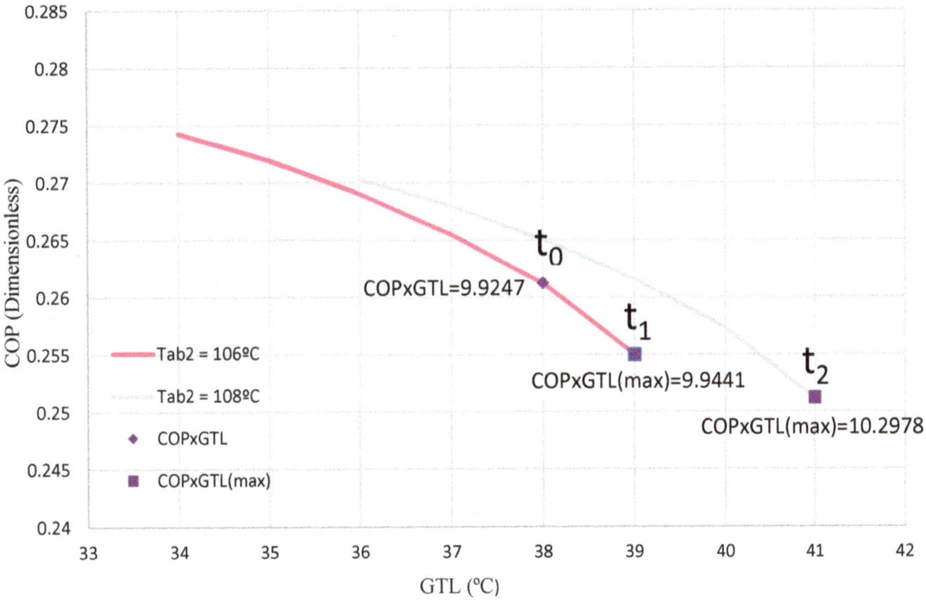


**Figure 12.** COP with respect to the GTL for Test 4.

Test 5:

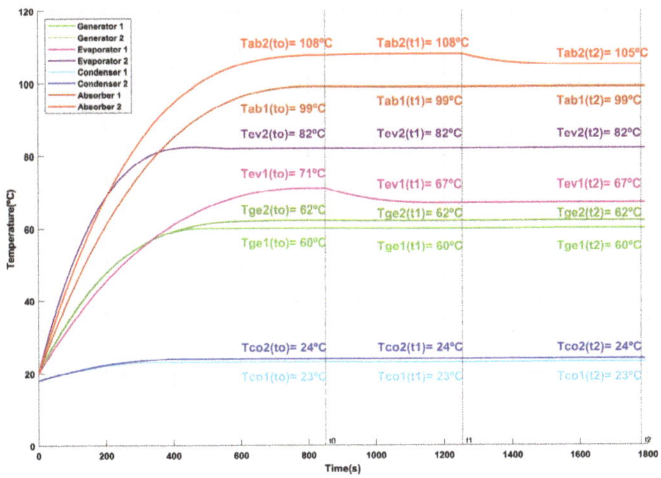


**Figure 13.** Behavior of DSHT temperatures over time for Test 5.

In Test 5, the operating conditions processed by the ANN reduce TEV1, thus maximizing the COP × GTL product in the t0–t1 range. In Figure 14, the pink line illustrates a TAB2 of 108 °C, while the purple diamond shows a COP × GTL of 9.5946. According to the ANN, the sweet spot corresponds to a maximum of 10.1096 (violet square). This condition will remain stable until TAB2 is adjusted to 105 °C, after which the ANN will modify the system in the t1–t2 range to ensure the new maximum of the COP × GTL product.

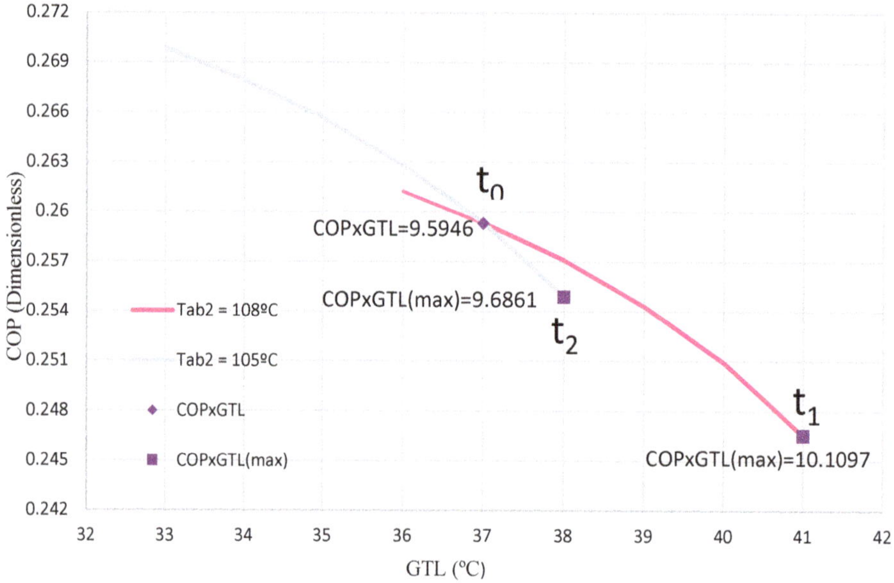


**Figure 14.** COP with respect to the GTL for Test 5.

Test 6:

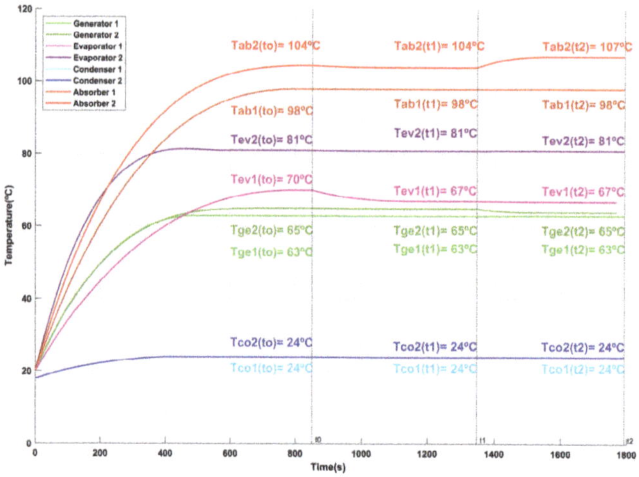


**Figure 15.** Behavior of DSHT temperatures over time for Test 6.

In Test 6, between t0–t1, the vector of conditions introduced in the ANN generates an adjustment in TEV1, optimizing the product COP × GTL. Figure 16 illustrates this relationship, showing the pink line for a TAB2 of 104 °C and a purple rhombus indicating a COP × GTL of 9.5716. The ideal scenario is reached with a maximum value of 10.2041 (violet square), according to the ANN. The DSHT system will remain in this optimal state until TAB2 is increased to 107 °C, which will trigger a new adaptation in the t1–t2 range to maintain maximum performance.

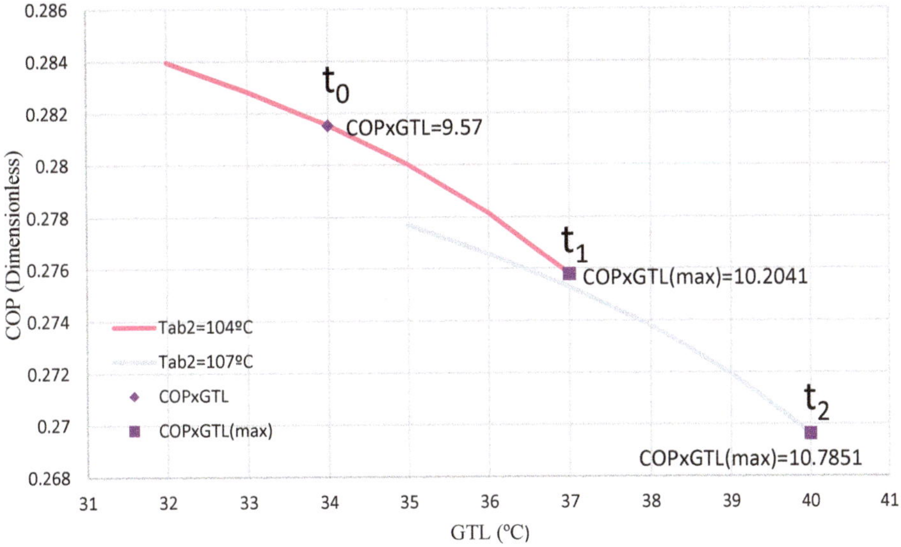


**Figure 16.** COP with respect to the GTL for Test 6.

Test 7:

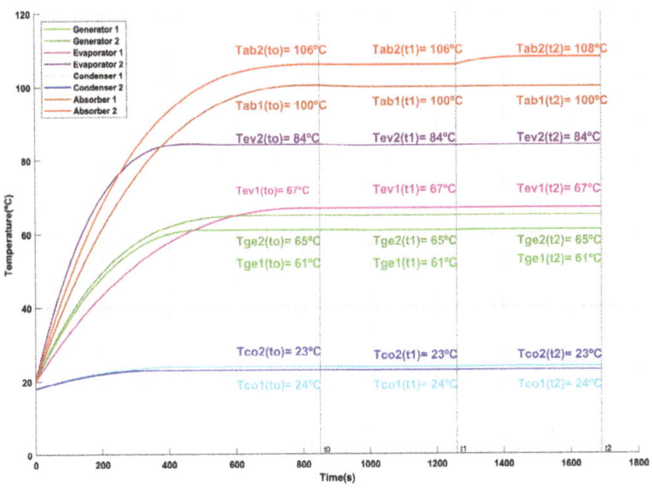


**Figure 17.** Behavior of DSHT temperatures over time for Test 7.

In Test 7, during the period t0–t1, the ANN suggests keeping the DSHT in this state, which is where the maximum COP × GTL product is found, with a value of 10.0191. This result, identified by a purple circle and a pink line (TAB2 set to 106 °C), can be seen in Figure 18. The DSHT will continue in this condition until the user modifies the TAB2, increasing it by 2 °C. Accordingly, the ANN will adjust the system again during t1–t2 to ensure the new maximum of COP × GTL.

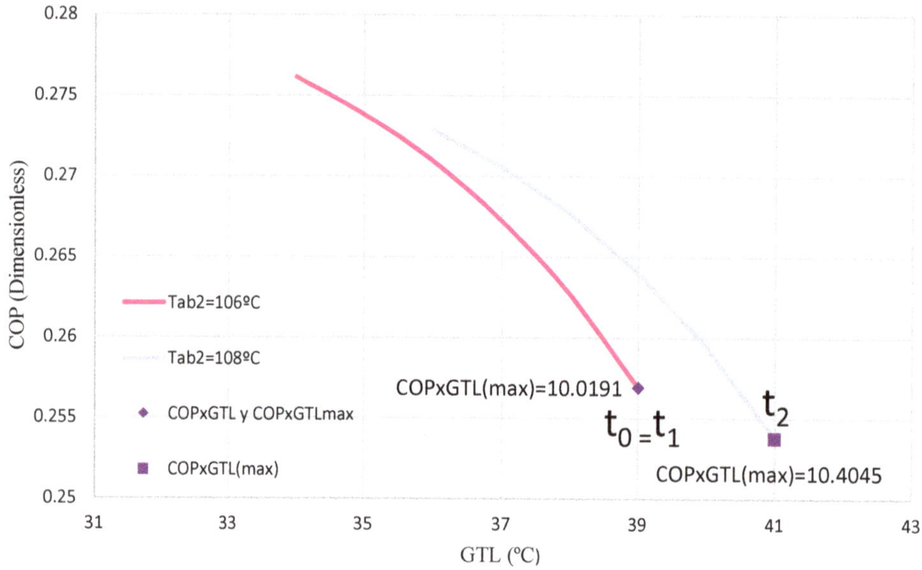


**Figure 18.** COP with respect to the GTL for Test 7.

It can be affirmed that using the Levenberg–Marquardt algorithm, we obtained higher values of R for training, validation, and testing. In the case of the scaled conjugate gradient algorithm, it can be seen in Table 10 that in our approximations, for 5, 10, 15, and 20 neurons, the R value for the Levenberg–Marquardt algorithm was always higher and even when we tested with 30 neurons the scaled conjugate gradient algorithm obtained its highest R values 0.99923, 0.999248, and 0.999249 for training, validation, and testing, respectively, without exceeding the Levenberg–Marquardt values of 0.9998414, 0.999826, and 0.999844 for training, validation, and testing, respectively, again.

**Table 10.** MSE and R values for the COP × GTL analyzed configurations.

| | | **Scaled Conjugate Gradient** | | **Levenberg–Marquardt** | |
|---|---|---|---|---|---|
| Neurons | Process | MSE | R | MSE | R |
| 5 | Training | 0.000439451 | 0.996133 | 0.000418619 | 0.996309 |
| | Validation | 0.000436066 | 0.996147 | 0.000197861 | 0.996306 |
| | Testing | 0.000432079 | 0.996179 | 0.000423703 | 0.996275 |
| 10 | Training | 0.000165692 | 0.99854 | $5.16531 \times 10^{-5}$ | 0.999545 |
| | Validation | 0.000165136 | 0.998552 | $5.83722 \times 10^{-5}$ | 0.999486 |
| | Testing | 0.000163748 | 0.99856 | $5.49637 \times 10^{-5}$ | 0.999516 |
| 15 | Training | 0.000116338 | 0.998976 | $4.43622 \times 10^{-5}$ | 0.999611 |
| | Validation | 0.000119767 | 0.998949 | $4.47101 \times 10^{-5}$ | 0.999604 |
| | Testing | 0.000116829 | 0.99897 | $4.88679 \times 10^{-5}$ | 0.999571 |
| 20 | Training | 0.000115385 | 0.998983 | $1.78592 \times 10^{-5}$ | 0.999841 |
| | Validation | 0.000114803 | 0.99899 | $1.97765 \times 10^{-5}$ | 0.999826 |
| | Testing | 0.000113515 | 0.999007 | $1.77207 \times 10^{-5}$ | 0.999844 |
| 25 | Training | $8.73692 \times 10^{-5}$ | 0.999230 | $2.84184 \times 10^{-5}$ | 0.999751 |
| | Validation | $8.56927 \times 10^{-5}$ | 0.999248 | $2.78101 \times 10^{-5}$ | 0.999754 |
| | Testing | $8.54462 \times 10^{-5}$ | 0.999249 | $2.78455 \times 10^{-5}$ | 0.999755 |
| 30 | Training | 0.000116442 | 0.998975 | | |
| | Validation | 0.000114514 | 0.998989 | | |
| | Testing | 0.000115232 | 0.998989 | | |

Comparing these values with the previous strategy [3] for calculating a first maximum COP × GTL in the AHT at the first stage and then based on the thermodynamic operating conditions, a second Levenberg–Marquardt for the DSHT was calculated, shown in Table 11, there is a variation with this new machine learning proposal. The previous Levenberg–Marquardt configuration is shown in Figure 19.

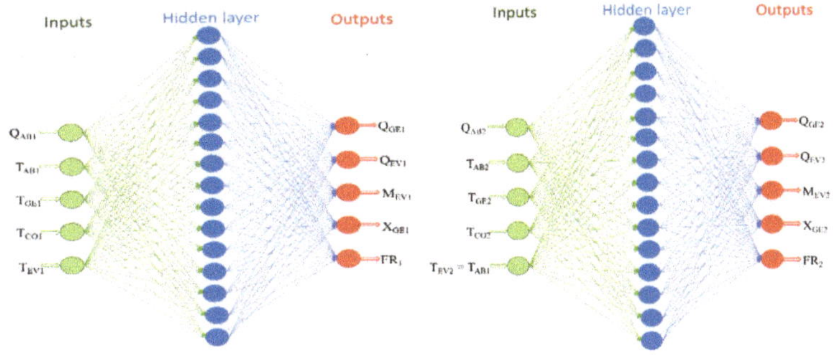


**Figure 19.** Previous ANN for Double Stage Heat Transformer [3].

**Table 11.** MSE and R values for the previous AHT and DSHT configuration.

| | | AHT | | | |
|---|---|---|---|---|---|
| | | Scaled Conjugated Gradient | | Levenberg–Marquardt | |
| Neurons | Process | MSE | R | MSE | R |
| 5 | Training | $8.2298 \times 10^{-4}$ | $9.9150 \times 10^{-1}$ | $6.8598 \times 10^{-4}$ | $9.9288 \times 10^{-1}$ |
| | Validation | $8.3759 \times 10^{-4}$ | $9.9184 \times 10^{-1}$ | $7.8749 \times 10^{-4}$ | $9.9178 \times 10^{-1}$ |
| | Testing | $8.9922 \times 10^{-4}$ | $9.9102 \times 10^{-1}$ | $8.1180 \times 10^{-4}$ | $9.9129 \times 10^{-1}$ |
| 10 | Training | $2.9817 \times 10^{-4}$ | $9.9637 \times 10^{-1}$ | $2.9638 \times 10^{-4}$ | $9.9691 \times 10^{-1}$ |
| | Validation | $3.2596 \times 10^{-4}$ | $9.9647 \times 10^{-1}$ | $1.3131 \times 10^{-4}$ | $9.9869 \times 10^{-1}$ |
| | Testing | $7.2386 \times 10^{-4}$ | $9.9267 \times 10^{-1}$ | $2.5201 \times 10^{-4}$ | $9.9752 \times 10^{-1}$ |
| 15 | Training | $2.7476 \times 10^{-4}$ | $9.9640 \times 10^{-1}$ | $3.3451 \times 10^{-5}$ | $9.9965 \times 10^{-1}$ |
| | Validation | $3.1573 \times 10^{-4}$ | $9.9683 \times 10^{-1}$ | $3.1256 \times 10^{-5}$ | $9.9969 \times 10^{-1}$ |
| | Testing | $1.3175 \times 10^{-4}$ | $9.9868 \times 10^{-1}$ | $3.0118 \times 10^{-5}$ | $9.9971 \times 10^{-1}$ |
| 20 | Training | $3.5319 \times 10^{-5}$ | $9.9963 \times 10^{-1}$ | $1.6566 \times 10^{-4}$ | $9.9833 \times 10^{-1}$ |
| | Validation | $4.5557 \times 10^{-5}$ | $9.9954 \times 10^{-1}$ | $1.2132 \times 10^{-4}$ | $9.9871 \times 10^{-1}$ |
| | Testing | $5.1862 \times 10^{-5}$ | $9.9948 \times 10^{-1}$ | $1.7321 \times 10^{-4}$ | $9.9819 \times 10^{-1}$ |
| | | DSHT | | | |
| | | Scaled Conjugated Gradient | | Levenberg–Marquardt | |
| Neurons | | MSE | R | MSE | R |
| 5 | Training | $1.9735 \times 10^{-3}$ | $9.8724 \times 10^{-1}$ | $1.1406 \times 10^{-3}$ | $9.9290 \times 10^{-1}$ |
| | Validation | $2.4229 \times 10^{-3}$ | $9.8774 \times 10^{-1}$ | $2.3185 \times 10^{-3}$ | $9.9638 \times 10^{-1}$ |
| | Testing | $2.6297 \times 10^{-3}$ | $9.8365 \times 10^{-1}$ | $2.0602 \times 10^{-3}$ | $9.8722 \times 10^{-1}$ |
| 10 | Training | $1.0946 \times 10^{-3}$ | $9.9305 \times 10^{-1}$ | $1.6282 \times 10^{-4}$ | $9.9898 \times 10^{-1}$ |
| | Validation | $1.3860 \times 10^{-3}$ | $9.9124 \times 10^{-1}$ | $1.5457 \times 10^{-4}$ | $9.9897 \times 10^{-1}$ |
| | Testing | $2.6100 \times 10^{-3}$ | $9.8411 \times 10^{-1}$ | $1.1681 \times 10^{-4}$ | $9.9929 \times 10^{-1}$ |
| 15 | Training | $1.0103 \times 10^{-3}$ | $9.9351 \times 10^{-1}$ | $5.1625 \times 10^{-5}$ | $9.9968 \times 10^{-1}$ |
| | Validation | $9.4817 \times 10^{-4}$ | $9.9403 \times 10^{-1}$ | $4.5519 \times 10^{-5}$ | $9.9945 \times 10^{-1}$ |
| | Testing | $1.6502 \times 10^{-3}$ | $9.9041 \times 10^{-1}$ | $4.9208 \times 10^{-5}$ | $9.9965 \times 10^{-1}$ |
| 20 | Training | $1.3008 \times 10^{-3}$ | $9.9166 \times 10^{-1}$ | $8.8756 \times 10^{-5}$ | $9.9944 \times 10^{-1}$ |
| | Validation | $6.2395 \times 10^{-4}$ | $9.9616 \times 10^{-1}$ | $8.7463 \times 10^{-5}$ | $9.9943 \times 10^{-1}$ |
| | Testing | $1.3258 \times 10^{-3}$ | $9.9210 \times 10^{-1}$ | $8.6782 \times 10^{-5}$ | $9.9946 \times 10^{-1}$ |

The results demonstrate that the R value for the new algorithm exceeds that of the AHT/DSHT two-step calculation, particularly for the maximum value of the coefficient of performance (COP) at the user-requested absorption temperature. A similar approach was applied for point-to-point network integration across multiple heat sources and users [30].

## 4. Discussion

In 2025, there are not enough data for controlling double-stage heat transformers based on lithium bromide absorption. There are some data for controlling the temperature in the single-stage heat pump, but the blend was ammonia–water from 80 °C close to 100 °C based on a one-dimensional heat exchanger falling film model [31–33], and there is no ANN proposal on that work. Another attempt to control energy recovery has added a compressor with a reduction of the COP and only a single stage [34–37]. Similar devices based on absorption compression were reported for control with genetic programming without optimal values [38].

In the literature [39], it has been established that the energy for the circulation of liquids in the thermodynamic cycle can be considered small and insignificant, and the flow relationship is always non-linear. Another approach to control a LiBr-$H_2O$ AHT is to control the flow [40]. The criterion for determining where a cycle with the highest waste heat recovery temperature can be operated to reintegrate it into the original process, with a circular economy approach, considers that the relationship between the energy that is recovered and the energy that is inputted, already established as COP [41] and that it is modulated between the Gross Temperature Lift (GTL) calculated as the differences in temperatures between the absorber and evaporator.

Reproducing with our ANN the methodology of [14] for the waste energy conditions, but at 70 °C, with an environment at 20 °C, it can be observed in Figure 20, that it only happens in the first stage of the thermodynamic cycle—the best condition to operate is not at the lowest absorption temperature (which obtains the highest COP) and not at the highest absorption temperature (which presents the lowest COP), but is at 114 °C, which is the highest value of the product COP × GTL.

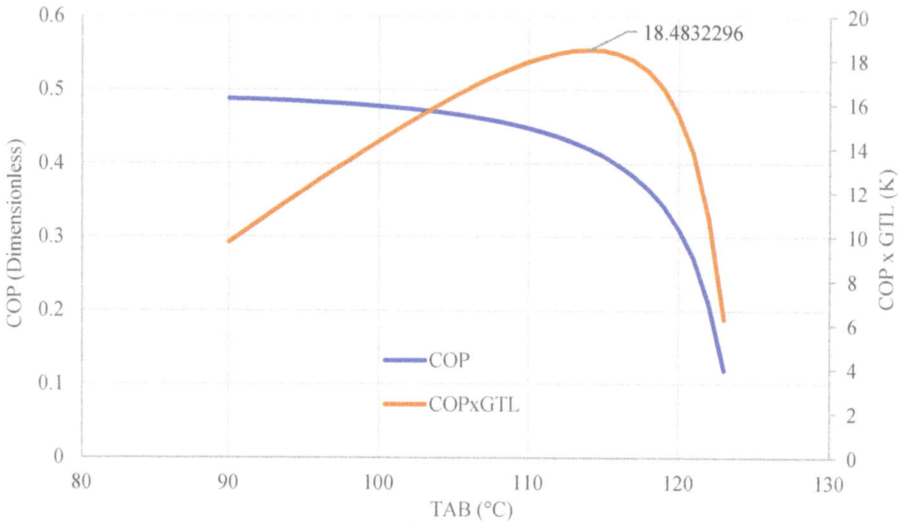


**Figure 20.** COP and COP × GTL based on the TAB for a one-stage heat recovery cycle.

In the case of a double stage, using our ANN, we can see the data in Figure 21 and confirm the nonlinear behavior, reported by [14]. Furthermore, it is not possible to identify where a DSHT should operate.

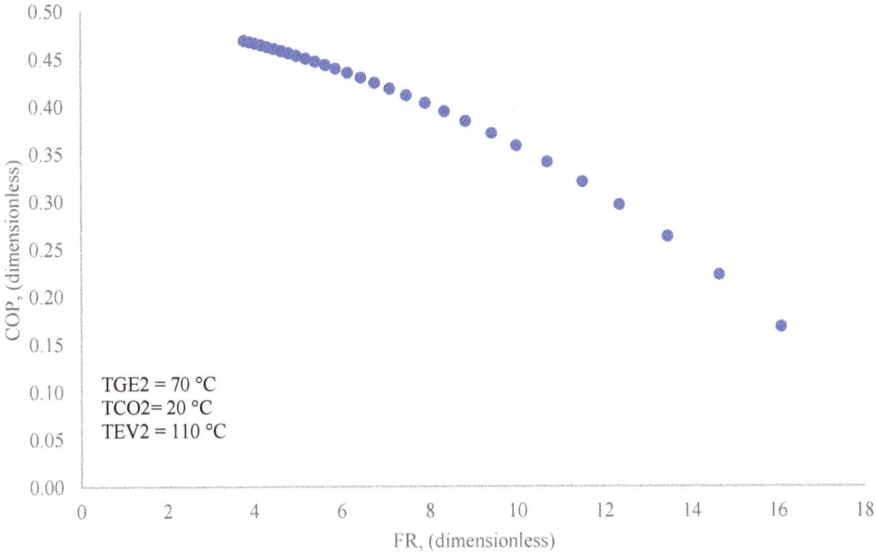


**Figure 21.** Performance coefficient as a function of the flow ratio for a DSHT from [14].

In Figure 22, it can be seen that the orange line, corresponding to the methodology presented in this work, allows the identification of the condition in which energy recovery for the circular economy can occur, using the proposed ANN strategy. The maximum TAB2 of the double-stage heat transformer the higher value in the blue line does not indicate the highest COP. Figure 21 shows how the highest value for FR is the lowest value for COP at operating conditions described in Figure 22.

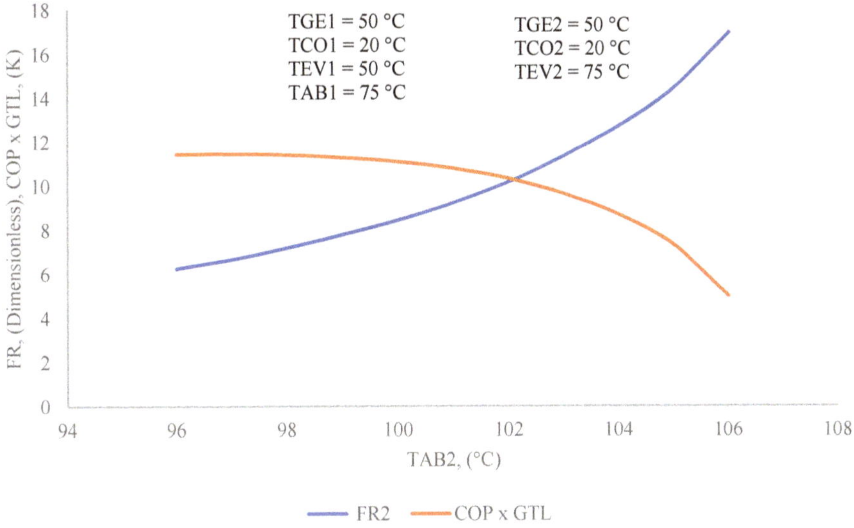


**Figure 22.** FR and COP × GTL as a function of the TAB2 of the second stage of a DSHT compared with previous data.

Figure 23 shows that with the data calculated by the ANN, it is possible to determine the optimized operating condition of a DSHT based not on the calculated COP [3]. The optimization on the COP includes the calculation of the energy that can be reintegrated into the process that disposes energy at 70 °C and transfers at 65 °C in the generators and evaporator 1. That energy in the first stage can revalue energy at 85 °C, which is transferred to evaporator 2 at 80 °C. The ANN calculation input determines that in the second stage, energy is added in a second evaporator (QEV2) and therefore the highest temperature of the DSHT is TAB2. Now, with this second stage, the energy will recover at 116 °C—this theoretical calculation shows that the maximum GTL value at the highest possible COP from waste heat is at 70 °C.

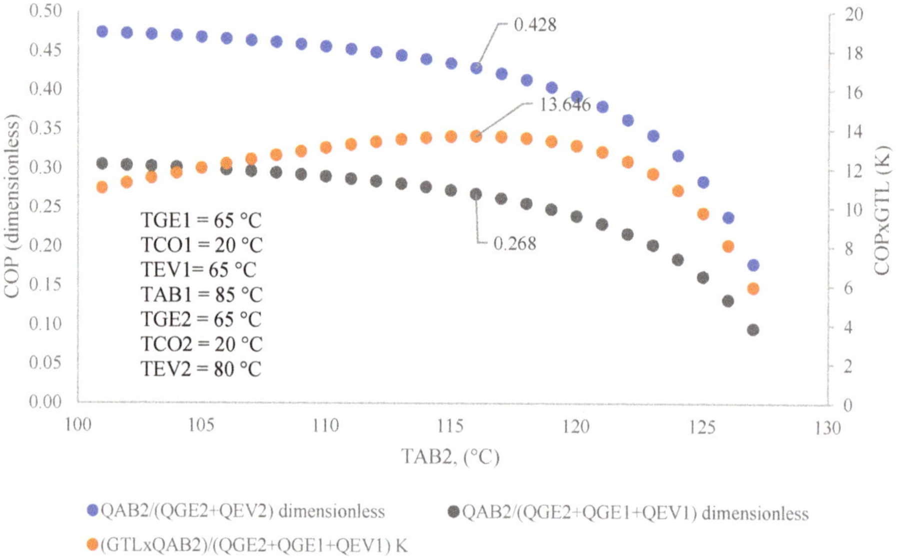


**Figure 23.** COP and COP × GTL as a function of the TAB2 of the second stage of a DSHT.

This prediction of the maximum simultaneous values for COP and GTL was achieved and found to be consistent with the thermodynamic values for future energy recycling. This was after evaluating the MSE and R values for the Levenberg–Marquardt (LM) and scaled conjugate gradient (SCG) methods, using five to thirty neurons for training, validation, and testing, as shown in Figure 24. The highest R value, with MSE in the E-05 range, was obtained using the Levenberg–Marquardt method with 15 neurons in the current ANN. In this figure, the lines of the same color were obtained and compared to get the highest R value, as Appendix A shows as a flow diagram. For the scaled conjugate gradient in our previous work, ref. [3] with five neurons, the R value for the training was close to 0.987, with ten being 0.993, fifteen being 0.994, and twenty being 0.992, respectively. Instead, for Levenberg–Marquardt for this work, from five neurons, the R value goes from 0.996 to 0.999 with ten neurons, 0.9996 with fifteen neurons, asymptotic to 1.0. It is remarkable that for 20 neurons, it is the highest R value: 0.999841, while for 25 neurons under training, R value diminishes to 0.999751. Levenberg–Marquardt is always greater than the scaled conjugate gradient from 0.02% to 0.10% with the same data for this study.

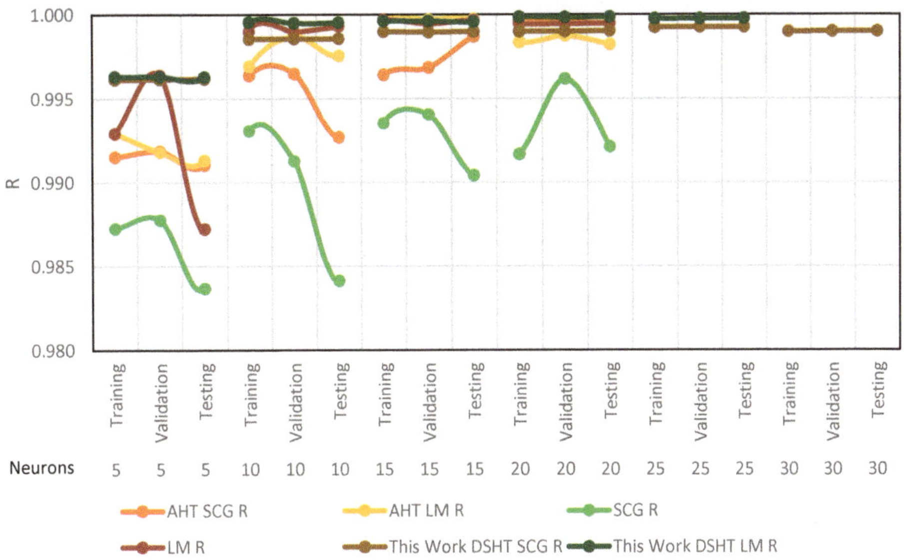


**Figure 24.** R values for scaled conjugated gradient and Levenberg–Marquardt algorithms obtained in this work and compared with a previous work [3].

The major improvement occurs when going from five to ten neurons for all cases, which represents a statistical improvement thirty-two times greater compared to increasing from ten to fifteen neurons in training, validation, and testing. From 15 to 20 neurons, the improvement is only two times, but training, validation, and testing from 20 to 25 neurons show a negative improvement, so the selection of neurons remains at 20 neurons.

There are several studies in the literature on the potential of absorption heat pumps in different applications within the industrial sector. In one of these, we work on a proposal integration of a single-state absorption heat pump in a textile industry process (ironing process) [6], without any artificial intelligent algorithm for control; but in this natural step, the implementation is derived from this work. Future work for this research on absorption heat pumps will consist of evaluating whether the algorithm used in this project can be applied to similar processes, where AHTs are already used as an alternative for energy recovery for circular economic processes.

## 5. Conclusions

An ANN has been designed for a dual-stage absorption heat transformer, configured with 20 neurons in the hidden layer, 360 weights, and 29 biases. The ANN reached a correlation coefficient of 0.9998 and presented MSE values of $1.78592 \times 10^{-5}$, $1.97765 \times 10^{-5}$, and $1.77207 \times 10^{-5}$ for the training, validation, and testing phases, respectively. This model allows calculating the optimal operating conditions to maximize the COP × GTL product.

A computer-aided simulator has been developed to analyze the transient and steady-state behavior of the DSHT temperature variables over time. The tests carried out show that the user-proposed change will cause the developed ANN to create an output vector containing the operating conditions of higher COP × GTL, leading to an MEV1 flow output that will mark the gradual change in the opening or closing of the servo valve.

Using the Levenberg–Marquardt algorithm, higher R values for training, validation, and tests of 0.061%, 0.058%, and 0.060%, respectively, have been obtained. This has resulted in an increase in the simultaneous highest values for COP and GTL. This improvement in energy recovery leads to taking waste energy from 70 °C to a useful circular economy.

**Author Contributions:** Conceptualization, S.V.-A. and R.J.R.; methodology, S.V.-A., L.D.-G., and R.J.R.; software, S.V.-A., R.J.R. and L.D.-G.; validation, S.V.-A., R.J.R., J.C., and M.M.-G.; formal analysis, S.V.-A., R.J.R., J.C., and M.M.-G.; investigation, S.V.-A. and L.D.-G.; resources, R.J.R.; data curation, S.V.-A. and R.J.R.; writing—original draft preparation, S.V.-A. and R.J.R.; writing—review and editing, S.V.-A., R.J.R., L.D.-G., M.M.-G., and J.C.; visualization, R.J.R. and J.C.; supervision, R.J.R.; project administration, R.J.R.; funding acquisition, R.J.R. All authors have read and agreed to the published version of the manuscript.

**Funding:** Secretaría de Ciencia Humanidades, Tecnología e Innovación: CVU 9391109.

**Data Availability Statement:** Research materials necessary to enable the reproduction of an experiment are indicated in Section 2.

**Acknowledgments:** To UAEM—IICBA—CIICAp Facilities.

**Conflicts of Interest:** The authors declare no conflicts of interest.

## Abbreviations

The following abbreviations are used in this manuscript:

| | |
|---|---|
| AHT | Absorption heat transformer |
| ANN | Artificial neural networks |
| COP | Coefficient of performance (dimensionless) |
| DSHT | Double-stage heat transformer |
| FR1 | Flow ratio in AHT (dimensionless) |
| FR2 | Flow ratio in DSHT (dimensionless) |
| GTL | Gross temperature lift (K) |
| MEV1 | Evaporator mass flow in AHT (kg/s) |
| MEV2 | Evaporator mass flow in DSHT (kg/s) |
| MSE | Mean squared error ($kg^2/s^2$) |
| QAB2 | Absorption thermal power in DSHT (kW) |
| QGE1 | Desorption thermal power in AHT (kW) |
| QGE2 | Desorption thermal power in DSHT (kW) |
| QEV1 | Evaporation thermal power in AHT (kW) |
| QEV2 | Evaporation thermal power in DSHT (kW) |
| TCO1 | Condenser temperature in AHT (°C) |
| TCO2 | Condenser temperature in DSHT (°C) |
| TEV1 | Evaporator temperature in AHT (°C) |
| TEV2 | Evaporator temperature in DSHT (°C) |
| TAB1 | Absorption temperature in AHT (°C) |
| TAB2 | Absorption temperature in DSHT (°C) |
| R | Strength of correlation (dimensionless) |

## Appendix A

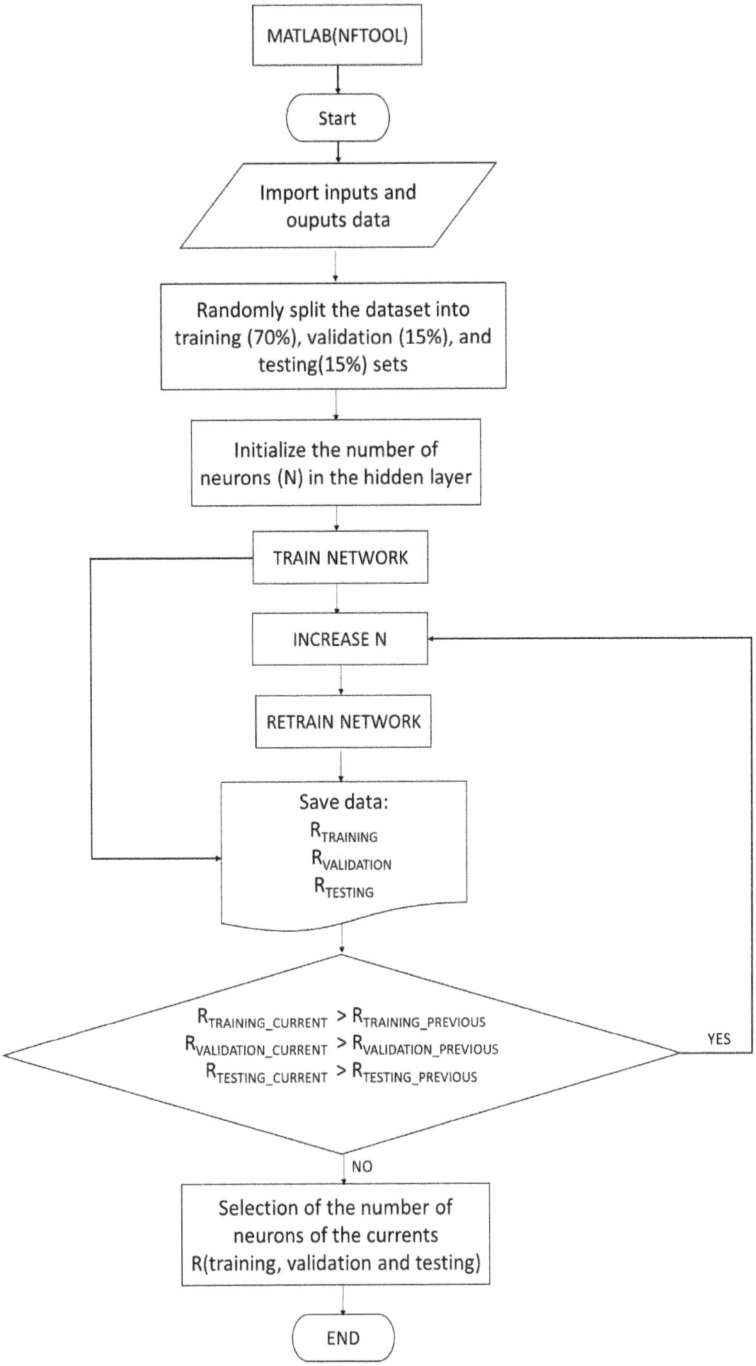


**Figure A1.** Flow diagram for obtaining the number of neurons in the hidden layer.

## Appendix B

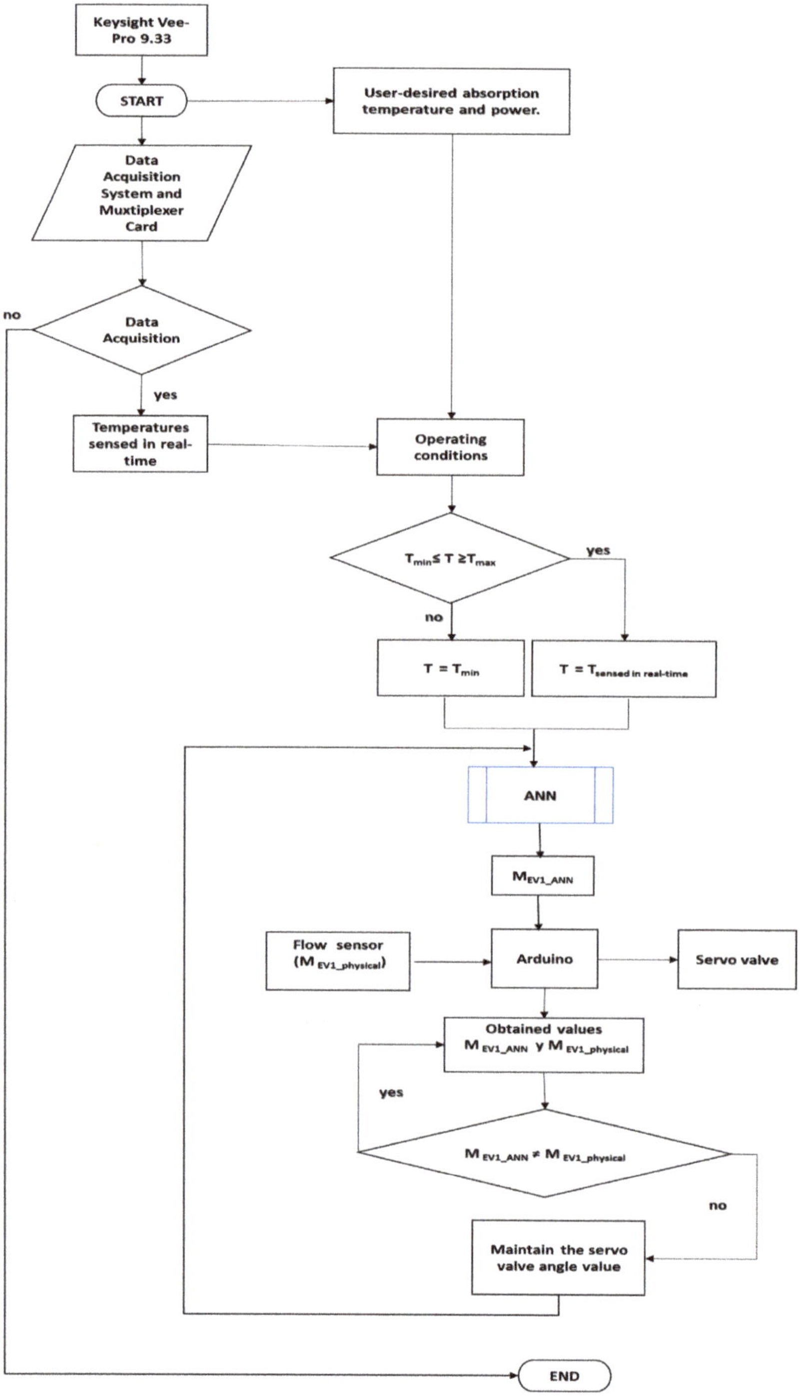


**Figure A2.** Flow control diagram MEV1.

## Appendix C

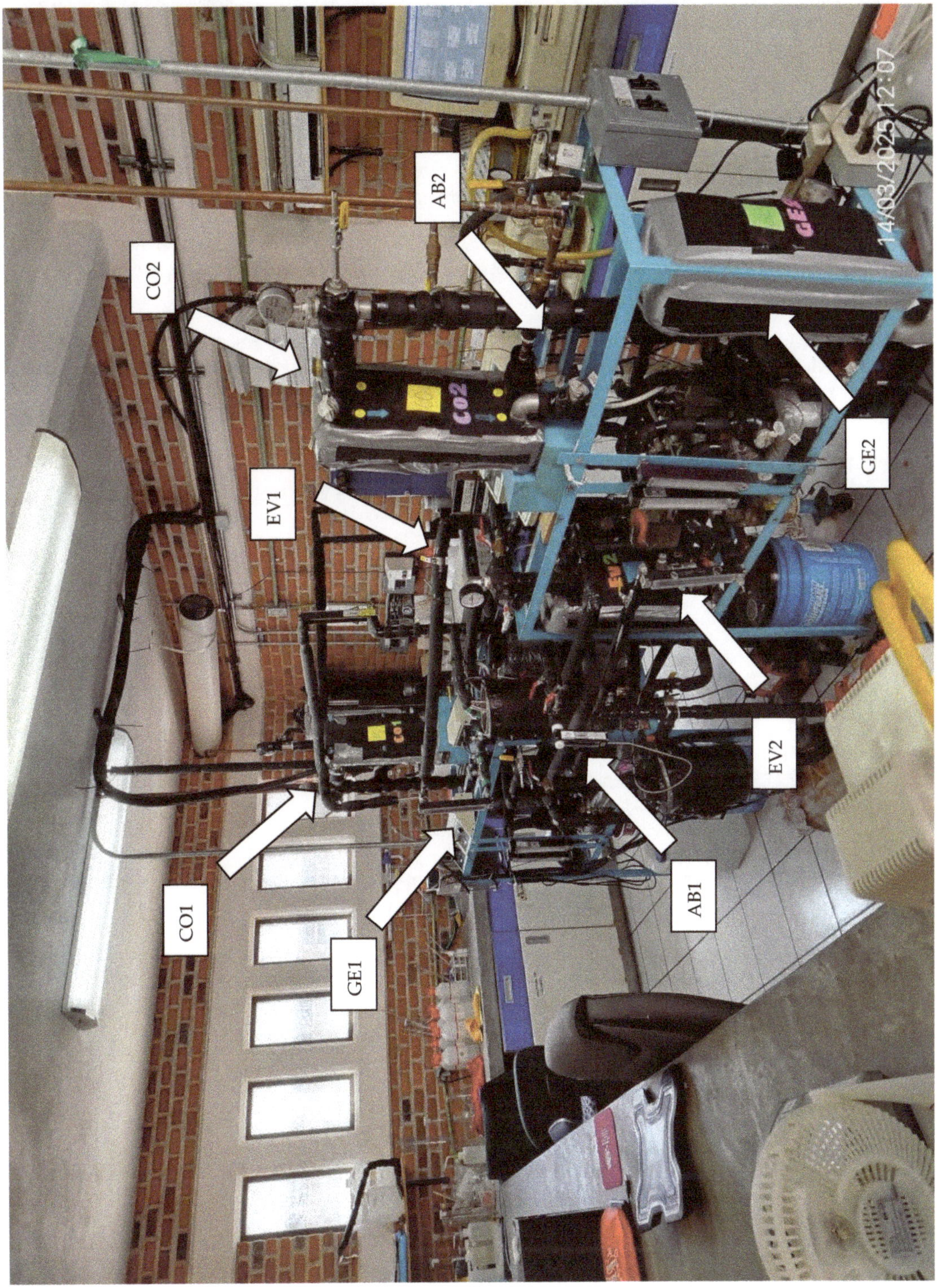

## References


1. Yuan, M.; Mathiesen, B.V.; Schneider, N.; Xia, J.; Zheng, W.; Sorknæs, P.; Lund, H.; Zhang, L. Renewable energy and waste heat recovery in district heating systems in China: A systematic review. *Energy* **2024**, *294*, 130788. [CrossRef]
2. IEA. International Energy Agency. Available online: https://www.iea.org/reports/energy-technology-perspectives-2024 (accessed on 5 November 2024).
3. Vázquez-Aveledo, S.; Romero, R.J.; Montiel-González, M.; Cerezo, J. Control Strategy Based on Artificial Intelligence for a Double-Stage Absorption Heat Transformer. *Processes* **2023**, *11*, 1632. [CrossRef]
4. Cudok, F.; Giannetti, N.; Ciganda, J.L.C.; Aoyama, J.; Babu, P.; Coronas, A.; Ziegler, F. Absorption heat transformer-state-of-the-art of industrial applications. *Renew. Sustain. Energy Rev.* **2021**, *141*, 110757. [CrossRef]
5. Romero, R.J.; Cerezo, J.; Rodríguez-Martínez, A.; Montiel, M. Absorption Heat Transformer for Solar Pond Energy Temperature Upgrading. *Chem. Eng. Trans.* **2021**, *86*, 703–708. [CrossRef]
6. Morales-Gómez, L.I.; Romero, R.J.; Vázquez-Aveledo, S.; Montiel-González, M.; Best, R. Energy and environmental study for the textile industry based on absorption heat transformer. *Energy Sources Part A Recovery Util. Environ. Eff.* **2023**, *45*, 5594–5607. [CrossRef]
7. Bora, R.; Richardson, R.; You, F. Resource recovery and waste-to-energy from wastewater sludge via thermochemical conversion technologies in support of circular economy: A comprehensive review. *BMC Chem. Eng.* **2020**, *2*, 8. [CrossRef]
8. Chen, H.; Song, X.; Jian, Y. Performance Assessment of a Municipal Solid Waste Gasification and Power Generation System Integrated with Absorption Heat Pump Drying. *Energies* **2024**, *17*, 6034. [CrossRef]
9. Cai, X.; Wang, Z.; Han, Y.; Su, W. Study on the Performance of a Novel Double-Section Full-Open Absorption Heat Pump for Flue Gas Waste Heat Recovery. *Processes* **2024**, *12*, 2181. [CrossRef]
10. Sun, D.; Liu, Z.; Zhang, H.; Zhang, X. Performance Analysis of a New Cogeneration System with Efficient Utilization of Waste Heat Resources and Energy Conversion Capabilities. *Energies* **2024**, *17*, 3347. [CrossRef]
11. Kabiesz, J.; Kubica, R. Optimizing the Recovery of Latent Heat of Condensation from the Flue Gas Stream through the Combustion of Solid Biomass with a High Moisture Content. *Energies* **2024**, *17*, 1670. [CrossRef]
12. Payá, J.; Cazorla-Marín, A.; Arpagaus, C.; Corrales Ciganda, J.L.; Hassan, A.H. Low-Pressure Steam Generation with Concentrating Solar Energy and Different Heat Upgrade Technologies: Potential in the European Industry. *Sustainability* **2024**, *16*, 1733. [CrossRef]
13. Abbas, T.; Chen, S.; Zhang, X.; Wang, Z. Coordinated Optimization of Hydrogen-Integrated Energy Hubs with Demand Response-Enabled Energy Sharing. *Processes* **2024**, *12*, 1338. [CrossRef]
14. Sotelo, S.S.; Romero, J.R.; Romero, J.R.; Rodríguez-Martínez, A. Double Stage Heat Transformer Controlled by Flow Ratio. In *Innovations in Computing Sciences and Software Engineering: Proceedings of the 2009 International Conference on Systems, Computing Sciences and Software Engineering (SCSS), CISSE 09, Bridgeport, CT, USA, 4–12 December 2009*; Springer: Dordrecht, The Netherlands, 2009. [CrossRef]
15. Sajid, M.; Tanveer, M.; Suganthan, P. Ensemble Deep Random Vector Functional Link Neural Network Based on Fuzzy Inference System. *IEEE Trans. Fuzzy Syst.* **2024**, *33*, 479–490. [CrossRef]
16. Dengiz, T.; Kleinebrahm, M. Imitation learning with artificial neural networks for demand response with a heuristic control approach for heat pumps. *Energy AI* **2024**, *18*, 100441. [CrossRef]
17. Rohrer, T.; Frison, L.; Kaupenjohann, L.; Scharf, K.; Hergenrother, E. Deep Reinforcement Learning for Heat Pump Control. In *Intelligent Computing. SAI 2023*; Arai, K., Ed.; Lecture Notes in Networks and Systems; Springer: Cham, Switzerland, 2023; Volume 711. [CrossRef]
18. Manjavacas, A.; Campoy-Nieves, A.; Jiménez-Raboso, J.; Molina-Solana, M.; Gómez-Romero, J. An experimental evaluation of deep reinforcement learning algorithms for HVAC control. *Artif. Intell. Rev.* **2024**, *57*, 173. [CrossRef]
19. Sajadi, P.; Rahmani, D.; Mostafa; Tang, Y.; Wang, G. Real-Time Two-Dimensional Temperature Field Prediction in Metal Additive Manufacturing Using Physics-Informed Neural Networks. *arXiv* **2024**, arXiv:2401.02403. [CrossRef]
20. Yarahmadi, A.M.; Breuß, M.; Hartmann, C. Long Short-Term Memory Neural Network for Temperature Prediction in Laser Powder Bed Additive Manufacturing. In *Intelligent Systems and Applications*; Arai, K., Ed.; Lecture Notes in Networks and Systems; Springer: Cham, Switzerland, 2023; Volume 544. [CrossRef]
21. Muravyev, N.V.; Luciano, G.; Ornaghi, H.L., Jr.; Svoboda, R.; Vyazovkin, S. Artificial Neural Networks for Pyrolysis, Thermal Analysis, and Thermokinetic Studies: The Status Quo. *Molecules* **2021**, *26*, 3727. [CrossRef]
22. Zhang, T.; Chen, L.; Wang, J. Multi-objective optimization of elliptical tube fin heat exchangers based on neural networks and genetic algorithm. *Energy* **2023**, *269*, 126729. [CrossRef]
23. Khan, J.; Lee, E.; Kim, K. A higher prediction accuracy–based alpha–beta filter algorithm using the feedforward artificial neural network. *CAAI Trans. Intell. Technol.* **2023**, *8*, 1124–1139. [CrossRef]
24. Villada, F.; Muñoz, N.; García-Quintero, E. Artificial Neural Networks applied to Gold Price Prediction. *Inf. Tecnol.* **2016**, *27*, 143–150. [CrossRef]

25. The MathWorks, Inc. Available online: https://es.mathworks.com/products/deep-learning.html (accessed on 10 May 2024).
26. Mishra, S.; Prusty, R.; Hota, P. Analysis of Levenberg-Marquardt and Scaled Conjugate gradient training algorithms for artificial neural network-based LS and MMSE estimated channel equalizers. In Proceedings of the International Conference on Man and Machine Interfacing, Bhubaneswar, India, 17–19 December 2015. [CrossRef]
27. Valdez, C.V. Design and Modelling of a Two-Stage Thermal Transformer for Waste Heat Recovery with Automatic Control Depending on the Energy to be Revalued. PhD Thesis, Autonomous University of the State of Morelos, Cuernavaca, MR, Mexic, 2019. Available online: http://riaa.uaem.mx/handle/20.500.12055/712 (accessed on 6 January 2025).
28. Mantech Electronics. Water Flow Sensor Tutorial. Available online: https://naylampmechatronics.com/sensores-liquido/352-sensor-de-flujo-de-agua-2-yf-dn50.html (accessed on 19 September 2024).
29. Heptro. Available online: https://hetpro-store.com/TUTORIALES/pines-arduino/ (accessed on 10 April 2024).
30. Wu, W.; Du, Y.; Qian, H.; Fan, H.; Jiang, Z.; Zhang, X.; Huang, S. Enhancing the waste heat utilization of industrial park: A heat pump-centric network integration approach for multiple heat sources and users. *Energy Convers. Manag.* **2024**, *306*, 118306. [CrossRef]
31. Collignon, R.; Demasles, H.; Phan, H.T. Modeling of an Ammonia/Water Absorption Heat Transformer to upgrade low-temperature industrial waste heat both at machine scale and at local scale inside the falling film absorber. *Therm. Sci. Eng. Prog.* **2025**, *59*, 103302.
32. Shen, Z.; Li, S.; Feng, L.; Jin, Z.; Du, K.; Li, Y.; Sheng, W. Performance research of a solution cross-type absorption-resorption heat transformer using $NH_3/H_2O$ work fluid. *Appl. Therm. Eng.* **2024**, *246*, 122874.
33. Jin, P.; Li, S.; Jin, Z.; Li, Y. Thermodynamic analysis of an ammonia-water double absorption-resorption heat transformer system. *Appl. Therm. Eng.* **2024**, *247*, 123130.
34. Gong, Y.; Liu, F.; Sui, J.; Wang, X.; Jin, H. Thermodynamic performance comparison of H2O/LiBr and ionic liquid working pairs in a novel absorption compression heat transformer system. *Therm. Sci. Eng. Prog.* **2025**, *57*, 103115.
35. Sun, X.; Liu, L.; Zhang, T.; Dai, Y. Multi-objective optimization of a Rectisol process integrated with compression-absorption cascade refrigeration system and ORC for waste heat recovery. *Appl. Therm. Eng.* **2024**, *244*, 122611. [CrossRef]
36. Ji, Q.; Yin, Y.; Huang, G.; Zhao, D.; Cao, B. An advanced cascade method for optimal industrial heating performance in hybrid heat pump. *Energy Convers. Manag.* **2024**, *303*, 118187. [CrossRef]
37. Liu, Y.; Qu, S.; Shen, S.; Feng, Y.; Sun, T.; Wang, C.; Xing, Z. Experimental investigation on the large temperature lift heat pump with an integrated two-stage independently variable frequency compressor. *Energy* **2025**, *314*, 134289. [CrossRef]
38. Wei, J.; Wu, D.; Wang, R. A Multi-Objective evolutionary algorithm-based optimization framework for hybrid absorption-compression heat pump systems. *Appl. Energy* **2025**, *382*, 125228.
39. Romero, R.J.; Cerezo, J.; Martínez, A.R.; Luna, G.H.; Montiel-González, M. On the dimensionless absorption heat pump widespread. *J. Adv. Therm. Sci. Res.* **2021**, *8*, 10–20. [CrossRef]
40. Liu, Z.; Lu, D.; Tao, S.; Chen, R.; Gong, M. Experimental study on using 85° C low-grade heat to generate < 120° C steam by a temperature-distributed absorption heat transformer. *Energy* **2024**, *299*, 131491. [CrossRef]
41. Valdez, V.; Romero, J.R. Optimal design criterion for Heat Transformer operating with Water Carrol. In Proceedings of the Fourth International Conference on Advances in Mechanical and Automation Engineering—MAE 2016, Rome, Italy, 19 August 2016; p. 63. [CrossRef]

machine learning & knowledge extraction

MDPI

*Review*

# Exploring the Intersection of Machine Learning and Big Data: A Survey

**Elias Dritsas * and Maria Trigka**

Industrial Systems Institute (ISI), Athena Research and Innovation Center, 26504 Patras, Greece
* Correspondence: dritsas@isi.gr

**Abstract:** The integration of machine learning (ML) with big data has revolutionized industries by enabling the extraction of valuable insights from vast and complex datasets. This convergence has fueled advancements in various fields, leading to the development of sophisticated models capable of addressing complicated problems. However, the application of ML in big data environments presents significant challenges, including issues related to scalability, data quality, model interpretability, privacy, and the handling of diverse and high-velocity data. This survey provides a comprehensive overview of the current state of ML applications in big data, systematically identifying the key challenges and recent advancements in the field. By critically analyzing existing methodologies, this paper highlights the gaps in current research and proposes future directions for the development of scalable, interpretable, and privacy-preserving ML techniques. Additionally, this survey addresses the ethical and societal implications of ML in big data, emphasizing the need for responsible and equitable approaches to harnessing these technologies. The insights presented in this paper aim to guide future research and contribute to the ongoing discourse on the responsible integration of ML and big data.

**Keywords:** machine learning; big data; data analytics; techniques; challenges

## 1. Introduction

The exponential growth of data generated by digital devices, social media platforms, sensors, and the Internet of Things (IoT) has ushered in the era of big data, profoundly transforming various industries and scientific fields. This deluge of data, often referred to as "big data", is characterized by its immense volume, diversity, high velocity, and uncertain veracity, posing significant challenges for traditional data processing and analysis methods. As organizations and researchers strive to harness the potential of these data, ML has emerged as a crucial tool, offering the ability to extract meaningful insights, make predictions, and drive decision-making processes in ways that were previously unimaginable [1,2].

ML, a subset of artificial intelligence (AI), involves the development of algorithms that can learn patterns from data and make decisions or predictions without being explicitly programmed to perform specific tasks. Combining ML with big data has led to groundbreaking applications across various domains, including healthcare, finance, transportation, and beyond. For instance, ML models are now capable of diagnosing diseases from medical images, detecting fraudulent transactions in financial systems, optimizing traffic flows in smart cities, and even predicting customer behavior in retail environments [3–5].

However, the convergence of big data and ML is not without challenges. The sheer scale and complexity of big data necessitate new approaches to data management, algorithm design, and computational infrastructure. Traditional ML algorithms, which were not designed to handle the vast amounts of data generated today, often struggle with the issues of scalability, efficiency, and accuracy. Additionally, the heterogeneous nature of big data—encompassing structured data from databases, unstructured data from text and images, and semi-structured data such as JavaScript object notation (JSON) files—further complicates the task of developing effective ML models [6–8].

Moreover, integrating ML into big data environments raises critical concerns about model interpretability, data privacy, and ethical considerations. As ML models become more complex, understanding how they arrive at their decisions becomes increasingly difficult, which can be problematic in high-stakes applications such as healthcare and finance. Furthermore, the use of personal and sensitive data in ML models raises significant privacy and security issues, necessitating the development of new techniques to protect individual rights while still enabling the use of large-scale data for analysis [9–12].

The present survey differentiates itself from the existing literature summarized in Table 1 by providing a more integrative and forward-looking perspective on the intersection of ML and big data. Unlike the surveys in Table 1, which primarily focus on domain-specific applications (e.g., energy, healthcare, and transportation) or challenges (e.g., scalability and interpretability), this survey adopts a broader framework. It systematically identifies critical challenges such as scalability, interpretability, data privacy, and ethical considerations while addressing their interconnections with ML techniques and frameworks.

**Table 1.** Summary of surveys that capture the intersection of ML and big data.

| Reference | Description |
|---|---|
| [13] | It discusses ML techniques for big data, including supervised, unsupervised, and semi-supervised learning, and their applications in fields like healthcare, agriculture, and robotics. It highlights challenges like data imbalance and offers remedies for researchers. |
| [14] | This survey explores ML methods tailored for big data applications. It addresses features, challenges, and practical uses of algorithms like classification and clustering, emphasizing their scalability and application in domains like healthcare and finance. |
| [15] | This is a paper providing an overview of ML methods for big data that examines challenges in processing large datasets and highlights promising approaches like distributed and parallel learning. The paper also discusses open research directions. |
| [16] | This is a survey focusing on big data and ML applications in the electrical power and energy sectors. It reviews challenges, solutions, and opportunities in applying ML for smart grid operations and energy management. |
| [17] | This paper compiles challenges associated with the use of ML and big data, categorizing them by the dimensions of big data (volume, velocity, variety, and veracity). It reviews emerging techniques and solutions, offering insights into research gaps and future directions. |
| [18] | This paper provides a detailed literature survey on ML for big data processing, covering techniques like deep learning (DL), representation learning, and their integration with signal processing. It highlights challenges like high dimensionality and discusses potential research trends. |
| [19] | This survey provides a discussion of opportunities and challenges associated with ML and big data. It introduces a framework that integrates ML phases (preprocessing, learning, and evaluation) with components like user input, the domain, and system architecture. |

A key differentiation is its focus on the ethical and societal implications of ML in big data, an area often overlooked in the reviewed surveys. Furthermore, this survey uniquely emphasizes the need for sustainable and privacy-preserving ML, proposing advanced solutions like federated learning and energy-efficient models. By consolidating insights across diverse applications and challenges, it highlights emerging research gaps, such as the integration of ML with legacy systems, the environmental impact of ML operations, and the scalability of algorithms for multi-modal data. This comprehensive perspective not only addresses existing gaps but also charts a roadmap for future research in responsible and scalable ML in big data contexts. In conclusion, this survey makes several key contributions to the understanding and advancement of ML in the context of big data:

- It provides an in-depth exploration of the diverse applications of ML in big data across multiple domains.
- It systematically identifies and analyzes the critical challenges that arise from the application of ML to big data.
- It reviews recent advancements in ML techniques and frameworks that have been developed to address the challenges posed by big data.
- It outlines key areas for future research, focusing on the continued development of scalable, interpretable, and privacy-preserving ML techniques.
- Recognizing the broader impact of ML and big data on society, the survey addresses the ethical challenges associated with bias, fairness, accountability, and the environmental impact of these technologies.

To provide a clear roadmap for the topics explored in this study, Figure 1 offers a visual overview of the key themes and their interconnections. This figure reflects the structure of the study and serves as a guide for the subsequent literature review, ensuring a comprehensive and cohesive exploration of ML applications and challenges in big data. More specifically, the remainder of this paper is structured as follows. Section 2 focuses on ML applications in big data. Section 3 explores the challenges associated with the use of big data with ML. Moreover, Section 4 notes recent advancements and future directions. Section 5 provides a discussion of the subject under consideration. Finally, Section 6 summarizes the findings of this survey.

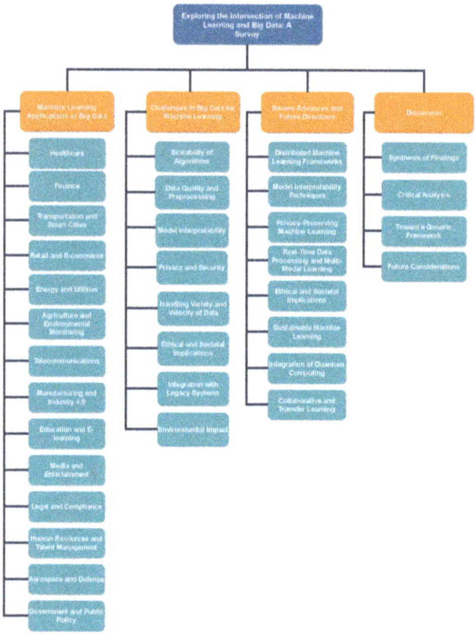


**Figure 1.** An overview of surveyed key topics: ML application and big data challenges.

## 2. Machine Learning Applications in Big Data

ML has emerged as a powerful tool for unlocking the vast potential of big data, enabling the extraction of meaningful insights from complex and voluminous datasets. Across various industries, ML applications drive significant advancements by leveraging big data to solve problems that were previously unsolvable. This section explores the diverse ways in which ML is applied to big data, transforming fields such as healthcare, finance, transportation, and beyond.

### 2.1. Healthcare

ML techniques, especially DL, reinforcement learning (RL), and ensemble methods, have demonstrated transformative potential in the healthcare sector, leveraging big data to revolutionize patient care, diagnostics, and treatment planning. One of the most prominent applications is predictive analytics. ML models forecast disease progression, patient outcomes, and potential complications by analyzing large datasets, including patient history, genetic information, and lifestyle factors. These models enable personalized medicine, allowing healthcare providers to tailor treatments to individual patients based on their unique data profiles [20–23].

Furthermore, ML is extensively used in medical imaging, where convolutional neural networks (CNNs) and other DL techniques have achieved state-of-the-art performance in detecting and diagnosing conditions from images such as X-ray, magnetic resonance imaging (MRI), and computed tomography (CT) scans. For instance, ML models can detect early signs of diseases like cancer, often more accurately than human radiologists, by training on vast datasets of labeled medical images. ML algorithms accelerate drug discovery by analyzing genomic data, chemical structures, and protein–ligand interactions to predict viable drug candidates efficiently. These techniques also enable virtual screening, molecular optimization, and drug repurposing, significantly reducing time and cost [24–27].

Additionally, natural language processing (NLP) techniques are employed to extract valuable insights from unstructured data such as clinical notes, research papers, and patient-reported outcomes. This enables the development of more comprehensive and context-aware healthcare models. Exploiting electronic health records (EHRs) with ML models facilitates real-time monitoring and decision support, enhancing the ability of clinicians to make informed decisions quickly. ML algorithms process diverse EHR data, including medical histories, imaging results, and lab reports, to predict patient outcomes, recommend treatments, and identify potential complications. For instance, NLP can extract critical information from clinical notes, while DL techniques analyze imaging data for timely diagnoses. By enabling real-time decision support, these applications not only improve patient outcomes but also reduce costs and enhance the overall efficiency of healthcare delivery [28–31].

ML-driven predictive analytics empowers healthcare providers to move from reactive to proactive care by forecasting disease risks, identifying complications early, and tailoring treatments to individual patients. This transformative capability not only enhances patient outcomes but also reduces operational costs, making ML a cornerstone of modern healthcare strategies [32–34].

### 2.2. Finance

In the finance industry, ML is transforming how financial institutions manage risks, detect fraud, and optimize investment strategies. The ability to analyze large volumes of transactional data, market trends, and customer behavior allows ML models to identify patterns and anomalies that may indicate fraudulent activities. While traditional data mining algorithms are proficient in analyzing structured datasets to detect fraud through rule-based pattern matching and historical data analysis, ML offers a transformative edge by handling both structured and unstructured data at scale. For instance, ML models can process transactional records alongside unstructured sources like customer complaints or social media signals to dynamically adapt to new fraud schemes [35–37].

Unlike static rule-based data-mining systems, ML models can generalize across scenarios, enabling real-time detection of anomalies in high-frequency financial transactions. An example is the deployment of DL techniques in credit card fraud detection, where models analyze transaction attributes (e.g., time, location, and amount) alongside behavioral patterns, thereby reducing false positives and improving detection accuracy. Building on these capabilities, ML-based fraud detection systems excel at analyzing millions of transactions in real time, identifying suspicious activities with high precision while minimizing false positives. Through continuous learning from newly observed data, these systems evolve to detect emerging fraud patterns and adapt to the ever-changing landscape of financial crime [38–41].

Risk management is another critical application where ML models assess credit, market risk, and operational risk by analyzing diverse datasets, including historical market data, financial statements, and economic indicators. These models help financial institutions predict potential losses, optimize capital allocation, and comply with regulatory requirements. In the realm of algorithmic trading, ML algorithms process vast amounts of financial data to predict stock prices, execute trades, and manage portfolios, often at speeds and accuracies unattainable by human traders. These models can adapt to changing market conditions in real time, making them invaluable in high-frequency trading environments [42–45].

Moreover, ML is increasingly used in customer relationship management (CRM) within the finance sector. By analyzing customer data, ML models can predict customer needs, personalize financial products, and optimize marketing strategies. These applications enhance customer satisfaction and retention by providing tailored financial services and improving the overall customer experience [46–49].

### 2.3. *Transportation and Smart Cities*

ML applications in transportation are reshaping urban mobility and the development of smart cities. Autonomous vehicles, one of the most significant advancements in this domain, rely on ML algorithms to process data from a multitude of sensors, including cameras, light detection and ranging (LiDAR), and global positioning systems (GPSs). These algorithms enable vehicles to perceive their environment, make real-time decisions, and navigate complex traffic conditions safely and efficiently. The continuous influx of data from millions of miles driven allows these models to learn and improve, reducing the likelihood of accidents and enhancing the reliability of self-driving cars [50–53].

In addition to autonomous driving, ML is applied to optimize traffic management systems in smart cities. By analyzing data from traffic sensors, surveillance cameras, and social media, ML models can predict traffic patterns, optimize traffic light sequences, and reduce congestion. This leads to more efficient use of infrastructure, lower emissions, and improved quality of life for urban residents [54–57].

ML is also crucial in the logistics and supply chain sectors, where it is used to optimize routing, inventory management, and demand forecasting. Companies use ML to predict delivery times, optimize delivery routes, and manage inventory levels in real time, reducing costs and improving customer satisfaction. The integration of ML with IoT devices in smart cities further enhances these capabilities by providing real-time data on traffic, weather conditions, and other factors that influence logistics operations [58–61].

### 2.4. Retail and E-Commerce

In the retail and e-commerce industries, ML plays a pivotal role in enhancing customer experience, optimizing operations, and driving sales. One of the most visible applications is in personalized recommendations, where ML algorithms analyze customer data, including browsing history, purchase patterns, and demographic information to recommend products tailored to individual preferences. Big companies have successfully implemented recommendation systems that significantly boost customer engagement and sales [62–65].

Predictive analytics is another critical application in retail, where ML models forecast demand, optimize pricing strategies, and manage inventory. By analyzing historical sales data, market trends, and external factors such as seasonality and economic conditions, these models can predict which products are likely to be in demand and adjust pricing accordingly to maximize revenue. ML also enables dynamic pricing, where prices are adjusted in real time based on factors such as competitor pricing, customer behavior, and inventory levels [66–69].

Besides personalization and predictive analytics, ML is used in supply chain management to optimize operations from production to delivery. By analyzing data from various sources, including suppliers, logistics providers, and point-of-sale systems, ML models can optimize inventory levels, reduce lead times, and minimize stockouts. This leads to more efficient operations, lower costs, and better customer service [70–73].

### 2.5. Energy and Utilities

The energy and utilities sector is increasingly leveraging ML to optimize operations, improve energy efficiency, and integrate renewable energy sources. One of the primary applications is in predictive maintenance, where ML models analyze data from sensors installed in power plants, wind turbines, and other infrastructure to predict equipment failures before they occur. This enables utilities to perform maintenance proactively, reducing downtime and maintenance costs [74–78].

Coupled with predictive maintenance, ML is applied to optimize energy consumption and improve grid stability. Smart grids, which use ML to analyze data from sensors and meters across the grid, can predict energy demand, optimize energy distribution, and integrate renewable energy sources more effectively. This leads to more efficient use of resources, lower energy costs, and reduced environmental impact [79–82].

ML also plays a crucial role in the integration of renewable energy sources, such as solar and wind, into the energy grid. By analyzing weather data, ML models can predict the availability of renewable energy, allowing utilities to optimize the use of renewable resources and reduce reliance on fossil fuels. This contributes to the development of a more sustainable and resilient energy system [83–85].

### 2.6. Agriculture and Environmental Monitoring

In agriculture, ML is driving the development of precision farming techniques that increase crop yields, reduce waste, and optimize resource use. By analyzing data from satellites, drones, and IoT devices, ML models can monitor crop health, predict yields, and optimize irrigation and fertilization schedules. These techniques enable farmers to make data-driven decisions that improve productivity and sustainability [86–89].

ML is also used in environmental monitoring to analyze data from sensors, satellites, and other sources to monitor air and water quality, predict natural disasters, and assess the impact of climate change. For example, ML models can analyze satellite images to detect deforestation, monitor changes in land use, and predict the impact of these changes on biodiversity and ecosystems. These applications are critical for managing natural resources and mitigating the effects of climate change [90–93].

In precision agriculture, ML algorithms analyze data from various sources, including soil sensors, weather stations, and drones, to optimize planting, irrigation, and harvesting schedules. This results in more efficient use of water, fertilizers, and pesticides, leading to higher crop yields and reduced environmental impact. Additionally, ML is used to develop disease and pest prediction models, enabling farmers to take preventive measures before outbreaks occur [94–97].

In environmental monitoring, ML is applied to analyze data from satellite imagery, weather models, and ground sensors to track changes in ecosystems, predict natural disasters, and monitor climate change. These models can detect patterns and trends that are not apparent to human observers, providing valuable insights for environmental management and policy making [98–101].

### 2.7. Telecommunications

The telecommunications industry has embraced ML to enhance network performance, improve customer experience, and optimize operations. One of the primary applications is in network optimization, where ML models analyze data from network sensors, user devices, and traffic patterns to optimize network performance, reduce latency, and improve service quality. These models can predict network congestion, optimize routing, and allocate resources dynamically based on real-time data [102–105].

Alongside network optimization, ML is used in CRM to analyze customer data, predict churn, and personalize marketing campaigns. By analyzing customer behavior, usage patterns, and feedback, ML models can identify customers at risk of leaving and develop targeted retention strategies. This leads to improved customer satisfaction and loyalty [106–109].

ML is also applied in fraud detection, where models analyze call data records, transaction data, and usage patterns to detect fraudulent activities such as subscriber identity module (SIM) card cloning, account takeovers, and identity theft. These models continuously learn from new data, improving their ability to detect and prevent fraud in real time [110–113].

### 2.8. Manufacturing and Industry 4.0

In manufacturing, ML is a key enabler of Industry 4.0, driving advancements in automation, predictive maintenance, and quality control. By analyzing data from sensors, machines, and production lines, ML models can predict equipment failures, optimize production schedules, and improve product quality. These applications lead to increased efficiency, reduced downtime, and lower production costs [114–116].

Predictive maintenance is one of the most widely adopted applications of ML in manufacturing. By analyzing data from sensors installed in machinery, ML models can predict when equipment is likely to fail and schedule maintenance before a breakdown occurs. This approach reduces unplanned downtime, extends equipment life, and lowers maintenance costs [117–119].

In quality control, ML models analyze data from production lines, including images, measurements, and sensor readings, to detect defects and ensure that products meet quality standards. These models can identify patterns and anomalies that human inspectors may miss, leading to higher-quality products and reduced waste [120–122].

Furthermore, ML is used in supply chain optimization, where models analyze data from suppliers, logistics providers, and customers to optimize inventory levels, reduce lead times, and improve supply chain resilience. This leads to more efficient operations, lower costs, and better customer service [123–125].

### 2.9. Education and E-Learning

In the education sector, ML is driving the development of personalized learning experiences, intelligent tutoring systems, and predictive analytics for student success. By analyzing data from students' interactions with learning platforms, assessments, and demographic information, ML models can create personalized learning paths that adapt to each student's strengths, weaknesses, and learning pace [126–128].

Intelligent tutoring systems use ML to provide real-time feedback and guidance to students, simulating one-on-one tutoring. These systems analyze student performance, identify areas where students struggle, and provide targeted interventions to help them improve. This leads to more effective learning and better educational outcomes [129–131].

Predictive analytics is also used in education to identify students at risk of dropping out or failing courses. By analyzing data such as attendance records, grades, and engagement with learning platforms, ML models can predict which students are likely to need additional support and recommend interventions to improve their chances of success [132–134].

ML is also applied in automated grading and assessment, where models analyze student responses to assignments and exams to provide grades and feedback. This approach reduces the workload for teachers, provides faster feedback to students, and enables more frequent assessments [135–137].

### 2.10. Media and Entertainment

In the media and entertainment industry, ML is transforming content recommendation, production, and distribution. Streaming platforms like Netflix and Spotify use ML algorithms to analyze user preferences, viewing habits, and social media activity to recommend personalized content. These recommendation systems drive user engagement, increase viewing time, and enhance customer satisfaction [138–141].

ML is also used in content creation and production, where models analyze trends, audience preferences, and historical data to predict the success of movies, TV shows, and music. These models help content creators and producers make data-driven decisions about what content to create, how to market it, and when to release it [142–144].

In addition to recommendation and content creation, ML is applied in media distribution to optimize the delivery of content across different platforms and devices. By analyzing data on network conditions, user preferences, and device capabilities, ML models can optimize video streaming quality, reduce buffering, and ensure a seamless viewing experience [145–147].

Moreover, ML is increasingly used in social media analytics, where models analyze vast amounts of user-generated content, including posts, comments, and likes, to understand trends, sentiment, and audience engagement. These insights help media companies tailor their content, marketing strategies, and user interactions to maximize engagement and revenue [148–150].

### 2.11. Legal and Compliance

In the legal industry, ML is driving advancements in legal research, contract analysis, and compliance monitoring. Legal research platforms use ML algorithms to analyze vast amounts of legal texts, case law, and statutes to provide relevant search results and legal insights. These tools enable lawyers and legal professionals to conduct research more efficiently and make more informed decisions [151–153].

Contract analysis is another critical application where ML models analyze contracts, agreements, and legal documents to identify key terms, obligations, and risks. These models can automate the review of large volumes of contracts, reducing the time and cost associated with contract analysis and ensuring compliance with legal requirements [154–156].

ML is also applied in compliance monitoring, where models analyze data from financial transactions, communications, and other sources to detect potential compliance violations, such as insider trading, money laundering, and regulatory breaches. These models help organizations comply with regulatory requirements, avoid legal penalties, and protect their reputations [157–159].

Alongside legal research and compliance, ML is used in e-discovery, where models analyze large volumes of electronic data, including emails, documents, and social media, to identify relevant information for legal cases. This approach reduces the time and cost associated with document review and improves the accuracy of e-discovery processes [160–162].

### 2.12. Human Resources and Talent Management

In human resources (HR) and talent management, ML is transforming recruitment, employee engagement, and workforce planning. Recruitment platforms use ML algorithms to analyze resumes, job descriptions, and candidate profiles to match the best candidates with job openings. These models can predict candidate success, optimize the hiring process, and reduce the time to hire [163–165].

ML is also applied in employee engagement, where models analyze data from employee surveys, performance reviews, and social media to understand employee sentiment, identify factors that drive engagement, and predict turnover. These insights help HR professionals develop strategies to improve employee satisfaction, reduce turnover, and enhance organizational performance [166–168].

Workforce planning is another critical application where ML models analyze data on workforce demographics, skills, and performance to predict future workforce needs and optimize talent management strategies. These models enable organizations to plan for succession, identify skills gaps, and develop targeted training programs to ensure that they have the talent needed to meet their business objectives [169–171].

Also, ML is increasingly used in performance management, where models analyze data on employee performance, productivity, and feedback to provide personalized recommendations for development and career growth. These models help organizations identify high-potential employees, provide targeted development opportunities, and improve overall workforce performance [172–174].

### 2.13. Aerospace and Defense

In the aerospace and defense sectors, ML is driving advancements in predictive maintenance, mission planning, and autonomous systems. Predictive maintenance is one of the most widely adopted applications, where ML models analyze data from aircraft sensors and maintenance records, as well as operational data, to predict equipment failures and optimize maintenance schedules. This approach reduces downtime, extends equipment life, and improves safety [175–177].

Mission planning is another critical application where ML models analyze data from satellite imagery, weather models, and operational data to optimize flight paths, mission objectives, and resource allocation. These models enable more efficient and effective mission planning, improving the success rate of military and aerospace operations [178–180].

ML is also applied in the development of autonomous systems, including unmanned aerial vehicles (UAVs), autonomous ships, and robotic systems. These models enable autonomous systems to perceive their environment, make real-time decisions, and execute complex tasks with minimal human intervention. The integration of ML with big data from sensors, cameras, and other sources enhances the capabilities of autonomous systems, enabling them to operate in dynamic and uncertain environments [181–184].

Moreover, ML is used in cybersecurity within the aerospace and defense sectors, where models analyze network traffic, user behavior, and threat intelligence data to detect and prevent cyberattacks. These models help organizations protect critical infrastructure, secure sensitive data, and ensure the integrity of their operations [185–187].

### 2.14. Government and Public Policy

In government and public policy, ML is being used to improve decision making, optimize resource allocation, and enhance public services. One of the primary applications is in predictive analytics, where ML models analyze data from various sources, including census data, economic indicators, and social media, to predict social, economic, and political trends. These insights help policymakers develop data-driven policies, allocate resources more effectively, and respond to emerging challenges [188–190].

ML is also applied in public safety and law enforcement, where models analyze crime data, social media activity, and other sources to predict crime hotspots, identify suspects, and optimize patrol routes. These models enable law enforcement agencies to prevent crime, allocate resources more effectively, and improve public safety [191–193].

In addition to predictive analytics and public safety, ML is used in public health to monitor and respond to outbreaks of diseases, such as COVID-19. By analyzing data from health records, social media, and other sources, ML models can predict the spread of diseases, identify at-risk populations, and recommend targeted interventions to control outbreaks [194,195].

ML is also applied in disaster response and emergency management, where models analyze data from satellite imagery, weather models, and social media to predict natural disasters, assess damage, and optimize response efforts. These models enable governments and humanitarian organizations to respond more quickly and effectively to disasters, saving lives and reducing the impact of disasters on communities [196,197].

Overall, the application of ML in government and public policy enhances the ability of governments to serve their citizens, improve public services, and respond to the challenges of the 21st century [198,199].

These diverse applications across industries underscore the extensive impact of ML in big data environments. To provide a clearer overview of the key studies referenced throughout this section, Table 2 categorizes the literature according to specific application domains, offering a structured guide to the wealth of research discussed.

**Table 2.** Structured summary of key studies across ML application domains.

| Topic | References | Description |
|---|---|---|
| Healthcare | [20–34] | ML applications in predictive analytics, medical imaging, drug discovery, and healthcare data management. |
| Finance | [35–49] | ML for risk management, fraud detection, algorithmic trading, and CRM. |
| Transportation & Smart Cities | [50–61] | ML applications in autonomous vehicles, traffic management, and smart city infrastructure. |
| Retail & E-commerce | [62–73] | ML for personalized recommendations, predictive analytics, dynamic pricing, and supply chain management. |
| Energy & Utilities | [74–85] | ML applications in predictive maintenance, energy optimization, smart grids, and integration of renewable energy sources. |

**Table 2.** *Cont.*

| Topic | References | Description |
|---|---|---|
| Agriculture & Environmental Monitoring | [86–101] | ML for precision farming, environmental monitoring, disaster prediction, and resource management. |
| Telecommunications | [102–113] | ML for network optimization, customer retention, fraud detection, and service quality improvement. |
| Manufacturing & Industry 4.0 | [114–125] | ML applications in predictive maintenance, quality control, supply chain optimization, and automation in manufacturing. |
| Education & E-learning | [126–137] | ML applications in personalized learning, intelligent tutoring systems, predictive analytics for student success, and automated grading. |
| Media & Entertainment | [138–150] | ML for content recommendation, media production, distribution, and social media analytics. |
| Legal & Compliance | [151–162] | ML applications in legal research, contract analysis, compliance monitoring, and e-discovery. |
| HR & Talent Management | [163–174] | ML applications in recruitment, employee engagement, workforce planning, and performance management. |
| Aerospace & Defense | [175–187] | ML for predictive maintenance, mission planning, autonomous systems, and cybersecurity in aerospace and defense. |
| Government & Public Policy | [188–199] | ML applications in predictive analytics, public safety, law enforcement, and public health monitoring. |

## 3. Challenges in Big Data for Machine Learning

The integration of ML with big data offers transformative potential across various domains, yet it also presents a unique set of challenges that must be addressed to fully realize its benefits. As the volume, variety, and velocity of data continue to grow exponentially, traditional ML techniques are often inadequate, necessitating the development of new approaches to tackle these complexities. This section explores the critical challenges that arise when applying ML to big data, focusing on scalability, data quality, model interpretability, privacy, and the management of diverse and high-velocity datasets.

### 3.1. *Scalability of Algorithms*

One of the most significant challenges in applying ML to big data is the scalability of algorithms. Traditional ML algorithms, many of which were developed when data volumes were orders of magnitude smaller, struggle to scale effectively in the face of today's massive datasets. As the size of data increases, both in terms of the number of samples and the dimensionality of features, the computational cost and memory requirements of these algorithms grow exponentially. This challenge is particularly pronounced in real-time applications, such as high-frequency trading or autonomous vehicles, where quick decision making is critical [200,201].

Many conventional ML algorithms, such as support vector machines (SVMs) and k-nearest neighbors (k-NN), are inherently limited by their reliance on operations like pairwise comparisons or matrix computations, which become computationally prohibitive as dataset sizes increase. Additionally, these algorithms are typically designed for static and structured datasets, making them ill-suited for the dynamic, heterogeneous, and unstructured nature of big data. For instance, big data environments often include continuous streams of diverse data types, such as text, images, and sensor readings, which require flexible and adaptive approaches [202–205].

To address these limitations, significant advancements have been made in distributed computing frameworks, such as Apache Hadoop and Apache Spark, which allow data to be processed in parallel across clusters of machines. Techniques like stochastic gradient descent (SGD) and mini-batch processing have also emerged, enabling scalable training of large models while reducing computational overhead. Furthermore, edge computing and federated learning are gaining traction as paradigms for the decentralization of computation, bringing data processing closer to its source and alleviating the bottlenecks of centralized processing [206–208].

Despite these advancements, achieving true scalability remains an ongoing challenge. Efficiently partitioning data across nodes, minimizing communication overhead, and ensuring fault tolerance are critical areas of research. As datasets continue to grow, developing algorithms capable of handling the scale, velocity, and variety of big data will remain a focal point of innovation in ML [209,210].

### 3.2. Data Quality and Preprocessing

Data quality is a critical concern in big data environments, and it directly impacts the performance and reliability of ML models. Big data are often characterized by their "messiness"—datasets can be incomplete, noisy, inconsistent, and riddled with errors. The presence of outliers, missing values, and duplicated data can lead to biased or inaccurate models if not properly addressed. Moreover, in many cases, big data sources are heterogeneous, combining structured data (such as relational databases) with unstructured data (such as text, images, and videos), each requiring different preprocessing techniques [211–214].

The process of cleaning and preparing big data for ML involves several complex steps, including data integration, transformation, normalization, and feature extraction. Given the scale of big data, these preprocessing steps can be computationally intensive and time-consuming. Automated data cleaning techniques often struggle with the diversity and complexity of real-world datasets, necessitating human intervention to ensure data integrity. Furthermore, data are often generated in real time, requiring continuous preprocessing to maintain data quality. This dynamic nature of big data presents an additional challenge, as models need to be continually retrained to adapt to new data, which may change in structure and distribution over time [215–218].

### 3.3. Model Interpretability

Model interpretability is a cornerstone of ML in high-stakes applications like healthcare, finance, and criminal justice, where decisions carry significant consequences. While complex models such as deep neural networks (DNNs) and ensemble methods offer high predictive accuracy, their "black-box" nature often obscures the reasoning behind their decisions. This lack of transparency can erode trust, impede accountability, and lead to ethical concerns when decisions adversely affect individuals or society [219,220].

Interpretability techniques such as SHAP (SHapley Additive Explanations), LIME (Local Interpretable Model-Agnostic Explanations), and Integrated Gradients (IGs) have emerged to address these challenges. These methods reveal how input features contribute to a model's output, allowing stakeholders to validate and understand predictions. For instance, in healthcare, interpretable models can explain why certain symptoms or tests lead to a diagnosis, enabling doctors to corroborate or challenge the recommendations. In finance, interpretability ensures that loan approvals or fraud detection decisions can be justified to regulators and affected parties [221,222].

High-stakes applications also demand actionable insights to guide decision making. Counterfactual explanations, which suggest minimal changes to inputs required to alter a prediction, provide clear and user-friendly feedback. For example, a counterfactual explanation might indicate that increasing an applicant's credit score by a specific amount would lead to loan approval, empowering users to take corrective actions. Similarly, Anchors offer localized, rule-based explanations that enhance the clarity and reliability of predictions in domains such as fraud detection [223–225].

Moreover, inherently interpretable models, such as generalized additive models (GAMs) with pairwise interactions, offer transparency by design, enabling stakeholders to understand how features influence outcomes without relying on post hoc explanations. Attention mechanisms in DL, particularly in transformers, further enhance interpretability by highlighting specific input elements, such as words or image regions, that drive predictions [226,227].

The importance of interpretability in high-stakes applications extends beyond technical validation; it fosters trust, supports compliance with regulatory requirements, and ensures ethical accountability. As ML systems become more pervasive in critical domains, interpretability remains a crucial factor in balancing model complexity with societal and operational demands [228,229].

### 3.4. Privacy and Security

The use of ML in big data environments raises significant privacy and security concerns, especially when dealing with sensitive information such as personal health records, financial data, or behavioral data. The integration of ML with big data often requires the collection, storage, and processing of vast amounts of personal information, which can be vulnerable to breaches and misuse. The challenge of ensuring data privacy is exacerbated by the fact that data are often distributed across multiple platforms and jurisdictions, each with its own set of privacy regulations [230–232].

Ensuring compliance with data protection regulations, such as the General Data Protection Regulation (GDPR) in Europe or the California Consumer Privacy Act (CCPA) in the United States, is a complex task. These regulations impose strict requirements on how data can be collected, stored, and used, and they grant individuals certain rights over their personal data, including the right to be forgotten. ML models, particularly those trained on sensitive data, must be designed to comply with these regulations while still delivering accurate and effective results [233–235].

Techniques such as differential privacy, which introduces noise to data to obscure individual identities, and federated learning, which allows models to be trained on decentralized data without the need to share raw data across parties, have been developed to address these privacy concerns. However, these techniques also introduce new challenges, such as increased computational complexity and potential trade-offs between privacy and model performance. Additionally, as ML models become more powerful, there is a growing risk of adversarial attacks, where malicious actors manipulate input data to deceive models, further complicating the security landscape [236–238].

### 3.5. Handling Variety and Velocity of Data

Big data are characterized not only by their sheer volume but also by their variety and velocity. Variety refers to the wide range of data types that must be processed, including structured data (e.g., databases), semi-structured data (e.g., XML files), and unstructured data (e.g., text, images, and video). Each of these data types requires a different processing technique, and integrating them into a cohesive analysis pipeline is a significant challenge. For example, combining numerical data from sensors with textual data from social media and visual data from surveillance cameras into a single predictive model requires sophisticated data fusion techniques [239,240].

Recent advancements in DL have introduced specialized architectures for addressing these challenges. Transformers, originally designed for NLP, have demonstrated exceptional versatility in handling unstructured data such as text and images. Models like BERT (Bidirectional Encoder Representations from Transformers) and GPT (Generative Pre-trained Transformer) use self-attention mechanisms to capture contextual relationships in sequential data, enabling state-of-the-art performance in tasks like machine translation, text summarization, and image captioning. Beyond NLP, transformers have been adapted to handle tabular data and multi-modal datasets, further expanding their applicability to semi-structured data scenarios [241–243].

For semi-structured data represented in graph formats, Graph Neural Networks (GNNs) have emerged as a powerful paradigm. GNNs such as Graph Convolutional Networks (GCNs) and Graph Attention Networks (GATs) leverage the structural relationships inherent in graph data to propagate and aggregate information across nodes and edges. This makes them particularly effective in domains such as social network analysis, molecular property prediction, and knowledge graph reasoning. For instance, GNNs can model complex relationships between entities in a knowledge graph, enhancing applications like recommendation systems and fraud detection [244–246].

The velocity of big data—the speed at which new data are generated and need to be processed—adds another layer of complexity. In many applications, such as real-time analytics, autonomous vehicles, and financial trading, decisions must be made within milliseconds of receiving new data. Traditional batch processing methods are often insufficient for these scenarios, necessitating the development of real-time data processing frameworks that can handle high-throughput data streams with low latency. Tools such as Apache Kafka and Apache Flink have made significant strides in this area. Furthermore, combining these real-time data frameworks with advanced models like transformers and GNNs has shown promise in enabling end-to-end pipelines that process, analyze, and make predictions on diverse datasets at unprecedented speeds. As a result, the integration of transformers and GNNs into big data analytics represents a significant advancement in the field, addressing the challenges of both variety and velocity. These models not only enhance the ability to process unstructured and semi-structured data but also pave the way for the development of more adaptable and robust systems capable of operating in dynamic environments [247–249].

### 3.6. Ethical and Societal Implications

The adoption of ML in big data applications introduces complex ethical challenges, particularly concerning justice, responsibility, and bias. Justice-related concerns arise when models trained on biased datasets reinforce or amplify existing inequities, such as in hiring or credit scoring, where under-represented groups often face systemic disadvantages. Addressing these issues requires fairness-aware algorithms, bias mitigation techniques in preprocessing, and continuous monitoring to ensure equitable performance [250–252].

Responsibility and accountability become critical in high-stakes domains like healthcare and finance, where decisions have significant implications for individuals and society. The opacity of many ML models complicates efforts to assign accountability for harmful outcomes. Clear governance frameworks, explainable AI (XAI) tools, and mechanisms for auditing model decisions are essential to maintain trust and transparency [253].

Bias in ML often stems from data imbalances, such as under-representation of certain demographics, leading to poorer performance for marginalized groups. For instance, facial recognition systems have been shown to exhibit higher error rates for minorities.

Techniques like reweighting, fairness constraints, and algorithmic debiasing are necessary to reduce discriminatory outcomes and ensure inclusivity [254,255].

Beyond these concerns, ML has broader societal implications, such as the displacement of workers due to automation and the misuse of AI in surveillance or disinformation campaigns. Proactively addressing these issues through collaborative policy making, ethical design principles, and robust regulatory frameworks will ensure that ML systems advance innovation while upholding societal values [256,257].

### 3.7. Integration with Legacy Systems

The integration of ML with existing legacy systems presents another significant challenge in the application of big data technologies. Many organizations rely on legacy systems that were not designed to handle the scale, complexity, or velocity of modern big data and ML applications. These systems often lack the computational power, data storage capabilities, and flexibility required for advanced analytics, making it difficult to incorporate ML models effectively [258–260].

Upgrading or replacing legacy systems is often costly and time-consuming, and it can introduce significant operational risks. Organizations must carefully plan the integration of new technologies with existing infrastructure to ensure compatibility and minimize disruption. This requires not only technical solutions but also strategic planning, including evaluating the cost–benefit of different integration approaches, ensuring data consistency across systems, and managing the transition process [261–263].

The combination of ML models with legacy systems can introduce additional challenges related to data interoperability and system compatibility. Different systems may use incompatible data formats, protocols, or standards, making it difficult to integrate data from multiple sources. Ensuring that ML models can seamlessly access and process data from legacy systems requires robust data integration frameworks, middleware solutions, and APIs that can bridge the gap between old and new technologies [264–266].

### 3.8. Environmental Impact

The environmental impact of big data and ML is an emerging challenge that is gaining increasing attention. The energy consumption associated with the training of large ML models, particularly DL models, is substantial. Data centers that power these computations require significant amounts of electricity, often leading to a large carbon footprint. As the demand for more powerful models and larger datasets grows, so does the environmental impact of ML [267–270].

Efforts to mitigate this impact include developing more energy-efficient algorithms, optimizing data center operations, and using renewable energy sources. Researchers are exploring techniques such as model pruning, quantization, and knowledge distillation to reduce the computational requirements of ML models without sacrificing performance. Additionally, there is a growing movement toward "green AI", which advocates for the development of sustainable ML practices that prioritize energy efficiency and environmental responsibility [271–273].

Organizations and researchers must also consider environmental impact when deciding on the scale and scope of their ML projects. This includes evaluating trade-offs between model complexity and energy consumption, exploring alternative data sources, and considering the broader environmental implications of deploying ML models at scale. By adopting more sustainable practices, the ML community can help reduce the environmental footprint of big data technologies and contribute to global efforts to combat climate change [274–276].

As we delve into the challenges posed by the use of ML with big data, it is essential to have a structured understanding of these complexities. Table 3 provides a clear categorization of the various obstacles identified in this section, offering a roadmap to the primary concerns that researchers and practitioners face.

**Table 3.** Categorization of challenges & key issues in big data for ML.

| Topic | References | Description |
|---|---|---|
| Scalability of Algorithms | [200–210] | Discusses challenges related to scaling ML algorithms to process massive datasets efficiently. This includes distributed computing and algorithm optimization techniques. |
| Data Quality and Preprocessing | [211–218] | Focuses on the importance of data quality in big data, including dealing with noise, missing values, and the complexity of preprocessing diverse datasets. |
| Model Interpretability | [219–229] | Addresses the difficulty in interpreting complex ML models, especially in high-stakes applications where transparency is crucial. |
| Privacy and Security | [230–238] | Explores privacy concerns, data security risks, and challenges related to ensuring compliance with data protection regulations while using big data. |
| Handling Variety and Velocity of Data | [239–249] | Discusses the challenges associated with the variety (structured, unstructured, and semi-structured) and velocity of big data, requiring real-time processing and integration. |
| Ethical and Societal Implications | [250–257] | Focuses on the ethical issues surrounding big data and ML, including bias, fairness, accountability, and the broader societal impact. |
| Integration with Legacy Systems | [258–266] | Discusses the challenges of integrating modern ML techniques and big data technologies with existing legacy systems. |
| Environmental Impact | [267–276] | Highlights the environmental concerns related to the high energy consumption of ML models and the need for sustainable AI practices. |

## 4. Recent Advances and Future Directions

The ML field, in conjunction with big data, has seen rapid advancements that have significantly enhanced its applications across various domains. As the challenges associated with big data continue to evolve, so do the innovations aimed at overcoming these hurdles, paving the way for future breakthroughs and more efficient, scalable solutions.

### *4.1. Distributed Machine Learning Frameworks*

Recent advancements in distributed ML frameworks have significantly enhanced the ability to process and analyze big data efficiently. Frameworks such as Apache Spark, TensorFlow, and PyTorch have been instrumental in scaling ML algorithms across large datasets by leveraging distributed computing resources. These frameworks allow for parallel processing, reducing the time required to train models on vast amounts of data. Innovations in data parallelism, model parallelism, and hybrid parallelism have further improved the scalability of ML models [277–281].

Recent advancements in DNNs have demonstrated that with the right architectures and optimizations, existing models can effectively handle large-scale data challenges. Techniques such as model parallelism and pipeline parallelism have been pivotal in distributing the computational workload across multiple nodes, reducing the training time required for large models. Furthermore, adaptive optimization algorithms like AdamW and RAdam improve convergence rates for high-dimensional data, enabling efficient training, even in resource-constrained environments [282–284].

Automated ML (AutoML) frameworks, including neural architecture search (NAS), have also been critical in identifying optimal network architectures tailored for specific datasets. These techniques automatically tune hyperparameters and design architectures that balance complexity and performance, making it possible to deploy DNNs in scenarios requiring low latency and high accuracy [285–287].

Moreover, advancements in hardware-aware model design, such as sparse networks and quantization-aware training, have further reduced the computational and memory requirements of DNNs, enabling their deployment in real-time and edge computing environments. These innovations ensure that large-scale DNNs can adapt to the growing demands of big data analytics, providing robust, scalable, and efficient solutions [288,289].

In addition to these frameworks, there has been a surge in the development of specialized hardware, such as graphics processing units (GPUs), tensor processing units (TPUs), and custom application-specific integrated circuits (ASICs), which are optimized for ML tasks. These hardware advancements, coupled with software innovations, have enabled the training of increasingly complex models, such as DNNs with billions of parameters. The integration of these technologies with cloud computing platforms like AWS, Google Cloud, and Azure has democratized access to high-performance computing, allowing researchers and businesses to scale their ML workflows without significant upfront infrastructure investments [290–293].

Looking forward, the continued evolution of distributed ML frameworks is expected to focus on improving the efficiency and usability of these systems. Areas such as automatic scaling, fault tolerance, and better support for heterogeneous computing environments (including edge devices) are likely to see significant advancements. Additionally, the development of more sophisticated orchestration tools that can seamlessly manage the life cycle of ML models—from data ingestion to deployment—will be crucial in enabling the widespread adoption of big data-driven ML applications [294–297].

### *4.2. Model Interpretability Techniques*

The challenge of interpreting complex ML models has driven the development of various techniques aimed at enhancing their transparency and trustworthiness. Widely recognized methods such as LIME and SHAP provide post hoc explanations by approximating the contribution of input features to model predictions. These techniques are essential in domains where understanding a model's decision-making process is critical for regulatory compliance, ethical considerations, and user trust [298–300].

Complementing these approaches, IGs address the attribution problem by integrating the gradients of a model's output with respect to its input features along a path from a baseline input to the actual input. This method ensures attribution scores are faithful to the model while maintaining completeness and sensitivity. IGs are particularly effective for DNNs, providing detailed insights into feature contributions in tasks such as image recognition and NLP. For example, in medical imaging, an IGs can highlight specific regions in an image that influence diagnostic predictions, enabling practitioners to better understand and validate the model's outputs [301–303].

In addition to feature attribution, anchors provide a rule-based approach to local interpretability by generating "if–then" rules that describe the key conditions under which model predictions remain consistent. Unlike general attribution methods, anchors offer highly precise and localized explanations that are both interpretable and generalizable across similar input data. These rules are particularly valuable in high-stakes applications such as fraud detection or medical diagnostics, where decision stability and clarity are paramount [304,305].

Beyond understanding feature contributions, counterfactual explanations focus on identifying the minimal changes to input data required to alter a model's output. This method provides actionable insights, making it intuitive and user-friendly for non-technical stakeholders. For example, in loan applications, a counterfactual explanation might suggest that increasing an applicant's income by a specific amount would lead to loan approval. By offering clear, actionable feedback, counterfactual explanations empower users to make informed decisions based on model outcomes and encourage model accountability [306,307].

Another promising area of research is the development of inherently interpretable models, which achieve transparency by design rather than relying on post hoc explanations. Models like GAMs with pairwise interactions offer a clear and intuitive understanding of how input features contribute to predictions. These models decompose complex relationships into additive components, allowing stakeholders to visualize and interpret the influence of individual features and promoting trust in model predictions [308,309].

Attention mechanisms in DL, particularly in architectures like transformers, have further advanced interpretability by revealing how models prioritize specific parts of the input data. Attention maps provide visual insights into what a model "focuses" on during decision making. For instance, in NLP, attention maps can highlight the words or phrases most influential to a prediction, such as identifying keywords in sentiment analysis. Similarly, in computer vision, attention mechanisms pinpoint regions of interest in an image, such as abnormalities in medical scans. In applications like healthcare, these insights are invaluable for validating AI-driven recommendations, while in autonomous systems, they clarify decision-making processes, improving reliability and safety [310–312].

Together, these advanced interpretability techniques—IGs, anchors, counterfactual explanations, inherently interpretable models, and attention mechanisms—extend the capabilities of traditional methods like LIME and SHAP. IGs excel in providing gradient-based attributions for complex neural networks, anchors generate precise rule-based insights for localized explanations, counterfactual explanations bridge transparency with actionable recommendations, inherently interpretable models offer built-in transparency by design, and attention mechanisms enhance model trust by revealing input priorities. Each method caters to specific interpretability needs, ensuring that models remain transparent and trustworthy across diverse domains [313–316].

Future research on model interpretability is likely to explore more sophisticated techniques that balance the trade-off between model complexity and transparency. Integrating interpretability directly into the model training process, rather than relying solely on post hoc explanations, holds great promise. As ML continues to be applied in critical areas such as healthcare, finance, and legal systems, the demand for interpretable and reliable models will drive further innovation and adoption in these fields [317–319].

### 4.3. *Privacy-Preserving Machine Learning*

With the growing concern over data privacy, especially in light of stringent regulations like the GDPR and CCPA, privacy-preserving ML has become a focal point of research and development. Techniques such as differential privacy, federated learning, and homomorphic encryption have been developed to protect individual privacy while still enabling the use of ML on sensitive data [320–323].

Federated learning, in particular, has gained significant traction, as it allows models to be trained on decentralized data sources such as smartphones or IoT devices, without the need to transfer raw data to a central server [324]. This approach not only enhances privacy but also reduces the risk of data breaches. For instance, companies like Google have employed federated learning in their mobile devices to improve predictive text algorithms without compromising user privacy. Homomorphic encryption, which allows computations to be performed on encrypted data, is another technique that is gaining attention. Although computationally intensive, advancements in this area are making it more feasible for practical applications [325–328].

Looking ahead, the future of privacy-preserving ML will likely focus on making these techniques more efficient and scalable. There is also growing interest in developing new cryptographic protocols that combine the strengths of different privacy-preserving techniques to provide robust and flexible solutions. Additionally, as more data move to the edge (e.g., in IoT and mobile devices), there will be a greater emphasis on ensuring that ML models can operate securely and privately in decentralized environments [329–332].

### 4.4. Real-Time Data Processing and Multi-Modal Learning

The increasing demand for real-time insights has driven significant advancements in real-time data processing and multi-modal learning. Real-time data processing frameworks, such as Apache Kafka and Apache Flink, have evolved to handle high-throughput data streams with low latency, enabling ML models to make predictions and decisions on the fly. These advancements are critical in applications such as autonomous driving, financial trading, and fraud detection, where delays in processing can lead to significant consequences [333–335].

Multi-modal learning, which involves the integration of various data types (e.g., text, images, audio, and video), has also seen considerable progress. Models that effectively combine information from different modalities can make more accurate and robust predictions. For example, in healthcare, multi-modal models can integrate medical images, genetic data, and clinical notes to provide more comprehensive diagnoses and treatment recommendations. In the entertainment industry, multi-modal learning is used to enhance user experiences by integrating data from video, audio, and user interactions to deliver personalized content [336–339].

The future of real-time data processing and multi-modal learning will likely involve further improvements in the efficiency and scalability of these systems. Additionally, as the amount of available data continues to grow, there will be a greater focus on developing models that can effectively learn from sparse or imbalanced multi-modal datasets. Advances in techniques such as transfer learning, domain adaptation, and meta-learning will play a crucial role in enabling these models to generalize across different domains and data types [340–342].

### 4.5. Ethical and Societal Implications

The ethical and societal implications of ML and big data are becoming increasingly prominent as these technologies become more pervasive. Concerns about bias, fairness, accountability, and the potential for misuse are driving the development of ethical frameworks and guidelines for the responsible use of ML [343,344].

Recent advancements in fairness-aware ML aim to address biases that may arise from training data or algorithmic design. Techniques such as adversarial debiasing, reweighting, and fairness constraints are being incorporated into ML pipelines to ensure that models make equitable decisions across different demographic groups. Additionally, there is growing interest in XAI, which seeks to make ML models more transparent and understandable, thereby enhancing accountability [345–347].

Another critical area of focus is the impact of ML on employment and society. As automation and AI technologies become more capable, there is a growing concern about job displacement and the widening of economic inequalities. Policy-makers, industry leaders, and researchers are increasingly collaborating to develop strategies to mitigate these impacts, such as workforce reskilling programs and policies that promote inclusive growth [348,349].

The future of ethical and societal considerations in ML will likely involve the development of more comprehensive frameworks that address not only technical issues but also the broader social, economic, and legal implications of these technologies. There is also a need for greater public engagement and dialogue about the role of ML in society, as well as for the establishment of regulatory bodies that can oversee the development and deployment of these technologies to ensure they are used responsibly [350–352].

### 4.6. Sustainable Machine Learning

As awareness of environmental issues grows, there is increasing emphasis on the sustainability of ML practices. The energy consumption associated with the training of large-scale models, particularly in DL, has prompted researchers to explore ways to reduce the environmental impact of ML. Recent advancements in energy-efficient algorithms, such as model pruning, quantization, and distillation, have shown promise in reducing the computational resources required without sacrificing model performance [353–355].

Another area of focus is the development of "green AI" practices that prioritize energy efficiency and sustainability in the design and deployment of ML models. This includes optimizing data center operations, leveraging renewable energy sources, and exploring alternative approaches to model training that are less resource-intensive. Researchers are also looking at ways to measure and report the carbon footprint of ML projects, enabling more informed decisions about the environmental trade-offs of different approaches [356–358].

The future of sustainable ML will likely involve a shift toward more environmentally conscious practices across the entire ML life cycle, from data collection and model training to deployment and maintenance. There will also be a growing emphasis on developing models that are not only accurate and efficient but also socially and environmentally responsible. As the field of ML continues to evolve, sustainability will become an increasingly important criterion for evaluating the success of new technologies [359–361].

### 4.7. Integration of Quantum Computing

Quantum computing represents one of the most exciting frontiers for the future of ML, particularly in the context of big data. Quantum computing offers the potential to solve certain types of problems much faster than classical computers, which could revolutionize fields such as cryptography, optimization, and complex simulations. In ML, quantum algorithms like quantum SVMs and quantum neural networks are being explored for their potential to handle high-dimensional data and perform computations that are infeasible for classical algorithms [362–365].

Recent advancements in quantum ML (QML) have demonstrated the feasibility of implementing basic quantum algorithms on existing quantum hardware. While current quantum computers are still in the early stages of development and are prone to errors, significant progress is being made in improving their stability and scalability. Hybrid quantum–classical algorithms, which combine quantum computing with classical ML methods, are also being developed to take advantage of quantum speedups where possible while relying on classical computation for tasks where quantum advantages are less clear [366–368].

Looking forward, integrating quantum computing with big data and ML is likely to become a major area of research. As quantum hardware continues to improve, the development of quantum ML frameworks and algorithms will accelerate, potentially leading to breakthroughs in areas that require the processing of large, complex datasets. The future will likely see a growing synergy between quantum computing and ML, opening up new possibilities in solving some of the most challenging problems in science, engineering, and beyond [369–372].

### 4.8. Collaborative and Transfer Learning

The concepts of collaborative and transfer learning are gaining importance in the context of big data, where the ability to leverage knowledge from different domains or collaborators can significantly enhance model performance and efficiency. Transfer learning allows models trained on one task to be adapted to another related task with limited data, reducing the need for extensive training datasets and computational resources. This is particularly useful in domains where labeled data are scarce or expensive to obtain [373–375].

Collaborative learning, which includes techniques like federated learning, enables multiple parties to collaboratively train models without sharing their data, preserving privacy and confidentiality. This approach is particularly relevant in industries such as healthcare and finance, where data privacy is paramount. Recent advancements in federated learning have improved the efficiency of these collaborative models, enabling them to scale to larger datasets and more complex tasks [376–379].

The future of collaborative and transfer learning will likely see further integration of these techniques with big data technologies, enabling more efficient and privacy-preserving ML across different domains. As the amount of generated data continues to grow, the ability to transfer knowledge across tasks and collaborate securely will become increasingly important for the scaling of ML applications and maximization of the value of big data [380–382].

The rapid evolution of ML technologies has led to significant advancements that address some of the core challenges discussed earlier. Table 4 highlights these cutting-edge developments, showcasing the innovative solutions paving the way for more effective and scalable ML applications. Finally, Table 5 outlines the most promising directions in the key areas discussed in this section, providing a forward-looking perspective on where the field is headed.

**Table 4.** Recent advances: charting the path for ML research and development.

| Focus Area | References | Description |
|---|---|---|
| Distributed ML Frameworks | [277–293] | Advances in distributed ML frameworks and specialized hardware, such as Apache Spark, TensorFlow, GPUs, TPUs, and custom ASICs, improving the scalability and performance of ML tasks. |
| Advancing Interpretability | [298–316] | Development of interpretability techniques such as SHAP, LIME, and inherently interpretable models (e.g., GAMs) to enhance the transparency and understanding of ML models. |
| Privacy-Preserving ML | [320–328] | Implementation of privacy-preserving techniques, including differential privacy, federated learning, and homomorphic encryption, to protect data privacy in ML applications. |
| Real-Time Data Processing | [333–339] | Enhancements in real-time data processing frameworks like Apache Kafka and Apache Flink and advancements in multi-modal learning integrating text, images, audio, and video for more accurate ML models. |

**Table 4.** *Cont.*

| Focus Area | References | Description |
| --- | --- | --- |
| Ethical and Societal Implications | [343–349] | Introduction of fairness-aware ML techniques and XAI to address ethical concerns, mitigate biases, and ensure the responsible use of ML in high-stakes domains. |
| Sustainable ML | [353–358] | Development of energy-efficient algorithms and sustainable ML practices to reduce the environmental impact of large-scale models, focusing on the creation of green AI. |
| Quantum Computing in ML | [362–368] | Early-stage research on quantum computing applications in ML, including quantum SVMs and quantum neural networks, showing potential for solving complex, high-dimensional data problems. |
| Collaborative and Transfer Learning | [373–379] | Advances in federated learning and collaborative ML models that enable distributed training across multiple entities without sharing raw data, enhancing privacy, efficiency, and cross-domain knowledge transfer in ML. |

**Table 5.** Future directions in ML research and development.

| Research & Development Areas | References | Description |
| --- | --- | --- |
| Scaling Distributed ML | [294–297] | Enhancing the scalability of distributed ML frameworks, with a focus on automatic scaling, fault tolerance, and edge computing support. |
| Advancing Interpretability | [317–319] | Developing more sophisticated techniques to ensure that ML models remain interpretable without compromising on complexity. |
| Enhancing Privacy Techniques | [329–332] | Research aimed at making privacy-preserving methods like differential privacy and federated learning more scalable and efficient for broader use. |
| Optimizing Real-Time Systems | [340–342] | Improving the efficiency and scalability of systems that process real-time data, which is crucial for time-sensitive applications in various fields. |
| Addressing Ethical Challenges | [350–352] | Formulating frameworks that address the ethical, social, and legal challenges posed by the increasing use of ML technologies. |
| Sustainable ML | [359–361] | Focusing on reducing the environmental impact of ML, with efforts to develop energy-efficient models and green AI practices. |
| Quantum Computing Integration | [369–372] | Pioneering the integration of quantum computing into ML, focusing on stability, scalability, and tackling complex data problems. |
| Innovations in Collaborative Learning | [380–382] | Advancing techniques in federated and transfer learning to improve efficiency, security, and privacy in collaborative ML applications. |

## 5. Discussion

The findings of this survey underline the transformative potential of ML in addressing the challenges posed by big data across various domains. However, while the paper identifies numerous applications, analysis reveals recurring patterns and broader themes that warrant deeper exploration. This section critically examines and summarizes these findings, identifies gaps in existing methodologies, proposes a unifying framework for ML applications in big data, and highlights considerations for further research and development.

### 5.1. Synthesis of Findings

The integration of ML with big data has enabled transformative advancements across numerous domains by leveraging the volume, variety, and velocity of modern datasets. ML's ability to process large-scale and complex data has revolutionized fields like healthcare, finance, and smart cities, enabling innovations such as predictive diagnostics, real-time fraud detection, and optimized urban traffic systems.

Scalable, interpretable, and privacy-preserving ML approaches play a crucial role in addressing the challenges posed by big data. Scalability allows ML models to handle the growing magnitude and complexity of data, facilitating real-time analytics in domains such as finance, where high-frequency trading requires near-instantaneous predictions, and healthcare, where predictive maintenance of medical equipment can save lives. Techniques like distributed computing and parallelism in frameworks such as Apache Spark and TensorFlow have been pivotal in achieving this scalability.

Interpretability enhances trust and accountability in ML models, particularly in high-stakes applications like medical diagnostics and loan approvals. Methods such as SHAP, IGs, and counterfactual explanations enable stakeholders to understand the rationale behind model predictions, ensuring ethical and informed decision making. This transparency is not only essential for regulatory compliance but also in fostering user trust, which is critical in sectors like healthcare and finance.

Privacy-preserving approaches, including federated learning and differential privacy, address the ethical and regulatory concerns associated with sensitive data. For instance, federated learning enables collaborative model training across decentralized data sources without exposing raw data, ensuring confidentiality in environments like healthcare, where patient data security is paramount. These advancements ensure that data-driven insights can be derived without compromising privacy, thereby balancing innovation with ethical responsibility.

Together, scalable, interpretable, and privacy-preserving ML approaches empower organizations to extract actionable insights from big data while adhering to ethical, legal, and technical standards. These advancements highlight the evolving synergy between technological capabilities and societal needs, underscoring ML's potential to drive impactful and responsible innovation across industries.

Finally, Table 6 presents case studies highlighting the successful application of ML techniques, which are being widely applied across a range of domains, demonstrating their capacity to address real-world challenges with innovative solutions and illustrating their practical utility and impact. These case studies emphasize the adaptability and transformative potential of ML in diverse fields. By connecting theoretical advancements with practical implementations, they provide valuable insights into the growing influence of ML across industries and domains.

**Table 6.** Case studies demonstrating successful applications of ML methods across various domains.

| Domain | Case Study | Methodology | Outcome |
|---|---|---|---|
| Healthcare | Detecting diabetic retinopathy | DL with CNNs | Improved diagnostic accuracy and clinician support |
| Finance | Fraud detection in high-frequency transactions | SHAP for feature attribution | Enhanced fraud detection and reduced false positives |

**Table 6.** *Cont.*

| Domain | Case Study | Methodology | Outcome |
|---|---|---|---|
| Transportation and Smart Cities | Traffic congestion prediction in urban areas | GNNs | Reduced travel times and optimized city planning |
| Retail & E-commerce | Personalized product recommendations | Collaborative filtering in recommender systems | Increased customer engagement and sales |
| Energy and Utilities | Smart grid energy optimization | GNN for load distribution | Reduced energy waste and optimized resource allocation |
| Agriculture and Environmental Monitoring | Crop yield prediction using satellite imagery | CNNs for remote sensing | Improved agricultural planning and yield optimization |
| Telecommunications | Network traffic forecasting | Recurrent neural networks | Improved quality of service and reduced network delays |
| Manufacturing and Industry 4.0 | Predictive maintenance in industrial equipment | Time-series analysis with LSTMs | Reduced downtime and maintenance costs |
| Education & E-learning | Personalized learning platforms | Adaptive learning algorithms | Improved learning outcomes and user engagement |
| Media and Entertainment | Content recommendation on streaming platforms | RL | Increased viewer retention and platform engagement |
| Legal and Compliance | Legal document classification and search | NLP with transformers | Faster case research and improved compliance tracking |
| HR and Talent Management | Resume screening and job matching | Decision trees and NLP | Accelerated recruitment process and better candidate matching |
| Aerospace and Defense | Aircraft fault detection using sensor data | Random forests and anomaly detection | Improved safety and reduced maintenance costs |
| Government and Public Policy | Predicting the spread of infectious diseases | Epidemiological modeling with ML | Informed policy decisions and effective resource allocation |

### *5.2. Critical Analysis*

The methodologies discussed in this paper, while effective in certain contexts, expose inherent trade-offs that must be critically evaluated. Supervised learning methods dominate structured data analysis but rely heavily on labeled datasets, which are often expensive or impractical to obtain at scale. In contrast, unsupervised learning and RL offer potential solutions for environments with limited or unstructured data but require more computational resources and sophisticated fine tuning.

Moreover, while distributed ML frameworks and cloud computing platforms address the challenge of scalability, they often overlook data privacy concerns. For instance, federated learning and differential privacy techniques have made strides in preserving individual anonymity, yet their computational overhead and reduced model accuracy remain barriers to widespread adoption. These trade-offs highlight the need for hybrid approaches that integrate the strengths of various methodologies while mitigating their limitations.

Additionally, this study reveals gaps in applying ML to domains with stringent real-time requirements. Applications such as autonomous driving and financial trading demand low-latency decision-making, where traditional batch-processing models often fail. The development of real-time learning algorithms that can adapt to dynamic data streams without significant retraining is, thus, an area of critical importance.

### 5.3. Toward a Generic Framework

To bridge these gaps and provide a structured approach to ML in big data, this paper proposes a generic framework categorizing applications based on three dimensions: data characteristics, learning methodologies, and domain-specific challenges. Data characteristics are divided into structured (e.g., transactional logs), semi-structured (e.g., XML data), and unstructured types (e.g., medical images and textual data). Each category requires distinct preprocessing techniques and model architectures, underscoring the importance of tailored solutions.

Learning methodologies are classified into supervised, unsupervised, and RL methods, each chosen based on the availability of labeled data, the need for predictive versus exploratory insights, and the adaptability of the application. Finally, domain-specific challenges such as scalability, interpretability, and ethical considerations are highlighted as critical components in designing effective ML pipelines.

For instance, in healthcare, unstructured data such as radiological images necessitate advanced DL models with explainable mechanisms to ensure trustworthiness. In contrast, financial applications often rely on semi-structured transactional data that benefit from scalable supervised learning frameworks. A detailed taxonomy aligning data types, methodologies, and domain challenges provides a roadmap for researchers and practitioners to navigate the complexities of ML applications in big data.

### 5.4. Future Considerations

While recent advancements in ML have addressed many of the challenges posed by big data, significant gaps remain, particularly in the areas of sustainability, fairness, and interdisciplinarity. The environmental impact of training large-scale models continues to grow, prompting a need for energy-efficient algorithms and "green AI" practices. Efforts such as model pruning, quantization, and the use of renewable energy sources in data centers are promising directions but require further refinement to balance performance with resource conservation.

Ethical considerations, including bias, fairness, and accountability, also demand sustained attention. Bias introduced during data collection and model development risks the perpetuation of systemic inequities, particularly in high-stakes domains like criminal justice and credit scoring. Techniques such as adversarial debiasing and fairness-aware ML must be integrated more comprehensively into the development life cycle of ML systems.

Finally, the integration of emerging paradigms, such as quantum ML and multi-modal learning, offers exciting opportunities to tackle the complexities of big data. Quantum computing holds the potential to address high-dimensional problems in cryptography and optimization, while multi-modal learning enables richer insights by combining disparate data sources such as text, audio, and video. However, these fields are still nascent and require collaborative efforts across disciplines to mature into practical solutions.

In conclusion, this discussion highlights the multifaceted challenges and opportunities at the intersection of ML and big data. By synthesizing findings, critically analyzing methodologies, and proposing a generic framework, this study provides a foundation to advance the responsible and effective use of ML in big data environments. Future work should prioritize sustainability, fairness, and interdisciplinary innovation to ensure that these technologies continue to benefit society.

## 6. Conclusions

The synergy between ML and big data has unlocked new possibilities across a wide range of domains, driving innovation and transforming industries. However, the full potential of this integration is tempered by several significant challenges that must be addressed to ensure the effective and responsible use of these technologies. This survey has provided a detailed exploration of the current landscape of ML applications in big data, highlighting the critical issues of scalability, data quality, model interpretability, privacy, and the handling of diverse and high-velocity data. While recent advancements have made substantial progress in addressing some of these challenges, there remains considerable work to be done.

Future research should focus on developing more scalable algorithms and frameworks that can efficiently process and analyze the ever-growing volumes of data. Additionally, improving model interpretability will be crucial for building trust in ML applications, particularly in high-stakes domains such as healthcare and finance. Privacy-preserving techniques must also be further refined to balance the need for data-driven insights with the protection of individual privacy rights.

Moreover, as the ethical and societal implications of ML and big data become increasingly apparent, it is essential to develop frameworks and guidelines that ensure these technologies are used in ways that are fair, transparent, and aligned with societal values. Addressing the environmental impact of large-scale ML models and promoting sustainable practices will also be key to the long-term viability of these technologies.

In conclusion, the integration of ML and big data presents both profound opportunities and complex challenges. By continuing to innovate and address the obstacles identified in this survey, researchers and practitioners can unlock the full potential of these technologies, driving progress across industries and contributing to the betterment of society as a whole. This survey serves as a comprehensive resource for understanding the current state of the field and as a guide for future research and development efforts at the intersection of ML and big data.

**Author Contributions:** E.D. and M.T. conceived of the idea, designed and performed the experiments, analyzed the results, drafted the initial manuscript, and revised the final manuscript. All authors have read and agreed to the published version of the manuscript.

**Funding:** This research received no external funding.

**Conflicts of Interest:** The authors declare no conflicts of interest.

## References

1. Naeem, M.; Jamal, T.; Diaz-Martinez, J.; Butt, S.A.; Montesano, N.; Tariq, M.I.; De-la Hoz-Franco, E.; De-La-Hoz-Valdiris, E. Trends and future perspective challenges in big data. In Proceedings of the Advances in Intelligent Data Analysis and Applications: Proceeding of the Sixth Euro-China Conference on Intelligent Data Analysis and Applications, Arad, Romania, 15–18 October 2019; Springer: Berlin/Heidelberg, Germany, 2022; pp. 309–325.
2. Krishnamurthi, R.; Kumar, A.; Gopinathan, D.; Nayyar, A.; Qureshi, B. An overview of IoT sensor data processing, fusion, and analysis techniques. *Sensors* **2020**, *20*, 6076. [CrossRef] [PubMed]
3. Habehh, H.; Gohel, S. Machine learning in healthcare. *Curr. Genom.* **2021**, *22*, 291. [CrossRef]
4. Ahmed, S.; Alshater, M.M.; El Ammari, A.; Hammami, H. Artificial intelligence and machine learning in finance: A bibliometric review. *Res. Int. Bus. Financ.* **2022**, *61*, 101646. [CrossRef]
5. Zamponi, M.E.; Barbierato, E. The dual role of artificial intelligence in developing smart cities. *Smart Cities* **2022**, *5*, 728–755. [CrossRef]
6. Kolisetty, V.V.; Rajput, D.S. A review on the significance of machine learning for data analysis in big data. *Jordanian J. Comput. Inf. Technol. (JJCIT)* **2020**, *6*, 155–171. [CrossRef]
7. Rahman, M.A.; Asyhari, A.T.; Leong, L.; Satrya, G.; Tao, M.H.; Zolkipli, M. Scalable machine learning-based intrusion detection system for IoT-enabled smart cities. *Sustain. Cities Soc.* **2020**, *61*, 102324. [CrossRef]

8. Cappuzzo, R.; Papotti, P.; Thirumuruganathan, S. Creating embeddings of heterogeneous relational datasets for data integration tasks. In Proceedings of the 2020 ACM SIGMOD International Conference on Management of Data, Portland, OR, USA, 14–19 June 2020; pp. 1335–1349.
9. Kaur, H.; Nori, H.; Jenkins, S.; Caruana, R.; Wallach, H.; Wortman Vaughan, J. Interpreting interpretability: Understanding data scientists' use of interpretability tools for machine learning. In Proceedings of the 2020 CHI Conference on Human Factors in Computing Systems, Honolulu, HI, USA, 25–30 April 2020; pp. 1–14.
10. Xu, R.; Baracaldo, N.; Joshi, J. Privacy-preserving machine learning: Methods, challenges and directions. *arXiv* **2021**, arXiv:2108.04417.
11. Rasheed, K.; Qayyum, A.; Ghaly, M.; Al-Fuqaha, A.; Razi, A.; Qadir, J. Explainable, trustworthy, and ethical machine learning for healthcare: A survey. *Comput. Biol. Med.* **2022**, *149*, 106043. [CrossRef] [PubMed]
12. Mhlanga, D. Financial inclusion in emerging economies: The application of machine learning and artificial intelligence in credit risk assessment. *Int. J. Financ. Stud.* **2021**, *9*, 39. [CrossRef]
13. Tyagi, A.K.; G, R. Machine learning with big data. In Proceedings of the International Conference on Sustainable Computing in Science, Technology and Management (SUSCOM), Amity University Rajasthan, Jaipur, India, 26–28 February 2019.
14. Vinothini, A.; Priya, S.B. Survey of machine learning methods for big data applications. In Proceedings of the 2017 International Conference on Computational Intelligence in Data Science (ICCIDS), Chennai, India, 2–3 June 2017; IEEE: Piscataway, NJ, USA, 2017; pp. 1–5.
15. Ruiz, Z.; Salvador, J.; Garcia-Rodriguez, J. A survey of machine learning methods for big data. In Proceedings of the Biomedical Applications Based on Natural and Artificial Computing: International Work-Conference on the Interplay Between Natural and Artificial Computation, IWINAC 2017, Corunna, Spain, 19–23 June 2017; Proceedings, Part II; Springer: Berlin/Heidelberg, Germany, 2017; pp. 259–267.
16. Salkuti, S.R. A survey of big data and machine learning. *Int. J. Electr. Comput. Eng.* **2020**, *10*, 575-580. [CrossRef]
17. L'heureux, A.; Grolinger, K.; Elyamany, H.F.; Capretz, M.A. Machine learning with big data: Challenges and approaches. *IEEE Access* **2017**, *5*, 7776–7797. [CrossRef]
18. Stewart, R.; Stone, L. A Survey of Machine Learning for Big Data Processing. *IEEE Trans. Knowl. Data Eng.* **2016**, *28*, 45–56.
19. Zhou, L.; Pan, S.; Wang, J.; Vasilakos, A.V. Machine learning on big data: Opportunities and challenges. *Neurocomputing* **2017**, *237*, 350–361. [CrossRef]
20. Li, W.; Chai, Y.; Khan, F.; Jan, S.R.U.; Verma, S.; Menon, V.G.; Kavita, F.; Li, X. A comprehensive survey on machine learning-based big data analytics for IoT-enabled smart healthcare system. *Mob. Netw. Appl.* **2021**, *26*, 234–252. [CrossRef]
21. Piccialli, F.; Di Somma, V.; Giampaolo, F.; Cuomo, S.; Fortino, G. A survey on deep learning in medicine: Why, how and when? *Inf. Fusion* **2021**, *66*, 111–137. [CrossRef]
22. Coronato, A.; Naeem, M.; De Pietro, G.; Paragliola, G. Reinforcement learning for intelligent healthcare applications: A survey. *Artif. Intell. Med.* **2020**, *109*, 101964. [CrossRef]
23. Javaid, M.; Haleem, A.; Singh, R.P.; Suman, R.; Rab, S. Significance of machine learning in healthcare: Features, pillars and applications. *Int. J. Intell. Netw.* **2022**, *3*, 58–73. [CrossRef]
24. Barragán-Montero, A.; Javaid, U.; Valdés, G.; Nguyen, D.; Desbordes, P.; Macq, B.; Willems, S.; Vandewinckele, L.; Holmström, M.; Löfman, F.; et al. Artificial intelligence and machine learning for medical imaging: A technology review. *Phys. Medica* **2021**, *83*, 242–256. [CrossRef]
25. Mawatari, T.; Hayashida, Y.; Katsuragawa, S.; Yoshimatsu, Y.; Hamamura, T.; Anai, K.; Ueno, M.; Yamaga, S.; Ueda, I.; Terasawa, T.; et al. The effect of deep convolutional neural networks on radiologists' performance in the detection of hip fractures on digital pelvic radiographs. *Eur. J. Radiol.* **2020**, *130*, 109188. [CrossRef] [PubMed]
26. Dara, S.; Dhamercherla, S.; Jadav, S.S.; Babu, C.M.; Ahsan, M.J. Machine learning in drug discovery: A review. *Artif. Intell. Rev.* **2022**, *55*, 1947–1999. [CrossRef] [PubMed]
27. Aggarwal, R.; Sounderajah, V.; Martin, G.; Ting, D.S.; Karthikesalingam, A.; King, D.; Ashrafian, H.; Darzi, A. Diagnostic accuracy of deep learning in medical imaging: A systematic review and meta-analysis. *NPJ Digit. Med.* **2021**, *4*, 65. [CrossRef] [PubMed]
28. Khanbhai, M.; Anyadi, P.; Symons, J.; Flott, K.; Darzi, A.; Mayer, E. Applying natural language processing and machine learning techniques to patient experience feedback: A systematic review. *BMJ Health Care Inform.* **2021**, *28*, e100262. [CrossRef] [PubMed]
29. Solares, J.R.A.; Raimondi, F.E.D.; Zhu, Y.; Rahimian, F.; Canoy, D.; Tran, J.; Gomes, A.C.P.; Payberah, A.H.; Zottoli, M.; Nazarzadeh, M.; et al. Deep learning for electronic health records: A comparative review of multiple deep neural architectures. *J. Biomed. Inform.* **2020**, *101*, 103337. [CrossRef] [PubMed]
30. Siddiq, M. Integration of Machine Learning in Clinical Decision Support Systems. *Eduvest-J. Univers. Stud.* **2021**, *1*, 1579–1591. [CrossRef]
31. Shilo, S.; Rossman, H.; Segal, E. Axes of a revolution: Challenges and promises of big data in healthcare. *Nat. Med.* **2020**, *26*, 29–38. [CrossRef] [PubMed]

32. Rahman, A.; Karmakar, M.; Debnath, P. Predictive Analytics for Healthcare: Improving Patient Outcomes in the US through Machine Learning. *Rev. Intel. Artif. Med.* **2023**, *14*, 595–624.
33. Ibrahim, M.S.; Saber, S. Machine learning and predictive analytics: Advancing disease prevention in healthcare. *J. Contemp. Healthc. Anal.* **2023**, *7*, 53–71.
34. Rehan, H. Artificial Intelligence and Machine Learning: The Impact of Machine Learning on Predictive Analytics in Healthcare. *Innov. Comput. Sci. J.* **2023**, *9*, 1–20.
35. Perols, J. Financial statement fraud detection: An analysis of statistical and machine learning algorithms. *Audit. A J. Pract. Theory* **2011**, *30*, 19–50. [CrossRef]
36. Aziz, S.; Dowling, M. Machine learning and AI for risk management. In *Disrupting Finance: FinTech and Strategy in the 21st Century*; Springer Nature, Palgrave Pivot: Cham, Switzerland, 2019; pp. 33–50.
37. Emran, A.; Rubel, M.T.H. Big Data Analytics and Ai-Driven Solutions for Financial Fraud Detection: Techniques, Applications, and Challenges. *Front. Appl. Eng. Technol.* **2024**, *1*, 269–285. [CrossRef]
38. Zhan, X.; Ling, Z.; Xu, Z.; Guo, L.; Zhuang, S. Driving efficiency and risk management in finance through AI and RPA. *Unique Endeavor Bus. Soc. Sci.* **2024**, *3*, 189–197.
39. Ali, A.; Abd Razak, S.; Othman, S.H.; Eisa, T.A.E.; Al-Dhaqm, A.; Nasser, M.; Elhassan, T.; Elshafie, H.; Saif, A. Financial fraud detection based on machine learning: A systematic literature review. *Appl. Sci.* **2022**, *12*, 9637. [CrossRef]
40. Bello, O.A.; Ogundipe, A.; Mohammed, D.; Adebola, F.; Alonge, O.A. AI-Driven approaches for real-time fraud detection in US financial transactions: Challenges and opportunities. *Eur. J. Comput. Sci. Inf. Technol.* **2023**, *11*, 84–102.
41. Li, X.; Sun, Y. Stock intelligent investment strategy based on support vector machine parameter optimization algorithm. *Neural Comput. Appl.* **2020**, *32*, 1765–1775. [CrossRef]
42. Moscato, V.; Picariello, A.; Sperlí, G. A benchmark of machine learning approaches for credit score prediction. *Expert Syst. Appl.* **2021**, *165*, 113986. [CrossRef]
43. Kumbure, M.M.; Lohrmann, C.; Luukka, P.; Porras, J. Machine learning techniques and data for stock market forecasting: A literature review. *Expert Syst. Appl.* **2022**, *197*, 116659. [CrossRef]
44. Kissell, R. *Algorithmic Trading Methods: Applications Using Advanced Statistics, Optimization, and Machine Learning Techniques*; Academic Press: Cambridge, MA, USA, 2020.
45. Mangat, M.K.; Reschenhofer, E.; Stark, T.; Zwatz, C. High-Frequency Trading with Machine Learning Algorithms and Limit Order Book Data. *Data Sci. Financ. Econ.* **2022**, *2*, 437–463. [CrossRef]
46. Venkataramanan, S.; Sadhu, A.K.R.; Gudala, L.; Reddy, A.K. Leveraging Artificial Intelligence for Enhanced Sales Forecasting Accuracy: A Review of AI-Driven Techniques and Practical Applications in Customer Relationship Management Systems. *Aust. J. Mach. Learn. Res. Appl.* **2024**, *4*, 267–287.
47. Lee, I.; Shin, Y.J. Machine learning for enterprises: Applications, algorithm selection, and challenges. *Bus. Horizons* **2020**, *63*, 157–170. [CrossRef]
48. Jajam, N.; Challa, N.P.; Prasanna, K.S.; Deepthi, C.V.S. Arithmetic optimization with ensemble deep learning SBLSTM-RNN-IGSA model for customer churn prediction. *IEEE Access* **2023**, *11*, 93111–93128. [CrossRef]
49. Chintala, S. Explore the impact of emerging technologies such as AI, machine learning, and blockchain on transforming retail marketing strategies. *Webology* **2021**, *18*, 2361–2375.
50. Yang, Q.; Fu, S.; Wang, H.; Fang, H. Machine-learning-enabled cooperative perception for connected autonomous vehicles: Challenges and opportunities. *IEEE Netw.* **2021**, *35*, 96–101. [CrossRef]
51. Yuan, T.; da Rocha Neto, W.; Rothenberg, C.E.; Obraczka, K.; Barakat, C.; Turletti, T. Machine learning for next-generation intelligent transportation systems: A survey. *Trans. Emerg. Telecommun. Technol.* **2022**, *33*, e4427. [CrossRef]
52. Cugurullo, F. Urban artificial intelligence: From automation to autonomy in the smart city. *Front. Sustain. Cities* **2020**, *2*, 38. [CrossRef]
53. Bjelica, M.Z.; Mrazovac, B. Reliability of self-driving cars: When can we remove the safety driver? *IEEE Intell. Transp. Syst. Mag.* **2023**, *15*, 46–54. [CrossRef]
54. Gamel, S.A.; Saleh, A.I.; Ali, H.A. Machine learning-based traffic management techniques for intelligent transportation system. *Nile J. Commun. Comput. Sci.* **2021**, *1*, 9–18.
55. Tchuitcheu, W.C.; Bobda, C.; Pantho, M.J.H. Internet of smart-cameras for traffic lights optimization in smart cities. *Internet Things* **2020**, *11*, 100207. [CrossRef]
56. George, S.; Santra, A.K. Traffic prediction using multifaceted techniques: A survey. *Wirel. Pers. Commun.* **2020**, *115*, 1047–1106. [CrossRef]
57. Boukerche, A.; Wang, J. Machine learning-based traffic prediction models for intelligent transportation systems. *Comput. Netw.* **2020**, *181*, 107530. [CrossRef]
58. Akbari, M.; Do, T.N.A. A systematic review of machine learning in logistics and supply chain management: Current trends and future directions. *Benchmarking Int. J.* **2021**, *28*, 2977–3005. [CrossRef]

59. Manoharan, G.; Kumar, V.; Karthik, A.; Asha, V.; Mohan, C.R.; Nijhawan, G. IoT-Based Smart Inventory Management System Using Machine Learning Techniques. In Proceedings of the 2024 International Conference on Advances in Computing, Communication and Applied Informatics (ACCAI), Chennai, India, 9–10 May 2024; IEEE: Piscataway, NJ, USA, 2024; pp. 1–5.
60. Abolghasemi, M.; Beh, E.; Tarr, G.; Gerlach, R. Demand forecasting in supply chain: The impact of demand volatility in the presence of promotion. *Comput. Ind. Eng.* **2020**, *142*, 106380. [CrossRef]
61. Chung, S.H. Applications of smart technologies in logistics and transport: A review. *Transp. Res. Part E Logist. Transp. Rev.* **2021**, *153*, 102455. [CrossRef]
62. Liu, L. e-Commerce Personalized Recommendation Based on Machine Learning Technology. *Mob. Inf. Syst.* **2022**, *2022*, 1761579. [CrossRef]
63. Fayyaz, Z.; Ebrahimian, M.; Nawara, D.; Ibrahim, A.; Kashef, R. Recommendation systems: Algorithms, challenges, metrics, and business opportunities. *Appl. Sci.* **2020**, *10*, 7748. [CrossRef]
64. Kliestik, T.; Zvarikova, K.; Lăzăroiu, G. Data-driven machine learning and neural network algorithms in the retailing environment: Consumer engagement, experience, and purchase behaviors. *Econ. Manag. Financ. Mark.* **2022**, *17*, 57–69.
65. Xu, K.; Zhou, H.; Zheng, H.; Zhu, M.; Xin, Q. Intelligent Classification and Personalized Recommendation of E-commerce Products Based on Machine Learning. *arXiv* **2024**, arXiv:2403.19345. [CrossRef]
66. Fildes, R.; Ma, S.; Kolassa, S. Retail forecasting: Research and practice. *Int. J. Forecast.* **2022**, *38*, 1283–1318. [CrossRef]
67. Ban, G.Y.; Keskin, N.B. Personalized dynamic pricing with machine learning: High-dimensional features and heterogeneous elasticity. *Manag. Sci.* **2021**, *67*, 5549–5568. [CrossRef]
68. Giri, C.; Chen, Y. Deep learning for demand forecasting in the fashion and apparel retail industry. *Forecasting* **2022**, *4*, 565–581. [CrossRef]
69. Wang, C.H. Considering economic indicators and dynamic channel interactions to conduct sales forecasting for retail sectors. *Comput. Ind. Eng.* **2022**, *165*, 107965. [CrossRef]
70. Tirkolaee, E.B.; Sadeghi, S.; Mooseloo, F.M.; Vandchali, H.R.; Aeini, S. Application of machine learning in supply chain management: A comprehensive overview of the main areas. *Math. Probl. Eng.* **2021**, *2021*, 1476043. [CrossRef]
71. Oyewole, A.T.; Okoye, C.C.; Ofodile, O.C.; Ejairu, E. Reviewing predictive analytics in supply chain management: Applications and benefits. *World J. Adv. Res. Rev.* **2024**, *21*, 568–574. [CrossRef]
72. Vanoy, R.J.A. Logistics 4.0: Exploring Artificial Intelligence Trends in Efficient Supply Chain Management. *Data Metadata* **2023**, *2*, 145. [CrossRef]
73. Tsai, F.M.; Bui, T.D.; Tseng, M.L.; Ali, M.H.; Lim, M.K.; Chiu, A.S. Sustainable supply chain management trends in world regions: A data-driven analysis. *Resour. Conserv. Recycl.* **2021**, *167*, 105421. [CrossRef]
74. Rangel-Martinez, D.; Nigam, K.; Ricardez-Sandoval, L.A. Machine learning on sustainable energy: A review and outlook on renewable energy systems, catalysis, smart grid and energy storage. *Chem. Eng. Res. Des.* **2021**, *174*, 414–441.
75. Pham, A.D.; Ngo, N.T.; Truong, T.T.H.; Huynh, N.T.; Truong, N.S. Predicting energy consumption in multiple buildings using machine learning for improving energy efficiency and sustainability. *J. Clean. Prod.* **2020**, *260*, 121082. [CrossRef]
76. Lai, J.P.; Chang, Y.M.; Chen, C.H.; Pai, P.F. A survey of machine learning models in renewable energy predictions. *Appl. Sci.* **2020**, *10*, 5975. [CrossRef]
77. Fausing Olesen, J.; Shaker, H.R. Predictive maintenance for pump systems and thermal power plants: State-of-the-art review, trends and challenges. *Sensors* **2020**, *20*, 2425. [CrossRef] [PubMed]
78. Hsu, J.Y.; Wang, Y.F.; Lin, K.C.; Chen, M.Y.; Hsu, J.H.Y. Wind turbine fault diagnosis and predictive maintenance through statistical process control and machine learning. *IEEE Access* **2020**, *8*, 23427–23439. [CrossRef]
79. Ahmed, W.; Ansari, H.; Khan, B.; Ullah, Z.; Ali, S.M.; Mehmood, C.A.A.; Qureshi, M.B.; Hussain, I.; Jawad, M.; Khan, M.U.S.; et al. Machine learning based energy management model for smart grid and renewable energy districts. *IEEE Access* **2020**, *8*, 185059–185078. [CrossRef]
80. Ahmad, T.; Madonski, R.; Zhang, D.; Huang, C.; Mujeeb, A. Data-driven probabilistic machine learning in sustainable smart energy/smart energy systems: Key developments, challenges, and future research opportunities in the context of smart grid paradigm. *Renew. Sustain. Energy Rev.* **2022**, *160*, 112128. [CrossRef]
81. Rathor, S.K.; Saxena, D. Energy management system for smart grid: An overview and key issues. *Int. J. Energy Res.* **2020**, *44*, 4067–4109. [CrossRef]
82. Aslam, S.; Herodotou, H.; Mohsin, S.M.; Javaid, N.; Ashraf, N.; Aslam, S. A survey on deep learning methods for power load and renewable energy forecasting in smart microgrids. *Renew. Sustain. Energy Rev.* **2021**, *144*, 110992. [CrossRef]
83. Sweeney, C.; Bessa, R.J.; Browell, J.; Pinson, P. The future of forecasting for renewable energy. *Wiley Interdiscip. Rev. Energy Environ.* **2020**, *9*, e365. [CrossRef]
84. Khan, P.W.; Byun, Y.C.; Lee, S.J.; Kang, D.H.; Kang, J.Y.; Park, H.S. Machine learning-based approach to predict energy consumption of renewable and nonrenewable power sources. *Energies* **2020**, *13*, 4870. [CrossRef]

85. Nam, K.; Hwangbo, S.; Yoo, C. A deep learning-based forecasting model for renewable energy scenarios to guide sustainable energy policy: A case study of Korea. *Renew. Sustain. Energy Rev.* **2020**, *122*, 109725. [CrossRef]
86. Shaikh, T.A.; Mir, W.A.; Rasool, T.; Sofi, S. Machine learning for smart agriculture and precision farming: Towards making the fields talk. *Arch. Comput. Methods Eng.* **2022**, *29*, 4557–4597.
87. Reddy, D.J.; Kumar, M.R. Crop yield prediction using machine learning algorithm. In Proceedings of the 2021 5th International Conference on Intelligent Computing and Control Systems (ICICCS), Madurai, India, 6–8 May 2021; IEEE: Piscataway, NJ, USA, 2021; pp. 1466–1470.
88. Akhter, R.; Sofi, S.A. Precision agriculture using IoT data analytics and machine learning. *J. King Saud Univ.-Comput. Inf. Sci.* **2022**, *34*, 5602–5618. [CrossRef]
89. Li, L.; Li, X.; Chong, C.; Wang, C.H.; Wang, X. A decision support framework for the design and operation of sustainable urban farming systems. *J. Clean. Prod.* **2020**, *268*, 121928. [CrossRef]
90. Ghannam, R.B.; Techtmann, S.M. Machine learning applications in microbial ecology, human microbiome studies, and environmental monitoring. *Comput. Struct. Biotechnol. J.* **2021**, *19*, 1092–1107. [CrossRef] [PubMed]
91. Vorotyntsev, P.; Gordienko, Y.; Alienin, O.; Rokovyi, O.; Stirenko, S. Satellite image segmentation using deep learning for deforestation detection. In Proceedings of the 2021 IEEE 3rd Ukraine Conference on Electrical and Computer Engineering (UKRCON), Lviv, Ukraine, 26–28 August 2021; IEEE: Piscataway, NJ, USA, 2021; pp. 226–231.
92. Albahri, A.; Khaleel, Y.L.; Habeeb, M.A.; Ismael, R.D.; Hameed, Q.A.; Deveci, M.; Homod, R.Z.; Albahri, O.; Alamoodi, A.; Alzubaidi, L. A systematic review of trustworthy artificial intelligence applications in natural disasters. *Comput. Electr. Eng.* **2024**, *118*, 109409.
93. Bayat, M.; Burkhart, H.; Namiranian, M.; Hamidi, S.K.; Heidari, S.; Hassani, M. Assessing biotic and abiotic effects on biodiversity index using machine learning. *Forests* **2021**, *12*, 461. [CrossRef]
94. Sharma, A.; Jain, A.; Gupta, P.; Chowdary, V. Machine learning applications for precision agriculture: A comprehensive review. *IEEE Access* **2020**, *9*, 4843–4873. [CrossRef]
95. Narra, N.; Nevavuori, P.; Linna, P.; Lipping, T. A data driven approach to decision support in farming. In *Information Modelling and Knowledge Bases XXXI*; IOS Press: Amsterdam, The Netherlands, 2020; pp. 175–185.
96. Dong, Y.; Xu, F.; Liu, L.; Du, X.; Ren, B.; Guo, A.; Geng, Y.; Ruan, C.; Ye, H.; Huang, W.; et al. Automatic system for crop pest and disease dynamic monitoring and early forecasting. *IEEE J. Sel. Top. Appl. Earth Obs. Remote Sens.* **2020**, *13*, 4410–4418. [CrossRef]
97. Abuzanouneh, K.I.M.; Al-Wesabi, F.N.; Albraikan, A.A.; Al Duhayyim, M.; Al-Shabi, M.; Hilal, A.M.; Hamza, M.A.; Zamani, A.S.; Muthulakshmi, K. Design of machine learning based smart irrigation System for precision Agriculture. *Comput. Mater. Contin.* **2022**, *72*, 109–124.
98. Uyeh, D.D.; Akinsoji, A.; Asem-Hiablie, S.; Bassey, B.I.; Osinuga, A.; Mallipeddi, R.; Amaizu, M.; Ha, Y.; Park, T. An online machine learning-based sensors clustering system for efficient and cost-effective environmental monitoring in controlled environment agriculture. *Comput. Electron. Agric.* **2022**, *199*, 107139. [CrossRef]
99. Burke, M.; Driscoll, A.; Lobell, D.B.; Ermon, S. Using satellite imagery to understand and promote sustainable development. *Science* **2021**, *371*, eabe8628. [CrossRef]
100. Khan, A.; Gupta, S.; Gupta, S.K. Multi-hazard disaster studies: Monitoring, detection, recovery, and management, based on emerging technologies and optimal techniques. *Int. J. Disaster Risk Reduct.* **2020**, *47*, 101642. [CrossRef]
101. Rolnick, D.; Donti, P.L.; Kaack, L.H.; Kochanski, K.; Lacoste, A.; Sankaran, K.; Ross, A.S.; Milojevic-Dupont, N.; Jaques, N.; Waldman-Brown, A.; et al. Tackling climate change with machine learning. *ACM Comput. Surv. (CSUR)* **2022**, *55*, 1–96.
102. Zhebka, V.; Gertsiuk, M.; Sokolov, V.; Malinov, V.; Sablina, M. Optimization of Machine Learning Method to Improve the Management Efficiency of Heterogeneous Telecommunication Network. *Cybersecur. Provid. Inf. Telecommun. Syst.* **2022**, *3288*, 149–155.
103. Abreu, R.B.; Pocovi, G.; Jacobsen, T.H.; Centenaro, M.; Pedersen, K.I.; Kolding, T.E. Scheduling enhancements and performance evaluation of downlink 5G time-sensitive communications. *IEEE Access* **2020**, *8*, 128106–128115. [CrossRef]
104. Akhtar, M.; Moridpour, S. A review of traffic congestion prediction using artificial intelligence. *J. Adv. Transp.* **2021**, *2021*, 8878011. [CrossRef]
105. Do-Duy, T.; Nguyen, L.D.; Duong, T.Q.; Khosravirad, S.R.; Claussen, H. Joint optimisation of real-time deployment and resource allocation for UAV-aided disaster emergency communications. *IEEE J. Sel. Areas Commun.* **2021**, *39*, 3411–3424. [CrossRef]
106. Reddy, S.G.; Sadhu, A.K.R.; Muravev, M.; Brazhenko, D.; Parfenov, M. Harnessing the Power of Generative Artificial Intelligence for Dynamic Content Personalization in Customer Relationship Management Systems: A Data-Driven Framework for Optimizing Customer Engagement and Experience. *J. AI-Assist. Sci. Discov.* **2023**, *3*, 379–395.
107. Fujo, S.W.; Subramanian, S.; Khder, M.A. Customer churn prediction in telecommunication industry using deep learning. *Inf. Sci. Lett.* **2022**, *11*, 185–198.
108. Al-Mashraie, M.; Chung, S.H.; Jeon, H.W. Customer switching behavior analysis in the telecommunication industry via push-pull-mooring framework: A machine learning approach. *Comput. Ind. Eng.* **2020**, *144*, 106476. [CrossRef]

109. Wu, S.; Yau, W.C.; Ong, T.S.; Chong, S.C. Integrated churn prediction and customer segmentation framework for telco business. *Ieee Access* **2021**, *9*, 62118–62136. [CrossRef]
110. Sanober, S.; Alam, I.; Pande, S.; Arslan, F.; Rane, K.P.; Singh, B.K.; Khamparia, A.; Shabaz, M. An enhanced secure deep learning algorithm for fraud detection in wireless communication. *Wirel. Commun. Mob. Comput.* **2021**, *2021*, 6079582. [CrossRef]
111. Murugalakshmi, S.; Robin, C.R. Advancements in Mobile Security: A Comprehensive Study of Sim Card Swapping and Cloning-Trends, Challenges and Innovative Solutions. *I-Manag. J. Mob. Appl. Technol.* **2023**, *10*, 23–29. . [CrossRef]
112. Bello, H.O.; Ige, A.B.; Ameyaw, M.N. Adaptive machine learning models: Concepts for real-time financial fraud prevention in dynamic environments. *World J. Adv. Eng. Technol. Sci.* **2024**, *12*, 021–034. [CrossRef]
113. Prabhu Kavin, B.; Karki, S.; Hemalatha, S.; Singh, D.; Vijayalakshmi, R.; Thangamani, M.; Haleem, S.L.A.; Jose, D.; Tirth, V.; Kshirsagar, P.R.; et al. Machine Learning-Based Secure Data Acquisition for Fake Accounts Detection in Future Mobile Communication Networks. *Wirel. Commun. Mob. Comput.* **2022**, *2022*, 6356152. [CrossRef]
114. Rai, R.; Tiwari, M.K.; Ivanov, D.; Dolgui, A. Machine learning in manufacturing and industry 4.0 applications. *Int. J. Prod. Res.* **2021**, *59*, 4773–4778. [CrossRef]
115. Zonta, T.; Da Costa, C.A.; da Rosa Righi, R.; de Lima, M.J.; da Trindade, E.S.; Li, G.P. Predictive maintenance in the Industry 4.0: A systematic literature review. *Comput. Ind. Eng.* **2020**, *150*, 106889. [CrossRef]
116. Silva, J.; Martínez, A. Machine Learning-Driven Quality Control in Supply Chains: Improving Product Integrity and Customer Satisfaction. *Innov. Comput. Sci. J.* **2023**, *9*, 1–8.
117. Çınar, Z.M.; Abdussalam Nuhu, A.; Zeeshan, Q.; Korhan, O.; Asmael, M.; Safaei, B. Machine learning in predictive maintenance towards sustainable smart manufacturing in industry 4.0. *Sustainability* **2020**, *12*, 8211. [CrossRef]
118. Pech, M.; Vrchota, J.; Bednář, J. Predictive maintenance and intelligent sensors in smart factory. *Sensors* **2021**, *21*, 1470. [CrossRef] [PubMed]
119. Shahin, M.; Chen, F.F.; Hosseinzadeh, A.; Zand, N. Using machine learning and deep learning algorithms for downtime minimization in manufacturing systems: An early failure detection diagnostic service. *Int. J. Adv. Manuf. Technol.* **2023**, *128*, 3857–3883. [CrossRef]
120. Wang, P.; Yang, Y.; Moghaddam, N.S. Process modeling in laser powder bed fusion towards defect detection and quality control via machine learning: The state-of-the-art and research challenges. *J. Manuf. Process.* **2022**, *73*, 961–984. [CrossRef]
121. Westphal, E.; Seitz, H. A machine learning method for defect detection and visualization in selective laser sintering based on convolutional neural networks. *Addit. Manuf.* **2021**, *41*, 101965. [CrossRef]
122. Pittino, F.; Puggl, M.; Moldaschl, T.; Hirschl, C. Automatic anomaly detection on in-production manufacturing machines using statistical learning methods. *Sensors* **2020**, *20*, 2344. [CrossRef]
123. Gayam, S.R.; Yellu, R.R.; Thuniki, P. Optimizing Supply Chain Management through Artificial Intelligence: Techniques for Predictive Maintenance, Demand Forecasting, and Inventory Optimization. *J. AI-Assist. Sci. Discov.* **2021**, *1*, 129–144.
124. Qi, M.; Shi, Y.; Qi, Y.; Ma, C.; Yuan, R.; Wu, D.; Shen, Z.J. A practical end-to-end inventory management model with deep learning. *Manag. Sci.* **2023**, *69*, 759–773. [CrossRef]
125. Belhadi, A.; Kamble, S.; Fosso Wamba, S.; Queiroz, M.M. Building supply-chain resilience: An artificial intelligence-based technique and decision-making framework. *Int. J. Prod. Res.* **2022**, *60*, 4487–4507. [CrossRef]
126. Pataranutaporn, P.; Danry, V.; Leong, J.; Punpongsanon, P.; Novy, D.; Maes, P.; Sra, M. AI-generated characters for supporting personalized learning and well-being. *Nat. Mach. Intell.* **2021**, *3*, 1013–1022. [CrossRef]
127. Mousavinasab, E.; Zarifsanaiey, N.; R. Niakan Kalhori, S.; Rakhshan, M.; Keikha, L.; Ghazi Saeedi, M. Intelligent tutoring systems: A systematic review of characteristics, applications, and evaluation methods. *Interact. Learn. Environ.* **2021**, *29*, 142–163. [CrossRef]
128. Muñoz, J.L.R.; Ojeda, F.M.; Jurado, D.L.A.; Peña, P.F.P.; Carranza, C.P.M.; Berríos, H.Q.; Molina, S.U.; Farfan, A.R.M.; Arias-Gonzáles, J.L.; Vasquez-Pauca, M.J. Systematic review of adaptive learning technology for learning in higher education. *Eurasian J. Educ. Res.* **2022**, *98*, 221–233.
129. Kochmar, E.; Vu, D.D.; Belfer, R.; Gupta, V.; Serban, I.V.; Pineau, J. Automated personalized feedback improves learning gains in an intelligent tutoring system. In Proceedings of the 21st International Conference on Artificial Intelligence in Education (AIED), Ifrane, Morocco, 6–10 July 2020; Springer: Berlin/Heidelberg, Germany, 2020; pp. 140–146.
130. Cavalcanti, A.P.; Barbosa, A.; Carvalho, R.; Freitas, F.; Tsai, Y.S.; Gašević, D.; Mello, R.F. Automatic feedback in online learning environments: A systematic literature review. *Comput. Educ. Artif. Intell.* **2021**, *2*, 100027. [CrossRef]
131. Kabudi, T.; Pappas, I.; Olsen, D.H. AI-enabled adaptive learning systems: A systematic mapping of the literature. *Comput. Educ. Artif. Intell.* **2021**, *2*, 100017. [CrossRef]
132. Doleck, T.; Lemay, D.J.; Basnet, R.B.; Bazelais, P. Predictive analytics in education: A comparison of deep learning frameworks. *Educ. Inf. Technol.* **2020**, *25*, 1951–1963. [CrossRef]

133. Del Bonifro, F.; Gabbrielli, M.; Lisanti, G.; Zingaro, S.P. Student dropout prediction. In Proceedings of the Artificial Intelligence in Education: 21st International Conference, AIED 2020, Ifrane, Morocco, 6–10 July 2020; Proceedings, Part I 21; Springer: Berlin/Heidelberg, Germany, 2020; pp. 129–140.
134. Adnan, M.; Habib, A.; Ashraf, J.; Mussadiq, S.; Raza, A.A.; Abid, M.; Bashir, M.; Khan, S.U. Predicting at-risk students at different percentages of course length for early intervention using machine learning models. *IEEE Access* **2021**, *9*, 7519–7539. [CrossRef]
135. Weegar, R.; Idestam-Almquist, P. Reducing workload in short answer grading using machine learning. *Int. J. Artif. Intell. Educ.* **2024**, *34*, 247–273. [CrossRef]
136. Li, K.C.; Wong, B.T.M.; Liu, M. Identification of Potential At-Risk Students Through an Intelligent Multi-model Academic Analytics Platform. In *Proceedings of the 7th International Conference on Technology in Education (ICTE), Hradec Kralove, Czech Republic, 2–5 December 2024*; Springer: Singapore, 2024; Volume 2330, pp. 199–209.
137. Lee, H.S.; Gweon, G.H.; Lord, T.; Paessel, N.; Pallant, A.; Pryputniewicz, S. Machine learning-enabled automated feedback: Supporting students' revision of scientific arguments based on data drawn from simulation. *J. Sci. Educ. Technol.* **2021**, *30*, 168–192. [CrossRef]
138. Choudhury, M.; Prabhu, S.; Sabri, A.K.; Marhoon, H.A. Impact of artificial intelligence (AI) in the media and entertainment industry. *AIP Conf. Proc.* **2023**, *2736*, 060012. [CrossRef]
139. Anderson, A.; Maystre, L.; Anderson, I.; Mehrotra, R.; Lalmas, M. Algorithmic effects on the diversity of consumption on spotify. In Proceedings of the Web Conference 2020, Taipei, Taiwan, 20–24 April 2020; pp. 2155–2165.
140. Stoldt, R. *Imagining the World: Personalization Algorithms and Global Media Flows on Netflix*; The University of Iowa: Iowa City, IA, USA, 2021.
141. Liu, X. Analyzing the impact of user-generated content on B2B Firms' stock performance: Big data analysis with machine learning methods. *Ind. Mark. Manag.* **2020**, *86*, 30–39. [CrossRef]
142. Balaji, T.; Annavarapu, C.S.R.; Bablani, A. Machine learning algorithms for social media analysis: A survey. *Comput. Sci. Rev.* **2021**, *40*, 100395.
143. Abidi, S.M.R.; Xu, Y.; Ni, J.; Wang, X.; Zhang, W. Popularity prediction of movies: From statistical modeling to machine learning techniques. *Multimed. Tools Appl.* **2020**, *79*, 35583–35617. [CrossRef]
144. Hallur, G.G.; Prabhu, S.; Aslekar, A. Entertainment in era of AI, big data & IoT. In *Digital Entertainment: The Next Evolution in Service Sector*; Springer Nature, Palgrave Macmillan: Singapore, 2021; pp. 87–109.
145. de Lima-Santos, M.F.; Ceron, W. Artificial intelligence in news media: Current perceptions and future outlook. *J. Media* **2021**, *3*, 13–26. [CrossRef]
146. Lekharu, A.; Moulii, K.; Sur, A.; Sarkar, A. Deep learning based prediction model for adaptive video streaming. In Proceedings of the 2020 International Conference on COMmunication Systems & NETworkS (COMSNETS), Bengaluru, India, 7–11 January 2020; IEEE: Piscataway, NJ, USA, 2020; pp. 152–159.
147. Kim, J.; Jung, Y.; Yeo, H.; Ye, J.; Han, D. Neural-enhanced live streaming: Improving live video ingest via online learning. In Proceedings of the Annual Conference of the ACM Special Interest Group on Data Communication on the Applications, Technologies, Architectures, and Protocols for Computer Communication, Virtual, 10–14 August 2020; pp. 107–125.
148. Islam, M.R.; Liu, S.; Wang, X.; Xu, G. Deep learning for misinformation detection on online social networks: A survey and new perspectives. *Soc. Netw. Anal. Min.* **2020**, *10*, 82. [CrossRef] [PubMed]
149. Smith, M.J.; Buckton, C.; Patterson, C.; Hilton, S. User-generated content and influencer marketing involving e-cigarettes on social media: A scoping review and content analysis of YouTube and Instagram. *BMC Public Health* **2023**, *23*, 530. [CrossRef] [PubMed]
150. Chakraborty, K.; Bhattacharyya, S.; Bag, R. A survey of sentiment analysis from social media data. *IEEE Trans. Comput. Soc. Syst.* **2020**, *7*, 450–464. [CrossRef]
151. Zakir, M.H.; Bashir, S.; Ali, R.N.; Khan, S.H. Artificial Intelligence and Machine Learning in Legal Research: A Comprehensive Analysis. *Qlantic J. Soc. Sci.* **2024**, *5*, 307–317. [CrossRef]
152. Xu, Y.; Hu, G.; You, L.; Cao, C. A novel machine learning-based analysis model for smart contract vulnerability. *Secur. Commun. Netw.* **2021**, *2021*, 5798033. [CrossRef]
153. Camilus, S.; Lee, Y.M. Automated hand hygiene compliance monitoring. In Proceedings of the 2020 2nd International Conference on Image, Video and Signal Processing, Marrakesh, Morocco, 4–6 June 2020; pp. 64–69.
154. Kushwaha, S.S.; Joshi, S.; Singh, D.; Kaur, M.; Lee, H.N. Ethereum smart contract analysis tools: A systematic review. *IEEE Access* **2022**, *10*, 57037–57062. [CrossRef]
155. Sleimi, A.; Sannier, N.; Sabetzadeh, M.; Briand, L.; Ceci, M.; Dann, J. An automated framework for the extraction of semantic legal metadata from legal texts. *Empir. Softw. Eng.* **2021**, *26*, 1–50. [CrossRef]
156. Amato, F.; Cozzolino, G.; Moscato, F.; Moscato, V.; Xhafa, F. A model for verification and validation of law compliance of smart contracts in IoT environment. *IEEE Trans. Ind. Inform.* **2021**, *17*, 7752–7759. [CrossRef]

157. Hamdani, R.E.; Mustapha, M.; Amariles, D.R.; Troussel, A.; Meeús, S.; Krasnashchok, K. A combined rule-based and machine learning approach for automated GDPR compliance checking. In Proceedings of the Eighteenth International Conference on Artificial Intelligence and Law, São Paulo, Brazil, 21–25 June 2021; pp. 40–49.
158. Pugliese, R.; Regondi, S.; Marini, R. Machine learning-based approach: Global trends, research directions, and regulatory standpoints. *Data Sci. Manag.* **2021**, *4*, 19–29. [CrossRef]
159. Bibal, A.; Lognoul, M.; De Streel, A.; Frénay, B. Legal requirements on explainability in machine learning. *Artif. Intell. Law* **2021**, *29*, 149–169. [CrossRef]
160. Scholtes, J.C.; van den Herik, H.J. Big data analytics for e-discovery. In *Research Handbook on Big Data Law*; Edward Elgar Publishing: Cheltenham, UK, 2021; pp. 253–284.
161. Ransbotham, S.; Overby, E.M.; Jernigan, M.C. Electronic trace data and legal outcomes: The effect of electronic medical records on malpractice claim resolution time. *Manag. Sci.* **2021**, *67*, 4341–4361. [CrossRef]
162. Amor, R.; Dimyadi, J. The promise of automated compliance checking. *Dev. Built Environ.* **2021**, *5*, 100039. [CrossRef]
163. Garg, S.; Sinha, S.; Kar, A.K.; Mani, M. A review of machine learning applications in human resource management. *Int. J. Product. Perform. Manag.* **2022**, *71*, 1590–1610. [CrossRef]
164. Pal, R.; Shaikh, S.; Satpute, S.; Bhagwat, S. Resume classification using various machine learning algorithms. In Proceedings of the ITM Web of Conferences. EDP Sciences, Tamil Nadu, India, 10–11 November 2022; Volume 44, p. 03011.
165. Edwards, M.R.; Edwards, K.; Jang, D. *Predictive HR Analytics: Mastering the HR Metric*; Kogan Page Publishers: London, UK, 2024.
166. Mer, A.; Srivastava, A. Employee engagement in the new normal: Artificial intelligence as a buzzword or a game changer? In *The Adoption and Effect of Artificial Intelligence on Human Resources Management, Part A*; Emerald Publishing Limited: Bingley, UK, 2023; pp. 15–46.
167. Lazzari, M.; Alvarez, J.M.; Ruggieri, S. Predicting and explaining employee turnover intention. *Int. J. Data Sci. Anal.* **2022**, *14*, 279–292. [CrossRef]
168. Lee, J.; Song, J.H. How does algorithm-based HR predict employees' sentiment?Developing an employee experience model through sentiment analysis. *Ind. Commer. Train.* **2024**, *56*, 273–289. [CrossRef]
169. Jain, P.; Tripathi, V.; Malladi, R.; Khang, A. Data-driven artificial intelligence (AI) models in the workforce development planning. In *Designing Workforce Management Systems for Industry 4.0*; CRC Press: Boca Raton, FL, USA, 2023; pp. 159–176.
170. Gurusinghe, R.N.; Arachchige, B.J.; Dayarathna, D. Predictive HR analytics and talent management: A conceptual framework. *J. Manag. Anal.* **2021**, *8*, 195–221. [CrossRef]
171. Atwood, C. *Succession Planning Basics*; Association for Talent Development: Alexandria, VA, USA, 2020.
172. Pessach, D.; Singer, G.; Avrahami, D.; Ben-Gal, H.C.; Shmueli, E.; Ben-Gal, I. Employees recruitment: A prescriptive analytics approach via machine learning and mathematical programming. *Decis. Support Syst.* **2020**, *134*, 113290. [CrossRef]
173. Fake, H.; Dabbagh, N. Personalized learning within online workforce learning environments: Exploring implementations, obstacles, opportunities, and perspectives of workforce leaders. *Technol. Knowl. Learn.* **2020**, *25*, 789–809. [CrossRef]
174. Williams, A.M.; Ford, P.R.; Drust, B. Talent identification and development in soccer since the millennium. *Sci. Footb.* **2023**, *38*, 1199–1210
175. Shukla, B.; Fan, I.S.; Jennions, I. Opportunities for explainable artificial intelligence in aerospace predictive maintenance. In Proceedings of the PHM Society European Conference, Virtual, 27–31 July 2020; Volume 5, p. 11.
176. Chen, J.; Sun, J.; Wang, G. From unmanned systems to autonomous intelligent systems. *Engineering* **2022**, *12*, 16–19. [CrossRef]
177. Li, C.; Zhang, Y.; Su, X.; Wang, X. An improved optimization algorithm for aeronautical maintenance and repair task scheduling problem. *Mathematics* **2022**, *10*, 3777. [CrossRef]
178. Kurunathan, H.; Huang, H.; Li, K.; Ni, W.; Hossain, E. Machine learning-aided operations and communications of unmanned aerial vehicles: A contemporary survey. *IEEE Commun. Surv. Tutorials* **2023**, *26*, 496–533. [CrossRef]
179. Fourati, F.; Alouini, M.S. Artificial intelligence for satellite communication: A review. *Intell. Converg. Netw.* **2021**, *2*, 213–243. [CrossRef]
180. Szabadföldi, I. Artificial intelligence in military application–opportunities and challenges. *Land Forces Acad. Rev.* **2021**, *26*, 157–165. [CrossRef]
181. Hawkins, R.; Paterson, C.; Picardi, C.; Jia, Y.; Calinescu, R.; Habli, I. Guidance on the assurance of machine learning in autonomous systems (AMLAS). *arXiv* **2021**, arXiv:2102.01564.
182. Yeong, D.J.; Velasco-Hernandez, G.; Barry, J.; Walsh, J. Sensor and sensor fusion technology in autonomous vehicles: A review. *Sensors* **2021**, *21*, 2140. [CrossRef] [PubMed]
183. Wang, J.; Meng, M.Q.H. Real-time decision making and path planning for robotic autonomous luggage trolley collection at airports. *IEEE Trans. Syst. Man Cybern. Syst.* **2021**, *52*, 2174–2183. [CrossRef]
184. Hu, J.; Wang, L.; Hu, T.; Guo, C.; Wang, Y. Autonomous maneuver decision making of dual-UAV cooperative air combat based on deep reinforcement learning. *Electronics* **2022**, *11*, 467. [CrossRef]

185. Garcia, A.B.; Babiceanu, R.F.; Seker, R. Artificial intelligence and machine learning approaches for aviation cybersecurity: An overview. In Proceedings of the 2021 Integrated Communications Navigation and Surveillance Conference (ICNS), Dulles, VA, USA, 19–23 April 2021; IEEE: Piscataway, NJ, USA, 2021; pp. 1–8.
186. Prasad, A.; Chandra, S. Machine learning to combat cyberattack: A survey of datasets and challenges. *J. Def. Model. Simul.* **2023**, *20*, 577–588. [CrossRef]
187. Kilincer, I.F.; Ertam, F.; Sengur, A. Machine learning methods for cyber security intrusion detection: Datasets and comparative study. *Comput. Netw.* **2021**, *188*, 107840. [CrossRef]
188. Carranza, J.P.; Piumetto, M.A.; Lucca, C.M.; Da Silva, E. Mass appraisal as affordable public policy: Open data and machine learning for mapping urban land values. *Land Use Policy* **2022**, *119*, 106211. [CrossRef]
189. Faridoon, L.; Liu, W.; Spence, C. The Impact of Big Data Analytics on Decision-Making Within the Government Sector. *Big Data* **2024**. Available online: https://www.liebertpub.com/doi/10.1089/big.2023.0019 (accessed on 1 December 2024).
190. Bejarano, J.; Barón, D.; González-Rojas, O.; Camargo, M. Discovering optimal resource allocations for what-if scenarios using data-driven simulation. *Front. Comput. Sci.* **2023**, *5*, 1279800. [CrossRef]
191. Jenga, K.; Catal, C.; Kar, G. Machine learning in crime prediction. *J. Ambient Intell. Humaniz. Comput.* **2023**, *14*, 2887–2913. [CrossRef]
192. Berk, R.A. Artificial intelligence, predictive policing, and risk assessment for law enforcement. *Annu. Rev. Criminol.* **2021**, *4*, 209–237. [CrossRef]
193. Nair, S.N.; Gopi, E. Deep learning techniques for crime hotspot detection. In *Optimization in Machine Learning and Applications*; Springer: Singapore, 2020; pp. 13–29.
194. Ahmad, F.; Almuayqil, S.N.; Humayun, M.; Naseem, S.; Khan, W.A.; Junaid, K. Prediction of COVID-19 cases using machine learning for effective public health management. *Comput. Mater. Contin.* **2020**, *66*, 2265–2282. [CrossRef]
195. Zeng, D.; Cao, Z.; Neill, D.B. Artificial intelligence–enabled public health surveillance—from local detection to global epidemic monitoring and control. In *Artificial Intelligence in Medicine*; Elsevier: Amsterdam, The Netherlands, 2021; pp. 437–453.
196. Linardos, V.; Drakaki, M.; Tzionas, P.; Karnavas, Y.L. Machine learning in disaster management: Recent developments in methods and applications. *Mach. Learn. Knowl. Extr.* **2022**, *4*, 446–473. [CrossRef]
197. Zheng, Z.; Zhong, Y.; Wang, J.; Ma, A.; Zhang, L. Building damage assessment for rapid disaster response with a deep object-based semantic change detection framework: From natural disasters to man-made disasters. *Remote Sens. Environ.* **2021**, *265*, 112636. [CrossRef]
198. Amarasinghe, K.; Rodolfa, K.T.; Lamba, H.; Ghani, R. Explainable machine learning for public policy: Use cases, gaps, and research directions. *Data Policy* **2023**, *5*, e5. [CrossRef]
199. Henman, P. Improving public services using artificial intelligence: Possibilities, pitfalls, governance. *Asia Pac. J. Public Adm.* **2020**, *42*, 209–221. [CrossRef]
200. Yogi, K.S.; Gowda, D.; Mouna, K.; Sujithra, L.; Prasad, K.; Midhun, P. Scalability and Performance Evaluation of Machine Learning Techniques in High-Volume Social Media Data Analysis. In Proceedings of the 2024 11th International Conference on Reliability, Infocom Technologies and Optimization (Trends and Future Directions) (ICRITO), Noida, India, 14–15 March 2024; IEEE: Piscataway, NJ, USA, 2024; pp. 1–6.
201. Deekshith, A. Scalable Machine Learning: Techniques for Managing Data Volume and Velocity in AI Applications. *Int. Sci. J. Res.* **2023**, *5*.
202. Potla, R.T. Scalable Machine Learning Algorithms for Big Data Analytics: Challenges and Opportunities. *J. Artif. Intell. Res.* **2022**, *2*, 124–141.
203. Triguero, I.; Maillo, J.; Luengo, J.; García, S.; Herrera, F. From big data to smart data with the k-nearest neighbours algorithm. In Proceedings of the 2016 IEEE International Conference on Internet of Things (iThings) and IEEE Green Computing and Communications (GreenCom) and IEEE Cyber, Physical and Social Computing (CPSCom) and IEEE Smart Data (SmartData), Chengdu, China, 15–18 December 2016; IEEE: Piscataway, NJ, USA, 2016; pp. 859–864.
204. Gaye, B.; Zhang, D.; Wulamu, A. Improvement of support vector machine algorithm in big data background. *Math. Probl. Eng.* **2021**, *2021*, 5594899. [CrossRef]
205. Wu, X.; Wu, Y.; Li, X.; Ye, Z.; Gu, X.; Wu, Z.; Yang, Y. Application of adaptive machine learning systems in heterogeneous data environments. *Glob. Acad. Front.* **2024**, *2*, 37–50.
206. Mishra, S.; Komandla, V.; Bandi, S. Leveraging in-memory computing for speeding up Apache Spark and Hadoop distributed data processing. *J. AI-Assist. Sci. Discov.* **2022**, *2*, 304–328.
207. Li, M.; Zhang, T.; Chen, Y.; Smola, A.J. Efficient mini-batch training for stochastic optimization. In Proceedings of the 20th ACM SIGKDD International Conference on Knowledge Discovery and Data Mining, New York, NY, USA, 24–27 August 2014; pp. 661–670.
208. Nguyen, D.C.; Ding, M.; Pham, Q.V.; Pathirana, P.N.; Le, L.B.; Seneviratne, A.; Li, J.; Niyato, D.; Poor, H.V. Federated learning meets blockchain in edge computing: Opportunities and challenges. *IEEE Internet Things J.* **2021**, *8*, 12806–12825. [CrossRef]

209. Koren, I.; Krishna, C.M. *Fault-Tolerant Systems*; Morgan Kaufmann: Burlington, MA, USA, 2020.
210. Gupta, P.; Sharma, A.; Jindal, R. Scalable machine-learning algorithms for big data analytics: A comprehensive review. *Wiley Interdiscip. Rev. Data Min. Knowl. Discov.* **2016**, *6*, 194–214. [CrossRef]
211. Elouataoui, W.; Alaoui, I.E.; Gahi, Y. Data quality in the era of big data: A global review. In *Big Data Intelligence for Smart Applications*; Springer: Cham, Switzerland, 2022; pp. 1–25.
212. Jain, A.; Patel, H.; Nagalapatti, L.; Gupta, N.; Mehta, S.; Guttula, S.; Mujumdar, S.; Afzal, S.; Sharma Mittal, R.; Munigala, V. Overview and importance of data quality for machine learning tasks. In Proceedings of the 26th ACM SIGKDD International Conference on Knowledge Discovery & Data Mining, Virtual, 6–10 July 2020; pp. 3561–3562.
213. Luengo, J.; Garcia-Gil, D.; Ramirez-Gallego, S.; Garcia, S.; Herrera, F. *Big Data Preprocessing*; Springer: Cham, Switzerland, 2020.
214. Shyshatskyi, A.; Zvieriev, O.; Salnikova, O.; Demchenko, Y.; Trotsko, O.; Neroznak, Y. Complex Methods of Processing Different Data in Intellectual Systems for Decision Support System. *Int. J.* **2020**, *9*. Available online: http://www.warse.org/IJATCSE/static/pdf/file/ijatcse206942020.pdf (accessed on 1 December 2024). [CrossRef]
215. Fan, C.; Chen, M.; Wang, X.; Wang, J.; Huang, B. A review on data preprocessing techniques toward efficient and reliable knowledge discovery from building operational data. *Front. Energy Res.* **2021**, *9*, 652801. [CrossRef]
216. Goyle, K.; Xie, Q.; Goyle, V. Dataassist: A machine learning approach to data cleaning and preparation. In Proceedings of the Intelligent Systems Conference, Amsterdam, The Netherlands, 5–6 September 2024; Springer: Cham, Switzerland, 2024; pp. 476–486.
217. Maharana, K.; Mondal, S.; Nemade, B. A review: Data pre-processing and data augmentation techniques. *Glob. Transitions Proc.* **2022**, *3*, 91–99. [CrossRef]
218. Chai, C.; Wang, J.; Luo, Y.; Niu, Z.; Li, G. Data management for machine learning: A survey. *IEEE Trans. Knowl. Data Eng.* **2022**, *35*, 4646–4667. [CrossRef]
219. Rudin, C. Stop explaining black box machine learning models for high stakes decisions and use interpretable models instead. *Nat. Mach. Intell.* **2019**, *1*, 206–215. [CrossRef] [PubMed]
220. Chaudhary, G. Unveiling the black box: Bringing algorithmic transparency to AI. *Masaryk Univ. J. Law Technol.* **2024**, *18*, 93–122. [CrossRef]
221. Srivastava, K.; Sorathiya, A.; Mehta, J.; Chotaliya, V. Enhancing Interpretability, Reliability and Trustworthiness: Applications of Explainable Artificial Intelligence in Medical Imaging, Financial Markets, and Sentiment Analysis. In Proceedings of the 2024 16th International Conference on Electronics, Computers and Artificial Intelligence (ECAI), Iasi, Romania, 27–28 June 2024; IEEE: Piscataway, NJ, USA, 2024; pp. 1–9.
222. Vishwarupe, V.; Joshi, P.M.; Mathias, N.; Maheshwari, S.; Mhaisalkar, S.; Pawar, V. Explainable AI and interpretable machine learning: A case study in perspective. *Procedia Comput. Sci.* **2022**, *204*, 869–876. [CrossRef]
223. Cheng, F.; Ming, Y.; Qu, H. Dece: Decision explorer with counterfactual explanations for machine learning models. *IEEE Trans. Vis. Comput. Graph.* **2020**, *27*, 1438–1447. [CrossRef] [PubMed]
224. Abam, E.B.; Webb, H.; Dowthwaite, L.; Triguero, I. Human Perceptions of Novel Visual and Non-Visual Explanations in High-Stakes Decision-Making Domains. In Proceedings of the International Conference on Human-Computer Interaction, Washington, DC, USA, 29 June–4 July 2024; Springer: Berlin/Heidelberg, Germany, 2024; pp. 3–13.
225. Arsic, S.; Mihic, M.; Petrovic, D.; Mitrovic, Z.; Kostic, S.C.; Mihic, O. Review of measures for improving ML model interpretability: Empowering decision makers with transparent insights. In Proceedings of the 2024 International Conference on Artificial Intelligence, Computer, Data Sciences and Applications (ACDSA), Victoria, Seychelles, 1–2 February 2024; IEEE: Piscataway, NJ, USA, 2024; pp. 1–5.
226. Yang, Z.; Zhang, A.; Sudjianto, A. GAMI-Net: An explainable neural network based on generalized additive models with structured interactions. *Pattern Recognit.* **2021**, *120*, 108192. [CrossRef]
227. Rigotti, M.; Miksovic, C.; Giurgiu, I.; Gschwind, T.; Scotton, P. Attention-based interpretability with concept transformers. In Proceedings of the International Conference on Learning Representations, Vienna, Austria, 4 May 2021.
228. Zytek, A.; Liu, D.; Vaithianathan, R.; Veeramachaneni, K. Sibyl: Understanding and addressing the usability challenges of machine learning in high-stakes decision making. *IEEE Trans. Vis. Comput. Graph.* **2021**, *28*, 1161–1171. [CrossRef]
229. Toreini, E.; Aitken, M.; Coopamootoo, K.; Elliott, K.; Zelaya, C.G.; Van Moorsel, A. The relationship between trust in AI and trustworthy machine learning technologies. In Proceedings of the 2020 Conference on Fairness, Accountability, and Transparency, Barcelona, Spain, 27–30 January 2020; pp. 272–283.
230. Josphineleela, R.; Kaliappan, S.; Natrayan, L.; Garg, A. Big Data Security through Privacy–Preserving Data Mining (PPDM): A Decentralization Approach. In Proceedings of the 2023 Second International Conference on Electronics and Renewable Systems (ICEARS), Tuticorin, India, 2–4 March 2023; IEEE: Piscataway, NJ, USA, 2023; pp. 718–721.
231. Xue, M.; Yuan, C.; Wu, H.; Zhang, Y.; Liu, W. Machine learning security: Threats, countermeasures, and evaluations. *IEEE Access* **2020**, *8*, 74720–74742. [CrossRef]

232. Singh, S.; Rathore, S.; Alfarraj, O.; Tolba, A.; Yoon, B. A framework for privacy-preservation of IoT healthcare data using Federated Learning and blockchain technology. *Future Gener. Comput. Syst.* **2022**, *129*, 380–388. [CrossRef]
233. Meurisch, C.; Muhlhauser, M. Data protection in AI services: A survey. *ACM Comput. Surv. (CSUR)* **2021**, *54*, 1–38. [CrossRef]
234. Goldsteen, A.; Ezov, G.; Shmelkin, R.; Moffie, M.; Farkash, A. Data minimization for GDPR compliance in machine learning models. *AI Ethics* **2022**, *2*, 477–491. [CrossRef]
235. Tanuwidjaja, H.C.; Choi, R.; Baek, S.; Kim, K. Privacy-preserving deep learning on machine learning as a service—A comprehensive survey. *IEEE Access* **2020**, *8*, 167425–167447. [CrossRef]
236. Ponomareva, N.; Hazimeh, H.; Kurakin, A.; Xu, Z.; Denison, C.; McMahan, H.B.; Vassilvitskii, S.; Chien, S.; Thakurta, A.G. How to dp-fy ml: A practical guide to machine learning with differential privacy. *J. Artif. Intell. Res.* **2023**, *77*, 1113–1201. [CrossRef]
237. Blanco-Justicia, A.; Domingo-Ferrer, J.; Martínez, S.; Sánchez, D.; Flanagan, A.; Tan, K.E. Achieving security and privacy in federated learning systems: Survey, research challenges and future directions. *Eng. Appl. Artif. Intell.* **2021**, *106*, 104468. [CrossRef]
238. Wang, Y.; Sun, T.; Li, S.; Yuan, X.; Ni, W.; Hossain, E.; Poor, H.V. Adversarial attacks and defenses in machine learning-empowered communication systems and networks: A contemporary survey. *IEEE Commun. Surv. Tutorials* **2023**, 25, 2245–2298. [CrossRef]
239. Dautov, R.; Distefano, S. Quantifying volume, velocity, and variety to support (Big) data-intensive application development. In Proceedings of the 2017 IEEE International Conference on Big Data (Big Data), Boston, MA, USA, 11–14 December 2017; IEEE: Piscataway, NJ, USA, 2017; pp. 2843–2852.
240. Tang, N.; Zhang, R.; Wei, Z.; Chen, X.; Li, G.; Song, Q.; Yi, D.; Wu, Y. Improving the performance of lung nodule classification by fusing structured and unstructured data. *Inf. Fusion* **2022**, *88*, 161–174. [CrossRef]
241. Xing, Y.; Lin, X.; Suh, N.; Song, Q.; Cheng, G. Benefits of transformer: In-context learning in linear regression tasks with unstructured data. *arXiv* **2024**, arXiv:2402.00743.
242. Liao, H.; Shen, H.; Li, Z.; Wang, C.; Li, G.; Bie, Y.; Xu, C. Gpt-4 enhanced multimodal grounding for autonomous driving: Leveraging cross-modal attention with large language models. *Commun. Transp. Res.* **2024**, *4*, 100116. [CrossRef]
243. Pan, F. *End-To-End Question Answering on Semi-Structured Tabular Data*; Rensselaer Polytechnic Institute: Troy, NY, USA, 2022.
244. Ma, H.; Bian, Y.; Rong, Y.; Huang, W.; Xu, T.; Xie, W.; Ye, G.; Huang, J. Cross-dependent graph neural networks for molecular property prediction. *Bioinformatics* **2022**, *38*, 2003–2009. [CrossRef]
245. Song, Y.; Wu, P.; Dai, D.; Gui, M.; Zhang, K. GATiT: An Intelligent Diagnosis Model Based on Graph Attention Network Incorporating Text Representation in Knowledge Reasoning. *Comput. Mater. Contin.* **2024**, *80*, 4767–4790. [CrossRef]
246. Dou, Y.; Liu, Z.; Sun, L.; Deng, Y.; Peng, H.; Yu, P.S. Enhancing graph neural network-based fraud detectors against camouflaged fraudsters. In Proceedings of the 29th ACM International Conference on Information & Knowledge Management, Virtual, 19–23 October 2020; pp. 315–324.
247. Saxena, S.; Gupta, S. *Practical Real-Time Data Processing and Analytics: Distributed Computing and Event Processing Using Apache Spark, Flink, Storm, and Kafka*; Packt Publishing Ltd.: Birmingham, UK, 2017.
248. Shehzad, A.; Xia, F.; Abid, S.; Peng, C.; Yu, S.; Zhang, D.; Verspoor, K. Graph transformers: A survey. *arXiv* **2024**, arXiv:2407.09777.
249. Manne, U.K. High-Availability Database Architectures for Autonomous Vehicles: Ensuring Real-Time Performance and Reliability. *Int. J. Res. Comput. Appl. Inf. Technol.* **2024**, *7*, 785–796.
250. Bird, S.; Kenthapadi, K.; Kiciman, E.; Mitchell, M. Fairness-aware machine learning: Practical challenges and lessons learned. In Proceedings of the Twelfth ACM International Conference on Web Search and Data Mining, Melbourne, VIC, Australia, 11–15 February 2019; pp. 834–835.
251. Ferrara, E. Fairness and bias in artificial intelligence: A brief survey of sources, impacts, and mitigation strategies. *Sci* **2023**, *6*, 3. [CrossRef]
252. Howe III, E.G.; Elenberg, F. Ethical challenges posed by big data. *Innov. Clin. Neurosci.* **2020**, *17*, 24.
253. Veale, M.; Van Kleek, M.; Binns, R. Fairness and accountability design needs for algorithmic support in high-stakes public sector decision-making. In Proceedings of the 2018 Chi Conference on Human Factors in Computing Systems, Montreal, QC, Canada, 21–26 April 2018; pp. 1–14.
254. Limantė, A. Bias in Facial Recognition Technologies Used by Law Enforcement: Understanding the Causes and Searching for a Way Out. *Nord. J. Hum. Rights* **2024**, *42*, 115–134. [CrossRef]
255. Nagpal, R.; Khan, A.; Borkar, M.; Gupta, A. A Multi-Objective Framework for Balancing Fairness and Accuracy in Debiasing Machine Learning Models. *Mach. Learn. Knowl. Extr.* **2024**, *6*, 2130–2148. [CrossRef]
256. Whittlestone, J.; Arulkumaran, K.; Crosby, M. The societal implications of deep reinforcement learning. *J. Artif. Intell. Res.* **2021**, *70*, 1003–1030. [CrossRef]
257. Bontridder, N.; Poullet, Y. The role of artificial intelligence in disinformation. *Data Policy* **2021**, *3*, e32. [CrossRef]
258. Hadge, S.; Shenoy, G.S. Drift Detection in Legacy Systems Using Machine Learning Techniques. In Proceedings of the 2024 3rd International Conference for Innovation in Technology (INOCON), Bangalore, India, 1–3 March 2024; IEEE: Piscataway, NJ, USA, 2024; pp. 1–6.

259. Khabouze, R. Modernization of Legacy Information Technology Systems. Ph.D. Thesis, Walden University, Minneapolis, MN, USA, 2022.
260. Serban, A.; Visser, J. Adapting software architectures to machine learning challenges. In Proceedings of the 2022 IEEE International Conference on Software Analysis, Evolution and Reengineering (SANER), Honolulu, HI, USA, 15–18 March 2022; IEEE: Piscataway, NJ, USA, 2022; pp. 152–163.
261. Ali, M.; Hussain, S.; Ashraf, M.; Paracha, M.K. Addressing software related issues on legacy systems—A review. *Int. J. Sci. Technol. Res.* **2020**, *9*, 3738–3742.
262. Munir, M.; Jajja, M.S.S.; Chatha, K.A.; Farooq, S. Supply chain risk management and operational performance: The enabling role of supply chain integration. *Int. J. Prod. Econ.* **2020**, *227*, 107667. [CrossRef]
263. Zhu, Q.; Leibowicz, B.D. A Markov Decision Process Approach for Cost-Benefit Analysis of Infrastructure Resilience Upgrades. *Risk Anal.* **2022**, *42*, 1585–1602. [CrossRef]
264. Lodato, T.; French, E.; Clark, J. Open government data in the smart city: Interoperability, urban knowledge, and linking legacy systems. *J. Urban Aff.* **2021**, *43*, 586–600. [CrossRef]
265. Huyen, C. *Designing Machine Learning Systems*; O'Reilly Media, Inc.: Sebastopol, CA, USA, 2022.
266. Stojanović, A.; Horvat, M.; Kovačević, Ž. An overview of data integration principles for heterogeneous databases. In Proceedings of the 45th Jubilee International Convention on Information, Communication and Electronic Technology (MIPRO), Opatija, Croatia, 23–27 May 2022; IEEE: Piscataway, NJ, USA, 2022; pp. 1111–1116.
267. Wu, C.J.; Raghavendra, R.; Gupta, U.; Acun, B.; Ardalani, N.; Maeng, K.; Chang, G.; Aga, F.; Huang, J.; Bai, C.; et al. Sustainable AI: Environmental implications, challenges and opportunities. *Proc. Mach. Learn. Syst.* **2022**, *4*, 795–813.
268. Liu, X.; Lu, D.; Zhang, A.; Liu, Q.; Jiang, G. Data-driven machine learning in environmental pollution: Gains and problems. *Environ. Sci. Technol.* **2022**, *56*, 2124–2133. [CrossRef]
269. Somu, N.; MR, G.R.; Ramamritham, K. A deep learning framework for building energy consumption forecast. *Renew. Sustain. Energy Rev.* **2021**, *137*, 110591. [CrossRef]
270. Cao, Z.; Zhou, X.; Hu, H.; Wang, Z.; Wen, Y. Toward a systematic survey for carbon neutral data centers. *IEEE Commun. Surv. Tutorials* **2022**, *24*, 895–936. [CrossRef]
271. Ding, Q.; Zhu, R.; Liu, H.; Ma, M. An overview of machine learning-based energy-efficient routing algorithms in wireless sensor networks. *Electronics* **2021**, *10*, 1539. [CrossRef]
272. Nishant, R.; Kennedy, M.; Corbett, J. Artificial intelligence for sustainability: Challenges, opportunities, and a research agenda. *Int. J. Inf. Manag.* **2020**, *53*, 102104. [CrossRef]
273. Thompson, N.C.; Greenewald, K.; Lee, K.; Manso, G.F. The computational limits of deep learning. *arXiv* **2020**, arXiv:2007.05558. [CrossRef]
274. Zhong, S.; Zhang, K.; Bagheri, M.; Burken, J.G.; Gu, A.; Li, B.; Ma, X.; Marrone, B.L.; Ren, Z.J.; Schrier, J.; et al. Machine learning: New ideas and tools in environmental science and engineering. *Environ. Sci. Technol.* **2021**, *55*, 12741–12754. [CrossRef] [PubMed]
275. Salama, R.; Altrjman, C.; Al-Turjman, F. A survey of machine learning (ML) in Sustainable Systems. *NEU J. Artif. Intell. Internet Things* **2023**, *2*. Available online: https://dergi.neu.edu.tr/index.php/aiit/article/view/726 (accessed on 1 December 2024).
276. Sarswatula, S.A.; Pugh, T.; Prabhu, V. Modeling energy consumption using machine learning. *Front. Manuf. Technol.* **2022**, *2*, 855208. [CrossRef]
277. Elgabli, A.; Park, J.; Bedi, A.S.; Bennis, M.; Aggarwal, V. GADMM: Fast and communication efficient framework for distributed machine learning. *J. Mach. Learn. Res.* **2020**, *21*, 1–39.
278. Sewal, P.; Singh, H. A critical analysis of apache hadoop and spark for big data processing. In Proceedings of the 2021 6th International Conference on Signal Processing, Computing and Control (ISPCC), Solan, India, 7–9 October 2021; IEEE: Piscataway, NJ, USA, 2021; pp. 308–313.
279. Caveness, E.; GC, P.S.; Peng, Z.; Polyzotis, N.; Roy, S.; Zinkevich, M. Tensorflow data validation: Data analysis and validation in continuous ml pipelines. In Proceedings of the 2020 ACM SIGMOD International Conference on Management of Data, Portland, OR, USA, 14–19 June 2020; pp. 2793–2796.
280. Park, J.H.; Yun, G.; Chang, M.Y.; Nguyen, N.T.; Lee, S.; Choi, J.; Noh, S.H.; Choi, Y.r. {HetPipe}: Enabling large {DNN} training on (whimpy) heterogeneous {GPU} clusters through integration of pipelined model parallelism and data parallelism. In Proceedings of the 2020 USENIX Annual Technical Conference (USENIX ATC 20), Boston, MA, USA, 15–17 July 2020; pp. 307–321.
281. Li, S.; Zhao, Y.; Varma, R.; Salpekar, O.; Noordhuis, P.; Li, T.; Paszke, A.; Smith, J.; Vaughan, B.; Damania, P.; et al. Pytorch distributed: Experiences on accelerating data parallel training. *arXiv* **2020**, arXiv:2006.15704. [CrossRef]
282. Huang, Y.; Cheng, Y.; Bapna, A.; Firat, O.; Chen, D.; Chen, M.; Lee, H.; Ngiam, J.; Le, Q.V.; Wu, Y.; et al. Gpipe: Efficient training of giant neural networks using pipeline parallelism. *Adv. Neural Inf. Process. Syst.* **2019**, *32*, 103–112.
283. Khaire, U.M.; Dhanalakshmi, R. High-dimensional microarray dataset classification using an improved adam optimizer (iAdam). *J. Ambient Intell. Humaniz. Comput.* **2020**, *11*, 5187–5204. [CrossRef]

284. Shen, L.; Sun, Y.; Yu, Z.; Ding, L.; Tian, X.; Tao, D. On Efficient Training of Large-Scale Deep Learning Models. *Acm Comput. Surv.* **2024**, *57*, 1–36.
285. Salehin, I.; Islam, M.S.; Saha, P.; Noman, S.; Tuni, A.; Hasan, M.M.; Baten, M.A. AutoML: A systematic review on automated machine learning with neural architecture search. *J. Inf. Intell.* **2024**, *2*, 52–81. [CrossRef]
286. van Stein, B.; Wang, H.; Bäck, T. Neural network design: Learning from neural architecture search. In Proceedings of the 2020 IEEE Symposium Series on Computational Intelligence (SSCI), Canberra, ACT, Australia, 1–4 December 2020; IEEE: Piscataway, NJ, USA, 2020; pp. 1341–1349.
287. Filippou, K.; Aifantis, G.; Papakostas, G.A.; Tsekouras, G.E. Structure learning and hyperparameter optimization using an automated machine learning (AutoML) pipeline. *Information* **2023**, *14*, 232. [CrossRef]
288. Shomron, G.; Gabbay, F.; Kurzum, S.; Weiser, U. Post-training sparsity-aware quantization. *Adv. Neural Inf. Process. Syst.* **2021**, *34*, 17737–17748.
289. Zhou, A.; Yang, J.; Qi, Y.; Shi, Y.; Qiao, T.; Zhao, W.; Hu, C. Hardware-aware graph neural network automated design for edge computing platforms. In Proceedings of the 2023 60th ACM/IEEE Design Automation Conference (DAC), San Francisco, CA, USA, 9–13 July 2023; IEEE: Piscataway, NJ, USA, 2023; pp. 1–6.
290. Nikolić, G.S.; Dimitrijević, B.R.; Nikolić, T.R.; Stojcev, M.K. A survey of three types of processing units: CPU, GPU and TPU. In Proceedings of the 2022 57th International Scientific Conference on Information, Communication and Energy Systems and Technologies (ICEST), Ohrid, North Macedonia, 16–18 June 2022; IEEE: Piscataway, NJ, USA, 2022; pp. 1–6.
291. Ren, J.; Xia, D. Deep Learning ASIC Design. In *Autonomous Driving Algorithms and Its IC Design*; Springer: Berlin/Heidelberg, Germany, 2023; pp. 201–224.
292. Sehgal, N.K.; Bhatt, P.C.P.; Acken, J.M. *Cloud Computing with Security and Scalability*; Springer: Berlin/Heidelberg, Germany, 2020.
293. Xu, H.; Song, S.; Mao, Z. Characterizing the performance of emerging deep learning, graph, and high performance computing workloads under interference. In Proceedings of the 2024 IEEE International Parallel and Distributed Processing Symposium Workshops (IPDPSW), San Francisco, CA, USA, 27–31 May 2024; IEEE: Piscataway, NJ, USA, 2024; pp. 468–477.
294. Nedic, A. Distributed gradient methods for convex machine learning problems in networks: Distributed optimization. *IEEE Signal Process. Mag.* **2020**, *37*, 92–101. [CrossRef]
295. Marino, R.; Wisultschew, C.; Otero, A.; Lanza-Gutierrez, J.M.; Portilla, J.; de la Torre, E. A machine-learning-based distributed system for fault diagnosis with scalable detection quality in industrial IoT. *IEEE Internet Things J.* **2020**, *8*, 4339–4352. [CrossRef]
296. Schlegel, M.; Sattler, K.U. Management of machine learning lifecycle artifacts: A survey. *ACM SIGMOD Rec.* **2023**, *51*, 18–35. [CrossRef]
297. Wang, M.; Fu, W.; He, X.; Hao, S.; Wu, X. A survey on large-scale machine learning. *IEEE Trans. Knowl. Data Eng.* **2020**, *34*, 2574–2594. [CrossRef]
298. Mane, D.; Magar, A.; Khode, O.; Koli, S.; Bhat, K.; Korade, P. Unlocking machine learning model decisions: A comparative analysis of LIME and SHAP for enhanced interpretability. *J. Electr. Syst.* **2024**, *20*, 1252–1267.
299. Vij, A.; Nanjundan, P. Comparing strategies for post-hoc explanations in machine learning models. In *Mobile Computing and Sustainable Informatics: Proceedings of ICMCSI 2021*; Springer: Berlin/Heidelberg, Germany, 2022; pp. 585–592.
300. Thunki, P.; Reddy, S.R.B.; Raparthi, M.; Maruthi, S.; Dodda, S.B.; Ravichandran, P. Explainable AI in Data Science-Enhancing Model Interpretability and Transparency. *Afr. J. Artif. Intell. Sustain. Dev.* **2021**, *1*, 1–8.
301. Goh, G.S.; Lapuschkin, S.; Weber, L.; Samek, W.; Binder, A. Understanding integrated gradients with smooth Taylor for deep neural network attribution. In Proceedings of the 25th International Conference on Pattern Recognition (ICPR), Milan, Italy, 10–15 January 2021; IEEE: Piscataway, NJ, USA, 2021; pp. 4949–4956.
302. Davydko, O.; Pavlov, V.; Biecek, P.; Longo, L. SRFAMap: A Method for Mapping Integrated Gradients of a CNN Trained with Statistical Radiomic Features to Medical Image Saliency Maps. In Proceedings of the World Conference on Explainable Artificial Intelligence, Valletta, Malta, 17–19 July 2024; Springer: Berlin/Heidelberg, Germany, 2024; pp. 3–23.
303. Kwon, H.J.; Koo, H.I.; Cho, N.I. Improving explainability of integrated gradients with guided non-linearity. In Proceedings of the 2020 25th International Conference on Pattern Recognition (ICPR), Milan, Italy, 10–15 January 2021; IEEE: Piscataway, NJ, USA, 2021; pp. 385–391.
304. Delaunay, J.; Galárraga, L.; Largouët, C. Improving anchor-based explanations. In Proceedings of the 29th ACM International Conference on Information & Knowledge Management, Virtual, 19–23 October 2020; pp. 3269–3272.
305. Watson, D.S.; Floridi, L. The explanation game: A formal framework for interpretable machine learning. In *Ethics, Governance, and Policies in Artificial Intelligence*; Springer: Berlin/Heidelberg, Germany, 2021; pp. 185–219.
306. Mothilal, R.K.; Sharma, A.; Tan, C. Explaining machine learning classifiers through diverse counterfactual explanations. In Proceedings of the 2020 Conference on Fairness, Accountability, and Transparency, Barcelona, Spain, 27–30 January 2020; pp. 607–617.

307. Singh, J.; Rani, S.; Srilakshmi, G. Towards Explainable AI: Interpretable Models for Complex Decision-making. In Proceedings of the 2024 International Conference on Knowledge Engineering and Communication Systems (ICKECS), Chikkaballapur, India, 18–19 April 2024; IEEE: Piscataway, NJ, USA, 2024; Volume 1, pp. 1–5.
308. Yang, Y.; Yi, Y.; Wang, W.; Zhou, Y.; Yang, Z. Generalized additive models for biomass simulation of submerged macrophytes in a shallow lake. *Sci. Total Environ.* **2020**, *711*, 135108. [CrossRef]
309. Agarwal, R.; Melnick, L.; Frosst, N.; Zhang, X.; Lengerich, B.; Caruana, R.; Hinton, G.E. Neural additive models: Interpretable machine learning with neural nets. *Adv. Neural Inf. Process. Syst.* **2021**, *34*, 4699–4711.
310. Tutek, M.; Šnajder, J. Toward practical usage of the attention mechanism as a tool for interpretability. *IEEE Access* **2022**, *10*, 47011–47030. [CrossRef]
311. Ekman, M. *Learning Deep Learning: Theory and Practice of Neural Networks, Computer Vision, Natural Language Processing, and Transformers Using TensorFlow*; Addison-Wesley Professional: Boston, MA, USA, 2021.
312. Dehimi, N.E.H.; Tolba, Z. Attention Mechanisms in Deep Learning: Towards Explainable Artificial Intelligence. In Proceedings of the 6th International Conference on Pattern Analysis and Intelligent Systems (PAIS), El Oued, Algeria, 24–25 April 2024; IEEE: Piscataway, NJ, USA, 2024; pp. 1–7.
313. Čík, I.; Rasamoelina, A.D.; Mach, M.; Sinčák, P. Explaining deep neural network using layer-wise relevance propagation and integrated gradients. In Proceedings of the 19th World Symposium on Applied Machine Intelligence and Informatics (SAMI), Herl'any, Slovakia, 21–23 January 2021; IEEE: Piscataway, NJ, USA, 2021; pp. 000381–000386.
314. Verma, S.; Boonsanong, V.; Hoang, M.; Hines, K.E.; Dickerson, J.P.; Shah C. Counterfactual explanations and Algorithmic Recourses for machine learning: A review. *Acm Comput. Surv.* **2024**, *56*. Available online: https://dl.acm.org/doi/pdf/10.1145/3677119 (accessed on 1 December 2024). [CrossRef]
315. Mohankumar, A.K.; Nema, P.; Narasimhan, S.; Khapra, M.M.; Srinivasan, B.V.; Ravindran, B. Towards transparent and explainable attention models. *arXiv* **2020**, arXiv:2004.14243.
316. Raufi, B.; Finnegan, C.; Longo, L. A Comparative Analysis of SHAP, LIME, ANCHORS, and DICE for Interpreting a Dense Neural Network in Credit Card Fraud Detection. In Proceedings of the World Conference on Explainable Artificial Intelligence, Valletta, Malta, 17–19 July 2024; Springer: Berlin/Heidelberg, Germany, 2024; pp. 365–383.
317. Rudin, C.; Chen, C.; Chen, Z.; Huang, H.; Semenova, L.; Zhong, C. Interpretable machine learning: Fundamental principles and 10 grand challenges. *Stat. Surv.* **2022**, *16*, 1–85. [CrossRef]
318. Bell, A.; Solano-Kamaiko, I.; Nov, O.; Stoyanovich, J. It's just not that simple: An empirical study of the accuracy-explainability trade-off in machine learning for public policy. In Proceedings of the 2022 ACM Conference on Fairness, Accountability, and Transparency, Seoul, Republic of Korea, 21–24 June 2022; pp. 248–266.
319. Murdoch, W.J.; Singh, C.; Kumbier, K.; Abbasi-Asl, R.; Yu, B. Interpretable machine learning: Definitions, methods, and applications. *arXiv* **2019**, arXiv:1901.04592. [CrossRef] [PubMed]
320. Fang, H.; Qian, Q. Privacy preserving machine learning with homomorphic encryption and federated learning. *Future Internet* **2021**, *13*, 94. [CrossRef]
321. Yang, M.; Guo, T.; Zhu, T.; Tjuawinata, I.; Zhao, J.; Lam, K.Y. Local differential privacy and its applications: A comprehensive survey. *Comput. Stand. Interfaces* **2023**, *89*, 103827. [CrossRef]
322. Li, Z.; Sharma, V.; Mohanty, S.P. Preserving data privacy via federated learning: Challenges and solutions. *IEEE Consum. Electron. Mag.* **2020**, *9*, 8–16. [CrossRef]
323. Dritsas, E.; Trigka, M.; Mylonas, P. A Survey on Privacy-Enhancing Techniques in the Era of Artificial Intelligence. In Proceedings of the Novel & Intelligent Digital Systems Conferences, Athens, Greece, 25–27 September 2024; Springer Nature: Cham, Switzerland, 2024; pp. 385–392.
324. Dritsas, E.; Trigka, M. Federated Learning for IoT: A Survey of Techniques, Challenges, and Applications. *J. Sens. Actuator Networks* **2025**, *14*, 9. [CrossRef]
325. Dash, B.; Sharma, P.; Ali, A. Federated learning for privacy-preserving: A review of PII data analysis in Fintech. *Int. J. Softw. Eng. Appl. (IJSEA)* **2022**, *13*. Available online: https://ssrn.com/abstract=4323967 (accessed on 1 December 2024). [CrossRef]
326. Ma, J.; Naas, S.A.; Sigg, S.; Lyu, X. Privacy-preserving federated learning based on multi-key homomorphic encryption. *Int. J. Intell. Syst.* **2022**, *37*, 5880–5901. [CrossRef]
327. Huang, Y.; Qiao, X.; Dustdar, S.; Zhang, J.; Li, J. Toward decentralized and collaborative deep learning inference for intelligent IoT devices. *IEEE Netw.* **2022**, *36*, 59–68. [CrossRef]
328. Dritsas, E.; Trigka, M. A Survey on Cybersecurity in IoT. *Future Internet* **2025**, *17*, 30. [CrossRef]
329. Liu, Z.; Guo, J.; Lam, K.Y.; Zhao, J. Efficient dropout-resilient aggregation for privacy-preserving machine learning. *IEEE Trans. Inf. Forensics Secur.* **2022**, *18*, 1839–1854. [CrossRef]
330. Qin, H.; He, D.; Feng, Q.; Khan, M.K.; Luo, M.; Choo, K.K.R. Cryptographic Primitives in Privacy-Preserving Machine Learning: A Survey. *IEEE Trans. Knowl. Data Eng.* **2023**, *36*, 1919–1934. [CrossRef]

331. Xu, H.; Chen, M.; Meng, Z.; Xu, Y.; Wang, L.; Qiao, C. Decentralized machine learning through experience-driven method in edge networks. *IEEE J. Sel. Areas Commun.* **2021**, *40*, 515–531. [CrossRef]
332. Wei, K.; Li, J.; Ding, M.; Ma, C.; Yang, H.H.; Farokhi, F.; Jin, S.; Quek, T.Q.; Poor, H.V. Federated learning with differential privacy: Algorithms and performance analysis. *IEEE Trans. Inf. Forensics Secur.* **2020**, *15*, 3454–3469. [CrossRef]
333. Mahrishi, M.; Hiran, K.K.; Meena, G.; Sharma, P. *Machine Learning and Deep Learning in Real-Time Applications*; IGI Global: Hershey, PA, USA, 2020.
334. Akhtar, M.S.; Chauhan, D.S.; Ekbal, A. A deep multi-task contextual attention framework for multi-modal affect analysis. *ACM Trans. Knowl. Discov. Data (TKDD)* **2020**, *14*, 1–27. [CrossRef]
335. Bozkurt, A.; Ekici, F.; Yetiskul, H. Utilizing Flink and Kafka Technologies for Real-Time Data Processing: A Case Study. *Eurasia Proc. Sci. Technol. Eng. Math.* **2023**, *24*, 177–183. [CrossRef]
336. Huang, Y.; Du, C.; Xue, Z.; Chen, X.; Zhao, H.; Huang, L. What makes multi-modal learning better than single (provably). *Adv. Neural Inf. Process. Syst.* **2021**, *34*, 10944–10956.
337. Guarascio, M.; Folino, G.; Chiaravalloti, F.; Gabriele, S.; Procopio, A.; Sabatino, P. A machine learning approach for rainfall estimation integrating heterogeneous data sources. *IEEE Trans. Geosci. Remote Sens.* **2020**, *60*, 1–11. [CrossRef]
338. Altameem, T.; Altameem, A. Facial expression recognition using human machine interaction and multi-modal visualization analysis for healthcare applications. *Image Vis. Comput.* **2020**, *103*, 104044. [CrossRef]
339. Goyal, P.; Sahu, S.; Ghosh, S.; Lee, C. Cross-modal learning for multi-modal video categorization. *arXiv* **2020**, arXiv:2003.03501.
340. Dhiman, G.; Kumar, A.V.; Nirmalan, R.; Sujitha, S.; Srihari, K.; Yuvaraj, N.; Arulprakash, P.; Raja, R.A. Multi-modal active learning with deep reinforcement learning for target feature extraction in multi-media image processing applications. *Multimed. Tools Appl.* **2023**, *82*, 5343–5367. [CrossRef]
341. Xu, W.; He, J.; Shu, Y. Transfer learning and deep domain adaptation. *Adv. Appl. Deep Learn.* **2020**, *45*.
342. Song, B.; Zhou, R.; Ahmed, F. Multi-modal machine learning in engineering design: A review and future directions. *J. Comput. Inf. Sci. Eng.* **2024**, *24*, 010801. [CrossRef]
343. Vesnic-Alujevic, L.; Nascimento, S.; Polvora, A. Societal and ethical impacts of artificial intelligence: Critical notes on European policy frameworks. *Telecommun. Policy* **2020**, *44*, 101961. [CrossRef]
344. Mehrabi, N.; Morstatter, F.; Saxena, N.; Lerman, K.; Galstyan, A. A survey on bias and fairness in machine learning. *ACM Comput. Surv. (CSUR)* **2021**, *54*, 1–35. [CrossRef]
345. Le Quy, T.; Roy, A.; Iosifidis, V.; Zhang, W.; Ntoutsi, E. A survey on datasets for fairness-aware machine learning. *Wiley Interdiscip. Rev. Data Min. Knowl. Discov.* **2022**, *12*, e1452. [CrossRef]
346. Petrović, A.; Nikolić, M.; Radovanović, S.; Delibašić, B.; Jovanović, M. FAIR: Fair adversarial instance re-weighting. *Neurocomputing* **2022**, *476*, 14–37. [CrossRef]
347. Rane, N.; Choudhary, S.; Rane, J. Explainable Artificial Intelligence (XAI) Approaches for Transparency and Accountability in Financial Decision-Making. *SSRN*. 2023. Available online: https://ssrn.com/abstract=4640316 (accessed on 5 December 2024). [CrossRef]
348. Tiwari, R. The impact of AI and machine learning on job displacement and employment opportunities. *Int. J. Eng. Technol. Manag. Res.* **2023**, *7*. [CrossRef]
349. Ramarajan, M.; Dinesh, A.; Muthuraman, C.; Rajini, J.; Anand, T.; Segar, B. AI-Driven Job Displacement and Economic Impacts: Ethics and Strategies for Implementation. In *Cases on AI Ethics in Business*; IGI Global: Hershey, PA, USA, 2024; pp. 216–238.
350. Prem, E. From ethical AI frameworks to tools: A review of approaches. *AI Ethics* **2023**, *3*, 699–716. [CrossRef]
351. Santosh, K.; Gaur, L. *Artificial Intelligence and Machine Learning in Public Healthcare: Opportunities and Societal Impact*; Springer Nature: Berlin/Heidelberg, Germany, 2022.
352. Loi, M.; Heitz, C.; Christen, M. A comparative assessment and synthesis of twenty ethics codes on AI and big data. In Proceedings of the 2020 7th Swiss Conference on Data Science (SDS), Luzern, Switzerland, 26–26 June 2020; IEEE: Piscataway, NJ, USA, 2020; pp. 41–46.
353. Li, F.; Yigitcanlar, T.; Nepal, M.; Nguyen, K.; Dur, F. Machine learning and remote sensing integration for leveraging urban sustainability: A review and framework. *Sustain. Cities Soc.* **2023**, *96*, 104653. [CrossRef]
354. Kumar, M.; Zhang, X.; Liu, L.; Wang, Y.; Shi, W. Energy-efficient machine learning on the edges. In Proceedings of the 2020 IEEE International Parallel and Distributed Processing Symposium Workshops (IPDPSW), New Orleans, LA, USA, 18–22 May 2020; IEEE: Piscataway, NJ, USA, 2020; pp. 912–921.
355. Issa, J.; Abdulrahman, L.M.; Abdullah, R.M.; Sami, T.M.G.; Wasfi, B. AI-powered Sustainability Management in Enterprise Systems based on Cloud and Web Technology: Integrating IoT Data for Environmental Impact Reduction. *J. Inf. Technol. Inform.* **2024**, *3*, 154.

356. Hassan, M.B.; Saeed, R.A.; Khalifa, O.; Ali, E.S.; Mokhtar, R.A.; Hashim, A.A. Green machine learning for green cloud energy efficiency. In Proceedings of the 2022 IEEE 2nd International Maghreb Meeting of the Conference on Sciences and Techniques of Automatic Control and Computer Engineering (MI-STA), Sabratha, Libya, 23–25 May 2022; IEEE: Piscataway, NJ, USA, 2022; pp. 288–294.
357. Bhuiyan, M. Carbon Footprint Measurement and Mitigation Using AI. *SSRN*. 2024. Available online: https://ssrn.com/abstract=4746446 (accessed on 5 December 2024).
358. Sapnken, F.E.; Hamed, M.M.; Soldo, B.; Tamba, J.G. Modeling energy-efficient building loads using machine-learning algorithms for the design phase. *Energy Build.* **2023**, *283*, 112807. [CrossRef]
359. de la Torre, R.; Corlu, C.G.; Faulin, J.; Onggo, B.S.; Juan, A.A. Simulation, optimization, and machine learning in sustainable transportation systems: Models and applications. *Sustainability* **2021**, *13*, 1551. [CrossRef]
360. Zhou, R.; Zheng, T.; Wang, X.; Wang, L.; Sirvent-Hien, E. Capability and Applicability of Measurement Tools for AI Model's Environmental Impact. *Comput. Tools* **2023**, *2023*, 1–8.
361. Mucha, T.; Ma, S.; Abhari, K. Sustainability of Machine Learning-based Solutions: A Lifecycle Perspective. In Proceedings of the Pacific Asia Conference on Information Systems. Association for Information Systems, Sydney, Australia, 5–9 July 2022; p. 1191.
362. Chakraborty, S.; Dey, L. Quantum Computing in Machine Learning. In *Computing for Data Analysis: Theory and Practices*; Springer: Berlin/Heidelberg, Germany, 2023; pp. 161–178.
363. Peters, E.; Caldeira, J.; Ho, A.; Leichenauer, S.; Mohseni, M.; Neven, H.; Spentzouris, P.; Strain, D.; Perdue, G.N. Machine learning of high dimensional data on a noisy quantum processor. *Npj Quantum Inf.* **2021**, *7*, 161. [CrossRef]
364. Kavitha, S.; Kaulgud, N. Quantum machine learning for support vector machine classification. *Evol. Intell.* **2024**, *17*, 819–828. [CrossRef]
365. Abbas, A.; Sutter, D.; Zoufal, C.; Lucchi, A.; Figalli, A.; Woerner, S. The power of quantum neural networks. *Nat. Comput. Sci.* **2021**, *1*, 403–409. [CrossRef]
366. Zhang, Y.; Ni, Q. Recent advances in quantum machine learning. *Quantum Eng.* **2020**, *2*, e34. [CrossRef]
367. Lubinski, T.; Granade, C.; Anderson, A.; Geller, A.; Roetteler, M.; Petrenko, A.; Heim, B. Advancing hybrid quantum–classical computation with real-time execution. *Front. Phys.* **2022**, *10*, 940293. [CrossRef]
368. Riel, H. Quantum computing technology. In Proceedings of the 2021 IEEE International Electron Devices Meeting (IEDM), San Francisco, CA, USA, 11–16 December 2021; IEEE: Piscataway, NJ, USA, 2021; pp. 1–3.
369. Mensa, S.; Sahin, E.; Tacchino, F.; Kl Barkoutsos, P.; Tavernelli, I. Quantum machine learning framework for virtual screening in drug discovery: A prospective quantum advantage. *Mach. Learn. Sci. Technol.* **2023**, *4*, 015023. [CrossRef]
370. Mallow, G.M.; Hornung, A.; Barajas, J.N.; Rudisill, S.S.; An, H.S.; Samartzis, D. Quantum computing: The future of big data and artificial intelligence in spine. *Spine Surg. Relat. Res.* **2022**, *6*, 93–98. [CrossRef]
371. Maheshwari, D.; Garcia-Zapirain, B.; Sierra-Soso, D. Machine learning applied to diabetes dataset using Quantum versus Classical computation. In Proceedings of the 2020 IEEE International Symposium on Signal Processing and Information Technology (ISSPIT), Louisville, KY, USA, 9–11 December 2020; IEEE: Piscataway, NJ, USA, 2020; pp. 1–6.
372. Ivanova, N.; Volkov, D.; Morozov, P.; Sokolova, O. Quantum Computing and Machine Learning Integration: Challenges and Opportunities. *J. Deep Learn. Genom. Data Anal.* **2024**, *4*, 42–58.
373. Anjos, J.C.D.; Matteussi, K.J.; Orlandi, F.C.; Barbosa, J.L.; Silva, J.S.; Bittencourt, L.F.; Geyer, C.F. A survey on collaborative learning for intelligent autonomous systems. *ACM Comput. Surv.* **2023**, *56*, 1–37. [CrossRef]
374. Pan, S.J. Transfer learning. *Learning* **2020**, *21*, 1–2.
375. Savelka, J.; Westermann, H.; Benyekhlef, K. Cross-domain generalization and knowledge transfer in transformers trained on legal data. *arXiv* **2021**, arXiv:2112.07870.
376. Li, Q.; Wen, Z.; Wu, Z.; Hu, S.; Wang, N.; Li, Y.; Liu, X.; He, B. A survey on federated learning systems: Vision, hype and reality for data privacy and protection. *IEEE Trans. Knowl. Data Eng.* **2021**, *35*, 3347–3366. [CrossRef]
377. Haraldseid-Driftland, C.; Billett, S.; Guise, V.; Schibevaag, L.; Alsvik, J.G.; Fagerdal, B.; Lyng, H.B.; Wiig, S. The role of collaborative learning in resilience in healthcare—A thematic qualitative meta-synthesis of resilience narratives. *BMC Health Serv. Res.* **2022**, *22*, 1091. [CrossRef] [PubMed]
378. Mammen, P.M. Federated learning: Opportunities and challenges. *arXiv* **2021**, arXiv:2101.05428.
379. Thapa, C.; Chamikara, M.A.P.; Camtepe, S.A. Advancements of federated learning towards privacy preservation: From federated learning to split learning. In *Federated Learning Systems: Towards Next-Generation AI*; Springer: Cham, Switzerland, 2021; pp. 79–109.
380. Tan, S.C.; Lee, A.V.Y.; Lee, M. A systematic review of artificial intelligence techniques for collaborative learning over the past two decades. *Comput. Educ. Artif. Intell.* **2022**, *3*, 100097. [CrossRef]

381. Qiu, M.; Li, P.; Wang, C.; Pan, H.; Wang, A.; Chen, C.; Jia, X.; Li, Y.; Huang, J.; Cai, D.; et al. Easytransfer: A simple and scalable deep transfer learning platform for NLP applications. In Proceedings of the 30th ACM International Conference on Information & Knowledge Management, Virtual, 1–5 November 2021; pp. 4075–4084.
382. Bozdemir, B. Privacy-Preserving Machine Learning Techniques. Ph.D. Thesis, Sorbonne Université, Paris, France, 2021.

machine learning & knowledge extraction

MDPI

*Article*

# Advancing Life Cycle Assessment of Sustainable Green Hydrogen Production Using Domain-Specific Fine-Tuning by Large Language Models Augmentation

**Yajing Chen [1,*], Urs Liebau [2], Shreyas Mysore Guruprasad [2], Iaroslav Trofimenko [2] and Christine Minke [1]**

[1] Institute of Mineral and Waste Processing, Recycling and Circular Economy Systems, Clausthal University of Technology, 38678 Clausthal-Zellerfeld, Germany; christine.minke@tu-clausthal.de
[2] Center for Digital Green Tech, August-Wilhelm-Scheer Institute, 38678 Clausthal-Zellerfeld, Germany; urs.liebau@aws-institut.de (U.L.); shreyas.mysoreguruprasad@aws-institut.de (S.M.G.)
* Correspondence: yajing.chen@tu-clausthal.de

**Abstract:** Assessing the sustainable development of green hydrogen and assessing its potential environmental impacts using the Life Cycle Assessment is crucial. Challenges in LCA, like missing environmental data, are often addressed using machine learning, such as artificial neural networks. However, to find an ML solution, researchers need to read extensive literature or consult experts. This research demonstrates how customised LLMs, trained with domain-specific papers, can help researchers overcome these challenges. By starting small by consolidating papers focused on the LCA of proton exchange membrane water electrolysis, which produces green hydrogen, and ML applications in LCA. These papers are uploaded to OpenAI to create the LlamaIndex, enabling future queries. Using the LangChain framework, researchers query the customised model (GPT-3.5-turbo), receiving tailored responses. The results demonstrate that customised LLMs can assist researchers in providing suitable ML solutions to address data inaccuracies and gaps. The ability to quickly query an LLM and receive an integrated response across relevant sources presents an improvement over manually retrieving and reading individual papers. This shows that leveraging fine-tuned LLMs can empower researchers to conduct LCAs more efficiently and effectively.

**Keywords:** life cycle assessment; green hydrogen; machine learning; customised large language model

## 1. Introduction

Green hydrogen is crucial for the future of renewable energy [1], and water electrolysis for hydrogen production is used to produce green hydrogen by utilising electricity generated from renewable energy sources [2]. Currently, the primary mature technologies for water electrolysis include Proton Exchange Membrane Water Electrolysis (PEMWE), Alkaline Water Electrolysis (AWE) and Solid Oxide Electrolysis Cells (SOEC) [2]. PEMWE boasts higher hydrogen production efficiency compared to AWE [3], while SOEC is not yet feasible for large-scale commercialisation [4]. Compared to AWE and SOEC, PEMWE offers greater adaptability to renewable energy sources [3] and is considered the most promising technology in terms of sustainability and environmental impact [4]. To measure the environmental impact of PEMWE in green hydrogen production, it is essential to assess its life cycle using the Life Cycle Assessment (LCA) approach. The LCA will comprehensively analyse the potential environmental impacts of PEMWE to optimise its application and improve overall sustainability [5,6].

However, conducting an LCA faces challenges, particularly related to data issues such as inaccuracies and missing environmental data [7]. Machine learning (ML) has emerged as a promising solution to address these challenges. Many studies have shown that it can effectively help solve the data-related challenges in LCA, such as using artificial neural networks (ANNs) to estimate the missing data or predict potential future environmental

*Mach. Learn. Knowl. Extr.* **2024**, *6*, 2494–2514. https://doi.org/10.3390/make6040122 https://www.mdpi.com/journal/make

impacts, thereby improving the accuracy and reliability of LCA [7]. However, finding these ML methods typically requires a significant time investment in reviewing the literature or consulting experts. Therefore, in this paper, the idea of using customised large language models (LLMs) to help find suitable ML solutions to address LCA challenges is presented.

Large Language Models (LLMs) have emerged as cutting-edge artificial intelligence systems that can process and generate text with coherent communication [8], and generalise to multiple tasks [9–11]. Although pre-trained LLMs have excellent generalisation capabilities, they must be fine-tuned to follow specific instructions and generate safe responses [12] for effective utilisation. Contextual augmentation helps LLMs to learn from the examples of concatenated inputs. This enables the LLMs to answer specific queries beyond the capacity acquired during training by producing factually correct and safe responses [9]. Studies such as [13,14] explore the strengths, weaknesses, risks and opportunities associated with leveraging LLMs to support LCA practitioners. These studies also evaluate the capability of generalised LLMs to perform various LCA tasks. Their findings suggest that LLMs have considerable potential to enhance the development of life cycle inventories and to effectively summarise and communicate LCA results. This, in turn, could lead to improved LCA quality while significantly reducing the time required to complete an assessment. LLMs are used in this study as they show significant potential for providing qualitative and quick research, which allows optimisation of time and resources spent in the drafting stage of an idea [15]. In this study, the LLM models were trained with research papers related to the LCA of PEMWE and the application of ML in LCA. When researchers query the customised LLM, the responses are tailored to specific queries. The results indicate that the customised LLMs significantly assist researchers in producing valuable outcomes by identifying appropriate ML solutions to address data inaccuracies and gaps. This underscores how leveraging LLMs empowers researchers to conduct LCAs more efficiently and effectively.

The Section 2 of the paper provides a brief theoretical background on LCA, PEMWE, and issues encountered in conducting LCA for PEMWE and LLMs. Section 3 extensively explains the methods used in the study, including the fine-tuning strategy of LLMs and prompt generation techniques. Section 4 presents the results and discussion of the customised LLMs' responses to five example questions. The Section 5 summarises all findings, highlighting how LLMs can significantly assist researchers in managing the complexities of LCA by offering qualitative insights and suggesting appropriate ML approaches to address data inaccuracies and deficiencies. The strengths and weaknesses of the customised LLMs are summarised along with a discussion of the approaches which are required to improve the results in the future.

## 2. Background

### 2.1. Life Cycle Assessment

LCA is a comprehensive methodology that evaluates the environmental impacts of all stages of a product's life cycle, from raw material extraction to production, use and disposal. The four phases for conducting an LCA as outlined by ISO 14040 and ISO 14044 are as follows [5,6]:

1. Goal and Scope Definition: Defining the assessment's purpose, scope and boundaries.
2. Life Cycle Inventory (LCI): Collecting data on the inputs and calculating the potential environmental outputs of the product system, collecting input data and calculating the product system's potential environmental outputs.
3. Life Cycle Impact Assessment (LCIA): Categorising and evaluating potential environmental impacts based on the LCI results.
4. Interpretation: Analysing results to make informed decisions.

### 2.2. General LCA Challenges and Application of ML Techniques

In this section, examples are used to showcase the challenges that exist in LCA studies and provide methods using ML that have been employed to address these challenges.

- Data Gaps: Environmental results generated from LCI databases frequently exhibit inconsistencies or gaps in data availability [7]. For example, Kalverkamp et al. [16] presented the issue of lacking suitable environmental data for different regions. Their case study showed that the ecoinvent database had limitations in providing environmental data for raw materials manufactured in China [16]. In this context, the only China-specific data used are for "electricity, medium voltage, at grid", "lithium hexafluorophosphate, at plant" and "ethylene carbonate, at plant" [16]. For other components and processes relevant to China, they had to rely on global average data provided by ecoinvent [16]. This data gap underscores the challenges in conducting accurate lifecycle assessments with incomplete regional. Furthermore, existing datasets often contain outdated information and require updates to reflect current practises, such as adjusting input data for solar panels based on the electricity source [17].
  To address these challenges, according to the literature review from Romeiko et al. [7], several studies about LCA have utilised approaches such as linear regression models, artificial neural networks (ANN) and random forest algorithms to predict or estimate environmental emissions, such as greenhouse gas emissions or the release of organic chemicals during the operational phase [7]. Additionally, these approaches are used to predict missing product characteristics, for example, forecasting biobased chemicals derived from hydrothermal treatment [7].
- Uncertainty: Variability in data sources and methods can introduce significant uncertainty into the LCA results. As summarised in Romeiko et al., challenges in interpreting LCA results include identifying where the highest impact lies (identifying hotspots), which involves conducting uncertainty and sensitivity analysis [7]. Questions arise regarding why these hotspots occur, what factors contribute to them and how they can be mitigated. ML approaches such as ANN, ANFIS, BRT, random forest, genetic algorithms, centroid-based clustering and logistic regression can be utilised for analysing the uncertainty and sensitivity of LCA results [7].

These examples only illustrate some of the challenges that arise in LCA and their corresponding ML solutions. In addition to these challenges, there are other issues in LCA, such as how to select LCI databases and LCIA methods.

The variability in environmental outcomes across different LCI databases poses a challenge in determining which database to prioritise, such as choosing between ecoinvent [18] and Sphera database (formerly known as the GaBi database) [19,20]. The reasons for making a choice include, as highlighted by Pauer et al. [19], that in many cases, the ecoinvent contains considerably more background processes (e.g., wear and tear of infrastructure, maintenance work, etc.) than Sphera [19]. For example, the generation of 1 kWh of electricity from nuclear energy in Germany shows that the result for "ionising radiation" in ecoinvent is twice as high as in Sphera [19]. This higher value in ecoinvent is mainly due to the dumping of overburden from uranium ore mining [19]. Furthermore, choosing between different databases also involves considering their data transparency and the flexibility to tailor the data according to users' requirements [21].

The variability in results can also be derived from different LCIA methods [19,22–24]. LCIA can be conducted at two assessment levels: midpoint and endpoint [25]. Different LCIA methods categorise LCI results differently, for example, ReCiPe 2016 normalised the characterisation factors (LCI results) into different midpoint environmental categories [26]. Normalisation allows users to see the relative contribution of each impact category to the overall system, which is particularly useful when addressing specific regional environmental challenges [25]. At the endpoint level assessments can be normalised or weighted, and only the EF v3.0 method can obtain weighted results at the midpoint level and the endpoint level and combine them into a single score [27]. For example, in the study by Domingo-Morcillo et al. [25] on the LCA of food loss and waste prevention and reduction, they aimed to clarify which impact categories are more significant through weighting, making it suitable for comparing and selecting the "best option", thereby providing a comprehensive basis for decision-making [25]. However, for non-LCA professionals, distinguishing between each LCIA method and selecting the most appropriate one based on their needs can be a challenging task.

### 2.3. LCA for PEMWE and Its Challenges

In this section, the different phases of LCA for PEMWE are introduced and the corresponding challenges identified are described. The life of a PEMWE can be divided into three main phases: construction, operation and end of life [28,29]. During the construction phase, the entire PEMWE plant will be built [28]. In the operation phase, the plant will produce hydrogen from electricity and water [28]. The end-of-life phase occurs when the plant reaches the end of its lifespan and faces either disposal or recycling [28]. To understand the potential environmental impact of the entire life cycle of a PEMWE plant, its LCA can be conducted in four phases according to ISO 14040 and 14044 [5,6].

Phase 1: This phase involves defining the system boundaries and the purpose of conducting the LCA. This includes specifying where the PEMWE plant is analysed (geographical boundary), the operational lifespan of PEMWE (time boundary), etc. [5,6]. Additionally, define the functional unit, which serves as a basis for all data collection, calculation and presentation of results [5,6,28].
Phase 2: The second phase is the LCI, where all the technical data of PEMWE are collected, such as the material inputs in the construction phase, energy demand in the operational phase, etc., and the life of PEMWE will be modelled using software (e.g., Umberto [30], Brightway [31] etc.) to generate LCI results showing various potential environmental results.
Phase 3: The third phase is LCIA, also conducted using software. Here, environmental results from the second phase, LCI, are categorised and summarised into different impact categories, such as human toxicity, resources, climate change, etc. [5,6]. Different LCIA methods categorise results differently, each using its distinct approach, such as ReCiPe, EF [32], etc. [33]
Phase 4: The final phase is interpretation, where the LCIA results are analysed. This includes conducting sensitivity analysis to understand the reasons behind PEMWE's varying environmental impacts at different life phases [5,6]. With this understanding, informed recommendations can be made to promote the more environmentally friendly development of PEMWE.

The primary challenge identified in current LCA studies on PEMWE lies in missing or inaccurate technical input data. For example, there is a notable absence of recycling potential data (e.g., recycling rate of specific material) in the end-of-life phase of PEMWE [28]. Additionally, there are data gaps for specific components in the Balance of Plant (BOP), such as technical specifications for hydrogen purification [28,34]. Moreover, in many cases, secondary data sources (e.g., data from literature) are predominantly used due to the limited availability of primary data (e.g., experimental data), particularly concerning renewable energy-based electrolytic technologies [35].

### 2.4. Large Language Models (LLMs)

An LLM is an advanced machine-learning model based on the transformer architecture. The transformer architecture was first proposed in the research paper "Attention is All You Need" [36]. The self-attention mechanism of this transformer architecture allows the models to weigh the significance of different words in a sentence, irrespective of their relative position. This feature enables the model to capture complex syntactic and semantic dependencies more effectively than previous architectures [37]. An LLM, like OpenAI's GPT (Generative pre-trained transformer) series, is specifically designed and trained for natural language processing tasks. These models contain tens to hundreds of billions of parameters pre-trained on vast amounts of text data and can generate human-like text, understand context, and answer questions. Examples of LLMs include BERT [38], RoBERTa [39], GPT-3, GPT-4 [40] and LLaMA [41]. The advanced capabilities of these models include (1) contextual learning, where LLMs can grasp and learn from a few examples provided during inference; (2) following instructions, where after being tuned with instructions, LLMs can perform new tasks based on guidelines without needing explicit examples; and (3) multistep reasoning, where LLMs solve intricate problems by breaking them down into intermediate reasoning steps, as seen in chain-of-thought prompting. In this framework, LLMs can aid engineers in conducting life cycle assessments by supplying domain-specific knowledge in natural language [42]. LLMs have demonstrated significant potential in scientific research, with applications ranging from literature review and code development to modelling complex biological sequences and parsing qualitative data [43]. In the medical domain, LLMs show promise in enhancing the quality and efficiency of research and scientific writing [44]. LLMs have been applied to textual knowledge, small molecules, macromolecular proteins and genomic sequences in the biological and chemical domains, focusing on model architectures, capabilities, datasets and evaluation [45]. LLMs such as ChatGPT, Gemini 1.5 and Claude 3.5 are designed to generate human-like text by analysing vast datasets of text data [46]. These models use deep learning techniques to understand and predict text patterns, making them capable of producing coherent and contextually relevant content. They have shown remarkable abilities in various tasks, including predicting electromagnetic spectra [47] and automating text analytics and generation [48]. However, they also pose significant challenges and risks, including perpetuating biases and the exclusion of non-majority languages [48]. The potential of LLMs to revolutionise research is significant, but their use must be transparent and ethical [15].

Most notably, LLMs can contribute to idea generation and drafting sections of research papers. However, their limitations in providing accurate citations and identifying genuine research gaps necessitate human oversight [49]. The integration of LLMs into scientific research offers both opportunities and challenges. LLMs can boost productivity and foster innovation by streamlining literature reviews, enhancing scientific writing and modelling complex biological sequences [43]. Researchers and peer reviewers require guidelines and norms to ensure their ethical application, especially regarding AI-generated content [50]. This study aims to help researchers find appropriate ML solutions to address their LCA challenges more effectively, utilising the capabilities of LLMs to achieve this goal. After gaining a particular understanding of the use of ML in LCA and the application of LLMs in the research field, in the next section, the progress of training the LLMs to find ML solutions for LCA challenges related to PEMWE is outlined.

## 3. Methodology

This section details a specific approach to using customised LLMs to discover ML solutions for LCA challenges. A visual representation of the methodology used in the paper is shown in Figure 1. The graphic shows the "classic human strategy" is based on reviewing papers with the help of human intelligence to find the solutions for the challenges of LCA for PEMWE. Furthermore, another strategy is the "classic LLM strategy", in which the questions of challenges are to directly query a pre-trained stock LLM to provide suitable responses to the challenges of the LCA without referring directly to papers related to the topic. A more effective approach is combining these two strategies into a fine-tuned, customised LLM trained with relevant scientific research papers. This tailored approach enables the LLM to provide more accurate and context-specific answers to the challenges. Further details of this approach are discussed in the following sections.

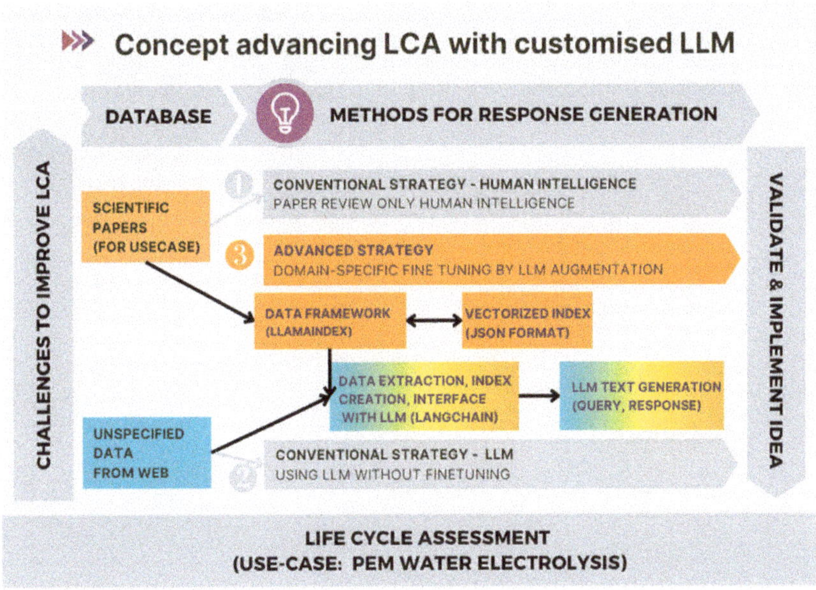


**Figure 1.** Concept advancing LCA with customised LLM. When challenges arise in LCA, in addition to using human intelligence (HI) by reading scientific papers (path 1) and employing non-finetuned LLMs (path 2) to find solutions and methods, path 3 is offered, where LLMs are fine-tuned and trained to address ideas of solutions for challenges that be encountered in the LCA of PEMWE. The fine-tuning process involves storing the relevant scientific papers into a data framework. These papers are vectorised using LlamaIndex within the LLMs, then integrated with other unspecified online resources (LangChain), providing LLMs with a broad information base to generate a customised response.

### 3.1. Fine-Tuning Strategy of LLM with Augmentation Techniques

The pre-trained LLMs can be used to generate desired outputs for various tasks. However, to exploit the full potential or to address their shortcomings, such as hallucinations, the augmentation of the models by providing domain-specific knowledge externally is needed [42]. In this contribution, stock LLMs are combined with the retrieval-augmented generation (RAG) approach to steer them towards more factual outputs. RAG is a methodology that integrates external data sources during inference, allowing the model to retrieve relevant information and generate more accurate responses. This approach simplifies data management and helps mitigate the inherent probabilistic nature of LLMs.

Another primary limitation of the stock pre-trained LLMs is their lack of up-to-date knowledge or access to private or use-case-specific information. Therefore, integrating an external database to the LLM to retrieve relevant information from the reference databank enables the model to generate a context-specific customised response to the questions. As mentioned earlier, OpenAI built the GPT LLM model series, including GPT-3 and GPT-4. ChatGPT is a web-based chatbot application that leverages the powerful GPT-3 model to facilitate fine-tuned optimal dialogue interactions. OpenAI also offers a feature for creating customised GPTs to harness the power of the LLMs using a custom dataset for augmentation. Subsequently, this customised GPT LLM is used in this work and can respond to inquiries based on the content within these research papers. The GPT models can be augmented with relevant research related to PEMWE and ML applications for LCA using this feature. The model retrieves specific documents from the curated corpus using LlamaIndex and LangChain and integrates these data into the LLM's output during inference, which is consistent with the RAG approach. OpenAI's customised GPT model is based on components such as LlamaIndex and LangChain, which provide a framework for interacting external data with LLMs. LlamaIndex is a data framework that provides a simple, flexible interface to connect the LLMs with external data. It creates a vectorised index of the document data to enable efficient queries. LangChain provides an application programming interface to access and interact with LLM and facilitate seamless integration for various use cases. The combination of the Llamaindex and LangChain provides the framework to augment context-specific GPT models with customised datasets and further develop applications. This approach is visually represented in Figure 1. The current approach consolidates the research papers that train the custom GPT model into a single folder. These files are uploaded into the OpenAI interface, forming the basis for constructing the LlamaIndex. These data are then vectorised, and the resulting index is saved as a repository for future reference. Once the index is generated, it can be stored and utilised for data querying. When a query is made, the system searches for relevant segments within the index. These identified document segments are matched with the user's query and transmitted to the GPT model (GPT-3.5-turbo) through the LangChain framework. This process ensures that the response generated by the model is tailored to the specific context of the query, providing personalised answers. The textual responses generated can then be compared in the subsequent step. In this case study, only five questions and answers are described and compared to illustrate the basic methodology. However, this approach is scalable and can be applied to a larger set of questions and an extensive collection of scientific papers, making it transferable to any LCA context.

### 3.2. *RAG-Based Document Retrieval and Augmentation*

To improve the results of LLMs, it is crucial to work qualitatively with input, and prompt engineering has been applied in this paper to achieve that. The significance of prompt engineering lies in its capacity to enhance the adaptability and applicability of LLMs across various sectors [51]. Figure 2 illustrates the components of prompt engineering. Techniques such as zero-shot prompting, where the model makes predictions for unseen tasks using general knowledge, and few-shot prompting, where the model generalises from a minimal number of examples, significantly boost model performance. More advanced methods like CoT prompting, which involves breaking down complex problems into intermediate reasoning steps, enable models to excel in various tasks [52].

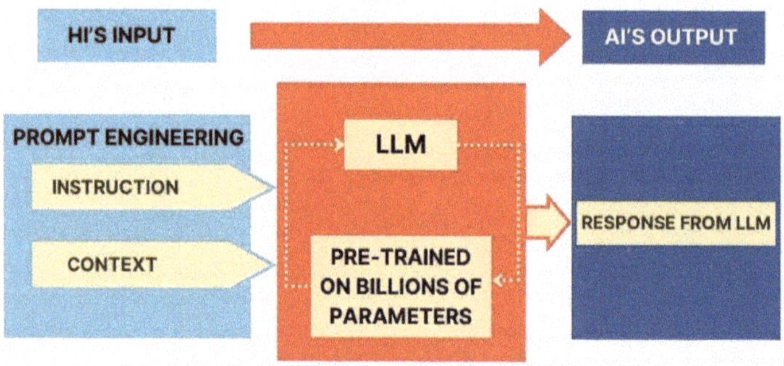


**Figure 2.** Prompt engineering components adapted from [51].

The CO-STAR framework is a structured approach to goal setting encompassing Context, Outcome, Scale, Time, Actor and Resources, providing clarity and direction in both organisational and personal settings. As per this framework, customised GPT is configured to provide a response based on the following prompt:

> **(Context)** *As a research analyst, you are now tasked with answering scientific questions using the literature at your disposal. This requires a deep understanding of the content, the ability to extract relevant information, and the capacity to synthesise this information*

*in a manner that directly addresses specific scientific inquiries.* ***(Objective)*** *Analyse the scientific papers provided to answer specific scientific questions. Use scientific language and methodologies to ensure your responses are evidence-based and grounded in current research.* ***(Style)*** *Employ a formal scientific writing style characterised by precision, clarity, and thoroughness. Structure your responses with clear argumentation supported by evidence from the literature. Use appropriate scientific terminology and citation practices.* ***(Tone)*** *Maintain a scholarly and objective tone throughout your responses. The tone should reflect the seriousness and rigour typical of scientific discourse, aiming to convey information in a factual and unbiased manner.* ***(Audience)*** *The intended audience for your responses includes scientists, researchers, and academics who are experts in the field. The language and style should cater to an informed audience that expects technical accuracy and depth. Begin each answer by clearly stating the scientific question being addressed.* ***(Response)*** *Review the relevant sections of the provided scientific papers to gather pertinent information and data, synthesise the findings and discuss how they relate to the question at hand, and ensure that all claims are supported by evidence, citing sources in the format: (Author's Name, Year, Article Title), conclude each response by summarising the key points made and their implications for the field of study, recheck the critical studies cited, ensuring that the data reported align with the conclusions drawn and that no crucial information has been misinterpreted or misrepresented in the summary.*

Chain of Verification (CoVe), introduced by Dhuliawala et al. in 2023 [52], aims to mitigate hallucinations in large language models (LLMs) through a systematic four-step process [52]. Initially, the model generates a response, after which it formulates verification questions to assess the accuracy of this response. The model then independently answers these verification questions and revises the initial response based on the verification answers. This process enhances the logical reasoning abilities of the LLM, thereby reducing errors even when faced with contradictory information [52]. This involves generating a baseline response, planning verification questions, answering verification questions independently and producing a revised response incorporating verification. By systematically generating and verifying information through tailored questions, the CoVe method ensures that the output is factual and relevant, significantly reducing the risk of producing hallucinated content. This approach mimics a human-like verification process, enhancing the LLM responses' coherence and reliability.

This method involves using the CO-STAR framework for structured prompt engineering to guide the prompt formulation and leveraging CoVe to enhance response reliability. The goal is to qualitatively assess the performance and answers of these LLMs in generating accurate, relevant and unbiased content for scientific research.

## 4. Experimental Results and Discussion

In this section, the results of the LLMs are presented, analysed and evaluated. In the first step, Section 4.1 describes the data corpus used for contextual augmentation of the customised ChatGPT in this experiment. Section 4.2 focuses on the questions, where Table 1 presents the responses from different LLMs (customised ChatGPT, ChatGPT-4, Gemini 1.5 and Claude 3.5). Section 4.3 provides an analysis of the responses. Here, the results are interpreted and compared; the comparison of the responses of the different LLMs provides information about the performance of the customised ChatGPT, which were tested by reviewing further questions (Section 4.4). The results from this further investigation, offering a deeper understanding of the customised model, are also presented in Section 4.4.

**Table 1.** Questions and their responses from LLMs. The table displays questions and corresponding answers from three LLMs compared with optimised GPT. Some of the answers in the table are represented by abbreviations of methods, with their full names listed in the last row of the table.

| | | |
|---|---|---|
| Question 1 | What Machine Learning (ML) Approaches are Suitable for Collecting Life Cycle Inventory (LCI) Data for a 5 MW Inverter Used in Proton Exchange Membrane Water Electrolysis (PEMWE) When Existing Databases Lack This Information? | |
| Customised Chat GPT | Answer | ANNs can model complex relationships and predict missing data by learning from available related datasets. In the context of PEMWE Life Cycle Assessment (LCA), where detailed and accurate LCI data are crucial, ANNs can fill gaps in the inventory, ensuring a more comprehensive and reliable environmental assessment of the PEMWE system. |
| | References | Khoshnevisan, B., Rafiee, S., Omid, M., Mousazadeh, H. and Sefeedpari, P. Prognostication of environmental indices in potato production using artificial neural networks. 2013 [53] |
| Chat GPT-4o | Answer | Data Augmentation: Regression analysis, support vector machines, or ANN with synthetic data generation or transfer learning.<br>Clustering: K-means or hierarchical clustering.<br>Hybrid approaches: support vector machines or generative models. |
| Gemini 1.5 | Answer | Regression or random forest |
| Claude 3.5 | Answer | Predictive modelling, transfer learning, generative adversarial networks, variational autoencoder and natural language processing. |
| Question 2 | What machine learning methods can be applied to rectify overestimated environmental impact data of copper in LCI databases? | |
| Customised Chat GPT | Answer | Support vector machines or random forest.<br>Machine learning methods such as support vector machines (SVM) or random forests can be applied to rectify overestimated copper environmental impact data in Life Cycle Inventory (LCI) databases. These techniques effectively identify and correct anomalies by learning from patterns within the data, leading to more accurate environmental assessments. |
| | References | Omidkar, A., Alagumalai, A., Li, Z. and Song, H. Machine learning assisted techno-economic and life cycle assessment of organic solid waste upgrading under natural gas. 2024 [54] |
| Chat GPT-4o | Answer | Data imputation: Linear regression, ridge regression or gradient boosting machines.<br>Anomaly detection: Isolation Forest, variational autoencoder or principal component analysis.<br>Ensemble learning: an ensemble of regression and anomaly detection models. |
| Gemini 1.5 | Answer | Regression model |
| Claude 3.5 | Answer | Isolation forest, support vector machines, random forest with gradient boosting machines, gaussian process regression, multi-task learning, Bayesian ML models with data or expert opinions. |
| Question 3: | Which Life Cycle Impact Assessment (LCIA) methods are recommended for conducting a Life Cycle Assessment (LCA) of Proton Exchange Membrane Water Electrolysis (PEMWE) systems, and why? | |

**Table 1.** *Cont.*

<table>
<tr><td>Question 1</td><td colspan="2">What Machine Learning (ML) Approaches are Suitable for Collecting Life Cycle Inventory (LCI) Data for a 5 MW Inverter Used in Proton Exchange Membrane Water Electrolysis (PEMWE) When Existing Databases Lack This Information?</td></tr>
<tr><td rowspan="2">Customised Chat GPT</td><td>Answer</td><td>CML 2001 provides a well-established framework for midpoint impact categories, allowing for detailed environmental impact analysis, especially in areas like resource depletion and global warming.<br>ReCiPe offers both midpoint and endpoint impact assessment, making it versatile for capturing various environmental impacts, including human health and ecosystem quality.<br>TRACI is particularly relevant for assessments within the United States. It focuses on region-specific impact categories, such as smog formation and acidification, which are important for evaluating PEMWE systems in that context.</td></tr>
<tr><td>References</td><td>Algren, M., Fisher, W. and Landis, A. E. Machine learning in life cycle assessment. 2021 [55]</td></tr>
<tr><td>Chat GPT-4o</td><td>Answer</td><td>ReCiPe, ILCD and TRACI</td></tr>
<tr><td>Gemini 1.5</td><td>Answer</td><td>CML, TRACI, ReCiPe and IMPACT 2002+</td></tr>
<tr><td>Claude 3.5</td><td>Answer</td><td>ReCiPe, CML, ILCD, USEtox, IPCC GWP</td></tr>
<tr><td>Question 4:</td><td colspan="2">How can machine learning be utilised to conduct a sensitivity analysis on the LCIA results of a PEMWE system?</td></tr>
<tr><td rowspan="2">Customised Chat GPT</td><td>Answer</td><td>Random Forest:<br>• Efficiently handles complex and non-linear relationships in LCIA data.<br>• Identifies and ranks the most influential factors affecting the environmental impact of PEMWE systems.<br>Gradient Boosting Machines:<br>• Provides precise sensitivity analysis by incrementally improving predictions on LCIA outcomes.<br>• Highlights key parameters that significantly influence the overall environmental performance of PEMWE systems, allowing for targeted optimisations.</td></tr>
<tr><td>References</td><td>Omidkar, A., Alagumalai, A., Li, Z. and Song, H. Machine learning assisted techno-economic and life cycle assessment of organic solid waste upgrading under natural gas. 2024 [54]<br>Zheng, L., Mueller, M., Luo, C. and Yan, X. Predicting whole-life carbon emissions for buildings using different machine learning algorithms: A case study on typical residential properties in Cornwall. 2024 [56]</td></tr>
<tr><td>Chat GPT-4o</td><td>Answer</td><td>ANN trained on monte-carlo simulation.<br>Random Forest or gradient boosting machines.</td></tr>
<tr><td>Gemini 1.5</td><td>Answer</td><td>Gaussian process regression and ANN</td></tr>
<tr><td>Claude 3.5</td><td>Answer</td><td>Random forest or gradient boosting machines, Sobol in-dices, variational autoencoders, optimise neural networks or Gaussian process, t-SNE (t-distributed Stochastic Neighbour Embedding) and UMAP (Uniform Manifold Approximation and Projection), polynomial chaos expansion or kriging.</td></tr>
<tr><td>Question 5:</td><td colspan="2">How can machine learning assist in generating optimised recommendations based on LCIA results for Proton Exchange Membrane Water Electrolysis (PEMWE) systems?</td></tr>
</table>

**Table 1.** *Cont.*

| Question 1 | | What Machine Learning (ML) Approaches are Suitable for Collecting Life Cycle Inventory (LCI) Data for a 5 MW Inverter Used in Proton Exchange Membrane Water Electrolysis (PEMWE) When Existing Databases Lack This Information? |
|---|---|---|
| Customised Chat GPT | Answer | Artificial Neural Networks (ANNs): Learn complex patterns in PEMWE performance and environmental impact data, enabling accurate predictions and optimisations.<br>Genetic Algorithms: Optimise the structure and parameters of ANNs, enhancing their ability to find the best PEMWE configurations for minimal environmental impact.<br>Bayesian Optimisation: Efficiently tunes ANN parameters by focusing on the most promising areas, improving PEMWE performance and reducing environmental impacts in line with LCIA findings. |
| | References | Omidkar, A., Alagumalai, A., Li, Z., and Song, H. Machine learning assisted techno-economic and life cycle assessment of organic solid waste upgrading under natural gas. 2024 [54]<br>Kaab, A., Sharifi, M., Mobli, H., Nabavi-Pelesaraei, A., and Chau, K. W. Combined life cycle assessment and artificial intelligence for prediction of output energy and environmental impacts of sugarcane production. 2019 [57] |
| Chat GPT-4o | Answer | Genetic algorithms, Particle swarm optimisation and simulated annealing.<br>Multi-objective evolutionary algorithms.<br>Predictive modelling with decision support systems. |
| Gemini 1.5 | Answer | Gaussian process regression and ANN |
| Claude 3.5 | Answer | Non-dominated sorting genetic algorithm II or multi-objective evolutionary algorithm based on decomposition.<br>Deep Q-networks; K-means or hierarchical clustering with support vector machines and random forest.<br>Gaussian process Bayesian optimisation, collaborative filtering, casual forest, Shapley additive explanations or local interpretable model-agnostic explanations. |

ILCD: The International Reference Life Cycle Data System, TRACI: Tool for Reduction and Assessment of Chemicals and Other Environmental Impacts, USEtox: The Toxicity Model from the Society of Environmental Toxicology and Chemistry of Environment Programme of United Nations.

### 4.1. Description of the Data Corpus for Augmentation

In this paper, the custom GPT model was tested against the responses from three other large language models: OpenAI's ChatGPT-4o, Gemini 1.5 and Claude 3.5 because they have demonstrated significant potential in scientific research. One of the unique features of OpenAI is the ability to create a customised GPT, which in turn provides the ability to apply a specific library of scientific literature to teach an LLM for a particular use case.

In this research, a customised ChatGPT model was developed to provide expert insights at the intersection of ML, LCA and hydrogen technologies. To train this model, a focused literature review was conducted using the Scholar database. The search targeted key areas using keywords such as "PEMWE", "Environmental impact" and "Machine learning in LCA". The final data corpus included 39 research papers, carefully selected for their relevance. This selection comprised 10 papers on LCA methodologies, 3 systematic reviews and 26 papers focused on the application of ML in LCA. The systematic reviews were particularly important, covering challenges and future needs in PEMWE technology, advancements in applying ML to LCA and the life-cycle assessment of hydrogen technologies. The information for these papers can be found in the Supplementary Materials.

The three selected review papers focus on key areas relevant to the intersection of machine learning, life cycle assessment and hydrogen technologies. The first paper discusses the challenges and future needs of PEMWEs, which are crucial for hydrogen production.

The second paper reviews the advancements in ML to LCA, highlighting current trends and challenges in this field. The third paper examines the LCA of hydrogen technologies, with an emphasis on critical raw materials and sustainability, particularly in the context of end-of-life strategies. The 26 papers focused on the application of ML in LCA were selected by using the keywords 'Machine Learning' AND 'Life cycle assessment', 'hydrogen production', 'PEMWE', 'Artificial Intelligence'. The 10 papers on LCA methods were selected by using the keywords 'LCA' AND 'PEMWE', 'LCA' AND 'hydrogen production'.

Gemini and Claude are not able to analyse many papers because they have limitations on the number of tokens. The customised LLM comprehends instructions by extracting relevant techniques, algorithms and methodologies from the provided literature. It then synthesises this information to provide practical recommendations for optimising LCA with ML algorithms, ensuring accuracy and efficiency improvements. This distinguishes it from other models and, therefore, requires separate consideration.

### 4.2. Formulation of Queries

One of the main objectives of this paper is to analyse the extent to which LLM can help solve complex challenges at the interface of ML, LCA and of ML, LCA and PEMWE. For this reason, the various questions asked to the LLMs arise from the challenges described in Sections 2.2 and 2.3. To enable a comparison of the answers, the four LLMs were asked the same questions. The questions were prompted into the pipeline and then evaluated, taking the reference answers into account. The list of questions is as follows:

1. What machine learning (ML) approaches are suitable for collecting Life Cycle Inventory (LCI) data for a 5 MW inverter used in Proton Exchange Membrane Water Electrolysis (PEMWE) when existing databases lack this information?
2. What machine learning methods can be applied to rectify overestimated environmental impact data of copper in LCI databases?
3. Which Life Cycle Impact Assessment (LCIA) methods are recommended for conducting a Life Cycle Assessment (LCA) of Proton Exchange Membrane Water Electrolysis (PEMWE) systems, and why?
4. How can machine learning be utilised to conduct a sensitivity analysis on the LCIA results of a PEMWE system?
5. How can machine learning assist in generating optimised recommendations based on LCIA results for Proton Exchange Membrane Water Electrolysis (PEMWE) systems?

The first question focuses on challenges that have already arisen in conducting an LCA for PEMWE in Section 2.3 and aims to explore which ML techniques can be provided by trained LLMs to address these challenges. The second question relates to the general challenges of data gaps, as described in Section 2.2. Questions three to five aim to check how LLMs can respond to and assist with general LCA problems when they occur in the context of PEMWE. For reasons of clarity, the five questions were formulated so that a comparison of the 20 answers from the different LLMs can be presented in a table. The answers of the different LLMs are shown in Table 1.

### 4.3. Analysis of the Responses

In this section, the analysis of the responses is conducted by interpreting and comparing the variations among the different answers.

In response to Q1, the customised GPT concludes that employing ANNs is a rational approach for estimating missing data in the LCI of PEMWE. Although the response initially draws from an agricultural example, the model adapts this knowledge to the context of PEMWE. This demonstrates the model's capability to synthesise insights across the three intersecting fields of ML, LCA and PEMWE. Upon manual fact-checking, the conclusion can be validated as accurate, since the application of ANNs in PEMWE is well-supported in the scientific literature [58]. In response to Q2, the customised GPT suggests using SVM or RF to rectify overestimated data. After manual verification, this suggestion is found to be valid, as it aligns with conclusions from relevant scientific articles in this domain [59,60]. For Q3, the model recommends three methods for assessing environmental impact: CML, ReCiPe and TRACI. However, it overlooks that the CML database has not been updated since 2017 [61] and TRACI has geographical limitations [62]. Furthermore, the model does not clearly define the boundaries between these methods, relying instead on listing them in succession from the cited article. While the recommendation is not entirely accurate, it still provides a useful starting point, as these are commonly applied methods. The answer to Q4 can be deemed correct, as it is consistent with current theories in the field, as noted previously. However, evaluating the correctness of the response to Q5 is more challenging, as it is primarily designed to offer recommendations. In this case, GPT synthesises information from both the uploaded data and its own internal databases, tailoring the output to the PEMWE context specified in the prompt. Overall, the customised GPT demonstrates the ability to generate answers by synthesising data from various sources, but the accuracy of its responses is dependent on the quantity of input data and the clarity of the questions posed. This underscores the importance of well-structured queries and sufficient data to guide the GPT in generating reliable and context-specific answers.

Notably, manual fact-checking is essential to verify the accuracy of LLM-generated responses, ensuring that the synthesis of information from heterogeneous sources—such as ML, LCA and PEMWE—corresponds to established facts. In this context, it is important to differentiate between two types of LLM responses: synthesised and generative. Synthesised responses strictly contain information extracted from the training data without modification, accurately reflecting the provided references. On the other hand, generative responses are derived from the given data, but GPT introduces additional connections or insights that extend beyond the explicit content of the training data, creating links between the provided information and the specific context of the task. These generative responses, while potentially insightful, require closer scrutiny, as they are not always directly grounded in the literature. Based on the above distinctions, the responses to question 1, 2 and 4 in Table 1 are generative, while the responses to question 3 and 5 are synthesised. As the results of comparing different types of responses show, purely synthesised responses are reliably answered through information extraction. However, for generative responses, the processing of information and the generation of links must be further tested to ensure the proposed answers.

The differences in the responses of LLMs can be attributed to their distinct training databases, fine-tuning techniques and intended application contexts. These variations impact their ability to provide practical details, categorise methods and cite literature. The customised ChatGPT provided specific examples of machine learning methods, emphasising their practical applications and summarising their documented uses in the literature. For example, random forests were suggested for correcting overestimated copper environmental impact data in LCI databases, and ANNs were recommended for estimating missing technical data in PEMWE systems. This customised ChatGPT is tailored to deliver example-driven explanations, indicating an optimisation for scenarios that require clear, direct demonstrations of ML methods. However, ChatGPT-4o categorised several machine learning methods, provided reasons for their selection, and illustrated one solution in an application context, but it lacked practical details and literature citations. For instance, it mentioned regression and random forest as methods for predicting missing technical data in PEMWE, but did not delve into the reasoning or processes behind these methods, as shown in Table 1. This approach is beneficial for users looking to understand the broader landscape of ML methods applied to the LCA of PEMWE, rather than for those seeking detailed application guidance. The absence of practical details and citations could reflect a focus on conceptual clarity and method variety over depth, or it might indicate a trade-off made to prioritise breadth over detailed practical guidance. Unlike customised GPT, other GPTs are trained on massive internet data, open sources such as Wikipedia articles and articles on various websites [63]. Gemini 1.5 referenced machine learning methods with citations but lacked practical explanations, suggesting its design prioritises providing quick references and illustrating applications through the literature. This version seems suited for users who need to rapidly locate relevant studies without requiring detailed explanations or step-by-step guidance. In contrast, Claude 3.5 categorised and explained various ML methods to address specific questions, especially emphasising practical approaches for questions 4 and 5. However, it did not include literature citations, indicating a focus on delivering immediate, actionable insights rather than academic references. This suggests Claude 3.5 is optimised for context-driven queries that prioritise practical solutions.

The customised ChatGPT is a RAG-LLM model, whose strength lies significantly in the quality of the curated documents used as the foundation for generating the responses. The customised GPT model provides answers by integrating various perspectives, methodologies and findings by synthesising across multiple documents. The curation process ensures that the LLM is equipped with highly relevant and domain-specific information, which inevitably contributes to its improved performance over off-the-shelf LLMs.

The customisation of LLMs described here is primarily user-centric, tailored to address specific problems and application needs rather than providing a broad academic overview. This customisation process involves trade-offs that are aligned with the user's particular requirements and the context of the application. The focus can vary, placing emphasis on practical details, the categorisation of methods or the citation of relevant literature, depending on the intended use case and user priorities. Understanding these focus areas is crucial for selecting the most appropriate LLM version for specific research and practical applications. It ensures that the model achieves an optimal balance between theoretical insight, practical utility, and academic rigour, thereby effectively meeting the needs of its intended users.

At this point, it should be noted that there are a variety of ways to ask questions about the challenges and that this can have an impact on the answers. However, as the focus is initially on comparing the different LLMs and the questions asked of the different LLMs remain the same, the specific nature of the question is less scrutinised in the responses to Table 1. Nevertheless, it must be recognised that this could present a limitation that must be considered. Given the assumptions that (1) a synthesised response will be generated based on the information in the training data, and (2) if the information is included in the training data, the customised GPT should be able to locate it and provide the corresponding source, the assumptions drawn from the answers to the five questions in Table 1 should be tested again in the next section with the help of additional questions.

### *4.4. Further Investigation LLM Responses*

In this section, the assumptions drawn from Section 4.3 are tested. The customised ChatGPT was trained on the same 39 research papers mentioned in Section 4.1. This time, however, five papers were randomly selected from this pool. After thoroughly reading these articles, the following five questions were formulated based on their content. The purpose of this approach was to ensure that the questions were designed such that the answers could be found within the articles. The questions posed were as follows:

1. What are the main differences between supervised and unsupervised machine learning, and how can each be applied to different stages of a Life Cycle Assessment (LCA)? Source [64]
2. How do machine learning models, such as Artificial Neural Networks (ANNs) handle non-linear relationships in environmental impact predictions, and what are their advantages over traditional regression models? Source [65]
3. In multi-objective optimisation using LCA, how does the Pareto-optimal solution help in balancing trade-offs between competing environmental and economic goals? Source [66]
4. What are the main limitations of using traditional LCA methods without the incorporation of machine learning, and how do ML approaches address these limitations? Source [64]

5. How does the use of ML algorithms, such as decision trees and deep learning, improve the characterisation factor (CF) estimations in LCAs involving complex and dynamic systems? Source [67]

The responses to these questions are presented in Table 2.

**Table 2.** The table shows the results of responses of the customised GPT to questions expecting a synthesised response from the training literature.

| Question 1S | What are the Main Differences Between Supervised and Unsupervised Machine Learning, and How Can Each be Applied to Different Stages of a Life Cycle Assessment (LCA)? | |
|---|---|---|
| Customised Chat GPT | Answer | Supervised learning uses labelled data to train models, making it ideal for predicting specific environmental impacts in LCA by associating inputs (e.g., material usage) with outputs (e.g., emissions). In contrast, unsupervised learning is applied to discover patterns or groupings in datasets without predefined labels, such as clustering similar products based on their environmental impact profiles. Both methods can be employed to improve data accuracy and interpret LCA results [64,68]. |
| Question 2S | How do machine learning models, such as Artificial Neural Networks (ANNs) handle non-linear relationships in environmental impact predictions, and what are their advantages over traditional regression models? | |
| Customised Chat GPT | Answer | Artificial Neural Networks (ANNs) excel at modelling complex, non-linear relationships between inputs and outputs in LCA due to their capacity to learn from large datasets and capture hidden dependencies. Traditional regression models, while useful for linear relationships, often fail to accurately predict environmental impacts when non-linearities are involved. ANNs and RF models are more flexible and can achieve higher prediction accuracy in such cases [65]. |
| Question 3S | In multi-objective optimisation using LCA, how does the Pareto-optimal solution help in balancing trade-offs between competing environmental and economic goals? | |
| Customised Chat GPT | Answer | The Pareto-optimal solution in multi-objective optimisation helps balance trade-offs by identifying a set of non-dominated solutions, where improving one objective (e.g., reducing environmental impact) cannot be achieved without worsening another (e.g., increasing costs). In LCA, Pareto-optimal solutions allow decision-makers to evaluate the trade-offs between environmental and economic goals and select the most balanced option [66,69]. |
| Question 4S | What are the main limitations of using traditional LCA methods without the incorporation of machine learning, and how do ML approaches address these limitations? | |
| Customised Chat GPT | Answer | Traditional LCA methods rely heavily on manual data processing and can struggle with incomplete datasets or complex systems with non-linear dependencies. ML approaches overcome these limitations by automating data processing, filling gaps in life cycle inventories and improving prediction accuracy for complex, non-linear systems. ML also allows faster processing of large datasets, which significantly reduces the time required for LCA computations [64,68]. |
| Question 5S | How does the use of ML algorithms, such as decision trees and deep learning, improve the characterisation factor (CF) estimations in LCAs involving complex and dynamic systems? | |
| Customised Chat GPT | Answer | ML algorithms like decision trees and deep learning improve CF estimations in LCAs by accurately modelling the relationships between various environmental factors, such as material usage, energy consumption and emissions. These algorithms can process large amounts of data and account for the dynamic interactions between different life cycle stages, leading to more precise CF estimations. They are especially useful in scenarios where traditional methods might oversimplify or miss key dependencies [67]. |

S—Synthesised Response.

The answers provided by the customised GPT demonstrate that it identified and located relevant sources for the previously asked questions. For example, in question 2S, the exact source [65], was correctly identified and cited in response to the question, confirming that the source being searched for was found. For question 5S, source [67] provided a detailed explanation of using decision trees and other methods to build ML models for estimating hazardous concentrations and determining ecotoxicity characterisation factors, which directly addressed the question. This structured approach shows how the customised GPT handled the questions and identified the relevant sources for most answers, while also highlighting areas where multiple sources were likely used to enhance the accuracy of the response. However, there were some anomalies in questions 1S, 3S and 4S. Initially, the answers did not directly reference a specific source. In the case of question 1S, source [64] was referenced, which primarily focuses on machine learning (ML) with only a minor section on life cycle assessment (LCA). It seems that source [68] was likely used to verify the LCA components of the response, ensuring the relevant aspects of the question were covered. In question 3, the response mentioned "improving one objective cannot be achieved without worsening another", which was directly linked to source [66]. Additionally, source [70] was cited for discussing the use of the Pareto front to visualise LCA. However, while source [70] mentions the Pareto front, its relevance to the question is much less significant compared to the insights from source [66]. Overall, the assumptions that were already made in Table 1 can be regarded as confirmed. The findings in Tables 1 and 2 indicate that LLMs have already contributed, to some extent, to assisting LCA professionals in using ML to provide new impulses to address potential challenges in LCA.

## 5. Conclusions

This study investigates using artificial intelligence as a customised, large-scale language model to improve LCA. The aim is to improve the challenges of environmental impact assessment, such as data gaps, as described in the use case of green hydrogen by PEMWE. By integrating advanced LLM capabilities, the method proposed in the study provides a robust tool for resolving specific and general issues within LCA practice. The applicability of this approach improves the reliability of LCA results and optimises the research process by reducing the time and resources required for data analysis. Additionally, the customised LLMs can offer problem-solving guidance through further queries and relevant citations, providing assistance to LCA researchers without a background in ML.

The findings of this paper indicate that customised LLMs can analyse and synthesise information from a diverse set of sources, significantly aiding researchers in navigating the complexities of LCA by providing qualitative insights and identifying suitable ML solutions. As demonstrated by the results, customised LLMs can offer advice on selecting LCIA methods, suggest ML techniques for sensitivity analysis and recommend environmental optimisation strategies for PEMWE. These contributions, using PEMWE as an example, demonstrate how LLMs can help to address the general challenges faced in LCA, as discussed in the paper, by providing clear, actionable insights and facilitating easy interaction with the LLM will enhance its utility for practitioners with varying levels of expertise.

This research also shows the importance of prompt engineering in optimising LLM performance. By tailoring the prompts for comparative analysis, it was ensured that the LLM-generated responses were precise, clear and grounded in current research, effectively catering to an informed audience of scientists and researchers. The questions in Section 4 were designed to directly address the challenges inherent in LCA, as well as those specific to PEMWE. Recognising that the formulation of prompts significantly influences responses, open-ended questions were deliberately chosen. This approach allows for a wide range of potential answers, providing a broad spectrum of insights. However, the trade-off is a reduced likelihood of receiving highly specific responses.

The results of the LLM customised with scientific articles were validated and verified against scientific research data in the specific field of PEMWE even though the original literature base did not include articles containing the inferences drawn. In contrast to customised models, non-customised models are not as reliable due to their underlying database, which often contains irrelevant data due to its shallow depth. Moreover, it is worth noting that, the customised LLM generates two types of responses in this study: synthesised responses and generative responses. Synthesised responses adhere to the information provided in the training data, making this type of response trustworthy. In contrast, generative responses are based on the training data but involve a certain level of inference by the LLM, indicating that these responses need to be re-evaluated by manually checking.

Future work can focus on refining the training of LLMs with more specific and up-to-date datasets related to PEMWE and other green hydrogen technologies, as well as fundamental LCA-related literature, such as the ILCD handbooks, the textbook from Hauschild et al. [71] etc. Also, future studies should consider training GPT on data from practical applications of machine learning in LCA to explore LLM as a tool to provide not only theoretical information but also practical guidance. Although RAG enhances the retrieval of the most pertinent sections from the curated corpus, future improvement might involve automating parts of the document selection process. This could lessen the dependence on manual curation, making the system more scalable and potentially reducing the need for highly selective document retrieval. To enhance the precision and relevance of the answers, future work should also focus on refining prompts through advanced prompt engineering techniques. For instance, tailoring questions to target specific LCA challenges with greater granularity can increase the likelihood of eliciting more focused and actionable responses from the LLM. Additionally, incorporating strategies such as Tree-of-Thought or Chain-of-Thought reasoning could further improve the depth and coherence of the model's responses, enabling it to address complex questions more effectively. Additionally, ongoing collaboration between AI and domain experts is essential to continuously validate and enhance the outputs generated by LLMs. By addressing the ethical considerations and biases inherent in AI models, the responsible and effective use of LLMs in scientific research can be further ensured.

In conclusion, integrating LLMs into the LCA process marks a significant step towards creating a solution for using ML in LCA and improving it. This approach demonstrates that AI can provide powerful tools for advancing research in renewable energy and sustainability.

**Supplementary Materials:** The following supporting information can be downloaded at: https://www.mdpi.com/article/10.3390/make6040122/s1. References [7,16,17,23,24,28,29,35,53–57,68,70,72–95] are cited in the supplementary materials.

**Author Contributions:** Conceptualization, Y.C. and U.L.; methodology, Y.C., U.L. and S.M.G.; validation, Y.C., U.L., S.M.G. and I.T.; formal analysis, Y.C., U.L., S.M.G. and I.T.; investigation, Y.C., U.L., S.M.G. and I.T.; resources, Y.C., U.L., S.M.G. and I.T.; data curation, Y.C., U.L., S.M.G. and I.T.; writing—original draft preparation, Y.C., U.L., S.M.G. and I.T.; writing—review and editing, Y.C., U.L., S.M.G. and I.T.; visualisation, Y.C. and U.L.; supervision, C.M.; project administration, Y.C., U.L. and S.M.G.; funding acquisition, Y.C. All authors have read and agreed to the published version of the manuscript.

**Funding:** This research received no external funding.

**Data Availability Statement:** No new data were created or analysed in this study. Data sharing is not applicable to this article.

**Acknowledgments:** We acknowledge financial support by the Open Access Publishing Fund of Clausthal University of Technology.

**Conflicts of Interest:** The authors declare no conflicts of interest.

## References

1. Hassan, Q.; Algburi, S.; Sameen, A.Z.; Salman, H.M.; Jaszczur, M. Green Hydrogen: A Pathway to a Sustainable Energy Future. *Int. J. Hydrogen Energy* **2024**, *50*, 310–333. [CrossRef]
2. Dang, J.; Yang, F.; Li, Y.; Zhao, Y.; Ouyang, M.; Hu, S. Experiments and Microsimulation of High-Pressure Single-Cell PEM Electrolyzer. *Appl. Energy* **2022**, *321*, 119351. [CrossRef]

3. Zhang, K.; Liang, X.; Wang, L.; Sun, K.; Wang, Y.; Xie, Z.; Wu, Q.; Bai, X.; Hamdy, M.S.; Chen, H.; et al. Status and Perspectives of Key Materials for PEM Electrolyzer. *Nano Res. Energy* **2022**, *1*, e9120032. [CrossRef]
4. Shiva Kumar, S.; Himabindu, V. Hydrogen Production by PEM Water Electrolysis—A Review. *Mater. Sci. Energy Technol.* **2019**, *2*, 442–454. [CrossRef]
5. *BS EN ISO 1404*; Environmental Management Life Cycle Assessment Principles and Framework. International Organization for Standartization: Geneva, Switzerland, 2006.
6. *DIN EN ISO 14044*; Environmental Management Life Cycle Assessment Requirements and Guidelines. International Organization for Standartizatio: Geneva, Switzerland, 2006.
7. Romeiko, X.X.; Zhang, X.; Pang, Y.; Gao, F.; Xu, M.; Lin, S.; Babbitt, C. A Review of Machine Learning Applications in Life Cycle Assessment Studies. *Sci. Total Environ.* **2024**, *912*, 168969. [CrossRef]
8. Y Arcas, B.A. Do Large Language Models Understand Us? *Daedalus* **2022**, *151*, 183–197. [CrossRef]
9. A Comprehensive Overview of Large Language Models. Available online: https://ar5iv.labs.arxiv.org/html/2307.06435 (accessed on 4 June 2024).
10. Brown, T.B.; Mann, B.; Ryder, N.; Subbiah, M.; Kaplan, J.; Dhariwal, P.; Neelakantan, A.; Shyam, P.; Sastry, G.; Askell, A.; et al. Language Models Are Few-Shot Learners. *arXiv* **2020**, arXiv:2005.14165.
11. Radford, A.; Wu, J.; Child, R.; Luan, D.; Amodei, D.; Sutskever, I. Language Models Are Unsupervised Multitask Learners. *OpenAI Blog* **2019**, *1*, 9.
12. Ouyang, L.; Wu, J.; Jiang, X.; Almeida, D.; Wainwright, C.L.; Mishkin, P.; Zhang, C.; Agarwal, S.; Slama, K.; Ray, A.; et al. Training Language Models to Follow Instructions with Human Feedback. *Adv. Neural Inf. Process. Syst.* **2022**, *35*, 27730–27744.
13. Cornago, S.; Ramakrishna, S.; Low, J.S.C. How Can Transformers and Large Language Models like ChatGPT Help LCA Practitioners? *Resour. Conserv. Recycl.* **2023**, *196*, 107062. [CrossRef]
14. Preuss, N.; Alshehri, A.S.; You, F. Large Language Models for Life Cycle Assessments: Opportunities, Challenges, and Risks. *J. Clean. Prod.* **2024**, *466*, 142824. [CrossRef]
15. Namvarpour, M.; Razi, A. Apprentices to Research Assistants: Advancing Research with Large Language Models. *arXiv* **2024**, arXiv:2404.06404. [CrossRef]
16. Kalverkamp, M.; Helmers, E.; Pehlken, A. Impacts of Life Cycle Inventory Databases on Life Cycle Assessments: A Review by Means of a Drivetrain Case Study. *J. Clean. Prod.* **2020**, *269*, 121329. [CrossRef]
17. Bareiß, K.; De La Rua, C.; Möckl, M.; Hamacher, T. Life Cycle Assessment of Hydrogen from Proton Exchange Membrane Water Electrolysis in Future Energy Systems. *Appl. Energy* **2019**, *237*, 862–872. [CrossRef]
18. Ecoinvent Database. Available online: https://ecoinvent.org/ (accessed on 24 October 2024).
19. Pauer, E.; Wohner, B.; Tacker, M. The Influence of Database Selection on Environmental Impact Results. Life Cycle Assessment of Packaging Using GaBi, Ecoinvent 3.6, and the Environmental Footprint Database. *Sustainability* **2020**, *12*, 9948. [CrossRef]
20. GaBi Database & Modelling Principles 2012. Available online: http://gabi-6-lci-documentation.gabi-software.com/xml-data/external_docs/GaBiModellingPrinciples.pdf (accessed on 24 October 2024).
21. Teng, Y.; Li, C.Z.; Shen, G.Q.P.; Yang, Q.; Peng, Z. The Impact of Life Cycle Assessment Database Selection on Embodied Carbon Estimation of Buildings. *Build. Environ.* **2023**, *243*, 110648. [CrossRef]
22. Su, D. (Ed.) *Sustainable Product Development: Tools, Methods and Examples*; Springer International Publishing: Berlin/Heidelberg, Germany, 2020; ISBN 978-3-030-39148-5.
23. Dreyer, L.C.; Niemann, A.L.; Hauschild, M.Z. Comparison of Three Different LCIA Methods: EDIP97, CML2001 and Eco-Indicator 99: Does It Matter Which One You Choose? *Int. J. Life Cycle Assess.* **2003**, *8*, 191–200. [CrossRef]
24. Lasvaux, S.; Achim, F.; Garat, P.; Peuportier, B.; Chevalier, J.; Habert, G. Correlations in Life Cycle Impact Assessment Methods (LCIA) and Indicators for Construction Materials: What Matters? *Ecol. Indic.* **2016**, *67*, 174–182. [CrossRef]
25. Domingo-Morcillo, E.; Escrig-Olmedo, E.; Rivera-Lirio, J.M.; Muñoz-Torres, M.J. Analyzing the Suitability of LCIA Methods to Foster the Most Beneficial Food Loss and Waste Prevention Action in Terms of Environmental Sustainability. *Environ. Impact Assess. Rev.* **2024**, *107*, 107575. [CrossRef]
26. Dekker, E.; Zijp, M.C.; Van De Kamp, M.E.; Temme, E.H.M.; Van Zelm, R. A Taste of the New ReCiPe for Life Cycle Assessment: Consequences of the Updated Impact Assessment Method on Food Product LCAs. *Int. J. Life Cycle Assess.* **2020**, *25*, 2315–2324. [CrossRef]
27. Commission Recommendation on the Use of the Environmental Footprint Methods 2021. Available online: https://environment.ec.europa.eu/publications/recommendation-use-environmental-footprint-methods_en (accessed on 24 October 2024).
28. Gerhardt-Mörsdorf, J.; Peterssen, F.; Burfeind, P.; Benecke, M.; Bensmann, B.; Hanke-Rauschenbach, R.; Minke, C. Life Cycle Assessment of a 5 MW Polymer Exchange Membrane Water Electrolysis Plant. *Adv. Energy Sustain. Res.* **2024**, *5*, 2300135. [CrossRef]
29. Lotrič, A.; Sekavčnik, M.; Kuštrin, I.; Mori, M. Life-Cycle Assessment of Hydrogen Technologies with the Focus on EU Critical Raw Materials and End-of-Life Strategies. *Int. J. Hydrogen Energy* **2021**, *46*, 10143–10160. [CrossRef]
30. iPoint Umberto. Available online: https://www.ifu.com/umberto/ (accessed on 24 October 2024).
31. Brightway Developers Brightway LCA Software Framework. Available online: https://docs.brightway.dev/en/latest/ (accessed on 24 October 2024).

32. European Commission European Platform on LCA—EPLCA—Environmental Footprint. Available online: https://eplca.jrc.ec.europa.eu/EnvironmentalFootprint.html (accessed on 24 October 2024).
33. Rosenbaum, R.K. Overview of Existing LCIA Methods—Annex to Chapter 10. In *Life Cycle Assessment*; Springer: Berlin/Heidelberg, Germany, 2018; ISBN 978-3-319-56475-3.
34. Krishnan, S.; Koning, V.; Theodorus De Groot, M.; De Groot, A.; Mendoza, P.G.; Junginger, M.; Kramer, G.J. Present and Future Cost of Alkaline and PEM Electrolyser Stacks. *Int. J. Hydrogen Energy* **2023**, *48*, 32313–32330. [CrossRef]
35. Bhandari, R.; Trudewind, C.A.; Zapp, P. Life Cycle Assessment of Hydrogen Production via Electrolysis—A Review. *J. Clean. Prod.* **2014**, *85*, 151–163. [CrossRef]
36. Vaswani, A.; Shazeer, N.; Parmar, N.; Uszkoreit, J.; Jones, L.; Gomez, A.N.; Kaiser, L.; Polosukhin, I. Attention Is All You Need. In Proceedings of the Advances in Neural Information Processing Systems 30 (NIPS 2017), Long Beach, CA, USA, 4–9 December 2017.
37. Chizhikova, A.; Murzakhmetov, S.; Serikov, O.; Shavrina, T.; Burtsev, M. Attention Understands Semantic Relations. In Proceedings of the Thirteenth Language Resources and Evaluation Conference, Marseille, France, 20–25 June 2022; Calzolari, N., Béchet, F., Blache, P., Choukri, K., Cieri, C., Declerck, T., Goggi, S., Isahara, H., Maegaard, B., Mariani, J., et al., Eds.; European Language Resources Association: Marseille, France, 2022; pp. 4040–4050.
38. Devlin, J.; Chang, M.-W.; Lee, K.; Toutanova, K. BERT: Pre-Training of Deep Bidirectional Transformers for Language Understanding. *arXiv* **2018**, arXiv:1810.04805.
39. Liu, Y.; Ott, M.; Goyal, N.; Du, J.; Joshi, M.; Chen, D.; Levy, O.; Lewis, M.; Zettlemoyer, L.; Stoyanov, V. RoBERTa: A Robustly Optimized BERT Pretraining Approach. *arXiv* **2019**, arXiv:1907.11692.
40. OpenAI; Achiam, J.; Adler, S.; Agarwal, S.; Ahmad, L.; Akkaya, I.; Aleman, F.L.; Almeida, D.; Altenschmidt, J.; Altman, S.; et al. GPT-4 Technical Report. *arXiv* **2023**, arXiv:2303.08774.
41. Touvron, H.; Lavril, T.; Izacard, G.; Martinet, X.; Lachaux, M.-A.; Lacroix, T.; Rozière, B.; Goyal, N.; Hambro, E.; Azhar, F.; et al. LLaMA: Open and Efficient Foundation Language Models. *arXiv* **2023**, arXiv:2302.13971.
42. Minaee, S.; Mikolov, T.; Nikzad, N.; Chenaghlu, M.; Socher, R.; Amatriain, X.; Gao, J. Large Language Models: A Survey. *arXiv* **2024**, arXiv:2402.06196. [CrossRef]
43. Boyko, J.; Cohen, J.; Fox, N.; Veiga, M.H.; Li, J.I.-H.; Liu, J.; Modenesi, B.; Rauch, A.H.; Reid, K.N.; Tribedi, S.; et al. An Interdisciplinary Outlook on Large Language Models for Scientific Research. *arXiv* **2023**, arXiv:2311.04929.
44. Abu-Jeyyab, M.; Alrosan, S.; Alkhawaldeh, I. Harnessing Large Language Models in Medical Research and Scientific Writing: A Closer Look to The Future: LLMs in Medical Research and Scientific Writing. *High Yield Med. Rev.* **2023**, *1*. [CrossRef]
45. Zhang, Q.; Ding, K.; Lyv, T.; Wang, X.; Yin, Q.; Zhang, Y.; Yu, J.; Wang, Y.; Li, X.; Xiang, Z.; et al. Scientific Large Language Models: A Survey on Biological & Chemical Domains. *arXiv* **2024**, arXiv:2401.14656. [CrossRef]
46. Routray, S.K.; Javali, A.; Sharmila, K.P.; Jha, M.K.; Pappa, M.; Singh, M. Large Language Models (LLMs): Hypes and Realities. In Proceedings of the 2023 International Conference on Computer Science and Emerging Technologies (CSET), Bangalore, India, 10–12 October 2023; IEEE: Bangalore, India, 2023; pp. 1–6.
47. Lu, D.; Deng, Y.; Malof, J.M.; Padilla, W.J. Can Large Language Models Learn the Physics of Metamaterials? An Empirical Study with ChatGPT. *arXiv* **2024**, arXiv:2404.15458. [CrossRef]
48. Head, C.B.; Jasper, P.; McConnachie, M.; Raftree, L.; Higdon, G. Large Language Model Applications for Evaluation: Opportunities and Ethical Implications. *New Dir. Eval.* **2023**, *2023*, 33–46. [CrossRef]
49. Doyal, A.S.; Sender, D.; Nanda, M.; Serrano, R.A. Chat GPT and Artificial Intelligence in Medical Writing: Concerns and Ethical Considerations. *Cureus* **2023**, *15*, e43292. [CrossRef]
50. Watkins, R. Guidance for Researchers and Peer-Reviewers on the Ethical Use of Large Language Models (LLMs) in Scientific Research Workflows. *AI Ethics* **2023**, 1–6. [CrossRef]
51. Sahoo, P.; Singh, A.K.; Saha, S.; Jain, V.; Mondal, S.; Chadha, A. A Systematic Survey of Prompt Engineering in Large Language Models: Techniques and Applications. *arXiv* **2024**, arXiv:2402.07927.
52. Dhuliawala, S.; Komeili, M.; Xu, J.; Raileanu, R.; Li, X.; Celikyilmaz, A.; Weston, J. Chain-of-Verification Reduces Hallucination in Large Language Models. *arXiv* **2023**, arXiv:2309.11495. [CrossRef]
53. Khoshnevisan, B.; Rafiee, S.; Omid, M.; Mousazadeh, H.; Sefeedpari, P. Prognostication of Environmental Indices in Potato Production Using Artificial Neural Networks. *J. Clean. Prod.* **2013**, *52*, 402–409. [CrossRef]
54. Omidkar, A.; Alagumalai, A.; Li, Z.; Song, H. Machine Learning Assisted Techno-Economic and Life Cycle Assessment of Organic Solid Waste Upgrading under Natural Gas. *Appl. Energy* **2024**, *355*, 122321. [CrossRef]
55. Algren, M.; Fisher, W.; Landis, A.E. Machine Learning in Life Cycle Assessment. In *Data Science Applied to Sustainability Analysis*; Elsevier: Amsterdam, The Netherlands, 2021; pp. 167–190, ISBN 978-0-12-817976-5.
56. Zheng, L.; Mueller, M.; Luo, C.; Yan, X. Predicting Whole-Life Carbon Emissions for Buildings Using Different Machine Learning Algorithms: A Case Study on Typical Residential Properties in Cornwall, UK. *Appl. Energy* **2024**, *357*, 122472. [CrossRef]
57. Kaab, A.; Sharifi, M.; Mobli, H.; Nabavi-Pelesaraei, A.; Chau, K. Combined Life Cycle Assessment and Artificial Intelligence for Prediction of Output Energy and Environmental Impacts of Sugarcane Production. *Sci. Total Environ.* **2019**, *664*, 1005–1019. [CrossRef] [PubMed]
58. Tawalbeh, M.; Shomope, I.; Al-Othman, A.; Alshraideh, H. Prediction of Hydrogen Production in Proton Exchange Membrane Water Electrolysis via Neural Networks. *Int. J. Thermofluids* **2024**, *24*, 100849. [CrossRef]

59. Saad, M.; Zhang, Y.; Jia, J.; Tian, J. Decision Tree-Based Approach to Extrapolate Life Cycle Inventory Data of Manufacturing Processes. *J. Environ. Manag.* **2024**, *360*, 121152. [CrossRef]
60. Camastra, F.; Capone, V.; Ciaramella, A.; Riccio, A.; Staiano, A. Prediction of Environmental Missing Data Time Series by Support Vector Machine Regression and Correlation Dimension Estimation. *Environ. Model. Softw.* **2022**, *150*, 105343. [CrossRef]
61. CML-IA Characterisation Factors. Available online: https://www.universiteitleiden.nl/en/research/research-output/science/cml-ia-characterisation-factors (accessed on 24 October 2024).
62. United Stated Environmental Protection Agency Tool for Reduction and Assessment of Chemicals and Other Environmental Impacts (TRACI). Available online: https://www.epa.gov/chemical-research/tool-reduction-and-assessment-chemicals-and-other-environmental-impacts-traci (accessed on 24 October 2024).
63. Gupta, M.R. ChatGPT-A Generative Pre-Trained Transformer. *Int. J. Adv. Res. Sci. Commun. Technol.* **2024**, 590–595. [CrossRef]
64. Abdella, G.M.; Kucukvar, M.; Onat, N.C.; Al-Yafay, H.M.; Bulak, M.E. Sustainability Assessment and Modeling Based on Supervised Machine Learning Techniques: The Case for Food Consumption. *J. Clean. Prod.* **2020**, *251*, 119661. [CrossRef]
65. Azari, R.; Garshasbi, S.; Amini, P.; Rashed-Ali, H.; Mohammadi, Y. Multi-Objective Optimization of Building Envelope Design for Life Cycle Environmental Performance. *Energy Build.* **2016**, *126*, 524–534. [CrossRef]
66. Nguyen, T.H.; Nong, D.; Paustian, K. Surrogate-Based Multi-Objective Optimization of Management Options for Agricultural Landscapes Using Artificial Neural Networks. *Ecol. Model.* **2019**, *400*, 1–13. [CrossRef]
67. Hou, P.; Jolliet, O.; Zhu, J.; Xu, M. Estimate Ecotoxicity Characterization Factors for Chemicals in Life Cycle Assessment Using Machine Learning Models. *Environ. Int.* **2020**, *135*, 105393. [CrossRef]
68. Cheng, F.; Luo, H.; Colosi, L.M. Slow Pyrolysis as a Platform for Negative Emissions Technology: An Integration of Machine Learning Models, Life Cycle Assessment, and Economic Analysis. *Energy Convers. Manag.* **2020**, *223*, 113258. [CrossRef]
69. Duprez, S.; Fouquet, M.; Herreros, Q.; Jusselme, T. Improving Life Cycle-Based Exploration Methods by Coupling Sensitivity Analysis and Metamodels. *Sustain. Cities Soc.* **2019**, *44*, 70–84. [CrossRef]
70. Slapnik, M.; Istenič, D.; Pintar, M.; Udovč, A. Extending Life Cycle Assessment Normalization Factors and Use of Machine Learning—A Slovenian Case Study. *Ecol. Indic.* **2015**, *50*, 161–172. [CrossRef]
71. Hauschild, M.Z.; Rosenbaum, R.K.; Olsen, S.I. *Life Cycle Assessment—Theory and Practice*; Springer: Berlin/Heidelberg, Germany, 2018; ISBN 978-3-319-56474-6.
72. Amasyali, K.; El-Gohary, N.M. A Review of Data-Driven Building Energy Consumption Prediction Studies. *Renew. Sustain. Energy Rev.* **2018**, 1192–1205. [CrossRef]
73. Yitmen, I.; Alizadehsalehi, S.; Akiner, L.; Akiner, M.E. An Adapted Model of Cognitive Digital Twins for Building Lifecycle Management. *Appl. Sci.* **2021**, *11*, 4276. [CrossRef]
74. Baduge, S.K.; Thilakarathna, S.; Perera, J.S.; Arashpour, M.; Sharafi, P.; Teodosio, B.; Shringi, A.; Mendis, P. Artificial Intelligence and Smart Vision for Building and Construction 4.0: Machine and Deep Learning Methods and Applications. *Autom. Constr.* **2022**, *141*, 104440. [CrossRef]
75. Wang, L.; Liu, Z.; Liu, A.; Tao, F. Artificial Intelligence in Product Lifecycle Management. *Int. J. Adv. Manuf. Technol.* **2021**, *114*, 771–796. [CrossRef]
76. D'Amico, A.; Ciulla, G.; Traverso, M.; Lo Brano, V.; Palumbo, E. Artificial Neural Networks to Assess Energy and Environmental Performance of Buildings: An Italian Case Study. *J. Clean. Prod.* **2019**, *239*, 117993. [CrossRef]
77. Long, F.; Liu, H. An Integration of Machine Learning Models and Life Cycle Assessment for Lignocellulosic Bioethanol Platforms. *Energy Convers. Manag.* **2023**, *292*, 117379. [CrossRef]
78. Markowska, A.; Krzywonos, M.; Culjak, M.; Walaszczyk, E.; Mialkowska, K.; Chojnacka-Komorowska, A.; Matouk, K.; Snierzynski, M. Machine Learning for Environmental Life Cycle Costing. *Procedia Comput. Sci.* **2022**, *207*, 4087–4096. [CrossRef]
79. Koyamparambath, A.; Adibi, N.; Szablewski, C.; Adibi, A.S.; Sonnemann, G. Implementing Artificial Intelligence Techniques to Predict Environmental Impacts: Case of Construction Products. *Sustainability* **2022**, *6*, 3699. [CrossRef]
80. Dinesh, A.; Rahul Prasad, B. Predictive Models in Machine Learning for Strength and Life Cycle Assessment of Concrete Structures. *Autom. Constr.* **2024**, *162*, 105412. [CrossRef]
81. Prioux, N.; Ouaret, R.; Hetreux, G.; Belaud, J.P. Environmental Assessment Coupled with Machine Learning for Circular Economy. *Clean Technol. Environ. Policy* **2023**, *25*, 689–702. [CrossRef]
82. Akhshik, M.; Bilton, A.; Tjong, J.; Singh, C.V.; Faruk, O.; Sain, M. Prediction of Greenhouse Gas Emissions Reductions via Machine Learning Algorithms: Toward an Artificial Intelligence-Based Life Cycle Assessment for Automotive Lightweighting. *Sustain. Mater. Technol.* **2022**, *31*, e00370. [CrossRef]
83. Hafdaoui, H.E.; Khallaayoun, A.; Bouarfa, I.; Ouazzani, K. Machine Learning for Embodied Carbon Life Cycle Assessment of Buildings. *J. Umm Al-Qura Univ. Eng. Archit.* **2023**, *14*, 188–200. [CrossRef]
84. Marvuglia, A.; Kanevski, M.; Benetto, E. Machine Learning for Toxicity Characterization of Organic Chemical Emissions Using USEtox Database: Learning the Structure of the Input Space. *Environ. Int.* **2015**, *83*, 72–85. [CrossRef]
85. Zhu, X.; Chi-Hung, H.; Wang, X. Application of Life Cycle Assessment and Machine Learning for High-Throughput Screening of Green Chemical Substitutes. *ACS Sustain. Chem. Eng.* **2020**, *8*, 11141–11151. [CrossRef]
86. Elomari, Y.; Mateu, C.; Marin-Genesca, M.; Boer, D. A Data-Driven Framework for Designing a Renewable Energy Community Based on the Integration of Machine Learning Model with Life Cycle Assessment and Life Cycle Cost Parameters. *Appl. Energy* **2024**, *358*, 122619. [CrossRef]

87. Nejad, M.S.; Almassi, M.; Ghahderijani, M. Life Cycle Energy and Environmental Impacts in Sugarcane Production: A Case Study of Amirkabir Sugarcane Agro-Industrial Company in Khuzestan Province. *Results Eng.* **2023**, *20*, 101545. [CrossRef]
88. Guinée, J. Handbook on Life Cycle Assessment—Operational Guide to the ISO Standards. *Int. J. Life Cycle Assess* **2001**, *6*, 255. [CrossRef]
89. Guo, G.; He, Y.; Jin, F.; Mašek, O.; Huang, Q. Application of Life Cycle Assessment and Machine Learning for the Production and Environmental Sustainability Assessment of Hydrothermal Bio-Oil. *Bioresour. Technol.* **2023**, *379*, 129027. [CrossRef] [PubMed]
90. Portolani, P.; Vitali, A.; Cornago, S.; Rovelli, D.; Brondi, C.; Low, J.S.C.; Ramakrishna, S.; Ballarino, A. Machine Learning to Forecast Electricity Hourly LCA Impacts Due to a Dynamic Electricity Technology Mix. *Front. Sustain.* **2022**, *3*, 1037497. [CrossRef]
91. Shirvanian, P.; Van Berkel, F. Novel Components in Proton Exchange Membrane (PEM) Water Electrolyzers (PEMWE): Status, Challenges and Future Needs. A Mini Review. *Electrochem. Commun.* **2020**, *114*, 106704. [CrossRef]
92. Ghoroghi, A.; Rezgui, Y.; Petri, I. Advances in Application of Machine Learning to Life Cycle Assessment: A Literature Review. *Int. J. Life Cycle Assess.* **2022**, *27*, 433–456. [CrossRef]
93. Takano, A.; Winter, S.; Hughes, M.; Linkosalmi, L. Comparison of Life Cycle Assessment Databases: A Case Study on Building Assessment. *Build. Environ.* **2014**, *79*, 20–30. [CrossRef]
94. Uekert, T.; Wikoff, H.M.; Badgett, A. Electrolyzer and Fuel Cell Recycling for a Circular Hydrogen Economy. *Adv. Sustain. Syst.* **2024**, *8*, 2300449. [CrossRef]
95. Bareiß, K. An Enhanced Methodology for Energy System Modeling Including Life-Cycle Analysis: Hydrogen as Power-to-X Element. Ph.D. Thesis, Technical University of Munich, Munich, Germany, 2020.

*machine learning & knowledge extraction*

MDPI

*Article*

# Balancing Results from AI-Based Geostatistics versus Fuzzy Inference by Game Theory Bargaining to Improve a Groundwater Monitoring Network

**Masoumeh Hashemi [1,*], Richard C. Peralta [2,*] and Matt Yost [1]**

[1] Plant, Soil & Climate Department, Utah State University, Logan, UT 84322, USA; matt.yost@usu.edu
[2] Civil and Environmental Engineering Department, Utah State University, Logan, UT 843322, USA
* Correspondence: masoumeh.hashemi@usu.edu (M.H.); richard.peralta@usu.edu (R.C.P.); Tel.: +1-435-470-7593 (M.H.); +1-435-881-4947 (R.C.P.)

**Abstract:** An artificial intelligence-based geostatistical optimization algorithm was developed to upgrade a test Iranian aquifer's existing groundwater monitoring network. For that aquifer, a preliminary study revealed that a Multi-Layer Perceptron Artificial Neural Network (MLP-ANN) more accurately determined temporally average water table elevations than geostatistical kriging, spline, and inverse distance weighting. Because kriging is usually used in that area for water table estimation, the developed algorithm used MLP-ANN to guide kriging, and Genetic Algorithm (GA) to determine locations for new monitoring well location(s). For possible annual fiscal budgets allowing 1–12 new wells, 12 sets of optimal new well locations are reported. Each set has the locations of new wells that would minimize the squared difference between the time-averaged heads developed by kriging versus MLP-ANN. Also, to simultaneously consider local expertise, the algorithm used fuzzy inference to quantify an expert's satisfaction with the number of new wells. Then, the algorithm used symmetric bargaining (Nash, Kalai–Smorodinsky, and area monotonic) to present an upgradation strategy that balanced professional judgment and heuristic optimization. In essence, the algorithm demonstrates the systematic application of relatively new computational practices to a common situation worldwide.

**Keywords:** bargaining theory; fuzzy inference system; groundwater monitoring; geostatistics; artificial neural network; optimization

## 1. Introduction

Groundwater level maps are crucial raster data that relate aquifer hydraulic conductivity, recharge zones, flow directions, velocity, and management strategies. They also assist in operations, i.e., their conservation policies. A groundwater level monitoring network is essential for managing groundwater [1,2]. However, installing observation wells throughout an aquifer is impractical [3,4]. Consequently, many researchers have focused on improving head estimation for unmonitored sites [5,6]. The accuracy of estimating groundwater heads at unmeasured locations depends on the number and location of monitoring wells and varies spatially with the surface fitting method [6,7].

The process of determining unknown values between known values is called interpolation. Surface fitting methods are used to interpolate the value at unknown points. These methods can be classified as follows: I: deterministic (e.g., spline, inverse distance weighting (IDW), etc.); II: geostatistical (e.g., kriging, universal kriging, etc.) [8]; and III: machine learning [6]. Of the geostatistical methods used to develop water table maps from observed water levels by surface fitting [9], kriging is the most common [10,11]. Machine learning has been applied to estimate or predict groundwater levels [6,12] and to predict other water-related variables [13].

The accuracy of interpolations depends on the number and spatial distribution of monitoring locations [11,14]. To improve the accuracy of estimation at unmonitored points, the importance of implementing observation well monitoring programs has attracted the attention of many authors [15,16]. Model fitting and interpolation methodologies can differ for site-specific conditions. Utilized optimization objective functions include reducing the long-term monitoring cost [5], maximizing spatial accuracy and minimizing temporal redundancy in head observations [16,17], minimizing standard deviations in predicted head error by adding new wells and eliminating wells [18,19], improving the reliability of groundwater simulation model predictions [20,21], and optimizing the number of monitoring stations and sampling intervals [22,23]. As far as the design of monitoring networks is concerned, there is no single right or wrong method, and often, judgment should be based on the expertise of the personnel designing the network rather than on statistical or modeling results [24,25].

Ideally, the design should employ (i) qualitative and quantitative hydrogeological information and statistical approach(es) that might include statistical analysis, interpolation methods, contaminant transport simulations, and/or numerical groundwater flow [24,26] and (ii) local experts' experience [24]. To represent an expert's opinion, a Fuzzy Inference System (FIS) uses fuzzy logic and set theory to convert fuzzy qualitative input values into crisp numeric values. Two types of widely used FIS [27] are Mamdani [28] and Sugeno [29]. To date, FIS has been used in groundwater management for estimating groundwater levels [30–32] but has not been utilized in improving a groundwater monitoring network.

The primary objective of this research was to integrate expert insights into a framework aimed at pinpointing optimal locations for new observation wells, thereby enhancing the precision of kriged groundwater level maps. Initially, it discerned the most precise surface fitting method for delineating groundwater levels within the study area, namely, the Qazvin plain in Iran. Subsequently, the study proposed strategies for augmenting groundwater level monitoring networks via heuristic optimization, which involved identifying prime sites for new wells and incorporating expert judgments through fuzzy logic. This study introduced an innovative methodology that orchestrated multiple processes concurrently and sequentially to systematically juxtapose and harmonize numerical optimization outcomes with expert-derived site-specific knowledge. Notably, this methodology introduced the inaugural FIS designed specifically to encapsulate expert judgment in enhancing groundwater level monitoring networks.

## 2. Materials and Methods

### 2.1. Study Area

Due to excessive groundwater extraction, over one-third of Iran's plains are now designated as prohibited zones for new well drilling [33,34]. In the 3919 km$^2$ Qazvin Aquifer, groundwater levels have steadily decreased over the years, leading to limitations on groundwater extraction in areas classified as prohibited plains where new extraction well drilling is prohibited [11,35]. This region has an annual mean temperature of 13 °C, an annual precipitation of about 320 mm, and a cold-dry climate (Figure 1). Groundwater levels, as monitored by 168 observation wells, exhibit an average monthly range between 1129.5 m and 1408.3 m.

Considering the aquifer's important role as a primary source of irrigation water, water managers are motivated to refine their estimations of groundwater volumes [11]. With a focus on aiding the Qazvin Regional Water Company (QRWC), this study aims to elucidate the most efficacious methodology for increasing the accuracy of widely utilized groundwater level data through the integration of additional groundwater level observation wells. Acknowledging the inherent temporal variability of groundwater, including fluctuations within each year, the study adopts the mean head derived from a comprehensive dataset encompassing 72 consecutive months of monthly measurements as the target water level at each pre-existing observation site.

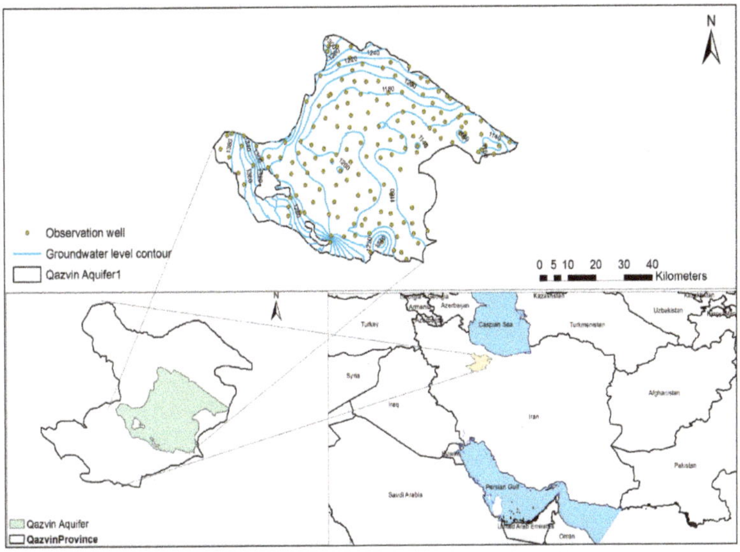


**Figure 1.** Groundwater level contours and observation wells in Qazvin Aquifer, Qazvin Province, Iran.

### 2.2. *Comparison of Groundwater Surface Mapping Methods for the Study Area*

In the study area, water managers have traditionally relied on kriging to generate water table maps [11]. Kriging head values are derived from an existing monitoring well network. There is commonly overestimation and underestimation of values for locations without observed data [36]. In our study, comparative analyses are performed between kriging [37], inverse distance weighting (IDW) [38,39], spline [40,41], and Multi-Layer Perceptron Artificial Neural Network (MLP-ANN) [42].

To conduct these analyses, a Kriging MATLAB toolbox [43] was added to the MATLAB toolboxes, and the neural network toolboxes were utilized for MLP-ANN. For spline and IDW methods, we used Arc GIS. Observed head values were divided into two groups: training and testing. The accuracy of each method was evaluated to estimate the heads of the testing sets.

#### 2.2.1. Kriging

Kriging is the most used technique for mapping geologic and hydrological surfaces [44,45]. To estimate a value at a specified location, kriging considers both the distance between known observation locations and the difference in their observed values. To estimate a value at a location without direct measurement, kriging employs observed data and weights as specified within Equation (1).

$$H^*(x) = \sum_{i=1}^{N_m} \frac{1}{2N(h)} \sum_{i=1}^{N(h)} (H(X_i) - H(X_i + h))\, H(x_i) \quad (1)$$

where $H^*(x)$ is the groundwater level estimated by kriging, $N_m$ is the number of observation wells, $H(X_i)$ is the groundwater level measured at the ith location, and N(h) is the total number of pairs of employed observation locations that are separated by a distance h. The weight is calculated by applying equations that use a site-specific semivariogram [37,39].

To adequately describe site-specific regional geologic trends, it is crucial to utilize an appropriate form of semivariogram. Within the study area, statistical indicators are employed to assess and contrast five types of theoretical variograms: spherical, exponential, Gaussian, linear, and power function. Within the outlined methodology, the semivariogram offering the most accurate estimation of head size is identified. For each semivariogram, the evaluation process involves dividing observed field data into 70% training and 30% testing sets, determining kriging that optimizes the agreement between observed and estimated (kriged) heads, applying these weights to estimate heads at testing dataset locations, and calculating statistical metrics.

### 2.2.2. Inverse Distance Weighting (IDW)

In IDW interpolation, a set of sample points is linearly weighted to determine a value for an unmeasured location. These weights are determined by the inverse distance between the measured and predicted locations, meaning that points closer to the predicted location exert more influence on its value compared to those farther away. The computation of the value for unmeasured points is performed using the following equation:

$$H^*(x_0) = \sum_{i=1}^{N_m} \frac{\frac{1}{d_i}}{\sum_{i=1}^{n}\left(\frac{1}{d_i}\right)} H(x_i) \tag{2}$$

where $d_i$ is the distance from the ith measured point ($x_i$) to the predicted point ($x_0$). The same evaluation process is applied to assess the performance of this method.

### 2.2.3. Spline

The spline interpolation method utilizes a mathematical function to minimize overall surface curvature, resulting in a smooth surface that precisely intersects the measured points. This function can be expressed as follows:

$$S(x,y) = T(x,y) + \sum_{i=1}^{N_m} \lambda_i R(r_i) \tag{3}$$

where $\lambda_i$ is the coefficient found by solving a system of linear equations, $r_i$ is the distance between the predicted point and the ith point, S(x,y) is the new point of interpolation, and $T(x,y)$ and $R(r_i)$ are defined differently based on the selected option, which is the regularized option in this study. For additional details, consult references [40,41]. To statistically evaluate the performance of the interpolation method, testing data that were not used for training are employed.

### 2.2.4. Artificial Neural Network (ANN)

Artificial Neural Networks (ANNs) use simple information to help describe a complex system [1,46]. Among machine learning algorithms, artificial neural networks stand out for their capacity to discern intricate patterns from data [6,47]. While a range of machine learning algorithms exists for estimating groundwater levels [6,48], this study aims to construct a model that requires minimal input data that are both easy and inexpensive to collect. Thus, a feed-forward back-propagation neural network algorithm featuring a Multi-Layer Perceptron (MLP-ANN) architecture is developed for estimating the water table at a designated location (Figure 2). A previously reported MLP-ANN [6] employed latitude and longitude as inputs, and one hidden layer was not as accurate as kriging. The new MLP-ANN presented here additionally employed ground elevation as input and incorporated more than one hidden layer, as suggested in [6], to improve interpolation accuracy.

An MLP-ANN having hidden layers is a function, $f : \mathbb{R}^I \to \mathbb{R}^O$, where $\mathbb{R}$ is the set of real numbers, I is the size of the input vector, and O is the size of the output vector $F_O(x)$, such that the matrix notation is as follows:

$$O(I) = F_O(b_O + w_O(F_H(b_H + w_H(I)))) \tag{4}$$

where $b_H$ and $b_O$ are the bias matrices of the hidden layer and output layer, respectively; $w_H$ and $w_O$ are the weight matrices of the hidden layer and output layer, respectively; and $F_H$ and $F_O$ are transfer functions.

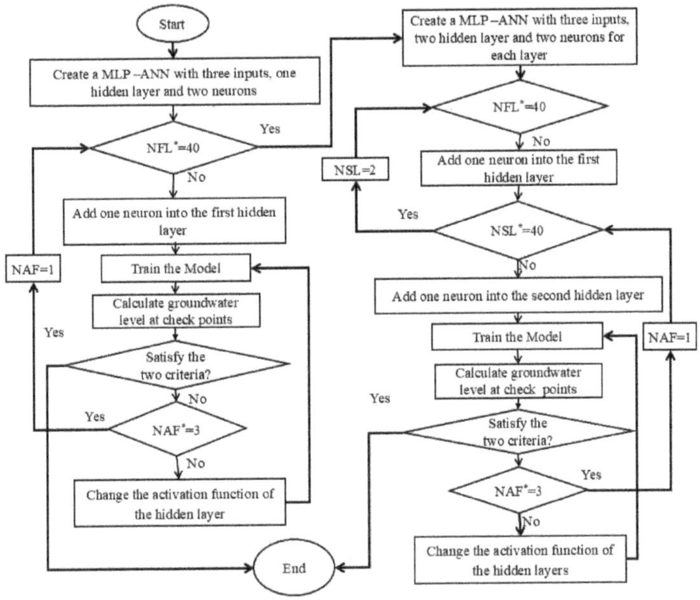


**Figure 2.** Conceptual architecture of employed hidden layer perceptron (NFL = number of neurons in the first layer; NSL = number of neurons in the second layer; NAF = number of activation functions).

The designed MLP-ANN calculated the groundwater level map using three inputs (longitude, latitude, and elevation) and used back-propagation to learn the network. The MPL-ANN is created using a neural network toolbox. To select an appropriate network, the data were randomly partitioned into two sets: 70% for training and 30% for testing. We selected the only MLP-ANN that satisfied two criteria: (i) a coefficient of determination higher than 0.9 and (ii) no estimated groundwater heads above the ground surface.

As shown in Figure 2, the first step started with a network that had one hidden layer and three neurons. The number of neurons was changed from 3 to 40. For each new number of neurons, three different activation functions—log-sigmoid, hyperbolic tangent sigmoid, and linear—were tested for the hidden layer. To evaluate each architecture, the same testing and training data were used. After that, the performance of each architecture was assessed based on the two criteria.

For the first criterion, the coefficient of determination ($R^2$) was calculated for the testing data. For the second criterion, 47,500 uniformly spaced check points that were 280 m apart (Figure 3) were provided. Groundwater levels at the check points were calculated and compared to the corresponding ground elevations. If no network met the two criteria, the number of neurons in the first layer could increase up to 40, and for each added neuron, the three activation functions could be evaluated. Following this step, one hidden layer could be added if the network did not still meet two criteria, so that the network was trained with two hidden layers. In this case, the first hidden layer had three neurons, and the second layer's neuron could change from 3 to 40. Furthermore, the activation function of hidden layers could be changed. Consequently, if it did not satisfy the criteria, one neuron could be added into the first hidden layer, making four neurons, and the second layer could change from 3 to 40 neurons to meet two criteria again. The cycle was continued until the created network satisfied both criteria.

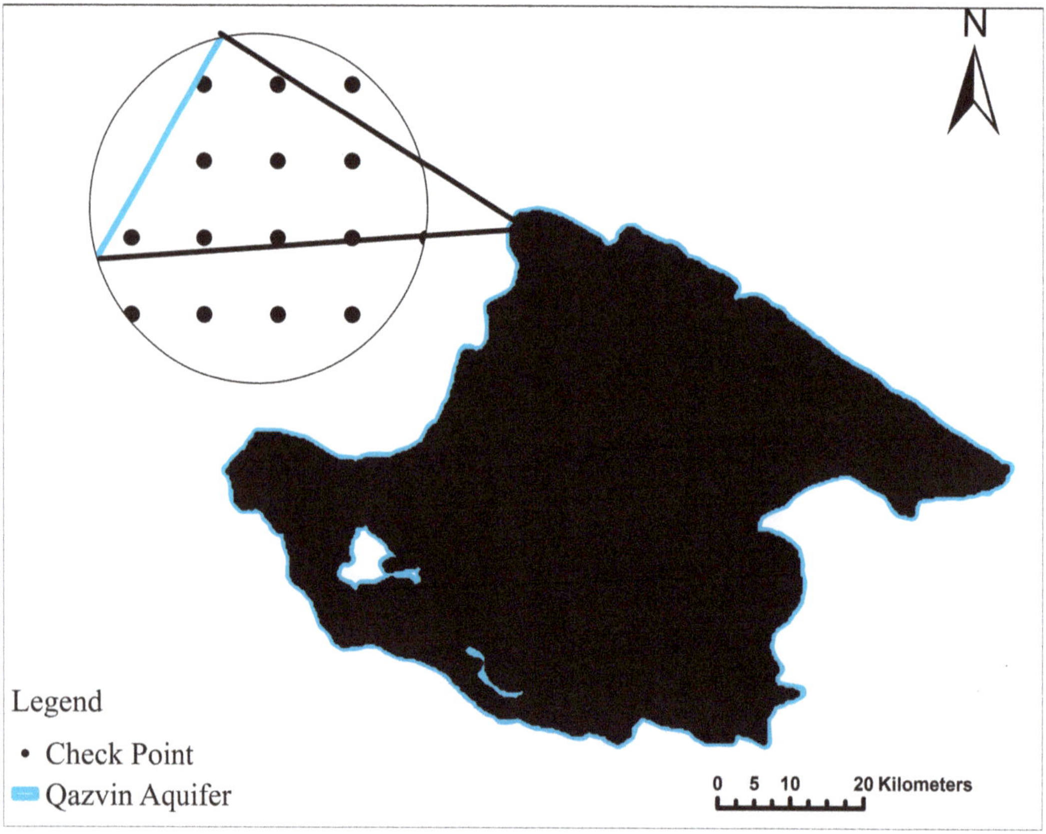


**Figure 3.** The check point locations (spaced 280 m apart).

2.2.5. Cross-Validation for Evaluation of Surface Fitting Methods

For each method, evaluation involves partitioning observed field head data into a training set and a testing set. Each method's training involves developing the set of weights or coefficients that cause the method's estimated heads to the best match observed training heads. Then, each trained method is used to estimate the heads of the testing dataset. The same testing and training sets have been used to evaluate the methods. The coefficient of determination ($R^2$), Root Mean Squared Error (RMSE), Mean Absolute Error (MAE), Root Mean Squared Logarithmic Error (RMSLE), and Relative Absolute Error (RAE) are used to evaluate how well each method estimates water levels at locations not used in training. Expressions of these parameters are shown in Equations (5)–(9):

$$R^2 = 1 - \frac{\sum_{i=1}^{N_{test}} \left(h_i^{obs} - h_i^{p}\right)^2}{\sum_{i=1}^{N_{test}} \left(h_i^{obs} - \overline{h}^{obs}\right)^2} \quad (5)$$

$$RMSE = \sqrt{\frac{\sum_{i=1}^{N_{test}} \left(h_i^{obs} - h_i^{p}\right)^2}{N_{test}}} \quad (6)$$

$$MAE = \frac{1}{N_{test}} \sum_{i=1}^{N_{test}} \left|h_i^{obs} - h_i^{p}\right| \quad (7)$$

$$\mathrm{RMSLE} = \sqrt{\frac{1}{\mathrm{N_{test}}} \sum_{i=1}^{\mathrm{N_{test}}} \left(\log\left(h_i^{obs}+1\right) - \log\left(h_i^{P}+1\right)\right)^2} \tag{8}$$

$$\mathrm{RAE} = \frac{\sum_{i=1}^{\mathrm{N_{test}}} \left|h_i^{P} - h_i^{obs}\right|}{\sum_{i=1}^{\mathrm{N_{test}}} \left|h_i^{P} - \overline{h}^{obs}\right|} \tag{9}$$

where $N_{test}$ is the number of elements within the testing subset, $h_i^{obs}$ is the observed groundwater level at the ith station, $h_i^P$ is the predicted groundwater level at the ith station, and $\overline{h}^{obs}$ is the average of observed groundwater levels.

The testing process outlined above identifies the method that offers the closest matches between estimated groundwater heads and observed groundwater heads. Subsequently, the novel methodology described below is employed to determine the requisite number and locations of additional observation well(s) necessary to achieve the study's objectives.

### 2.3. Designed Methodology and Model

The procedural goal is to determine the number and locations of new observation wells to be added to an existing observation network. To maximize simultaneously both quantitative accuracy improvement and qualitative Satisfaction of the Expert, the presented procedure uses multiple tools simultaneously, iteratively, and sequentially to develop trade-off curves, and then applies game theory to select a compromise strategy. Figure 4 illustrates the flowchart of the proposed model.

Overall, the user is first requested to enter the Maximum Number of Added Wells (MNAWs) to be considered for addition to the monitoring network. The subsequent process is divided into two main phases:

- Phase 1: This phase is executed MNAW times to construct a Pareto optimum trade-off curve. It is further subdivided as follows:
    - Phase 1a: For each specified Number of Additional Wells (NOAWs) (ranging from 1 to MNAW), the model employs kriged groundwater level, the most accurate interpolation method, combined with a heuristic optimization algorithm. This phase aims to identify new well location(s) that will maximize the improvement in water level representation achieved through the kriging method.
    - Phase 1b: This phase utilizes an FIS to incorporate local expert opinions regarding the preferred number of a new well(s) and the unit cost of a new well.
    - Phase 1c: After executing phases 1a and 1b MNAW times, phase 1c constructs the Pareto optimum curve. This curve visualizes the trade-off between accuracy improvement from phase 1a vs. the expert opinion from phase 1b. It provides a comprehensive view of potential conflicts and compromises between numerical optimization and experiential input.
- Phase 2: In this phase, three game theory techniques are applied to the Pareto optimum curve to identify equilibrium strategies. By applying these game theory techniques, the model identifies the most balanced and effective strategies for well placement, considering both numerical accuracy and expert opinions. These strategies help ensure that the final decision on the number and location of new wells is both optimal and equitable.

Based on the outcomes of Phase 1 and Phase 2, the model user selects the number of new wells to be installed at the locations specified by the model. The detailed procedures and methodologies employed in each phase are explained in the following sections.

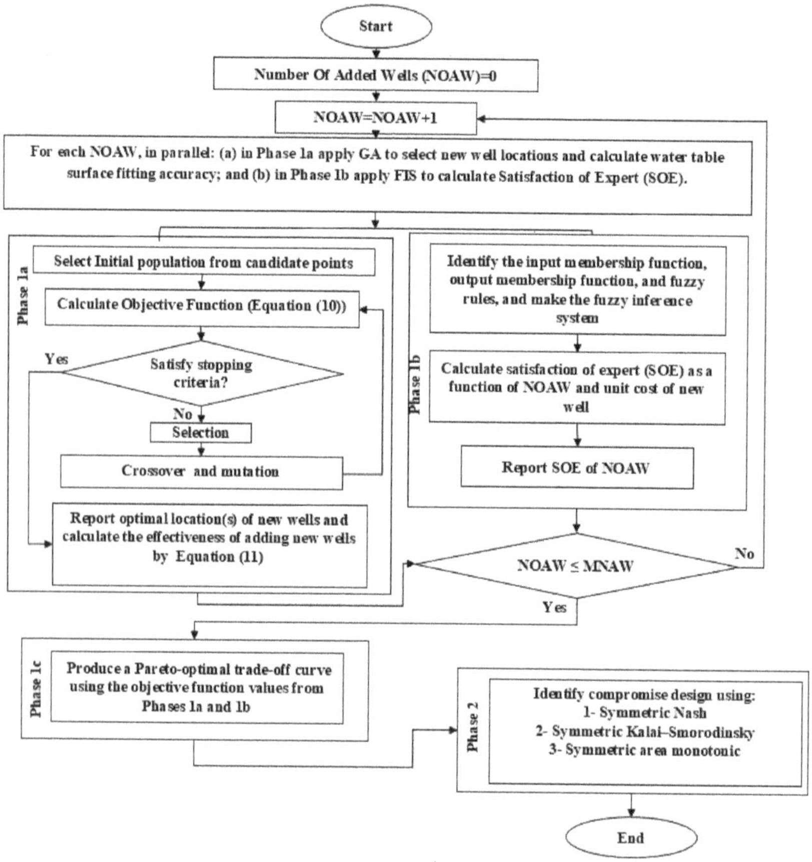


**Figure 4.** Algorithm for improving existing monitoring networks (NOAW: Number of Additional Observation Well(s); MNAWs: Maximum Number of Added Wells; GA: Genetic Algorithm; SOE: Satisfaction of the Expert; and FIS: Fuzzy Inference System).

### 2.3.1. Phase 1 (Produce Heuristic and Experiential Solutions)

Phases 1a and 1b run once for each specified Number of Additional Wells (NOAWs). NOAW values range from 1 to MNAWs (the MNAWs in this study is 12 wells). For each NOAW, within Phase 1a, a Genetic Algorithm (GA) identifies the optimal location(s) of added well(s) by maximizing the inverse of the mean sum of squared differences between the Most Accurate Interpolated Method (MAIM) and a newly kriged surface (the kriging weights change with additional well(s)). In the separate Phase 1b, a Fuzzy Inference System (FIS) calculates the Satisfaction of the Expert (SOE) for each NOAW. Phases 1a and 1b both run MNAW times. Then, Phase 1c prepares a trade-off curve reflecting tension between the results of Phases 1a and 1b.

#### Phase 1a (Produce and Apply Genetic Algorithm (GA))

GA is an iterative optimization technique inspired by the natural genetic processes of living organisms [49,50]. It is particularly useful for solving complex, nonlinear problems with multiple local optima, making it ideal for search and optimization tasks [7,51].

In the context of hydrology, GA excels in handling the inherent uncertainty and complexity of surface and subsurface water systems [50,52]. One of its key features is adaptability; by adjusting the mutation and crossover rates in response to changes in the average fitness value, GA can introduce randomness to avoid local minima or increase the crossover rate for more informed reproduction when there are significant changes in fitness. This adaptability enhances its ability to find optimal solutions in dynamic and complex environments [25]. Consequently, this study employed the GA due to its proven success and widespread application in water resources, as demonstrated by [7,20]. Other optimization algorithms could substitute for the GA in the presented procedure.

The flowchart in Figure 5 illustrates the Genetic Algorithm (GA) process utilized in this study. Each optimization uses a different NOAW, ranging from one to MNAWs. In each optimization, the number of observation well(s) to be added to the existing network and the search area need to be specified. To provide the GA with feasible options, around 1000 uniformly spaced candidate well locations are provided (Figure 6). Then, the most accurate interpolation method is used to simulate groundwater levels for them.

As explained, the intent of this study was to identify the optimal locations for adding NOAW new wells to improve the accuracy of the kriged groundwater level map. To begin an optimization, the model randomly selects NOAW locations from Figure 6 candidate coordinate points. This location or set of locations can be termed a coordinate point strategy. In a NOAW 2 optimization, an individual strategy of the population of strategies identifies two new coordinate points or locations. Each location has two optimization variables, the x coordinate and y coordinate, that are adjusted within each iteration. For example, for NOAW 2, each individual has two x and two y coordinates.

Kriging is then executed using just the heads from a new monitoring network that includes the existing wells plus the NOAWs of randomly selected wells. Next, the objective function Equation (10) is used to calculate the fitness value of that monitoring network. Each optimization sought to select the NOAW location(s) that would maximize the inverse of the mean squared error difference between the kriged surface from the new monitoring network and the heads from most accurate interpolation method (MAIM) at all N locations shown in Figure 6. Each optimization stops iterating when (1) the best objective function value remains unchanged for 1000 consecutive iterations and (2) the best fitness value (BFV) is better than or equal to the best previous fitness value (BPFV). BPFV is the BFV for "NOAW-1".

$$\text{maximize } Z_{\text{NOAW}} = \left( \frac{\sum_{i=1}^{N} \left( h_i^{\text{AIM}} - h_i^{\text{Kriged}} \right)^2}{N} \right)^{-1} \quad \text{for NOAW} = 1, 2, \ldots, \text{MNAW} \quad (10)$$

In Equation (10), NOAWs is the number of additional observation wells for a particular optimization; i is the index of the center of a cell within a uniform grid covering the Qazvin Aquifer; N is the number of cells in the grid; $h_i^{\text{AIM}}$ is the interpolated head at the *i*th location computed by the most accurate interpolation method; and $h_i^{\text{kriged}}$ is the head at the ith location that was estimated by kriging that used heads from NOAWs and existing wells.

If the stopping criteria are not satisfied, individuals are selected using the tournament selection method to crossover parents. After crossing the parents, the new locations are replaced with the points from the search space (Figure 6) that are closest to those locations. Then, mutation occurs with a specific mutation probability.

Individual fitness values are determined (Equation (10)) and compared with the previous best fitness. If the best fitness is the same as the previous best fitness, the best repetition fitness value is increased by one; otherwise, the best fitness value is replaced with the new fitness and the counter is reset to zero. The optimization continues until both stopping criteria are met. Phase 1a ends when NOAWs equal MNAWs.

For a specified NOAW, Equation (10) minimizes the MSE of differences between the most accurately interpolated potentiometric surface elevations and newly kriged values resulting from adding new observation well(s). Equation (11) divides Root Mean Square Error (RMSE) by NOAW. If the objective function values of NOAW and NOAW-1 are equal, the design using NOAW-1 provides the higher efficiency ($Ef_{NOAW}$). Thus, $Ef_{NOAW}$ is a measure of the effectiveness per additional new well, and the larger the value, the better.

$$Ef_{NOAW} = \frac{\left(\frac{\sum_{i=1}^{N}\left(h_i^{ANN}-h_i^{kriging}\right)^2}{N}\right)^{0.5}}{NOAW} \quad (11)$$

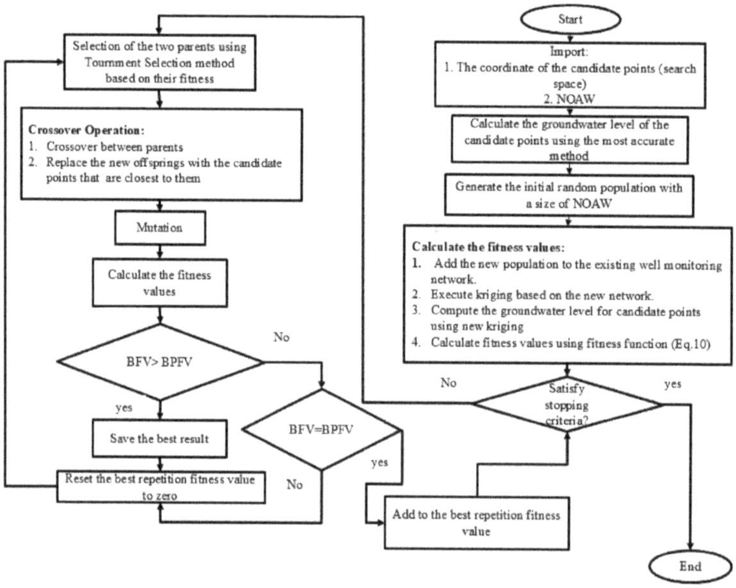


**Figure 5.** Flowchart of Genetic Algorithm model (BFV: the best fitness value; BPFV: the best previous fitness value).

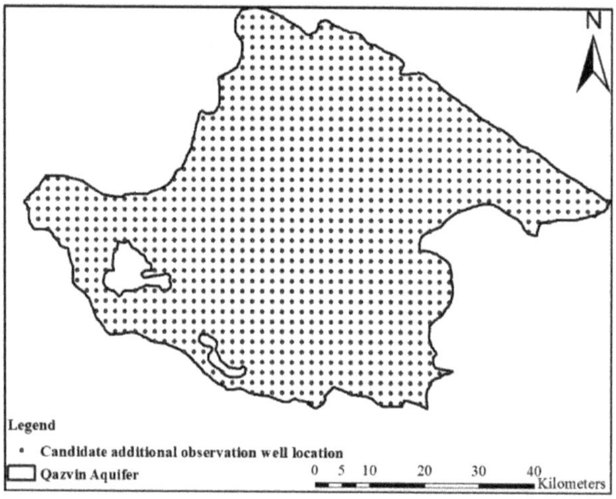


**Figure 6.** Qazvin Aquifer candidate additional observation well locations (search space of Genetic Algorithm).

Phase 1b (Produce and Apply Fuzzy Inference System, FIS)

Recently, fuzzy systems have been extensively utilized to address environmental issues [53,54], effectively overcoming the shortcomings of traditional methods [24,54]. Fuzzy inference supports consistent decision making using linguistic terms, similar to how decisions are made in everyday situations while remaining aligned with the principles established by the decision maker in advance. Fuzzy inference systems employ approximate reasoning, a mathematical framework developed by [55], to manage information heterogeneity and linguistic ambiguity.

The importance of incorporating an expert's knowledge in optimizing groundwater monitoring is emphasized by [24]. FIS was used in this study to achieve expert satisfaction in optimizing the monitoring network and to overcome the limitations of conventional methods. The Satisfaction of the Expert (SOE) regarding the addition of wells to the existing network is formulated using the Mamdani Fuzzy Inference System (MFIS). The MFIS was developed using the Fuzzy Logic Toolbox in MATLAB. As shown in Figure 7, the FIS consists of three main components: fuzzification, the fuzzy inference mechanism, and defuzzification.

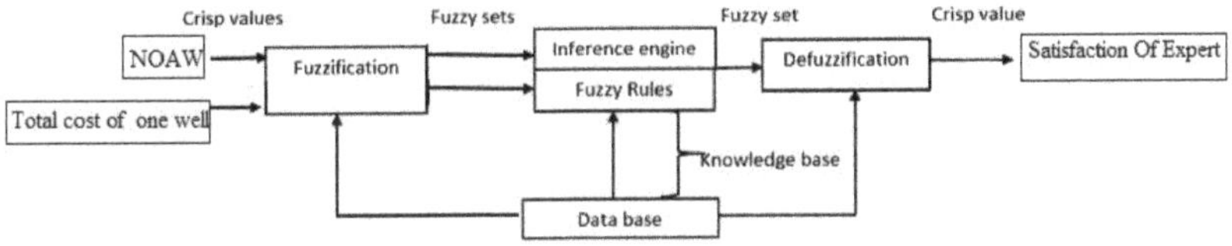


**Figure 7.** Fuzzy Inference System (FIS) process.

The process began assigning membership functions to all inputs and outputs and fuzzifying all variables. The Mamdani FIS in this study takes NOAWs and the unit cost of well installation as inputs and expert opinions as outputs. Figures 8–10, respectively, illustrate FIS development of membership functions for NOAWs, well installation cost, and the Satisfaction of the Expert (SOE) in the case study.

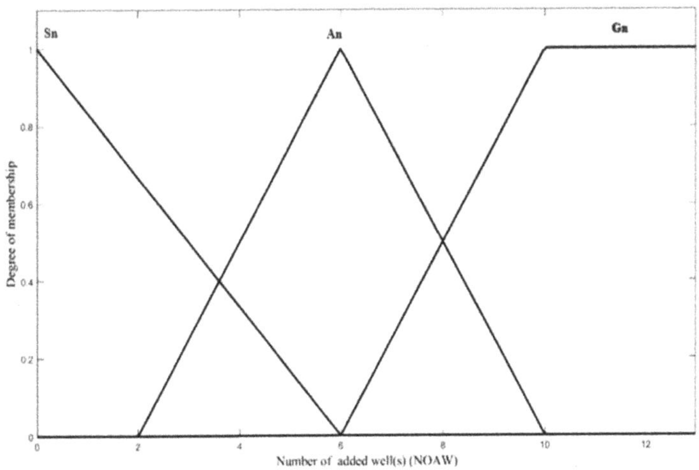


**Figure 8.** Membership function for NOAWs.

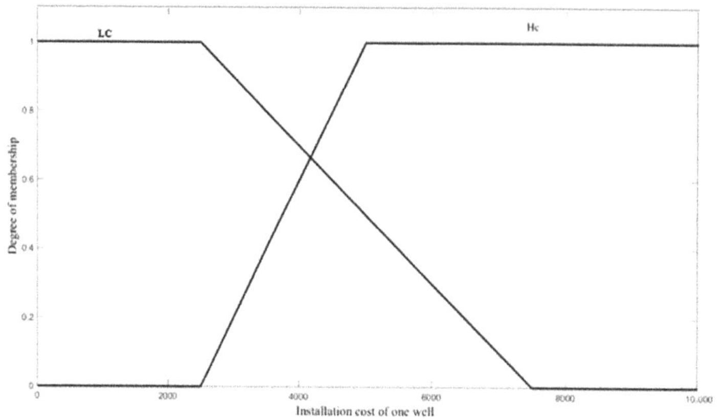


**Figure 9.** Membership function for installation cost of one well.

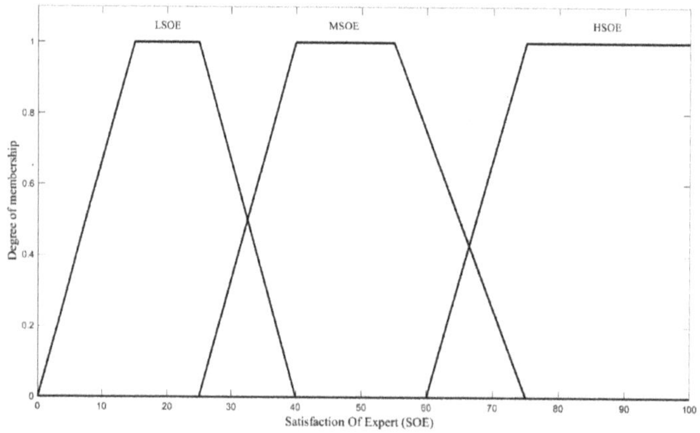


**Figure 10.** Membership function for satisfaction of expert.

Figure 8 shows NOAW fuzzification using triangular and trapezoidal membership functions to represent the number of monitoring wells being added: small number (Sn), average number (An), and great number (Gn). Zero wells, six wells, and from ten to twelve wells have the highest degree of memberships in groups "Sn", "An", and "Gn", respectively. The NOAWs for "Sn" changes from 0 to 5 new wells, set "An" ranges from 3 to 9 new wells, and set "Gn" ranges from 7 to 12 new wells.

Figure 9 shows unit well installation cost fuzzification into low cost (Lc) and high cost (Hc) sets, using trapezoidal membership functions. USD 0 to USD 2500 and USD 5000 and above, respectively, define membership in cost sets "LC" and "HC".

The FIS uses trapezoidal membership functions to calculate the Satisfaction of the Expert (SOE) for each NOAW ($SOE_{NOAW}$). Figure 10 shows the fuzzification of SOE with the number of added wells into three linguistic values: Low Satisfaction of the Expert (LSOE), Medium Satisfaction of the Expert (MSOE), and High Satisfaction of the Expert (HSOE).

After fuzzifying the variables, inference rules are applied to link the input variables to the output. Fuzzy inference is the process of formulating the mapping from a given input to an output using fuzzy logic. Table 1 presents the specific inference rules used in the developed FIS. There are three sets of inference rules that describe NOAWs and two sets that describe the unit cost of a new well, resulting in a total of six FIS model inference rules.

**Table 1.** Fuzzy inference system rules for determining the satisfaction of the expert with a NOAW based on the unit cost of the NOAW.

| Unit Cost of New Well | | NOAW | | |
|---|---|---|---|---|
| | | Small | Average | Great |
| | Low cost | LSOE | MSOE | HSOE |
| | High cost | MSOE | LSOE | LSOE |

Then, during the inference step, these fuzzy inputs are processed using the inference operations and rules. In implementing the Mamdani approach to formulate the FIS, a maximization fuzzy operator, a minimization implication method, a maximization aggregation method, and a center of area defuzzification method are applied.

Finally, the defuzzification process converts the fuzzy output sets back into crisp values, providing a clear, actionable output. For each NOAW, the FIS application provided the SOE, effectively translating the fuzzy inputs and rules into a meaningful output that reflects expert opinions. Phase 1b ends when NOAWs equal MNAWs.

Phase 1c (Normalized Pareto Curve Production and Application)

A conflict between two objectives is quantified as the rate of change in one optimal objective value with respect to the other optimal objective value within the feasible solution space ($S \subseteq \Re^2$, where $\Re^2$ refers to two dimensions in real number space). The Phase 1a goal conflicts with the Phase 1b goal of maximizing $SOE_{NOAW}$. Assuming a maximization objective (in which the largest objective function value is the best), Phase 1c uses Equation (12) to normalize the optimal $Ef_{NOAW}$ and $SOE_{NOAW}$ values. A unit normalized value represents the best objective function value, and a zero value represents the worst.

$$o_{n,i} = \frac{o_i - o_{m,i}}{o_{x,i} - o_{m,i}} \tag{12}$$

In Equation (12), $o_{n,i}$ is the normalized ith objective function value; $o_i$ is the ith objective function value; $o_{x,i}$ is the maximum objective value; and $o_{m,i}$ is the minimum objective value.

2.3.2. Phase 2 (Produce and Use Symmetric Conflict Resolution Methods)

To identify equilibrium or compromise solutions that consider the two objectives resulting from GA and FIS, Phase 2 applies three symmetric bargaining theory methods: (1) Nash, (2) Kalai–Smorodinsky, and (3) area monotonic. An Excel Workbook was used to calculate comparison solutions for each method.

- Method 1: Nash solution

The approach of Nash requires that a two-party conflict resolution solution satisfies four specific conditions or axioms [56,57]. As formulated in Equation (13) to address the current problem, the resulting symmetric Nash ($SOE_{NORM}{}^*$, $Ef_{NORM}{}^*$) solution lies on the Pareto frontier and maximizes the product of positive changes from the minimum feasible objective function values of the two objective functions:

$$\begin{aligned} &\text{Maximize } (SOE_{NORM} - d_1)(Ef_{NORM} - d_2) \\ &\text{Subject to the following:} \\ &d_1 \le SOE_{NORM} \le m_1 \\ &d_2 \le Ef_{NORM} = g(SOE_{NORM}) \le m_2 \end{aligned} \tag{13}$$

where $Ef_{NORM}$ is the normalized improvement effectiveness of optimal locations selected by GA for each NOAW; $SOE_{NORM}$ is the normalized Satisfaction of the Expert determined via MFIS for each NOAW; $d_1$ and $d_2$ are the normalized minimum acceptable objective values; $m_1$ is the normalized maximum effectiveness improvement achievable according to the GA; and $m_2$ is the normalized maximum satisfaction of the expert achievable for the assumed new well unit cost, according to the MFIS. $d_1$ and $d_2$ equal zero (their least achievements), and $m_1$ and $m_2$ equal one (their highest achievements).

- Method 2: Kalai—Smorodinsky solution

Kalai and Smorodinsky (1975) showed that by replacing Nash's axiom of independence of irrelevant alternatives with an axiom of monotonicity, the resulting solution is monotonic and linear. Assuming a linear solution segment exists between a point of disagreement and the best point, then the best solution is at the interception of this segment with the Pareto frontier [58]. For a situation in which the mathematical optimization results and the expert's satisfaction ($Ef_{NORM}$ = SOE $_{NORM}$) have equal weight, the solution of Equation (14) yields the compromise strategy in the normalized space.

$$\begin{gathered} d_2 + \left[\frac{(m_2 - d_2)}{(m_1 - d_1)}\right](\text{SOE}_{\text{NORM}} - d_1) - Ef_{\text{NORM}} = 0 \\ \text{Subject to the following:} \\ d_1 \le \text{SOE}_{\text{NORM}} \le m_1 \\ Ef_{\text{NORM}} = g(\text{SOE}_{\text{NORM}}) \end{gathered} \tag{14}$$

Rearranging Equation (9) as $(Ef_{NORM} - d^2)/(m_2 - d_2)$ = $(SOE_{NORM} - d_1)/(m_1 - d_1)$ shows that on the line both objective function values are the same proportional distance above their minimum within their respective ranges. The compromise strategy is at the intersection of that line with the Pareto curve.

- Method 3: symmetric area monotonic solution

A solution to Nash's cooperative bargaining problem is for a linear segment starting at the disagreement point that divides the area under the curve into two subsets of equal areas [58]. The solution is the root of the nonlinear equation, as seen in Equation (15):

$$\begin{aligned} &\left[\int_{d1}^{x} g(t)dt - \tfrac{1}{2}(x - d_1)(g(\text{SOE}_{\text{NORM}}) + d_2)\right] \\ &= \left[\int_{x}^{m1} g(t)dt - (m_1 - \text{SOE}_{\text{NORM}})d_2 + \tfrac{1}{2}(x - d_1)(g(\text{SOE}_{\text{NORM}}) - d_2)\right] \end{aligned} \tag{15}$$

## 3. Results

### 3.1. Water Table Estimation

As previously discussed, the accuracies of the four surface fitting methods for the Qazvin Aquifer were evaluated. This process commenced by partitioning the total observed head and location data into separate training and testing datasets. Subsequently, each of the four methods underwent training using the identical training dataset and testing using the same testing dataset. A comparative analysis of the performance of each method is presented in Table 2.

**Table 2.** Testing cross-validation results of the best of each surface fitting method.

| Statistical Parameter | Method | | | | | | | |
|---|---|---|---|---|---|---|---|---|
| | IDW | | Kriging | | MLP-ANN | | Spline | |
| | Train | Test | Train | Test | Train | Test | Train | Test |
| $R^2$ | 1.00 | 0.75 | 1.00 | 0.81 | 0.97 | 0.93 | 1.00 | 0.79 |
| RMSE | 0.09 | 26.80 | 0.00 | 24.53 | 10.77 | 13.70 | 0.04 | 26.52 |
| MAE | 0.04 | 13.44 | 0.00 | 11.93 | 4.50 | 6.62 | 0.02 | 12.10 |
| RMSLE | 0.000 | 0.009 | 0.000 | 0.009 | 0.004 | 0.005 | 0.000 | 0.009 |
| ARE | 0.001 | 0.496 | 0.000 | 0.423 | 0.155 | 0.279 | 0.001 | 0.457 |

The results indicated that the MLP-ANN provided the most accurate estimation of groundwater levels at testing locations, while ensuring that no water table heads were estimated above the ground surface. This was evidenced by its highest $R^2$ value and lowest RMSE, MAE, RMSLE, and ARE values in the test dataset. In addition to our findings, refs. [8,59] also demonstrated that the ANN method had the best performance in their studies. Their results corroborated our conclusion that machine learning excels in predictive accuracy and generalization capability, further reinforcing our favorable conclusion concerning the effectiveness of this method for groundwater level predictions.

The optimal MLP-ANN structure comprised a feed-forward neural network with two hidden layers, featuring 6 and 33 neurons, respectively. Sigmoid tangent activation functions were employed in the hidden layers, while a linear transfer function was used in the output layer. Consequently, Phase 1a utilized this MLP-ANN to estimate groundwater levels at candidate locations for adding well(s).

Kriging demonstrated the highest accuracy after MLP-ANN. However, it incorrectly produced some water table heads above the ground surface. Regardless of its accuracy, kriging requires defining the spatial correlation structure using a parameterized but unknown variogram model. This process is complicated and requires making numerous assumptions, such as stationarity, isotropy, and multivariable normality. These conditions are not easily verifiable and require expert knowledge of spatial statistics. Another study noted that the accuracy of kriging can be significantly affected by the assumptions and conditions needed for its implementation [6,14]. Their simulated data followed a Gaussian distribution with a specified variogram model, likely contributing to kriging's minimal prediction error in that context.

By applying MLP-ANN, the data do not need to assume a specific distribution, and more input data can be used to increase accuracy. The training process is also more flexible, and various methods can be utilized to enhance accuracy and control error, as demonstrated in this study. Additionally, the spatial relationships between hydrogeological variables are poorly understood due to their inherent complexity and nonlinearity. Therefore, integrating soft computing models with each other or with numerical methods (creating hybrid models) significantly enhances our comprehension of these intricate relationships. This approach leads to superior modeling accuracy, as previously demonstrated [25,52].

Here, the best kriging option used a Gaussian distribution semivariogram, which was then applied in Phase 1a. While both IDW and spline methods showed good training results, they did not generalize as effectively as MLP-ANN and kriging. In line with that, [60,61] showed that kriging was more accurate than IDW, and the spline was less accurate compared to kriging was shown by [62,63]

### 3.2. *Phase 1a (GA Application)*

Because MLP-ANN most closely matched observed heads during testing, the purpose of this phase is to cause kriged heads to match more closely the MLP-ANN heads for GA-selected locations. To execute the designed GA, a code has been written in MATLAB 2016a.

Within each optimization, the GA provides the locations of the NOAW wells that will most improve the overall accuracy of the kriged surface. The red line in Figure 11 shows the change in RMSE as new wells are added. As demonstrated, RMSE decreases as the number of added wells increases. The RMSE for each NOAW was lower than the RMSE from the previous iteration, demonstrating that the algorithm's performance improved as it progressed. Without adding a new well, the RMSE was 20.42 m. By adding wells, the improvement in RMSE ranged from 0.73 m for one well to 2 m for twelve wells.

Figure 11 illustrates the effectiveness per added well ($Ef_{NOAW}$), computed by Equation (11), versus RMSE. Increasing NOAWs to improve accuracy (by decreasing RMSE), asymptotically decreased the per-well effectiveness ($Ef_{NOAW}$). Adding one well had the most significant impact compared to other NOAW scenarios. However, as more wells were added, the intensity of RMSE change fluctuated. For example, the change in

RMSE for one well was 3.56%. For four wells, it was 0.1%, and it increased to 0.45% for six wells. Then, it started to decrease again, and for twelve wells, the RMSE increased by 1.40%. The effectiveness changes also decreased, similar to the trend in RMSE. A significant change was observed with the addition of the first well, about 50%, and from NOAW 10 onwards, the effectiveness remained almost constant. The initial result was presented at the 12th International Conference on Hydro Informatics [64]. A similar trend and concerns were observed in the study by [5].

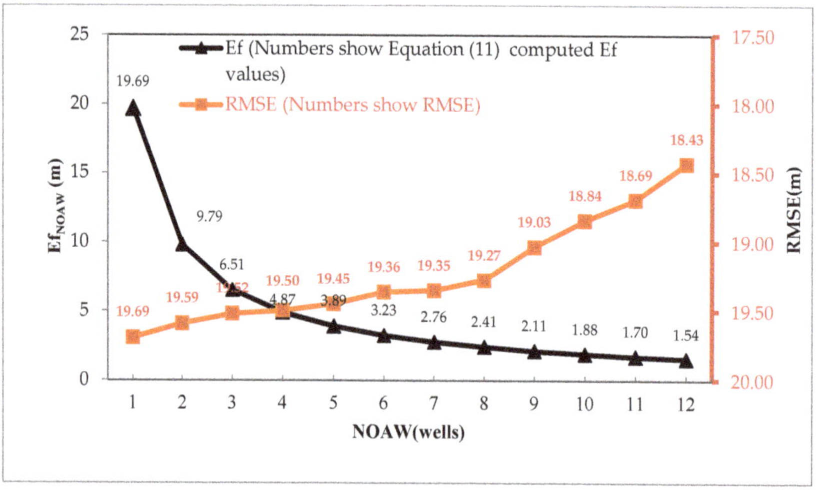


**Figure 11.** Ef and RMSE as functions of NOAWs.

A trade-off between increasing accuracy and efficiency occurred at NOAW 5, where the lines intersected. In other words, a designer can determine the number of wells to add by considering the intersection of two lines as well as the percent change in efficiency resulting from adding an additional well. Decision making can be aided by considering the trade-off between accuracy and efficiency in adding wells.

Although the GA is designed to find the optimal locations for NOAWs to improve accuracy, Figure 11 shows that the amount of improvement becomes less significant or even increases slightly in some cases. This suggests that adding more wells might not always be cost-effective, as the change in RMSE diminishes with additional wells. Following this section, we demonstrated how the application of FIS can enable experts' opinions to assist decision making further.

### 3.3. *Phase 1b (FIS Application)*

To address the concerns mentioned in the previous section and to overcome the limitations of using only conventional methods for hydrologic decision making, an MFIS was developed [24]. In this MFIS, NOAWs and the unit cost of well installation were considered to evaluate expert satisfaction and incorporate expert opinions into the optimization process. The proposed model is flexible enough to incorporate additional information that could impact expert opinions concerning their satisfaction. However, in this study, we focused on demonstrating how considering only the cost and NOAWs can involve decision makers in the numerical optimization model.

Figure 12 demonstrates the inference mechanism for specific inputs, such as NOAW 9, and a unit well cost of USD 4000. This figure illustrates how the features are applied to map the input variables to the output. The MFIS was run for three different well costs, as presented in Table 3. The result showed that as the cost increased, expert satisfaction decreased. The proposed model utilized the result of MFIS for a cost of USD 4000.

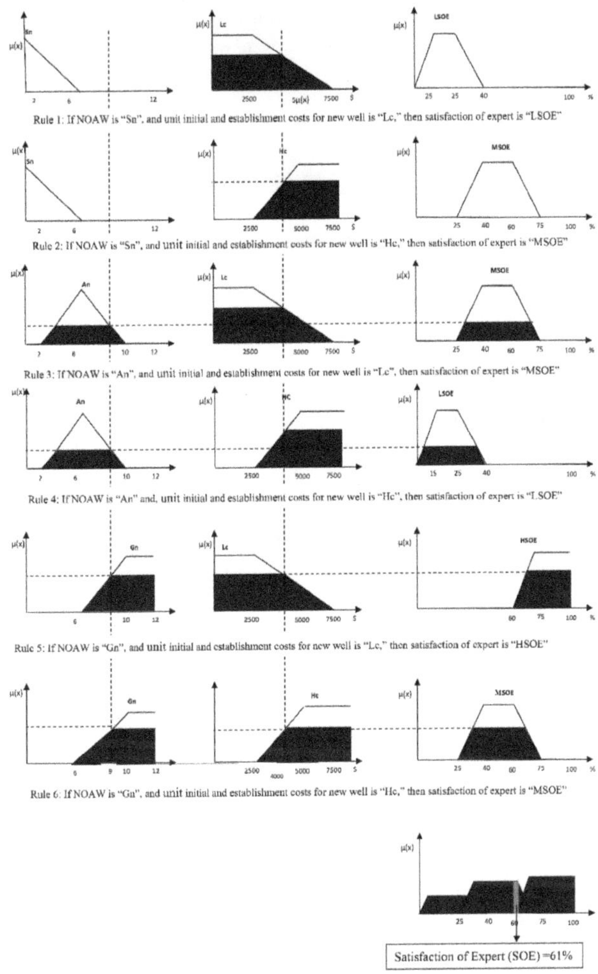

**Figure 12.** Fuzzification, inference, and defuzzification processes in determining the Satisfaction of the Expert (SOE) for each NOAW (for NOAWs = 9 and unit well cost = USD 4000, SOE = 61%).

**Table 3.** Satisfaction of the expert (SOE) with each NOAW, as a function of unit well installation cost.

| Number of Additional Wells (NOAWs) | Satisfaction of the Expert (SOE) for USD 4000/Well | Satisfaction of the Expert (SOE) for USD 6000/Well | Satisfaction of the Expert (SOE) for USD 8000/Well |
|---|---|---|---|
| **1** | 35 | 44 | 49 |
| **2** | 36 | 44 | 49 |
| **3** | 37 | 42 | 43 |
| **4** | 37 | 31 | 31 |
| **5** | 39 | 27 | 24 |
| **6** | 39 | 25 | 20 |
| **7** | 44 | 27 | 20 |
| **8** | 52 | 30 | 20 |
| **9** | 61 | 27 | 20 |
| **10** | 68 | 25 | 20 |
| **11** | 68 | 25 | 20 |
| **12** | 68 | 25 | 20 |

For a unit well cost of USD 4000, the results showed that increasing NOAWs led to an increase in expert satisfaction. However, the amount of SOE remained constant from NOAW 10 onwards. To combine the results from both Phases 1a and 1b, conflict resolution methods were applied.

### 3.4. Phase 1c (Pareto Curve Production)

In this step, the application of Equation (11) to the results from Phases 1a and 1b produces a Pareto curve (Figure 13). Figure 13 Pareto curve does not show values for NOAWs of 4, 6, 11, and 12 because they are inferior to adjacent solutions for NOAWs 3, 5, and 10, respectively (they have the same $SOE_{NOAW}$ but a smaller $Ef_{NOAW}$ than an adjacent solution). In Figure 10, the normalized point $(d_1, d_2) \in R^2$ has the worst possible payoff values for both objectives. The best normalized SOE and Ef values are, respectively, at points $(m_1, d_2)$ and $(d_1, m_2)$. The equation assigned a value of 1 to the best result from each phase and a value of 0 to the worst result for both phases. Graphically, human supporters of a particular strategy often want their achieved objective function value to be as much above $d_1$ and $d_2$ as possible. Incorporating expert opinions into the results, initially suggested solely based on the GA, highlighted how integrating expert input can lead to more feasible and practical solutions.

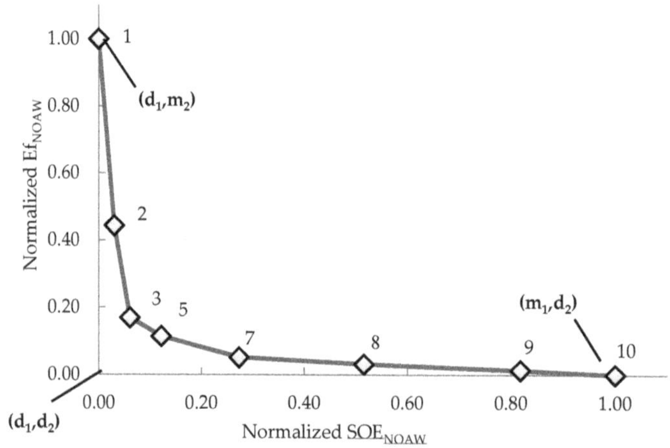


**Figure 13.** Normalized Pareto optimum curve of Ef versus SOE for USD 4000 unit well cost (labels show NOAWs).

### 3.5. Phase 2

To find the equilibrium strategies, three bargaining theory methods were used. The symmetric Nash, symmetric Kalai–Smorodinsky, and the symmetric area monotonic methods, respectively, specified eight, five, and five wells as the compromise numbers of wells to add (NOAWs) to the Qazvin Aquifer monitoring network. Figure 14 shows kriged groundwater contour maps prepared for each compromise strategy. Each map employed existing wells plus the NOAW wells specified by the bargaining game. The average design recommendation of the three Phase 2 gaming methods was six wells. However, a five-well solution dominates over a six-well solution (they have the same $SOE_{NOAW,}$ but a five-well solution has a greater $Ef_{NOAW}$ than a six-well solution).

Otherwise, because conflict resolution aims to find a state where all objectives are acceptably satisfied, strategies having a $Ef_{NORM}/SOE_{NORM}$ ratio that is close to 1 in normalized space is preferable. A ratio close to one showed that both objectives are close to equally achieved. A five-well NOAW strategy yielded an $Ef_{NORM}/SOE_{NORM}$ value closest to 1. The symmetric Kalai–Smorodinsky and the symmetric area monotonic picked the optimal compromise NOAWs. Therefore, adding five wells to the aquifer is recommended to the water agency. This study reveals that FIS is a reliable tool for integrating expert opinions into mathematics and statistical methods for optimizing monitoring networks. This finding is consistent with the results of [53,65] that underscore the effectiveness of FIS in enhancing decision making processes.

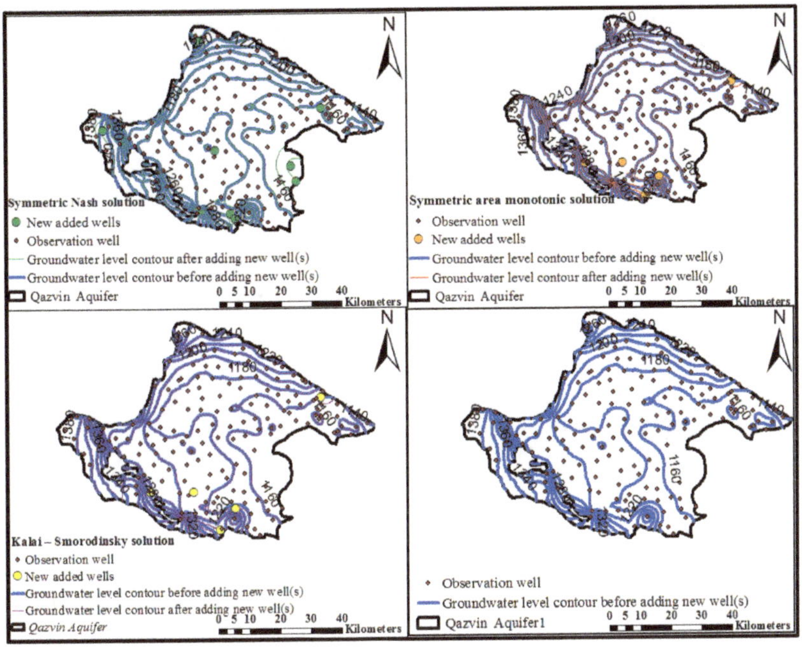


**Figure 14.** The groundwater level contour maps based on bargaining game results.

Regarding the results of the three bargaining methods, five and eight observation wells were selected to be added to the aquifer. The five wells are mainly distributed along the southern boundary of the aquifer. Most of the southern aquifer relies on groundwater as the primary water resource for the agricultural sector and does not have a significant surface water supply. The study by [66] showed that this region, where most observation wells are added, experiences more severe drought during drought years than other parts of the aquifer, leading to significant fluctuations in water levels and thus requiring more wells for monitoring. Additionally, kriging showed greater error near the aquifer's boundaries due to a lack of known data points in these areas, particularly in the southern part. This suggests that the GA successfully identified optimal locations to support kriging, thereby enhancing the accuracy of groundwater level predictions.

However, when the number of wells increases beyond five, some wells are also added to the center of the aquifer, where the groundwater is more stable than at the boundary. Regardless of the number of added wells, the areas that show severe drought consistently remain the priority for well placement. When the number of added wells is lower, they are mostly placed in areas with more significant water level fluctuations. As the number increases, the locations extend to other parts of the aquifer that are not as variable.

## 4. Discussion

A novel approach to monitoring network expansion is presented here that uses encapsulated fuzzy expert opinions to negotiate between quantitative results from artificial intelligence-guided optimization and fuzzy expert opinions. A methodology was developed in the present study to address Rosen's statement [24] that expert opinion information and mathematical–statistical information ought to be incorporated simultaneously into the development of a potentiometric surface monitoring well network. First, the evaluation shows that MLP-ANN produces more accurate potentiometric surface maps than spline, IDW, and the commonly used kriging. Accordingly, the methodology provides a guide to the placement of new observation wells so that kriging values will become more like those generated by MLP-ANN. In order to minimize the total difference between heads from kriging and heads from MLP-ANN, the Genetic Algorithm (GA) optimization determines the locations of new observation wells for each set of candidate new observation wells. Results from the GA showed that the rate of decreasing RMSE per additional well decreases as NOAWs increase. Decision makers can select one of two criteria to decide when to stop adding wells: minimum acceptable RMSE and minimum acceptable RMSE reduction per well. Efficiency and accuracy of intersection lines can also be critical factors in choosing NOAWs that balance both.

Along with the optimization process, a Fuzzy Inference System (FIS) is created by incorporating the opinions of local experts regarding well installation costs and the practical number of monitoring wells to be installed. The MFIS quantifies the Satisfaction of the Expert with each possible number of new monitoring wells up to 12.

In their determination of the optimal number of new wells, GA and FIS differ. The conflict is resolved by utilizing three game theory symmetric techniques (Nash, Kalai–Smorodinsky, and area monotonic) after preparing a normalized Pareto optimum curve. In their respective approaches, the three approaches suggest adding eight, five, and five monitoring wells. On average, the three approaches propose six monitoring wells. According to Figure 13, the six-well design is inferior and dominated by the five-well design; therefore, the average of the bargaining methods for a six-well design is five wells.

The limitation of the model in the context of application to other situations lies in its computational complexity, especially when scaling up for very large problems. As the number of wells increases, this complexity could require significant processing power and time. The time required to tune and train an artificial neural network increases with network complexity and the volume of data. Without access to advanced CPU or GPU technology, these limitations could hinder the application [6].

Future work should focus on several key areas to enhance the transferability and applicability of the model. Assigning weights to additional observation candidates based on their perceived importance, particularly in areas experiencing severe declines in groundwater levels, could provide increased accuracy in those areas. Incorporating the location of the new well(s) into the Fuzzy Inference System (FIS) is another potential enhancement. Exploring alternative metaheuristic algorithms and evaluating their impact on the optimization process, especially when adding many wells, could further improve the model's effectiveness and efficiency.

In summary, a novel technique is presented to predict where and how many observation wells should be installed to improve the accuracy of groundwater level monitoring networks. Both sophisticated computational results and critically important situation-specific hydrogeologic and other field experiences are appropriately considered in this technique. The developed algorithm is designed to be easily upgraded to suit the contexts of other areas. Additionally, these hybrid technologies can also be adapted to map other variables such as groundwater quantity, soil sensors, climatology stations, and other sampling data.

**Author Contributions:** Conceptualization, M.H. and R.C.P.; methodology, M.H. and R.C.P.; software, M.H. and R.C.P.; validation, M.H., R.C.P., and M.Y.; formal analysis, M.H. and R.C.P.; investigation, M.H. and R.C.P.; resources, R.C.P. and M.Y.; data curation, M.H.; writing—original draft preparation, M.H. and R.C.P.—review and editing, M.H., R.C.P., and M.Y.; visualization, M.H., R.C.P., and M.Y.; supervision, R.C.P. and M.Y.; project administration, R.C.P. and M.Y.; funding acquisition, M.H. and R.C.P. All authors have read and agreed to the published version of the manuscript.

**Funding:** This research was funded by Qazvin Regional Water Company 2019, grant number 95/28590/101, and Utah Agricultural Experiment Station 2019, grant number UAES #9210.

**Data Availability Statement:** The dataset can be found at http://www.hydroshare.org/resource/84bf350e46de412fbf09a69369f4a686 (accessed on 15 May 2024).

**Conflicts of Interest:** The authors declare no conflicts of interest. The funders had no role in the design of the study; in the collection, analyses, or interpretation of data; in the writing of the manuscript; or in the decision to publish the results.

## References

1. Rajaee, T.; Ebrahimi, H.; Nourani, V. A Review of the Artificial Intelligence Methods in Groundwater Level Modeling. *J. Hydrol.* **2019**, *572*, 336–351. [CrossRef]
2. Amiri, S.; Rajabi, A.; Shabanlou, S.; Yosefvand, F.; Izadbakhsh, M.A. Prediction of Groundwater Level Variations Using Deep Learning Methods and GMS Numerical Model. *Earth Sci. Inform.* **2023**, *16*, 3227–3241. [CrossRef]
3. Todd, D.K.; Mays, L.W. *Groundwater Hydrology*; John Wiley & Sons: Hoboken, NJ, USA, 2005; ISBN 0471452548.
4. Narany, T.S.; Ramli, M.F.; Aris, A.Z.; Sulaiman, W.N.A.; Fakharian, K. Spatial Assessment of Groundwater Quality Monitoring Wells Using Indicator Kriging and Risk Mapping, Amol-Babol Plain, Iran. *Water* **2014**, *6*, 68–85. [CrossRef]
5. Kavusi, M.; Khashei Siuki, A.; Dastourani, M. Optimal Design of Groundwater Monitoring Network Using the Combined Election-Kriging Method. *Water Resour. Manag.* **2020**, *34*, 2503–2516. [CrossRef]
6. Tavassoli, A.; Waghei, Y.; Nazemi, A. Comparison of Kriging and Artificial Neural Network Models for the Prediction of Spatial Data. *J. Stat. Comput. Simul.* **2022**, *92*, 352–369. [CrossRef]
7. Majedi-Asl, M.; Fuladipanah, M.; Mahmoudpour, H.; Ebrahimpour, E.; Kisi, O. Optimization Design of Quality Monitoring Network of Urmia Plain Using Genetic Algorithm and Vulnerability Map. *Geocarto Int.* **2023**, *38*, 2152492. [CrossRef]
8. Abdi, E.; Ali, M.; Santos, C.A.G.; Olusola, A.; Ghorbani, M.A. Enhancing Groundwater Level Prediction Accuracy Using Interpolation Techniques in Deep Learning Models. *Groundw. Sustain. Dev.* **2024**, *26*, 101213. [CrossRef]
9. Uyan, M.; Cay, T. Spatial Analyses of Groundwater Level Differences Using Geostatistical Modeling. *Environ. Ecol. Stat.* **2013**, *20*, 633–646. [CrossRef]
10. Rabah, F.K.J.; Ghabayen, S.M.; Salha, A.A. Effect of GIS Interpolation Techniques on the Accuracy of the Spatial Representation of Groundwater Monitoring Data in Gaza Strip. *J. Environ. Sci. Technol.* **2011**, *4*, 579–589. [CrossRef]
11. Amini, H.; Ashrafzadeh, A.; Khaledian, M. Enhancing Groundwater Salinity Estimation through Integrated GMDH and Geostatistical Techniques to Minimize Kriging Interpolation Error. *Earth Sci. Inform.* **2024**, *17*, 283–297. [CrossRef]
12. Jithendra, T.; Basha, S.S. Analyzing Groundwater Level with Hybrid ANN and ANFIS Using Metaheuristic Optimization. *Earth Sci. Inform.* **2023**, *16*, 3323–3353. [CrossRef]
13. Hashemi, M.; Sepaskhah, A.R. Evaluation of Artificial Neural Network and Penman–Monteith Equation for the Prediction of Barley Standard Evapotranspiration in a Semi-Arid Region. *Theor. Appl. Climatol.* **2020**, *139*, 275–285. [CrossRef]
14. Tirol Kirçiçek, N.; Baba, A.; Koçbay, A.; Toklu, M.M. Evaluation of GIS-Based Spatial Interpolation Methods for Groundwater Level: A Case Study of Türkiye. *Turk. J. Earth Sci.* **2024**, *33*, 576–591. [CrossRef]
15. Aceves-De-Alba, J.; ENRIQUE Júnez, H.; González-Trinidad, J.; Cardona-Benavides, A.; Bautista-Capetillo, C. Methodology for the Optimization of Groundwater Quality Monitoring Networks Oriented to Satisfy a Specific Spatial Coverage. *Appl. Ecol. Environ. Res.* **2019**, *17*, 10861–10882. [CrossRef]
16. Nunes, L.M.; Cunha, M.C.; Ribeiro, L. Groundwater Monitoring Network Optimization with Redundancy Reduction. *J. Water Resour. Plan. Manag.* **2004**, *130*, 33–43. [CrossRef]
17. Ohmer, M.; Liesch, T.; Wunsch, A. Spatiotemporal Optimization of Groundwater Monitoring Networks Using Data-Driven Sparse Sensing Methods. *Hydrol. Earth Syst. Sci.* **2022**, *26*, 4033–4053. [CrossRef]
18. Abedian, H.; Mohammadi, K.; Rafiee, R. Optimizing Monitoring Network of Water Table by Geostatistical Methods. *J. Geol. Min. Res.* **2013**, *5*, 223–231. [CrossRef]
19. Teimoori, S.; Olya, M.H.; Miller, C.J. Groundwater Level Monitoring Network Design with Machine Learning Methods. *J. Hydrol.* **2023**, *625*, 130145. [CrossRef]
20. Mirzaie-Nodoushan, F.; Bozorg-Haddad, O.; Loaíciga, H.A. Optimal Design of Groundwater-Level Monitoring Networks. *J. Hydroinform.* **2017**, *19*, 920–929. [CrossRef]
21. Ayvaz, M.T.; Elçi, A. Identification of the Optimum Groundwater Quality Monitoring Network Using a Genetic Algorithm Based Optimization Approach. *J. Hydrol.* **2018**, *563*, 1078–1091. [CrossRef]
22. Hosseini, M.; Kerachian, R. A Data Fusion-Based Methodology for Optimal Redesign of Groundwater Monitoring Networks. *J. Hydrol.* **2017**, *552*, 267–282. [CrossRef]
23. Amiri, H.; Azadi, S.; Javadpour, S.; Naghavi, A.A.; Boczkaj, G. Selecting Wells for an Optimal Design of Groundwater Monitoring Network Based on Monitoring Priority Map: A Kish Island Case Study. *Water Resour. Ind.* **2022**, *27*, 100172. [CrossRef]
24. Rosen, M.R. Groundwater monitoring networks, in Groundwater. In *Encyclopedia of Life Support Systems (EOLSS)*; Silveira, L., Ed.; Eolss Publishers: Oxford, UK, 2003; Available online: https://www.eolss.net/ebooklib/bookinfo/groundwater.aspx#chapters (accessed on 15 May 2024).
25. Kraft, B.; Jung, M.; Körner, M.; Reichstein, M. Hybrid Modeling: Fusion of a Deep Approach and Physics-Based Model for Global Hydrological Modeling. *Int. Arch. Photogramm. Remote Sens. Spat. Inf. Sci.* **2020**, *43*, 1537–1544. [CrossRef]

26. Fisher, J. *Optimization of Water-Level Monitoring Networks in the Eastern Snake River Plain Aquifer Using a Kriging-Based Genetic Algorithm Method*; Scientific Investigations Report 2013-5120; US Geological Survey: Reston, VA, USA, 2013.
27. Firat, M.; Turan, M.E.; Yurdusev, M.A. Comparative Analysis of Fuzzy Inference Systems for Water Consumption Time Series Prediction. *J. Hydrol.* **2009**, *374*, 235–241. [CrossRef]
28. Mamdani, E.H.; Assilian, S. An Experiment in Linguistic Synthesis with a Fuzzy Logic Controller. *Int. J. Hum. Comput. Stud.* **1973**, *51*, 135–147. [CrossRef]
29. Takagi, T.; Sugeno, M. Fuzzy Identification of Systems and Its Applications to Modeling and Control. *IEEE Trans. Syst. Man Cybern.* **1985**, *1*, 116–132. [CrossRef]
30. Dhar, A.; Patil, R.S. Multiobjective Design of Groundwater Monitoring Network Under Epistemic Uncertainty. *Water Resour. Manag.* **2012**, *26*, 1809–1825. [CrossRef]
31. Masoumi, Z.; Rezaei, A.; Maleki, J. Improvement of Water Table Interpolation and Groundwater Storage Volume Using Fuzzy Computations. *Environ. Monit. Assess.* **2019**, *191*, 401. [CrossRef]
32. Nourani, V.; Maleki, S.; Najafi, H.; Baghanam, A.H. A Fuzzy Logic-Based Approach for Groundwater Vulnerability Assessment. *Environ. Sci. Pollut. Res.* **2024**, *31*, 18010–18029. [CrossRef]
33. Noori, R.; Maghrebi, M.; Mirchi, A.; Tang, Q.; Bhattarai, R.; Sadegh, M.; Noury, M.; Haghighi, A.T.; Kløve, B.; Madani, K. Anthropogenic Depletion of Iran's Aquifers. *Proc. Natl. Acad. Sci. USA* **2021**, *118*, e2024221118. [CrossRef]
34. Moridi, A. State of Water Resources in Iran. *Int. J. Hydrol.* **2017**, *1*, 111–114. [CrossRef]
35. Hashemi, M.; Zadeh, H.M.; Zarghami, M.; Demeke, B.W.; Delgarm, R.T. An Analysis of Why Rehabilitation and Balancing Programs for Aquifers Do Not Meet Water Organizations' Targets (a Case Study of the Qazvin Aquifer in Iran). *Agric. Water Manag.* **2023**, *281*, 108258. [CrossRef]
36. Yao, L.; Huo, Z.; Feng, S.; Mao, X.; Kang, S.; Chen, J.; Xu, J.; Steenhuis, T.S. Evaluation of Spatial Interpolation Methods for Groundwater Level in an Arid Inland Oasis, Northwest China. *Environ. Earth Sci.* **2014**, *71*, 1911–1924. [CrossRef]
37. Mair, A.; Fares, A. Comparison of Rainfall Interpolation Methods in a Mountainous Region of a Tropical Island. *J. Hydrol. Eng.* **2011**, *16*, 371–383. [CrossRef]
38. Ohmer, M.; Liesch, T.; Goeppert, N.; Goldscheider, N. On the Optimal Selection of Interpolation Methods for Groundwater Contouring: An Example of Propagation of Uncertainty Regarding Inter-Aquifer Exchange. *Adv. Water Resour.* **2017**, *109*, 121–132. [CrossRef]
39. Boumpoulis, V.; Michalopoulou, M.; Depountis, N. Comparison between Different Spatial Interpolation Methods for the Development of Sediment Distribution Maps in Coastal Areas. *Earth Sci. Inform.* **2023**, *16*, 2069–2087. [CrossRef]
40. Franke, R. Smooth Interpolation of Scattered Data by Local Thin Plate Splines. *Comput. Math. Appl.* **1982**, *8*, 273–281. [CrossRef]
41. Mitáš, L.; Mitášová, H. General Variational Approach to the Interpolation Problem. *Comput. Math. Appl.* **1988**, *16*, 983–992. [CrossRef]
42. Safavi, H.R.; Ahmadi, K.M. Prediction and Assessment of Drought Effects on Surface Water Quality Using Artificial Neural Networks: Case Study of Zayandehrud River, Iran. *J. Environ. Health Sci. Eng.* **2015**, *13*, 68. [CrossRef]
43. Lophaven, S.N.; Nielsen, H.B.; Sondergaard, J.; Dace, A. *A Matlab Kriging Toolbox*; Technical Report No. IMM-TR-2002-12; Technical University of Denmark: Copenhagen, Denmark, 2002.
44. Tomassi, A.; Trippetta, F.; de Franco, R.; Ruggieri, R. From Petrophysical Properties to Forward-Seismic Modeling of Facies Heterogeneity in the Carbonate Realm (Majella Massif, Central Italy). *J. Pet. Sci. Eng.* **2022**, *211*, 110242. [CrossRef]
45. Shexo, A.H.M.; Abdullah, T.H. Robust Estimation Based on Lognormal Kriging Technique for Some Soil Data. *Math. Model. Eng. Probl.* **2024**, *11*, 5. [CrossRef]
46. Rajabi, F.; Faraji, N.; Hashemi, M. An Efficient Video-Based Rainfall Intensity Estimation Employing Different Recurrent Neural Network Models. *Earth Sci. Inform.* **2024**, *17*, 2367–2380. [CrossRef]
47. Shadkani, S.; Hashemi, S.; Pak, A.; Lahijan, A.B. Random Forest and Multilayer Perceptron Hybrid Models Integrated with the Genetic Algorithm for Predicting Pan Evaporation of Target Site Using a Limited Set of Neighboring Reference Station Data. *Earth Sci. Inform.* **2024**, *17*, 1261–1280. [CrossRef]
48. Mirarabi, A.; Nassery, H.R.; Nakhaei, M.; Adamowski, J.; Akbarzadeh, A.H.; Alijani, F. Evaluation of Data-Driven Models (SVR and ANN) for Groundwater-Level Prediction in Confined and Unconfined Systems. *Environ. Earth. Sci.* **2019**, *78*, 489. [CrossRef]
49. Magalhães-Mendes, J. A Comparative Study of Crossover Operators for Genetic Algorithms to Solve the Job Shop Scheduling Problem. *WSEAS Trans. Comput.* **2013**, *12*, 164–173.
50. Mahmoudpour, H.; Janatrostami, S.; Ashrafzadeh, A. Optimal Design of Groundwater Quality Monitoring Network Using Aquifer Vulnerability Map. *Water Resour. Manag.* **2023**, *37*, 797–818. [CrossRef]
51. Hashemi, M.; Mazandarani Zadeh, H.; Daneshkare Arasteh, P.; Zarghami, M. Economic and Environmental Impacts of Cropping Pattern Elements Using Systems Dynamics. *Civ. Eng. J.* **2019**, *5*, 1020–1032. [CrossRef]
52. Gladish, D.W.; Pagendam, D.E.; Janardhanan, S.; Gonzalez, D. Geostatistical Based Optimization of Groundwater Monitoring Well Network Design. *Front. Earth Sci.* **2023**, *11*, 1188316. [CrossRef]
53. Loganathan, S.; Ramakrishnan, D.; Sathiyamoorthy, M.; Azamathulla, H.M. Assessment of Irrigational Suitability of Groundwater in Thanjavur District, Southern India Using Mamdani Fuzzy Inference System. *Results Eng.* **2024**, *21*, 101789. [CrossRef]
54. Kambalimath, S.; Deka, P.C. A Basic Review of Fuzzy Logic Applications in Hydrology and Water Resources. *Appl. Water Sci.* **2020**, *10*, 191. [CrossRef]

55. Zadeh, L.A. Fuzzy Sets. *Inf. Control.* **1965**, *8*, 338–353. [CrossRef]
56. Nash, J.F. The Bargaining Problem. *Econometrica* **1950**, *18*, 155–162. [CrossRef]
57. Kalai, E.; Smorodinsky, M. Other Solutions to Nash's Bargaining Problem. *Econometrica* **1975**, *43*, 513–518. [CrossRef]
58. Salazar, R.; Szidarovszky, F.; Coppola, E.; Rojano, A. Application of Game Theory for a Groundwater Conflict in Mexico. *J. Environ. Manag.* **2007**, *84*, 560–571. [CrossRef]
59. Chitsazan, M.; Rahmani, G.; Neyamadpour, A. Groundwater Level Simulation Using Artificial Neural Network: A Case Study from Aghili Plain, Urban Area of Gotvand, South-West Iran. *Geopersia* **2013**, *3*, 35–46.
60. Dewana, B.R.; Prasetyo, S.Y.J.; Hartomo, K.D. Comparison of IDW and Kriging Interpolation Methods Using Geoelectric Data to Determine the Depth of the Aquifer in Semarang, Indonesia. *J. Ilm. Tek. Elektro Komput. Dan Inform.* **2022**, *8*, 215. [CrossRef]
61. Njeban, H.S. Comparison and Evaluation of GIS-Based Spatial Interpolation Methods for Estimation Groundwater Level in AL-Salman District—Southwest Iraq. *J. Geogr. Inf. Syst.* **2018**, *10*, 362–380. [CrossRef]
62. Arkoc, O. Modeling of Spatiotemporal Variations of Groundwater Levels Using Different Interpolation Methods with the Aid of GIS, Case Study from Ergene Basin, Turkey. *Model. Earth Syst. Environ.* **2022**, *8*, 967–976. [CrossRef]
63. Noori, S.; Ebrahimi, K.; Liaghat, A.-M.; Hoorfar, A.-H. Comparison of Different Geostatistical Methods to Estimate Groundwater Level at Different Climatic Periods. *Water Environ. J.* **2013**, *27*, 10–19. [CrossRef]
64. Hashemi Tameh, M.A.; Mazandarani Zadeh, H.; Arasteh Daneshkar, P. A Novel Solution to Define the Optimum Number and Location of New Wells to Improve Groundwater Level Map. *Procedia Eng.* **2016**, *154*, 252–259. [CrossRef]
65. Chang, L.-C.; Chu, H.-J.; Chen, Y.-W. A Fuzzy Inference System for the Conjunctive Use of Surface and Subsurface Water. *Adv. Fuzzy Syst.* **2013**, *2013*, 128393. [CrossRef]
66. Isazade, V.; Qasimi, A.B.; Toomanian, A.; Isazade, E. The Effect of Drought Phenomenon on the Surface of Groundwater Aquifer in Qazvin Plain in Iran. *J. Appl. Sci. Technol. Trends* **2023**, *4*, 80–85. [CrossRef]

*machine learning & knowledge extraction*

MDPI

*Article*

# Enhancing Visitor Forecasting with Target-Concatenated Autoencoder and Ensemble Learning

**Ray-I Chang [1], Chih-Yung Tsai [1,2,*] and Yu-Wei Chang [3]**

[1] Department of Engineering Science and Ocean Engineering, National Taiwan University, Taipei 10617, Taiwan; rayichang@ntu.edu.tw

[2] Department of Education, University of Taipei, Taipei 100234, Taiwan

[3] Doctorate Program on Cybersecurity, Department of Electrical Engineering, National Taiwan University, Taipei 10617, Taiwan; b01505025@ntu.edu.tw

* Correspondence: cytsai@utaipei.edu.tw; Tel.: +886-2-23113040

**Abstract:** Accurate forecasting of inbound visitor numbers is crucial for effective planning and resource allocation in the tourism industry. Preceding forecasting algorithms primarily focused on time series analysis, often overlooking influential factors such as economic conditions. Regression models, on the other hand, face challenges when dealing with high-dimensional data. Previous autoencoders for feature selection do not simultaneously incorporate feature and target information simultaneously, potentially limiting their effectiveness in improving predictive performance. This study presents a novel approach that combines a target-concatenated autoencoder (TCA) with ensemble learning to enhance the accuracy of tourism demand predictions. The TCA method integrates the prediction target into the training process, ensuring that the learned feature representations are optimized for specific forecasting tasks. Extensive experiments conducted on the Taiwan and Hawaii datasets demonstrate that the proposed TCA method significantly outperforms traditional feature selection techniques and other advanced algorithms in terms of the mean absolute percentage error (MAPE), mean absolute error (MAE), and coefficient of determination ($R^2$). The results show that TCA combined with XGBoost achieves MAPE values of 3.3947% and 4.0059% for the Taiwan and Hawaii datasets, respectively, indicating substantial improvements over existing methods. Additionally, the proposed approach yields better $R^2$ and MAE metrics than existing methods, further demonstrating its effectiveness. This study highlights the potential of TCA in providing reliable and accurate forecasts, thereby supporting strategic planning, infrastructure development, and sustainable growth in the tourism sector. Future research is advised to explore real-time data integration, expanded feature sets, and hybrid modeling approaches to further enhance the capabilities of the proposed framework.

**Keywords:** autoencoder; ensemble learning; forecasting; feature selection; tourism

## 1. Introduction

Tourism has become an essential industry in an increasingly interconnected world, significantly driving economic expansion and progress [1]. Precise predictions of inbound tourist arrivals are crucial for efficient planning and resource management within the tourism sector. These forecasts guide various strategic decisions, including infrastructure development and marketing initiatives. They are essential for optimizing the economic advantages of tourism while minimizing adverse effects on local communities and the environment.

Recent studies have proposed various methods to improve tourism demand forecasting. Xin Li et al. [2] introduced a comprehensive decomposition algorithm that effectively handles seasonality, trends, and outliers, outperforming existing methods. Shilin Xu et al. [3] developed the temporal fusion encoder–decoder (TFED) network, which enhances interpretability and accuracy through deep learning and attention mechanisms. Another

*Mach. Learn. Knowl. Extr.* **2024**, *6*, 1673–1698. https://doi.org/10.3390/make6030083 https://www.mdpi.com/journal/make

study by Xin Li et al. [4] presented a transformer-based framework that integrates decomposition and Bayesian optimization for improved reliability and accuracy. Zhixue Liao et al. [5] combined empirical mode decomposition (EMD) with cooperative training to optimize neural networks for complex, nonlinear data, demonstrating superior stability and accuracy. Yunxuan Dong et al. [6] created the deep spatial–temporal enhancement tourism demand forecasting (DSTE-TDF) model, which uses convolutional filters to capture intricate spatial–temporal features, significantly outperforming traditional methods.

Despite their widespread adoption, previous tourism forecasting methods demonstrate significant drawbacks. Although proficient at detecting temporal trends, time series analysis techniques often overlook external factors such as economic indicators, social trends, and policy changes, which can substantially affect tourism demand. Conversely, regression models, while able to incorporate multiple features, often face challenges with high-dimensional data, resulting in problems like overfitting and increased computational complexity [7]. This makes models expensive to run and obscures which features are critical, complicating the interpretation and application of forecasts. These limitations underscore the need for more advanced models that integrate various influencing factors while effectively managing high-dimensional datasets.

Conventional methods like principal component analysis (PCA), non-negative matrix factorization (NMF), independent component analysis (ICA), and genetic algorithms (GAs) each have their uses but also distinct limitations in handling complex, non-linear tourism data [8]. PCA reduces dimensionality by transforming features into linearly uncorrelated components; however, it often misses non-linear relationships [9]. NMF, which produces parts-based, non-negative representations, struggles with data containing negative values, potentially missing intricate interdependencies [10]. ICA separates signals into independent subcomponents but assumes statistical independence and requires large data samples [11]. GAs optimize feature subsets through natural evolution simulation but are computationally intensive and dependent on the choice of fitness function and genetic operators [12].

Related studies on autoencoder-based feature selection have introduced innovative frameworks for enhancing supervised learning. Lei Wang et al. [13] proposed a video classification system using the loss switching fusion network (LSFNet), which combines a five-layer autoencoder with a multilayer perceptron (MLP) classifier, alternating between mean squared error (MSE) and cross-entropy to produce discriminative feature vectors. Jarrett et al. [14] introduced target-embedding autoencoders (TEAs) for high-dimensional target spaces, where the autoencoder learns latent representations that are both predictable from features and predictive of targets, improving generalization through joint optimization. Another study by Yigit et al. [15] presented a novel autoencoder-based feature selection method for predicting drug–target interactions This method focuses on human-interpretable feature weights. It effectively addresses high-dimensional data challenges, enhancing prediction accuracy and outperforming traditional methods. Thus, this method is valuable for drug discovery and design.

However, it is crucial to note that the compressed representation obtained from an autoencoder does not necessarily improve the performance of subsequent classification and regression tasks. The effectiveness of the latent representation depends on how well it captures the underlying structure of the data relevant to the specific predictive task. If the autoencoder fails to encapsulate the critical features needed for prediction, the resulting model may perform poorly. Furthermore, a notable drawback of the previous autoencoders used for feature selection is their inability to integrate both feature and target information concurrently, leading to suboptimal representations for supervised learning tasks.

To address the limitations of previous tourism forecasting algorithms and autoencoders for feature selection, this study proposes a novel target-concatenated autoencoder (TCA) combined with ensemble learning for tourism visitor forecasting. This approach effectively integrates the prediction target into the training process, ensuring that the learned feature representations are optimized for specific forecasting tasks. By doing so, it overcomes the common issues of high-dimensional data and the inability of traditional methods to consider diverse influencing factors simultaneously.

Numerous factors influence inbound tourism, including economic conditions, sociopolitical stability, exchange rates, visa policies, and flight availability [16]. Economic prosperity in a tourist's home country typically boosts travel, while downturns reduce discretionary spending. Additionally, cultural attractions, natural landscapes, and safety perceptions are vital in attracting visitors. Seasonal trends and special events cause fluctuations in visitor numbers, necessitating dynamic tourism strategies. Emerging trends like eco-tourism and wellness tourism further evolve travel preferences and demand.

The proposed TCA method tackles the challenges of autoencoders for feature selection by concatenating the target variable with the features during the autoencoder training. This ensures that the compressed representations retain the most relevant information for the predictive task. Furthermore, by incorporating ensemble learning algorithms such as XGBoost, LightGBM, and deep neural networks (DNNs), the approach leverages the strengths of multiple models to enhance prediction accuracy and reliability. This integration effectively handles complex, high-dimensional data, leading to more accurate and reliable tourism forecasts.

The experimental results demonstrate the superior performance of the proposed TCA combined with ensemble learning algorithms in forecasting inbound tourism demand. The TCA method consistently achieved a lower mean absolute percentage error (MAPE) across various datasets, significantly outperforming traditional feature selection techniques and other advanced models. For instance, TCA combined with XGBoost achieved a MAPE of 3.39% for the Taiwan dataset and 4.00% for the Hawaii dataset, indicating substantial improvements in predictive accuracy. These results underscore the efficacy of integrating target information into the feature selection process, thereby enhancing the relevance and quality of the compressed representations. Moreover, the computational efficiency of the TCA method, along with its resilience to different hyperparameter configurations, makes it a practical solution for real-world applications. The implications of these findings are far-reaching, enabling tourism managers and policymakers to make more informed decisions regarding infrastructure development, marketing strategies, and resource allocation. This, in turn, supports the sustainable growth of the tourism sector by optimizing economic benefits while minimizing adverse impacts on local communities and environments.

The contributions of this study are threefold.

- Integration of Diverse Influencing Factors: This study addressed the challenges of previous tourism forecasting algorithms by integrating economic conditions, sociopolitical stability, and other external factors into the forecasting model. This comprehensive approach enhanced the model's ability to capture and predict tourism demand accurately, overcoming the limitations of time series and regression models that often fail to consider these diverse influencing factors.
- Introduction of TCA for Feature Selection: This study resolved the limitations of related autoencoders for feature selection by introducing the TCA. Unlike traditional autoencoders that do not incorporate target information, TCA integrates the prediction target during the training process, ensuring that the learned representations are optimized for the specific forecasting task. This leads to more relevant and informative feature selection, improving the model's predictive performance.
- Significant Implications for the Tourism Industry: By achieving lower MAPE and demonstrating computational efficiency, the proposed method provides a practical tool for tourism managers and policymakers. It enables accurate forecasts; facilitates better infrastructure development, marketing strategies, and resource allocation; supports sustainable growth; and minimizes negative impacts on local communities and environments.

The remainder of this paper is organized into five main sections to thoroughly explore and evaluate the proposed model. Section 2 reviews the existing literature on tourism forecasting and feature selection techniques, highlighting their applications and limitations.

Section 3 details the framework of the proposed approach. Section 4, presents a comprehensive analysis of the model's performance using a realistic tourism dataset, comparing it with conventional methods to underscore its efficacy and efficiency. Section 5 delves into the implications of the findings, addressing potential challenges and limitations of the model within broader forecasting applications. Lastly, Section 6 summarizes the key contributions of this study and suggests directions for future research in terms of improving feature selection and dimension reduction for predictive modeling in tourism and other complex domains.

## 2. Related Work

This section reviews the existing literature in several key areas relevant to the proposed work. First, it examines tourism demand factors and forecasting algorithms, including traditional time series analysis methods and regression models such as linear regression, support vector machines (SVMs), XGBoost, LightGBM, and various deep learning approaches. Then, it discusses the use of autoencoders for feature selection.

### 2.1. Tourism Demand Factors

Tourism demand is influenced by various factors. Economic indicators are significant, as an economic boom with positive consumption trends can lead to more people willing to spend on travel. Therefore, economic indicators objectively reflect economic prospects and expected consumption trends. The exchange rate plays a crucial role in the number of tourists. One study [17] noted that a country's exchange rate system (volatility) can have both positive and negative impacts on tourism flows. Lower exchange rate volatility has a greater positive impact on tourism flows [18], especially since currency depreciation can affect inbound tourism prices [19]. Additionally, [20] used the gross domestic product (GDP), relative consumer price index (CPI), population, trade volume, and foreign exchange rate of the country of origin to predict changes in the number of arrivals. Another study [21] utilized the Purchasing Managers Index (PMI), Consumer Confidence Index (CCI), and Real Effective Exchange Rate Index (REERI) to predict the number of cruise tourists in China.

The quality and price of tourism resources significantly impact tourism motivations and destinations. One article [22] pointed out that service quality positively impacts the number of tourists; [23] highlighted that ski resort size, terrain elevation, ski lift capacity, ski lift quality, average annual snowfall, ticket costs, and accommodation costs all affect the number of tourists. One study [24] emphasized that hotel service quality has an important impact on the number of tourists, indicating that tourists consider the quality and price of hotels when choosing travel destinations [25]. The authors of [26] forecasted tourism demand using accommodation and food service prices.

Weather is a crucial condition for travel and a key attraction [27]. Generally, climate and weather conditions can motivate people to travel to resorts for vacations [28], and weather can affect the profitability of the tourism industry by influencing customer satisfaction and loyalty to the destination [29,30]. Negative weather experiences have a greater impact on tourist satisfaction than positive weather experiences [28,31].

People often search online before choosing a travel destination, resulting in a strong positive correlation between the number of online searches for a travel destination and the number of visitors to that destination. Trend data from Google and Baidu are currently used to predict the number of tourists at destinations [32–34] and tourist attractions [35], as well as hotel room demand [36,37]. The authors of [36] used Google to search for travel-related keywords to predict hotel room demand, while [38] used 211 Google and 45 Baidu keywords to obtain search engine data and predict travel demand in Macau.

Based on the above, numerous factors affect tourism demand. This study used the official statistics of the Republic of China as the main basis for predicting the number of tourists in Taiwan. This study refers to the exchange rate, CPI, GDP, price index, and other economic indicators; accommodation capacity; and climate factors as the main variables in predicting tourist arrivals.

### 2.2. Tourism Forecasting Algorithm

The accurate prediction of inbound visitor numbers significantly depends on the selection of suitable forecasting methods. Various approaches have been utilized in the literature, ranging from time series analysis to machine learning models.

Common time series techniques include exponential smoothing [39], which assigns exponentially decreasing weights to past observations, making it responsive to recent changes while considering historical data. Weighted moving average assigns different weights to past data points to smooth out short-term fluctuations and emphasize longer-term trends [40]. The grey model (GM), suitable for forecasting with limited and uncertain data, has been applied in diverse fields including tourism [41]. The autoregressive integrated moving average (ARIMA) model, which integrates autoregression, differencing, and moving average components to capture various data patterns, is widely recognized for its reliability [41].

In addition to time series methods, regression or associative models are employed in tourism forecasting [42]. SVMs are effective for both classification and regression tasks, modeling complex relationships between input features and tourism demand. Ensemble learning methods like XGBoost [43] and LightGBM [44] enhance performance through gradient-boosted decision trees, efficiently and accurately handling large-scale data. Neural networks, particularly deep learning models, excel in learning complex non-linear relationships, making them highly suitable for forecasting tourism demand [42].

Xin Li et al. [2] introduced a comprehensive decomposition algorithm for tourism demand forecasting, dividing data into sub-series and applying suitable models. The framework, tested on monthly tourist arrivals in Hong Kong, outperforms existing methods in terms of accuracy, effectively handling seasonality, trends, and outliers.

Shilin Xu et al. [3] proposed the TFED network with Bayesian optimization for daily tourism demand forecasting. This deep learning model uses an encoder–decoder architecture and attention mechanisms to enhance interpretability and accuracy by analyzing factors like weather and search queries, demonstrating significant improvements in empirical studies.

Xin Li et al. [4] presented a transformer-based framework for tourism demand forecasting, integrating the tree-structured Parzen estimator, a decomposition method, and Bayesian optimization. This model improves accuracy and reliability, effectively handling outliers and enhancing interpretability with attention mechanisms, making it valuable for tourism managers.

Zhixue Liao et al. [5] introduced a framework combining EMD and a cooperative training mechanism, optimizing neural networks for each decomposed sub-series. The model, tested on tourism demand data, shows superior accuracy and stability, effectively handling complex, nonlinear time series data.

Yunxuan Dong et al. [6] developed the DSTE-TDF model, which enhances spatial–temporal features by converting data into images using convolutional filters. Tested with Zhuhai tourism data, this model outperforms traditional methods in accuracy, capturing intricate spatial–temporal features and effectively predicting dynamic tourism demand.

Despite their widespread use, previous tourism forecasting algorithms exhibit notable limitations. While effective at observing temporal patterns, time series analysis methods fail to consider external influencing factors such as economic indicators, social trends, and policy changes, which can significantly impact tourism demand. On the other hand, regression models, although capable of incorporating various features, often struggle with high-dimensional data, leading to issues like overfitting and increased computational complexity. These limitations highlight the need for more effective models that can integrate diverse influencing factors while efficiently handling high-dimensional datasets.

### 2.3. Autoencoder for Feature Selection

Autoencoders, a type of artificial neural network, provide a powerful non-linear feature selection and dimensionality reduction method. An autoencoder consists of an encoder and a decoder, where the encoder condenses input data into a latent-space representation and the decoder reconstructs the input from this condensed form. By learning to compress and reconstruct data, autoencoders can identify the most critical features, effectively reducing dimensionality.

Variational autoencoders (VAEs) introduce a probabilistic perspective, offering a structured latent space that is beneficial for generating new data points and enhancing feature representation [45]. Sparse autoencoders apply a sparsity constraint on hidden units, prompting the network to learn a more efficient and compact representation.

Lei Wang et al. [13] proposed a video classification system using a lightweight LSFNet that integrated a five-layer autoencoder with an MLP classifier, sharing the encoder component. Using MSE for reconstruction and cross-entropy for classification performance, the LSFNet produced discriminative feature vectors. The system processes fused spatiotemporal descriptors through similarity search and soft voting, achieving superior results on industry datasets.

Jarrett et al. [14] introduced TEA for supervised representation learning for high-dimensional target spaces. They proposed a framework where the autoencoder learns an intermediate latent representation that is predictable from features and predictive of targets. This joint optimization, minimizing both prediction and reconstruction errors, regulates and improves generalization. The TEA framework shows advantages in multivariate sequence forecasting through theoretical validation and empirical experiments.

Yigit et al. [15] introduced a novel autoencoder-based feature selection method for predicting drug–target interactions, emphasizing human-interpretable feature weights. The method addresses the challenge of high-dimensional data by using an autoencoder to identify the most relevant features, thereby enhancing prediction accuracy. This approach offers superior performance compared to traditional feature selection methods, making it a valuable tool for drug discovery and design.

However, it is important to note that the compressed representation learned by an autoencoder does not necessarily enhance the performance of subsequent classification and regression tasks. The quality of the latent representation depends on how effectively it captures the underlying structure of the data pertinent to the specific predictive task. If the autoencoder fails to encapsulate essential features required for the predictive task, the resulting model may underperform. Additionally, a significant limitation of previous autoencoders for feature selection is their simultaneous incorporation of features and target information, leading to suboptimal representation for supervised learning tasks.

## 3. Proposed Method: Target-Concatenated Autoencoder and Ensemble Learning

This study proposes a TCA and ensemble learning as a novel approach to enhance the performance of predictive models in tourism forecasting by combining the strengths of feature selection techniques and autoencoders. This method addresses the limitations of traditional autoencoders in feature selection by incorporating the prediction target into the training process, ensuring that the learned representations are optimized for specific forecasting tasks.

### *3.1. Overview of the Target-Concatenated Autoencoder and Ensemble Learning Approach*

Figure 1 illustrates a step-by-step workflow of the TCA and ensemble learning approach for visitor forecasting.

- Start and Obtain Data: The process begins with data collection, encompassing key variables such as the number of tourist arrivals, economic factors, tourism resources, and other influencing factors. These data points form the foundation for the forecasting model.
- Target-Concatenated Autoencoder Feature Selection: The TCA is employed at this stage. The encoder component of the autoencoder compresses the input data into a latent representation, while the decoder attempts to reconstruct the original input from this compressed form. By incorporating the target variable (e.g., visitor num-

bers) during training, the autoencoder learns features that represent the input data and predict the target, ensuring that the encoded features are highly relevant to the forecasting task.

- Feature Importance and Encoded Features: The encoded features generated by the autoencoder are then analyzed for their importance in predicting the target variable. This step helps identify and select the most significant features, which reduces dimensionality and enhances model interpretability.
- Ensemble Learning Algorithm: The selected encoded features are subsequently fed into an ensemble learning algorithm. Ensemble learning methods, such as XGBoost, LightGBM, or a combination of neural networks, aggregate the predictions of multiple models to improve overall prediction accuracy and reliability.
- Model Evaluation: The final step involves evaluating the performance of the ensemble model using various metrics (e.g., mean absolute error, root mean squared error, mean absolute percentage error). This evaluation ensures that the model meets the desired accuracy and reliability standards.
- Finish: The process concludes with the finalization of the model, which is ready to be deployed for forecasting visitor numbers accurately.

Combining the strengths of autoencoders and ensemble learning, this structured approach aims to provide a comprehensive solution for accurate and reliable visitor forecasting.

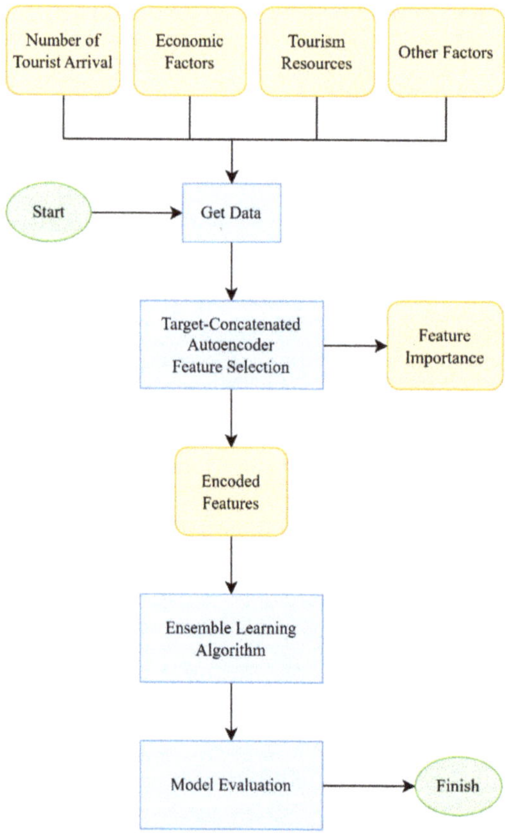


**Figure 1.** Flowchart of the TCA and ensemble learning approach for enhanced visitor forecasting.

### 3.2. Architecture of Target-Concatenated Autoencoder

The architecture of the TCA was designed to enhance the representation of input features by incorporating target information during the training process. This integration ensured that the learned features represented the input data and predicted the target, leading to improved performance in forecasting tasks.

Figure 2 illustrates the detailed architecture of the TCA. The process began with the model input, which included various features relevant to visitor forecasting, such as economic factors, tourism resources, and other influencing variables.

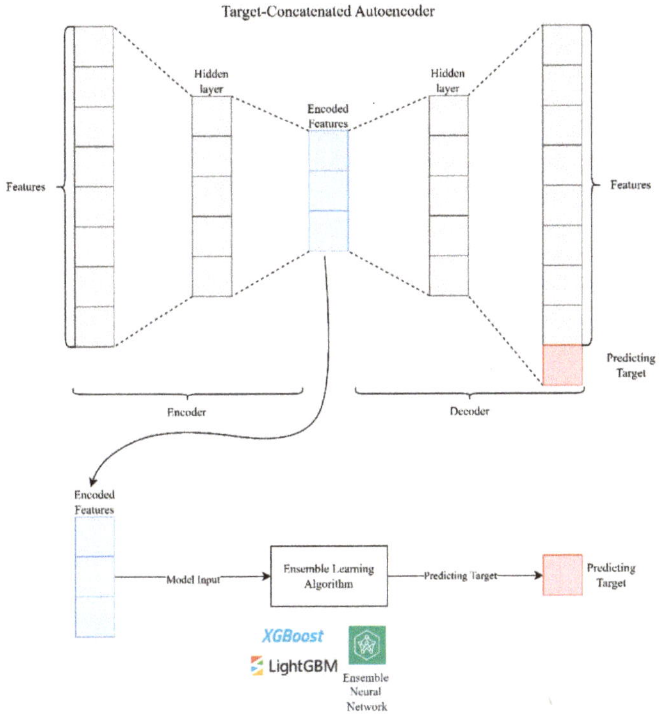


**Figure 2.** The TCA architecture for enhanced visitor forecasting.

- Encoder: The encoder component of the autoencoder compresses the input features into a latent representation. This process involves multiple layers:
    - The first layer processes the original input features through a dense layer with activation functions to capture non-linear relationships.
    - Subsequent layers further compress the data, reducing its dimensionality while retaining essential information.
- Target Concatenation: At a specific stage within the encoding process, the target variable (e.g., the number of tourist arrivals) is concatenated with the intermediate features. This step ensures that the autoencoder considers the target information while learning the compressed representation. By doing so, the model learns to emphasize features that are more predictive of the target, enhancing the quality of the latent representation.
- Decoder: The decoder reconstructs the original input from the latent representation, ensuring that the encoded features retain enough information to reconstruct the input accurately. This reconstruction process helps the model learn a compact yet informative data representation.

- Feature Extraction: The encoded features are extracted from the autoencoder and used for further analysis. These features are now optimized to represent the input and predict the target, making them highly valuable for subsequent modeling tasks.

In summary, the architecture of the TCA integrates the target variable during the encoding process, ensuring that the learned features are optimized for prediction tasks. Combined with ensemble learning, this approach provides a comprehensive framework for accurate and reliable visitor forecasting.

### *3.3. Feature Importance with Target-Concatenated Autoencoder*

The TCA not only aids in dimensionality reduction and feature selection but also provides a mechanism to determine the importance of each feature in the context of the target prediction. This is achieved by analyzing the weights learned by the autoencoder during the training process.

Figure 3 illustrates the process of calculating feature importance using the TCA. The workflow begins with the input features, which include various factors relevant to visitor forecasting, such as economic indicators, tourism resources, and other influencing variables.

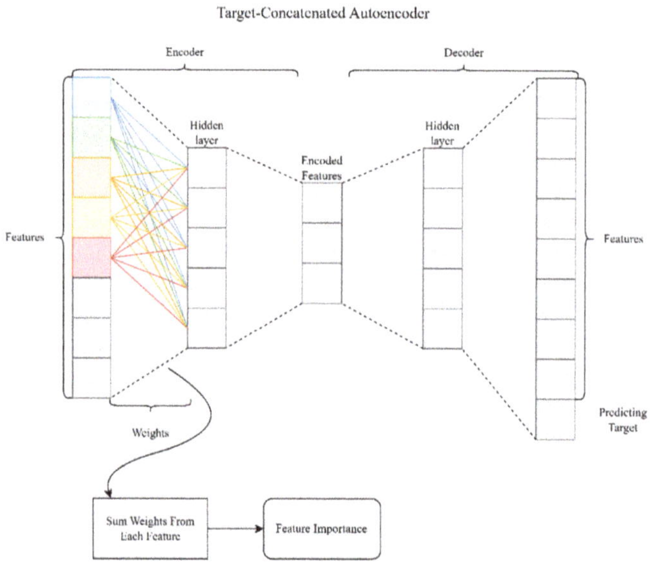


**Figure 3.** Visualization of feature importance calculation in the TCA.

- Encoder: As the input features pass through the encoder, they are transformed into a lower-dimensional latent space. During this transformation, the network learns weights that capture the relationships between the input features and the target variable. These weights are crucial as they reflect the contribution of each input feature to the encoded representation.
- Weight Analysis: To determine feature importance, this study analyzed the weights connecting the input layer to the first hidden layer of the encoder. By summing the absolute values of these weights for each feature, the impact of each feature on the latent representation could be quantified. This sum represented the overall importance of the feature in predicting the target variable.
- Feature Importance Calculation: The summed weights were then normalized to provide a relative measure of feature importance. Features with higher summed weights were deemed more significant, indicating their crucial role in the prediction task. Conversely, features with lower weights had a lesser impact.

- Output: The final output was a ranked list of features based on their importance scores. This ranking helped identify the most relevant forecasting predictor, allowing for a more focused and efficient modeling process.

To summarize, the TCA facilitates the calculation of feature importance by leveraging the weights learned during the encoding process. This method provides a clear and interpretable measure of which features are most influential in predicting the target variable, thereby enhancing the overall effectiveness of the forecasting model.

## 4. Experiment and Results

This section presents a detailed examination of the experiments conducted to assess the efficacy of the TCA and ensemble learning approach. It encompasses a description of the datasets utilized, the hyperparameters and experimental configuration, the evaluation metrics applied, an ablation study, and a comparison of the results with related works. The aim is to showcase the reliability and efficiency of the TCA and ensemble learning in forecasting inbound visitor numbers.

### *4.1. Dataset*

Two datasets were employed in this study: the Taiwan Visitor Dataset and the Hawaii Visitor Dataset.

The Taiwan Visitor Dataset used in this study was sourced from various open and governmental data repositories:

- Taiwan National Statistics Database
- Taiwan Ministry of Transportation and Communications: Tourism Statistics
- Ministry of Transportation and Communications: Visitor Statistics
- Ministry of Transportation and Communications: Transportation Statistics
- Google Trends
- Data Taiwan

The study period spanned from 1 January 2001 to 1 December 2023, as shown in Figure 4a. Initially, 145 features were considered, covering various economic, tourism resource, and other factors potentially influencing the number of tourists arriving in Taiwan.

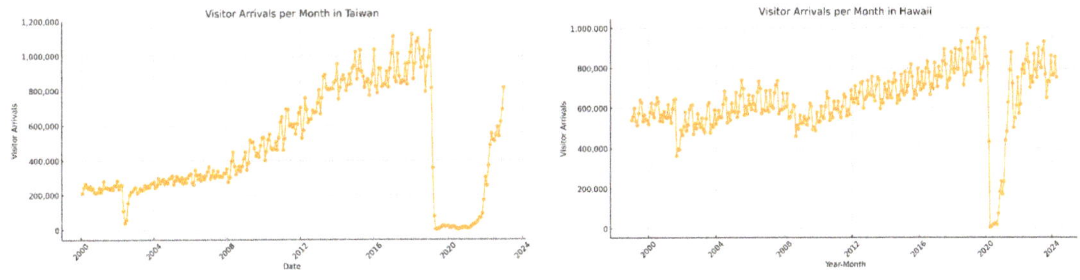


(a) (b)

**Figure 4.** Time series of visitor arrivals per month. (**a**) Visitor arrivals per month in Taiwan (2001–2023). (**b**) Visitor arrivals per month in Hawaii (1999–2024).

The features were categorized into three main classes: Economic Factors, Tourism Resource Factors, and Other Factors. Table 1 lists the ten most important features of each category.

These classifications influence tourism for various reasons:

- Economic Factors: Economic stability and growth directly affect tourists' disposable income and purchasing power, influencing their ability to travel. Exchange rates impact the cost of traveling to a destination, while GDP and GNI provide an overall economic context [46].

- Tourism Resources: The availability and quality of accommodation, transport infrastructure, and tourism facilities are crucial for attracting and retaining tourists. High occupancy rates indicate a healthy tourism sector, while the number of tourist establishments reflects the capacity to accommodate visitors [47,48].
- Other Factors: Weather conditions (e.g., precipitation days), crime rates, and economic indicators (e.g., export and import growth rates) also play significant roles. Favorable weather and safety enhance a destination's appeal, while economic indicators reflect overall market conditions that can influence travel decisions.

The Hawaii Visitor Dataset sourced from the Department of Business, Economic Development & Tourism, covered the period from 1999 to April 2024, as shown in Figure 4b.

**Table 1.** Classification of features influencing the number of tourists arriving in Taiwan.

| Factor Class | Feature Name |
|---|---|
| Economic Factors | Average Exchange Rate NTD/USD, Economic Growth Rate, GDP Nominal Value Million NTD, Average GDP per Capita NTD, GNI Nominal Value Million NTD, Average GNI per Person NTD, National Income Million NTD, Basic Consumer Price Index, CPI Food, Export Annual Growth Rate, Import Annual Growth Rate, Taiwan Weighted Index, Taiwan Annual Growth Rate |
| Tourism Resources | Overview of Hotels and B&Bs, Number of Rooms, International Tourist Hotel Number, International Tourist Hotel Rooms, General Hotels Guesthouse Rooms, Tourist Hotel Occupancy Rate, International Tourist Hotel Occupancy Rate, General Tourist Hotel Occupancy Rate, Number of Passengers, Total Number of Tourist Hotels, Total Number of Tourist Hotel Rooms, International Tourist Hotels Houses, General Tourist Hotels Rooms |
| Other Factors | Number of Precipitation Days Taipei, Number of Occurrences Including Supplementary Reports, Monthly Indicators (Is January, Is February, Is March, etc.), Criminal Case Incidence Rate |

### 4.2. Hyperparameters and Experimental Setup

The experiments evaluating the TCA and ensemble learning approach were conducted on two comprehensive datasets, incorporating various features from economic indicators to tourism statistics. Data preprocessing involved several critical steps to ensure that the datasets were complete and standardized for analysis. Missing values were imputed using the median value of each column, an effective method for handling missing data. The datasets were then normalized to a feature range of 0 to 1, ensuring uniformity in the scale of all features contributing to the model training process. Following normalization, the data were split into training and testing sets at a 90:10 ratio, providing a substantial portion of data for model training while reserving a part for unbiased evaluation.

Dimensionality reduction was performed using PCA, NMF, and ICA, with the Taiwan dataset reduced to 64 components and the Hawaii dataset reduced to 12 components. This step was essential for mitigating the complexity of the datasets while retaining their most informative features.

A genetic algorithm (GA) was employed with specific settings to optimize the feature set effectively for feature selection. The GA was configured using the DEAP library [49], where attributes, individuals, population, evaluation functions, mating, mutation, and selection operators were registered. The initial population comprised 50 individuals, each represented by a binary vector indicating the presence or absence of features. Individuals were evaluated based on a custom function assessing model performance. The GA utilized a two-point crossover with a probability of 0.5 and a bit-flip mutation with a probability of 0.2 to maintain genetic diversity. Tournament selection with a size of three was employed to choose individuals for the next generation, and the algorithm ran for 40 generations to iteratively optimize the feature set. The essential hyperparameters for the GA included a population size of 50, a crossover probability of 0.5, and a mutation probability of 0.2, with the number of generations set to 40.

Linear regression, support vector machines (SVMs), XGBoost, LightGBM, and deep neural networks (DNNs) are widely used regression models for tourism demand forecasting, each offering unique strengths and challenges. Linear regression is a fundamental technique that models the relationship between independent and dependent variables linearly, but it often struggles with non-linear data patterns. Support vector machines, on the other hand, can handle non-linear relationships by using kernel functions, although they can be computationally intensive and require careful parameter tuning. XGBoost and LightGBM are gradient-boosting frameworks that build ensembles of decision trees, known for their high accuracy and efficiency, particularly in handling large-scale datasets with complex patterns. Deep neural networks excel at capturing intricate non-linear relationships due to their multi-layered architectures, but they demand substantial computational resources and risk overfitting.

To optimize the performance of these models, this study employed a grid search to tune their hyperparameters systematically. A grid search exhaustively explores the hyperparameter space, adjusting settings such as the learning rate, number of trees, maximum depth for XGBoost and LightGBM, and the number of layers and neurons for DNNs, to minimize the mean absolute percentage error (MAPE). This rigorous tuning process ensures that each model operates at its best, providing the most accurate and reliable forecasts.

The computation time for the experiments was measured on an Ubuntu 18.04.6 LTS machine equipped with a 56-core Intel(R) Xeon(R) CPU E5-2690 v4 @ 2.60 GHz. Each program that was run was repeated ten times, and the average and standard deviation of the computation time were reported to ensure reliability and consistency.

This comprehensive experimental setup provided an effective framework for evaluating the effectiveness of the TCA and ensemble learning approach in forecasting inbound visitor numbers, integrating advanced preprocessing, feature selection, and predictive modeling techniques.

### 4.3. Evaluation Metric

The performance of the predictive models was assessed using widely recognized evaluation metrics for tourism forecasting: the MAPE, MAE, MSE, and coefficient of determination ($R^2$). These metrics offered a comprehensive understanding of the model's accuracy and reliability.

- Mean absolute percentage error (MAPE) quantifies prediction accuracy as a percentage, providing a scale-independent measure of error. It is computed as the average absolute percentage difference between the predicted and actual values, represented by the below formula:

$$\text{MAPE} = \frac{100\%}{n}\sum_{i=1}^{n}\left|\frac{y_i - \hat{y}_i}{y_i}\right|$$

  MAPE is particularly useful in scenarios where understanding the relative size of errors is essential. However, it can be sensitive to small actual values, potentially resulting in extremely high percentage errors.
- Mean absolute error (MAE) measures the average magnitude of errors in a set of predictions, without considering their direction. It is calculated as the average absolute difference between the predicted and actual values, represented by the below formula:

$$\text{MAE} = \frac{1}{n}\sum_{i=1}^{n}|y_i - \hat{y}_i|$$

  MAE provides a straightforward interpretation of prediction errors, reflecting the average error magnitude in the same units as the data.
- Mean squared error (MSE) is a quadratic scoring rule that measures the average magnitude of errors. It squares the differences between predicted and actual values, averages them, and then takes the square root, represented by the below formula:

$$\text{MSE} = \frac{1}{n}\sum_{i=1}^{n}(y_i - \hat{y}_i)^2$$

MSE is particularly useful for identifying larger errors due to its quadratic nature, which penalizes significant deviations more than smaller ones. This makes MSE sensitive to outliers and provides a comprehensive measure of model accuracy.

- The coefficient of determination ($R^2$) indicates the proportion of the variance in the dependent variable that is predictable from the independent variables, represented by the below formula:

$$R^2 = 1 - \frac{\sum_{i=1}^{n}(y_i - \hat{y}_i)^2}{\sum_{i=1}^{n}(y_i - \overline{y})^2}$$

where $\overline{y}$ is the mean of the observed data. $R^2$ values range from 0 to 1, with higher values indicating better model performance.

These evaluation metrics were selected to provide a balanced assessment of model performance, capturing both absolute and relative prediction errors and highlighting the models' ability to handle large deviations while offering reliable forecasts. By employing MAPE, MAE, MSE, and $R^2$, this study ensured a thorough evaluation of the predictive model's effectiveness in forecasting inbound visitor numbers.

### 4.4. Ablation Study

This study conducted a series of ablation experiments to evaluate the contributions of various components in the TCA and ensemble learning approach. These experiments involved varying the encoding dimension of the target-concatenated autoencoder to assess the impact of different latent space sizes on model performance. Additionally, this study explored different learning rates to determine the optimal balance between training speed and stability for the autoencoder. Furthermore, various modifications to the autoencoder structures were tested, incorporating batch normalization and adjusting dropout rates to assess their impact on the model's accuracy and reliability. Through these ablation studies, this study aimed to isolate and identify the most effective configurations for enhancing visitor forecasting.

#### 4.4.1. Impact of Encoding Dimensions on Model Performance

This section discusses the impact of varying encoding dimensions on the performance of the predictive models, as illustrated in Figure 5. The figure compares the MAPE and $R^2$ across different encoding dimensions for three models: XGBoost, LightGBM, and an ensemble deep neural network (DNN) on the Taiwan and Hawaii datasets.

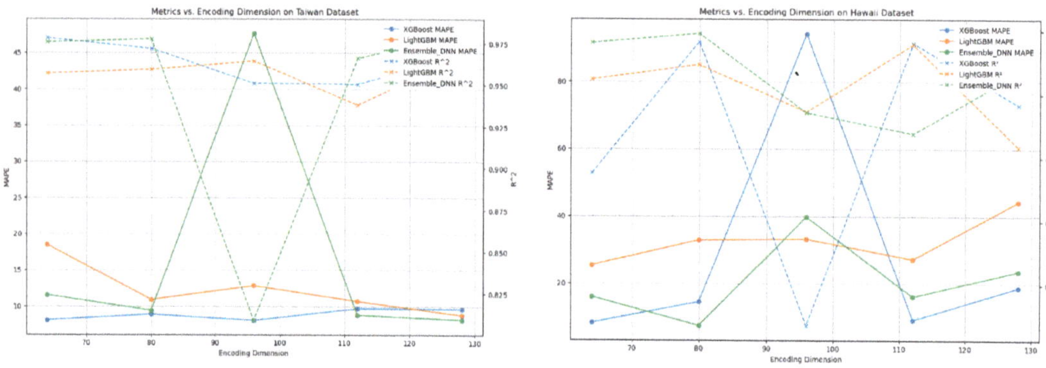


(a) (b)

**Figure 5.** Metrics vs. encoding dimension of target-concatenated autoencoder. (**a**) Metrics vs. encoding dimension on the Taiwan dataset for various models. (**b**) Metrics vs. encoding dimension on the Hawaii dataset for various models.

Figure 5a shows that the MAPE for XGBoost remained relatively stable across different encoding dimensions, indicating effective utilization of the encoded features irrespective of the latent space size. LightGBM exhibited more variability, with noticeable peaks and troughs, suggesting moderate sensitivity to encoding dimensions. The ensemble DNN exhibited significant fluctuations in MAPE, with a sharp increase around an encoding dimension of approximately 85, indicating poor performance at this size. However, its performance stabilized at higher dimensions, aligning more closely with the other models. The $R^2$ values for XGBoost were consistently high, showing that it maintained a strong fit across encoding dimensions, whereas LightGBM and the ensemble DNN exhibited more variability, especially at lower encoding dimensions.

Figure 5b illustrates the MAPE and $R^2$ for the Hawaii dataset across varying encoding dimensions. XGBoost displayed significant variability, with a sharp spike around an encoding dimension of 85, where MAPE exceeded 90%, indicating substantial performance degradation. In contrast, LightGBM demonstrated more consistent performance, with MAPE values generally ranging between 20% and 40%, indicating better stability across different encoding dimensions. The ensemble DNN exhibited fluctuations peaking around an encoding dimension of 100 but achieved lower errors beyond 110. The $R^2$ values reflected this trend, with the ensemble DNN showing improved $R^2$ at higher dimensions, indicating better predictive accuracy when the encoding dimension was suitably tuned.

Both figures highlight the critical role of selecting appropriate encoding dimensions to achieve optimal model performance. XGBoost's performance was highly variable, requiring careful tuning to avoid significant errors. LightGBM exhibited greater stability but still benefited from attention to encoding dimensions. The ensemble DNN demonstrated the potential for lower errors and higher $R^2$ with precise tuning of encoding dimensions, emphasizing the importance of finetuning to enhance the accuracy and reliability of visitor forecasting models. These findings indicate that while some models are more sensitive to encoding dimensions than others, all models can benefit from the careful selection of encoding dimensions to optimize performance.

### 4.4.2. Impact of Learning Rate on Model Performance

This section discusses the impact of varying learning rates on the performance of the predictive models, as shown in Figure 6. The figure compares the MAPE and $R^2$ across different learning rates for three models: XGBoost, LightGBM, and an ensemble DNN on the Taiwan and Hawaii datasets.

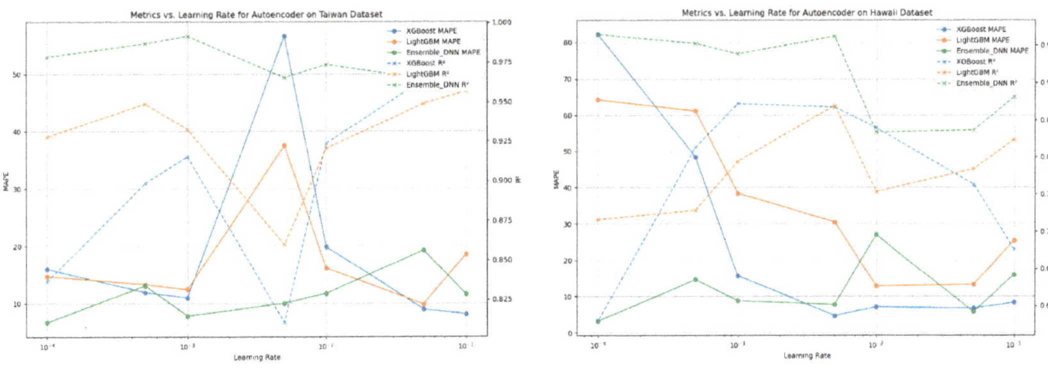


(a) (b)

**Figure 6.** Metrics vs. learning rate for TCA. (**a**) Metrics vs. learning rate for autoencoder on Taiwan dataset for various models. (**b**) Metrics vs. learning rate for autoencoder on Hawaii dataset for various models.

Figure 6a shows that the performance of XGBoost demonstrated significant sensitivity to learning rate variations. A sharp increase in MAPE occurred at a learning rate of $10^{-2}$, where the error exceeded 50%, indicating that a higher learning rate leads to severe performance degradation for XGBoost. Conversely, lower learning rates ($10^{-4}$ to $10^{-3}$) resulted in a more stable and lower MAPE, suggesting that XGBoost benefits from smaller learning rates for optimal performance. The $R^2$ values followed an inverse trend, decreasing with higher learning rates, highlighting the model's decreased accuracy.

LightGBM also showed variability in performance across different learning rates. Higher errors were observed at intermediate learning rates, while both lower ($10^{-4}$) and higher ($10^{-1}$) learning rates yielded better performance. This indicated moderate sensitivity to learning rate changes, emphasizing the need for careful tuning to achieve consistent results. The $R^2$ values for LightGBM remained relatively stable across the learning rates but tended to improve at the lower and higher extremes.

The ensemble DNN, on the other hand, demonstrated the least variability in MAPE across different learning rates. It maintained relatively stable performance, with MAPE values generally below 20% across learning rates from $10^{-4}$ to $10^{-1}$. This stability suggested that the ensemble DNN was less sensitive to changes in the learning rate, indicating reliability in its training process. The $R^2$ values for the ensemble DNN also showed stability, reinforcing its consistent performance.

Figure 6b shows a similar trend for the Hawaii dataset. XGBoost exhibited a steep decline in MAPE as the learning rate decreased. At higher learning rates ($10^{-1}$), the MAPE was significantly high, around 80%, indicating poor performance. As the learning rate decreased to $10^{-4}$, the MAPE stabilized at around 10%, suggesting that XGBoost performs optimally at lower learning rates. The $R^2$ values increased with lower learning rates, corroborating the improved performance.

LightGBM also showed a declining trend in MAPE with decreasing learning rates. At higher learning rates, the MAPE started at around 60% and gradually decreased, with the lowest MAPE observed at lower learning rates ($10^{-4}$), stabilizing at around 10–20%. This indicated that LightGBM benefits from smaller learning rates for better performance. The $R^2$ values for LightGBM also improved with lower learning rates, indicating enhanced predictive accuracy.

The ensemble DNN continued to demonstrate the most stable performance across different learning rates. The MAPE remained consistently low, ranging from 10% to 20%, regardless of the learning rate. This stability further underscored the reliability of the ensemble DNN model in handling varying training conditions. The $R^2$ values remained high and stable, further emphasizing the model's resilience.

Both figures highlight the critical role of selecting suitable learning rates for achieving optimal model performance. XGBoost and LightGBM showed significant improvements in MAPE with lower learning rates, indicating their sensitivity to this hyperparameter. In contrast, the ensemble DNN demonstrated stable performance across all learning rates, highlighting its reliability. These findings emphasize that while tuning the learning rate is critical for models like XGBoost and LightGBM, the ensemble DNN offers a more resilient alternative, performing well even without extensive hyperparameter tuning. This insight is crucial for ensuring reliable and accurate visitor forecasting in practical applications.

#### 4.4.3. Impact of Autoencoder Configurations on Model Performance

This section discusses the impact of varying ablation configurations on the performance of the predictive models, as illustrated in Figure 7. The figure compares the MAPE and $R^2$ across different ablation configurations for three models: XGBoost, LightGBM, and an ensemble DNN on the Taiwan and Hawaii datasets.

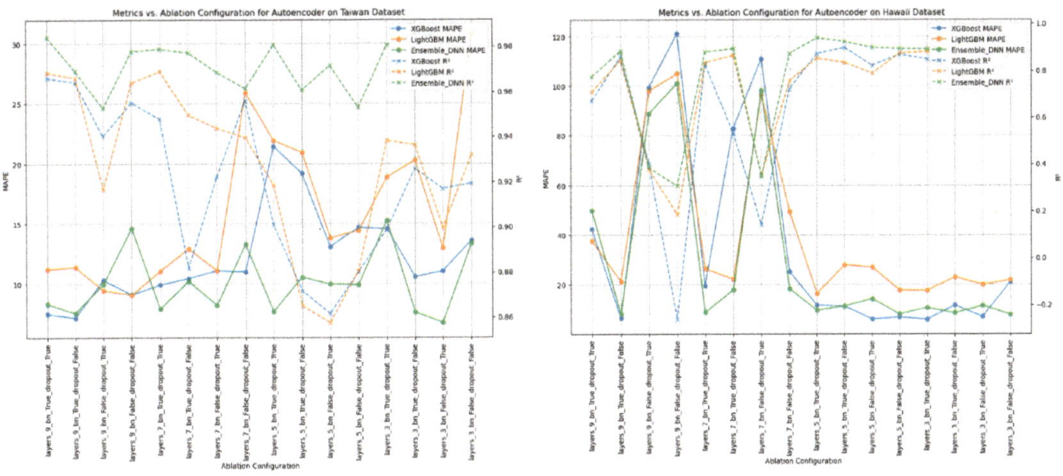


(**a**) (**b**)

**Figure 7.** Metrics vs. ablation configuration for TCA. (**a**) Metrics vs. ablation configuration for autoencoder on Taiwan dataset for various models. (**b**) Metrics vs. ablation configuration for autoencoder on Hawaii Dataset for various models.

Figure 7a shows that XGBoost's performance was highly variable across different ablation configurations, with MAPE ranging from around 10% to 30%. This indicated that the model was sensitive to changes in the autoencoder configuration. The $R^2$ values for XGBoost followed a similar trend, fluctuating with the different configurations, which highlighted the importance of selecting appropriate configurations for optimal performance.

LightGBM also showed variability in performance with different ablation configurations. The MAPE ranged between approximately 10% and 25%, with the highest errors observed in configurations with fewer layers and without dropout. The $R^2$ values for LightGBM also exhibited variability, improving with configurations that included more layers and dropout, suggesting that these configurations helped stabilize the model's performance.

The ensemble DNN demonstrated the most stability across different ablation configurations. The MAPE remained relatively low, generally below 15%, regardless of the configuration, indicating reliability to changes in the autoencoder structure. The $R^2$ values for the ensemble DNN were consistently high, further emphasizing the model's ability to maintain performance across varying configurations.

Figure 7b shows similar trends for the Hawaii dataset. XGBoost's MAPE varied significantly, with peaks reaching as high as 120%, indicating poor performance for certain configurations. The $R^2$ values for XGBoost were correspondingly low for these configurations, underscoring the model's sensitivity.

Similarly, LightGBM displayed a more consistent performance on the Hawaii dataset, with MAPE values mostly between 20% and 40%. The $R^2$ values for LightGBM were relatively stable, though they improved with configurations that included dropout and more layers, indicating that these settings enhanced model reliability.

In contrast, the ensemble DNN continued to show the most consistent performance, with MAPE values generally below 20% across all configurations. The $R^2$ values for the ensemble DNN remained high, reinforcing the model's resilience to different ablation settings.

Both figures highlight the importance of selecting suitable ablation configurations to optimize model performance. XGBoost and LightGBM showed significant variability in performance with different configurations, indicating the need for careful tuning. Conversely, the ensemble DNN demonstrated stable performance across all configurations, demonstrating resilience even without extensive hyperparameter tuning. These findings emphasize that tuning the learning rate is critical for models like XGBoost and LightGBM. This insight is essential for ensuring reliable and accurate visitor forecasting in practical applications.

#### 4.4.4. Performance Evaluation of the TCA + XGBoost Model on the Taiwan Dataset

Figure 8a illustrates the performance of the TCA combined with the XGBoost model in predicting the number of tourists in Taiwan. The scatter plot compares the true values of tourist arrivals ($x$-axis) against the predicted values ($y$-axis), with the dashed line representing perfect predictions (where true values equaled predicted values). The close alignment of data points along the dashed line indicates the model's high accuracy and effectiveness in forecasting tourism demand.

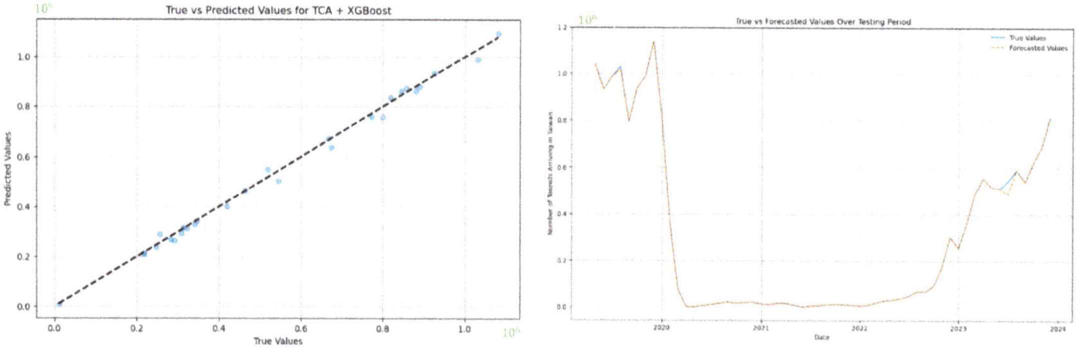


(**a**) (**b**)

**Figure 8.** (**a**) True vs. predicted values for the TCA + XGBoost model on the Taiwan dataset. (**b**) True vs. forecasted values over the testing period for the Taiwan dataset.

Figure 8b displays the comparison between the actual number of tourists arriving in Taiwan (blue line) and the forecasted values (orange dashed line) by the TCA + XGBoost model over the testing period. The $x$-axis represents the date, while the $y$-axis shows the number of tourists arriving in Taiwan. The close alignment between the true and forecasted values demonstrates the model's ability to accurately predict tourism demand over time.

These figures illustrate the accuracy and reliability of the TCA combined with XGBoost in predicting tourism demand. The Figure 8a demonstrates a high correlation between the predicted and true values, indicating the model's precision in capturing the underlying patterns of the data. The Figure 8b shows the model's performance over the testing period, with the forecasted values closely aligning with the actual number of tourists arriving in Taiwan. These visualizations confirm that the TCA + XGBoost model effectively generalizes and accurately forecasts future visitor numbers, proving its utility for strategic planning in the tourism sector.

### *4.5. Comparison Result*

This section comprehensively evaluates the proposed TCA and ensemble learning method against various benchmarks. This section presents a detailed comparison with non-ensemble algorithms and traditional feature selection techniques, highlighting the advantages of the proposed approach. Additionally, it presents a computation time analysis of ensemble learning after applying different feature selection methods, demonstrating the efficiency of the proposed method. Furthermore, this section compares the performance of the proposed method with existing tourism forecasting algorithms, underscoring its effectiveness in predicting tourism. Lastly, a comparison with other autoencoder-based feature selection algorithms is provided, showcasing the superior performance and resilience of the TCA in enhancing forecasting accuracy.

#### 4.5.1. Comparison with Non-Ensemble and Feature Selection Algorithm

Table 2 compares the MAPE, $R^2$, MAE, and MSE across different machine learning algorithms and feature selection techniques for the Taiwan and Hawaii datasets. The table is divided into two main sections: non-ensemble algorithms and ensemble algorithms, showcasing the performance of linear regression, SVR, XGBoost, LightGBM, and an ensemble DNN under various feature selection methods.

For the non-ensemble algorithms, linear regression and SVR, the results indicate that both algorithms generally performed poorly compared to ensemble methods. Linear regression showed a high MAPE across most feature selection methods, with significant errors observed for both datasets. SVR, in particular, exhibited exceptionally high MAPE values, especially for the Taiwan dataset without any feature selection. The $R^2$ values for these algorithms were relatively low, further indicating their limited effectiveness.

Among the ensemble algorithms, XGBoost, LightGBM, and the ensemble DNN revealed markedly better performance. XGBoost demonstrated the lowest MAPE values with the GA and the proposed TCA on the Taiwan dataset, achieving 3.97% and 3.39%, respectively. Similarly, LightGBM and the ensemble DNN exhibited improved performance with the proposed TCA method, indicating their effectiveness in reducing prediction errors. For instance, LightGBM achieved a MAPE of 4.01% on the Taiwan dataset with TCA, while the ensemble DNN achieved 3.82%. These models also displayed higher $R^2$ values, signifying better predictive accuracy and model fit.

The table also highlights the variability in performance across different feature selection methods. For instance, PCA and ICA generally resulted in higher MAPE values for ensemble algorithms, suggesting that these traditional dimension reduction techniques may not be as effective in this context. In contrast, the proposed TCA consistently provided lower MAPE values across both datasets and all ensemble algorithms, demonstrating its reliability and superiority. This was further supported by lower MAE and MSE values, which indicated fewer prediction errors and better overall model performance.

Additionally, the table includes results for NMF and autoencoder-based feature selection (AE), which illustrated mixed performance. NMF yielded relatively high MAPE values for the ensemble methods, while AE provided better results, though not as consistently as the proposed TCA. The $R^2$ values for AE were also comparatively lower, indicating less reliable predictive power.

Overall, the table underscores the significant improvements in forecasting accuracy achieved by the proposed TCA, particularly when used with ensemble learning algorithms. These findings highlight the importance of effective feature selection in enhancing the performance of predictive models in tourism demand forecasting.

**Table 2.** Metrics for various machine learning algorithms and feature selection methods on Taiwan and Hawaii datasets.

| ML Algorithm | | Non-Ensemble Algorithm | | | | Ensemble Algorithm | | | | | |
|---|---|---|---|---|---|---|---|---|---|---|---|
| | | Linear Regression | | Support Vector Regression | | XGBoost | | LightGBM | | Ensemble DNN | |
| | Metrics | Taiwan Dataset | Hawaii Dataset | Taiwan Dataset | Hawaii Dataset | Taiwan Dataset | Hawaii Dataset | Taiwan Dataset | Hawaii Dataset | Taiwan Dataset | Hawaii Dataset |
| N/A | MAPE(%) | 44.37 | 16.21 | 153.95 | 106.46 | 6.30 | 5.48 | 10.71 | 34.71 | 6.45 | 7.62 |
| | $R^2$ | 0.96 | 0.95 | 0.44 | 0.01 | 0.98 | 0.92 | 0.97 | 0.78 | 0.99 | 0.96 |
| | MAE | 48,191.56 | 29,607.05 | 272,444.50 | 127,291.25 | 30,176.27 | 35,045.92 | 33,087.99 | 53,033.07 | 19,708.60 | 20,488.88 |
| | MSE | 3,580,592,919.74 | 1,428,550,200.08 | 122,502,556,231.60 | 29,136,902,542.55 | 1,545,737,496.62 | 2,431,270,227.28 | 1,810,755,913.05 | 6,306,689,740.96 | 686,173,563.94 | 10,444,29,832.88 |
| PCA | MAPE(%) | 30.98 | 116.07 | 153.95 | 106.45 | 8.47 | 98.02 | 10.80 | 93.79 | 7.68 | 93.14 |
| | $R^2$ | 0.97 | 0.02 | 0.44 | 0.01 | 0.96 | 0.02 | 0.98 | 0.42 | 0.99 | 0.42 |
| | MAE | 44,413.17 | 88,792.58 | 272,445.54 | 127,291.36 | 45,902.30 | 76,612.07 | 37,033.22 | 64,840.58 | 19,781.80 | 61,009.96 |
| | MSE | 2,876,436,756.27 | 29,295,102,232.71 | 122,502,714,091.85 | 29,137,198,570.28 | 3,778,180,675.34 | 28,133,109,043.76 | 2,072,797,773.85 | 16,577,496,052.83 | 618,026,385.05 | 16,697,134,852.70 |
| NMF | MAPE(%) | 10.00 | 113.10 | 153.95 | 106.46 | 13.87 | 110.64 | 22.65 | 88.71 | 22.05 | 103.59 |
| | $R^2$ | 0.98 | 0.06 | 0.44 | 0.01 | 0.96 | 0.01 | 0.97 | 0.44 | 0.98 | 0.33 |
| | MAE | 35,905.75 | 78,195.33 | 272,448.92 | 127,295.17 | 40,632.38 | 88,337.42 | 42,452.38 | 62,554.41 | 26,025.87 | 62,003.89 |
| | MSE | 1,763,518,534.39 | 27,017,646,693.74 | 122,506,951,824.28 | 29,138,263,565.44 | 3,155,862,181.89 | 28,544,686,820.03 | 2,790,969,394.51 | 16,273,102,607.65 | 1,310,598,482.89 | 19,442,662,498.81 |
| ICA | MAPE(%) | 30.98 | 116.07 | 153.95 | 106.46 | 96.35 | 10.79 | 105.08 | 42.43 | 17.00 | 64.84 |
| | $R^2$ | 0.97 | 0.02 | 0.44 | 0.01 | 0.58 | 0.84 | 0.65 | 0.75 | 0.99 | 0.40 |
| | MAE | 44,413.17 | 88,792.58 | 272,467.79 | 127,293.88 | 142,846.21 | 42,586.48 | 139,005.58 | 55,865.14 | 26,311.08 | 62,962.40 |
| | MSE | 2,876,436,756.27 | 29,295,102,232.71 | 122,516,110,191.73 | 29,137,926,008.70 | 36,115,301,305.40 | 4,671,807,062.51 | 30,189,483,312.54 | 7,101,395,924.60 | 1,169,826,432.83 | 16,180,779,860.68 |
| GA | MAPE(%) | 15.88 | 12.82 | 153.94 | 87.58 | 3.97 | 13.49 | 10.07 | 87.14 | 5.94 | 85.61 |
| | $R^2$ | 0.99 | 0.82 | 0.44 | 0.02 | 0.98 | 0.85 | 0.98 | 0.86 | 0.99 | 0.94 |
| | MAE | 18,597.52 | 49,775.85 | 272,440.82 | 114,824.03 | 26,015.40 | 42,986.75 | 31,416.39 | 44,144.06 | 17,685.21 | 29,444.51 |
| | MSE | 579,034,917.90 | 4,512,793,296.79 | 122,500,280,086.79 | 25,690,312,566.67 | 1,336,329,997.87 | 4,163,766,490.20 | 1,689,813,130.69 | 4,057,405,850.44 | 542,619,854.65 | 1,661,177,597.14 |
| AE | MAPE(%) | 13.85 | 16.43 | 153.94 | 106.46 | 8.87 | 5.73 | 17.24 | 12.29 | 8.30 | 11.15 |
| | $R^2$ | 0.90 | 0.72 | 0.44 | 0.01 | 0.97 | 0.88 | 0.98 | 0.81 | 0.96 | 0.90 |
| | MAE | 632,82.15 | 518,83.72 | 272,443.50 | 127,294.46 | 40,602.58 | 38,273.52 | 37,472.40 | 45,745.87 | 34,241.51 | 33,786.79 |
| | MSE | 8,606,617,153.48 | 8,122,755,005.22 | 122,502,875,176.51 | 29,137,715,139.45 | 2,958,574,653.26 | 3,495,323,416.13 | 2,024,845,387.51 | 5408,841,511.93 | 2,076,884,185.44 | 2871,565,836.54 |
| Proposed TCA | MAPE(%) | 23.60 | 100.90 | 153.96 | 106.46 | **3.39** | **4.01** | **4.20** | 12.24 | **3.82** | **5.40** |
| | $R^2$ | 0.93 | 0.35 | 0.44 | 0.01 | 0.99 | 0.94 | 0.99 | 0.95 | 0.99 | 0.93 |
| | MAE | 57,597.40 | 71,267.4 | 272,423.22 | 127,292.40 | 17,546.36 | 24,622.89 | 20,411.49 | 26,424.88 | 20,265.13 | 32,021.74 |
| | MSE | 5,305,466,415.67 | 18,828,240,838.64 | 122,484,233,648.75 | 29,137,155,794.53 | 572,043,855.45 | 1,511,766,621.07 | 704,602,763.48 | 1,410,040,762.55 | 797,674,876.20 | 1,939,227,582.49 |

The bold numbers are MAPE below 10.

#### 4.5.2. Computation Time Comparison of Ensemble Learning after Feature Selection Techniques

Table 3 presents the computation time required for various ensemble learning algorithms—XGBoost, LightGBM, and a DNN—when using different feature selection methods. The table compares the performance without any feature selection (N/A), with GA, autoencoder-based feature selection (AE), and the proposed TCA.

**Table 3.** Computation time (in seconds) for ensemble learning algorithms with different feature selection methods.

| Feature Selection Algorithm (sec) | XGBoost | LightGBM | DNN |
|---|---|---|---|
| N/A | 0.6702 | 0.0582 | 28.073 |
| GA | 0.2656 | 0.0514 | 26.3374 |
| AE | 0.3321 | 0.0413 | 22.4690 |
| Proposed TCA | 0.2429 | 0.0410 | 20.6280 |

The results indicate that the proposed TCA method consistently provided the shortest computation times across all three algorithms. For XGBoost, the computation time with TCA was 0.2429 s, which was significantly lower than the time of 0.6702 s without any feature selection. Similarly, LightGBM also demonstrated reduced computation times with TCA, clocking in at 0.0410 s compared to 0.0582 s without feature selection. The most substantial reduction in computation time was observed for the DNN, where TCA achieved a time of 20.6280 s, which was significantly lower than the time of 28.073 s without feature selection.

The table demonstrates that GA also improved computation efficiency, particularly for XGBoost and LightGBM, though not as effectively as the TCA. The AE method provided moderate improvements in computation times but still fell short of the efficiency achieved by the TCA.

These findings highlight the efficiency of the proposed TCA in reducing the computational overhead of ensemble learning algorithms. By selecting and reducing the dimensionality of features more effectively, the TCA enhances prediction accuracy and accelerates the training process, making it a valuable method for large-scale and time-sensitive predictive modeling tasks, such as tourism demand forecasting.

#### 4.5.3. Comparison with Tourism Forecasting Algorithms

Table 4 provides a comparative analysis of the MAPE, $R^2$, MAE, and MSE for different forecasting algorithms applied to the Taiwan and Hawaii datasets. The table includes results from several studies, such as those by Xin Li et al. [2], Shilin Xu et al. [3], Xin Li et al. [4], Zhixue Liao et al. [5], and Yunxuan Dong et al. [6], alongside the proposed TCA combined with XGBoost.

**Table 4.** Comparison of various forecasting algorithms on Taiwan and Hawaii datasets.

| Forecasting Algorithm | Dataset | | | | | | | |
|---|---|---|---|---|---|---|---|---|
| | Taiwan Dataset | | | | Hawaii Dataset | | | |
| Metric | MAPE(%) | $R^2$ | MAE | MSE | MAPE(%) | $R^2$ | MAE | MSE |
| Xin Li et al. [2] | 11.7960 | 0.59 | 502759.63 | 350522908752.52 | 8.2054 | 0.62 | 650606.63 | 450379091178.05 |
| Shilin Xu et al. [3] | 18.7761 | 0.42 | 160452.71 | 56406622541.15 | 14.7302 | 0.05 | 109171.56 | 25844328174.50 |
| Xin Li et al. [4] | 15.9470 | 0.40 | 188488.32 | 58782250414.49 | 16.2598 | 0.11 | 102129.15 | 23907956381.84 |
| Zhixue Liao et al. [5] | 56.3386 | 0.26 | 123353.41 | 34060171896.04 | 16.1864 | 0.12 | 200205.85 | 57409595119.83 |
| Yunxuan Dong et al. [6] | 32.5634 | 0.08 | 264340.13 | 105147294705.17 | 13.9422 | 0.07 | 130939.70 | 28906322391.38 |
| Proposed TCA + XGBoost | 3.3947 | 0.99 | 17546.36 | 572043855.45 | 4.0059 | 0.95 | 24622.89 | 1511766621.07 |

The proposed TCA + XGBoost method significantly outperformed the other algorithms, achieving the lowest MAPE values for both datasets. Specifically, it recorded a MAPE of 3.3947% for the Taiwan dataset and 4.0059% for the Hawaii dataset, demonstrating its superior accuracy in forecasting visitor numbers. Additionally, the proposed method yielded high $R^2$ values of 0.99 for the Taiwan dataset and 0.95 for the Hawaii dataset, indicating excellent predictive accuracy. The MAE and MSE values for the proposed method were also significantly lower, at 17,546.36 and 572,043,855.45 for the Taiwan dataset and 24,622.89 and 1,511,766,621.07 for the Hawaii dataset, respectively, highlighting the model's reliability and precision.

In contrast, the other algorithms exhibited higher MAPE values, indicating less accurate predictions. For example, Xin Li et al. [2] reported MAPE values of 11.7960% for the Taiwan dataset and 8.2054% for the Hawaii dataset, with corresponding $R^2$ values of 0.59 and 0.62. The MAE and MSE for their method were substantially higher, reflecting poorer performance. In contrast, Shilin Xu et al. [3] reported even higher errors, with MAPE values of 18.7761% and 14.7302%, and relatively low $R^2$ values of 0.42 and 0.05, further emphasizing the limitations of their approach.

The performance of Xin Li et al. [4] and Zhixue Liao et al. [5] varied significantly, with MAPE values ranging from 15.9470% to 56.3386%, indicating substantial room for improvement. Their methods also showed lower $R^2$ values and higher MAE and MSE, underscoring the challenges in achieving accurate forecasts with these approaches.

Yunxuan Dong et al. [6] also reported moderate performance, with MAPE values of 32.5634% for the Taiwan dataset and 13.9422% for the Hawaii dataset, which are higher than those of the proposed method. Their $R^2$ values were also lower, indicating less reliable predictions.

Overall, the table underscores the effectiveness of the proposed TCA + XGBoost method in delivering more accurate forecasts. The proposed approach consistently achieves lower error rates by integrating advanced feature selection with ensemble learning, higher $R^2$ values, and lower MAE and MSE, highlighting its potential as a robust solution for tourism demand forecasting. These results emphasize the importance of incorporating sophisticated feature selection techniques like TCA to enhance the predictive power of machine learning models in real-world applications.

#### 4.5.4. Comparison with Autoencoder for Feature Selection Algorithms

Table 5 compares the MAPE, $R^2$, MAE, and MSE for different feature selection algorithms when used with various ensemble learning models: XGBoost, LightGBM, and a DNN. The table includes results from LSFNet [13], TEA [14], and Yigit et al. [15], alongside the proposed TCA.

**Table 5.** Comparison of various autoencoders for feature selection algorithms with ensemble models.

| Autoencoder for Feature Selection Algorithm | Ensemble Algorithm | | | | | | | | | | | |
|---|---|---|---|---|---|---|---|---|---|---|---|---|
| | XGboost | | | | LightGBM | | | | DNN | | | |
| Metric | MAPE(%) | $R^2$ | MAE | MSE | MAPE(%) | $R^2$ | MAE | MSE | MAPE(%) | $R^2$ | MAE | MSE |
| LSFNet [13] | 8.1555 | 0.95 | 42525.26 | 4341837554.26 | 20.0276 | 0.91 | 52919.48 | 7471447265.09 | 11.4890 | 0.97 | 28609.67 | 2430952014.99 |
| TEA [14] | 6.2099 | 0.98 | 26631.71 | 1319270923.18 | 5.0711 | 0.99 | 21020.31 | 685203513.18 | 7.7560 | 0.99 | 19770.87 | 584301475.34 |
| Yigit et al. [15] | 14.5297 | 0.88 | 62040.50 | 9989434231.52 | 22.5313 | 0.94 | 52751.88 | 5495490699.08 | 7.7506 | 0.94 | 34930.77 | 5338013378.45 |
| Proposed TCA | 3.3947 | 0.99 | 17546.36 | 572043855.45 | 4.1990 | 0.99 | 20855.41 | 767308943.62 | 3.8246 | 0.99 | 20265.13 | 797674876.20 |

The proposed TCA method consistently achieved the lowest MAPE values across all three ensemble algorithms, demonstrating its superior performance. Specifically, TCA recorded a MAPE of 3.3947% for XGBoost, 4.1990% for LightGBM, and 3.8246% for the DNN. These results highlight the effectiveness of the TCA in enhancing the predictive accuracy of ensemble models. Furthermore, the TCA showed high $R^2$ values (0.99 across all models), indicating excellent predictive accuracy, with significantly lower MAE and MSE values compared to other methods.

TEA [14] also performed well, particularly with LightGBM, where it achieved a MAPE of 5.0711% and an $R^2$ of 0.99. However, its performance for XGBoost and DNN, with MAPE values of 6.2099% and 7.7560%, respectively, was not as strong as the TCA. TEA also showed lower MAE and MSE compared to other methods but was still higher than the TCA.

LSFNet [13] exhibited higher MAPE values across all ensemble models, particularly with LightGBM, where it recorded a MAPE of 20.0276%. This indicates that while LSFNet is useful, it is less effective than the TCA in reducing prediction errors. LSFNet also had higher MAE and MSE values, reflecting its lower accuracy.

Yigit et al. [15] reported mixed performance, with a notable MAPE of 7.7506% for DNN, which was competitive but still higher than the results achieved by the TCA. However, its performance with XGBoost and LightGBM was less impressive, with MAPE values of 14.5297% and 22.5313%, respectively. The corresponding $R^2$, MAE, and MSE values further underscored the variability in its performance.

Overall, the table clearly demonstrates the advantages of the proposed TCA method in improving the accuracy of ensemble learning algorithms. By providing lower MAPE values consistently across different models, along with high $R^2$ and lower MAE and MSE values, the TCA proves to be a more reliable and effective feature selection technique for enhancing tourism demand forecasting. These findings underscore the potential of integrating advanced feature selection methods like the TCA to optimize the performance of machine learning models in various predictive tasks.

### 4.6. Feature Importance Analysis Using Target-Concatenated Autoencoder

Table 6 provides a detailed list of feature importance scores calculated from the TCA. These scores reflect the significance of each feature in predicting the target variable, which was the number of tourist arrivals.

**Table 6.** Feature importance calculated from target-concatenated autoencoder.

| Feature | Importance |
|---|---|
| General_tourist_hotel_occupancy_rate_ | 980.2686 |
| Tourist_hotel_occupancy_rate_ | 890.6157 |
| International_tourist_hotel_occupancy_rate_ | 880.665 |
| Hualien_Port_Vessel_Number | 606.4426 |
| US_NAS_Annual_Growth_Rate_ | 593.4832 |
| _International_Number_of_tourist_hotel_rooms_rooms_ | 586.5709 |
| Tourist_hotelsaverage_room_rateinternational_hotels_NTD | 549.1753 |
| Midterm_population_person | 547.4845 |
| Singapore_Annual_Growth_Rate_ | 528.6199 |
| Revenue_NT1000 | 524.0346 |
| Is_December | 517.9967 |
| International_tourist_hotel_number_of_rooms | 517.4117 |
| Total_Number_of_tourist_hotel_rooms_rooms | 516.4645 |
| _Taichung_Port_Vessel_Number | 503.0249 |
| International_Number_of_tourist_hotels_houses | 498.6601 |
| Taiwan_Annual_Growth_Rate_ | 492.6557 |
| Shenzhen_Composite_Index | 489.9534 |
| Is_November | 485.3672 |
| Is_January | 485.2595 |
| International_tourist_hotel_number | 480.1551 |

The top three features with the highest importance scores were related to hotel occupancy rates: General Tourist Hotel Occupancy Rate (980.2686), Tourist Hotel Occupancy Rate (890.6157), and International Tourist Hotel Occupancy Rate (880.665). These high scores indicate that the occupancy rates of various types of hotels are critical factors in predicting tourism demand, likely because they directly reflect tourism activity and infrastructure utilization.

Following the occupancy rates, the Hualien Port Vessel Number (606.4426) was identified as another significant feature, suggesting that maritime activity at Hualien Port is a strong indicator of tourism trends, possibly due to the port's role in facilitating tourist access.

Economic indicators also play a crucial role, as evidenced by the U.S. NAS Annual Growth Rate (593.4832) and the Singapore Annual Growth Rate (528.6199). These features likely capture the broader economic conditions that influence international travel decisions.

Other essential features included the number of tourist hotel rooms, average room rates, and midterm population figures. For instance, the International Number of Tourist Hotel Rooms (586.5709) and Tourist Hotels Average Room Rate (549.1753) were crucial, highlighting the significance of accommodation capacity and pricing in tourism forecasting.

Seasonal indicators such as " Is December" (517.9967), " Is November" (485.3672), and " Is January" (485.2595) were also prominent. These variables underscore the seasonal patterns in tourism, with certain months showing higher or lower tourist arrivals.

Additionally, stock indices like the Shenzhen Composite Index (489.9534) and revenue figures (524.0346) were included, suggesting that financial market conditions and business revenues are relevant for predicting tourism demand.

Overall, the table highlights the diverse factors, from hotel occupancy and room numbers to economic growth rates and seasonal indicators, which the TCA identified as significant for forecasting tourist arrivals. This comprehensive approach ensured that the model captured a broad spectrum of influences, leading to more accurate and reliable predictions.

## 5. Discussion and Future Works

The experimental results presented in this study highlight the effectiveness of the proposed TCA combined with ensemble learning algorithms for forecasting tourist arrivals. A comprehensive comparison of MAPE across various models and feature selection techniques highlights the TCA's consistent superiority, significantly improving predictive accuracy.

### *5.1. Performance Comparison*

Tables 4 and 5 demonstrate that the TCA achieves lower MAPE values compared to other forecasting algorithms and feature selection methods. For instance, TCA combined with XGBoost achieved a MAPE of 3.3947% for the Taiwan dataset and 4.0059% for the Hawaii dataset, significantly outperforming other state-of-the-art methods such as those proposed by Xin Li et al. [2], Shilin Xu et al. [3], and Yunxuan Dong et al. [6]. This highlights the TCA's ability to effectively capture and leverage relevant features for accurate predictions.

### *5.2. Computational Efficiency*

Table 3 illustrates that the TCA enhances computational efficiency, achieving the shortest computation times across XGBoost, LightGBM, and the DNN. This efficiency is crucial for real-world applications demanding quick and accurate forecasts.

### *5.3. Ablation Study*

Figures 5 and 6, which analyze the impact of different encoding dimensions, learning rates, and autoencoder configurations on MAPE, respectively, reinforce the reliability of the TCA. The ensemble DNN, in particular, demonstrated stable performance across various configurations, highlighting the TCA's resilience to hyperparameter variations. Furthermore, the ablation study on autoencoder configurations (Figure 7) confirmed that the TCA maintained low error rates, even with different architectural setups, further validating its reliability.

### *5.4. Feature Importance Analysis*

The feature importance scores derived from the TCA, as shown in Table 6, underscore the critical role of hotel occupancy rates, maritime activity, economic growth indicators, and seasonal factors in tourism demand prediction. High importance scores for features like General Tourist Hotel Occupancy Rate, Tourist Hotel Occupancy Rate, and International Tourist Hotel Occupancy Rate emphasize the criticality of accommodation availability and utilization for accurate tourism forecasting. Additionally, indicators such as port vessel numbers and economic growth rates from the U.S. and Singapore highlight the influence of infrastructure and macroeconomic conditions on tourist arrivals.

### *5.5. Future Work*

Based on these promising results, future research could explore several avenues to further enhance the proposed method:

- Integration with Real-Time Data: Incorporating real-time data streams and online learning techniques could further improve the responsiveness and accuracy of tourism forecasts. This approach could enable more dynamic and adaptive models.
- Expanded Feature Sets: Exploring additional features, such as social media trends, global travel advisories, and tourist sentiment analysis, could provide deeper insights into the factors influencing tourism demand. Incorporating these features could enhance the model's predictive capabilities.
- Cross-Region and Cross-Sector Applications: Extending the application of the TCA to other regions and sectors, such as hospitality, retail, and transportation, could validate its versatility and effectiveness in different contexts. This broader application could uncover unique insights and improve forecasting accuracy across various domains.
- Hybrid Models: Combining the TCA with other advanced techniques, such as reinforcement learning and hybrid neural network architectures, could further improve prediction accuracy and reliability. These hybrid approaches could leverage the strengths of different methodologies to optimize forecasting performance.
- Explainability and Transparency: Developing methods to enhance the interpretability of the model's predictions is valuable for stakeholders. Techniques like SHAP (SHapley Additive exPlanations) values could be integrated to provide clearer insights into feature importance and model decision-making processes. By addressing these areas, future research can continue to refine and extend the capabilities of the TCA and ensemble learning framework, solidifying its role as a powerful tool for tourism demand forecasting and beyond.

## 6. Conclusions

The accurate prediction of inbound visitor arrivals is crucial for the tourism industry, facilitating effective planning and resource allocation. Enhanced forecasting models empower tourism managers and policymakers to make informed decisions on infrastructure development, marketing strategies, and service provision. The benefits of precise predictions extend beyond immediate economic gains, fostering strategic planning and ensuring long-term sustainability in tourism development. For instance, understanding visitor trends can guide investments in new tourist attractions, improve disaster preparedness and response strategies, and promote the growth of eco-tourism initiatives that prioritize environmental conservation.

The proposed TCA combined with ensemble learning algorithms demonstrated superior performance in forecasting tourism demand. The experimental results highlight the TCA's ability to achieve a lower MAPE than traditional methods and other advanced algorithms. Moreover, the TCA's computational efficiency and reliability make it a valuable tool for real-world applications where timely and accurate forecasts are essential.

Future research should focus on integrating real-time data, expanding feature sets, applying the method to different regions and sectors, developing hybrid models, and improving the interpretability of predictions. Pursuing these avenues will allow the TCA and ensemble learning framework to further enhance the accuracy and applicability of tourism demand forecasting, thereby fostering sustainable growth in the tourism industry.

**Author Contributions:** Conceptualization, R.-I.C. and C.-Y.T.; methodology, C.-Y.T.; software, Y.-W.C.; validation, C.-Y.T. and Y.-W.C.; formal analysis, C.-Y.T.; investigation, C.-Y.T. and Y.-W.C.; resources, R.-I.C.; data curation, Y.-W.C.; writing—original draft preparation, C.-Y.T. and Y.-W.C.; writing—review and editing, C.-Y.T. and Y.-W.C.; visualization, C.-Y.T. and Y.-W.C.; supervision, R.-I.C.; project administration, R.-I.C.; funding acquisition, R.-I.C. All authors have read and agreed to the published version of the manuscript.

**Funding:** This research was funded by National Science and Technology Council grant number 103-2511-S-845-006-.

**Data Availability Statement:** No new data were created.

**Conflicts of Interest:** The authors declare no conflict of interest.

## References

1. Nguyen, L.Q.; Fernandes, P.O.; Teixeira, J.P. Analyzing and forecasting tourism demand in Vietnam with artificial neural networks. *Forecasting* **2021**, *4*, 36–50. [CrossRef]
2. Li, X.; Zhang, X.; Zhang, C.; Wang, S. Forecasting tourism demand with a novel robust decomposition and ensemble framework. *Expert Syst. Appl.* **2024**, *236*, 121388. [CrossRef]
3. Xu, S.; Liu, Y.; Jin, C. Forecasting daily tourism demand with multiple factors. *Ann. Tour. Res.* **2023**, *103*, 103675. [CrossRef]
4. Li, X.; Xu, Y.; Law, R.; Wang, S. Enhancing tourism demand forecasting with a transformer-based framework. *Ann. Tour. Res.* **2024**, *107*, 103791. [CrossRef]
5. Liao, Z.; Ren, C.; Sun, F.; Tao, Y.; Li, W. EMD-based model with cooperative training mechanism for tourism demand forecasting. *Expert Syst. Appl.* **2024**, *244*, 122930. [CrossRef]
6. Dong, Y.; Zhou, B.; Yang, G.; Hou, F.; Hu, Z.; Ma, S. A novel model for tourism demand forecasting with spatial–temporal feature enhancement and image-driven method. *Neurocomputing* **2023**, *556*, 126663. [CrossRef]
7. Subbiah, S.S.; Chinnappan, J. Opportunities and challenges of feature selection methods for high dimensional data: A review. *Ing. Syst. d'Information* **2021**, *26*, 67. [CrossRef]
8. Jia, W.; Sun, M.; Lian, J.; Hou, S. Feature dimensionality reduction: A review. *Complex Intell. Syst.* **2022**, *8*, 2663–2693. [CrossRef]
9. Zebari, R.; Abdulazeez, A.; Zeebaree, D.; Zebari, D.; Saeed, J. A comprehensive review of dimensionality reduction techniques for feature selection and feature extraction. *J. Appl. Sci. Technol. Trends* **2020**, *1*, 56–70. [CrossRef]
10. Peng, X.; Xu, D.; Chen, D. Robust distribution-based nonnegative matrix factorizations for dimensionality reduction. *Inf. Sci.* **2021**, *552*, 244–260. [CrossRef]
11. Liu, X.; Yang, W.; Meng, F.; Sun, T. Material recognition using robotic hand with capacitive tactile sensor array and machine learning. *IEEE Trans. Instrum. Meas.* **2024**, *73*, 1–9. [CrossRef]
12. Feng, G. Feature selection algorithm based on optimized genetic algorithm and the application in high-dimensional data processing. *PLoS ONE* **2024**, *19*, e0303088. [CrossRef] [PubMed]
13. Wang, L.; Huynh, D.Q.; Mansour, M.R. Loss switching fusion with similarity search for video classification. In Proceedings of the 2019 IEEE International Conference on Image Processing (ICIP), Taipei, Taiwan, 22–25 September 2019; IEEE: New York, NY, USA, 2019; pp. 974–978.
14. Jarrett, D.; van der Schaar, M. Target-embedding autoencoders for supervised representation learning. *arXiv* **2020**, arXiv:2001.08345.
15. Yigit, G.O.; Baransel, C. A novel autoencoder-based feature selection method for drug-target interaction prediction with human-interpretable feature weights. *Symmetry* **2023**, *15*, 192. [CrossRef]
16. Gidebo, H.B. Factors determining international tourist flow to tourism destinations: A systematic review. *J. Hosp. Manag. Tour.* **2021**, *12*, 9–17.
17. Chang, C.-L.; McAleer, M. Aggregation, heterogeneous autoregression and volatility of daily international tourist arrivals and exchange rates. *Jpn. Econ. Rev.* **2012**, *63*, 397–419. [CrossRef]
18. Santana-Gallego, M.; Ledesma-Rodríguez, F.J.; Pérez-Rodríguez, J.V. Exchange rate regimes and tourism. *Tour. Econ.* **2010**, *16*, 25–43. [CrossRef]
19. Chao, C.-C.; Lu, L.-J.; Lai, C.-C.; Hu, S.-W.; Wang, V. Devaluation, pass-through and foreign reserves dynamics in a tourism economy. *Econ. Model.* **2013**, *30*, 456–461. [CrossRef]
20. Goh, C.; Law, R. Incorporating the rough sets theory into travel demand analysis. *Tour. Manag.* **2003**, *24*, 511–517. [CrossRef]
21. Xie, G.; Qian, Y.; Wang, S. Forecasting chinese cruise tourism demand with big data: An optimized machine learning approach. *Tour. Manag.* **2021**, *82*, 104208. [CrossRef]
22. Albaladejo, I.; González-Martínez, M. A nonlinear dynamic model for international tourism demand on the Spanish Mediterranean coasts. *Econ. Manag.* **2018**, *21*, 65–78. [CrossRef]
23. Englin, J.; Moeltner, K. The value of snowfall to skiers and boarders. *Environ. Resour. Econ.* **2004**, *29*, 123–136. [CrossRef]
24. Kandampully, J.; Juwaheer, T.D.; Hu, H.-H. The influence of a hotel firm's quality of service and image and its effect on tourism customer loyalty. *Int. J. Hosp. Tour. Adm.* **2011**, *12*, 21–42. [CrossRef]

25. Huybers, T. Modelling short-break holiday destination choices. *Tour. Econ.* **2003**, *9*, 389–405. [CrossRef]
26. Ongan, S.; Işik, C.; Ozdemir, D. The effects of real exchange rates and income on international tourism demand for the USA from some European Union countries. *Economies* **2017**, *5*, 51. [CrossRef]
27. Pan, B.; Yang, Y. Forecasting destination weekly hotel occupancy with big data. *J. Travel Res.* **2017**, *56*, 957–970. [CrossRef]
28. Falk, M. Impact of weather conditions on tourism demand in the peak summer season over the last 50 years. *Tour. Manag. Perspect.* **2014**, *9*, 24–35.
29. Becken, S. Measuring the effect of weather on tourism: A destination and activity-based analysis. *J. Travel Res.* **2013**, *52*, 156–167. [CrossRef]
30. Bi, J.-W.; Liu, Y.; Li, H. Daily tourism volume forecasting for tourist attractions. *Ann. Tour. Res.* **2020**, *83*, 102923. [CrossRef]
31. Álvarez-Díaz, M.; Rosselló-Nadal, J. Forecasting British tourist arrivals in the Balearic Islands using meteorological variables. *Tour. Econ.* **2010**, *16*, 153–168. [CrossRef]
32. Bangwayo-Skeete, P.F.; Skeete, R.W. Can google data improve the forecasting performance of tourist arrivals? Mixed-data sampling approach. *Tour. Manag.* **2015**, *46*, 454–464. [CrossRef]
33. Yang, X.; Pan, B.; Evans, J.A.; Lv, B. Forecasting Chinese tourist volume with search engine data. *Tour. Manag.* **2015**, *46*, 386–397. [CrossRef]
34. Li, S.; Chen, T.; Wang, L.; Ming, C. Effective tourist volume forecasting supported by PCA and improved BPNN using Baidu index. *Tour. Manag.* **2018**, *68*, 116–126. [CrossRef]
35. Li, K.; Lu, W.; Liang, C.; Wang, B. Intelligence in tourism management: A hybrid FOA-BP method on daily tourism demand forecasting with web search data. *Mathematics* **2019**, *7*, 531. [CrossRef]
36. Pan, B.; Wu, D.C.; Song, H. Forecasting hotel room demand using search engine data. *J. Hosp. Tour. Technol.* **2012**, *3*, 196–210. [CrossRef]
37. Zhang, B.; Pu, Y.; Wang, Y.; Li, J. Forecasting hotel accommodation demand based on LSTM model incorporating internet search index. *Sustainability* **2019**, *11*, 4708. [CrossRef]
38. Law, R.; Li, G.; Fong, D.K.C.; Han, X. Tourism demand forecasting: A deep learning approach. *Ann. Tour. Res.* **2019**, *75*, 410–423. [CrossRef]
39. Gardner, E.S., Jr. Exponential smoothing: The state of the art. *J. Forecast.* **1985**, *4*, 1–28. [CrossRef]
40. Holt, C.C. Forecasting seasonals and trends by exponentially weighted moving averages. *Int. J. Forecast.* **2004**, *20*, 5–10. [CrossRef]
41. Lee, Y.-S.; Tong, L.-I. Forecasting energy consumption using a grey model improved by incorporating genetic programming. *Energy Convers. Manag.* **2011**, *52*, 147–152. [CrossRef]
42. Chang, Y.-W.; Tsai, C.-Y. Apply deep learning neural network to forecast number of tourists. In Proceedings of the 2017 31st International Conference on Advanced Information Networking and Applications Workshops (WAINA), Taipei, Taiwan, 27–29 March 2017; IEEE: New York, NY, USA, 2017; pp. 259–264.
43. Chen, T.; Guestrin, C. XGBoost: A scalable tree boosting system. In Proceedings of the 22nd ACM SIGKDD International Conference on Knowledge Discovery and Data Mining, San Francisco, CA, USA, 13–17 August 2016; pp. 785–794.
44. Ke, G.; Meng, Q.; Finley, T.; Wang, T.; Chen, W.; Ma, W.; Ye, Q.; Liu, T.-Y. LightGBM: A highly efficient gradient boosting decision tree. In Proceedings of the 31st Conference on Neural Information Processing Systems (NIPS 2017), Long Beach, CA, USA, 4–9 December 2017; Volume 30.
45. Vahdat, A.; Kautz, J. NVAE: A deep hierarchical variational autoencoder. *Adv. Neural Inf. Process. Syst.* **2020**, *33*, 19667–19679.
46. Khan, N.; Hassan, A.U.; Fahad, S.; Naushad, M. Factors affecting tourism industry and its impacts on global economy of the world. *SSRN Electron. J.* **2020**, *1*, 1–32. [CrossRef]
47. Sapkota, P.; Vashisth, K.K.; Ranabhat, D. A systematic literature review on factors affecting rural tourism. In *International Conference on Intelligent Computing & Optimization*; Springer: Cham, Switzerland, 2023; pp. 45–55.
48. Luo, Y.; Yi, X. Tourism industry resilience and its influencing factors: An experience from 60 countries. *E3S Web Conf.* **2023**, *409*, 06005.
49. De Rainville, F.-M.; Fortin, F.-A.; Gardner, M.-A.; Parizeau, M.; Gagne, C. DEAP: A python framework for evolutionary algorithms. In Proceedings of the 14th Annual Conference Companion on Genetic and Evolutionary Computation, Philadelphia, PA, USA, 7–11 July 2012; pp. 85–92.

*machine learning & knowledge extraction*

MDPI

*Article*

# Towards AI Dashboards in Financial Services: Design and Implementation of an AI Development Dashboard for Credit Assessment

**Mustafa Pamuk * and Matthias Schumann**

Faculty of Business and Economics, University of Goettingen, 37073 Goettingen, Germany; mschuma1@uni-goettingen.de
* Correspondence: mustafa.pamuk@uni-goettingen.de

**Abstract:** Financial institutions are increasingly turning to artificial intelligence (AI) to improve their decision-making processes and gain a competitive edge. Due to the iterative process of AI development, it is mandatory to have a structured process in place, from the design to the deployment of AI-based services in the finance industry. This process must include the required validation and coordination with regulatory authorities. An appropriate dashboard can help to shape and structure the process of model development, e.g., for credit assessment in the finance industry. In addition, the analysis of datasets must be included as an important part of the dashboard to understand the reasons for changes in model performance. Furthermore, a dashboard can undertake documentation tasks to make the process of model development traceable, explainable, and transparent, as required by regulatory authorities in the finance industry. This can offer a comprehensive solution for financial companies to optimize their models, improve regulatory compliance, and ultimately foster sustainable growth in an increasingly competitive market. In this study, we investigate the requirements and provide a prototypical dashboard to create, manage, compare, and validate AI models to be used in the credit assessment of private customers.

**Keywords:** credit assessment; dashboard design; artificial intelligence; financial services

## 1. Introduction

For the assessment of financial credit risk, the use of AI to accelerate, automate, and improve the credit assessment process is becoming increasingly attractive [1]. Moreover, increased computational power has made it possible to analyze vast amounts of data and to recognize behavioral patterns relating to loans. The example of credit risk assessment illustrates how AI must be utilized in the financial services industry, demonstrating the necessity for precision, efficiency, and the ability to handle large datasets to identify and evaluate potential risks accurately. Therefore, the integration of AI in financial services has become a transformative force in research and practice [2]. However, previous research has primarily focused on testing AI techniques to increase the predictive accuracy of credit assessment [3,4] (Appendix B). However, the integration of AI is leading to a paradigm shift in the way that financial institutions should develop, maintain, and operate AI and concurrently cooperate with regulators [5,6]. Therefore, in the long term, it is important to derive concepts or dashboards for model development to operate, monitor, and maintain AI models with suitable and compliant processes [7].

These challenges to the use of AI in financial services are increasingly being addressed by politicians, as they attempt to define regulations for the use of AI to promote trust, manage risks appropriately, and encourage AI innovations [8,9]. According to the European Commission's "AI Act" [10], the entire process of model creation, including the data used and all measures taken, must comply with various quality guidelines and must be documented in detail. For example, the processes of data cleaning and preprocessing must be fully documented to prove that the underlying dataset has been prepared appropriately and compliantly with the AI Act, e.g., taking account of biases in the dataset [10]. Moreover, the problem of masking the internal decision-making process is addressed by regulatory requirements so that the explainability, interpretability, traceability, transparency, and security of AI-based services is increased [9,11,12]. To address the challenges identified in the integration of AI for credit risk assessment, various commercial tools have been developed to facilitate the creation and management of AI-driven credit risk dashboards. Leading examples, such as FICO, Zest AI, and CreditVidya, provide comprehensive analytics and visualization capabilities. However, financial companies must define iterative and compliant processes in model development for regulatory adherence in financial services, ensuring accuracy and transparency. Furthermore, all these aspects must be comprehensively considered during the design of AI-based services and associated processes to fulfill regulatory requirements.

Furthermore, previous research on AI in credit assessment indicates that AI-based models can deliver more accurate and performant results than traditional statistical models [7,13,14]. However, AI models add complexity and require an iterative approach over the long term. This creates a conflict where higher performance often comes at the cost of lower explainability, and vice versa. The development of these models corresponds to a data mining process and is associated with many phases and steps, ranging from the data preprocessing to the implementation of the model. Such a process is highly time-consuming and can take between 9 and 18 months [15–18]. Moreover, these datasets face challenges such as an uneven distribution of "good" and "bad" loans, and a time lag between data collection and model application.

Problems with the datasets can lead to a decrease in performance and intensify over time, a phenomenon known as concept shift or model shift [19]. Serious incidents like the 2007 financial crisis and the COVID-19 pandemic significantly trigger such conceptual shifts, requiring banks to continually validate and adjust their models to maintain functionality and accuracy [20–22]. This involves regular and ad-hoc validations, potentially leading to recalibrations or new models [21]. Furthermore, standardized procedures and comprehensive documentation are essential for structured control by financial companies and regulators [21]. Therefore, AI dashboards can assist in these iterative analyses by systematically evaluating datasets, developing and monitoring models, and enabling swift actions to ensure system accuracy for customer safety.

Moreover, mandatory cooperation with supervisory authorities and the lack of structure in model development and validation need to be addressed, as scoring model evaluations are often inadequate. To effectively analyze and monitor datasets and AI models, it is essential to structure and foster iterative processes like data analysis and model evaluation and comparison. Identifying and addressing concept-shift issues requires analyzing the performance of existing or new AI models with incoming data. A dashboard supporting these iterative analyses and documentation can enhance the development, maintenance, and evaluation of AI models [13]. This study addresses the research gap in structuring and systematizing the development, training, testing, comparison, evaluation, and deployment of AI models for credit assessment. The following research questions (RQs) aim to bring more structure to the field through automated documentation and clearly defined procedures:

**RQ$_1$**: What are the requirements for an AI dashboard to develop and maintain AI models for credit assessment?
**RQ$_2$**: How should an AI dashboard for credit assessment be designed and the model development process structured?

In the following, we first introduce the related research into AI-based services. Subsequently, we present the underlying methodology of the conducted design science research framework [23] and the employed cross-industry standard process for data mining (CRISP-DM) [24]. We then derive the requirements before presenting the design and development process leading to the final dashboard design. After the demonstration of the artifact, we discuss our results, mention limitations, and state a conclusion with an outlook on future research.

## 2. Related Research for the Use of AI in the Finance Industry

The accurate assessment of creditworthiness, prediction of bankruptcy, and detection or prevention of fraud are crucial for informed financial decision making, influencing access to loans, insurance, and other products. Moreover, while many of these processes have traditionally relied on established statistical models, the rise of AI has introduced a new paradigm with significant implications. For example, rule-based traditional models for credit assessment such as FICO scores are based on factors that are easy to understand, such as income, debt, and payment history. Thanks to this transparency, borrowers can understand how their score is calculated and can take action to improve it [25]. Therefore, the rule-based conventional models adhere to established regulations and guidelines and ensure fairness and consistency in credit assessment, with the logic behind them being relatively simple and making it easier for human analysts to understand and explain decisions. However, the governance of data-driven AI models strongly differs from the conventional models and requires a customized governance process to focus more on AI-specific criteria and risks [26,27]. Understanding trained AI models can be significantly enhanced through the extraction of patterns from datasets. The European Commission's Artificial Intelligence Act highlights the necessity of distinguishing between so-called *Weak AI*, which focuses on specific tasks, and *Strong AI*, which exhibits more generalized cognitive capabilities [28].

Ensuring the trustworthiness of AI requires that datasets are free from biases and protect individual privacy. Adhering to these principles not only aids in the development of robust and versatile AI systems but also ensures they are ethical and secure, fostering greater public confidence and societal advantages. Furthermore, the problem of customized governance has also been considered by regulatory authorities in many European countries [20,21,29–33]. For example, the French Prudential Supervision and Resolution Authority (ACPR) published the first discussion paper in 2020, considering the issues with explainability and governance of AI [29]. ACPR defined four evaluation principles to design and develop AI algorithms and models: appropriate data management, performance, stability, and explainability. These four principles include the required structure and characteristics of AI-based services in financial services that must be defined, developed, and deployed in a compliant structure to ensure customers' safety. However, due to the potential to increase automation in financial services with AI, all underlying and related processes and systems to develop and maintain these AI models must also be accelerated [34]. Therefore, the complexity of implementation and quality assurance issues become major obstacles preventing financial institutions from adopting AI-based services [34].

Thus, a balance must be struck between innovation and risk when using AI in financial services. Accordingly, it is necessary to develop not only accurate AI models but also systems or dashboards to maintain, develop, and monitor these models. Nevertheless, the existing literature aims to develop suitable and highly accurate models for datasets [35]. These approaches cannot guide the financial industry forward if there is no combination of well-defined systems and processes to maintain the models to ensure continued system security, as an AI model cannot operate properly forever [36]. In addition, the operational quality and robustness of the models must be monitored and validated regularly [10]. In case of adjustments required due to model or data drift, e.g., caused by changing economic conditions, financial companies or providers of these AI-based services must be equipped with potential solutions through increased automation, integration, and mitigation measures [26]. However, all the specific governance needs vary depending on the use case [37].

Furthermore, existing regulatory bases and recommendations from the OECD [38] focus on responsibility for trustworthy AI and require proactivity and sustainable development. Therefore, it is necessary to foster a regulatory environment that supports a flexible transition from research to the development, deployment, and operation of AI-based services [9]. Consideration of a controlled environment, e.g., an AI dashboard, is necessary to be able to test and scale up the proposed models [37,38]. Moreover, this interactivity between financial firms and regulators needs to be improved to promote entrepreneurship and productivity and ensure the benefits of AI [29,38,39].

## 3. Research Design

To target the research gap outlined in the first section, we employed a problem-oriented design science research approach (DSR) according to Peffers et al. [23] in combination with CRISP-DM [24] to structure and support the process of model development for credit assessment with an AI dashboard. DSR helps us to structure the research process while identifying the problem, analyzing requirements, and developing artifacts (Figure 1). Moreover, due to the structure of CRISP-DM across industries for data mining processes, it provides a fundamental and appropriate basis on which to structure the process of model development and model evaluation for credit assessment with an associated understanding of business and data.

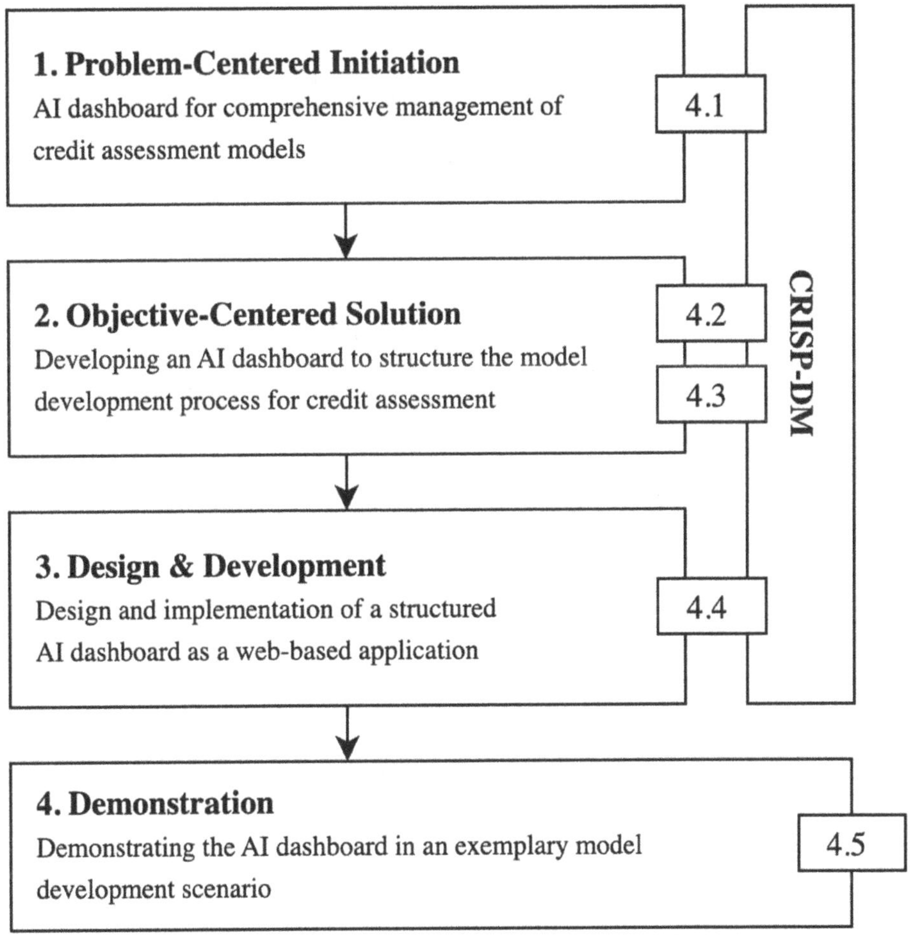


**Figure 1.** Process of the problem-centered design science research approach in Sections 4.1–4.5.

We followed the CRISP-DM approach to implement a standardized, non-iterative process that significantly reduces lengthy iterations. CRISP-DM's established structure allows for extensions and simplifies the model development process for an AI dashboard for financial companies, developers, and regulators. The first step, business understanding, determined the requirements for an AI dashboard in credit assessment. As already outlined, with CRISP-DM, it is necessary to investigate the underlying dataset for a practical and useful orientation to propose an appropriate list of requirements.

The process of requirements analysis, which is based on four steps of the CRSIP-DM, is described in Section 4.1 (Figure 2). First, we investigate the requirements for business and data understanding based on the credit assessment dataset. Second, we identify the requirements for data preprocessing and preparation including data analysis. Third, we gather the requirements for modeling to support the process of model development on the AI dashboard. Lastly, we identify the requirements for the evaluation and comparison of models.

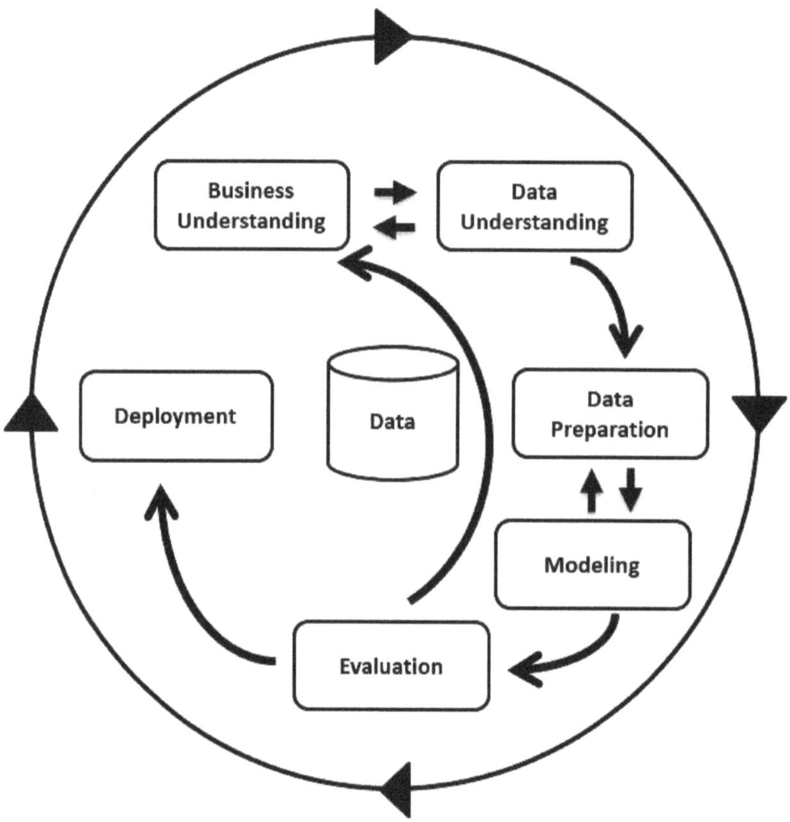


**Figure 2.** CRISP-DM process model.

In Section 4.2, we derive the functionalities to fulfill the identified requirements based on the use-case analysis. Moreover, due to the regulations in the finance industry, it is necessary to analyze and consider regulatory requirements to select appropriate modeling techniques for an AI dashboard (Section 4.3). Based on the analysis of the requirements, use cases, and regulatory basis, we designed and developed the proposed artifact for the development and maintenance of AI models, as described in Section 4.4. As the last step of problem-centered DSR, the demonstration of the artifact "AIDash" is described in

Section 4.5, using an exemplary scenario in which a new model for credit assessment is developed and evaluated.

## 4. AI Dashboard for Model Development in Credit Assessment

We start with analysis of the problem and requirements, to structure the development process of the meta-artifact to support the iterative processes of data understanding, data preprocessing, model development, and model evaluation based on CRISP-DM.

### 4.1. Problem Identification and Requirement Analysis

For the development of an artifact for credit assessment, it is necessary to consider the existing approaches. Therefore, we conducted a structured literature review based on the methodological guidelines of Cooper [40] and vom Brocke et al. [41]. The search was conducted in established scientific databases JSTOR, AIS Electronic Library, Emerald Insight, and IEEE Xplore with the following search terms: "Credit Scoring", "Credit Assessment", "Artificial Intelligence", and "Machine Learning", from 2014 onwards. We initially found 1301 publications, of which 61 appeared to be relevant for AI-based credit assessment after analyzing the titles and abstracts of the accessible publications (Appendix B). Relevant articles were those that dealt with AI-based credit assessment, dashboards for model development, provided literature reviews or interview studies, or considered respective regulations.

Based on the conducted literature review, we first examined the existing studies dealing with AI-based credit assessment. As identified from the literature review, CRISP-DM can help to structure the process of model development for credit assessment. Here, however, it is not possible to cover all the phases of CRISP-DM. In this study, the phases of business understanding, and deployment were not in our focus, as they set the prerequisites for the planned dashboard and require further strategic decisions depending on the companies' service infrastructure (Table 1). In the following, we go through the four phases of CRISP-DM, conduct a requirement analysis for credit assessment, and summarize the gathered requirements and derived functionalities in a table.

**Table 1.** CRISP-DM process model.

| Business Understanding | Data Understanding | Data Preparation | Modeling | Evaluation | Deployment |
|---|---|---|---|---|---|
| Determine business objectives | Collect initial data | Select data | Select modeling techniques | Evaluate results | Plan deployment |
| Assess situation | Describe data | Clean data | Generate test design | Review process | Plan monitoring and maintenance |
| Determine data mining goals | Explore data | Construct data | Build model | Determine Next Steps | Produce final report |
| Produce project plan | Verify data quality | Integrate data | Assess model | | Review project |
| | | Format data | | | |

#### 4.1.1. Data Understanding of Credit Assessment

Datasets to train and build AI models consist of credit applications with positive and negative decisions based on several features such as previous payment behavior, deposits in bank accounts, bonds, and duration of employment. For this study, we used an exemplary dataset from Fahrmeir and Hamerle [42] including 1095 credit applications from private customers with 21 features, 300 rejections, and 795 approvals (Appendix A). The CRISP-DM approach consists of multiple steps distributed over phases. The first step of data understanding begins with the initial collection of data and includes functions to gain first insights about the dataset [24]. This involves determining the quality of the data, gaining initial impressions, and/or recognizing groups in the dataset from which hypotheses can later be formed. We first started gathering requirements from the second step of CRISP-DM, i.e., data understanding, for the analysis and management of datasets for credit assessment. The ability to manage datasets is crucial, as all subsequent steps are based on this data ($R_{DU}$ 1). This step also includes loading (or uploading) the dataset into the dashboard, which enables the available dataset for analysis ($F_{1.1}$). Moreover, to work and integrate the datasets in the next steps, the prototype should provide an overview of the existing datasets [24]. As the datasets are possibly available in different formats, it is necessary to have the option of changing the parameters for import so that datasets can be integrated homogeneously and thus processed consistently (Table 2).

**Table 2.** List of requirements and derived functionalities from CRISP-DM for the artifact.

| Block | Requirements | Function Identifier | Derived Functions for Credit Assessment |
|---|---|---|---|
| **Data Understanding** $R_{DU}$ | $R_{DU}$ 1 Data collection | $F_1$ | Managing datasets |
| | | $F_{1.1}$ | Uploading datasets |
| | | $F_{1.2}$ | Changing parameters for import |
| | $R_{DU}$ 2 Data description | $F_{1.3}$ | Describing datasets |
| | $R_{DU}$ 3 Explore data | $F_2$ | Analyzing datasets |
| | | $F_{2.1}$ | Plotting datasets |
| | | $F_{2.2}$ | Comparing datasets |
| | $R_{DU}$ 4 Data assessment | - | - |
| **Data Preprocessing** $R_{DP}$ | $R_{DP}$ 1 Data selection | $F_{1.4}$ | Managing features |
| | $R_{DP}$ 2 Data cleaning | $F_{1.2}$ | Changing parameters for import |
| | | $F_{1.4.2}$ | Cleaning outliers |
| | $R_{DP}$ 3 Data construction | - | - |
| | $R_{DP}$ 4 Data integration | - | - |
| | $R_{DP}$ 5 Data formatting | $F_{1.2}$ | Changing parameters for import |
| | | $F_{1.4.1}$ | Coding features |
| **Modeling** $R_M$ | $R_M$ 1 Model selection | $F_{1.4}$ | Managing features |
| | $R_M$ 2 Model preparation and tests | $F_{3.1.1}$ | Training a model |
| | | $F_{3.1.2}$ | Balancing (training) classes |
| | $R_M$ 3 Model creation | $F_3$ | Managing models |
| | | $F_{3.1}$ | Creating a model |
| | | $F_{3.2}$ | Saving and downloading a model |
| | | $F_{3.3}$ | Deleting a model |
| | | $F_{3.4}$ | Uploading a model |
| | | $F_{3.5}$ | Re-training a model |
| | $R_M$ 4 Model assessment | $F_4$ | Comparing models |
| | | $F_6$ | Exporting results |

**Table 2.** *Cont.*

| Block | Requirements | Function Identifier | Derived Functions for Credit Assessment |
|---|---|---|---|
| Evaluation $R_{EV}$ | $R_{EV}$ 1 Evaluation of results | $F_6$ | Exporting results |
| | | $F_5$ | Testing models |
| | | $F_{5.1}$ | Checking a credit decision |
| | | $F_{5.2}$ | Testing model performance with other datasets |
| | | $F_{3.2}$ | Downloading a model |
| | $R_{EV}$ 2 Evaluation of processes | $F_6$ | Exporting results |
| | $R_{EV}$ 3 Determine the next steps | - | - |

The second part of data understanding is data description ($R_{DU}$ 2), which must include the functionalities to check "gross" or "surface" properties of the acquired dataset and to report on the results. Furthermore, the third part consists of data exploration ($R_{DU}$ 3) to gain more insights for data preprocessing with the help of plots and reports ($F_2$ and $F_{2.1}$). Based on the nature of credit assessment, it is necessary to consider periodical changes, so the ability to compare multiple datasets must be provided to gain deeper insights for pre-processing datasets later in model training ($F_{2.2}$). The use of plots is ideal for supporting this task, as they provide a quick and intuitive understanding of the distribution of the data. Plots such as bar charts, correlation matrices, or boxplots are common types that are used to examine the datasets in data mining. The last step of data understanding is data assessment to verify the quality of the data by checking it for completeness, missing values, and errors ($F_{1.2}$ and $F_{1.3}$). No function is derived for the data assessment, as this check should be performed most easily by examining and making individual queries away from the artifact.

4.1.2. Data Preprocessing

The pre-processing consists of all the steps required to construct the final dataset. The tasks in this step are usually conducted more than once in a non-linear process. The first step consists of data selection ($R_{DP}$ 1), which includes the functionality for the selection of features based on criteria such as relevancy, quality, quantity, and technical characteristics like data scope or type. Therefore, it is necessary to extend the functionality of $F_1$ to allow users to manage the features ($F_{1.4}$). The selected dataset must be clean of any missing values and outliers based on the conducted feature selection ($F_{1.2}$ and $F_{1.4.2}$).

Furthermore, the next part of data preprocessing consists of data construction ($R_{DP}$ 3) to derive further metrics from a dataset using mathematical operations. However, the credit assessment dataset is ordinal, i.e., its values are subject to a sequence, and numbers are assigned to the different values. Therefore, the dataset does not require any conventions that are needed for other use cases dealing with more complex datasets, such as insolvency forecasting. Likewise, the integration of datasets, e.g., from multiple tables or records to create new records or values, is not required for the scope of the prototypical implementation of the AI dashboard for credit assessment. Moreover, the formatting of the dataset consists of syntactical modifications such as delimiter in CSV files or the position of the target variable ($F_{1.2}$). Therefore, it is necessary to have the option to change parameters for importing the dataset, so that the dataset can be imported properly. Furthermore, in the case of metrical data records, it is necessary to have the option of converting them into an ordinal structure ($F_{1.4.1}$), which extends the derived function $F_{1.4}$.

#### 4.1.3. Modeling

The artifact must provide the structure for AI modeling, which includes the application of various techniques and the discovery of the (hyper-)parameterization leading to optimal values. It is important to consider that the performance of a model depends strongly on the dataset. Hence, modeling techniques require certain pre-processing measures, which is why it is essential to be able to go back to an upstream phase. The first step for modeling begins with the selection ($R_{MB}$ 1) of modeling techniques, such as neural networks, decision trees, support vector classifier, XG Boost, etc. To evaluate the quality and validity of the model, it is necessary to develop a mechanism that tests the performance of the model ($R_{MB}$ 2). For a credit assessment, it is common to determine the error rates of classification. Therefore, it is necessary to be able to split the dataset into training and test sets. Credit assessment datasets usually contain more approvals than rejections, which is why a balancing function must be offered to avoid any bias in the trained models.

The creation of a model ($R_{MB}$ 3) consists of the determination of many parameters ($F_3$). Moreover, this step involves several iterations, including creating ($F_{3.1}$), saving ($F_{3.2}$), deleting ($F_{3.3}$), uploading ($F_{3.4}$), and re-training ($F_{3.5}$) an AI model. As a result, models can be evaluated based on the performance metrics. As the decision structure and therefore the datasets for credit assessment can change periodically, it is necessary to compare different datasets and models. For the assessment of the model ($R_{MB}$ 4), many technical areas usually come together to evaluate the results. There is a large overlap between this step and the subsequent evaluation phase. First, the data mining engineer or data scientist interprets the results using their knowledge and the success criteria. In addition, business analysts and experts in their respective fields are consulted to discuss the results from the company's perspective. In most projects, the data scientist/data mining engineer needs to create several models so that they can be compared with each other. Therefore, the functionality to compare the models and export the results is required to assess the models.

#### 4.1.4. Evaluation

This step provides the functionality to evaluate the quality of the models and the approach, including data preparation and data quality. It is important to check whether the business-related problems of credit assessment, the proposed solution, and the AI model have been sufficiently considered. Previous assessment steps ($R_M$ 4) deal with factors that affect the performance of the models, in which context the objective of this phase is to evaluate whether a model contributes to the achievement of the company's objectives and whether it fulfills the business-related requirements ($R_{EV}$ 1). It is therefore necessary to view ($F_5$) and export ($F_6$) the results. This makes it possible to check and compare all the specifications of the models. In addition, the models should be able to be tested with both real as well as hypothetical credit applications ($F_{5.1}$) or using another dataset ($F_{5.2}$) to simulate the model behavior. The function of downloading the model ($F_{3.2}$) is ultimately to integrate it into a production environment or to make further adjustments ($R_{EV}$ 2).

The entire process up to model creation should be documented for evaluation, both to fulfill regulatory requirements and to ensure the traceability of the procedure. This requires that all model parameters and features can be exported in a report. In the final step of the evaluation phase, it then remains to be defined how to continue with the defined AI models. Hereafter, the development process is finished if the model performance is good enough and all requirements have been met, so that the deployment can begin. In addition, further iterations or new model development processes can be initiated if the model behavior needs to be tested regularly with new or revised datasets. However, although the artifact can help to make final decisions about the proposed AI models, it cannot provide any functionality to determine the next steps. An overview of identified requirements and derived functionalities is shown in Table 2.

### 4.2. Analysis of Use Cases of AI Dashboard for Credit Assessment

To structure the process based on the identified requirements and functions, it is necessary to analyze the use cases (Figure 3) and UML activity diagrams (Appendix C). This can promote the understanding of the requirements and functions when designing the artifact. Moreover, the individual modules do not correspond to the individual phases of the CRISP-DM process. The reasons for this relate to the iterative nature of CRISP-DM. For example, the first phase to be supported, data understanding, includes the steps of describing and examining the dataset. However, these steps cannot be completed before the dataset can be imported into the prototype correctly. Therefore, the function to change the parameters for import ($F_{1.2}$), which is assigned to the second phase (pre-processing) according to CRISP-DM, must have already been carried out previously.

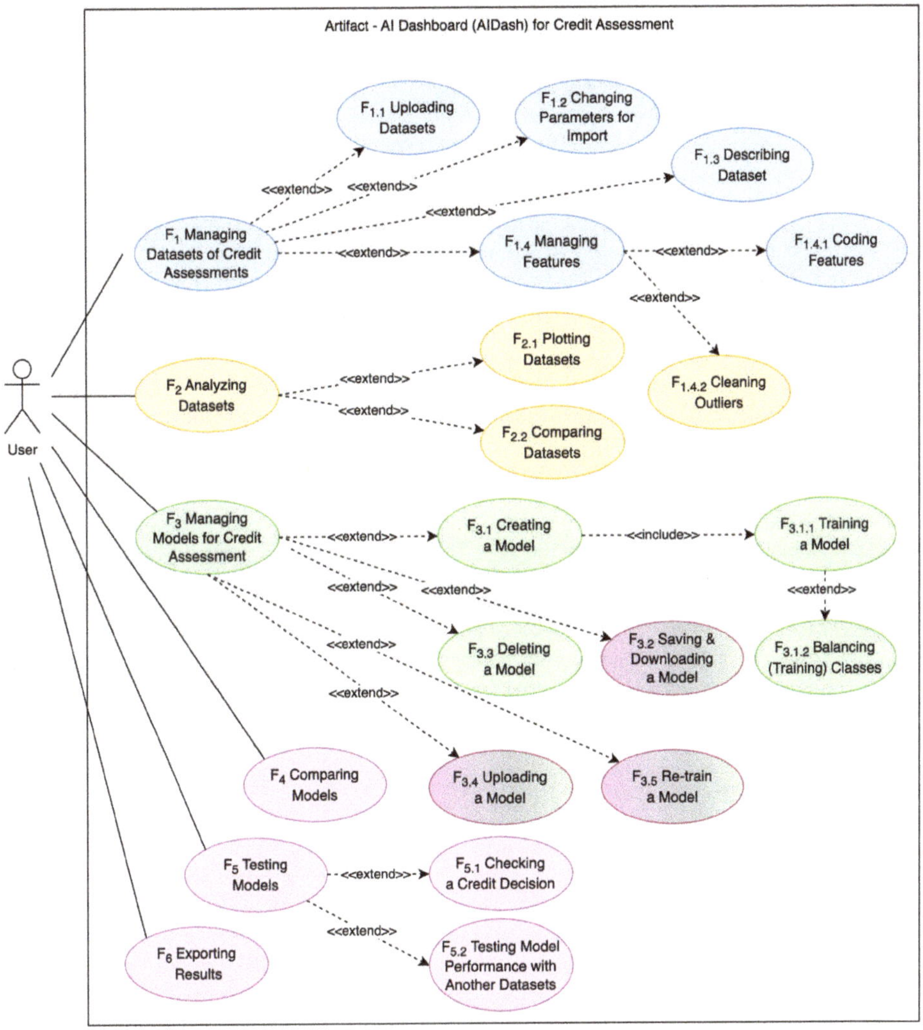


**Figure 3.** The use-case diagram of the artifact.

The artifact's functional scope is illustrated with a UML use-case diagram divided into four CRISP-DM phases (Figure 3), using colors (blue, yellow, green, purple) corresponding to four modules: upload, plot, model, and dashboard. The upload module assists with preprocessing and data understanding by allowing dataset uploads and formatting. The plot module enables graphical evaluation and detailed statistical analysis of datasets. The modeling module supports various modeling techniques and parameter optimization. The dashboard module visualizes and compares model performance, allowing new models to be uploaded or existing ones retrained. It also allows periodic testing of model behavior with new datasets or individual credit applications.

### 4.3. Selection of Modeling Techniques

The regulatory principles determine the criteria for the use of AI models in financial services. The European Commission regulation for the use of AI [10] stipulates that these models must have good forecasting capability and no systematic errors or distortions. In addition, regulatory principles for processes related to data quality as well as model validation are defined [21]. However, these are not considered in detail, as they must be implemented individually by the respective institutions for each specific application. For instance, they do not specify what can be considered good forecasting capability.

Moreover, the supervisory authorities define further country-specific regulations for the use of AI-based models. For example, the Federal Financial Supervisory Authority (BaFin) of Germany defines conditions for the selection of methods and techniques, requiring that companies must be able to justify the decisions and the underlying assumptions comprehensibly [20]. The use of models with increased complexity and so-called "black box" structure is critical for supervisory authorities, as they are concerned about the problem of limited insight into the model decision structure. Moreover, approaches such as LIME (local interpretable model-agnostic explanation) provide insights into the inner structures of AI models and so reveal the underlying decision structures of AI models [43]. However, the required explainability relates not only to the model but also to the associated process for its development, so documentation is essential to bring more transparency to the underlying development process. Therefore, the supervisory authorities provide no general approval for algorithms, so companies must ensure that the models produce correct, robust, and reproducible results.

The modeling techniques for credit assessment must provide a high level of explainability, transparency, and performance [10]. Nevertheless, for prototypical implementation, the modeling process must allow the use of different approaches that can be evaluated and compared. Therefore, the artifact should be expandable to integrate further modeling techniques. However, users should be aware that complex models such as neural networks cannot be used in credit assessment without further elaboration by supervisory authorities due to the hidden black box structure. We derived the given categorization and techniques, i.e., statistical and intelligent learning models and ensemble methods, from the literature [13,15,44–48] to provide algorithms that were as representative and efficient as possible (Table 3). However, a clear categorization of the selected techniques was not possible since semi-parametric methods represent a bridge between statistical and intelligent learning models.

**Table 3.** Selected modeling techniques for credit assessment dashboard.

| | |
|---|---|
| **Intelligent methods** | Artificial neural network |
| | Decision tree |
| | Support vector classifier |
| | K-nearest neighbors classifier |
| **Statistical models** | Linear regression |
| | Logistic regression |
| **Ensemble methods** | XGB classifier |
| | Random forest |

To appropriately compare models, it is necessary to provide functionality for model assessment based on performance metrics. Graphs and tables can support this assessment process by visualizing extracted performance metrics [49–51]. A suitable representation of model performance is the confusion matrix, which visualizes performance using actual and predicted values, aiding in decision making [49]. Additionally, the receiver operating characteristic (ROC) curve effectively illustrates model performance by plotting the true positive rate (TPR) against the false positive rate (FPR) at various threshold settings. A steeper curve closer to the 0.0/1.0 coordinate indicates a better model, whereas a bisector-like ROC curve suggests random classification [52]. It is crucial to use statistical and appropriate metrics to present performance neutrally without distortion [13,53–55]. Chen et al. [13] define relevant performance metrics for binary classification or regression, such as in credit assessment. Moreover, including the negative prediction value (NPV) is essential for assessing the predictive quality of negative classifications, particularly in credit assessment, where an AI model could inaccurately achieve high accuracy by classifying all applications as positive if the dataset has few bad credit applications.

Moreover, it is essential to include these metrics as a part of the exported reports (Table 4) and to export training and testing datasets for further assessment, e.g., by responsible regulatory authorities or managers [13,51,56–58]. Documentation and export of all model-related information can promote development and evaluation processes that are as transparent and comprehensible as possible. Due to the required model assessment ($R_M$4), it is crucial to be able to compare these performance metrics of several models with drill-down functionality to identify and highlight their differences [50,59–61]. Thereby, the grid structure of a table can provide a simple, clear comparison of the different performance metrics. The possibility of adding different models to the table allows the user the necessary interactivity [62].

**Table 4.** Metrics for the assessment of the model performance of a binary classification.

| Value | Name | Description | Calculation |
|---|---|---|---|
| Acc | Accuracy | - | $\frac{TP+TN}{n}$ |
| RSME | Root mean squared error | Equivalent to the Brier score for one-dimensional predictions | $\sqrt{\frac{\Sigma(P(x)-T(x))^2}{n}}$ |
| TPR | True positive rate | Recall, sensitivity, hit rate | $\frac{TP}{TP+FN}$ |
| TNR | True negative rate | Specificity, selectivity | $\frac{TN}{TN+FP}$ |
| FPR | False positive rate | Fall-out | $\frac{FP}{TN+FP}$ |
| FNR | False negative rate | Miss rate | $\frac{FN}{TP+FN}$ |
| PPV | Positive prediction value | Precision | $\frac{TP}{TP+FN}$ |
| F | F-score | Harmonic mean of precision and recall | $2 * \frac{PPV*TPR}{PPV+TPR}$ |
| AUC | The area under the ROC curve | - | - |
| NPV | Negative prediction value | - | $\frac{TN}{TN+FN}$ |

### 4.4. Design and Development

To fulfill the specified requirements to assist the process of AI development, we designed and developed the web-based artifact *AIDash*. Web-based applications enhance transparency and traceability in the development process by providing easy access to artifacts for operational employees, managers, and regulators [63]. They facilitate real-time collaboration, ensure accountability through detailed logs and version control, and improve communication via centralized information and interactive dashboards. However, these benefits come with challenges such as increased security risks, dependence on internet connectivity, complex implementation, and compliance with data privacy regulations. Balancing these advantages and disadvantages is essential for effectively utilizing web-based applications while mitigating potential risks. For the development of the artifact, we opted for the Python-based Django framework, which provides sufficient AI modules and a modern development architecture for data mining processes [64,65] (Appendix H).

As described in Section 4.2, the artifact consists of four modules (upload, plot, model, and dashboard), that guide the user through the entire model creation process (Figure 3). Below, a possible sequence of use is modeled using UML activity diagrams for each of the modules (Appendix C). However, as the procedure and the required processes are strongly dependent on the respective case and the stage of the project, completely different sequences are also possible. For instance, the data format check can be skipped if it has already been carried out manually.

#### 4.4.1. Upload Module

The first module provides the functionalities to support the data understanding and preprocessing aspects of CRISP-DM. First, a new dataset can be uploaded in CSV format or selected from the list of already uploaded datasets (Figure 4). The artifact provides an overview of the uploaded or selected dataset so that the user can change the parameters for the import if there is incorrect formatting, e.g., caused by an incorrectly selected delimiter. Then, once the file has been read correctly, the target variable must be specified. The selected delimiter, the position of the header line, and the name of the target feature in the dataset are saved in the database.

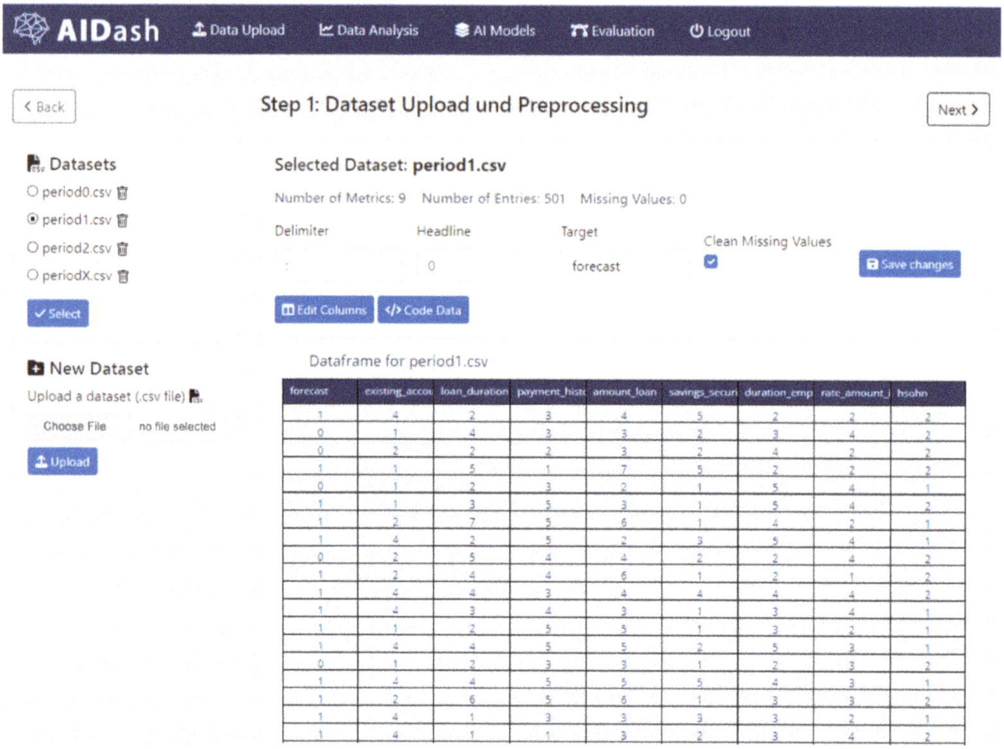


**Figure 4.** Data upload module in AIDash.

Furthermore, it is possible to check, rename, or delete the columns if any changes are necessary for training an AI model (Appendices A and D). However, the management of the dataset ($F_1$) also provides functionality for coding the dataset ($F_{1.4.1}$), with the conversion of the metric characteristics into ordinal values such as credit ratings (AAA, AA+, . . ., D). In addition, there is another option for setting the value ranges for the assignment of ordinal values, which helps to exclude outliers in the selected columns by entering minimum and maximum values. For additional insights to be able to make necessary changes in import parameters, such as value ranges to exclude outliers or for an appropriate selection of features, the user can navigate to the plot module and generate graphical impressions with interactive bar charts and boxplots or can check the correlations between the features. Therefore, multiple iterations may be necessary to finalize the parameters and the selection of features.

#### 4.4.2. Plot Module

The plot module serves as a graphical representation of the selected dataset (Figure 5). It thus enables in-depth analysis and comparison between, for example, the periodic datasets (e.g., $D_t$ and $D_{t-1}$) to determine the possible conceptual or model changes. The potential deviations in datasets can lead to changes in the model structure, meaning that it is no longer possible to continue training existing models. Initially, the user decides whether only one dataset should be viewed or a comparison is desired. Depending on the decision, a second dataset from the user can be selected or removed from the view. The default view is a bar chart, so that the frequencies of each feature are displayed. The user can also select a pie chart to analyze the distribution of the feature values.

However, the primary focus on percentage composition (Appendix E) can be explored in more detail using the boxplot diagram, which provides a precise overview of the distribution, quantiles, and medians (Figure A9). Moreover, the boxplot diagram also shows outliers and provides an opportunity to remove them. As another important part of the data analysis, a correlation matrix can be selected to obtain the pairwise correlation coefficients of the features in the form of a table (Figure A11). AIDash allows us to make an easy comparison with a second dataset for each diagram type. Further arrangements of datasets based on the graphical analysis can be carried out in the upload module.

#### 4.4.3. Model Module

The model module serves the management of models so that the user can create or upload new models and also delete or download existing models (Figure 6). The buttons for deleting or downloading are located on the left-hand side of the module. A new model can also be created using the corresponding button, whereupon a dialog window opens and allows the user to specify a title for the model. Once the desired model has been selected, individual hyperparameters for the model can be determined manually by the user (Appendix F). Furthermore, the ratio of "good" and "bad" credit applications in the selected dataset is plotted on a doughnut chart (Figure A12). Significant imbalances in the dataset can have a strong negative impact on model accuracy and distort the results by simply predicting the majority class and so providing poor recognition of bad credit applications [13].

Therefore, AIDash provides two options to balance the dataset by adjusting the ratio of "good" and "bad" credit applications (Figure A12). First, the random removal function allows the selection of the desired ratio between "good" and "bad" credit applications, so that credit applications are randomly selected and removed. As a second option, SMOTE–Tomek provides a combination of over- and undersampling techniques to balance the dataset [66]. Datasets for credit assessment contain a very small number of bad loans by default [67–69]. The SMOTE–Tomek algorithm randomly selects entries from the minority class and generates synthetic entries using the K-nearest neighbor algorithm until the desired ratio between the minority and majority class is reached [66]. Subsequently, so-called Tomek links are removed, which are defined as entries of the majority class whose nearest neighbor is an entry from the minority class and vice versa. In the implementation of the prototype, oversampling is carried out until a balanced ratio (50:50) between the majority and minority classes is reached. Once the desired adjustments have been made, the model can be trained (Figure A12).

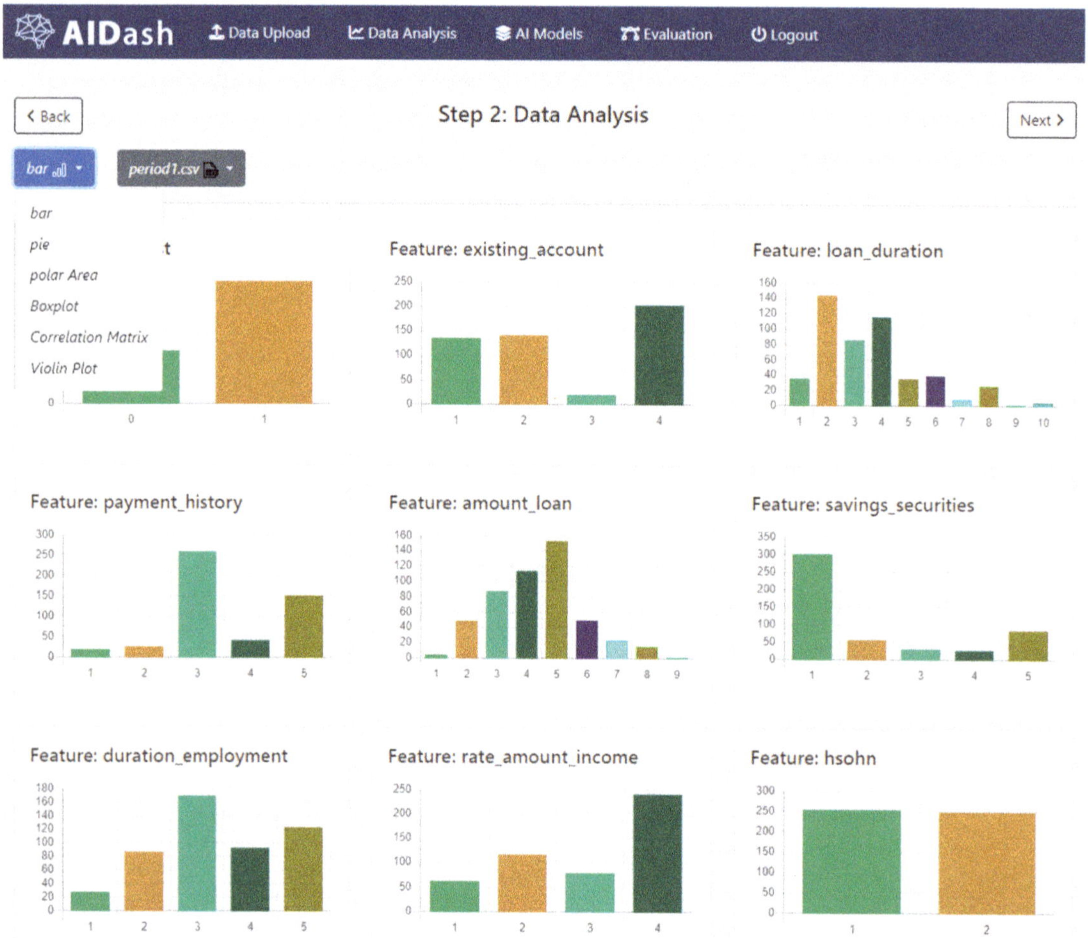


**Figure 5.** Plot module in AIDash.

In case of a need to evaluate or compare a model created independently (outside the prototype), it is possible to upload models (Figure 6). For this, a dialog window opens in which the title, description, model name, and model type can be specified. Furthermore, the associated training and test datasets must be uploaded. These must be serialized (e.g., using the Pickle library of Python) so that they can be imported and saved as a new object in the database. However, before the model is saved in the database, the performance metrics can be calculated. Once all relevant models are available, it is possible to navigate to the dashboard module for the evaluation of multiple models.

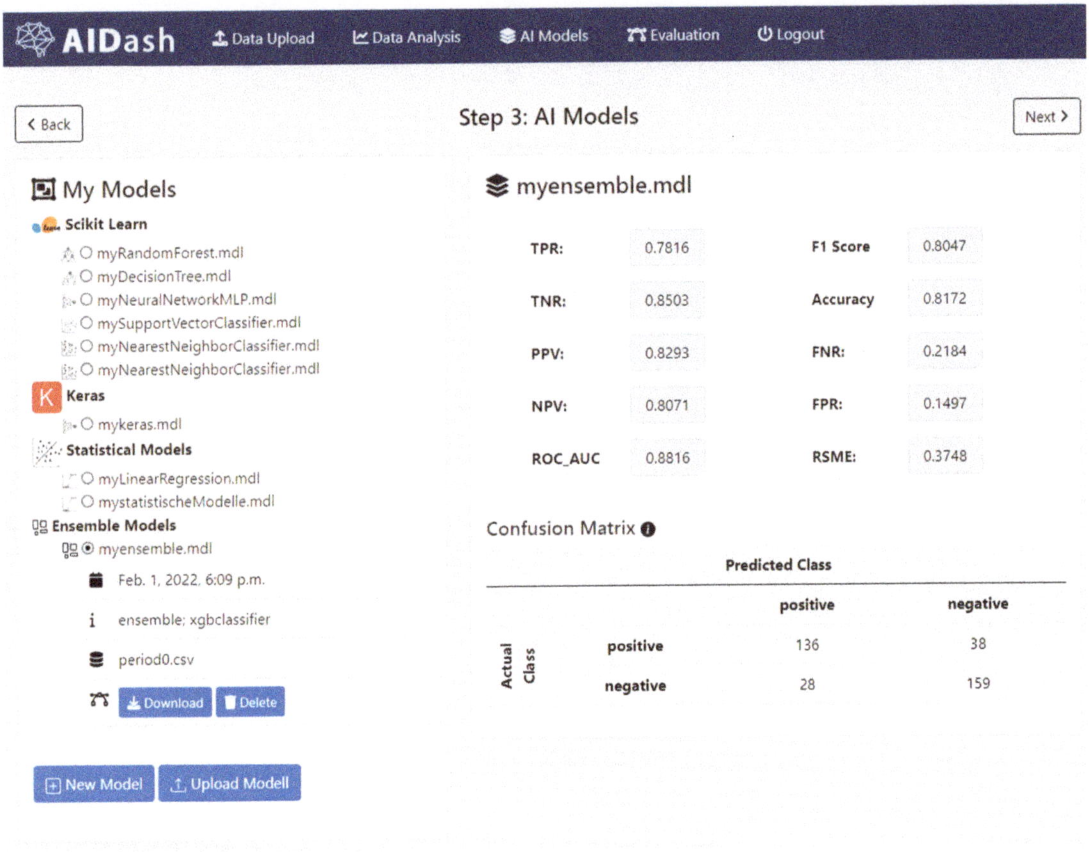


**Figure 6.** Model module in AIDash.

4.4.4. Dashboard Module

The dashboard module is the core of the prototype (Figure 7) and provides the necessary functionality to evaluate prepared or existing AI models (Figure 6). All previous steps and modules are used to build the model so that it can be evaluated in this module. Moreover, it also includes additional features, such as re-training, testing with another dataset, or creating a report (Appendix G). By default, the dashboard contains a single model including all key performance metrics for the evaluation. However, it is possible to add further models for comparison with the key performance metrics using the plus symbol in the top right corner of the table (Figure 7).

**Figure 7.** Dashboard module in AIDash.

In addition, AIDash provides the option of downloading each model and the associated training/test sets via the corresponding button in the last row of the table. A full report can be created via the third icon, containing model performance based on metrics, metadata about the model, classifications made, training/test datasets, graphs, and the selected hyperparameters of the model (Figure A15). The dashboard module itself provides step-by-step documentation of the modeling process with the specific operations performed. Thus, documentation of the tests and analyses performed is provided either via the dashboard itself or by downloading reports for internal or regulatory approval.

Furthermore, each model contained in the view can be retrained via a drop-down menu by uploading new training and test datasets in serialized format (Figure A13). This function allows users to test existing models with new datasets to conduct further adjustments directly on the dashboard module. For this, a new model is created in the background so that new credit applications can be assessed. Moreover, the model performance can be tested either by entering credit applications manually via a drop-down menu or by file upload (Figure A14), so that the predictions for each entry can be calculated. Moreover, there is a binary prediction option in which the model classifies the application as "good" or "bad" (1—good; 0—bad). Alternatively, it is possible to generate and export the probabilities of the classification (between 0 and 1).

In case of a need to test already trained models with new datasets (e.g., for periodic comparisons between $D_t$ and $D_{t-1}$) to determine whether the model performance is sufficient, or any adjustments are necessary, by selecting "Test model with another dataset" in the drop-down menu, the corresponding dialog window is opened (Appendix G) so that a title can be specified for the new object and a new corresponding testing dataset can be uploaded. Subsequently, the prototype generates the predictions and provides the performance metrics of the model.

### 4.5. Demonstration of AIDash

Following the implementation of the artifact, the functional correctness of the AIDash was validated by applying it to an application scenario. The demonstration of AIDash consisted of two consecutive periods and the datasets of these. Due to the necessary change of datasets, it was necessary to check whether there was data or model drift, so that a new AI model could be trained, tested, compared, and prepared for deployment.

Based on the periodic nature of credit scoring datasets, the first module (Section 4.4.1) provides the functionality to upload a new dataset to compare multiple datasets (between $D_{period1.csv}$ and $D_{period2.csv}$) and model behavior. Moreover, after the final selection of features from the dataset (see Figure A5), the coding process of features can be conducted (see Figure A6). Since both datasets were already coded, it was not necessary to make further adjustments to the features, and the next step began with the comparison of the feature distributions between datasets, e.g., the current and the next period, on the plot module before training the model (Appendix A).

By using the comparison view, it was possible to identify possible data drifts that affected the model performance and the model behavior (Figure 8). Firstly, the ratio between "good" and "bad" credit applications was similar in the two datasets. However, the second feature (existing_account) showed that the third (for more than 200 monetary units or salary accounts for at least one year in the bank) and fourth types (for no current account) of customers were associated with an upward trend in credit applications compared with the previous period. In addition, we observed a new set of loan durations, with 10 loan applications between 54 and 60 months. In addition, an increased loan duration was also reflected in the amount of the loan applied for (9: $1500 < \ldots \leq 20{,}000$). These significant changes indicated a data drift that may have led to incorrect assessment by the models.

Due to the identified changes in the new dataset, it was necessary to develop a new model to assess the performance and ensure system safety. To do this, the model module (Figure 6) provided the functionality to manage the modeling process. The definition of a new model with AIDash is assisted by the predefined parameters, which can be further refined if necessary. However, the new dataset contained more "good" than "bad" loans, which was balanced out during the development of the new models (Figure A12). To enable a comparison on the dashboard module to find the best among all existing modeling techniques, we created several models from the list of techniques provided by AIDash.

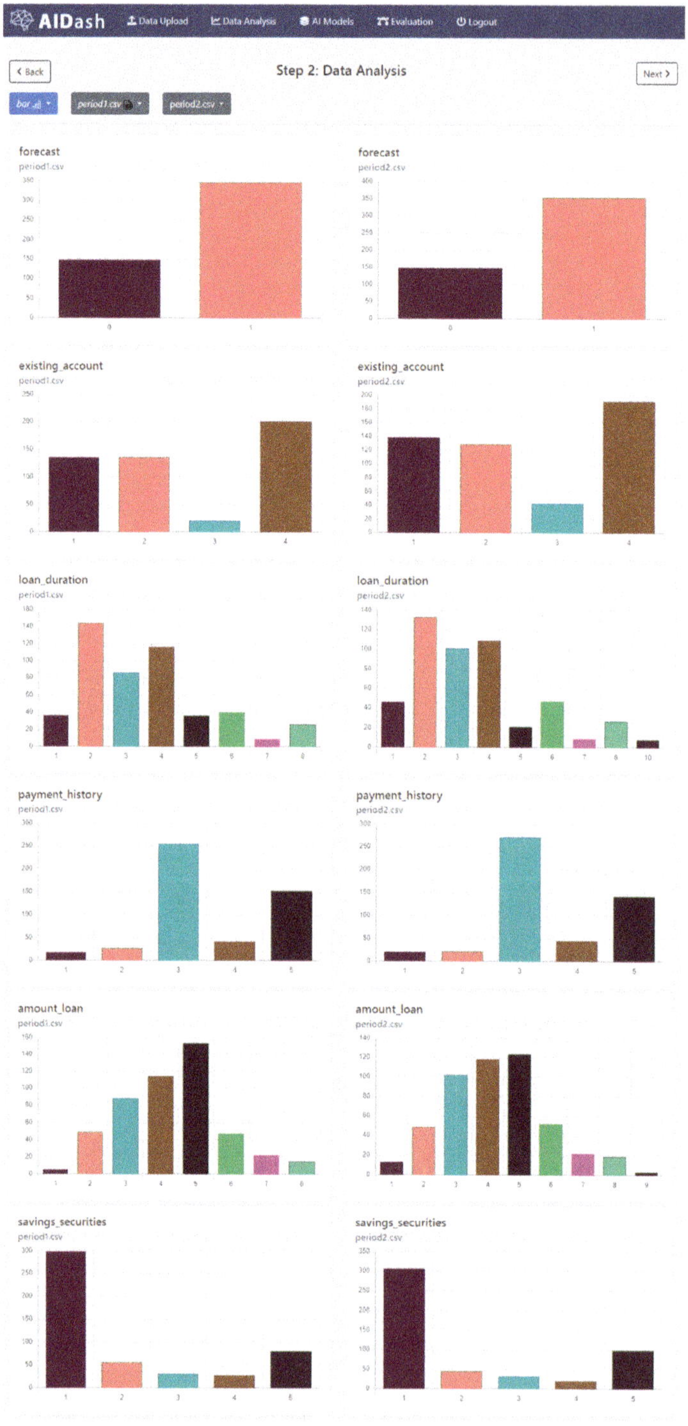


**Figure 8.** Data analysis in AIDash.

In the last step of the process, AIDash provides a comparison view of multiple models. In order to demonstrate the model evaluation process, XGB, and DT models trained with $D_{period2.csv}$ and $D_{period1.csv}$ were added so that the performance of each model could be analyzed (Figure 9). Thus, AIDash was able to promote a periodical comparison between the existing and newly trained models. However, in this step, it was necessary to iteratively add/remove models to/from this view for comparison before the final decision was made. In this case, the XGB and DT models allowed us to assess the transition in model performance between the two periods and datasets.

**Figure 9.** Evaluation of new models.

First, the ROC curve indicated that the XGB models overperformed the DT models from this and the previous period. We observed that the curve for the new XGB model with $D_{period2.csv}$ rapidly extended towards the upper right-hand corner of the graph. Second, the new XGB model with the performance metrics in the table below showed that a change or modification of the existing model made sense due to its superior performance. In addition, the performance metrics showed the better quality of the XGB model that was trained with the new dataset, with higher accuracy, higher F1 score, and lower Brier score. The metrics are highlighted with specific colors to make it easy to identify changes in performance. Moreover, AIDash provides the functionality to test the model with another dataset, allowing monitoring of the performance of existing models on new datasets to identify model drift (Figure A13). Lastly, it was necessary to export the model's train and test datasets and the documentation report to make final adjustments for deployment. In case of a need for any regulatory assessment, the model behavior can be assessed by checking individual credit applications (Figure A13).

## 5. Discussion and Limitations

The implemented artifact provides an exemplary structure based on the gathered requirements from CRISP-DM to develop, maintain, evaluate, and monitor AI models for financial services. Table 5 provides an overview of the functional scope of the artifact AIDash. Comparing the scope of requirements and functions (Section 4.1) with the steps from CRISP-DM, the feasibility is visualized as follows: the green cells in the table are supported steps, while the yellow cells indicate the partial coverage, and the orange cells are the unsupported steps. The business understanding and deployment phases cannot be supported with the artifact as they require more strategic, conceptional thinking, as well as practical action and integration beyond the artifact. Assuming that the fundamental and strategic requirements are in place, the steps marked in green and yellow can be facilitated and improved within the scope of the artifact.

As in the first research question addressed, the derived functionalities from CRISP-DM outline the functional requirements in Table 2 [$F_1$–$F_6$]. In addition, these requirements can help to develop an artifact for other similar use cases working with quantitative datasets in financial services. Moreover, due to the regulatory requirements for the use of AI in financial services, it is necessary to extend the artifact with further explainability, traceability, and transparency approaches throughout the development process—from data preparation to model development. The regulations do not clearly define any criteria for a suitable level of explainability. The artifact provides decision tree and logistic regression models that include explainability by design (Section 4.3). However, for black box models such as NN, it is necessary to extend the artifact with XAI techniques such as LIME or Shapley to provide the required explainability for these models.

The existing research gap in appropriate structures and systems for the development of AI models including training, testing, comparison, evaluation, deployment, and documentation mechanisms was investigated in this study. The requirements identified from the CRISP-DM stages addressed the problem of long development times and concept shifts. The structure of the artifact was formed from the functions derived from the requirements and mapped into four modules (upload, plot, model, and dashboard). The AI models identified in Section 4.3 and legal requirements confirm that models cannot be permitted or prohibited in general. Therefore, dashboards must provide a structure that ensures that the models and the associated processes are transparent, explainable, performant, and individually assessable.

**Table 5.** Overview of the functional scope of the developed artifact based on CRISP-DM.

| Steps | Business Understanding | Data Understanding | Data Preparation | Modeling | Evaluation | Deployment |
|---|---|---|---|---|---|---|
| 1. | Determine business objectives | Collect initial data | Select data | Select modeling techniques | Evaluate results | Plan deployment |
| 2. | Assess situation | Describe data | Clean data | Generate test design | Review process | Plan monitoring and maintenance |
| 3. | Determine data mining goals | Explore data | Construct data | Build model | Determine next steps | Produce final report |
| 4. | Produce project plan | Verify data quality | Integrate data | Assess model | | Review project |
| 5. | | | Format data | | | |

Green: full coverage; yellow: partial coverage; orange: No coverage.

The problem of the occurrence of concept shifts and the associated decline in model performance can impair a model's ability to classify credit applications based on factual characteristics. Corresponding models are often based on datasets from up to three years in the past, as the development of new models by data analysts is time-consuming [15]. This high level of effort comes from the fact that there are high quality requirements for these models and the documentation both from credit institutions and the regulators, in order to increase transparency and ensure customers' safety and trust. Therefore, the adaptability of AI-based services must be ensured due to the dynamic macroeconomic environment, so that possible concept shifts can be recognized at an early stage and measures can be taken to ensure good predictive capability of the models (Section 5).

Furthermore, the performance of a model depends significantly on the dataset used, so multiple iterations are relevant for the preparation of datasets and models for determining the best set of configurations [13,70]. Therefore, the possibility to analyze, compare, test, and evaluate datasets and models in detail is provided in the four modules. Furthermore, the export function makes it possible to document systemically the reports on conducted analyses. A potential conceptual shift can easily be detected by testing the already trained models with datasets from a different period. A reduction or improvement in model performance can then easily be discovered using the calculated performance metrics. If further assessments are required, the user can create or upload new models directly.

All these factors lead to lengthy model development and therefore cost-intensive processes that are usually carried out by experts in the field of data science, which is exactly the problem addressed by the developed artifact AIDash. The four outlined modules (upload, plot, model, and dashboard) enable the rapid development or maintenance of AI models. Thanks to the graphical user interface, even non-experts in the field of data science can develop or evaluate AI models. However, it should be noted that these models are not considered final or optimal. Rather, they can serve as a first iteration, as a performance comparison, or for control of the performance of existing or used models.

Moreover, the plot module provides the functionalities to identify deviations from the previous datasets, based on different graphical representations. The function for comparing data records enables assessment and observation of features to determine whether any strong variations or imbalances exist. The corresponding graphical representations from the available datasets help to rapidly identify periodical changes in the datasets that may lead to a conceptual shift. Furthermore, proposed models must be configured on the model module, which provides the functionality to address the imbalances between "good" and "bad" loans in the selected dataset. In addition, the artifact provides the basic functionality for creating models and balancing the selected dataset, which can be extended in fine granularity depending on the objective and required complexity.

The AI dashboard for financial services has significant implications for regulatory authorities, especially under frameworks like the European AI Act. While it enhances transparency and traceability by documenting every step from data preparation to model development, the explainability requirements of the models need to be further investigated based on the specific modeling technique. Therefore, requirements for a model- and case-specific degree of explainability must first be investigated. Furthermore, regulatory authorities demand high levels of transparency and traceability, and the AI dashboard aids compliance by providing detailed documentation of all actions taken during the model development process, supporting regulatory reviews and helping maintain compliance with documentation standards.

Additionally, the dashboard's functionalities to detect and address conceptual shifts are crucial for maintaining model performance, which is essential for compliance. Systematically analyzing and testing models with new datasets helps to identify shifts early, allowing timely corrective actions. This proactive approach ensures AI models remain accurate and reliable, aligning with regulatory expectations for ongoing validation and performance monitoring. Furthermore, the dashboard promotes standardization in AI model development, ensuring all processes are consistent and well-documented, which is essential for regulatory approval. This streamlined development process reduces time and costs, making AI model development more accessible, aligning with regulatory goals of accessibility and inclusivity, and enabling even non-experts to develop and evaluate models.

Moreover, documenting data preprocessing, modeling, and sampling enhances transparency for regulatory authorities. Sharing prepared models with all documentation and datasets will aid regulatory control and review. This documentation justifies decisions to use or change AI models. It lacks features for recalculating or combining new model features, which could improve prediction quality. Research indicates that splitting datasets to train multiple models can enhance predictions, suggesting that the artifact could benefit from this functionality to reduce bias and improve accuracy [19,71]. Lastly, the problem-centered DSR process should include practical evaluations and expert interviews to refine requirements, concepts, and prototypes based on practical insights [23].

## 6. Conclusions

This study investigates the development of an AI dashboard to structure and support the development process of AI models for private credit assessment. We identified 13 requirements as part of the first research question and derived 28 key functionalities from them, distributed across four blocks of CRISP-DM (Table 5): data understanding, data preprocessing, modeling, and evaluation. Due to the underlying dataset and corresponding use case of credit assessment, four identified requirements [$R_{DU}$ 1, $R_{DP}$ 3, $R_{DP}$ 4, and $R_{EV}$ 3] were not considered for deriving any functionalities. To provide a structured process of modeling, the proposed artifact consists of four modules equipped with the identified functionalities. To address the second research question, we structured the model development process and implemented an artifact that enables multiple iterations between these modules, allowing numerous corrections for models and datasets. Moreover, the provided workflow defines a useful and structured method for data preprocessing to avoid any bias in datasets. Automated documentation makes it possible to track the design process and thus brings more transparency into the field.

The AI dashboard for financial services significantly impacts financial regulations, particularly under frameworks like the European AI Act. It enhances transparency and traceability by meticulously documenting each step of the model development process, aiding regulatory reviews and compliance. This ensures all actions during data preparation, model training, testing, and evaluation are transparent and traceable, essential for regulatory scrutiny. The dashboard's ability to detect and address concept shifts maintains model performance, aligning with regulatory requirements for ongoing validation and performance monitoring. It promotes standardization in AI model development, ensuring consistent and well-documented processes crucial for regulatory approval. This streamlines development reduces time and costs and supports regulatory goals of accessibility and inclusivity, enabling even non-experts to develop and evaluate models. While the dashboard addresses many current regulatory requirements, further enhancements are needed to fully comply with evolving European AI Act standards, to make it a comprehensive tool for regulatory compliance in AI in financial services.

The artifact AIDash goes beyond the functionalities of a typical dashboard and addresses several problems of model creation and validation in credit assessment. In particular, the prototype addresses the problem of concept shifts (Section 5). Users can recognize a decrease in model performance by testing an existing model with a new dataset, e.g., from a subsequent period. Furthermore, thanks to the graphical presentation (plot module), changes in the dataset can be recognized and countermeasures can thus be undertaken. The dashboard as a web application enables simplified analysis and evaluation of datasets and models so that even non-experts in the field of data science can perform regular analyses and monitor already developed models.

Extensive support for the phases and steps of CRISP-DM enables initial models to be developed quickly and easily. These models can be used, for example, as a performance comparison or can also be further developed so that they can subsequently be deployed in a productive environment. The AI dashboard stores all data relevant for the documentation of model creation. These data can be exported and thus also stored externally so that they can be used for the mandatory documentation for the supervisory authorities. In addition, the explainability desired by regulators must be addressed so that the artifact can be extended by XAI techniques to allow more complex models such as neural networks to be used in financial services. This study has made it clear that further research is needed to define compliant approaches to design, develop, maintain, document, and deploy AI models.

**Author Contributions:** Conceptualization, M.P. and M.S.; methodology, M.P.; formal analysis, M.P.; data curation, M.P.; writing—original draft preparation, M.P.; writing—review and editing, M.P. and M.S.; visualization, M.P.; validation, M.P.; project administration, M.S. All authors have read and agreed to the published version of the manuscript.

**Funding:** This research received no external funding.

**Data Availability Statement:** No new data were created or analyzed in this study. Data sharing is not applicable to this article.

**Acknowledgments:** We would like to thank the reviewers for their thoughtful comments and efforts toward improving our manuscript.

**Conflicts of Interest:** The authors declare no conflicts of interest.

## Appendix A. Dataset

**Table A1.** Coding of the underlying dataset.

| Feature | Description | Coding |
|---|---|---|
| **Y** | Target | 0: Bad loan<br>1: Good loan |
| **X1** | Type of existing account with the bank | 1: No account or debit balance<br>2: 0 ≤ … < 200<br>3: ≥200 or salary account for at least 1 year<br>4: No current account |
| **X2** | Duration of the loan in months | 1: ≤6<br>2: 6 < … ≤ 12<br>3: 12 < … ≤ 18<br>4: 18 < … ≤ 24<br>5: 24 < … ≤ 30<br>6: 30 < … ≤ 36<br>7: 36 < … ≤ 42<br>8: 42 < … ≤ 48<br>9: 48 < … ≤ 54<br>10: 54 < … ≤ 60 |
| **X3** | Previous payment performance | 1: No loans to date/all loans duly repaid<br>2: Previous loans processed properly at the bank<br>3: Loans still outstanding with the bank<br>4: Previously hesitant credit management<br>5: Critical account/there are other loans (not with the bank) |
| **X4** | Amount of the loan | 1: ≤500<br>2: 500 < … ≤ 1000<br>3: 1000 < … ≤ 1500<br>4: 1500 < … ≤ 2500<br>5: 2500 < … ≤ 5000<br>6: 5000 < … ≤ 7500<br>7: 7500 < … ≤ 10,000<br>8: 10,000 < … 15,000<br>9: 15,000 < … ≤ 20,000<br>10: >20,000 |

**Table A1.** *Cont.*

| Feature | Description | Coding |
|---|---|---|
| **X5** | Savings account or securities | 1: <100<br>2: 100 ≤ ... < 500<br>3: 500 ≤ ... < 1000<br>4: ≥1000<br>5: Not available/no savings account |
| **X6** | Duration of employment with the current employer | 1: Unemployed<br>2: <1 Years<br>3: 1 ≤ ... < 4 Years<br>4: 4 Years ≤ ...< 7 Years<br>5: ≥7 Years |
| **X7** | Amount of rates as % of disposable income | 1: ≥35%<br>2: 25 ≤ ... < 35%<br>3: 20 ≤ ... < 25%<br>4: <20% |
| **X8** | Duration at current residence | 1: 1 Year<br>2: 1 ≤ ... < 4 Year(s)<br>3: 4 ≤ ... < 7 Years<br>4: ≥7 Years |
| **X9** | Type of existing assets | 1: Owning a house or land<br>2: If not 1: Home loan and savings contract/life insurance<br>3: If not 1 or 2: Car or other<br>4: Not available/no assets |

## Appendix B. Literature Review

**Table A2.** List of relevant literature from the literature review.

| Sources | AI-Based Credit Assessment | Dashboards for Model Development | Literature Review | Interview Study | Financial Regulations |
|---|---|---|---|---|---|
| **Addi and Souissi [72]** | | x | | | |
| **Adisa et al. [73]** | x | | x | | |
| **Arner et al. [74]** | x | | | | |
| **Baier et al. [75]** | x | | x | | |
| **Baldo et al. [76]** | x | | | | |
| **Berrada et al. [77]** | x | | x | | |
| **Cao et al. [78]** | x | | | | |
| **Chornous and Nikolskyi [79]** | | | | | x |
| **Dastile and Celik [80]** | x | | | | |
| **Devi and Chezian [81]** | x | | | | |
| **Devos et al. [82]** | x | | | | |
| **Dyczkowski et al. [83]** | x | | x | | |
| **Guntay et al. [84]** | x | | x | | |
| **Hassan and Jayousi [85]** | x | | x | | |
| **Hentzen et al. [4]** | x | | | | |
| **Hooman et al. [86]** | x | | | | |
| **Hoover [87]** | | | x | x | |
| **Ismawati and Faturohman [88]** | | x | | | |

Table A2. *Cont.*

| Sources | AI-Based Credit Assessment | Dashboards for Model Development | Literature Review | Interview Study | Financial Regulations |
|---|---|---|---|---|---|
| Jemai et al. [89] | x | | | | |
| Jin [90] | x | | | | |
| Karim et al. [91] | | | | | x |
| Khemakhem et al. [69] | x | | x | | |
| Khemakhem and Boujelbene [92] | x | | | | |
| Kossow et al. [93] | x | | x | | |
| Kothandapani [94] | x | | | | |
| Kruse et al. [34] | x | | | | |
| Kurshan et al. [26] | x | | | | |
| Li [95] | x | | | | x |
| Lombardo [9] | x | | | | x |
| Luo [96] | x | | x | | |
| Maurya and Gaur [97] | x | | | | |
| Mirza and Ogrenci [98] | x | | | | |
| Mittal et al. [99] | x | | | | |
| Moula et al. [68] | x | | | | |
| Nieto [100] | | | x | | |
| Ordabayeva et al. [101] | | | x | | |
| Pamuk et al. [19] | x | | x | | |
| Pan et al. [102] | x | | | | |
| Paul et al. [103] | x | | | | |
| Pincovsky et al. [3] | x | | | | |
| Punniyamoorthy and Sridevi [104] | x | | | | x |
| Qiu et al. [105] | | | x | | |
| Ranpara and Patel [106] | x | | | | |
| Sadok et al. [107] | x | | | | |
| Safiya Parvin and Saleena [108] | x | | | | |
| Septama et al. [109] | x | x | x | | |
| Shoumo et al. [110] | | x | | | |
| Soares de Melo Junior et al. [111] | x | | | | |
| Solow-Niederman et al. [112] | x | | | | |
| Virág and Nyitrai [113] | x | | | | |
| Wang et al. [114] | x | | | | |
| Wei [115] | x | | | | |
| Wilson Drakes [116] | x | | x | | |
| Xiao and Wang [117] | x | | | | |
| Xiao et al. [118] | x | | | | |
| Yotsawat et al. [119] | x | | | | |
| Yu et al. [120] | x | | | | |

**Table A2.** *Cont.*

| Sources | AI-Based Credit Assessment | Dashboards for Model Development | Literature Review | Interview Study | Financial Regulations |
|---|---|---|---|---|---|
| **Zhang et al. [121]** | x | | | | |
| **Zhao et al. [67]** | x | | | | |
| **Zhong and Wang [122]** | | | | | x |
| **Zhu et al. [123]** | | | | | x |

## Appendix C. UML Activity Diagrams

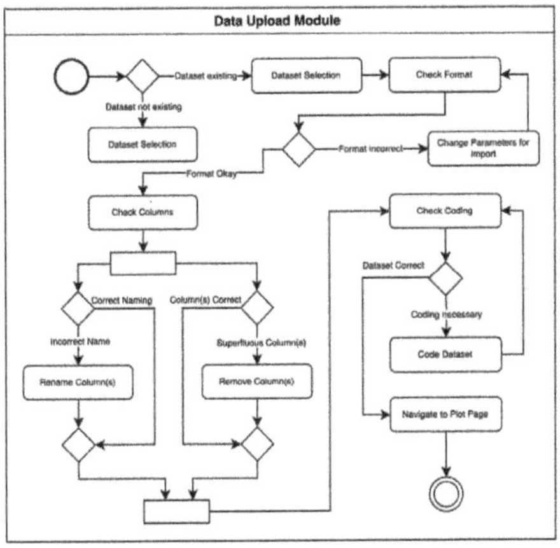


**Figure A1.** UML activity diagram of upload module.

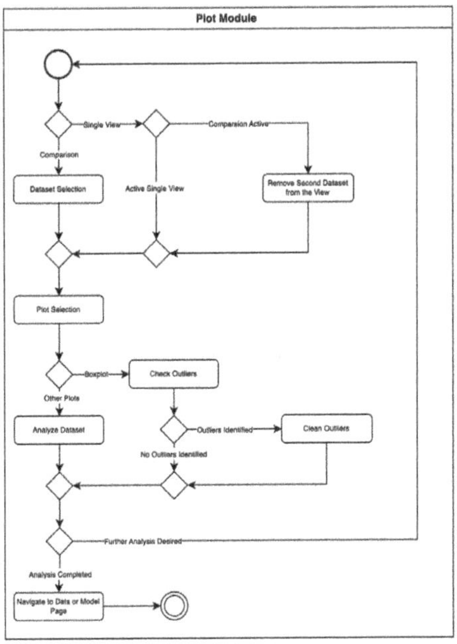


**Figure A2.** UML activity diagram of plot module.

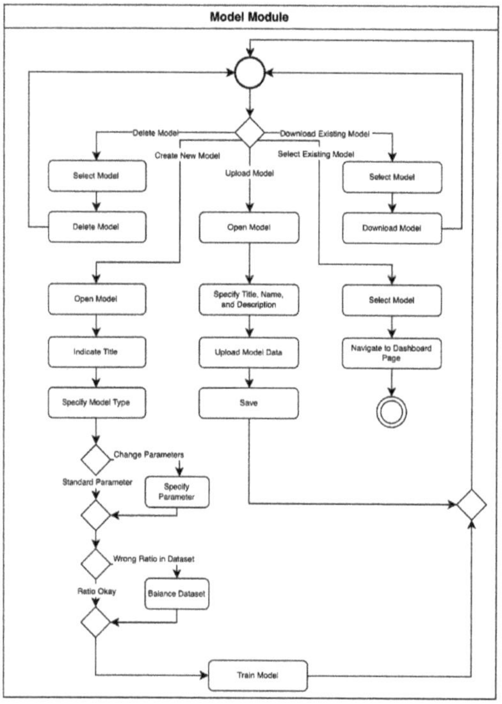


**Figure A3.** UML activity diagram of model module.

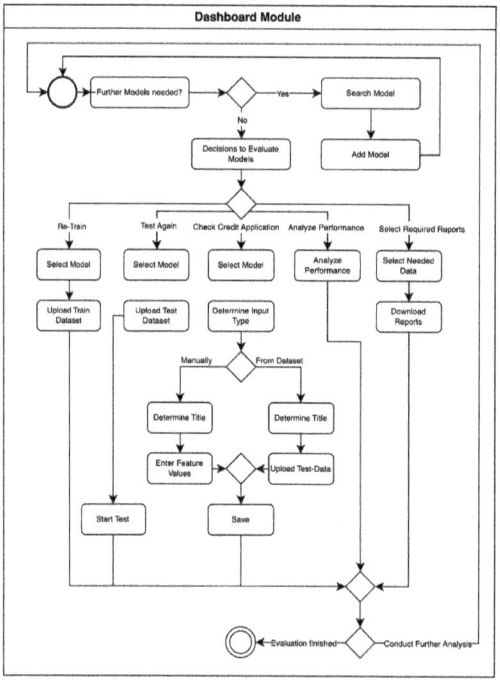


**Figure A4.** UML activity diagram for dashboard module.

## Appendix D. Upload Module

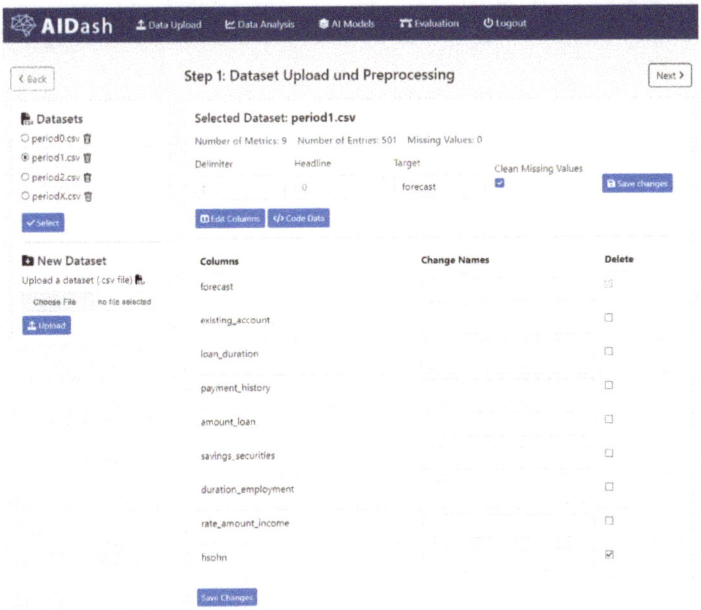

**Figure A5.** Change and selection of columns.

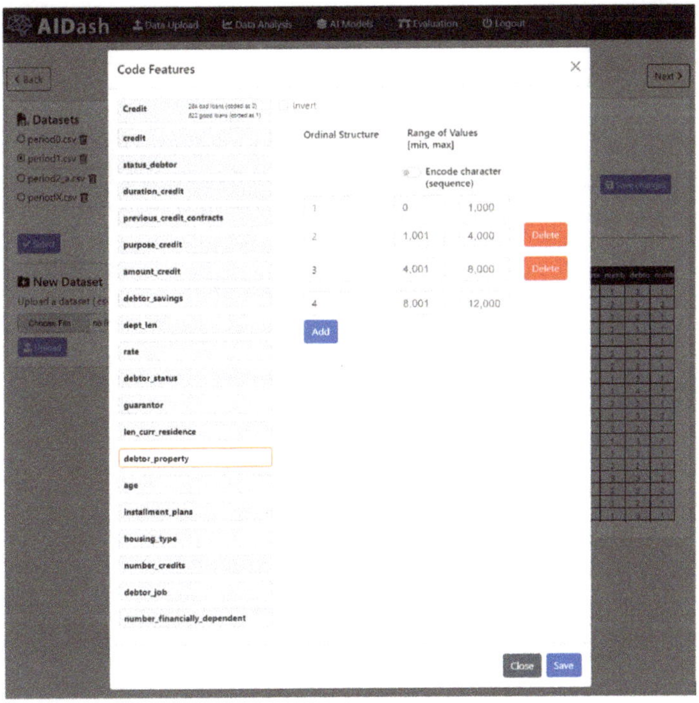

**Figure A6.** Coding features.

## Appendix E. Interactive Plot Module

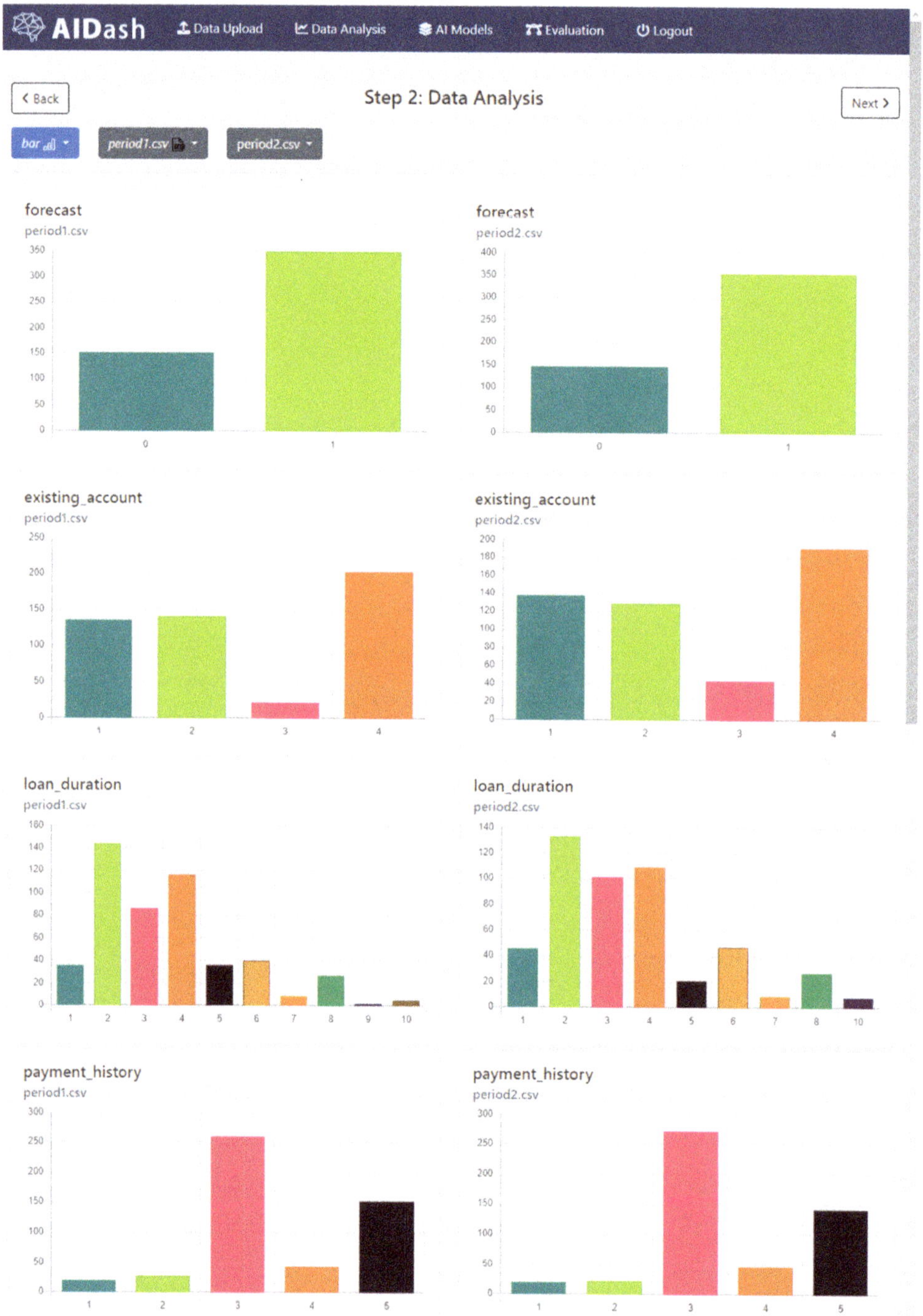


**Figure A7.** Bar plot comparing two datasets.

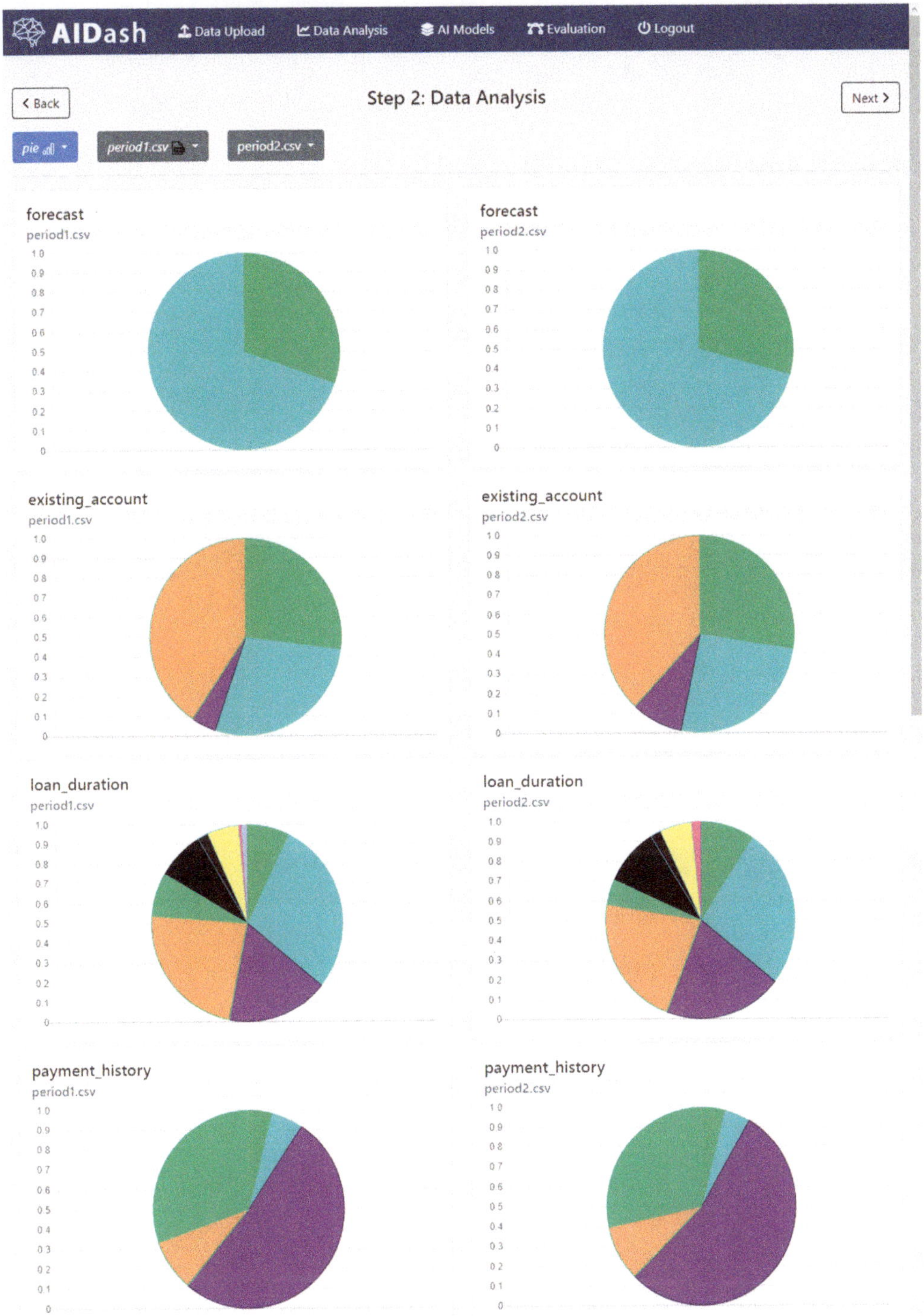


**Figure A8.** Pie plot comparing two datasets.

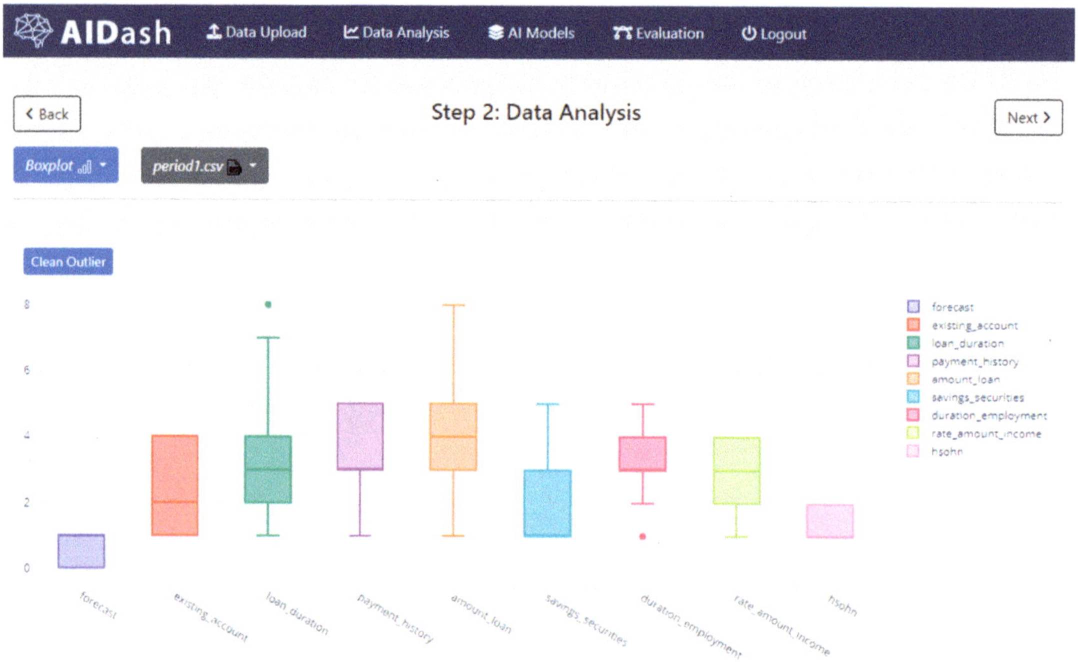


**Figure A9.** Boxplot to clean outliers in selected dataset.

**Figure A10.** Violin plots.

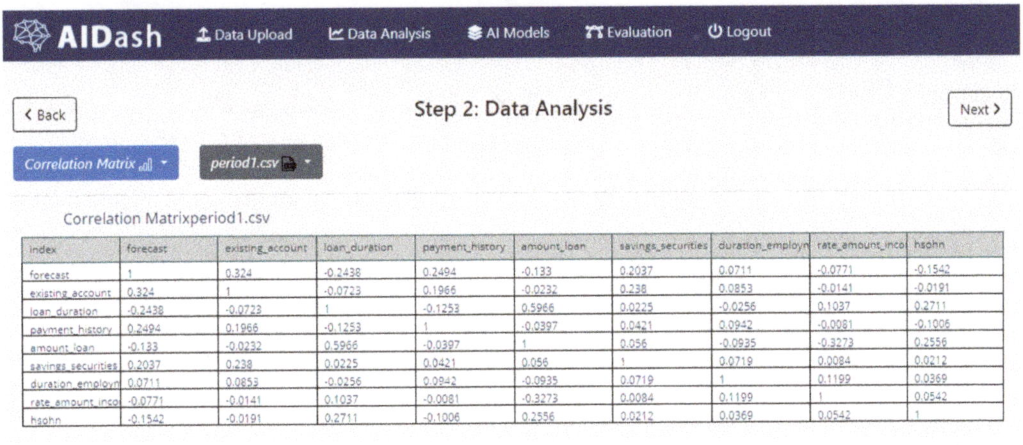


| index | forecast | existing_account | loan_duration | payment_history | amount_loan | savings_securities | duration_employ | rate_amount_inco | hsohn |
|---|---|---|---|---|---|---|---|---|---|
| forecast | 1 | 0.324 | -0.2438 | 0.2494 | -0.133 | 0.2037 | 0.0711 | -0.0771 | -0.1542 |
| existing_account | 0.324 | 1 | -0.0723 | 0.1966 | -0.0232 | 0.238 | 0.0853 | -0.0141 | -0.0191 |
| loan_duration | -0.2438 | -0.0723 | 1 | -0.1253 | 0.5966 | 0.0225 | -0.0256 | 0.1037 | 0.2711 |
| payment_history | 0.2494 | 0.1966 | -0.1253 | 1 | -0.0397 | 0.0421 | 0.0942 | -0.0081 | -0.1006 |
| amount_loan | -0.133 | -0.0232 | 0.5966 | -0.0397 | 1 | 0.056 | -0.0935 | -0.3273 | 0.2556 |
| savings_securities | 0.2037 | 0.238 | 0.0225 | 0.0421 | 0.056 | 1 | 0.0719 | 0.0084 | 0.0212 |
| duration_employ | 0.0711 | 0.0853 | -0.0256 | 0.0942 | -0.0935 | 0.0719 | 1 | 0.1199 | 0.0369 |
| rate_amount_inco | -0.0771 | -0.0141 | 0.1037 | -0.0081 | -0.3273 | 0.0084 | 0.1199 | 1 | 0.0542 |
| hsohn | -0.1542 | -0.0191 | 0.2711 | -0.1006 | 0.2556 | 0.0212 | 0.0369 | 0.0542 | 1 |

**Figure A11.** Confusion matrix of the dataset from Appendix A.

## Appendix F. Model Module

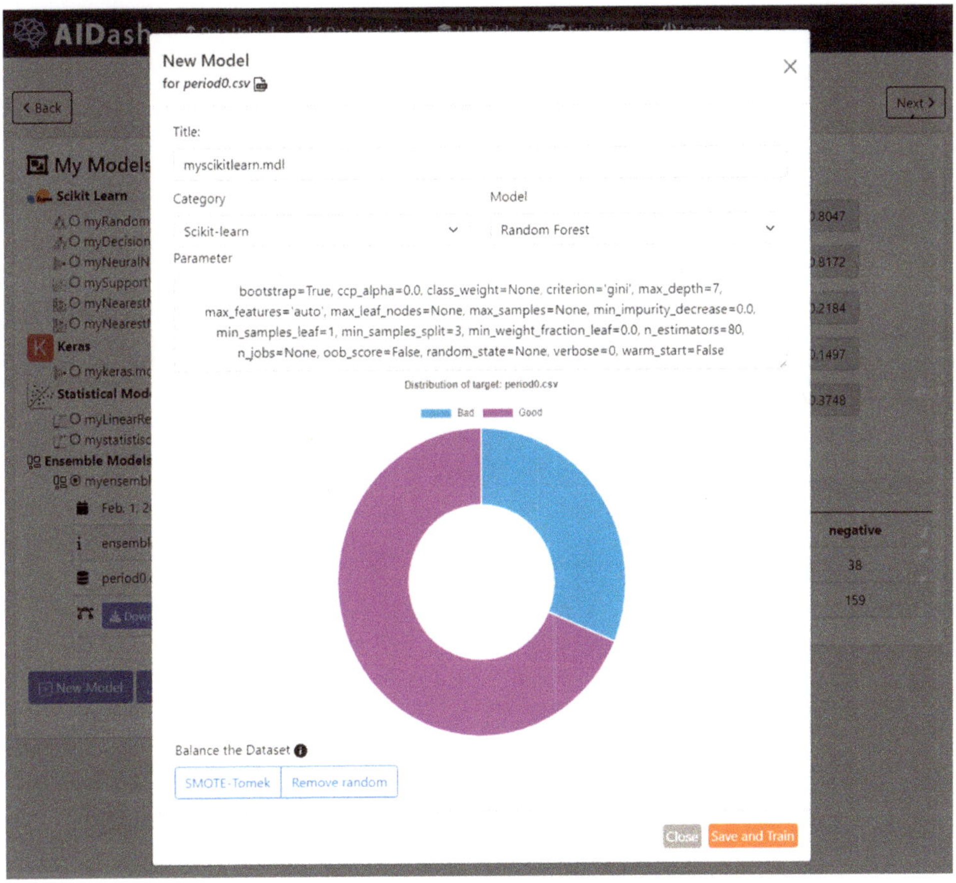


**Figure A12.** Creating a new model with the selected dataset.

## Appendix G. Dashboard Module

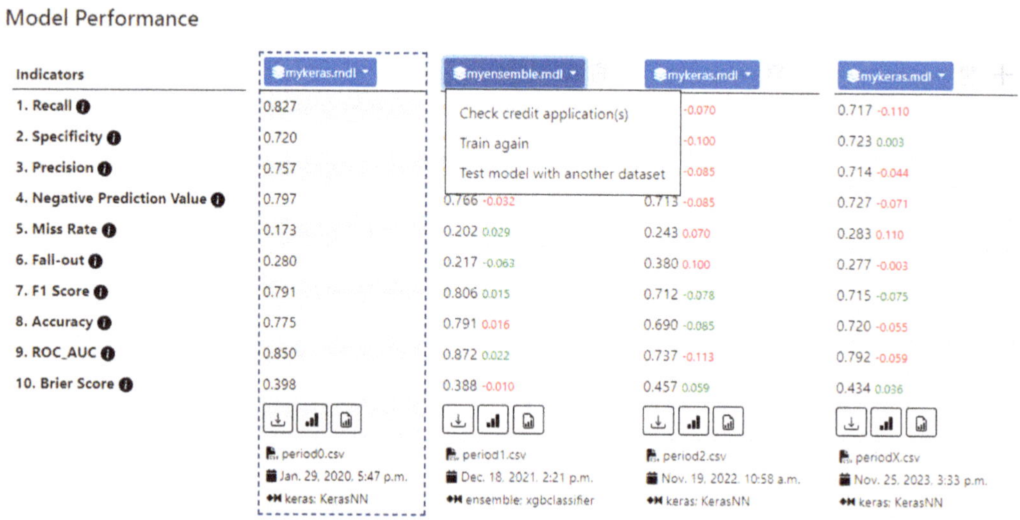

**Figure A13.** Evaluation functions in a comparison view of multiple models.

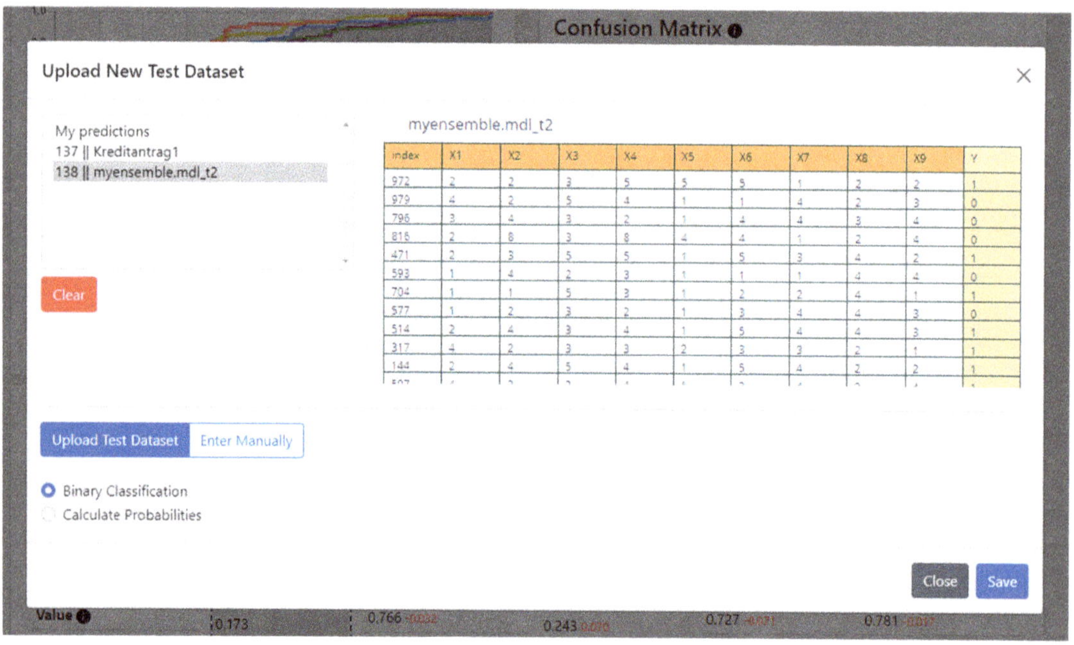

**Figure A14.** Testing model decisions for credit applications directly in AIDash.

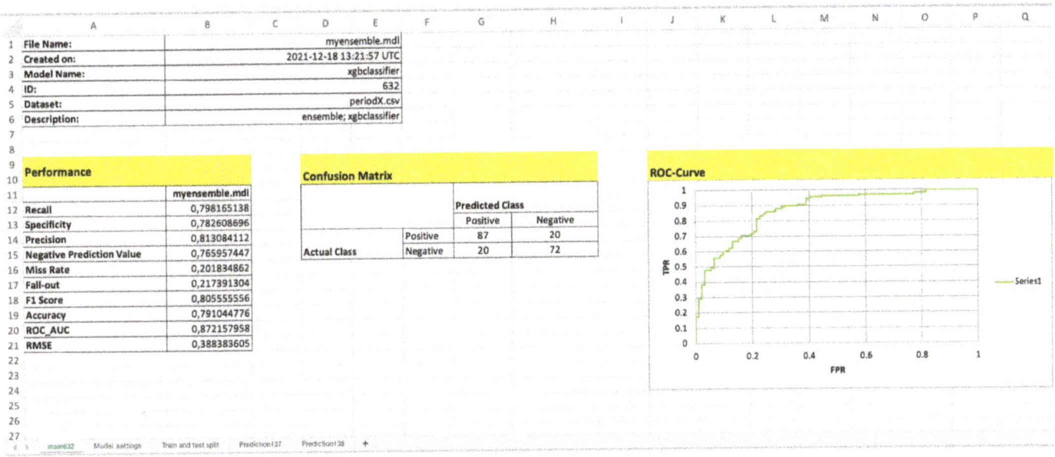

**Figure A15.** An example report of a trained model.

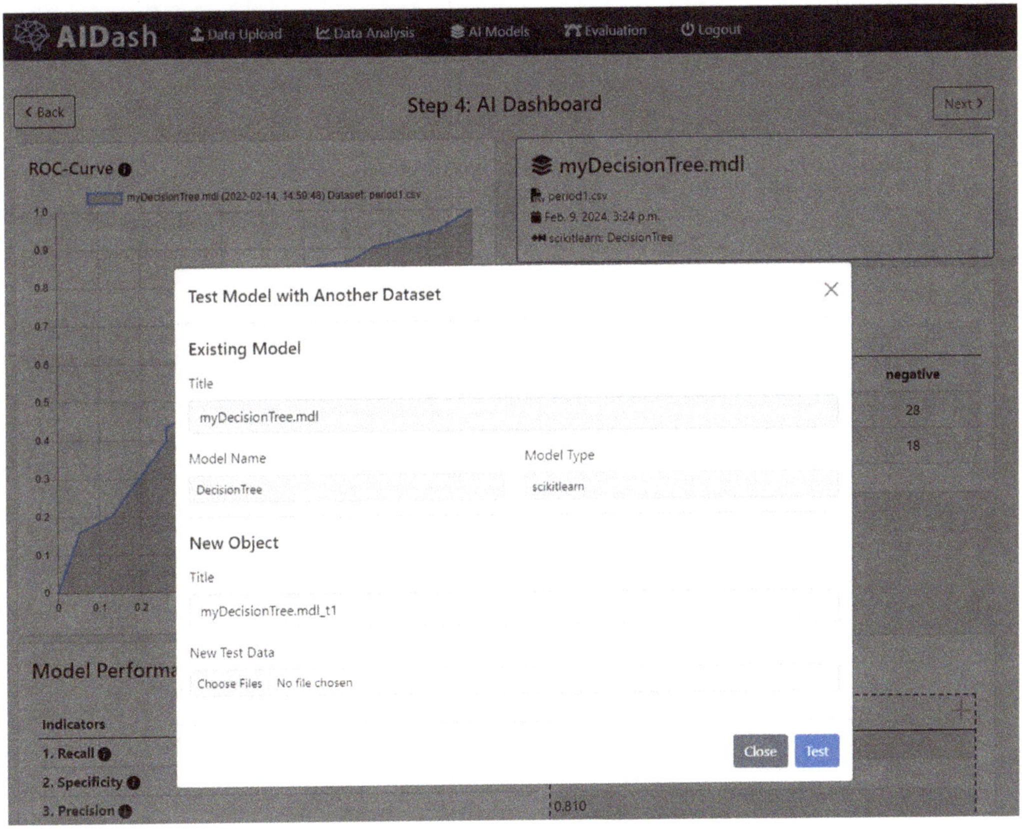

**Figure A16.** Testing model with another dataset in AIDash.

## Appendix H. Technical Details of AIDash

**Table A3.** List of Requirements for the Artifact "AIDash".

| Name | Version |
|---|---|
| Python | 3.8.6 |
| Django | 3.1.3 |
| djangorestframework | 3.12.4 |
| django-reset-migrations | 0.4.0 |
| h5py | 3.1.0 |
| imbalanced_learn | 0.8.0 |
| imblearn | 0.0 |
| matplotlib | 3.3.3 |
| numpy | 1.20.1 |
| openpyxl | 3.0.7 |
| pandas | 1.1.4 |
| plotly | 4.14.3 |
| scikit_learn | 1.0.1 |
| scipy | 1.5.4 |
| seaborn | 0.11.0 |
| setuptools | 49.2.1 |
| tensorflow | 2.5.0 |
| xgboost | 1.4.2 |

## References


1. Giudici, P.; Raffinetti, E. SAFE Artificial Intelligence in finance. *Financ. Res. Lett.* **2023**, *56*, 104088. [CrossRef]
2. Lee, J. Access to Finance for Artificial Intelligence Regulation in the Financial Services Industry. *Eur. Bus. Org. Law. Rev.* **2020**, *21*, 731–757. [CrossRef]
3. Pincovsky, M.; Falcao, A.; Nunes, W.N.; Paula Furtado, A.; Cunha, R.C. Machine Learning applied to credit analysis: A Systematic Literature Review. In Proceedings of the 2021 16th Iberian Conference on Information Systems and Technologies (CISTI), Chaves, Portugal, 23–26 June 2021; pp. 1–5, ISBN 978-989-54659-1-0.
4. Hentzen, J.K.; Hoffmann, A.; Dolan, R.; Pala, E. Artificial intelligence in customer-facing financial services: A systematic literature review and agenda for future research. *Int. J. Bank Mark.* **2022**, *40*, 1299–1336. [CrossRef]
5. Cao, L. AI in Finance: Challenges, Techniques, and Opportunities. *ACM Comput. Surv.* **2023**, *55*, 64. [CrossRef]
6. Cao, L. AI in Finance: A Review. *SSRN J.* **2020**, *2020*, 3647625. [CrossRef]
7. Loyola-Gonzalez, O. Black-Box vs. White-Box: Understanding Their Advantages and Weaknesses from a Practical Point of View. *IEEE Access* **2019**, *7*, 154096–154113. [CrossRef]
8. ZVEI. ZVEI Comments on the European AI Regulation ("AI Act"). Available online: https://www.zvei.org/en/press-media/publications/zvei-comments-on-the-european-ai-regulation-ai-act (accessed on 9 February 2024).
9. Lombardo, G. The AI industry and regulation: Time for implementation? In *Ethical Evidence and Policymaking*, 1st ed.; Iphofen, R., O'Mathúna, D., Eds.; Bristol University Press: Bristol, UK, 2022; pp. 185–200, ISBN 9781447363958.
10. European Commission. Regulation of the European Parliament and of the Council: Laying Down Harmonised Rules on Artificial Intelligence (Artificial Intelligence Act) and Amending Certain Union Legislative Acts. Available online: https://eur-lex.europa.eu/legal-content/EN/TXT/HTML/?uri=CELEX:52021PC0206 (accessed on 28 December 2023).
11. Covington. Artificial Intelligence in Financial Services in Europe. Available online: https://www.knplaw.com/wp-content/uploads/2022/02/Artificial-Intelligence-in-Financial-Services-in-Europe-2022.pdf (accessed on 5 December 2023).
12. ECB. Opinion of the European Central Bank of 29 December 2021 on a Proposal for a Regulation Laying down Harmonised Rules on Artificial Intelligence. Available online: https://eur-lex.europa.eu/legal-content/EN/TXT/PDF/?uri=CELEX:52021AB0040 (accessed on 10 May 2023).
13. Chen, N.; Ribeiro, B.; Chen, A. Financial credit risk assessment: A recent review. *Artif. Intell. Rev.* **2016**, *45*, 1–23. [CrossRef]

14. Bank of England; Prudential Regulation Authority; Financial Conduct Authority. DP5/22—Artificial Intelligence and Machine Learning. Available online: https://www.bankofengland.co.uk/prudential-regulation/publication/2022/october/artificial-intelligence (accessed on 10 May 2023).
15. Sousa, M.R.; Gama, J.; Brandão, E. A new dynamic modeling framework for credit risk assessment. *Expert Syst. Appl.* **2016**, *45*, 341–351. [CrossRef]
16. Son, H.; Hyun, C.; Phan, D.; Hwang, H.J. Data analytic approach for bankruptcy prediction. *Expert Syst. Appl.* **2019**, *138*, 112816. [CrossRef]
17. Gabrielli, G.; Melioli, A.; Bertini, F. High-dimensional Data from Financial Statements for a Bankruptcy Prediction Model. In Proceedings of the 2023 IEEE 39th International Conference on Data Engineering Workshops (ICDEW), Anaheim, CA, USA, 3–7 April 2023; pp. 1–7, ISBN 979-8-3503-2244-6.
18. Tsai, C.-F. Two-stage hybrid learning techniques for bankruptcy prediction. *Stat. Anal.* **2020**, *13*, 565–572. [CrossRef]
19. Pamuk, M.; Grendel, R.O.; Schumann, M. Towards ML-based Platforms in Finance Industry-An ML Approach to Generate Corporate Bankruptcy Probabilities based on Annual Financial Statements. In Proceedings of the 2021 IEEE/ACIS 20th International Fall Conference on Computer and Information Science (ICIS Fall), Xi'an, China, 13–15 October 2021.
20. BaFin. Big Data and Artificial Intelligence: Principles for the Use of Algorithms in Decision-Making Processes. Available online: https://www.bafin.de/dok/16185950 (accessed on 31 January 2023).
21. Deutsche Bundesbank; BaFin. Machine Learning in Risk Models—Characteristics and Supervisory Priorities: Consultation Paper. Available online: https://www.bundesbank.de/resource/blob/793670/61532e24c3298d8b24d4d15a34f503a8/mL/2021-07-15-ml-konsultationspapier-data.pdf (accessed on 11 September 2022).
22. AMF. Artificial Intelligence in Finance: Recommendations for Its Responsible Use. Available online: https://lautorite.qc.ca/fileadmin/lautorite/grand_public/publications/professionnels/rapport-intelligence-artificielle-finance-an.pdf (accessed on 5 December 2023).
23. Peffers, K.; Tuunanen, T.; Rothenberger, M.A.; Chatterjee, S. A Design Science Research Methodology for Information Systems Research. *J. Manag. Inf. Syst.* **2007**, *24*, 45–77. [CrossRef]
24. Chapman, P. *CRISP-DM 1.0: Step-by-Step Data Mining Guide*; SPSS: Southall, UK, 2000.
25. Bazarbash, M. *FinTech in Financial Inclusion: Machine Learning Applications in Assessing Credit Risk*; International Monetary Fund: Washington, DC, USA, 2019; ISBN 9781498314428.
26. Kurshan, E.; Shen, H.; Chen, J. Towards self-regulating AI. In Proceedings of the ICAIF '20: ACM International Conference on AI in Finance, New York, NY, USA, 15–16 October 2020; Balch, T., Ed.; ACM: New York, NY, USA, 2020; pp. 1–8, ISBN 9781450375849.
27. LeCun, Y.; Bengio, Y.; Hinton, G. Deep learning. *Nature* **2015**, *521*, 436–444. [CrossRef] [PubMed]
28. Bertini, F. Artificial Intelligence and data privacy. *Sist. Intelligenti* **2023**, *35*, 477–484. [CrossRef]
29. ACPR. Governance of Artificial Intelligence in Finance. Available online: https://acpr.banque-france.fr/en/governance-artificial-intelligence-finance (accessed on 14 February 2024).
30. De Nederlandsche Bank. General Principles for the Use of Artificial Intelligence in the Financial Sector. Available online: https://www.dnb.nl/media/voffsric/general-principles-for-the-use-of-artificial-intelligence-in-the-financial-sector.pdf (accessed on 25 May 2023).
31. Banca D'Italia. Artificial Intelligence in Credit Scoring: An Analysis of Some Experiences in the Italian Financial System. Available online: https://www.bancaditalia.it/pubblicazioni/qef/2022-0721/QEF_721_EN.pdf?language_id=1 (accessed on 5 December 2023).
32. Banca D'Italia. Legal Framework. Available online: https://www.bancaditalia.it/compiti/vigilanza/normativa/index.html?com.dotmarketing.htmlpage.language=1 (accessed on 16 May 2023).
33. Banco de España. Machine Learning in Credit Risk: Measuring the Dilemma between Prediction and Supervisory Cost. *Documentos de Trabajo N.° 2032*. Available online: https://www.bde.es/f/webbde/SES/Secciones/Publicaciones/PublicacionesSeriadas/DocumentosTrabajo/20/Files/dt2032e.pdf (accessed on 24 May 2023).
34. Kruse, L.; Wunderlich, N.; Beck, R. Artificial Intelligence for the Financial Services Industry: What Challenges Organizations to Succeed. In Proceedings of the 52nd Hawaii International Conference on System Sciences, Maui, HI, USA, 8–11 January 2019; Bui, T., Ed.; 2019.
35. Pamuk, M.; Schumann, M.; Nickerson, R.C. What Do the Regulators Mean? A Taxonomy of Regulatory Principles for the Use of AI in Financial Services. *Make* **2024**, *6*, 143–155. [CrossRef]
36. Sanz, J.L.C.; Zhu, Y. Toward Scalable Artificial Intelligence in Finance. In Proceedings of the 2021 IEEE International Conference on Services Computing (SCC), Chicago, IL, USA, 5–10 September 2021; pp. 460–469, ISBN 978-1-6654-1683-2.
37. OECD. SAFE (Sustainable, Accurate, Fair and Explainable). Available online: https://oecd.ai/en/catalogue/metrics/safe-(sustainable-accurate-fair-and-explainable) (accessed on 28 December 2023).
38. OECD. OECD Legal Instruments: Recommendation of the Council on Artificial Intelligence. Available online: https://legalinstruments.oecd.org/en/instruments/OECD-LEGAL-0449#backgroundInformation (accessed on 28 November 2023).
39. OECD. Artificial Intelligence, Machine Learning and Big Data in Finance—OECD. Available online: https://www.oecd.org/finance/artificial-intelligence-machine-learning-big-data-in-finance.htm (accessed on 5 October 2023).
40. Cooper, H.M. Organizing knowledge syntheses: A taxonomy of literature reviews. *Knowl. Soc.* **1988**, *1*, 104–126. [CrossRef]

41. vom Brocke, J.; Simons, A.; Riemer, K.; Niehaves, B.; Plattfaut, R.; Cleven, A. Standing on the Shoulders of Giants: Challenges and Recommendations of Literature Search in Information Systems Research. *Commun. Assoc. Inf. Syst.* **2015**, *37*, 9. [CrossRef]
42. Fahrmeir, L.; Hamerle, A. *Multivariate Statistische Verfahren*; Walter de Gruyter: Berlin, NY, USA, 1984; ISBN 9783110085099.
43. Ribeiro, M.T.; Singh, S.; Guestrin, C. Why Should I Trust You? In Proceedings of the KDD '16: The 22nd ACM SIGKDD International Conference on Knowledge Discovery and Data Mining, San Francisco, CA, USA, 13–17 August 2016; Krishnapuram, B., Shah, M., Smola, A., Aggarwal, C., Shen, D., Rastogi, R., Eds.; ACM: New York, NY, USA, 2016; pp. 1135–1144, ISBN 9781450342322.
44. Leo, M.; Sharma, S.; Maddulety, K. Machine Learning in Banking Risk Management: A Literature Review. *Risks* **2019**, *7*, 29. [CrossRef]
45. Yu, L.; Zhang, X.; Yin, H. An extreme learning machine based virtual sample generation method with feature engineering for credit risk assessment with data scarcity. *Expert Syst. Appl.* **2022**, *202*, 117363. [CrossRef]
46. Liu, W.; Fan, H.; Xia, M. Step-wise multi-grained augmented gradient boosting decision trees for credit scoring. *Eng. Appl. Artif. Intell.* **2021**, *97*, 104036. [CrossRef]
47. Wang, Y.; Zhang, Y.; Lu, Y.; Yu, X. A Comparative Assessment of Credit Risk Model Based on Machine Learning—A case study of bank loan data. *Procedia Comput. Sci.* **2020**, *174*, 141–149. [CrossRef]
48. Fan, S.; Shen, Y.; Peng, S. Improved ML-Based Technique for Credit Card Scoring in Internet Financial Risk Control. *Complexity* **2020**, *2020*, 8706285. [CrossRef]
49. Yigitbasioglu, O.M.; Velcu, O. A review of dashboards in performance management: Implications for design and research. *Int. J. Account. Inf. Syst.* **2012**, *13*, 41–59. [CrossRef]
50. Few, S. *Information Dashboard Design: The Effective Visual Communication of Data*, 1st ed.; O'Reilly & Associates: Sebastopol, CA, USA, 2006; ISBN 978-0-596-10016-2.
51. Noonpakdee, W.; Khunkornsiri, T.; Phothichai, A.; Danaisawat, K. A framework for analyzing and developing dashboard templates for small and medium enterprises. In Proceedings of the 2018 5th International Conference on Industrial Engineering and Applications (ICIEA), Singapore, 26–28 April 2018; pp. 479–483, ISBN 978-1-5386-5747-8.
52. Hoo, Z.H.; Candlish, J.; Teare, D. What is an ROC curve? *Emerg. Med. J.* **2017**, *34*, 357–359. [CrossRef] [PubMed]
53. Pace, A.; Buttigieg, S.C. Can hospital dashboards provide visibility of information from bedside to board? A case study approach. *J. Health Organ. Manag.* **2017**, *31*, 142–161. [CrossRef] [PubMed]
54. Ghazisaeidi, M.; Safdari, R.; Torabi, M.; Mirzaee, M.; Farzi, J.; Goodini, A. Development of Performance Dashboards in Healthcare Sector: Key Practical Issues. *Acta Inform. Med.* **2015**, *23*, 317–321. [CrossRef] [PubMed]
55. Maheshwari, D.; Janssen, M. Dashboards for supporting organizational development. In Proceedings of the ICEGOV2014: 8th International Conference on Theory and Practice of Electronic Governance, Guimaraes, Portugal, 27–30 October 2014; Estevez, E., Janssen, M., Barbosa, L.S., Eds.; ACM: New York, NY, USA, 2014; pp. 178–185, ISBN 9781605586113.
56. Fischer, M.J.; Kourany, W.M.; Sovern, K.; Forrester, K.; Griffin, C.; Lightner, N.; Loftus, S.; Murphy, K.; Roth, G.; Palevsky, P.M.; et al. Development, implementation and user experience of the Veterans Health Administration (VHA) dialysis dashboard. *BMC Nephrol.* **2020**, *21*, 136. [CrossRef] [PubMed]
57. Rahman, A.A.; Adamu, Y.B.; Harun, P. Review on dashboard application from managerial perspective. In Proceedings of the 2017 5th International Conference on Research and Innovation in Information Systems (ICRIIS), Langkawi, Malaysia, 16–17 July 2017; pp. 1–5, ISBN 978-1-5090-3035-4.
58. Maury, E.; Boldi, M.-O.; Greub, G.; Chavez, V.; Jaton, K.; Opota, O. An Automated Dashboard to Improve Laboratory COVID-19 Diagnostics Management. *Front. Digit. Health* **2021**, *3*, 773986. [CrossRef] [PubMed]
59. Büdel, V.; Fritsch, A.; Oberweis, A. Integrating sustainability into day-to-day business. In Proceedings of the ICT4S2020: 7th International Conference on ICT for Sustainability, Bristol, UK, 21–26 June 2020; Chitchyan, R., Schien, D., Moreira, A., Combemale, B., Eds.; ACM: New York, NY, USA, 2020; pp. 56–65, ISBN 9781450375955.
60. Pauwels, K.; Ambler, T.; Clark, B.H.; LaPointe, P.; Reibstein, D.; Skiera, B.; Wierenga, B.; Wiesel, T. Dashboards as a Service. *J. Serv. Res.* **2009**, *12*, 175–189. [CrossRef]
61. Lin, C.-Y.; Liang, F.-W.; Li, S.-T.; Lu, T.-H. 5S Dashboard Design Principles for Self-Service Business Intelligence Tool User. *J. Big Data Res.* **2018**, *1*, 5–19. [CrossRef]
62. Presthus, W.; Canales, C.A. Business Intelligence Dashboard Design. A Case Study of a Large Logistics Company. *Norsk Konferanse for Organisasjoners Bruk av IT*. 2015. Available online: https://www.semanticscholar.org/paper/BUSINESS-INTELLIGENCE-DASHBOARD-DESIGN.-A-CASE-OF-A-Presthus-Canales/fc49fcfc4f345c748246d24dc47b5972323d1791 (accessed on 1 May 2024).
63. Cankaya, E.C.; Odekirk, D. Creating Effective and Efficient User Dashboards through Dynamic Customization and Well-Designed Webpage Visualization. Available online: https://huichawaii.org/wp-content/uploads/2019/06/Cankaya-Ebru-Celikel-2019-STEM-HUIC.pdf (accessed on 1 February 2024).
64. Liawatimena, S.; Hendric Spits Warnars, H.L.; Trisetyarso, A.; Abdurahman, E.; Soewito, B.; Wibowo, A.; Gaol, F.L.; Abbas, B.S. Django Web Framework Software Metrics Measurement Using Radon and Pylint. In Proceedings of the 2018 Indonesian Association for Pattern Recognition International Conference (INAPR), Jakarta, Indonesia, 7–8 September 2018; pp. 218–222, ISBN 978-1-5386-9422-0.
65. Elliott, T. The State of the Octoverse: Machine learning. Available online: https://github.blog/2019-01-24-the-state-of-the-octoverse-machine-learning/ (accessed on 9 February 2024).

66. Batista, G.E.; Bazzan, A.L.; Monard, M.C. Balancing Training Data for Automated Annotation of Keywords: A Case Study. *Wob* **2003**, *3*, 10–18.
67. Zhao, J.; Wu, Z.; Wu, B. An AdaBoost-DT Model for Credit Scoring. In Proceedings of the 20th Wuhan International Conference on E-Business, WHICEB 2021, Wuhan, China, 28–30 May 2021.
68. Moula, F.E.; Guotai, C.; Abedin, M.Z. Credit default prediction modeling: An application of support vector machine. *Risk Manag.* **2017**, *19*, 158–187. [CrossRef]
69. Khemakhem, S.; Ben Said, F.; Boujelbene, Y. Credit risk assessment for unbalanced datasets based on data mining, artificial neural network and support vector machines. *J. Model. Manag.* **2018**, *13*, 932–951. [CrossRef]
70. Kouki, M.; Elkhaldi, A. Toward a Predicting Model of Firm Bankruptcy: Evidence from the Tunisian Context. *Middle East. Financ. Econ.* **2011**, *14*, 26–43.
71. Pamuk, M.; Schumann, M. Opening a New Era with Machine Learning in Financial Services? Forecasting Corporate Credit Ratings Based on Annual Financial Statements. *Int. J. Financial Stud.* **2023**, *11*, 96. [CrossRef]
72. Addi, K.B.; Souissi, N. An Ontology-Based Model for Credit Scoring Knowledge in Microfinance: Towards a Better Decision Making. In Proceedings of the 2020 IEEE 10th International Conference on Intelligent Systems (IS), Varna, Bulgaria, 28–30 August 2020; pp. 380–385, ISBN 978-1-7281-5456-5.
73. Adisa, J.; Ojo, S.; Owolawi, P.; Pretorius, A.; Ojo, S.O. Credit Score Prediction using Genetic Algorithm-LSTM Technique. In Proceedings of the 2022 Conference on Information Communications Technology and Society (ICTAS), Durban, South Africa, 9–10 March 2022; pp. 1–6, ISBN 978-1-6654-4019-6.
74. Arner, D.W.; Zetzsche, D.A.; Buckley, R.P.; Barberis, J.N. FinTech and RegTech: Enabling Innovation While Preserving Financial Stability. *Georget. J. Int. Aff.* **2017**, *18*, 47–58. [CrossRef]
75. Baier, L.; Jöhren, F.; Seebacher, S. Challenges in the deployment and operation of machine learning in practice. *Res. Pap.* **2019**, 1–15.
76. Baldo, D.R.; Regio, M.S.; Manssour, I.H. Visual analytics for monitoring credit scoring models. *Inf. Vis.* **2023**, *22*, 340–357. [CrossRef]
77. Berrada, I.R.; Barramou, F.Z.; Alami, O.B. A review of Artificial Intelligence approach for credit risk assessment. In Proceedings of the 2022 2nd International Conference on Artificial Intelligence and Signal Processing (AISP), Vijayawada, India, 12–14 February 2022; pp. 1–5, ISBN 978-1-6654-4290-9.
78. Cao, N.T.; Tran, L.H.; Ton-That, A.H. Using machine learning to create a credit scoring model in banking and finance. In Proceedings of the 2021 IEEE Asia-Pacific Conference on Computer Science and Data Engineering (CSDE), Brisbane, Australia, 8–10 December 2021; pp. 1–5, ISBN 978-1-6654-9552-3.
79. Chornous, G.; Nikolskyi, I. Business-Oriented Feature Selection for Hybrid Classification Model of Credit Scoring. In Proceedings of the 2018 IEEE Second International Conference on Data Stream Mining & Processing (DSMP), Lviv, Ukraine, 21–25 August 2018; pp. 397–401, ISBN 978-1-5386-2874-4.
80. Dastile, X.; Celik, T. Making Deep Learning-Based Predictions for Credit Scoring Explainable. *IEEE Access* **2021**, *9*, 50426–50440. [CrossRef]
81. Devi, C.R.D.; Chezian, R.M. A relative evaluation of the performance of ensemble learning in credit scoring. In Proceedings of the 2016 IEEE International Conference on Advances in Computer Applications (ICACA), Coimbatore, India, 24 October 2016; pp. 161–165, ISBN 978-1-5090-3769-8.
82. Devos, A.; Dhondt, J.; Stripling, E.; Baesens, B.; Broucke, S.v.; Sukhatme, G. Profit Maximizing Logistic Regression Modeling for Credit Scoring. In Proceedings of the 2018 IEEE Data Science Workshop (DSW), Lausanne, Switzerland, 4–6 June 2018; pp. 125–129, ISBN 978-1-5386-4410-2.
83. Dyczkowski, M.; Korczak, J.; Dudycz, H. Multi-criteria Evaluation of the Intelligent Dashboard for SME Managers based on Scorecard Framework. In Proceedings of the 2014 Federated Conference on Computer Science and Information Systems, Warsaw, Poland, 7–10 September 2014; pp. 1147–1155.
84. Guntay, L.; Bozan, E.; Tigrak, U.; Durdu, T.; Ozkahya, G.E. An Explainable Credit Scoring Framework: A Use Case of Addressing Challenges in Applied Machine Learning. In Proceedings of the 2022 IEEE Technology and Engineering Management Conference (TEMSCON EUROPE), Izmir, Turkey, 25–29 April 2022; pp. 222–227, ISBN 978-1-6654-8313-1.
85. Hassan, A.; Jayousi, R. Financial Services Credit Scoring System Using Data Mining. In Proceedings of the 2020 IEEE 14th International Conference on Application of Information and Communication Technologies (AICT), Tashkent, Uzbekistan, 7–9 October 2020; pp. 1–7, ISBN 978-1-7281-7386-3.
86. Hooman, A.; Marthandan, G.; Yusoff, W.F.W.; Omid, M.; Karamizadeh, S. Statistical and Data Mining Methods in Credit Scoring. *J. Dev. Areas* **2016**, *50*, 371–381. [CrossRef]
87. Hoover, S. California Credit Dashboard. California Policy Lab [Online]. 19 November 2023. Available online: https://www.capolicylab.org/california-credit-dashboard/ (accessed on 7 March 2024).
88. Ismawati, I.Y.; Faturohman, T. Credit Risk Scoring Model for Consumer Financing: Logistic Regression Method. In *Comparative Analysis of Trade and Finance in Emerging Economies*; Barnett, W.A., Sergi, B.S., Eds.; Emerald Publishing Limited: Leeds, UK, 2023; pp. 167–189, ISBN 978-1-80455-759-4.

89. Jemai, J.; Chaieb, M.; Zarrad, A. A Big Data Mining Approach for Credit Risk Analysis. In Proceedings of the 2022 International Symposium on Networks, Computers and Communications (ISNCC), Shenzhen, China, 19–22 July 2022; pp. 1–6, ISBN 978-1-6654-8544-9.
90. Jin, S. Research on Bank Credit Risk Assessment Model based on artificial intelligence algorithm. In Proceedings of the 2022 2nd International Symposium on Artificial Intelligence and its Application on Media (ISAIAM), Xi'an, China, 10–12 June 2022; pp. 128–134, ISBN 978-1-6654-8541-8.
91. Karim, M.; Samad, M.F.; Muntasir, F. Improving Performance Factors of an Imbalanced Credit Risk Dataset Using SMOTE. In Proceedings of the 2022 4th International Conference on Electrical, Computer & Telecommunication Engineering (ICECTE), Rajshahi, Bangladesh, 29–31 December 2022; pp. 1–4, ISBN 979-8-3503-2054-1.
92. Khemakhem, S.; Boujelbene, Y. Predicting credit risk on the basis of financial and non-financial variables and data mining. *Rev. Account. Financ.* **2018**, *17*, 316–340. [CrossRef]
93. Kossow, N.; Windwehr, S.; Jenkins, M. Algorithmic Transparency and Accountability. 2024. Available online: http://www.jstor.org/stable/resrep30838 (accessed on 8 March 2024).
94. Kothandapani, H.P. Drivers and Barriers of Adopting Interactive Dashboard Reporting in the Finance Sector: An Empirical Investigation. *Rev. Contemp. Bus. Anal.* **2019**, *2*, 45–70.
95. Li, Y. Credit Risk Prediction Based on Machine Learning Methods. In Proceedings of the 2019 14th International Conference on Computer Science & Education (ICCSE), Toronto, ON, Canada, 19–21 August 2019; pp. 1011–1013, ISBN 978-1-7281-1846-8.
96. Luo, C. A comprehensive decision support approach for credit scoring. *Ind. Manag. Data Syst.* **2020**, *120*, 280–290. [CrossRef]
97. Maurya, A.; Gaur, S. A Decision Tree Classifier Based Ensemble Approach to Credit Score Classification. In Proceedings of the 2023 International Conference on Computing, Communication, and Intelligent Systems (ICCCIS), Greater Noida, India, 3–4 November 2023; pp. 620–624, ISBN 979-8-3503-0611-8.
98. Mirza, F.K.; Ogrenci, A.S. Using Hybrid Approaches for Credit Application Scoring. In Proceedings of the 2023 IEEE 23rd International Symposium on Computational Intelligence and Informatics (CINTI), Budapest, Hungary, 20–22 November 2023; pp. 111–116, ISBN 979-8-3503-4294-9.
99. Mittal, A.; Shrivastava, A.; Saxena, A.; Manoria, M. A Study on Credit Risk Assessment in Banking Sector using Data Mining Techniques. In Proceedings of the 2018 International Conference on Advanced Computation and Telecommunication (ICACAT), Bhopal, India, 28–29 December 2018; pp. 1–5, ISBN 978-1-5386-5367-8.
100. Nieto, M.J. Banks, climate risk and financial stability. *J. Financ. Regul. Compliance* **2019**, *27*, 243–262. [CrossRef]
101. Ordabayeva, Z.; Moldagulova, A.; Riza, I. Building a Credit Scoring Model Based on the Type of Target Variable. In Proceedings of the 2023 IEEE International Conference on Smart Information Systems and Technologies (SIST), Astana, Kazakhstan, 4–6 May 2023; pp. 31–36, ISBN 979-8-3503-3504-0.
102. Pan, J.-S.; Wu, Y.-Q.; Lv, Y.; Lin, Q.-Y.; Peng, J.-R.; Ye, M.; Cai, X.-F.; Huang, W. Domain-adversarial neural network with joint-distribution adaption for credit risk classification. In Proceedings of the International Conference on Electronic Business, Chiayi, Taiwan, 19–23 October 2023.
103. Paul, S.; Gupta, A.; Kar, A.K.; Singh, V. An Automatic Deep Reinforcement Learning Based Credit Scoring Model using Deep-Q Network for Classification of Customer Credit Requests. In Proceedings of the 2023 IEEE International Symposium on Technology and Society (ISTAS), Swansea, UK, 13–15 September 2023; pp. 1–8, ISBN 979-8-3503-2486-0.
104. Punniyamoorthy, M.; Sridevi, P. Identification of a standard AI based technique for credit risk analysis. *Benchmarking Int. J.* **2016**, *23*, 1381–1390. [CrossRef]
105. Qiu, Z.; Li, Y.; Ni, P.; Li, G. Credit Risk Scoring Analysis Based on Machine Learning Models. In Proceedings of the 2019 6th International Conference on Information Science and Control Engineering (ICISCE), Shanghai, China, 20–22 December 2019; pp. 220–224, ISBN 978-1-7281-5712-2.
106. Ranpara, R.D.; Patel, P.S. An Ensemble Learning Approach to Improve Credit Scoring Accuracy for Imbalanced Data. In Proceedings of the 2023 International Conference on Integrated Intelligence and Communication Systems (ICIICS), Kalaburagi, India, 24–25 November 2023; pp. 1–5, ISBN 979-8-3503-1545-5.
107. Sadok, H.; Mahboub, H.; Chaibi, H.; Saadane, R.; Wahbi, M. Applications of Artificial Intelligence in Finance: Prospects, Limits and Risks. In Proceedings of the 2023 International Conference on Digital Age & Technological Advances for Sustainable Development (ICDATA), Casablanca, Morocco, 3–5 May 2023; pp. 145–149, ISBN 979-8-3503-1111-2.
108. Safiya Parvin, A.; Saleena, B. An Ensemble Classifier Model to Predict Credit Scoring—Comparative Analysis. In Proceedings of the 2020 IEEE International Symposium on Smart Electronic Systems (iSES) (Formerly iNiS), Chennai, India, 14–16 December 2020; pp. 27–30, ISBN 978-1-6654-0478-5.
109. Septama, H.D.; Yulianti, T.; Budiyanto, D.; Mulyadi, S.M.; Cahyana, A.H. A Comparative Analysis of Machine Learning Algorithms for Credit Risk Scoring using Chi-Square Feature Selection. In Proceedings of the 2023 International Conference on Converging Technology in Electrical and Information Engineering (ICCTEIE), Bandar Lampung, Indonesia, 25–26 October 2023; pp. 32–37, ISBN 979-8-3503-7064-5.
110. Shoumo, S.Z.H.; Dhruba, M.I.M.; Hossain, S.; Ghani, N.H.; Arif, H.; Islam, S. Application of Machine Learning in Credit Risk Assessment: A Prelude to Smart Banking. In Proceedings of the TENCON 2019—2019 IEEE Region 10 Conference (TENCON), Kochi, India, 17–20 October 2019; pp. 2023–2028, ISBN 978-1-7281-1895-6.

111. Soares de Melo Junior, L.; Nardini, F.M.; Renso, C.; Fernandes de Macedo, J.A. An Empirical Comparison of Classification Algorithms for Imbalanced Credit Scoring Datasets. In Proceedings of the 2019 18th IEEE International Conference On Machine Learning And Applications (ICMLA), Boca Raton, FL, USA, 16–19 December 2019; pp. 747–754, ISBN 978-1-7281-4550-1.
112. Solow-Niederman, A.; Choi, Y.J.; van den Broeck, G. The Institutional Life of Algorithmic Risk Assessment. *Berkeley Technol. Law J.* **2019**, *34*, 705–744.
113. Virág, M.; Nyitrai, T. Is there a trade-off between the predictive power and the interpretability of bankruptcy models? The case of the first Hungarian bankruptcy prediction model. *Acta Oeconomica* **2014**, *64*, 419–440. [CrossRef]
114. Wang, H.; Li, C.; Gu, B.; Min, W. Does AI-based Credit Scoring Improve Financial Inclusion? Evidence from Online Payday Lending. In Proceedings of the International Conference on Information Systems (ICIS) 2019 Conference, Munich, Germany, 15–18 December 2019.
115. Wei, Y. Application of Machine Learning and Artificial Intelligence in Credit Risk Assessment. In Proceedings of the 2023 2nd International Conference on Artificial Intelligence and Autonomous Robot Systems (AIARS), Bristol, UK, 29–31 July 2023; pp. 150–156, ISBN 979-8-3503-2435-8.
116. Wilson Drakes, C.-A. Algorithmic decision-making systems: Boon or bane to credit risk assessment? In Proceedings of the 29th European Conference on Information Systems–Human Values Crisis in a Digitizing World, ECIS 2021, Morocco, Africa, 14–16 June 2021.
117. Xiao, J.; Wang, R. A Triplet Deep Neural Networks Model for Customer Credit Scoring. In Proceedings of the 2023 3rd International Conference on Consumer Electronics and Computer Engineering (ICCECE), Guangzhou, China, 6–8 January 2023; pp. 511–514, ISBN 979-8-3503-3157-8.
118. Xiao, J.; Xie, L.; Liu, D.; Xiao, Y.; Hu, Y. A clustering and selection based transfer ensemble model for customer credit scoring. *Filomat* **2016**, *30*, 4015–4026. [CrossRef]
119. Yotsawat, W.; Wattuya, P.; Srivihok, A. A Novel Method for Credit Scoring Based on Cost-Sensitive Neural Network Ensemble. *IEEE Access* **2021**, *9*, 78521–78537. [CrossRef]
120. Yu, L.; Li, X.; Tang, L.; Gao, L. An ELM-based Classification Algorithm with Optimal Cutoff Selection for Credit Risk Assessment. *Filomat* **2016**, *30*, 4027–4036. [CrossRef]
121. Zhang, X.; Yang, Y.; Zhou, Z. A novel credit scoring model based on optimized random forest. In Proceedings of the 2018 IEEE 8th Annual Computing and Communication Workshop and Conference (CCWC), Las Vegas, NV, USA, 8–10 January 2018; pp. 60–65, ISBN 978-1-5386-4649-6.
122. Zhong, Y.; Wang, H. Internet Financial Credit Scoring Models Based on Deep Forest and Resampling Methods. *IEEE Access* **2023**, *11*, 8689–8700. [CrossRef]
123. Zhu, B.; Yang, W.; Wang, H.; Yuan, Y. A hybrid deep learning model for consumer credit scoring. In Proceedings of the 2018 International Conference on Artificial Intelligence and Big Data (ICAIBD), Chengdu, China, 26–28 May 2018; pp. 205–208, ISBN 978-1-5386-6987-7.

machine learning & knowledge extraction

MDPI

*Article*

# Birthweight Range Prediction and Classification: A Machine Learning-Based Sustainable Approach

**Dina A. Alabbad [1], Shahad Y. Ajibi [1], Raghad B. Alotaibi [1], Noura K. Alsqer [1], Rahaf A. Alqahtani [1], Noor M. Felemban [1], Atta Rahman [2,*], Sumayh S. Aljameel [2], Mohammed Imran Basheer Ahmed [1] and Mustafa M. Youldash [1]**

1 Department of Computer Engineering, College of Computer Science and Information Technology, Imam Abdulrahman Bin Faisal University, P.O. Box 1982, Dammam 31441, Saudi Arabia; daalabbad@iau.edu.sa (D.A.A.); 2190005368@iau.edu.sa (R.B.A.); 2180000479@iau.edu.sa (N.K.A.); 2180001113@iau.edu.sa (R.A.A.); mmzyouldash@iau.edu.sa (M.M.Y.)

2 Department of Computer Science, College of Computer Science and Information Technology, Imam Abdulrahman Bin Faisal University, P.O. Box 1982, Dammam 31441, Saudi Arabia

* Correspondence: aaurrahman@iau.edu.sa

**Abstract:** An accurate prediction of fetal birth weight is crucial in ensuring safe delivery without health complications for the mother and baby. The uncertainty surrounding the fetus's birth situation, including its weight range, can lead to significant risks for both mother and baby. As there is a standard birth weight range, if the fetus exceeds or falls below this range, it can result in considerable health problems. Although ultrasound imaging is commonly used to predict fetal weight, it does not always provide accurate readings, which may lead to unnecessary decisions such as early delivery and cesarian section. Besides that, no supporting system is available to predict the weight range in Saudi Arabia. Therefore, leveraging the available technologies to build a system that can serve as a second opinion for doctors and health professionals is essential. Machine learning (ML) offers significant advantages to numerous fields and can address various issues. As such, this study aims to utilize ML techniques to build a predictive model to predict the birthweight range of infants into low, normal, or high. For this purpose, two datasets were used: one from King Fahd University Hospital (KFHU), Saudi Arabia, and another publicly available dataset from the Institute of Electrical and Electronics Engineers (IEEE) data port. KFUH's best result was obtained with the Extra Trees model, achieving an accuracy, precision, recall, and F1-score of 98%, with a specificity of 99%. On the other hand, using the Random Forest model, the IEEE dataset attained an accuracy, precision, recall, and F1-score of 96%, respectively, with a specificity of 98%. These results suggest that the proposed ML system can provide reliable predictions, which could be of significant value for doctors and health professionals in Saudi Arabia.

**Keywords:** machine learning; sustainable approach; birthweight range; classification; fetal weight

## 1. Introduction

At delivery, the transition from embryo to newborn (also known as neonate) is a complex process that must occur quickly for successful survival [1]. Every day, nearly 800 women die from conditions related to pregnancy and childbirth that could have been avoided [2]. Every year, more than 20 million low birth weight (LBW) babies are born [3]. LBW babies are more prone to complications that can lead to death. In Saudi Arabia, infant mortality rates have increased to where the prevalence is around 5.497 deaths per 1000 live births [4]. A few high-risk births have been reported in the early stages of pregnancy, so optimal obstetric care may not be provided in Saudi Arabia. Early intervention and timely medical attention can help mitigate the long-term risks associated with birth weight. Prenatal fetal weight classification can play a significant role in saving the lives of both mothers and newborns. Hence, developing new technologies to accurately predict the classification of newborns' weight ranges is crucial. Accurate prediction of a newborn infant's weight is of great importance for the safety and well-being of both the mother and baby. Knowledge of the expected weight range of newborns can help healthcare professionals quickly identify any potential issues that may arise during labor and delivery. According to the World Health Organization (WHO) [5], neonates with a birth weight between 2500 g (about 5.51 lb) and 4000 g (about 8.82 lb) are typically considered to be of average healthy weight. In comparison, a baby weight of less than 2500 g (about 5.51 lb) is classified as LBW, and those above 4000 g (about 8.82 lb) are overweight. So, it is crucial to identify the factors that affect the baby's birth weight. Based on previous research, those factors are commonly identified as genetics, parents' age, weight gains during pregnancy, length of gestation, gender, and the number of babies.

Low birth weight (LBW) babies are at an increased risk of a variety of complications, including infant mortality, labor complications, neonatal survival, and multiple birth complications [1]. Additionally, LBW babies are more likely to die within the first 28 days (about four weeks) of life due to a variety of illnesses and other medical problems. As such, LBW babies must receive proper care and attention to ensure their health and well-being. On the other hand, overweight infants are associated with a variety of adverse outcomes such as dystocia, increased risk for neonatal hypoglycemia, and higher rates of cesarean section deliveries due to fetal distress or other labor-related difficulties. Also, there are many risks associated with their health later in life, including obesity, diabetes, and heart defects, to name a few; all of which have long-term implications for child and mother alike if not appropriately addressed early on in the development stages. When it comes to pregnant women with abnormal infant weight, they are at risk for several complications, including an increased risk of infection, preterm labor, and postpartum depression. Additionally, the mother may be at risk for hemorrhaging, blood clots, and other health problems.

As evidenced by the challenges identified above, there is a need for a reliable prediction technique that can accurately determine the birth weight range of each child. Machine learning (ML) algorithms are well-suited for this task, as they can learn and improve with experience and data [6]. ML models can be employed to create forecasts without requiring explicit programming and are commonly used in various fields, such as health, education, and agriculture. This research aims to utilize ML technologies to develop a model for predicting a baby's birth weight class with minimal errors and cost-effectiveness. Understanding the features of both mother and baby that contribute to birth weight prediction is essential for improving prenatal care and reducing complications during labor and delivery. Features such as maternal age, weight, height, blood pressure, blood sugar levels, and hemoglobin levels provide crucial insights into maternal health and potential risk factors for low or high birth weight. Additionally, factors related to the newborn, such as gender, height, and weight, play a significant role in determining birth weight ranges. By leveraging machine learning (ML) algorithms, healthcare professionals can analyze these features to develop predictive models that assist in identifying potential issues early on, thereby enabling timely interventions and mitigating adverse outcomes. Integrating such predictive tools into clinical practice holds promise for enhancing maternal and neonatal care by facilitating personalized and proactive healthcare strategies. Through the utilization of comprehensive datasets containing these diverse features, ML algorithms can effectively learn patterns and relationships to accurately predict birth weight ranges, ultimately leading to improved outcomes for both mothers and babies.

The proposed model is intended to provide a reliable and efficient tool for predicting a baby's birth weight range using ML, which potentially benefits healthcare and mitigating the negative consequences of false birthweight estimation. This study utilizes and compares two datasets of pregnant mothers' clinical data. First, the Saudi private dataset provided by King Fahd University Hospital (KFUH) consists of 639 pregnant women and 15 attributes of the mother's features. Second, a purchased public dataset is available from the Institute of Electrical and Electronics Engineers (IEEE) [7]. The dataset consists of 1801 records combined with 18 features of the mother and baby. Various ML algorithms were utilized to identify the best performance technique for the research purpose, including Support Vector Machine (SVM), Decision Tree (DT), Random Forest (RF), Extra Trees (ET), Gaussian Naive Bayes (GaussianNB), Extreme Gradient Boosting (XGBoost), Adaptive Boosting (AdaBoost), and Light Gradient Boosting Machine (LGBM). The results show that the Extra Trees model outperformed the other algorithms with an accuracy, precision, and recall score of 98% and a specificity of 99% on the KFUH dataset. In contrast, using the Random Forest classifier, the IEEE dataset attained an accuracy, precision, recall, and F1-score of 96%, respectively, with a specificity of 98%. These models would greatly benefit the medical community, providing an accurate and reliable means of predicting a baby's birth weight.

This paper is structured as follows: Section 2 presents the related works and studies. Section 3 presents the materials and methods used, including the dataset description, statistical analysis, a description of the employed ML algorithms, the performance measures used to assess the developed models, and, finally, the optimization strategy chosen. The findings of this paper are explained in Section 4, and the results of the models are described in Section 5. Finally, conclusions and future work are discussed in Section 6.

## 2. Related Work

Over the past few years, machine learning has become increasingly popular in healthcare. Also, researchers have examined the utilization of machine learning algorithms for fetal weight estimation. For this purpose, multiple studies implemented various ML and DL techniques to create classifier models using clinical data, besides other genetic and environmental factors. Below are some literature reviews that identify potential areas for improvement in this research.

The work presented in [8] proposed a method to predict the weight range of infants using a machine learning approach. Their motivation for this study was to reduce the mortality risk in the first year, since it is directly related to the infant's weight. The dataset contained around 500 records for pregnant women in the first six months. They defined 16 attributes that affect an infant's birth weight, such as blood group, the pregnant woman's age, a history of abortion, and blood sugar. The researchers applied five machine learning models: artificial neural networks (ANNs), Naïve Bayes (NB), Support Vector Machine (SVM), Logistic Regression, and Decision Tree (DT). The obtained accuracy with ANNs and NB is 70%, and it is 60% for SVM and Logistic Regression. In contrast, DT was below 60%. Moreover, the authors in [9] intended to estimate infant birth weight and low birth weight in the United Arab Emirates using machine learning algorithms. The predictions were performed with and without feature selection techniques by combining multiple subsets of features. Moreover, the SMOTE technique was employed to oversample the minority class. Thirty ML algorithms were used for infant BW estimation and LBW classification. The experiments were conducted on a self-created dataset with 88 features.

Furthermore, the dataset was obtained from 821 women from three hospitals in the United Arab Emirates (UAE). The best weight estimation was obtained using the Random Forest algorithm, with a mean absolute error of 294.53 g using five-fold cross-validation. In contrast, the best classification performance was obtained using Logistic Regression with SMOTE oversampling techniques, which achieved an accuracy, precision, recall, and F1-score of 90.24%, 87.6%, 90.2%, and 0.89, respectively.

The research in [10] provided a classification model to group infants born to mothers with hypertension according to their estimated weights. The Weka platform was used to implement the Naive Bayes NB classification model by three testing techniques: supplied test, cross-validation, and split percentage. The researchers collected a dataset of 219 pregnant women from Muhammadiyah Palembang Hospital. The outcomes demonstrated that NB and cross-validation achieved the best results, with accuracy, recall, and precision reaching 82.45%, 69.5%, and 79.67%, respectively.

Moreover, the authors in [11] aimed to estimate fetal birth weight in high-risk pregnancies through machine learning techniques. This paper compared several ML techniques: Tree, Support Vector Machine (SVM), k-Nearest Neighbor (kNN), Boosted Trees, Bagged Trees, and Subspace KNN. Data were acquired by supplying a form to pregnant women who suffered from some hypertensive disorder during pregnancy at the Maternity School Assis Chateaubriand of the municipality of Fortaleza, Ceara, Brazil, from May to September 2017. The results show that hybrid methods based on ensemble learning can efficiently predict the fetus's expected weight at birth. The accuracy achieved for Tree, K-NN, Boosted Trees, and Subspace KNN was 83%, while it was 79% for SVM and 84% for Bagged Trees. Likewise, the study in [12] investigates machine learning for estimating fetal weight at varying gestational ages. For this purpose, the researchers used ensemble methods in machine learning that create multiple models for a robust prediction, since these models can increase the diversity of algorithms and reduce generalization errors to improve the accuracy of the results. The dataset was from Shenzhen Bao'an Maternity and Child Healthcare Hospital. A total number of 5000 samples were randomly selected, with no gynecology and other general medical histories regarding prenatal care screened out. The implemented algorithms were Random Forest, XGBoost, and LightGBM. The accuracy results were 69%, 62%, and 61%, respectively. Furthermore, for the ensemble model, it was 65%. The authors in [13] also aimed to design a model to predict early fetal weight using Support Vector Regression (SVR). The dataset was obtained in the first trimester of pregnancy, and birth weight was taken after delivery, for a total of 250 pregnant women. To test various prediction algorithms, the study used four different SVR variants: Linear, Polynomial (Poly), Radial Basis Function (RBF), and Nu. In addition, a 10–fold cross-validation was carried out during the training and validation. Compared to other study methods, the results of this study showed that the obtained errors were competitive, achieving relative errors of less than 3% with SVR-RBF.

Apart from that, the author in [14] proposed a model to estimate newborn babies' low birth weight (LBW). The dataset was gathered from the Ethiopia Demographic and Health Survey (EDHS) 2016, consisting of 10,641 instances. The implemented classification model classes are LBW and normal, the SMOTE technique is applied to the resampling of imbalanced data, and randomized search cross-validation is employed; the dataset was 2110 records and 25 features on preprocessing; the data was split 80:20 for training and testing sets; the training models used in the study were Logistic Regression (LR), Decision Tree (DT), Naive Bayes (NB), K-Nearest Neighbor (K-NN), Random Forest (RF), Support Vector Machine (SVM), Gradient Boosting (GB), and Extreme Gradient Boosting (XGB). The experiments indicated that RF offered the best results, with 91.6% for all (accuracy, recall, and F1-score) and 96.8% for the ROC-AUC.

Similarly, the authors of [15] aimed to estimate and classify the low birth weight of newborns using prediction and classification machine learning models. Several machine learning techniques were utilized to build this model: Binary Logistic Regression and Random Forest (RF). The authors used data from 45,607 women from the Indonesian Demographic and Health Survey (IDH) 2012. The results revealed that the Binary Logistic Regression accuracy was 0.937 for prediction and classification; it was weakly supported by the AUC value = 0.505; however, Random Forest had an accuracy of 93%. The work in [16] aimed to develop a mathematical model for predicting infant weight using un-medical variables: ethnicity, education level, smoking habit, baby weight, and duration of gestation. The dataset contained data on 1113 pregnant women. Researchers determined which factors are essential for prediction using Multivariate Linear Regression. The model predicts birth weight based on the factors determined. The results showed that the regression could explain 65% of the variation in the newborn weights. Nevertheless, there has been increasing attention to developing methods of fetal weight classification using ultrasound data.

In [17], the researchers used hybrid data from electronic medical records with the B-ultrasonic examination of pregnant women to build a predicting birth weight classifier model based on long short-term memory (LSTM) networks. The data have been collected from a clinical dataset at a hospital in Eastern China. As a result, they used the accuracy rate of the prediction model by using a Back Propagation Neural Network (BPNN), Random Forest (RF), Convolutional Neuron Networks (CNNs), Linear Regression (LR), Support Vector Regression (SVR), and the proposed hybrid LSTM. According to a comparison between the machine learning models, the hybrid LSTM model obtained the mean relative error (MRE) and the best accuracy of 0.933. Using the same techniques, in [18], the authors used the data for 80 women collected from a Chinese hospital. Therefore, this study aims to create a prediction model for fetal weight using the genetic algorithm to improve the Back Propagation Neural Network (GA-BPNN) to deal with the continuous change in the signs of pregnant women. The GA-BPNN model achieved a prediction rate of control error within 6%, and the accuracy was 76.3%, 14.5% higher than the traditional methods. According to the results, we can estimate that the GA-BPNN model can predict fetal weight effectively and with high accuracy.

Various ML approaches have been investigated in [19] to predict LBW. In this regard, five ML techniques were used, including DT, RF, ANN, SVM, and LR, with five evaluation criteria applied to evaluate their performance. A dataset comprising 741 mother–newborn pairs and 13 potential features obtained from Fatemieh Hospital has been investigated. The outcome showed a 7% occurrence of LBW. The LR method provided a sensitivity, specificity, positive likelihood ratio, negative likelihood ratio, and accuracy of 74%, 89%, 7.04%, 29%, and 88%, respectively. Moreover, using LR, the gestational age, number of abortions, gravida, consanguinity, maternal age at delivery, and neonatal sex were observed as the six most essential features related to LBW. Similarly, in [20], authors investigated around eight ML and DL algorithms, including LR, DT, RF, DL Feed Forward, Extreme Gradient Boost (XGBoost), Light Gradient Boost (LGBoost), SVM, and permutation feature classification with kNN. A real-life dataset named IMaN Net was considered, and a highest accuracy of 79%, a precision of 87%, recall of 69%, and F1-score of 77% was obtained using XGBoost. Likewise, a study in [21] proposed an ML-based prediction of LBW and assessed the impact of data-balancing approaches and associated risks. The study investigates a huge dataset of 266,687 samples over six years, where 8.63% (23,019 of the records) were labeled as LBW. Seven ML algorithms with various balancing techniques were investigated, and XGBoost obtained the highest recall value of 70%.

Based on the literature reviews related to this study, it has been noted that most studies achieved their best outcomes with the RF algorithm. Likewise, most reviewed papers have confined their categorization to the low and normal weight range, while neglecting the high weight classification category. Similarly, no studies have used Extra Trees (ET) or Adaptive Boosting (AdaBoost) to forecast birth weight. However, only one study utilized the optimizer for tuning the hyperparameters with Gride search. Moreover, studies were only found in the literature on the Saudi Arabia dataset, namely the kingdom's eastern province, considering the effect of demographical location on many features for women. Therefore, this research proposed a three-category classifier model using the local Saudi dataset and a public dataset, besides the grid search optimizer, to compare findings to determine the optimal direction for advancing fetal weight prognostication.

## 3. Materials and Methods

This work developed a model for classifying a birth weight range using Python programming through the Jupiter Notebook, Visual Studio Code, and Google Colab. The preprocessing methods used on both datasets are depicted in Figure 1. The best features were selected utilizing the SelectKBest method for the KFUH dataset K = 4 and K = 12 in the IEEE dataset. Moreover, the datasets were divided into 80% for training and 20% for testing the proposed models. The Synthetic Minority Oversampling Technique SMOTE was applied to balance the classes. Additionally, the data features were scaled using the standard scaler technique. Furthermore, the chosen features were used to train eight ML algorithms: SVM, DT, RF, ET, GaussianNB, XGBoost, AdaBoost, and LGBM. GridSearchCV was then employed to find the optimal hyperparameters of the trained models. Various performance metrics were used to evaluate the models, including accuracy, precision, recall,

F1-score, sensitivity, and confusion matrix. Finally, the best model was then interpreted by applying SHAP techniques. Figure 1 summarizes the steps used in developing the prediction models.

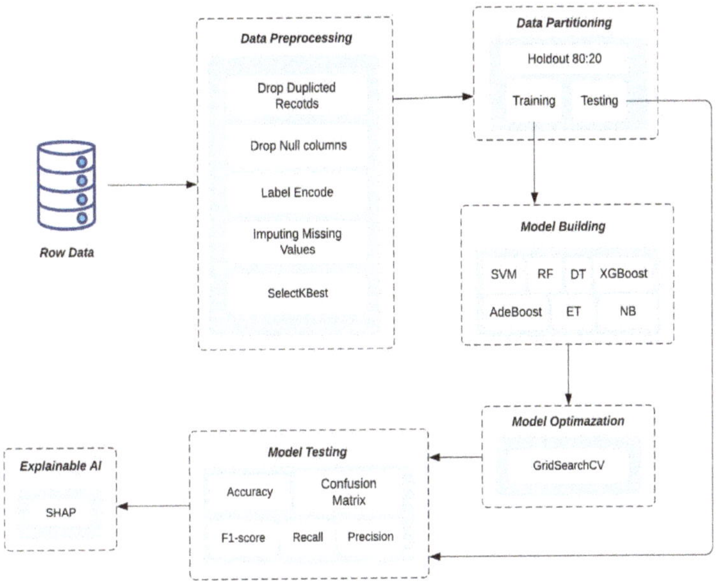


**Figure 1.** Proposed methodology.

### 3.1. Datasets Description

This study employed two datasets of pregnant mothers' clinical data: genome and maternal. The first dataset was obtained from the King Fahd University Hospital (KFUH) in Dammam, Saudi Arabia. This dataset consisted of 4335 records from 639 pregnant women and 16 attributes of the mother's features and details of several test results. After data preprocessing, the final dataset had 639 records and 23 attributes. The second is a public dataset obtained from IEEE [7], consisting of 1801 records and 18 features of pregnant mothers' clinical data. Table 1 illustrates the features of each dataset. In both datasets utilized in this study, the feature sets were obtained through systematic collection processes overseen by medical professionals, ensuring that the variables analyzed were not arbitrarily chosen. The IEEE dataset is meticulously curated by medical professionals. This ensures the inclusion of clinically relevant features that are widely recognized in the medical community for their significance in health assessments. Furthermore, the feature set employed in this dataset is derived from established medical guidelines and protocols, thereby emphasizing its robustness and reliability. On the other hand, the KFUH dataset represents a valuable source of real-world data collected by medical staff with expertise in patient care in the specified triage rooms. The feature set utilized in this dataset is carefully selected based on the insights and recommendations of medical practitioners who possess firsthand knowledge of the clinical context and the variables most pertinent to patient health assessments. In this study, we meticulously compared our dataset with previously published works, ensuring its relevance and reliability. The primary goal was to closely examine the features between maternal and fetal data. This focused approach allowed us to employ a technique tailored specifically to meet the demands of our research objectives. By implementing this streamlined approach, we efficiently navigated through the extensive array of data points, pinpointing those most crucial to our investigation. This deliberate strategy empowered us to delve deeply into the fundamental aspects of our study, facilitating a more profound and insightful analysis of maternal–fetal features.

**Table 1.** KFUH and IEEE datasets feature descriptions.

| Public (IEEE) Dataset | | | KFUH Dataset | | |
|---|---|---|---|---|---|
| **Attribute** | **Data Type** | **Description** | **Attribute** | **Data Type** | **Description** |
| SEC | Categorical | Economic condition | Sex | Categorical | The baby's gender |
| Age (years) | Numerical | Age of mother | Nb Height | Numerical | The newborn baby's height |
| Height (cm) | Numerical | Height of mother | Nb Weight | Numerical | The newborn baby's weight |
| Bgroup | Categorical | Blood group of the mother | Remark | Categorical | Description of the ID and date |
| Parity | Numerical | No. of previous pregnancy | Age (Years) | Numerical | The mother's age |
| ANC | Numerical | Antenatal check | Height (cm) | Numerical | The mother's height |
| Iwt (kg) | Numerical | The initial weight of the mother | Weight | Numerical | The mother's weight |
| FBP_dias | Numerical | Final diastolic blood pressure | Random glucose | Numerical | The measured random glucose of the mother |
| IBP_sys | Numerical | Initial systolic blood pressure | Hemoglobin | Numerical | The measured hemoglobin of the mother |
| IBP_dias | Numerical | Initial diastolic blood pressure | LabTest Item Flag for random glucose | Categorical | If the glucose results are normal or abnormal |
| FBP_sys | Numerical | Final systolic blood pressure | Lab Test Item Flag for hemoglobin | Categorical | If the hemoglobin results are normal or abnormal |
| IHb (gm%) | Numerical | Initial hemoglobin level | Order Comment | Categorical | The instructions and the procedures to be done |
| FHb (gm%) | Numerical | Final hemoglobin level | H-V0 | Numerical | H-V0's measured value |
| BS(RBS) | Numerical | Blood sugar | H-V1 | Numerical | H-V1's measured value |
| Term/Preterm | Categorical | 37 to 40 weeks, or <37 weeks. | H-V2 | Numerical | H-V2's measured value |
| Sex | Categorical | Sex of newborn baby | Patient MRN | Numerical | The mother's ID |
| LNH | Categorical | Class label name | Resulted By | Categorical | The name of the test performer |
| FWt (kg) | Numerical | The final weight of the mother | Interpretation | Categorical | If it is rechecked or not |

## 3.2. Statistical Analysis

Statistical analysis is the process of using mathematical techniques to analyze and interpret data. In machine learning, statistical analysis is commonly used to identify patterns, relationships, and trends in datasets for preprocessing the data according to the analysis results. The first step in preprocessing any dataset is to investigate its features. Thus, Table 2 shows the statical characteristics of the numerical features for both the KFUH and IEEE datasets, including the count, mean, standard deviation (std), and the minimum, Q1, median, Q3, maximum values, and missing values count.

**Table 2.** KFUH and IEEE dataset statistical characteristics.

| | Count | Mean | Std | Min | 25% | 50% | 75% | Max | Null_Count |
|---|---|---|---|---|---|---|---|---|---|
| | | | | **KFUH Dataset** | | | | | |
| NB_Gender | 639.0 | 0.478873 | 0.499945 | 0.0 | 0.00 | 0.0 | 1.00 | 1.0 | 0 |
| Mother_Age | 639.0 | 31.566510 | 5.780592 | 16.0 | 28.00 | 32.0 | 36.00 | 47.0 | 0 |
| Random Glucose (mg/dL) | 84.0 | 119.619048 | 36.228493 | 71.0 | 90.00 | 108.5 | 141.25 | 215.0 | 555 |
| Hemoglobin A1c | 67.0 | 5.580597 | 0.636334 | 4.0 | 5.25 | 5.6 | 5.90 | 7.8 | 572 |
| Lab Test Item Flag G | 66.0 | 0.272727 | 0.448775 | 0.0 | 0.00 | 0.0 | 1.00 | 1.0 | 573 |
| Lab Test Item Flag H | 59.0 | 0.220339 | 0.418033 | 0.0 | 0.00 | 0.0 | 0.00 | 1.0 | 580 |
| Weight_Range | 639.0 | 1.003130 | 0.519214 | 0.0 | 1.00 | 1.0 | 1.00 | 2.0 | 0 |
| | | | | **Public (IEEE) Dataset** | | | | | |
| Age (years) | 1786.0 | 22.986002 | 4.050843 | 8.0 | 20.0 | 22.0 | 25.0 | 55.0 | 14 |
| Height (cm) | 1527.0 | 143.785855 | 19.702879 | 10.0 | 135.0 | 150.0 | 150.0 | 195.0 | 273 |
| Parity | 1767.0 | 0.667233 | 0.993277 | 0.0 | 0.0 | 0.0 | 1.0 | 6.0 | 33 |
| ANC | 1781.0 | 3.423358 | 0.889005 | 1.0 | 3.0 | 4.0 | 4.0 | 4.0 | 19 |
| Lwt (kg) | 1751.0 | 45.749857 | 6.655457 | 30.0 | 41.0 | 45.0 | 50.0 | 93.0 | 49 |
| FWt (kg) | 1739.0 | 51.645371 | 6.905943 | 30.0 | 47.0 | 51.0 | 55.0 | 100.0 | 61 |
| IBP_sys | 1760.0 | 108.032386 | 12.021658 | 10.0 | 100.0 | 110.0 | 112.0 | 197.0 | 40 |
| IBP_dias | 1760.0 | 66.091477 | 8.263232 | 14.0 | 60.0 | 66.0 | 70.0 | 100.0 | 40 |
| FBP_sys | 1749.0 | 111.819325 | 11.809435 | 10.0 | 110.0 | 110.0 | 120.0 | 160.0 | 51 |
| FBP_dias | 1748.0 | 69.405606 | 9.249682 | 10.0 | 60.0 | 70.0 | 78.0 | 117.0 | 52 |
| IHb (gm%) | 1395.0 | 9.919398 | 1.052058 | 6.0 | 9.2 | 10.0 | 10.6 | 13.0 | 405 |
| FHb (gm%) | 1393.0 | 10.401651 | 0.989487 | 1.5 | 10.0 | 10.4 | 11.0 | 13.2 | 407 |
| BS(RBS) | 608.0 | 100.898026 | 17.251874 | 12.0 | 93.0 | 100.0 | 109.0 | 240.0 | 1192 |
| LNH | 1072.0 | 1.871269 | 0.346026 | 1.0 | 2.0 | 2.0 | 2.0 | 3.0 | 728 |

Table 3 presents the correlation coefficient of each feature with the target class on the two datasets used in this project. To explain the analysis more profoundly, the correlation will help to understand and measure the strength and the direction of the relationship between the features and the fetal weight.

**Table 3.** KFUH and IEEE correlations tables.

| **KFUH Dataset** | | **Public (IEEE) Dataset** | |
|---|---|---|---|
| **Attribute** | **Correlation with Target Class** | **Attribute** | **Correlation with Target Class** |
| NB_Gender | −0.078 | BS(RBS) | 0.14 |
| | | ANC | 0.1 |
| Mother_Age | 0.083 | FBP_sys | 0.071 |
| | | FWt (kg) | 0.054 |
| Random Glucose (mg/dL) | −0.047 | FBP_dias | 0.042 |
| | | Age (years) | 0.034 |
| Hemoglobin A1c | −0.012 | Lwt (kg) | 0.0058 |
| | | IBP_sys | −0.0075 |
| Lab Test Item Flag G | −0.017 | Parity | −0.012 |
| | | IBP_dias | −0.032 |
| Lab Test Item Flag H | 0.018 | Height (cm) | −0.1 |
| | | FHb (gn%) | −0.11 |
| | | IHb (gm%) | −0.13 |

### 3.3. Data Preprocessing

One of the critical and sensitive processes of transforming raw data and making it suitable in terms of quality is the derivation of information to influence the learning ability of the model, which is called the data preprocessing process [22,23]. The preprocessing techniques used in this study were from the Python Sklearn and Pandas packages. The KFUH dataset initially included 4335 records from 639 pregnant women and 16 features. In contrast, the dataset from Public IEEE contains 1801 records and 20 features. There were often null values in the two datasets. Therefore, features with 500 or more deficiencies in the KFUH dataset and Public IEEE were deleted using the drop () method, and the duplicated rows were removed using the duplicated () method. Accordingly, 639 instances and 23 features from the KFUH data and 1300 instances with 19 features from the IEEE data remained. Moreover, the Sklearn LabelEncoder() method was used to convert categorical data into a numerical format before the training and evaluating models.

Missing values are an unavailable entity, an incomplete feature, or a wrong entry in the data, so the results of the machine learning model may be affected by low statistical power, inaccurate parameter estimation, and difficulty in preprocessing the data. Thus, we may need to process these fields and convert them to use them in the analysis and modeling. As a result, the fillna() method is provided in the Python programming language to solve this problem; it replaces the new object in the DataFrame, while the in-place parameter is not set to True, in which case the fillna() method performs an overwrite into the original DataFrame instead. This study checks the skewed data to observe how the data are distributed to impute the numerical null values. Whenever the skewness is symmetrical, the data are nearly between −0.5 and 0.5; therefore, the null values are filled using the mean, as shown below in Equation (1), where $n$ represents the total number of values in a column. $x_i$ represents a single data point [24].

$$Mean = \overline{x} = \frac{\sum_{i=1}^{n} x_i}{n} \tag{1}$$

In contrast, if the skewness is slight, the data are nearly between −1 and −0.5 negatively skewed or between 0.5 and 1 positively skewed. The null data are filled with the median, as shown below in Equation (2). For a dataset $x$ of $n$ elements arranged in ascending order [25]:

$$\begin{aligned} Median\ (x) &= \frac{x_{(n+1)}}{2},\ if\ n\ is\ odd \\ Median\ (x) &= \frac{x_{(n/2)} + x_{(n+1/2)}}{2},\ if\ n\ is\ even \end{aligned} \tag{2}$$

Moreover, when the skewness is extreme, the data lower than −1 are negatively skewed, or the data greater than one are positively skewed. The null data are filled with the mode, as shown below in Equation (3). If $\boldsymbol{X}$ is a discrete random variable, the mode is the value $x$ at which the probability mass function takes its maximum value. It is the most probable value to be sampled [26].

$$Mode = x = \text{argmax}_{xi}\text{P}(\boldsymbol{X} = xi) \tag{3}$$

Next, each dataset was split into two stratified sets: 80% for training and validation and 20% for testing. The first dataset, KFUH, comprised a total of 639 records. Within this dataset, 511 records were assigned for training and validation, with the remaining 128 earmarked for testing. The second dataset, IEEE, consisted of 1801 records. From these, 930 were designated for training and validation, leaving 360 for testing. This ensures that the model learns from a significant portion of the data, while retaining a separate portion to assess its generalization ability on unseen data.

The KFUH and public IEEE datasets values were scaled using StandardScaler to standardize a feature by subtracting the mean and then scaling to unit variance, which has been fitted to the training set and transformed into the testing set using Equation (4).

$$y = \frac{\chi - mean}{standard\ deviation} \tag{4}$$

### 3.4. Description of Utilized Machine Learning Algorithms

This study utilized several machine learning algorithms to classify the weight of newborn babies into three categories: low, normal, and high. The algorithms used include Adaptive Boosting, Decision Tree, and Random Forest. These algorithms have been chosen due to their efficiency and accuracy in classification tasks for similar purposes. Due to the different nature of the two datasets used in terms of features, the number of records, and the nature and content of the data, the lazy classifier was applied, which provided the performance of more than 20 prediction models for the given datasets, in which the top-performing five models for each dataset were used.

#### 3.4.1. Random Forest (RF)

RF is a supervised ensemble learning algorithm for classification and regression problems. It works by creating a set of decision trees on random subsets of the training data and then combining their outputs through a voting mechanism. It helps to reduce overfitting and improve accuracy. It can handle high-dimensional data with many features, missing data, and outliers. On the other hand, it can be computationally expensive, time-consuming, and not good with imbalanced data [27].

#### 3.4.2. Gaussian Naive Bayes (NB)

It is a probabilistic machine learning algorithm for binary or multi-classification tasks. It assumes that the features are independent of each other given the class label and that the probability distribution of each feature given the class label is Gaussian (i.e., normal distribution). During training, the algorithm estimates each feature's mean and standard deviation for each class label. During prediction, it calculates the likelihood of each class label given the input features using Bayes' theorem and selects the class label with the highest probability as the prediction. Gaussian Naive Bayes is simple, efficient, and often works well in practice, especially for high-dimensional datasets. Although the features are not always independent nor normally distributed, they can suffer from the zero probabilities problem [28].

#### 3.4.3. Extremely Randomized Trees (ET)

Extra Trees, or Extremely Randomized Trees, is an ensemble machine learning algorithm for classification and regression tasks. It is similar to Random Forest but with an additional randomization step. During training, Extra Trees randomly selects a subset of features and thresholds for each decision tree, making the trees more diverse and less correlated. It helps to reduce overfitting and improve accuracy. At prediction time, the outputs of all the trees are averaged or combined to produce the final prediction. Extra Trees is simple, efficient, and often works well in practice, especially for high-dimensional datasets. The main disadvantages of Extra Trees are a higher bias and more complex tuning [29].

#### 3.4.4. Support Vector Machines (SVMs)

SVMs are powerful machine learning algorithms for classification, regression, and outlier detection tasks. SVMs find the optimal hyperplane that separates two classes of data with a maximum margin, called the maximum margin hyperplane. During training, SVMs optimize a convex objective function, using the input features to find the hyperplane that maximizes the margin. If the classes are not linearly separable, SVMs use a kernel function to map the input features to a higher-dimensional space where the classes can be separated. SVMs are effective in high-dimensional spaces and often work well in practice. However, SVMs can be computationally expensive to train and sensitive to imbalance [30].

#### 3.4.5. Adaptive Boosting (AdaBoost)

AdaBoost is an ensemble machine learning algorithm used for classification and regression tasks. It works by iteratively training a series of weak models on weighted versions of the dataset, where the weights are adjusted to focus on misclassified instances. The weak models are then combined into a strong model by assigning weights to their predictions based on their performance during training. AdaBoost is particularly effective for boosting the performance of decision trees, and it can be used with various base models. AdaBoost is known for its ability to improve accuracy, reduce overfitting, and handle imbalanced datasets. AdaBoost is sensitive to noisy data [31].

#### 3.4.6. Extreme Gradient Boosting (XGBoost)

XGBoost is a gradient-boosting machine learning algorithm used for classification, regression, and ranking tasks. It works by iteratively training decision trees to minimize a loss function, using a gradient descent optimization approach. XGBoost also includes several regularization techniques, such as L1 and L2 regularization, to prevent overfitting. It also supports parallel processing and distributed computing to improve efficiency on large datasets. XGBoost is a popular and powerful algorithm that has won numerous machine learning competitions and is widely used in the industry for various applications. XGBoost requires significant computational resources [32].

#### 3.4.7. Light Gradient Boosting (LGBM)

LGBM is an ensemble machine learning algorithm used for classification and regression tasks. It is similar to XGBoost but uses a different approach to build decision trees, and it utilizes histogram-based algorithms to speed up the training process. LightGBM also includes techniques such as gradient-based one-side sampling (GOSS) and exclusive feature bundling (EFB) to further improve performance and reduce memory usage. It is known for its scalability, speed, and high accuracy, making it a popular choice in the industry for large-scale machine learning tasks. However, it requires careful tuning and validation to achieve the best performance, and its interpretability may be limited, especially for complex models [33].

#### 3.4.8. Decision Tree (DT)

Decision Tree is a machine learning algorithm used for classification and regression tasks. It works by constructing a tree-like model of decisions and their possible consequences, with each internal node representing a test on a feature and each leaf node representing a class or a value. During training, the algorithm selects the best feature to split the data based on a certain criterion, such as information gain or Gini impurity. During prediction, the input data traverse through the decision tree, and the prediction is based on the leaf node that the input data reach. Decision Trees are simple, interpretable, and can work well in practice, especially for small to medium-sized datasets. But it requires careful tuning and validation to prevent overfitting and instability, and its performance may be limited by its bias toward certain features [34].

### 3.5. Performance Measure

The performance of the developed models will be assisted using a confusion matrix and several performance measures derived from it. The confusion matrix in Table 4 summarizes the actual and predicted classifications of a model on a dataset for one class used to evaluate the performance of the ML's model, which consists of True Positive (TP), False Positive (FP), True Negative (TN), and False Negative (FN), where (P) is Placed and (N) Not Placed.

**Table 4.** Confusion matrix.

| | | **The Actual** | |
|---|---|---|---|
| | | **P** | **N** |
| **The predicted** | **P** | TP | FP |
| | **N** | FN | TN |

True Positive (TP): The model predicted that the newborn's weight was in a certain class, and the actual weight of the newborn fell into the same class. False Positive (FP): The model predicted that the newborn's weight was in a certain class, but the actual weight of the newborn falls into a different class. False Negative (FN): The model failed to predict that the newborn's weight was in a certain class, but the actual weight of the newborn falls into that class. True Negative (TN): The model correctly predicted that the newborn's weight was not in a certain class, and the actual weight of the newborn also fell outside that class.

The performance metrics that will mainly be used in this classification model are accuracy, precision, recall, specificity, and F1-score. Accuracy works to define the ratio between the correctly classified results and the total number of all results. As for precision and recall, both will measure the correctly predicted positives, but precision aims to show the number of weights that were positively placed, whereas recall helps to understand how many positively placed weights the model was able to detect. In addition, specificity is the percentage of true negative samples that were accurately predicted out of all real negative samples. The F1-score can be seen as the harmonic mean of both precision and recall. Using a variety of metrics will significantly help in defining the performance of this model [35]. The equations of the previously mentioned measures are [36–38]:

$$\text{Accuracy} = (\text{TP} + \text{TN})/(\text{TP} + \text{TN} + \text{FP} + \text{FN}) \quad (5)$$

$$\text{precision} = \text{TP}/(\text{TP} + \text{FP}) \quad (6)$$

$$\text{Recall} = \text{TP}/(\text{TP} + \text{FN}) \quad (7)$$

$$\text{Specificity} = \text{TN}/\text{TN} + \text{FP} \quad (8)$$

$$\text{F1-score} = (2 \times \text{Precision} \times \text{Recall})/(\text{Precision} + \text{Recall}) \quad (9)$$

### 3.6. Optimization Strategy

#### 3.6.1. Hyperparameters Tuning

Using a model hyperparameter, the model seeks to search for the best optimal values for the learning algorithm. Furthermore, it describes the external architecture of the model, which cannot be determined by the values from the data but must be selected before the learning process. To realize better results, the model is trained by integrating hyperparameters to maximize model performance and minimize the predetermined loss function [39,40].

### 3.6.2. GridSearchCV

GridSearchCV searches for optimal parameters based on a grid of parameters, and Sklearn's model_selection package also utilizes it. Furthermore, the training data fit the estimator model based on a predefined set of hyperparameters. Thus, you can select the best hyperparameters from the list [41,42]. Tables 5 and 6 show the optimal values for each parameter in both datasets used.

**Table 5.** The optimal values of hyperparameters.

| | **KFUH Dataset** | |
|---|---|---|
| **Classifier** | **Hyperparameter** | **Optimal Value** |
| Random Forest | Max_depth | 12 |
| | Min_samples_leaf | 1 |
| | Min_samples_split | 2 |
| | N_estimators | 200 |
| Extra Trees | min_samples_leaf | 1 |
| | Max_depth | 30 |
| | N_estimators | 200 |
| | Min_samples_split | 2 |
| LGBM | Boosting_type | Gbdt |
| | Learning_rate | 0.05 |
| | N_estimators | 1000 |
| | Num_leaves | 100 |
| Decision Tree | Max_depth | 25 |
| | Min_samples_leaf | 1 |
| | Min_samples_split | 2 |
| XGB | Learning_rate | 0.1 |
| | N_estimators | 150 |
| | Gamma | 0 |
| | Booster | Gbtree |

**Table 6.** The optimal values of hyperparameters.

| | **Public (IEEE) Dataset** | |
|---|---|---|
| **Classifier** | **Hyperparameter** | **Optimal Value** |
| Random Forest | Max_depth | 12 |
| | Min_samples_leaf | 2 |
| | Min_samples_split | 2 |
| | N_estimators | 300 |
| Extra Trees | Min_samples_leaf | 1 |
| | Max_depth | 8 |
| | N_estimators | 200 |
| | Min_samples_split | 2 |
| XGB | Learning_rate | 0.1 |
| | N_estimators | 150 |
| | Gamma | 0 |
| | Booster | Gbtree |
| SVM | C | 1 |
| | Gamma | Scale |
| | Kernel | Rbf |
| GaussianNB | Priors | None |
| | var_smoothing | $1 \times 10^{-7}$ |
| AdaBoost | Learning_rate | 0.01 |
| | N_estimators | 1000 |

## 4. Results

The models developed were evaluated based on various performance criteria, using the most suitable hyperparameters and feature subsets generated separately by the GridSearchCV and SelectKBest methods, and the results are presented in Table 7. On the KFUH dataset, the evaluation matrices revealed that the ET classifier outperformed the other four algorithms, achieving an accuracy, precision, recall, and F1-score of 98%. The LGBM classifier followed closely with an accuracy of 93%, precision of 94%, recall of 93%, and F1-score of 93%. Following that, the RF algorithm achieved an accuracy of 91%, a precision of 92%, recall of 91%, and F1-score of 91%. In contrast, the XGBoost model demonstrated a relatively lower performance, with an accuracy of 90%, precision of 92%, recall of 90%, and F1-score of 90%. Finally, the Decision Tree algorithm achieved the lowest performance, with an accuracy of 90.5%, precision of 91%, recall of 90%, and F1-score of 90%. Figure 2 illustrates the confusion matrices for the optimized conducted models.

**Table 7.** The results of the proposed models.

| | | | KFUH Dataset | | |
|---|---|---|---|---|---|
| **Classifier** | **Precision** | **Recall** | **Specificity** | **F1-Score** | **Accuracy** |
| ET | 0.98 | 0.98 | 0.99 | 0.98 | 0.98 |
| LGBM | 0.94 | 0.93 | 0.96 | 0.93 | 0.93 |
| RF | 0.92 | 0.91 | 0.95 | 0.91 | 0.91 |
| XGBoost | 0.92 | 0.90 | 0.94 | 0.90 | 0.90 |
| DT | 0.91 | 0.90 | 0.94 | 0.90 | 0.90 |
| | | | **IEEE Dataset** | | |
| **Classifier** | **Precision** | **Recall** | **Specificity** | **F1-Score** | **Accuracy** |
| RF | 0.96 | 0.96 | 0.98 | 0.96 | 0.96 |
| XGBoost | 0.95 | 0.95 | 0.97 | 0.95 | 0.95 |
| ET | 0.93 | 0.92 | 0.95 | 0.92 | 0.93 |
| SVM | 0.91 | 0.91 | 0.96 | 0.91 | 0.91 |
| AdaBoost | 0.91 | 0.91 | 0.96 | 0.91 | 0.91 |
| NB | 0.81 | 0.81 | 0.91 | 0.81 | 0.81 |

In experimenting with the IEEE dataset, six different algorithms were investigated. The results indicated that the RF classifier was the best-performing model, achieving an accuracy, precision, recall, and F1-score of 96%. The XGBoost model was a close second, achieving an accuracy, precision, recall, and F1-score of 95%. The ET classifier also demonstrated good performance, with an accuracy of 93%, precision of 93%, recall of 92%, and F1-score of 92%. However, the SVM, AdaBoost, and NB models had a lower performance compared to the other models. The confusion matrices for the optimized models are shown in Figure 3.

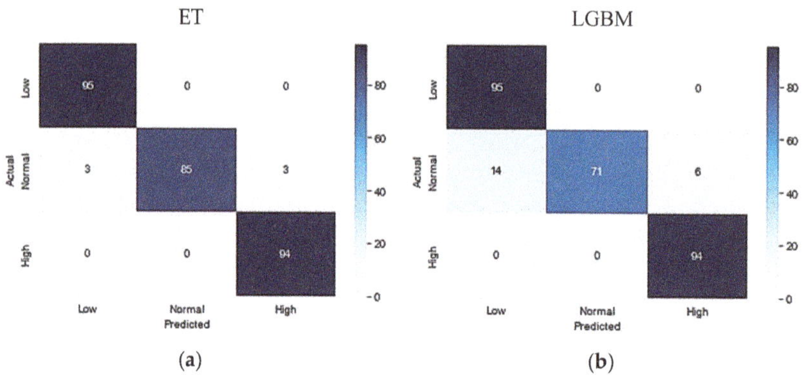


**Figure 2.** *Cont.*

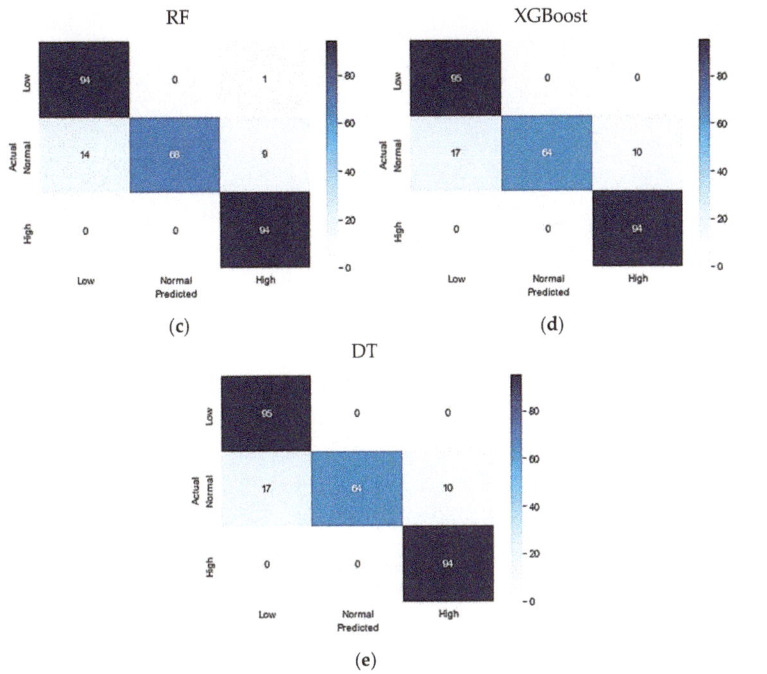


**Figure 2.** Confusion matrices for KFUH data: (**a**) ET, (**b**) LGBM, (**c**) RF, (**d**) XGBoost, (**e**) DT.

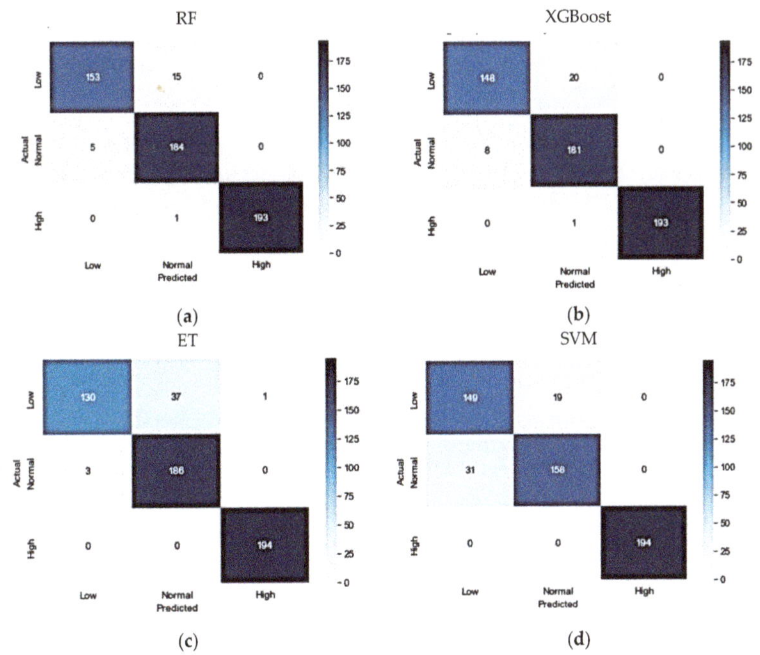


**Figure 3.** *Cont.*

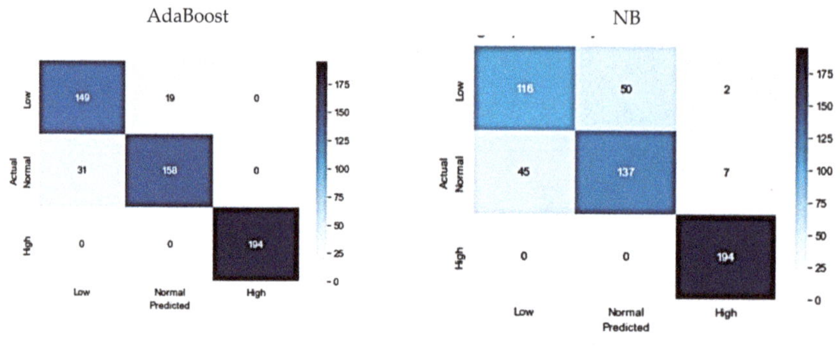


(e) (f)

**Figure 3.** Confusion matrices for IEEE data: (**a**) RF, (**b**) XGBoost, (**c**) ET, (**d**) SVM, (**e**) Adaboost, (**f**) NB.

Overall, the results showed that the ET classifier achieved the highest accuracy, precision, recall, and F1-score on the KFUH dataset, followed by the LGBM and RF algorithms. For the IEEE dataset, the RF classifier performed the best, followed closely by the XGBoost model and the ET classifier. The confusion matrices for the optimized models are presented for both datasets, providing a clear visualization of the models' performance. Hence, this study showed promising results in using machine learning for fetal weight range classification, with potential applications in improving prenatal care and outcomes.

*Explainable AI (XAI) and Shapley Additive Explanation (SHAP)*

Explainable Artificial Intelligence (XAI) is a critical area of research in machine learning, aimed at providing insights into the inner workings of black box models. One of the most promising XAI techniques is the Shapley Additive Explanation (SHAP). SHAP is an approach that provides a unified explanation of the output of a model by attributing each feature's importance to the final prediction [43]. SHAP builds upon game theory concepts to provide explanations for individual predictions. By defining a "game" between a feature and a set of features, SHAP measures the contribution of each feature to the prediction. This approach allows for global and local feature importance measures, which can be used to understand how the model arrived at a particular decision. SHAP has been applied to a wide range of machine learning applications, from image classification to natural language processing. Its use has shown promising results in increasing the interpretability and trustworthiness of black box models. However, there are still challenges in applying SHAP to complex models, such as deep neural networks, due to the large number of features involved. Research in this area is ongoing to develop more efficient and scalable SHAP algorithms for such models [44]. Figure 4 demonstrates the impact of selected features on the model performance for both the KFUH and IEEE datasets. As is evident from Figure 4a, the selected features in the KFUH dataset have a significant impact on the model performance for all three classes when using the best-performing model, which is the Extra Trees algorithm, with mother weight as the most important feature that significantly affects the prediction. On the other hand, Figure 4b presents feature impact in the IEEE dataset using the Random Forest classifier, and the most significant features in the model performance are the initial diastolic blood pressure (IBP-dia), number of previous pregnancies (Parity), and final weight of the mother (Fwt). Notably, Fwt is also the most important feature in the KFUH dataset, as the data were collected for women in their last month.

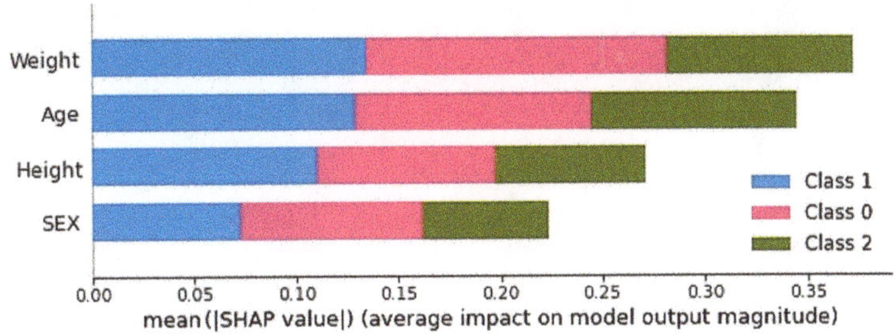


(a)

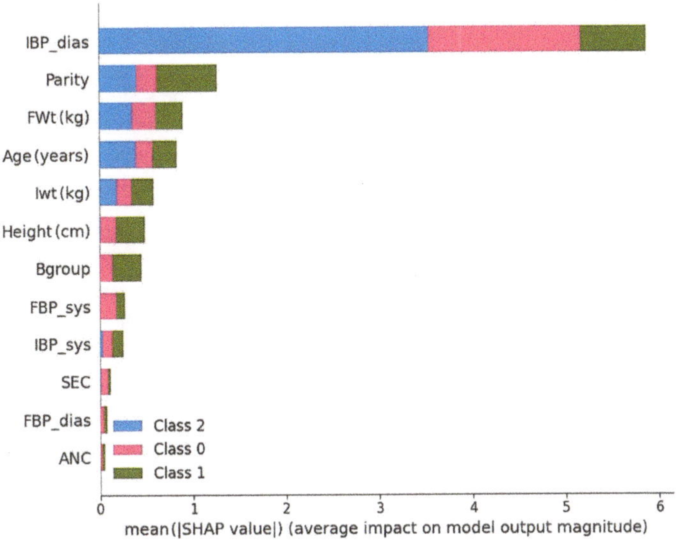


(b)

**Figure 4.** Shapley values: (**a**) ET model with KFUH dataset, (**b**) RF model with IEEE dataset.

## 5. Discussion

Several studies have utilized ML methods to classify the weight of fetuses at birth, yielding promising results. However, these studies only differentiate between low and normal birth weights, while paying less attention to the potential risks associated with a high birth weight. Additionally, many of these successful studies have relied on ultrasound imaging, which necessitates a large sample size and a high cost, besides the expected errors associated with machine readings. The diagnostic imaging sector in Saudi Arabia was valued at USD 353.97 million in the base year and is expected to increase at a CAGR of 4.1% to reach USD 453.17 million by the end of the forecast period [45]. As such, obtaining ultrasound images is both expensive and time-consuming. Therefore, it is necessary to develop an appropriate alternative model for classifying fetal weight at birth as an aid to ultrasound images, which would be less invasive and more cost-effective.

The main goal of this research was to develop an ML model capable of predicting fetal birth weight from clinical data collected from pregnant women. To achieve this, two datasets, the KFUH and IEEE datasets, were examined to identify the essential characteristics for effectively anticipating the weight range. Several ML algorithms were created and analyzed, and despite minor variations in their performance indicators, all the models exhibited similar levels of performance. However, the best model was the ET model, which obtained a 98% accuracy, precision, recall, and F1-score using 4 attributes on the

KFUH dataset, while the IEEE dataset achieved a 96% accuracy, precision, recall, and F1-score using only 12 attributes with the RF model. The SHAP technique demonstrated that attributes such as age, weight, height, and sex had a significant influence on the model's prediction.

The prediction of fetal weight at birth is based on the analysis of different characteristics of the fetus and mother. Some of the characteristics that are classified as the most important features include the sex of the fetus, the age of the mother, height, weight, and the length of the pregnancy [46]. This research has shown that increasing the mother's weight during pregnancy increases the weight of the fetus at birth. Besides, taller mothers tend to give birth to larger babies. Moreover, it turns out that the second most important feature is the age of the mother, because older mothers may give birth to heavier babies compared to younger mothers.

The consistency of the SHAP results with numerous other studies indicates the dependability of the proposed model. In addition, high weight was included in the classification of fetal weight along with low weight and normal weight, in contrast to previous studies. Moreover, unlike earlier literature studies, which relied on ultrasound imaging, this research centered on estimating fetal birth weight utilizing clinical data, thereby ensuring the model's computational and budget-friendly aspects. Upcoming research will broaden the dataset's scope by acquiring diverse maternal and fetal features and increasing the number of data points. This measure is intended to enhance the predictive capability of our proposed models for fetal birth weight classification.

## 6. Conclusions

The accurate prediction of a newborn's weight is of paramount importance for ensuring the safety and health of both the mother and child. The present study aimed to improve the precision of such predictions by utilizing machine learning algorithms. Specifically, two datasets were analyzed using a range of algorithms, including the Decision Tree, Extremely Randomized Tree, Random Forest, Light Gradient Boosting Machine, and AdaBoost models. The results indicated that the ET model achieved a 98% accuracy rate when applied to the KFUH dataset, while Random Forest achieved 96% accuracy in the IEEE dataset. Furthermore, this study identified factors such as maternal age, pregnancy weight gain, initial diastolic blood pressure (IBP-dia), and infant gender that directly impact birth weight, enabling healthcare professionals to provide better care to expectant mothers and their newborns. Furthermore, it would be beneficial to expand the size of the datasets used in this study to increase the robustness and generalizability of the machine learning models. Additionally, employing deep learning techniques, such as convolutional neural networks and recurrent neural networks, may further improve the accuracy of birth weight predictions by capturing more complex patterns and relationships within the data. Another area of future work could be investigating the potential impact of additional maternal and fetal health factors, such as maternal nutrition status or fetal heart rate, on birth weight prediction. Ultimately, these efforts could lead to the development of more sophisticated and accurate models that could significantly enhance the quality of care for pregnant women and their infants.

**Author Contributions:** Conceptualization, D.A.A. and S.S.A.; Data curation, R.B.A.; Formal analysis, N.M.F., M.M.Y. and A.R.; Investigation, M.M.Y., N.K.A. and M.I.B.A.; Methodology, D.A.A., N.M.F., S.S.A., S.Y.A. and R.A.A.; Project administration, M.I.B.A.; Resources, M.I.B.A.; Software, S.Y.A., N.K.A., R.B.A. and R.A.A.; Supervision, D.A.A. and S.S.A.; Validation, N.M.F., M.M.Y. and A.R.; Writing—original draft, S.Y.A., N.K.A., R.B.A. and R.A.A.; Writing—review and editing, A.R. All authors have read and agreed to the published version of the manuscript.

**Funding:** This research received no external funding.

**Data Availability Statement:** The dataset is available with the corresponding author and can be provided on a reasonable request.

**Conflicts of Interest:** The authors declare no conflict of interest.

## References


1. Segni, M. Disorders of the Thyroid Gland in Infancy, Childhood and Adolescence. *Endotext*, March 2017. [Online]. Available online: https://www.ncbi.nlm.nih.gov/books/NBK279032/ (accessed on 25 April 2023).
2. Maternal Mortality. Available online: https://www.who.int/news-room/fact-sheets/detail/maternal-mortality (accessed on 25 April 2023).
3. Newborn Health. Available online: https://www.who.int/teams/maternal-newborn-child-adolescent-health-and-ageing/newborn-health/preterm-and-low-birth-weight/ (accessed on 25 April 2023).
4. Saudi Arabia (SAU)-Demographics, Health & Infant Mortality-UNICEF DATA. Available online: https://data.unicef.org/country/sau/ (accessed on 25 April 2023).
5. UN Yearbook. Available online: https://www.unmultimedia.org/yearbook/page.jsp?volume=1984&bookpage=1228 (accessed on 25 April 2023).
6. Rzig, D.E.; Hassan, F.; Kessentini, M. An empirical study on ML DevOps adoption trends, efforts, and benefits analysis. *Inf. Softw. Technol.* **2022**, *152*, 107037. [CrossRef]
7. Child Birth Weight Dataset | IEEE DataPort. Available online: https://ieee-dataport.org/documents/child-birth-weight-dataset (accessed on 25 April 2023).
8. Adeeba, S.; Kuhaneswaran, B.; Kumara, B.T.G.S. Prediction of Weight Range of Neonate Using Machine Learning Approach. In Proceedings of the 2022 International Conference on Innovations in Science, Engineering and Technology (ICISET), Chittagong, Bangladesh, 26–27 February 2022; pp. 427–432. [CrossRef]
9. Khan, W.; Zaki, N.; Masud, M.M.; Ahmad, A.; Ali, L.; Ali, N.; Ahmed, L.A. Infant birth weight estimation and low birth weight classification in United Arab Emirates using machine learning algorithms. *Sci. Rep.* **2022**, *12*, 12110. [CrossRef]
10. Desiani, A.; Primartha, R.; Arhami, M.; Orsalan, O. Naive Bayes classifier for infant weight prediction of hypertension mother. *J. Phys. Conf. Ser.* **2019**, *1282*, 012005. [CrossRef]
11. Moreira, M.W.L.; Rodrigues, J.J.P.C.; Furtado, V.; Mavromoustakis, C.X.; Kumar, N.; Woungang, I. Fetal Birth Weight Estimation in High-Risk Pregnancies through Machine Learning Techniques. In Proceedings of the ICC 2019-2019 IEEE International Conference on Communications (ICC), Shanghai, China, 20–24 May 2019. [CrossRef]
12. Lu, Y.; Zhang, X.; Fu, X.; Chen, F.; Wong, K.K.L. Ensemble Machine Learning for Estimating Fetal Weight at Varying Gestational Age. *Proc. AAAI Conf. Artif. Intell.* **2019**, *33*, 9522–9527. [CrossRef]
13. Trujillo, O.C.; Perez-Gonzalez, J.; Medina-Bañuelos, V. Early Prediction of Weight at Birth Using Support Vector Regression. *IFMBE Proc.* **2020**, *75*, 37–41. [CrossRef]
14. Bekele, W.T. Machine learning algorithms for predicting low birth weight in Ethiopia. *BMC Med. Inform. Decis. Mak.* **2022**, *22*, 232. [CrossRef] [PubMed]
15. Faruk, A.; Cahyono, E.S.; Eliyati, N.; Arifieni, I. Prediction and Classification of Low Birth Weight Data Using Machine Learning Techniques. *Indones. J. Sci. Technol.* **2018**, *3*, 18–28. [CrossRef]
16. Pathak, R.; Faraz, S.; Jain, M.; Gaurav, K. Infant Weight Prediction Using Multivariate Linear Regression. *Int. J. Res. Anal. Rev.* **2018**, *5*, 158–164. Available online: http://ijrar.com/ (accessed on 25 April 2023).
17. Tao, J.; Yuan, Z.; Sun, L.; Yu, K.; Zhang, Z. Fetal birthweight prediction with measured data by a temporal machine learning method. *BMC Med. Inform. Decis. Mak.* **2021**, *21*, 26. [CrossRef]
18. Gao, H.; Wu, C.; Huang, D.; Zha, D.; Zhou, C. Prediction of fetal weight based on back propagation neural network optimized by genetic algorithm. *Math. Biosci. Eng.* **2021**, *18*, 4402–4410. [CrossRef]
19. Arayeshgari, M.; Najafi-Ghobadi, S.; Tarhsaz, H.; Parami, S.; Tapak, L. Machine Learning-based Classifiers for the Prediction of Low Birth Weight. *Healthc. Inform. Res.* **2023**, *29*, 54–63. [CrossRef]
20. Ranjbar, A.; Montazeri, F.; Farashah, M.V.; Mehrnoush, V.; Darsareh, F.; Roozbeh, N. Machine learning-based approach for predicting low birth weight. *BMC Pregnancy Childbirth* **2023**, *23*, 803. [CrossRef] [PubMed]
21. Ren, Y.; Wu, D.; Tong, Y.; López-DeFede, A.; Gareau, S. Issue of Data Imbalance on Low Birthweight Baby Outcomes Prediction and Associated Risk Factors Identification: Establishment of Benchmarking Key Machine Learning Models with Data Rebalancing Strategies. *J. Med. Internet Res.* **2023**, *25*, e44081. [CrossRef] [PubMed]
22. Kumar, D. Introduction to Data Preprocessing in Machine Learning. *Towards Data Sci.* **2018**, *25*, 48. Available online: https://towardsdatascience.com/introduction-to-data-preprocessing-in-machine-learning-a9fa83a5dc9d (accessed on 25 April 2023).
23. Data Preprocessing in Machine Learning-Javatpoint. Available online: https://www.javatpoint.com/data-preprocessing-machine-learning (accessed on 25 April 2023).
24. Kumar, A.; Ogunkeye, F.; Singh, S. Python-Replace Missing Values with Mean, Median & Mode-Data Analytics. Available online: https://vitalflux.com/pandas-impute-missing-values-mean-median-mode/ (accessed on 25 April 2023).
25. Kartik, M. The Complete Guide to Skewness and Kurtosis | Simplilearn. Available online: https://www.simplilearn.com/tutorials/statistics-tutorial/skewness-and-kurtosis (accessed on 25 April 2023).
26. Mode | Mode in Statistics (Definition, How to Find Mode, Examples). Available online: https://byjus.com/maths/mode/ (accessed on 25 April 2023).
27. Alghamdi, A.S.; Rahman, A. Data Mining Approach to Predict Success of Secondary School Students: A Saudi Arabian Case Study. *Educ. Sci.* **2023**, *13*, 293. [CrossRef]

28. Gollapalli, M.; Rahman, A.; Alkharraa, M.; Saraireh, L.; AlKhulaifi, D.; Salam, A.A.; Krishnasamy, G.; Alam Khan, M.A.; Farooqui, M.; Mahmud, M.; et al. SUNFIT: A Machine Learning-Based Sustainable University Field Training Framework for Higher Education. *Sustainability* **2023**, *15*, 8057. [CrossRef]
29. Geurts, P.; Ernst, D.; Wehenkel, L. Extremely randomized trees. *Mach. Learn.* **2006**, *63*, 3–42. [CrossRef]
30. Musleh, D.A.; Olatunji, S.O.; Almajed, A.A.; Alghamdi, A.S.; Alamoudi, B.K.; Almousa, F.S.; Aleid, R.A.; Alamoudi, S.K.; Jan, F.; Al-Mofeez, K.A.; et al. Ensemble Learning Based Sustainable Approach to Carbonate Reservoirs Permeability Prediction. *Sustainability* **2023**, *15*, 14403. [CrossRef]
31. AdaBoost Algorithm: Understand, Implement and Master AdaBoost. Available online: https://www.analyticsvidhya.com/blog/2021/09/adaboost-algorithm-a-complete-guide-for-beginners/ (accessed on 25 April 2023).
32. What is XGBoost? | Introduction to XGBoost Algorithm in ML. Available online: https://www.analyticsvidhya.com/blog/2018/09/an-end-to-end-guide-to-understand-the-math-behind-xgboost/ (accessed on 25 April 2023).
33. XGBoost vs. LightGBM: How Are They Different. Available online: https://neptune.ai/blog/xgboost-vs-lightgbm (accessed on 25 April 2023).
34. Qureshi, M.A.; Asif, M.; Anwar, S.; Shaukat, U.; Khan, M.A.; Mosavi, A. Aspect Level Songs Rating Based upon Reviews in English. *Comput. Mater. Contin.* **2023**, *74*, 2589–2605.
35. Abbas, S.; Raza, S.A.; Khan, M.A.; Rahman, A.; Sultan, K.; Mosavi, A. Automated File Labeling for Heterogeneous Files Organization Using Machine Learning. *Comput. Mater. Contin.* **2023**, *74*, 3263–3278. [CrossRef]
36. Ahmed, M.S.; Rahman, A.; AlGhamdi, F.; AlDakheel, S.; Hakami, H.; AlJumah, A.; AlIbrahim, Z.; Youldash, M.; Alam Khan, M.A.; Basheer Ahmed, M.I. Joint Diagnosis of Pneumonia, COVID-19, and Tuberculosis from Chest X-ray Images: A Deep Learning Approach. *Diagnostics* **2023**, *13*, 2562. [CrossRef]
37. Jan, F.; Rahman, A.; Busaleh, R.; Alwarthan, H.; Aljaser, S.; Al-Towailib, S.; Alshammari, S.; Alhindi, K.R.; Almogbil, A.; Bubshait, D.A.; et al. Assessing Acetabular Index Angle in Infants: A Deep Learning-Based Novel Approach. *J. Imaging* **2023**, *9*, 242. [CrossRef]
38. Khan, T.A.; Fatima, A.; Shahzad, T.; Rahman, A.U.; Alissa, K.; Ghazal, T.M.; Al-Sakhnini, M.M.; Abbas, S.; Khan, M.A.; Ahmed, A. Secure IoMT for Disease Prediction Empowered with Transfer Learning in Healthcare 5.0, the Concept and Case Study. *IEEE Access* **2023**, *11*, 39418–39430. [CrossRef]
39. Navas, J. What Is Hyperparameter Tuning | Anyscale. Available online: https://www.anyscale.com/blog/what-is-hyperparameter-tuning (accessed on 25 April 2023).
40. Brownlee, J. What Is the Difference between a Parameter and a Hyperparameter? Available online: https://machinelearningmastery.com/difference-between-a-parameter-and-a-hyperparameter/ (accessed on 25 April 2023).
41. Grid Search for Hyperparameter Tuning | by Mathanraj Sharma | Towards Data Science. Available online: https://towardsdatascience.com/grid-search-for-hyperparameter-tuning-9f63945e8fec (accessed on 25 April 2023).
42. An Introduction to GridSearchCV | What Is Grid Search | Great Learning. Available online: https://www.mygreatlearning.com/blog/gridsearchcv/ (accessed on 25 April 2023).
43. Lundberg, S.M.; Erion, G.; Chen, H.; DeGrave, A.; Prutkin, J.M.; Nair, B.; Katz, R.; Himmelfarb, J.; Bansal, N.; Lee, S.-I. From local explanations to global understanding with explainable AI for trees. *Nat. Mach. Intell.* **2020**, *2*, 56–67. [CrossRef] [PubMed]
44. GitHub-Slundberg/Shap: A Game Theoretic Approach to Explain the Output of Any Machine Learning Model. Available online: https://github.com/slundberg/shap (accessed on 25 April 2023).
45. Saudi Arabia Diagnostic Imaging Market Size & Share Analysis-Industry Research Report-Growth Trends. Available online: https://www.mordorintelligence.com/industry-reports/saudi-arabia-diagnostic-imaging-equipment-market-industry (accessed on 25 April 2023).
46. Gaillard, R.; Steegers, E.A.P.; de-Jongste, J.C.; Hofman, A.; Jaddoe, V.W.V. Tracking of fetal growth characteristics during different trimesters and the risks of adverse birth outcomes. *Int. J. Epidemiol.* **2014**, *43*, 1140–1153. [CrossRef] [PubMed]

machine learning & knowledge extraction

MDPI

*Article*

# Effective Detection of Epileptic Seizures through EEG Signals Using Deep Learning Approaches

**Sakorn Mekruksavanich [1] and Anuchit Jitpattanakul [2,3,*]**

1 Department of Computer Engineering, School of Information and Communication Technology, University of Phayao, Phayao 56000, Thailand; sakorn.me@up.ac.th
2 Department of Mathematics, Faculty of Applied Science, King Mongkut's University of Technology North Bangkok, Bangkok 10800, Thailand
3 Intelligent and Nonlinear Dynamic Innovations Research Center, Science and Technology Research Institute, King Mongkut's University of Technology North Bangkok, Bangkok 10800, Thailand
* Correspondence: anuchit.j@sci.kmutnb.ac.th

**Abstract:** Epileptic seizures are a prevalent neurological condition that impacts a considerable portion of the global population. Timely and precise identification can result in as many as 70% of individuals achieving freedom from seizures. To achieve this, there is a pressing need for smart, automated systems to assist medical professionals in identifying neurological disorders correctly. Previous efforts have utilized raw electroencephalography (EEG) data and machine learning techniques to classify behaviors in patients with epilepsy. However, these studies required expertise in clinical domains like radiology and clinical procedures for feature extraction. Traditional machine learning for classification relied on manual feature engineering, limiting performance. Deep learning excels at automated feature learning directly from raw data sans human effort. For example, deep neural networks now show promise in analyzing raw EEG data to detect seizures, eliminating intensive clinical or engineering needs. Though still emerging, initial studies demonstrate practical applications across medical domains. In this work, we introduce a novel deep residual model called ResNet-BiGRU-ECA, analyzing brain activity through EEG data to accurately identify epileptic seizures. To evaluate our proposed deep learning model's efficacy, we used a publicly available benchmark dataset on epilepsy. The results of our experiments demonstrated that our suggested model surpassed both the basic model and cutting-edge deep learning models, achieving an outstanding accuracy rate of 0.998 and the top F1-score of 0.998.

**Keywords:** electroencephalography; epileptic seizure detection; deep learning; deep residual network; efficient channel attention

## 1. Introduction

Epilepsy is an enduring neurological disorder that primarily impacts the central nervous system, with its primary expression manifesting in the brain. It is characterized by the occurrence of sudden and repetitive seizures [1]. This ailment is recognized as the third most prevalent neurological condition, ranking closely behind stroke and Alzheimer's disease [2]. An epileptic seizure is a temporary event characterized by unusual and exaggerated activity of brain neurons, leading to the presence of signs or symptoms [3]. Seizures can be identified by observing and analyzing various physiological indicators, such as brain and muscle activities, heart rate, oxygen levels, synthetic speech, or visual patterns. Techniques like electroencephalography (EEG), electrocardiogram (ECG), electromyography (EMG), movement tracking, or video capturing on a person's head and body are used for this purpose [4].

To detect anomalous behaviors and enable early detection of epileptic seizures before they escalate into more severe states, human activity recognition (HAR) can be effectively applied [5]. Recent scholarly investigations have explored a range of techniques for identifying anomalous behaviors [6], including wearable technologies, sensor-based approaches, and ambient instrument methodologies. The activated notification system ensures the verification of action identification. However, the accuracy of detecting these behaviors depends on the thorough analysis and precise acquisition of feature patterns [7].

EEG signals are preferred for their cost-effectiveness, portability, and ability to exhibit distinct frequency-dependent patterns [8]. The EEG is a measurement technique that captures the brain's bioelectric activities by recording voltage fluctuations resulting from the ionic flow of neurons [9]. To identify epileptic seizures accurately, capturing signals over an extended duration is necessary, which can introduce complexity due to multiple channels used for storage. Studies have also raised concerns over wearable devices' energy use and data storage limits posing challenges for creating seizure forecasting tools [10]. These portable gadgets tend to swiftly drain batteries and lack capacity to save the huge data flows needed to reliably predict seizures over extended periods. Overcoming these power and memory roadblocks to enable precise ambulatory monitoring and algorithms will require further innovations going forward. Nonetheless, EEG signals can be influenced by disturbances arising from different origins, including the main power supply, movement of electrodes, and muscular vibrations [11]. The presence of noisy EEG signals poses a significant challenge for healthcare professionals in diagnosing epileptic seizures effectively. To address these difficulties, extensive research is currently being conducted to detect and forecast epileptic seizures through the utilization of EEG methods, alongside tools like magnetic resonance imaging (MRI) and artificial intelligence (AI) methodologies [12]. The realm of diagnosing epileptic seizures has been incorporating traditional machine learning (ML) and deep learning (DL) techniques within the framework of AI methods [13].

Numerous ML algorithms have been established for epileptic seizure identification, incorporating statistical, temporal, spectral, time–frequency domain, and nonlinear features [14]. Traditional ML approaches involve a trial-and-error method for selecting features and classifiers [15]. A thorough grasp of signal processing and data mining techniques is essential for constructing accurate models. A recent study [16] utilized three ML models—support vector machines, linear discriminant analysis, and multilayer perceptrons—to differentiate resting state EEG data between healthy subjects and those with psychogenic non-epileptic seizures. Specifically, these algorithms aimed to uncover connections between measures of functional brain connectivity and the eventual categorical diagnosis. By modeling these complex relationships, the systems classified individual data points as belonging to either the healthy control group or the psychogenic seizure group. Initial findings demonstrated promise in using patterns of functional connectivity derived from EEGs to accurately predict which subjects were suffering from non-epileptic events via completely automated ML. However, further validation is still needed, particularly around generalizability to diverse patient subgroups. While these models perform well with small data sets, the field has also implemented sophisticated DL techniques for epileptic seizure identification [17]. DL models, unlike traditional ML methods, require a substantial amount of data during training due to their complex feature mapping spaces. This phenomenon leads to overfitting challenges when confronted with insufficient data.

The primary objective of this research is to utilize DL networks to detect epilepsy by automatically processing EEG signals and recognizing patterns. The aim is to identify the spatial distribution and temporal characteristics of spikes and seizures. Convolutional neural networks (CNN), long short-term memory (LSTM), and gated recurrent unit (GRU) are among the methods employed in this research. We introduce a new deep residual model, ResNet-BiGRU-ECA, to accurately identify epileptic seizures by analyzing EEG data.

To evaluate the performance of our model, we utilized a publicly available epilepsy dataset. This benchmark compilation contained EEG readings segmented into five distinct health categories—one representing active epileptic seizures and the remaining four encompassing normal, non-seizure brain activity. Leveraging this diverse test set enabled robust assessment of the model's ability to accurately differentiate between the pathological seizure state and healthy function. Through this analysis, we aim to demonstrate several key contributions of the current research, summarized as follows:

- This research presents a framework for epileptic seizure detection (ESD) using EEG data to assess the performance of various DL structures within this particular domain.
- The suggested method introduces a deep residual model that incorporates residual blocks, an efficient channel attention (ECA) module, and a bidirectional GRU (Bi-GRU). This model adeptly captures extended data sequences, extracts spatio-temporal features, and carries out EEG classification.

The paper's organization is as follows: Section 2 offers a summary of pertinent literature and prior studies. Section 3 outlines the proposed DL-based framework for epileptic seizure recognition. The results are showcased and examined in Section 4, and Section 5 wraps up and deliberates on potential avenues for future research.

## 2. Related Work

In this section, we review several studies that have used DL to classify epileptic and non-epileptic activities. One study introduced a DL model called the pyramidal one-dimensional CNN. This CNN model uses improved parameters that are less amenable to training than those used in conventional CNNs. The model achieved a remarkable accuracy of 99.1% when used to distinguish between different behaviors, including typical behaviors such as eyes closed, eyes open, and pre-ictal, as well as unusual behaviors such as inter-ictal and ictal [18].

Conventional DL models struggle to process lengthy, variable input data like text, sensor readings over time, or video [19]. Yet these sequential data types represent abundant real-world information. Recurrent neural networks (RNNs) have emerged to enable DL on such ordered series with temporal dynamics. Through internal state units retaining context, RNNs can analyze signals that change over timescales like EEG—gaining widespread use in physiology. Standard deep networks fail on such variable, redundant sequential inputs. But by propagating context, RNNs overcome challenges of long inputs with fluctuations and redundancy across temporal or spatial dimensions [7]. This unique feedback architecture provides short-term memory lacking in feedforward networks to better extract patterns from sequential data like measurements over time.

The primary limitation of a basic RNN lies in its inability to retain information effectively over short periods of time. This is mainly because RNNs struggle to propagate information from earlier time steps to later ones, especially when dealing with long sequential data [20]. Another challenge faced by RNNs is the vanishing gradient problem [21], which occurs when the gradients diminish significantly during backpropagation. To overcome the short-term memory issue, researchers devised a solution in the form of LSTM neural networks [22]. LSTM networks address the problem by allowing the model to selectively store and access relevant information, making them more adept at handling long sequences and retaining essential details.

In their study, Golmohammadi et al. [23] evaluated two LSTM designs: one with three layers and the other with four layers, both combined with the Softmax classifier. The researchers reported that their findings were considered appropriate. In another study [24], a three-layer LSTM architecture was used for feature extraction and classification. The final fully connected layer commonly employed the sigmoid activation function for classification purposes. Furthermore, in a study conducted by another group [25], two structures, LSTM and GRU, were investigated. The structure of the LSTM/GRU model included a reshaped layer, succeeded by four layers of LSTM/GRU with an activation function, and, ultimately, a fully connected layer featuring a sigmoid activation function. In summary, these studies explored various LSTM designs and activation functions to improve feature extraction and classification accuracy.

In the realm of sophisticated DL models, it has been observed that employing more intricate and deeper architectures leads to enhanced accuracy compared to the feature learning approach discussed earlier. These prototypes employ CNNs to identify features autonomously [26]. In particular, the CNN feature extractor is often denoted as the backbone when it comes to object recognition, setting it apart from the complete model architecture. In this investigation, we adopt a CNN-based feature extractor as the foundational framework. DL techniques, such as CNNs and RNNs, have demonstrated their ability to obtain state-of-the-art performance by autonomously learning the underlying characteristics from raw sensor data. The concept of deepening neural networks has evolved with the emergence of hybrid networks. These hybrid models combine diverse architectural designs, leading to improved feature representation and enhancing both computing and network achievements. Moreover, this development opens up opportunities for DL-based techniques in portable electronics.

## 3. Methodology

In this section, we delineate the structure applied in our study to assess the importance of EEG signals concerning epileptic seizures. The suggested ESD framework encompasses four separate phases: (i) collecting data, (ii) preparing data, (iii) processing data, and (iv) performing classification. To visually represent the approach used to detect seizures, refer to Figure 1.

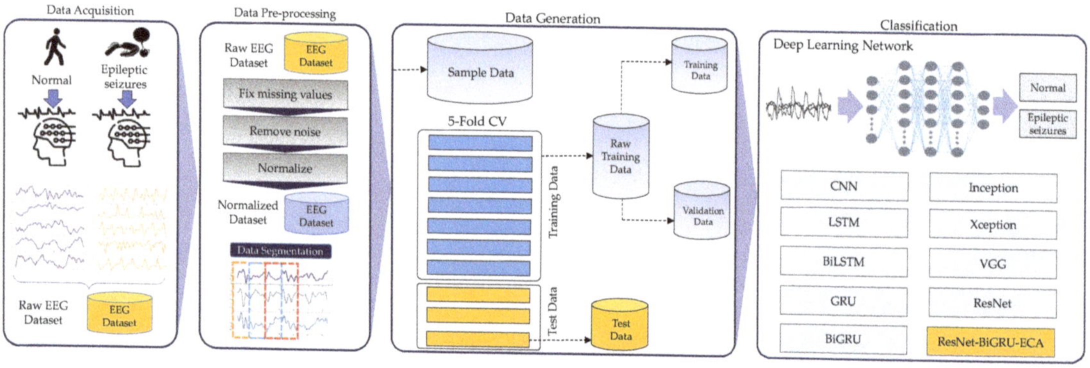


**Figure 1.** The epileptic seizure detection (ESD) framework proposed in this study.

### 3.1. Data Acquisition

Data acquisition refers to the systematic process of collecting and preserving digital or numerical data to incorporate it into our mathematical framework. This can be done either in its original, unprocessed state or after undergoing preliminary processing, depending on data accessibility. Therefore, it is crucial to have a comprehensive understanding of the dataset before obtaining the data.

To develop and test our model, we employed the epileptic seizures recognition dataset (ESRD), a publicly accessible benchmark widely utilized for detecting seizures [27]. This compilation contains EEG readings from multiple patients, acquired through a standardized 128-channel system and averaged reference methodology. The analogue signals were digitized via 12-bit analog-to-digital conversion and continuously saved onto a computer at 173.61 Hz sampling frequency. Understanding such data collection and processing details is crucial for appropriate methodology. The ESRD dataset comprises data from 500 individuals, including 11,500 instances of time-series EEG signals specifically designed for investigating EEG signal alterations during seizure events. Before being made available online, the initial dataset undergoes preliminary processing by the university of California Irvine (UCI). Each dataset sample in our study consists of 4097 data points, further divided into 23 parts, with each part comprising 178 data points representing one second of data. These 23 components are shuffled in a random manner, yielding a collective count of 11,500 time-series EEG signal samples sourced from the 500 individuals in the study group. The UCI dataset for recognizing epileptic seizures encompasses five distinct medical conditions, with one being explicitly linked to epileptic seizures, while the remaining four conditions pertain to individuals displaying no signs of epilepsy. More information about these five categories and their respective samples can be found in Table 1.

**Table 1.** Summarized details of the epileptic seizures recognition dataset (ESRD).

| Class | No. of Samples | ESR Classes | Details |
|---|---|---|---|
| 1 | 2300 | Ictal | Recordings made during epileptic episodes |
| 2 | 2300 | Pre-ictal | Recording obtained prior to the onset of a single-site seizure |
| 3 | 2300 | Inter-ictal | Recording obtained prior to the onset of the consecutive seizure |
| 4 | 2300 | Healthy (close eye) | An individual in good health with their eyes shut |
| 5 | 2300 | Healthy (open eye) | An individual in good health with their eyes open |

Numerous analyses have recommended simplifying the multi-class categorization challenge embodied in the UCI seizure dataset, which segregates EEG data into five unique groups as shown in Figure 2. Rather than attempting to draw boundaries between all categories, they propose concentrating specifically on discriminating class one—representing active epileptic seizures—from aggregate signals of the other classes signifying ordinary non-seizure brain states. This binary framework focuses model resources on the most vital differentiation between pathological and healthy function. Though it sacrifices granularity within normal activity subtypes, enhanced accuracy and reliability in identifying the central seizure condition demonstrate the sensibility of this targeted approach.

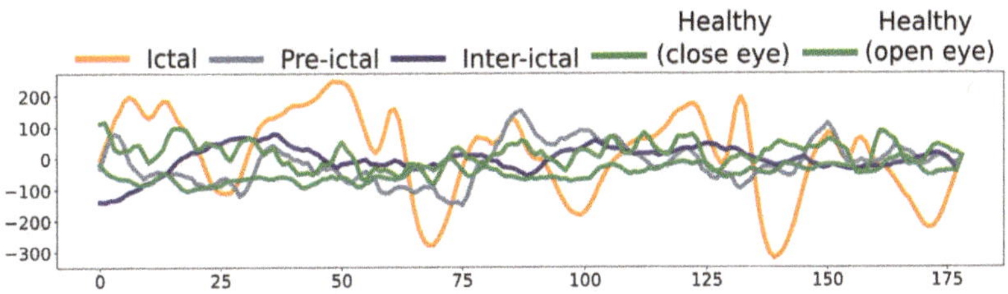


**Figure 2.** Electroencephalography (EEG) waveforms of five epileptic seizures recognition (ESR) classes from the epileptic seizures recognition dataset (ESRD).

### 3.2. Data Pre-Processing

During this phase, the EEG data undergo filtering and normalization procedures. The goal is to generate a dataset that is uniform and appropriate for training a detection model. In this approach, any incomplete or anomalous data values are removed from the dataset according to the following procedure:

- We used the linear interpolation procedure for imputation to address the issue of incomplete values in sensor data. This helped eliminate any existing noises. To reduce noise that could obscure relevant EEG patterns, we implemented sequential low and median pass filtering. Initially, a third-order Butterworth filter eliminated high frequency artifacts over 20 Hz. Next, a third-order median filter replaced each point with the regional median value, calculated from surrounding data. By emphasizing the median, sporadic outliers and anomalies get rejected in favor of the less skewed central tendency. This substitutes misleading erratic spikes with smoothed waveforms reflecting underlying dynamics. The process removes irrelevant deviations so key shape features needed for model training remain, without distortion from sporadic spikes that misrepresent normal or pathological brain activity.

- In addition, we standardized each individual segment of EEG data using a normalization method that involved calculating the mean and standard deviation. This step was crucial in ensuring consistency and comparability across the data.

The normalization process entails using the min–max method to adjust the unprocessed EEG data linearly. After the data are cleaned and normalized, they become the input for the subsequent data preparation and classification procedures. To facilitate the training of the classifier, the data are partitioned based on the chosen methodology. The second group is subsequently employed as a test set to assess the performance of the classifier that has been trained.

### 3.3. The Proposed ResNet-BiGRU-ECA Model

This study introduces the ResNet-BiGRU-ECA model that utilizes EEG signals to identify epileptic seizures accurately. The model demonstrated in this study can autonomously extract distinctive features from the input sensor data. Figure 3 provides a depiction of the ResNet-BiGRU-ECA architecture, comprising a convolutional block (ConvB) and eight hybrid residual blocks designed for extracting spatial features with unique characteristics. These features are further processed through a global average pooling (GAP) layer and a fully connected (FC) layer.

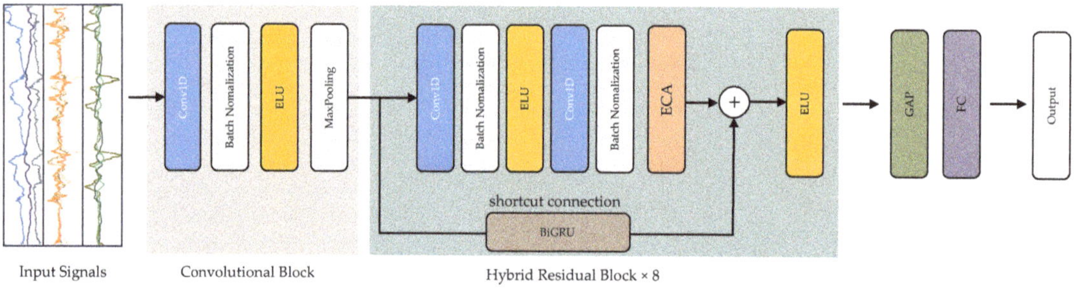


**Figure 3.** The structure of the ResNet-BiGRU-ECA model introduced in this study.

#### 3.3.1. Convolutional Block

CNNs are a type of neural network commonly used in supervised learning. CNNs have a specific architecture in which each neuron in one layer is connected to every neuron in the next layer. The input to each neuron is transformed into an output via an activation function [28]. Two key properties of the activation function that impact CNN performance are sparsity (having many zeros) and ability to propagate gradients to lower layers during backpropagation. Overall, CNNs leverage their specialized architecture with sparse activation functions to effectively learn representations of data like images for classification and other supervised learning tasks [29]. In CNNs, pooling operations are frequently employed to reduce dimensionality. Two frequently employed pooling functions include max-pooling and average-pooling, both of which aid in extracting the most significant features from the data.

In this research, ConvB is employed to extract foundational features from unprocessed sensor data. The ConvB structure comprises four components: 1D-convolutional (Conv1D), batch normalization (BN), exponential linear unit (ELU), and max-pooling (MP) layers, as visualized in Figure 3. The Conv1D layer utilizes multiple trainable convolutional kernels to detect distinct features, generating a feature map for each kernel. The BN layer is applied to improve stability and accelerate the training process. Additionally, the ELU layer is integrated to enhance the model's expressive capacity. Furthermore, the MP layer is used to downsize the feature map's dimensions while retaining the most salient features. This amalgamation of layers within the ConvB architecture assists in extracting valuable foundational features from the raw sensor data.

#### 3.3.2. Bidirectional Gated Recurrent Unit

GRU was introduced to address the issue of gradients either growing too large or vanishing in RNNs. However, the incorporation of memory cells in the GRU design elevates the memory resource requirements [30]. Unlike the LSTM model, the GRU is a more streamlined version, lacking a separate memory cell in its architecture [31]. Instead, the GRU network integrates update and reset gates, which play a role in determining the adjustments made to each hidden state. These gates control the information that should be propagated to the following state and the data deemed unnecessary, as illustrated in Figure 4a.

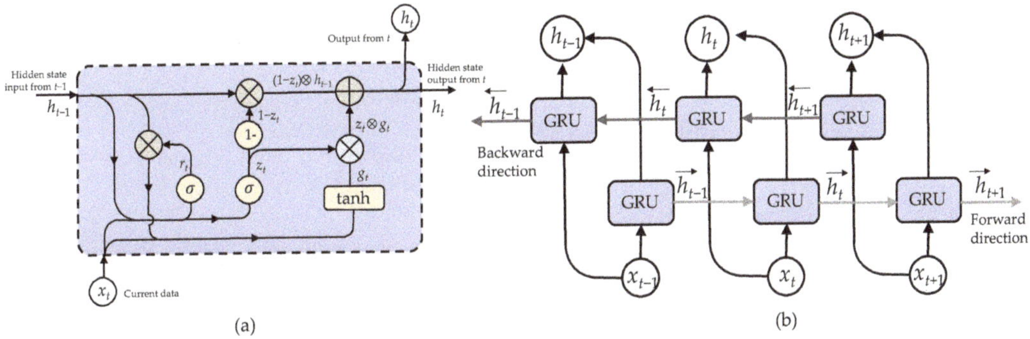


**Figure 4.** The structure of the ResNet-BiGRU-ECA model introduced in this study: (**a**) GRU cell and (**b**) unroll BiGRU.

The calculation of the hidden state $h_t$ at time $t$ in a GRU model involves utilizing the update gate $z_t$, reset gate $r_t$, current input $x_t$, and the prior hidden state $h_{t-1}$. These components work together to manage the flow of information in the GRU network efficiently.

$$z_t = s(W_z x_t \oplus U_z h_{t-1}) \tag{1}$$

$$r_t = s(W_r x_t \oplus U_r h_{t-1}) \tag{2}$$

$$g_t = \tanh(W_g x_t \oplus U_g(r_t \otimes h_{t-1})) \tag{3}$$

$$h_t = ((1 - z_t) \otimes h_{t-1}) \oplus (z_t \otimes g_t) \tag{4}$$

where $s$ denotes a sigmoid function, $\oplus$ denotes an elementary addition operation, and $\otimes$ denotes an elementary multiplication operation.

In 1997, Schuster and Paliwal [32] introduced the bidirectional RNN (BiRNN) to address limitations of traditional unidirectional RNNs. The key innovation was to have the outputs at each time step incorporate contextual information not just from preceding time steps but also future time steps. This is achieved by training two separate hidden states, one processing the inputs in a forward direction and the other processing in reverse. The outputs at each time step are then computed based on the hidden states from both directions. By leveraging future context as well as past, BiRNNs can better model sequential data like text or speech compared to unidirectional RNNs. This bidirectional architecture has become widely adopted for sequence modeling tasks.

Within this BiRNN framework, the neurons in a standard RNN are segregated into two separate components: one dedicated to processing information in the forward direction and the other focused on information from the opposite direction. Notably, the output of positive neurons is independent of negative neurons, and vice versa. This arrangement gives rise to a general structure illustrated in Figure 4b. The underlying computational processes are outlined by the equations provided below.

$$\overrightarrow{h_t} = GRU(x_t, \overrightarrow{h_{t-1}}) \tag{5}$$

$$\overleftarrow{h_t} = GRU(x_t, \overleftarrow{h_{t+1}}) \tag{6}$$

$$h_t = [\overrightarrow{h_t}, \overleftarrow{h_t}] \tag{7}$$

#### 3.3.3. ECA Mechanism

The ECA strategy holds great promise for boosting the effectiveness of deep CNNs. However, most current approaches focus on developing intricate attention components to enhance effectiveness, inadvertently leading to more complex models and increased processing demands. A solution known as ECA has been proposed to address the challenges of overfitting and high computational needs [33]. This ECA module determines weights for individual channels and captures interrelationships among different channels.

In time series data, the norm involves assigning higher weights to crucial features while assigning lower weights to less relevant ones. Herein, the ECA method takes on the responsibility of prioritizing pertinent information, thus bolstering the network's capacity to discern and respond to pivotal characteristics. The configuration of the ECA module is visually represented in Figure 5. The channel weights in ECA are generated by applying a 1D convolution with a creative choice of kernel size ($k$) to the aggregated data obtained through GAP. The choice of the value for $k$ is decided by mapping the channel dimensions (C).

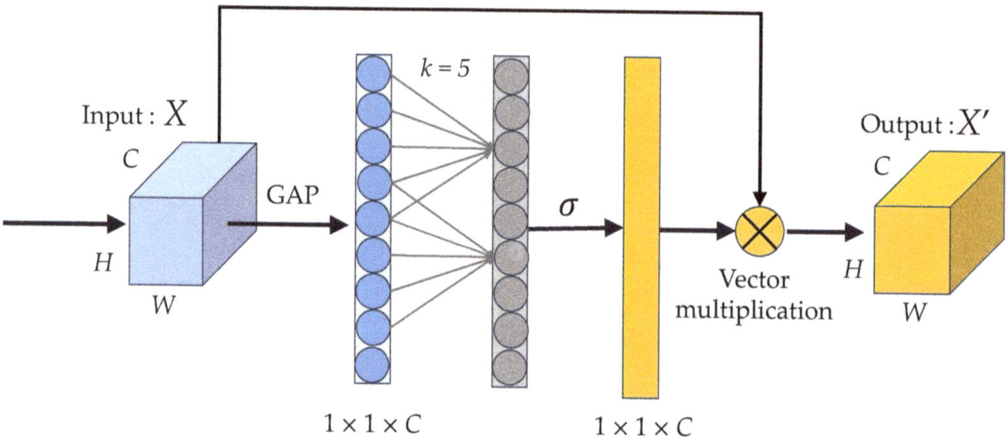


**Figure 5.** The structure of the efficient channel attention (ECA) block.

#### 3.3.4. Training and Hyperparameters

Model performance hinges critically on sufficient volumes of representative, varied data for training along with properly tuned architectural design parameters called hyperparameters, like iteration counts, learning rates, batch size, activation logic, etc. We applied a standardized approach separating data into training (for hyperparameter optimization) and holdout validation sets (for independent comparative testing). Guided by trial and error, the following settings maximized eventual accuracy: 128 batch size, $1 \times 10^{-3}$ learning rate, 200 epoch count, plus adaptive logic to cut the learning rate by 25% after 10 stagnant epochs lacking improvement. Beyond tuning, we enabled data shuffling before each epoch for robustness. For model specification, we utilized an Adam optimizer for weight adjustments and cross-entropy error quantification. Refer to Table 2 for full architectural details, including all set hyperparameters for our customized ResNet-BiGRU-ECA framework.

**Table 2.** The summary of hyperparameters of the ResNet-BiGRU-ECA used in this work.

| Stage | Hyperparameters | | Values |
|---|---|---|---|
| Architecture | Convolutional Block | | |
| | 1D-Convolution | Kernel Size | 5 |
| | | Stride | 1 |
| | | Filters | 64 |
| | Batch Normalization | | - |
| | Activation | | ELU |
| | Max Pooling | | 2 |
| | Hybrid Residual Block × 8 | | |
| | Main Path | | |
| | 1D-Convolution | Kernel Size | 5 |
| | | Stride | 1 |
| | | Filters | 32 |
| | Batch Normalization | | - |
| | Activation | | ELU |
| | 1D-Convolution | Kernel Size | 5 |
| | | Stride | 1 |
| | | Filters | 64 |
| | Batch Normalization | | - |
| | ECA Module | | - |
| | Parallel Path | | |
| | BiGRU Unit | | 128 |
| | Global Average Pooling | | - |
| | Flatten | | - |
| | Dense | | 128 |
| Training | Loss Function | | Cross-entropy |
| | Optimizer | | Adam |
| | Batch Size | | 64 |
| | Number of Epochs | | 200 |

### 3.4. Cross Validation

The k-fold cross-validation ($k$-CV) procedure is a technique employed to assess the performance of a classification model [34]. This method entails partitioning a dataset, collected from one or more sources, into approximately equal-sized, distinct, and non-overlapping subsets of $k$. Each of these subsets is then utilized to evaluate the model, which is trained on the remaining $k-1$ subsets. The overall performance of the model is determined by computing the mean of various performance metrics, such as accuracy, precision, recall, and F-measure, all derived from the $k$-CV process [35].

Nonetheless, it is important to acknowledge that this method can pose significant computational demands, particularly when working with extensive datasets or when $k$ is set to a high value. In our study, we have employed the $k$-CV procedure with a chosen value of $k = 5$, as depicted in Figure 6, to assess the effectiveness of our models.

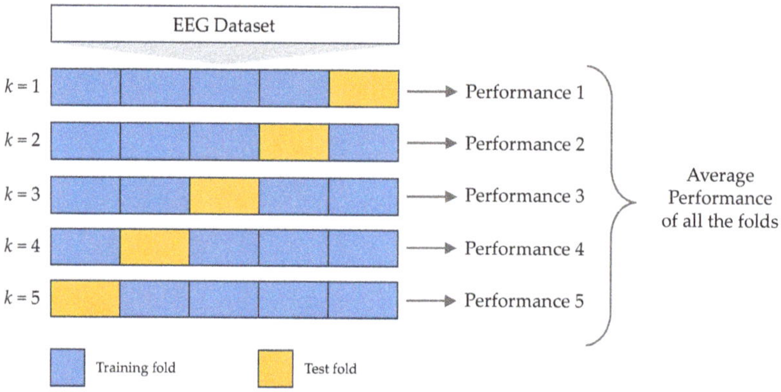


**Figure 6.** The 5-fold cross validation.

## 4. Experimental Results and Discussion

In this section, we will detail the experimental setup and showcase the outcomes acquired through our assessment of DL models for the purpose of identifying epileptic seizures.

### 4.1. Experiments

The experiments in this study were conducted using Google Colab Pro, which provides access to Tesla V100 GPUs. The implementation was done in Python 3.6.9, utilizing key libraries, including TensorFlow 2.2.0 for building the neural network models, Keras 2.3.1 for the high-level API, Scikit-Learn for machine learning utilities, Numpy 1.18.5 for numerical processing, and Pandas 1.0.5 for data manipulation. By leveraging Google Colab and these state-of-the-art libraries, the experiments could be efficiently run on powerful hardware, enabling the exploration of deep neural network architectures for the research questions under investigation.

This empirical study compared four main DL architectures for the application of ESD on the ESRD dataset. The models tested were CNNs, LSTMs, bidirectional LSTMs (BiLSTMs), GRUs, and BiGRUs. These represented the state-of-the-art approaches. Our proposed model, called ResNet-BiGRU-ECA, was benchmarked against these models to assess its performance at identifying seizures relative to conventional architectures. By evaluating both unidirectional and bidirectional variants of LSTM and GRU models, we aimed to thoroughly compare our novel approach to existing methods using these epileptic seizure data.

Additionally, we conducted an in-depth investigation into various CNN backbone models. Specifically, we examined VGG16 [36], ResNet18 [37], Pyramid-Net18 [38], Inception [39], and Xception [40] to perform a comprehensive experimental comparison analysis. These models were considered as potential solutions for addressing the challenge of time-series classification. Consequently, we restructured each model to suit the context of ESR.

In this study, we conducted research on two distinct scenarios involving EEG data for ESRD. In each of these scenarios, we utilized separate datasets for both training and testing DL models, as detailed in Table 3.

**Table 3.** A compilation of experiments applied in this study.

| Scenario | Description |
|---|---|
| I | Subjects in category 1 exclusively experience epileptic seizures, whereas those in category 3 are strictly categorized as non-epileptic. |
| II | Subjects in category 1 are the sole ones with epileptic seizures, whereas subjects in the remaining classes are designated as non-epileptic. |

### 4.2. Experimental Results

In each of our experiments, we used the ESRD dataset for training DL models. To assess these models, we employed a 5-CV approach. Our study centered on assessing the effectiveness of five core DL models (CNN, LSTM, BiLSTM, GRU, and BiGRU), in addition to cutting-edge DL models, within the framework of the two situations outlined in Tables 4 and 5.

**Table 4.** Experimental results of the deep learning (DL) networks trained and tested using electroencephalography (EEG) from scenario I.

| Model | Recognition Performance | | |
|---|---|---|---|
| | **Accuracy** | **Loss** | **F1-Score** |
| CNN | 0.882 (±0.1911) | 0.245 (±0.2322) | 0.849 (±0.0258) |
| LSTM | 0.982 (±0.0019) | 0.142 (±0.0487) | 0.982 (±0.0019) |
| BiLSTM | 0.982 (±0.0016) | 0.138 (±0.0467) | 0.982 (±0.0016) |
| GRU | 0.988 (±0.0041) | 0.081 (±0.0465) | 0.988 (±0.0041) |
| BiGRU | 0.985 (±0.0016) | 0.116 (±0.0240) | 0.985 (±0.0016) |
| ResNet-BiGRU-ECA | 0.998 (±0.0007) | 0.008 (±0.0021) | 0.998 (±0.0008) |

The DL models underwent training and testing using EEG data from scenario I, as detailed in Table 4. Our experiments revealed that the ResNet-BiGRU-ECA model, as proposed, demonstrated exceptional efficiency, boasting an average accuracy of 0.998 and an average F1-score of 0.998.

**Table 5.** Experimental results of the deep learning (DL) networks trained and tested using electroencephalography (EEG) from scenario II.

| Model | Recognition Performance | | |
|---|---|---|---|
| | **Accuracy** | **Loss** | **F1-Score** |
| CNN | 0.973 (±0.0075) | 0.140 (±0.0284) | 0.957 (±0.0132) |
| LSTM | 0.985 (±0.0023) | 0.095 (±0.0280) | 0.976 (±0.0039) |
| BiLSTM | 0.983 (±0.0032) | 0.132 (±0.0436) | 0.973 (±0.0051) |
| GRU | 0.985 (±0.0027) | 0.104 (±0.0388) | 0.977 (±0.0042) |
| BiGRU | 0.985 (±0.0042) | 0.113 (±0.0367) | 0.977 (±0.0065) |
| ResNet-BiGRU-ECA | 0.996 (±0.0010) | 0.020 (±0.0059) | 0.994 (±0.0016) |

The DL models underwent training and testing with EEG data sourced from scenario II, as specified in Table 5. Upon analyzing the experiment results, it became evident that the ResNet-BiGRU-ECA model, as initially proposed, displayed the highest level of effectiveness. Its impressive performance supports this conclusion, boasting an average accuracy rate of 0.996 and an average F1-score of 0.994.

### 4.3. Comparative Results with ML Models

Guided by prior analyses [5], we selected leading ML classifiers for comparative benchmarking, including k-nearest neighbors (KNN), naive Bayes (NB), logistic regression (LR), random forest (RF), decision trees (DT), stochastic gradient boosting (SGDC), and gradient boosting (GB). Recent studies confirm the utility of these algorithms paired with neurologists in accurately detecting seizures and characterizing epileptiform EEG dynamics [41,42]. Our experiments leveraged the standard ESRD dataset under equivalent scenarios to examine model performance variability when using raw EEG readings versus extracted feature sets as inputs. Table 6 presents accuracy outcomes with our proposed deep ResNet-BiGRU-ECA architecture versus these widely adopted shallow ML approaches. By evaluating on equal inputs, we aimed to isolate the performance gains stemming solely from algorithmic and architectural optimizations rather than data pre-processing.

**Table 6.** Comparative results of the proposed model and machine learning (ML) models using electroencephalography (EEG) data from the epileptic seizures recognition dataset (ESRD).

| Model | Scenario I | | Scenario II | |
|---|---|---|---|---|
| | Accuracy | F1-Score | Accuracy | F1-Score |
| KNN | 0.870 | 0.836 | 0.890 | 0.851 |
| NB | 0.950 | 0.878 | 0.950 | 0.878 |
| LR | 0.790 | 0.878 | 0.790 | 0.878 |
| RF | 0.922 | 0.892 | 0.937 | 0.901 |
| DT | 0.910 | 0.787 | 0.910 | 0.787 |
| SGDC | 0.810 | 0.719 | 0.810 | 0.726 |
| GB | 0.800 | 0.799 | 0.834 | 0.819 |
| ResNet-BiGRU-ECA | 0.998 | 0.998 | 0.996 | 0.994 |

Results showed NB reached 95% accuracy, the sole ML technique with comparable proficiency. However, our deep ResNet-BiGRU-ECA architecture significantly exceeded all benchmark methods under both data scenarios. Surpassing 99% accuracy and 99% F1, the optimized network architecture demonstrated superior feature extraction and pattern recognition even from raw EEG readings. This substantial performance gap despite shared inputs suggests deep networks intrinsically outperform shallow ML at derives nuanced relationships within complex physiological signals. Rather than relying on predefined assumptions in simplified models, DL constructs intricate representations via hierarchical data transformations. Though some conventional methods approach sufficiency for classification tasks, deep neural networks attain state-of-the-art performance by learning intricate embeddings uniquely tuned to the intricacies of the data through backpropagation and gradient descent optimization.

### 4.4. Comparative Results with DL Models

The ResNet-BiGRU-ECA model under examination is subjected to a comparative analysis alongside previously developed models using the same dataset, specifically the ESDR dataset. Prior research studies [36–40] have consistently shown that leveraging CNN-based DL architectures yields remarkable results in the field of time-series classification. The existing literature introduced the 5-CV methodology, which we also employed in our study. The summary of comparative results can be found in Tables 7 and 8. These outcomes reveal that the ResNet-BiGRU-ECA model, as presented here, exhibits superior accuracy compared to the earlier models across the majority of actions.

**Table 7.** A side-by-side comparison of the outcomes achieved by the proposed model and state-of-the-art deep learning (DL) networks, all trained and tested using electroencephalography (EEG) data from scenario I.

| Model | Recognition Effectiveness | | |
|---|---|---|---|
| | Accuracy | Loss | F1-Score |
| Inception | 0.995 (±0.0021) | 0.03 (±0.01) | 0.995 (±0.0021) |
| Xception | 0.984 (±0.0213) | 0.10 (±0.14) | 0.984 (±0.0021) |
| VGG11 | 0.975 (±0.0065) | 0.35 (±0.18) | 0.975 (±0.0065) |
| VGG13 | 0.980 (±0.0059) | 0.27 (±0.23) | 0.980 (±0.0059) |
| VGG16 | 0.985 (±0.0039) | 0.15 (±0.07) | 0.985 (±0.0039) |
| VGG19 | 0.989 (±0.0048) | 0.08 (±0.05) | 0.989 (±0.0048) |
| ResNet16 | 0.995 (±0.0017) | 0.02 (±0.01) | 0.995 (±0.0017) |
| ResNet18 | 0.994 (±0.0018) | 0.03 (±0.01) | 0.994 (±0.0018) |
| ResNet34 | 0.994 (±0.0029) | 0.04 (±0.01) | 0.994 (±0.0029) |
| ResNet-BiGRU-ECA | 0.998 (±0.0007) | 0.01 (±0.01) | 0.998 (±0.0008) |

**Table 8.** A side-by-side comparison of the outcomes achieved by the proposed model and state-of-the-art deep learning (DL) networks, all trained and tested using electroencephalography (EEG) data from scenario II.

| Model | Recognition Effectiveness | | |
|---|---|---|---|
| | Accuracy | Loss | F1-Score |
| Inception | 0.994 (±0.0018) | 0.03 (±0.01) | 0.991 (±0.0028) |
| Xception | 0.962 (±0.0663) | 0.22 (±0.39) | 0.952 (±0.0808) |
| VGG11 | 0.985 (±0.0019) | 0.20 (±0.11) | 0.975 (±0.0031) |
| VGG13 | 0.984 (±0.0023) | 0.23 (±0.10) | 0.975 (±0.0038) |
| VGG16 | 0.989 (±0.0035) | 0.12 (±0.05) | 0.982 (±0.0056) |
| VGG19 | 0.991 (±0.0030) | 0.11 (±0.06) | 0.986 (±0.0047) |
| ResNet16 | 0.995 (±0.0023) | 0.03 (±0.01) | 0.991 (±0.0037) |
| ResNet18 | 0.883 (±0.2065) | 1.39 (±2.60) | 0.877 (±0.2052) |
| ResNet34 | 0.990 (±0.0071) | 0.21 (±0.36) | 0.984 (±0.0117) |
| ResNet-BiGRU-ECA | 0.996 (±0.0010) | 0.02 (±0.01) | 0.994 (±0.0016) |

### 4.5. Effect of BiGRU and ECA Modules

Additional investigations were conducted to provide a more comprehensive assessment of the BiGRU and ECA modules within the proposed ResNet-BiGRU-ECA architecture. As depicted in Table 9, the findings obviously indicate that both the BiGRU module and the ECA module contribute significantly to enhancing the model's efficiency in identifying datasets from two distinct situations.

**Table 9.** A comparative analysis of ResNet-based models, with and without the bidirectional gated recurrent unit (BiGRU) and efficient channel attention (ECA) modules.

| BiGRU | ECA | Accuracy | |
|---|---|---|---|
| | | Scenario I | Scenario II |
| - | - | 0.9904 (±0.0116) | 0.9924 (±0.0011) |
| ✓ | - | 0.9965 (±0.0017) | 0.9948 (±0.0007) |
| - | ✓ | 0.9926 (±0.0080) | 0.9935 (±0.0045) |
| ✓ | ✓ | 0.9980 (±0.0007) | 0.9960 (±0.0010) |

A checkmark (✓) indicates that the module is included in the given variation of the ResNet model and a dash (-) indicates that it is not included in that ResNet model variation.

## 5. Conclusions and Future Work

Epilepsy, a neurological disorder, can be significantly mitigated if detected early. This study introduces a novel hybrid DL model named ResNet-BiGRU-ECA, designed to accurately identify epileptic seizures using EEG signals. This model combines residual blocks, an ECA module, and a BiGRU to recognize epileptic seizures in pre-processed multichannel EEG recordings. To gauge the efficiency of our suggested model, we carried out a thorough assessment by contrasting it with five fundamental DL models and leading time-series classification models, all applied to the same publicly available dataset. The DL models underwent training and evaluation using a 5-CV approach. We analyzed model performance using standard evaluation metrics, and the ResNet-BiGRU-ECA model consistently outperformed other models, achieving an average accuracy of 0.998 and an F1-score of 0.998. Furthermore, our model surpassed most existing systems in terms of effectiveness when compared using the same dataset. The objective of this research is to make a meaningful contribution to the field of neurology by investigating the potential benefits of employing EEG data in the context of epilepsy detection and related matters. Our primary goal is to investigate the possibility of reducing examination duration while simultaneously improving diagnostic efficiency and effectiveness.

In future research, we intend to employ the ResNet-BiGRU-ECA model to address other detection issues relying on EEG signals. Additionally, we plan to delve into the explainability of our model to gain insights into the mechanisms and reasoning behind its accurate decision-making process.

**Author Contributions:** Conceptualization, S.M. and A.J.; methodology, S.M.; software, A.J.; validation, A.J.; formal analysis, S.M.; investigation, S.M.; resources, A.J.; data curation, A.J.; writing—original draft preparation, S.M.; writing—review and editing, A.J.; visualization, S.M.; supervision, A.J.; project administration, A.J.; funding acquisition, S.M. and A.J. All authors have read and agreed to the published version of the manuscript.

**Funding:** This research was funded by Thailand Science Research and Innovation Fund; University of Phayao (Grant No. FF67-UoE-Sakorn); National Science, Research and Innovation Fund (NSRF); and King Mongkut's University of Technology North Bangkok with Contract no. KMUTNB-FF-67-B-09.

**Data Availability Statement:** All data were presented in the main text.

**Conflicts of Interest:** The authors declare no conflict of interest.

## Abbreviations

The following abbreviations are used in this manuscript:

| | |
|---|---|
| AI | Artificial intelligence |
| BiGRU | Bidirectional gated recurrent unit |
| BiLSTMs | Bidirectional long short-term memory |
| BiRNN | Bidirectional recurrent neural network |
| BN | Batch normalization |
| CNN | Convolutional neural network |
| Conv1D | 1D-convolutional |
| ConvB | Convolutional block |
| DL | Deep learning |
| DT | Decision trees |
| ECA | Efficient channel attention |
| ECG | Electrocardiogram |
| EEG | Electroencephalography |
| ELU | Exponential linear unit |
| EMG | Electromyography |
| ESD | Epileptic seizure detection |
| ESR | Epileptic seizures recognition |
| ESRD | Epileptic seizures recognition dataset |
| FC | Fully connected |
| GAP | Global average pooling |
| GB | Gradient boosting |
| GRU | Gated recurrent unit |
| HAR | Human activity recognition |
| (*k*-CV) | k-fold cross-validation |
| KNN | k-nearest neighbors |
| LR | Logistic regression |
| LSTM | Long short-term memory |
| ML | Machine learning |
| MRI | Magnetic resonance imaging |
| MP | Max-pooling |
| NB | Naive Bayes |
| RF | Random forest |
| RNN | Recurrent neural network |
| SGDC | Stochastic gradient boosting |
| UCI | The university of California Irvine |

## References


1. Siddiqui, M.K.; Morales-Menendez, R.; Huang, X.; Hussain, N. A review of epileptic seizure detection using machine learning classifiers. *Brain Inform.* **2020**, *7*, 1–18. [CrossRef] [PubMed]
2. Sharma, R.; Pachori, R.B.; Sircar, P. Seizures classification based on higher order statistics and deep neural network. *Biomed. Signal Process. Control* **2020**, *59*, 101921. [CrossRef]
3. Fisher, R.S.; Boas, W.V.E.; Blume, W.; Elger, C.; Genton, P.; Lee, P.; Engel, J., Jr. Epileptic Seizures and Epilepsy: Definitions Proposed by the International League Against Epilepsy (ILAE) and the International Bureau for Epilepsy (IBE). *Epilepsia* **2005**, *46*, 470–472. [CrossRef] [PubMed]
4. Kim, T.; Nguyen, P.; Pham, N.; Bui, N.; Truong, H.; Ha, S.; Vu, T. Epileptic Seizure Detection and Experimental Treatment: A Review. *Front. Neurol.* **2020**, *11*, 701. [CrossRef]
5. Ayman, U.; Zia, M.S.; Okon, O.D.; Rehman, N.U.; Meraj, T.; Ragab, A.E.; Rauf, H.T. Epileptic Patient Activity Recognition System Using Extreme Learning Machine Method. *Biomedicines* **2023**, *11*, 816. [CrossRef]
6. Mekruksavanich, S.; Phaphan, W.; Hnoohom, N.; Jitpattanakul, A. Attention-Based Hybrid Deep Learning Network for Human Activity Recognition Using WiFi Channel State Information. *Appl. Sci.* **2023**, *13*, 8884. [CrossRef]
7. Shoeibi, A.; Khodatars, M.; Ghassemi, N.; Jafari, M.; Moridian, P.; Alizadehsani, R.; Panahiazar, M.; Khozeimeh, F.; Zare, A.; Hosseini-Nejad, H.; et al. Epileptic Seizures Detection Using Deep Learning Techniques: A Review. *Int. J. Environ. Res. Public Health* **2021**, *18*, 5780. [CrossRef]
8. Shoka, A.; Dessouky, M.; El-Sayed, A.; Hemdan, E.E.D. EEG seizure detection: Concepts, techniques, challenges, and future trends. *Multimed. Tools Appl.* **2023**, *82*, 42021–42051. [CrossRef]
9. Sharma, R.; Pachori, R.B. Classification of epileptic seizures in EEG signals based on phase space representation of intrinsic mode functions. *Expert Syst. Appl.* **2015**, *42*, 1106–1117. [CrossRef]
10. Wang, Z.; Yang, J.; Wu, H.; Zhu, J.; Sawan, M. Power efficient refined seizure prediction algorithm based on an enhanced benchmarking. *Sci. Rep.* **2021**, *11*, 23498. [CrossRef]
11. Sheoran, M.; Kumar, S.; Chawla, S. Methods of denoising of electroencephalogram signal: A review. *Int. J. Biomed. Eng. Technol.* **2015**, *18*, 385–395. [CrossRef]
12. Romaine, J.B.; Pereira Martín, M.; Salvador Ortiz, J.R.; Manzano Crespo, J.M. EEG—Single-Channel Envelope Synchronisation and Classification for Seizure Detection and Prediction. *Brain Sci.* **2021**, *11*, 516. [CrossRef] [PubMed]
13. Tang, X.; Zhang, X. Conditional Adversarial Domain Adaptation Neural Network for Motor Imagery EEG Decoding. *Entropy* **2020**, *22*, 96. [CrossRef] [PubMed]
14. Alickovic, E.; Kevric, J.; Subasi, A. Performance evaluation of empirical mode decomposition, discrete wavelet transform, and wavelet packed decomposition for automated epileptic seizure detection and prediction. *Biomed. Signal Process. Control* **2018**, *39*, 94–102. [CrossRef]
15. Bou Assi, E.; Nguyen, D.K.; Rihana, S.; Sawan, M. Towards accurate prediction of epileptic seizures: A review. *Biomed. Signal Process. Control* **2017**, *34*, 144–157. [CrossRef]
16. Varone, G.; Boulila, W.; Lo Giudice, M.; Benjdira, B.; Mammone, N.; Ieracitano, C.; Dashtipour, K.; Neri, S.; Gasparini, S.; Morabito, F.C.; et al. A Machine Learning Approach Involving Functional Connectivity Features to Classify Rest-EEG Psychogenic Non-Epileptic Seizures from Healthy Controls. *Sensors* **2022**, *22*, 129. [CrossRef] [PubMed]
17. Craik, A.; He, Y.; Contreras-Vidal, J.L. Deep learning for electroencephalogram (EEG) classification tasks: A review. *J. Neural Eng.* **2019**, *16*, 031001. [CrossRef] [PubMed]
18. Ullah, I.; Hussain, M.; ul Haq Qazi, E.; Aboalsamh, H. An automated system for epilepsy detection using EEG brain signals based on deep learning approach. *Expert Syst. Appl.* **2018**, *107*, 61–71. [CrossRef]
19. Goodfellow, I.J.; Bengio, Y.; Courville, A. *Deep Learning*; MIT Press: Cambridge, MA, USA, 2016
20. Bengio, Y.; Simard, P.; Frasconi, P. Learning long-term dependencies with gradient descent is difficult. *IEEE Trans. Neural Netw.* **1994**, *5*, 157–166. [CrossRef]
21. Yu, D.; Deng, L. Deep Learning and Its Applications to Signal and Information Processing [Exploratory DSP]. *IEEE Signal Process. Mag.* **2011**, *28*, 145–154. [CrossRef]
22. Hochreiter, S.; Schmidhuber, J. Long Short-Term Memory. *Neural Comput.* **1997**, *9*, 1735–1780. [CrossRef] [PubMed]
23. Golmohammadi, M.; Ziyabari, S.; Shah, V.; de Diego, S.L.; Obeid, I.; Picone, J. Deep Architectures for Automated Seizure Detection in Scalp EEGs. *arXiv* **2017**, arXiv:1712.09776.
24. Chen, X.; Ji, J.; Ji, T.; Li, P. Cost-sensitive deep active learning for epileptic seizure detection. In Proceedings of the 2018 ACM International Conference on Bioinformatics, Computational Biology, and Health Informatics, BCB '18, New York, NY, USA, 29 August–1 September 2018; pp. 226–235. [CrossRef]
25. Fukumori, K.; Thu Nguyen, H.T.; Yoshida, N.; Tanaka, T. Fully Data-driven Convolutional Filters with Deep Learning Models for Epileptic Spike Detection. In Proceedings of the ICASSP 2019—IEEE International Conference on Acoustics, Speech and Signal Processing (ICASSP), Brighton, UK, 12–17 May 2019; pp. 2772–2776. [CrossRef]
26. Gu, J.; Wang, Z.; Kuen, J.; Ma, L.; Shahroudy, A.; Shuai, B.; Liu, T.; Wang, X.; Wang, G.; Cai, J.; et al. Recent advances in convolutional neural networks. *Pattern Recognit.* **2018**, *77*, 354–377. [CrossRef]

27. Andrzejak, R.G.; Lehnertz, K.; Mormann, F.; Rieke, C.; David, P.; Elger, C.E. Indications of nonlinear deterministic and finite-dimensional structures in time series of brain electrical activity: Dependence on recording region and brain state. *Phys. Rev. E* **2001**, *64*, 061907. [CrossRef] [PubMed]
28. Varone, G.; Boulila, W.; Driss, M.; Kumari, S.; Khan, M.K.; Gadekallu, T.R.; Hussain, A. Finger pinching and imagination classification: A fusion of CNN architectures for IoMT-enabled BCI applications. *Inf. Fusion* **2023**, *101*, 102006. [CrossRef]
29. Van Doorn, J. Analysis of deep convolutional neural Network architectures. In Proceedings of the 21st Twente Student Conference on IT (TScIT 21), Enschede, The Netherlands, 21–24 June 2014.
30. Cho, K.; van Merriënboer, B.; Bahdanau, D.; Bengio, Y. On the Properties of Neural Machine Translation: Encoder–Decoder Approaches. In Proceedings of the SSST-8, 8th Workshop on Syntax, Semantics and Structure in Statistical Translation, Doha, Qatar, 25 October 2014; pp. 103–111. [CrossRef]
31. Chung, J.; Gulcehre, C.; Cho, K.; Bengio, Y. Empirical evaluation of gated recurrent neural networks on sequence modeling. In Proceedings of the NIPS 2014 Workshop on Deep Learning, Montreal, QC, Canada, 8–13 December 2014.
32. Schuster, M.; Paliwal, K. Bidirectional recurrent neural networks. *IEEE Trans. Signal Process.* **1997**, *45*, 2673–2681. [CrossRef]
33. Yang, Z.; He, X.; Gao, J.; Deng, L.; Smola, A. Stacked attention networks for image question answering. In Proceedings of the 2016 IEEE Conference on Computer Vision and Pattern Recognition (CVPR), Los Alamitos, CA, USA, 27–30 June 2016; pp. 21–29. [CrossRef]
34. Wong, T.T. Performance evaluation of classification algorithms by k-fold and leave-one-out cross validation. *Pattern Recognit.* **2015**, *48*, 2839–2846. [CrossRef]
35. Bragança, H.; Colonna, J.G.; Oliveira, H.A.B.F.; Souto, E. How Validation Methodology Influences Human Activity Recognition Mobile Systems. *Sensors* **2022**, *22*, 2360. [CrossRef]
36. Simonyan, K.; Zisserman, A. Very Deep Convolutional Networks for Large-Scale Image Recognition. *arXiv* **2015**, arXiv:cs.CV/1409.1556.
37. He, K.; Zhang, X.; Ren, S.; Sun, J. Deep Residual Learning for Image Recognition. *arXiv* **2015**, arXiv:cs.CV/1512.03385.
38. Han, D.; Kim, J.; Kim, J. Deep Pyramidal Residual Networks. In Proceedings of the 2017 IEEE Conference on Computer Vision and Pattern Recognition (CVPR), Honolulu, HI, USA, 21–26 July 2017; pp. 6307–6315. [CrossRef]
39. Szegedy, C.; Vanhoucke, V.; Ioffe, S.; Shlens, J.; Wojna, Z. Rethinking the Inception Architecture for Computer Vision. In Proceedings of the 2016 IEEE Conference on Computer Vision and Pattern Recognition (CVPR), Las Vegas, NV, USA, 27–30 June 2016; pp. 2818–2826. [CrossRef]
40. Chollet, F. Xception: Deep Learning with Depthwise Separable Convolutions. In Proceedings of the 2017 IEEE Conference on Computer Vision and Pattern Recognition (CVPR), Los Alamitos, CA, USA, 21–26 July 2017; pp. 1800–1807. [CrossRef]
41. Elghamry, H.; Ghoneim, M.; Abo Haggag, A.; Saeed Darweesh, M.; Ismail, T. Comparative Analysis of Various Machine Learning Techniques for Epileptic Seizures Detection and Prediction Using EEG Data. In Proceedings of the 2020 2nd Novel Intelligent and Leading Emerging Sciences Conference (NILES), Giza, Egypt, 24–26 October 2020; pp. 175–180. [CrossRef]
42. Torse, D.A.; Khanai, R.; Desai, V.V. Classification of Epileptic Seizures using Recurrence Plots and Machine Learning Techniques. In Proceedings of the 2019 International Conference on Communication and Signal Processing (ICCSP), Tamil Nadu, India, 4–6 April 2019; pp. 611–615. [CrossRef]

MDPI AG
Grosspeteranlage 5
4052 Basel
Switzerland
Tel.: +41 61 683 77 34

*Machine Learning and Knowledge Extraction* Editorial Office
E-mail: make@mdpi.com
www.mdpi.com/journal/make

www.ingramcontent.com/pod-product-compliance
Lightning Source LLC
Chambersburg PA
CBHW041945260926
51850CB00018B/886
*9783725871766*